American Experiences

Readings in American History

Third Edition

■

Randy Roberts
Purdue University

■

James S. Olson
Sam Houston State University

D1312220

HarperCollins*CollegePublishers*

Executive Editor: Bruce Borland
Project Coordination and Text Design: Proof Positive/Farrowlyne Associates, Inc.
Cover Design: Kay Petronio
Cover Illustration: John H. Howard
Photo Researcher: Leslie Coopersmith
Production Manager: Kewal Sharma
Compositor: Proof Positive/Farrowlyne Associates, Inc.
Printer and Binder: R. R. Donnelley & Sons Company
Cover Printer: R. R. Donnelley & Sons Company

Credits: 3 Library of Congress 8 *Harper's Weekly*, October 26, 1874 20 Library of Congress 22 The Kansas State Historical Society, Topeka 27 Library of Congress 34 Culver Pictures 59 Culver Pictures 64 Countway Library, Harvard Medical School 77 Culver Pictures 79 Library of Congress 89 Illinois Labor History Society 92 Stock Montage, Chicago 104 Brown Brothers 113 Brown Brothers 126 Trustees of the Imperial War Museum, London 131 © JB & R Inc., *Old Life* 135 Culver Pictures 149 UPI/Bettmann 159 Culver Pictures 169 UPI/Bettmann 181 Dorothea Lange, The Oakland Museum 185 Brown Brothers 193 Austin History Center, Austin (Texas) Public Library 213 Wide World Photos 219 U. S. Army 241 Kobal Collection 247 U. S. Navy 250 UPI/Bettmann 272 Wayne Miller/Magnum Photos 283 Wide World Photos 293 The Lester Glassner Collection 299 *The Chicago Tribune*, photo by Michael Budrys 310 Wide World Photos 329 Moondog's, Incorporated, Elk Grove Village, IL 340 Susan Meiselas/Magnum Photos 350 Peter Menzel/Stock, Boston

American Experiences: Readings in American History, Volume II, 1877 to the Present, Third Edition
Copyright © 1994 by HarperCollins College Publishers

All rights reserved. Printed in the United States of America. No part of this book may be used or reproduced in any manner whatsoever without written permission, except in the case of brief quotations embodied in critical articles and reviews. For information address HarperCollins College Publishers, 10 East 53rd Street, New York, NY 10022.

Library of Congress Cataloging-in-Publication Data
American Experiences: readings in American history/[edited by]
    Randy Roberts, James S. Olson. —3rd ed.
        p. cm.
    Includes bibliographical references.
    Contents: v. 1. 1607-1877 — v. 2. 1877 to the present
    ISBN 0-673-46737-6
    1. United States—History. I. Roberts, Randy, 1951– .
II. Olson, James Stuart, 1946– .
E178.6.A395 1994
973—dc20   93-32508
                                            CIP

95 96 9 8 7 6 5 4

Contents

Part Four

HEROES AND SOCIETY IN THE 1920s ••
page 130

Part Five

•• DEPRESSION AND WAR ••
page 180

Part Seven

COMING APART: 1960–1990
page 298

Preface

American History instructors enjoy talking about the grand sweep of the American past. Many note the development of unique traditions such as the American political tradition and the American diplomatic tradition. They employ the article *the* so often that they depict history as a seamless garment and Americans as all cut from the same fabric. Nothing could be further from the truth. America is a diverse country, and its population is the most ethnically varied in the world—white and black, Indian and Chicano, rich and poor, male and female. No single tradition can encompass this variety. *American Experiences* shows the complexity and richness of the nation's past by focusing on the people themselves—how they coped with, adjusted to, or rebelled against America. The readings examine them as they worked and played, fought and made love, lived and died.

We designed *American Experiences* as a supplement to the standard textbooks used in college survey classes in American History. Unlike other readers, it covers ground not usually found in textbooks. For example, instead of an essay on the effect of the New Deal, it includes a selection on life in the Hill Country of Texas before rural electrification. Instead of a discussion of the political impact of the Populist movement, it explores the *Wizard of Oz* as a Populist parable. In short, it presents different slants on standard and not-so-standard topics.

We have tested each essay in classrooms so that *American Experiences* reflects not only our interest in social history but also student interests in American history in general. We selected essays that are readable, interesting, and help illuminate important aspects of America's past. For example, to show the nature of the class system in the South and to introduce the topic of southern values, we selected one essay on gambling and horse racing in the Old South and another on gouging matches in the southern backcountry. As an introduction to the conventional and medical view of women in the late nineteenth century, we selected an essay about Lizzie Borden. Each essay, then, serves at least two purposes: to tell a particular story well, and to help illuminate the social or political landscape of America.

This reader presents a balanced picture of the experiences of Americans. The characters in these volumes are not exclusively white males from the Northeast, whose eyes are continually focused on Boston, New York, and Washington. Although their stories are certainly important, so, too, are the stories of blacks adjusting with dignity to a barbarous labor system, Chicanos coming to terms with Anglo society, and women striving for increased opportunities in a sexually restrictive society. We have looked at all of these stories and, in doing so, we have assumed that Americans express themselves in a variety of ways, through work, sex, and games, as well as politics and diplomacy.

During the last three years, we have solicited a variety of opinions, from colleagues and students, about the selections for *American Experiences*. Based on that feedback we have made a number of changes in the third edition, always with the intention of selecting articles that undergraduate students will find interesting and informative. The new articles for this second volume of *American Experiences* Third Edition, include James C. Mohr's "The Physicians' Crusade Against Abortion, 1857–1880," Dean Smith's "The Black Sox Scandal," Edward Oxford's "Night of the Martians," Randy Roberts's "John Wayne Goes to War," David Burner and Thomas R. West on "Kennedy Liberalism," and Bradford Wright's "Vietnam in the Comic Books."

Each volume of *American Experiences* is divided into standard chronological and topical parts. Each part is introduced by a brief discussion of the major themes of the period or topic. In turn, each individual selection is preceded by a short discussion of how it fits into the part's general theme. We employed this method to give students some guidance through the complexity of the experiences of Americans. At the conclusion of each selection is a series of study questions and a brief bibliographic essay. These are intended to further the usefulness of *American Experiences* for students as well as teachers.

We would like to thank our reviewers, who read the manuscript carefully and provided many invaluable suggestions.

Terry Bilhartz, Sam Houston State University

Ron Fritze, Lamar University

Cathy Lively, Blinn Junior College

Max Reichard, Delgado Community College

Larry Watson, Texas A&M University and Blinn Junior College—College Station, Texas

Randy Roberts
James S. Olson

Volume II   1877 to the Present

American Experiences

Readings in American History

Third Edition

Part One

RECONSTRUCTION
AND
THE WEST

Although the Civil War did not begin as a crusade against slavery, it ended that way. The Emancipation Proclamation and Thirteenth Amendment to the Constitution destroyed human bondage in the United States, and during Reconstruction Republicans worked diligently to extend full civil rights to southern blacks. Despite the concerted opposition of President Andrew Johnson, the Radical Republicans in Congress pushed through a strong legislative program. The Civil Rights Act of 1866 and the Fourteenth and Fifteenth Amendments to the Constitution were all basically designed to bring the emancipated slaves into the political arena and build a respectable Republican party in the South. Both of those goals were still-born. When Congress removed the troops from the last southern states in 1877, the old planter elite resumed its control of southern politics. They disfranchised and relegated blacks to second-class citizenship, and the South became solidly Democratic. The South had indeed been brought back into the Union, but the grandiose hopes for a true reconstruction of southern life would not be realized for more than a century.

Genuine change in the southern social structure required more than most Northerners could accept. Confiscation and redistribution of the plantations among poor whites and former slaves was too brazen an assault on property rights; northern

businessmen feared that someday their own workers might demand similar treatment. Nor were Northerners prepared for real social change. Advocating political rights for blacks was one thing; true social equality was quite another. Prejudice ran deep in the American psyche, too deep in the 1870s to allow for massive social change. Finally, most Americans were growing tired of the debate over civil rights and becoming preoccupied with business, money, and economic growth. Heavy industry in the East and vacant land in the West were absorbing their energies.

Just as Reconstruction was coming to an end, out west, ambitious farmers were rapidly settling the frontier, anxious to convert the land into an agricultural empire. Civilization was forever replacing a wilderness mentality with familiar political, economic, and social institutions. Already the "Old West" was becoming the stuff of which nostalgia is made. Normal, if somewhat eccentric, people were being transformed into larger-than-life heroes as American society tried to maintain its rural, individualistic roots. Back East, cities and factories were announcing a future of bureaucracies, interest groups, crowds, and enormous industrial production. America would never be the same again. The cult of Western heroes helped people forget the misery of the Civil War and vicariously preserve a disappearing way of life.

THE KNIGHTS OF THE RISING SUN

Allen W. Trelease

The Civil War, which started in 1861 and ended in 1865, was like a nightmare come true for most Americans. More than 600,000 young men were dead, countless others wounded and permanently maimed, and the South a prostrate ruin. For the next twelve years, northern Republicans tried to "reconstruct" the South in a chaotic crusade mixing retribution, corruption, and genuine idealism. Intent on punishing white Southerners for their disloyalty, northern Republicans, especially the Radicals, tried to extend full civil rights—via the Fourteenth and Fifteenth Amendments—to the former slaves. For a variety of reasons, the attempt at giving equality to southern blacks failed, and by 1877 political power in the South reverted to the white elite.

A major factor in the failure of Radical Republicans to "reconstruct" the South was the rise of the Ku Klux Klan. Enraged at the very thought of black political power, Klansmen resorted to intimidation and violence, punishing southern blacks even suspected of sympathizing with Radicals' goals for the South. In "The Knights of the Rising Sun," historian Allen W. Trelease describes Klan activities in Texas during the late 1860s. Isolated from the main theaters of the Civil War, much of Texas remained unreconstructed, and the old white elite, along with their Klan allies, succeeded in destroying every vestige of black political activity and in eliminating the Republican party from the political life of the state.

Large parts of Texas remained close to anarchy through 1868. Much of this was politically inspired despite the fact that the state was not yet reconstructed and took no part in the national election. In theory the Army was freer to take a direct hand in maintaining order than was true in the states which had been readmitted, but the shortage of troops available for this duty considerably lessened that advantage. At least twenty counties were involved in the Ku Klux terror, from Houston north to the Red River. In Houston itself Klan activity was limited to the holding of monthly meetings in a gymnasium and posting notices on lampposts, but in other places there was considerable violence.

By mid-September disguised bands had committed several murders in Trinity County, where two lawyers and both justices of the peace in the town of Sumter were well known as Klansmen. Not only did the crimes go unpunished, but Conservatives used them to force a majority of the Negroes to swear allegiance to the Democratic party; in return they received the familiar protection papers supposedly guaranteeing them against further outrage. "Any one in this community opposed to the Grand Cyclops and his imps is in danger of his life," wrote a local Republican in November. In Washington County the Klan sent warning notices to Republicans and committed at least one murder. As late as January 1869 masked parties were active around Palestine, shaving heads, whipping, and shooting among the black population, as well as burning down their houses. The military arrested five or six men for these offenses, but the Klan continued to make the rounds of Negroes' and Union men's houses, confiscating

both guns and money. Early in November General J. J. Reynolds, military commander in the state, declared in a widely quoted report that "civil law east of the Trinity river is almost a dead letter" by virtue of the activities of Ku Klux Klans and similar organizations. Republicans had been publicly slated for assassination and forced to flee their homes, while the murder of Negroes was too common to keep track of. These lawless bands, he said, were "evidently countenanced, or at least not discouraged, by a majority of the white people in the counties where [they] are most numerous. They could not otherwise exist." These statements did not endear the general to Conservative Texans, but they were substantially true.

The worst region of all, as to both Klan activity and general banditry, remained northeast Texas. A correspondent of the Cincinnati *Commercial* wrote from Sulphur Springs early in January 1869:

Armed bands of banditti, thieves, cut-throats and assassins infest the country; they prowl around houses, they call men out and shoot or hang them, they attack travellers upon the road, they seem almost everywhere present, and are ever intent upon mischief. You cannot pick up a paper without reading of murders, assassinations and robbery. . . . And yet not the fourth part of the truth has been told; not one act in ten is reported. Go where you will, and you will hear of fresh murders and violence. . . . The civil authority is powerless—the military insufficient in number, while hell has transferred its capital from pandemonium to Jefferson, and the devil is holding high carnival in Gilmer, Tyler, Canton, Quitman, Boston, Marshall and other places in Texas.

Judge Hardin Hart wrote Governor Pease in September to say that on account of "a regularly organized band which has overrun the country" he could not hold court in Grayson, Fannin, and Hunt counties without a military escort.

Much of this difficulty was attributable to

"Texas: The Knights of the Rising Sun" from *White Terror: The Ku Klux Klan Conspiracy and Southern Reconstruction* by Allen W. Trelease. Copyright © 1971 by Allen W. Trelease. Reprinted by permission of the author.

outlaw gangs like those of Ben Bickerstaff and Cullen Baker, but even their activities were often racially and politically inspired, with Negroes and Union men the chief sufferers. Army officers and soldiers reported that most of the population at Sulphur Springs was organized into Ku Klux clubs affiliated with the Democratic party and some of the outlaws called themselves Ku Klux Rangers. At Clarksville a band of young men calling themselves Ku Klux broke up a Negro school and forced the teacher to flee the state.

White Conservatives around Paris at first took advantage of Klan depredations among Negroes by issuing protection papers to those who agreed to join the Democratic party. But the marauding reached such proportions that many freedmen fled their homes and jobs, leaving the crops untended. When a body of Klansmen came into town early in September, apparently to disarm more blacks, some of the leading citizens warned them to stop. The freedmen were not misbehaving, they said, and if they needed disarming at a later time the local people would take care of it themselves. Still the raiding continued, and after a sheriff's posse failed to catch the culprits the farmers in one neighborhood banded together to oppose them by force. (Since the Klan had become sacred among Democrats, these men claimed that the raiding was done by an unauthorized group using its name. They carefully denied any idea of opposing the Klan itself.) Even this tactic was ineffective so far as the county as a whole was concerned, and the terror continued at least into November. The Freedmen's Bureau agent, Colonel DeWitt C. Brown, was driven away from his own farm thirty miles from Paris and took refuge in town. There he was subjected to constant threats of assassination by Klansmen or their sympathizers. From where he stood the Klan seemed to be in almost total command.

The Bureau agent at Marshall (like his predecessor in the summer) suspected that the planters themselves were implicated in much of the terrorism. By driving Negroes from their homes just before harvest time the Klan enabled many landowners to collect the crop without having to pay the laborers' share.

Jefferson and Marion County remained the center of Ku Klux terrorism, as the Cincinnati reporter pointed out. A garrison of twenty-six men under Major James Curtis did little to deter violence. Bands of hooded men continued to make nocturnal depredations on Negroes in the surrounding countryside during September and October as they had for weeks past. "Whipping the freedmen, robbing them of their arms, driving them off plantations, and murdering whole families are of daily, and nightly occurrence," wrote the local Bureau agent at the end of October, "all done by disguised parties whom no one can testify to. The civil authorities never budge an inch to try and discover these midnight marauders and apparently a perfect apathy exists throughout the whole community regarding the general state of society. Nothing but martial law can save this section as it is at present. . . ." Inside town, Republicans hardly dared go outdoors at night, and for several weeks the county judge, who was afraid to go home even in the daytime, slept at the Army post. The local Democratic newspapers, including the *Ultra Ku Klux*, encouraged the terror by vying with one another in the ferocity of their denunciations of Republicans.

Major Curtis confirmed this state of affairs in a report to General Reynolds:

Since my arrival at the Post . . . [in mid-September] I have carefully observed the temper of the people and studied their intentions. I am constrained to say that neither are pacific. The amount of unblushing fraud and outrage perpetrated upon the negroes is hardly to be believed unless witnessed. Citizens who are esteemed respectable do not hesitate to take every unfair advantage. My office is daily visited by large numbers of unfortunates who have had money owing them, which they have been unable to obtain. The moral sense of the community appears blunted and gray headed apologists for such men as Baker and Bickerstaff can be met on all the street corners. . . . The right of franchise in this section is a farce. Numbers of negroes have been killed for daring to be Radicals, and their houses have so often been broken into by their Ku Klux neighbors in search of arms that they are now pretty well defenceless. The civil officers cannot and will not punish these outrages. Calvary armed with double barrelled shotguns would soon scour the country and these desperadoes be met on their own ground. They do not fear the arms that the troops now have, for they shoot from behind hedges and fences or at night and then run. No more notice is taken here of the death of a Radical negro than of a mad dog. A democratic negro however, who was shot the other day by another of his stripe, was followed to his grave through the streets of this city by a long procession in carriages, on horseback, and on foot. I saw some of the most aristocratic and respectable white men in this city in the procession.

On the same night that Curtis wrote, the new Grand Officers of the Knights of the Rising Sun were installed in the presence of a crowd of 1,200 or 1,500 persons. "The town was beautifully illuminated," a newspaper reported, "and the Seymour Knights and the Lone Star Club turned out in full uniform, with transparencies and burners, in honor of the occasion." Sworn in as Grand Commander for the ensuing twelve months was Colonel William P. Saufley, who doubled as chairman of the Marion County Democratic executive committee. Following the installation "able and patriotic speeches" were delivered by several notables, including a Democratic Negro.

As usual, the most hated Republican was the one who had the greatest Negro following. This was Captain George W. Smith, a young Union army veteran from New York who had settled in Jefferson as a merchant at the end of the war. His business failed, but the advent of Radical Reconstruction opened the prospect of a successful political career; at the age of twenty-four Smith was elected to the state constitu-

tional convention by the suffrage of the Negro majority around Jefferson. At the convention, according to a perhaps overflattering posthumous account, he was recognized as one of the abler members. "In his daily life he was correct, almost austere. He never drank, smoked, chewed, nor used profane language." However, "he was odious as a negro leader, as a radical, as a man who could not be cowed, nor scared away." Smith may also have alienated his fellow townspeople by the strenuous efforts he made to collect debts they owed him. Even a few native Republicans like Judge Charles Caldwell, who was scarcely more popular with Conservatives, refused to speak from the same platform with him. As his admirer pointed out, Smith "was ostracized and his life often threatened. But he refused to be scared. He sued some of his debtors and went to live with colored people." One day, as he returned from a session of the convention, his carpetbag—perhaps symbolically—was stolen, its contents rifled, and a list of them published in a local newspaper.

The beginning of the end for Smith came on the night of October 3, after he and Anderson Wright, a Negro, had spoken at a Republican meeting. As he opened the door of a Negro cabin to enter, Smith was fired upon by four men outside including Colonel Richard P. Crump, one of Jefferson's leading gentry. Smith drew his revolver and returned the fire, wounding two of the assailants and driving them away. He then went to Major Curtis at the Army post. Here Crump, with the chief of police and others, soon arrived bearing a warrant for his arrest on a charge of assault. The attackers' original intention to kill Smith now assumed greater urgency because he and several Negroes present had recognized their assailants. Smith objected strenuously to their efforts to get custody of him, protesting that it was equivalent to signing his death warrant. Nevertheless Curtis turned him over to the civil authorities on their assurance of his safety. Smith was taken off to jail and a small civilian guard was posted around it. The major was uneasy, however, and requested reinforcements from his superior, but they were refused.

The next day there were signs in Jefferson of an assembling of the Knights of the Rising Sun. Hoping to head off a lynching, Curtis dispatched sixteen soldiers (the greater part of his command) to help guard the jail. At 9 P.M., finally, a signal was sounded—a series of strokes on a bell at the place where the Knights held their meetings. About seventy members now mobilized under the command of Colonel Saufley and proceeded to march in formation toward the jail; they were in disguise and many carried torches. The jail building lay in an enclosed yard where at that time four black men were confined for a variety of petty offenses. One of the prisoners was Anderson Wright, and apparently the real reason for their being there was that they had witnessed the previous night's attempt to murder Smith; they may even have been fellow targets at that time. When the Knights reached this enclosure they burst through it with a shout and overpowered the guard, commanded by a young Army lieutenant. The invaders then turned to the Negro prisoners and dragged them into some adjoining woods. Wright and a second man, Cornelius Turner, managed to escape from them, although Wright was wounded; the other two prisoners were shot nearly to pieces. As soon as Major Curtis heard the shooting and firing he came running with his remaining soldiers; but they too were quickly overpowered. Repeatedly the major himself tried to prevent the mob from entering the jail building in which Smith was confined, only to be dragged away from the door each time. They had no trouble unlocking the door, for city marshall Silas Nance, who possessed the key, was one of the conspirators.

At first Smith tried to hold the door shut against their entry. Eventually failing at this, he caught the foremost man, pulled him into the room, and somehow killed him. "It is common

■■■ *Terrorist activities by Ku Klux Klansmen, such as those related in this article, convinced many Republicans that conditions for southern blacks and their white supporters were "worse than slavery." as this cartoon from* Harper's Weekly *(October 26, 1874) graphically depicts.*

talk in Jefferson now," wrote a former Bureau agent some months later, "that Capt. Smith killed the first man who entered—that the Knights of the Rising Sun afterward buried him secretly with their funeral rites, and it was hushed up, he being a man from a distance. It is an established fact that one Gray, a strong man, who ventured into the open door, was so beaten by Capt. Smith that he cried, 'Pull me out! He's killing me!' and he was dragged out backward by the leg." All this took place in such darkness that the Knights could not see their victim. Some of them now went outside and held torches up to the small barred window of Smith's cell. By this light they were able to shoot him four times. "The door was burst open and the crowd surged in upon him as he fell, and then, man after man, as they filed around fired into the dying body. This refinement of barbarity was continued while he writhed and after his limbs had ceased to quiver, that each one might participate in the triumph."

Once the mob had finished its work at the jail it broke up into squads which began patrolling the town and searching for other Republican leaders. County Judge Campbell had anticipated trouble earlier in the evening and taken refuge as usual at Major Curtis' headquarters. Judge Caldwell was hated second only to Smith after his well-publicized report as chairman of the constitutional convention's committee on lawlessness. Hearing the shooting around the jail, he fled from his home into the woods. In a few moments twenty-five or thirty Knights appeared at the house, looking for him. Some of the party were for killing him, and they spent two hours vainly trying to learn his whereabouts from his fifteen-year-old son, who refused to tell. Another band went to the house of G. H. Slaughter, also a member of the convention, but he too escaped.

The next day the few remaining white Republicans in town were warned by friends of a widely expressed desire to make a "clean sweep" of them. Most of them stayed at the Haywood House hotel the following night under a military guard. Meanwhile the KRS scoured the city looking for dangerous Negroes, including those who knew too much about the preceding events for anyone's safety. When Major Curtis confessed that the only protection he could give the white Republicans was a military escort out of town, most of them decided to leave. At this point some civic leaders, alarmed at the probable effects to the town and themselves of such an exodus under these circumstances, urged them to stay and offered their protection. But the Republicans recalled the pledge to Smith and departed as quickly as they could, some openly and others furtively to avoid ambush.

White Conservatives saw these events—or at least their background and causes—in another light. They regarded Smith as "a dangerous, unprincipled carpet-bagger" who "lived almost entirely with negroes, on terms of perfect equality." Whether there was evidence for it or not, they found it easy to believe further that this "cohabitation" was accompanied by "the most unbridled and groveling licentiousness"; according to one account he walked the streets with Negroes in a state of near-nudity. For at least eighteen months he had thus "outraged the moral sentiment of the city of Jefferson," defying the whites to do anything about it and threatening a race war if they tried. This might have been overlooked if he had not tried repeatedly to precipitate such a collision. As head of the Union League he delivered inflammatory speeches and organized the blacks into armed mobs who committed assaults and robberies and threatened to burn the town. When part of the city did go up in flames earlier in the year Smith was held responsible. Overlooking the well-attested white terrorism which had prevailed in the city and county for months, a Democratic newspaper claimed that all had been peace and quiet during Smith's absence at the constitutional convention. But on his return he resumed his incendiary course and made it necessary for the whites to arm in self-defense.

According to Conservatives the initial shooting affray on the night of October 3 was precipitated by a group of armed Negroes with Smith at their head. They opened fire on Crump and his friends while the latter were on their way to protect a white man whom Smith had threatened to attack. Democrats did not dwell overlong on the ensuing lynching, nor did they bother to explain the killing of the Negro prisoners. In fact the affair was made deliberately mysterious and a bit romantic in their telling. According to the Jefferson *Times*, both the soldiers and the civilians on guard at the jail characterized the lynch party as "entirely sober and apparently well disciplined." (One of the party later testified in court that at least some of them had put on their disguises while drinking at a local saloon.) "After the accomplishment of their object," the *Times* continued, "they all retired as quietly and mysteriously as they came—none knowing who they were or from whence they came." (This assertion, it turned out, was more hopeful than factual.)

The *Times* deplored such proceedings in general, it assured its readers, but in this case lynching "had become . . . an unavoidable necessity. The sanctity of home, the peace and safety of society, the prosperity of the country, and the security of life itself demanded the removal of so base a villain." A month later it declared: "Every community in the South will do well to relieve themselves [*sic*] of their surplus Geo. Smiths, and others of like ilk, as Jefferson rid herself of hers. This is not a healthy locality for such incendiaries, and no town in the South should be." Democratic papers made much of Judge Caldwell's refusal to appear publicly with Smith—which was probably inspired by his Negro associations. They claimed that Smith's fellow Republicans were also glad to have him out of the way, and noted that the local citizens had assured them of protection. But there was no mention of the riotous search and the threats upon their lives which produced that offer, nor of their flight from the city anyway.

The Smith affair raises problems of fact and interpretation which appeared in almost every Ku Klux raid across the South. Most were not so fully examined or reported as this, but even here it is impossible to know certainly where the truth lay. Republican and Democratic accounts differed diametrically on almost every particular, and both were colored by considerations of political and personal interest. But enough detailed and impartial evidence survives to sustain the Republican case on most counts. Negro and Republican testimony concerning the actual events in October is confirmed by members of the KRS who turned state's evidence when they were later brought to trial. Smith's prior activities and his personal character are less clear. Republicans all agreed later that he was almost puritanical in his moral code and that he was hated

because of his unquestioned social associations and political influence with the blacks. He never counseled violence or issued threats to burn the town, they insisted; on the contrary, the only time he ever headed a Negro crowd was when he brought a number of them to help extinguish the fire which he was falsely accused of starting.

As elsewhere in the South, the logic of some of the charges against Smith is not convincing. Whites had a majority in the city and blacks in the county. Theoretically each could gain by racial violence, offsetting its minority status. But Conservatives always had the advantage in such confrontations. They were repeatedly guilty of intimidating the freedmen, and in case of an open collision everyone (including Republicans) knew they could win hands down. Democrats were certainly sincere in their personal and political detestation of Smith; almost as certainly they were sincere in their fears of his political activity and what it might lead to. From their viewpoint an open consorter with and leader of Negroes was capable of anything. It was easy therefore to believe the worst and attribute the basest motives without clear evidence. If some Negroes did threaten to burn the town—often this was a threat to retaliate for preceding white terrorism—it was easy to overlook the real cause and attribute the idea to Smith. The next step, involving hypocrisy and deliberate falsehood in some cases, was to charge him with specific expressions and activities which no other source substantiates and which the logic of the situation makes improbable. Men who practiced or condoned terrorism and murder in what they conceived to be a just cause would not shrink from character assassination in the same cause.

Interestingly enough, most of the character assassination—in Smith's case and generally—followed rather than preceded Ku Klux attacks. This did not arise primarily from a feeling of greater freedom or safety once the victim was no longer around to defend himself; some victims, unlike Smith, lived to speak out in their own behalf. Accusations after the fact were intended rather to rationalize and win public approval of the attack once it had occurred; since these raids were the product of at least semisecret conspiracy there was less need to win public approval beforehand. Sometimes such accusations were partially true, no doubt, and it was never easy for persons at a distance to judge them; often it is no easier now. Democrats tended to believe and Republicans to reject them as a matter of course. The *Daily Austin Republican* was typical of Radical papers in its reaction to Democratic newspaper slurs against Smith after his death: "We have read your lying sheets for the last *eighteen* months, and this is the first time you have made any such charges. . . ." It was surely justified in charging the Democratic editors of Texas with being accessories after the fact in Smith's murder.

The military authorities had done almost nothing to stop KRS terrorism among the Negroes before Smith's murder, and this violence continued for at least two months afterward. Similar conditions prevailed widely, and there were too few troops—especially cavalry—to patrol every lawless county. But the murder of a white man, particularly one of Smith's prominence and in such a fashion, aroused officials to unwonted activity. The Army recalled Major Curtis and sent Colonel H. G. Malloy to Jefferson as provisional mayor with orders to discover and bring to justice the murderers of Smith and the two freedmen killed with him. More troops were also sent, amounting ultimately to nine companies of infantry and four of cavalry. With their help Malloy arrested four of Jefferson's leading men on December 5. Colonel W. P. Saufley, whom witnesses identified as the organizer of the lynching, would have been a fifth, but he left town the day before on business, a Democratic newspaper explained, apparently unaware that he was wanted. (This business was to take him into the Cherokee Indian Nation and perhaps as far as New York, detaining him so long that the authorities never succeeded in apprehending him.) That night the KRS held an emergency meeting and about twenty men left town for parts unknown while others prepared to follow.

General George P. Buell arrived soon afterward as commandant, and under his direction the arrests continued for months, reaching thirty-seven by early April. They included by common repute some of the best as well as the worst citizens of Jefferson. Detectives were sent as far as New York to round up suspects who had scattered in all directions. One of the last to leave was General H. P. Mabry, a former judge and a KRS leader who was serving as one of the counsel for the defense. When a soldier revealed that one of the prisoners had turned state's evidence and identified Mabry as a leader in the lynching, he abruptly fled to Canada.

The authorities took great pains to recover Anderson Wright and Cornelius Turner, the Negro survivors of the lynching, whose testimony would be vital in the forthcoming trials. After locating Wright, General Buell sent him with an Army officer to find Turner, who had escaped to New Orleans. They traveled part of the way by steamboat and at one point, when the officer was momentarily occupied elsewhere, Wright was set upon by four men. He saved himself by jumping overboard and made his way to a nearby Army post, whence he was brought back to Jefferson. Buell then sent a detective after Turner, who eventually was located, and both men later testified at the trial.

The intention of the authorities was to try the suspects before a military commission, as they were virtually sure of acquittal in the civil courts. Defense counsel (who consisted ultimately of eleven lawyers—nearly the whole Jefferson bar) made every effort to have the case transferred; two of them even went to Washington to appeal personally to Secretary of War Schofield, but he refused to interfere. R. W. Loughery, the editor of both the Jefferson

Times and the *Texas Republican* in Marshall, appealed to the court of public opinion. His editorials screamed indignation at the "terrible and revolting ordeal through which a refined, hospitable, and intelligent people are passing, under radical rule," continually subject to the indignity and danger of midnight arrest. He also sent requests to Washington and to Northern newspapers for intercession against Jefferson's military despotism. The prisoners, he said, were subject to brutal and inhuman treatment. Loughery's *ex parte* statement of the facts created a momentary ripple but no reversal of policy. In reality the prisoners were treated quite adequately and were confined in two buildings enclosed by a stockade. Buell released a few of them on bond, but refused to do so in most cases for the obvious reason that they would have followed their brothers in flight. Although they seem to have been denied visitors at first, this rule was lifted and friends regularly brought them extra food and delicacies. The number of visitors had to be limited, however, because most of the white community regarded them as martyrs and crowded to the prison to show their support.

After many delays the members of the military commission arrived in May and the trial got under way; it continued into September. Although it proved somewhat more effective than the civil courts in punishing Ku Klux criminals, this tribunal was a far cry from the military despotism depicted by its hysterical opponents. The defense counsel presented their case fully and freely. Before long it was obvious that they would produce witnesses to swear alibis for most or all of the defendants. Given a general public conspiracy of this magnitude, and the oaths of KRS members to protect each other, this was easy to do; and given the dependence of the prosecution by contrast on Negro witnesses whose credibility white men (including Army officers) were accustomed to discounting, the tactic was all too effective. The results were mixed. At least fourteen persons arrested at one time or another

never went to trial, either for lack of evidence or because they turned state's evidence. Seventeen others were tried and acquitted, apparently in most cases because of sworn statements by friends that they were not present at the time of the lynching. Only six were convicted. Three of these were sentenced to life terms, and three to a term of four years each in the Huntsville penitentiary. General Reynolds refused to accept the acquittal of Colonel Crump and three others, but they were released from custody anyway, and the matter was not raised again. Witnesses who had risked their lives by testifying against the terrorists were given help in leaving the state, while most of the defendants returned to their homes and occupations. The arrests and trials did bring peace to Jefferson, however. The Knights of the Rising Sun rode no more, and the new freedom for Radicals was symbolized in August by the appearance of a Republican newspaper.

Relative tranquillity came to northeast Texas generally during the early part of 1869. Some Republicans attributed this to the election of General Grant, but that event brought no such result to other parts of the South. Both Ben Bickerstaff and Cullen Baker were killed and their gangs dispersed, which certainly helped. The example of military action in Jefferson likely played a part; it was accompanied by an increase of military activity throughout the region as troops were shifted here from the frontier and other portions of the state. Immediately after the Smith lynching in October, General Reynolds ordered all civil and military officials to "arrest, on the spot any person wearing a mask or otherwise disguised." Arrests did increase, but it was probably owing less to this order than to the more efficient concentration of troops. In December the Bureau agent in Jefferson had cavalry (for a change) to send out after men accused of Ku Klux outrages in Upshur County. Between October 1868 and September 1869 fifty-nine cases were tried before military commissions in Texas, chiefly involving murder or aggravated assault; they resulted in twenty-nine convictions. This record was almost breathtaking by comparison with that of the civil courts.

The Texas crime rate remained high after 1868. Organized Ku Klux activity declined markedly, but it continued in sporadic fashion around the state for several years. A new state government was elected in November 1869 and organized early the next year under Republican Governor E. J. Davis. In his first annual message, in April 1870, Davis called attention to the depredations of disguised bands. To cope with them he asked the legislature to create both a state police and a militia, and to invest him with the power of martial law. In June and July the legislature responded affirmatively on each count. The state police consisted of a mounted force of fewer than 200 men under the state adjutant general; in addition, all county sheriffs and their deputies and all local marshals and constables were considered to be part of the state police and subject to its orders. In November 1871 a law against armed and disguised persons followed. Between July 1870 and December 1871 the state police arrested 4,580 persons, 829 of them for murder or attempted murder. Hundreds of other criminals probably fled the state to evade arrest. This activity, coupled with occasional use of the governor's martial law powers in troubled localities, seems to have diminished lawlessness by early 1872. There still remained the usual problems of prosecuting or convicting Ku Klux offenders, however, and very few seem to have been punished legally.

■■■

STUDY QUESTIONS

1. Why was Klan terrorism so rampant in Texas? Did the federal government possess the means of preventing it?

2. What was the relationship between the Ku Klux Klan in Texas and the Democratic party?

3. How did well-to-do white planters respond to the Ku Klux Klan?

4. What were the objectives of the Ku Klux Klan in Texas?

5. Who were the White Conservatives? How did they interpret Klan activities?

6. Why did the state government try to curtail Klan activities in the early 1870s? Did state officials succeed?

BIBLIOGRAPHY

The standard work on Reconstruction, one which created two generations of stereotypes by vindicating the South and indicting the North, is William A. Dunning, *Reconstruction, Political and Economic* (1907). The first major dissent from Dunning was W. E. B. DuBois's classic work *Black Reconstruction* (1935). It was not until the social changes of the 1960s, triggered by the civil rights movement, that historians took a new look at Reconstruction. John Hope Franklin's *Reconstruction After the Civil War* (1961) first questioned the Dunning view, arguing that northern intentions toward the South were humanitarian as well as political. Kenneth Stampp's *The Era of Reconstruction* (1965) carried that argument further, restoring the reputation of "carpetbaggers" and "scalawags," describing the successes of black politicians, and criticizing the Ku Klux Klan. Also see Allen Trelease, *White Terror* (1967); Sarah Wiggins, *The Scalawag in Alabama Politics, 1865–1881* (1977); L. N. Powell, *New Masters: Northern Planters During the Civil War and Reconstruction* (1980); and Paul D. Escott, *Many Excellent People* (1985).

For studies of Andrew Johnson, see Howard K. Beale, *The Critical Year: A Study of Andrew Johnson and Reconstruction* (1930), which takes the traditional point of view. A very critical view is Eric McKitrick, *Andrew Johnson and Reconstruction* (1960). Also see Michael Benedict, *The Impeachment of Andrew Johnson* (1973).

DAY OF THE LONGHORNS

Dee Brown

The Texas Longhorn looked slightly unbalanced, as if it were about to fall over. Its body often appeared thin, and its horns stretched out like the curved balancing rod of a high-wire performer. And its face—only another Longhorn or a Texan could love it. Nevertheless, this rugged breed of steer was the focus of the long drives during the dusty, golden age of cowboys.

Ironically, this era of the cowboy was made possible by the westward push of railroad builders. After the Civil War, a three- or four-dollar Texas Longhorn could be sold in the upper Mississippi region for forty dollars. If Texas entrepreneurs could drive the steers to the railheads, they could earn a $100,000 profit from 3,000 head of cattle. And so the drive was on, first to Sedalia, Missouri, and later, as railways extended west, to the Kansas cow towns of Newton, Abilene, Ellsworth, and Dodge City. During the late 1860s and 1870s, a total of over four million cattle survived the heat, dust, Indian attacks, and other problems and reached the Kansas railroads. Dee Brown describes the difficult journey and the Longhorns, and the cowboys who drove them to the railheads.

When Coronado marched northward from Mexico in 1540, searching for the mythical golden cities of Cibola, he brought with his expedition a number of Spanish cattle. These were the first of the breed to enter what is now the United States. Over the next century other Spanish explorers and missionaries followed, most of them bringing at least "a bull and a cow, a stallion and a mare." From these seed stocks, Longhorns and mustangs and cowboys and ranching slowly developed in the Southwest, the Spanish cattle mutating and evolving, the vaquero perfecting his costume and the tools of his trade.

The Longhorns, which also came to be known as Texas cattle, took their name from their wide-spreading horns which sometimes measured up to eight feet across, and there are legends of horn spreads even more extensive. From their mixed ancestry of blacks, browns, reds, duns, slates, and brindles the Longhorns were varicolored, the shadings and combinations of hues so differentiated that, as J. Frank Dobie pointed out, no two of these animals were ever alike in appearance. "For all his heroic stature," said Dobie, "the Texas steer stood with his body tucked up in the flanks, his high shoulder-top sometimes thin enough to split a hailstone, his ribs flat, his length frequently so extended that his back swayed."

Ungraceful though they were, the Longhorns showed more intelligence than domesticated cattle. They were curious, suspicious, fierce, and resourceful. After all, by the mid-19th century they were the survivors of several generations which had lived under wild or semiwild conditions. They possessed unusually keen senses of smell, sight, and hearing; their voices were powerful and penetrating; they could survive extreme heat or cold; they could exist on the sparest of vegetation and water; they could outwalk any other breed of cattle. It was this last attribute that brought the Texas Longhorns out of their native habitat and onto the pages of history to create the romantic era of the cowboys, the long drives, and riproaring trail towns of the Great Plains.

The drives began even before Texas became a state. A few enterprising adventurers occasionally would round up a herd out of the brush and drive them overland to Galveston or Shreveport where the animals were sold mainly for their hides and tallow. After the California gold rush of 1849 created a demand for meat, a few daring young Texans drove herds all the way to the Pacific coast. W.H. Snyder put together an outfit that moved out of Texas into New Mexico, and then crossed Colorado, Wyoming, Utah, and Nevada. After two years Snyder finally got his Longhorns to the miners. Captain Jack Cureton of the Texas Rangers followed a southern route across New Mexico and Arizona, dodging Apaches all the way, but from the meat-hungry goldseekers Cureton took a profit of $20,000, a considerable fortune in those days.

In the early 1850s a young English emigrant named Tom Candy Ponting probably established the record for the longest trail drive of Longhorns. Ponting was engaged in the livestock business in Illinois when he learned of the easy availability of Longhorns in Texas. Late in 1852 he and his partner traveled there on horseback, carrying a small bag of gold coins. They had no trouble assembling a herd of 700 bawling Longhorns at nine dollars or less a head. Early in 1853 they headed north for Illinois. It was a rainy spring and Ponting and his partner had to hire Cherokees to help swim the cattle across the Arkansas River. "I sat on my horse every night while we were crossing through the Indian country," said Ponting. "I was so afraid I could not sleep in the tent, but we had no stampede." Missouri was still thinly settled, and there was plenty of vegetation to

Dee Brown, "Day of the Longhorns." From *American History Illustrated* 9 (January 1975), pp. 4–9, 42–48. Reprinted through the courtesy of Cowles Magazines, publisher of *American History Illustrated*.

keep the Longhorns from losing weight. At St. Louis the animals were ferried across the Mississippi, and on July 26, Ponting and his cattle reached Christian County, Illinois.

There through the winter months he fed them on corn, which cost him fifteen cents a bushel. He sold off a few scrubs to traveling cattle buyers, and then in the spring he cut out the best of the herd and started trail driving again, this time toward the East. At Muncie, Ponting found that railroad cars were available for livestock transport to New York. "We made arrangements and put the cattle on the cars. We unloaded them at Cleveland, letting them jump out on the sand banks. We unloaded them next to Dunkirk, then at Harnesville, and then at Bergen Hill." On July 3, 1854, from Bergen Hill in New Jersey, Ponting ferried the much-traveled Longhorns across the Hudson to the New York cattle market, completing a two-year journey of 1,500 miles on foot and 600 miles by rail. They were the first Texas Longhorns to reach New York City.

"The cattle are rather long-legged though finehorned, with long taper horns, and something of a wild look," reported the New York *Tribune*. "The expense from Texas to Illinois was about two dollars a head, the owners camping all the way. From Illinois to New York, the expense was seventeen dollars a head." To the New York buyers the Longhorns were worth eighty dollars a head. Tom Ponting had more than doubled his investment.

About this same time another young adventurer from Illinois, Charles Goodnight, was trying to build up his own herd of Longhorns in the Brazos River country. As a young boy Goodnight had journeyed to Texas with his family, riding much of the way bareback. When he was 21, he and his stepbrother went to work for a rancher, keeping watch over 400 skittish Longhorns and branding the calves. Their pay for this work was one-fourth of the calves born during the year. "As the end of the first year's branding resulted in only thirty-two calves for our share," Goodnight recalled after-

ward, "and as the value was about three dollars per head, we figured out that we had made between us, not counting expenses, ninety-six dollars."

Goodnight and his partner persevered, however, and after four years of hard work they owned a herd of 4,000. Before they could convert many of their animals into cash, however, the Civil War began. Goodnight soon found himself scouting for a company of Confederate mounted riflemen and spent most of the war disputing control of the upper Brazos and Red River country with Comanches and Kiowas instead of with blue-coated Yankees. At the war's end his makeshift uniform was worn out, his Confederate money was worthless, and his Longhorn herd had virtually disappeared. "I suffered great loss," Goodnight said. "The Confederate authorities had taken many of my cattle without paying a cent. Indians had raided our herds and cattle thieves were branding them, to their own benefit without regard to our rights." He was 30 years old and financially destitute.

Almost every other Texan returning from the war found himself in the same situation. When rumors reached the cattle country early in the spring of 1866 that meat was in short supply in the North, hundreds of young Texans began rounding up Longhorns. Huge packing houses were being constructed in Northern cities, and on a 345-acre tract where nine railroads converged, the Chicago Union Stock Yards was opened for business. A Longhorn steer worth five dollars in useless Confederate money in Texas would bring forty dollars in good U.S. currency in the Chicago market.

From the brush country, the plains, and the coastal regions of Texas, mounted drivers turned herd after herd of cattle northward across Indian Territory. Their goal was the nearest railhead, Sedalia, in west-central Missouri. Following approximately the route used by Tom Ponting thirteen years earlier, the trail drivers forded Red River and moved on to

Fort Gibson, where they had to cross the more formidable Arkansas. Plagued by unseasonable cold weather, stampedes, and flooded streams, they pushed their Longhorns on into southeastern Kansas.

Here they encountered real trouble. From Baxter Springs northward to Sedalia railhead, the country was being settled by small farmers, many of them recent battlefield enemies of the Texans. The settlers did not want their fences wrecked and their crops trampled, and they used force in stopping the Texans from driving cattle across their properties. By summer's end, over 100,000 stalled cattle were strung out between Baxter Springs and Sedalia. The grass died or was burned off by defiant farmers. Dishonest cattle buyers from the North bought herds with bad checks. The unsold cattle died or were abandoned, and the great drives of 1866 came to an end. For many of the Texans it had been a financial bust.

A less optimistic folk might have gone home defeated, but not the cattlemen of Texas. By the spring of 1867 many were ready to drive Longhorns north again. And in that year, thanks to an enterprising Yankee stockman, a convenient shipping point was waiting to welcome their coming. At the end of the Civil War, Joseph McCoy of Springfield, Illinois, had started a business of buying livestock for resale to the new packinghouses in Chicago. Appalled by the Baxter Springs–Sedalia debacle of 1866, McCoy was determined to find a railroad shipping point somewhere at the end of an open trail from Texas. He studied the maps of new railroads being built westward and chose a town in Kansas—Abilene, near the end of the Kansas Pacific Railroad.

"Abilene in 1867 was a very small, dead place," McCoy admitted. But it met all the requirements for a cattle-shipping town. It was west of the settled farming country; it had a railroad, a river full of water for thirsty steers, and a sea of grass for miles around for holding and fattening livestock at the end of the drives. And nearby was Fort Riley, offering protection from possible Indian raids.

Within sixty days McCoy managed to construct a shipping yard, a barn, an office, and a hotel. From the Kansas Pacific he wheedled railroad ties to build loading pens sturdy enough to hold wild Longhorns. Meanwhile, he had sent messengers southward to inform the cattlemen of Texas that Abilene was "a good safe place to drive to, where they could sell, or ship cattle unmolested to other markets."

Over what soon became known as the Chisholm Trail, thousands of Texas cattle began moving into Abilene. Although the 1867 season got off to a late start and rail shipments did not begin until September, 36,000 Longhorns were marketed that first year. In 1868 the number doubled, and in 1870 the Kansas Pacific could scarcely find enough cars to handle the 300,000 Longhorns sold to Northern packing houses. Abilene in the meantime had grown into a boom town of stores, hotels, saloons, and honkytonks where Texas cowboys celebrated the end of their trail drive and engendered the legends of gunmen, lawmen, shootouts, and exotic dance hall girls.

One Texas cowman who did not make the long drive north to Abilene was Charles Goodnight. Back in the spring of 1866 when most of his neighbors were driving herds across Indian Territory for the Sedalia railhead, Goodnight was still trying to round up his scattered Longhorns. By the time he was ready to move out, he suspected that there was going to be a glut of cattle in Kansas and Missouri. Instead of heading north, he combined his Longhorns with those of Oliver Loving and they started their herd of 2,000 west toward New Mexico. Cattle were reported to be in great demand there by government agents who bought them for distribution to reservation Indians.

To reach New Mexico, Goodnight and Loving followed the abandoned route of the Butterfield Overland Stage along which waterholes and wells had been dug by the stage company. For this arduous journey, Goodnight constructed what was probably the first chuckwagon. Obtaining an old military wagon, he rebuilt it with the toughest wood he knew, a wood used by Indians for fashioning their bows—Osage orange or *bois d'arc*. At the rear he built a chuckbox with a hinged lid to which a folding leg was attached so that when it was lowered it formed a cook's work table. Fastened securely in front of the wagon was a convenient spigot running through to a barrel of water. Beneath the driver's seat was a supply of necessary tools such as axes and spades, and below the wagon was a cowhide sling for transporting dry wood or buffalo chips to be used in making cooking fires. A generation of trail drivers would adopt Goodnight's chuckwagon for long drives and roundups, and variations of it are still used today.

Goodnight's and Loving's first drive to New Mexico was uneventful until they began crossing the lower edge of the Staked Plains, where the water holes had gone dry. For three days the rangy Longhorns became almost unmanageable from thirst, and when they scented the waters of the Pecos they stampeded, piling into the river, some drowning under the onrush of those in the rear. The partners succeeded, however, in driving most of the herd into Fort Sumner, where several thousand Navajos confined in the Bosque Redondo were near starvation.

A government contractor took more than half the Longhorns, paying Goodnight and Loving $12,000 in gold. By the standards of the day they had suddenly become prosperous. While Loving drove the remainder of the cattle to the Colorado mining country, Goodnight returned to Texas to round up another herd of Longhorns.

In the years immediately following the disruptions of the Civil War, thousands of unbranded Longhorns roamed wild in the Texas brush country. The cowboys soon discovered that the easiest way to round up these cattle was to lure them out of the chaparral with tame decoys. James H. Cook, an early trail driver who later became a leading cattleman of the West, described such a wild Longhorn roundup:

"About sunrise we left the corral, taking with us the decoy herd, Longworth leading the way. After traveling a mile or more he led the herd into a dense clump of brush and motioned us to stop driving it. Then, telling two men to stay with the cattle he rode off, signaling the other men and myself to follow him . . . in the brush ahead I caught a glimpse of some cattle. A few minutes later I heard voices singing a peculiar melody without words. The sounds of these voices indicated that the singers were scattered in the form of a circle about the cattle. In a few moments some of the cattle came toward me, and I recognized a few of them as belonging to the herd which we had brought from our camp. In a few seconds more I saw that we had some wild ones, too. They whirled back when they saw me, only to find a rider wherever they might turn. The decoy cattle were fairly quiet, simply milling around through the thicket, and the wild ones were soon thoroughly mingled with them." Cook and the other cowboys now had little difficulty driving the combined tame and wild Longhorns into a corral where they were held until time to start an overland drive to market.

The work of rounding up Longhorns gradually developed into an organized routine directed by a man who came to be known as the range boss. During a roundup, his authority was as ironclad as that of a ship's captain. At the beginning of a "gather" the range boss would assemble an outfit of about twenty cowhands, a horse wrangler to look after the mounts and, most important of all, a camp cook. Roundups began very early in the spring because every cattleman was eager to be the first to hit the trail before the grass overgrazed along the route to Kansas.

On the first morning of a roundup the men would be up before sunrise to eat their breakfasts hurriedly at the chuckwagon; then in the

■ ■ *Texas Longhorns are herded across a stream during an 1867 cattle drive. Between 1867 and 1887, a total of 5.5 million head of Texas Longhorns were trailed north.*

gray light of dawn they would mount their best ponies and gather around the range boss for orders. As soon as he had outlined the limits of the day's roundup, the boss would send his cowhands riding out in various directions to sweep the range. When each rider reached a specified point, he turned back and herded all the cattle within his area back into the camp center.

After a herd was collected, the second operation of a roundup began. This next step was to separate the young stock which were to be branded for return to the range from the mature animals which were to be driven overland to market. "Cutting out" it was fittingly called, and this performance was, and still is, the highest art of the cowboy. Cutting out required a specially trained pony, one that

could "turn on a dime," and a rider who had a sharp eye, good muscular reflexes, and who was an artist at handling a lariat. After selecting an animal to be separated from the herd, the rider and his horse would begin a quick-moving game of twisting and turning, of sudden stops and changes of pace.

Roping, the final act of the cutting out process, also required close cooperation between pony and rider. Forming an oval-shaped noose six or seven feet in diameter, the cowboy would spin it over his head with tremendous speed. A second before making the throw, he would draw his arm and shoulder back, then shoot his hand forward, aiming the noose sometimes for the animal's head, sometimes for its feet. As the lariat jerked tight, the rider instantly snubbed it around his saddle horn. At the same moment the pony had to be stopped short. The position of the pony at the moment of throw was important; a sudden jerk of a taut lariat could spill both horse and rider.

As soon as the unbranded animal was roped, it was immediately herded or dragged to the nearest bonfire where branding irons were kept heated to an orange red. In Texas, all branding was done in a corral, a legal requirement devised to prevent hasty and illegal branding by rustlers on the open range. The first brands in Texas were usually the initials of the owners, and if two cattlemen had the same initials, a bar or a circle distinguished one from the other. Law required that brands be publicly registered by counties in Texas; other Western states had state brand books. In the early years when ranches were unfenced and land boundaries poorly marked, friction over unbranded cattle caused many a gunfight. To discourage rustlers who could easily change a "C" to an "O," an "F" to an "E," a "V" to a "W," ranchers designed unusual brands, some of the more famous being the Stirrup, Andiron, Scissors, Frying Pan, and Dinner Bell.

As soon as the work of branding was completed, preparations for the trail drive began in earnest. The owner of the cattle was responsible for food and other supplies, but each cowboy assembled the personal gear he would need on the journey. Every item he wore or carried was designed for utility. Tents were seldom taken along, two blankets being considered sufficient shelter from the elements. If the weather was warm, the cowboys shed their coats, and if they wore vests they rarely buttoned them because of the rangeland belief that to do so would bring on a bad cold. Most wore leather chaps to protect their legs from underbrush and weather. They put high heels on their boots to keep their feet from slipping through the stirrups, and they wore heavy leather gloves because the toughest palms could be burned raw by the lariats they used constantly in their work. They paid good

money for wide-brimmed hats because they served as roofs against rain, snow, and sun. They used bandannas for ear coverings, as dust masks, as strainers when drinking muddy water, for drying dishes, as bandages, towels, slings for broken arms, to tie hats on in very windy weather, and for countless other purposes.

Getting the average trail herd of about 3,000 cattle underway was as complicated an operation as starting a small army on a march across country. Each rider needed several spare mounts for the long journey, and this herd of horses accompanying a cow column was known as the remuda—from a Spanish word meaning replacement. A trail boss, sixteen to eighteen cowboys, a cook and chuckwagon, and a horse wrangler for the remuda made up the personnel of an average drive.

It was necessary to move slowly at first until the restive Longhorns grew accustomed to daily routines. To keep a herd in order a wise trail boss would search out a huge dominating animal and make it the lead steer. Charles Goodnight had one called Old Blue which he considered so valuable as a leader that after every long drive he brought the animal back to the home ranch. Two or three quiet days on the trail was usually long enough to calm a herd of Longhorns. After that the cattle would fall into place each morning like infantrymen on the march, each one keeping the same relative position in file as the herd moved along.

Cattleman John Clay left a classic description of an early trail herd in motion: "You see a steer's head and horns silhouetted against the skyline, and then another and another, till you realize it is a herd. On each flank is a horseman. Along come the leaders with a swinging gait, quickening as they smell the waters of the muddy river." The pattern of trail driving soon became as routinized as that of roundups—the trail boss a mile or two out in front, horse herd and chuckwagon following, then the point riders directing the lead steers, and strung along the widening flow of the herd the swing and

■ ■ *In 1878, Dodge City was the "king of the trail towns." Longhorns and cattlemen made the city what it was, but their day of glory ended during Dodge's long reign.*

flank riders, until at the rear came the drag riders in clouds of dust, keeping the weaker cattle moving.

Not many trail drivers had time to keep diaries, that of George Duffield being one of the rare survivors. From it a reader can feel the tensions and weariness, the constant threats of weather, the difficult river crossings, and dangers of stampedes.

MAY 1: Big stampede. Lost 200 head of Cattle.
MAY 2: Spent the day hunting & found but 25 Head. It has been Raining for three days. These are dark days for me.
MAY 3: Day spent in hunting Cattle. Found 23. Hard rain and wind. Lots of trouble.
MAY 8: Rain pouring down in torrents. Ran my horse into a ditch & got my Knee badly sprained—15 miles.
MAY 9: Still dark and gloomy. River up. Everything looks Blue to me.
MAY 14: Swam our cattle & Horses & built Raft & Rafted our provisions & blanket & covers. Lost Most of our Kitchen furniture such as camp Kittles Coffee Pots Cups Plates Canteens &tc &tc.
MAY 17: No Breakfast. Pack & off is the order.
MAY 31: Swimming Cattle is the order. We worked all day in the River & at dusk got the last Beefe over—I am now out of Texas—This day will long be remembered by me—There was one of our party Drowned today.

George Duffield made his drive along the eastern edge of Indian Territory in 1866. Ten years later the drives were still as wearisome and dangerous, but the trails had shifted much farther westward and there had been a swift succession of trail towns. A new railroad, the Sante Fe, pushed sixty-five miles south of Abilene in 1871, and Newton became the main cattle-shipping town. Newton's reign was brief, however; it was replaced by Ellsworth and Wichita. Although the advancing railroad tracks were a boon to cattlemen seeking shorter routes to markets, they also brought settlers west by the thousands. By 1876 the life of the Chisholm Tail was ending and the Western Trail, or Dodge City Trail, had taken its place.

Dodge City was the king of the trail towns, the "cowboy capital," a fabulous town of innumerable legends for a golden decade. The names survive in history: Long Branch Saloon, the Lady Gay, the Dodge Opera House, Delmonico's, Wyatt Earp, Doc Holliday, Boot Hill, Bat Masterson, Clay Allison, Luke Short, and Big Nose Kate. But it was Longhorns and cattlemen that made Dodge City, and it was during Dodge's long reign that the Longhorns came to the end of their day of glory.

One of the men responsible for the change was Charles Goodnight. In the year that Dodge opened as a cow town, 1875, Goodnight found himself financially destitute for the second time in his life. He had made a fortune with Texas cattle, bought a ranch in Colorado, become a banker, and then lost everything in the Panic of 1873. All he had left in 1875 was a small herd of unmarketable Longhorns, and he decided it was time to return to Texas and start all over again.

He chose an unlikely region, the Texas Panhandle, and area long shunned by cattlemen because it was supposed to be a desert. Goodnight, however, recalled the immense herds of buffalo which had roamed there for centuries, and he reasoned that wherever buffalo could thrive so could Longhorns. He found a partner, John Adair, to furnish the capital and drove his Longhorns into the heart of the Panhandle, to the Palo Duro Canyon, where he discovered plenty of water and grass. There he founded the JA Ranch. Soon after starting operations, Goodnight began introducing Herefords and shorthorns, cross-breeding them at first with Longhorns so that his cattle produced more and better beef, yet retained the ability to flourish on the open range and endure long drives to Dodge City.

Other ranchers soon followed his example, and "White Faces" instead of "Longhorns" gradually became the symbol of trail cattle. After a continuing flood of homesteaders, brought west by the proliferating railroads, made it necessary to close the trail to Dodge City, one more overland route—the National Trail to Wyoming and Montana—saw the last treks of the Longhorns.

As the 19th century came to an end, so did open range ranching and trail driving. There was no longer any place for rangy Longhorns. Until the day he died, however, Charles Goodnight kept a small herd of them to remind him of the old days. A few specimens survive today in wildlife refuges and on larger ranches as curiosities, or for occasional use in parades and Western movies. But most of these animals are descendants of crossbreds. The day of the genuine Texas Longhorn—with his body tucked up in the flanks, his high shoulder-top thin enough to split a hail stone, his ribs flat, his back swayed, his ability to outwalk any other breed of cattle—now belongs to history.

■■■

STUDY QUESTIONS

1. What were the origins of the Texas Longhorns? Why were they so well suited for the long drive?

2. How did the Civil War affect the cattle business?

3. Why did Joseph McCoy choose to drive cattle to Abilene?

4. What was life like on the long drive?

5. Why did the drive end?

BIBLIOGRAPHY

Ray Allen Billington's *The Far Western Frontier* (1963) and *Westward Expansion* (1974) are excellent introductions to the westward movement. Ernest S. Osgood, *The Day of the Cattlemen* (1929) is a classic work on the subject, and Lewis Atherton, *The Cattle Kings* (1961) is a more recent study. Gene M. Gressley, *Bankers and Cattlemen* (1966) deals with Eastern as well as Western interests. Wayne Gard, *The Chisholm Trail* (1954) is an outstanding study of the Long Drive, and J. Frank Dobie *The Longhorns* (1941) tells the story delightfully well. Robert R. Dykstra, *The Cattle Town* (1968) and Joe B. Frantz and J. E. Choate, *The American Cowboy* (1981) remove the myths that surround their subjects.

Part Two

THE GILDED AGE

Change dominated the American scene during the last quarter of the nineteenth century. Noted throughout most of the century for its agricultural output, America suddenly became an industrial giant, and by the 1900 it lead the world in industrial production. Unfettered by governmental codes and regulations, industrialists created sprawling empires. In 1872, Scottish immigrant Andrew Carnegie built his first steel mill, and his holdings steadily expanded until, almost thirty years later, he sold his steel empire to J. Pierpont Morgan for close to a half-billion dollars. In oil, meat packing, and other industries, the pattern was the same—a handful of ruthless, efficient, and farsighted men dominated and directed America's industrial growth.

Just as important as the ambitious industrialists were the millions of men and women who provided the muscle that built the industries and ran the machines. Some came from the country's farmlands, victims of dropping agricultural prices or the loneliness and boredom of farm life. Others were immigrants who came to the United States to escape poverty and political oppression. Crowded into booming cities, the workers— native and immigrant alike—labored long and hard for meager rewards.

The changes wrought by industrial growth and urban expansion created an atmosphere characterized by excitement and confusion. Some people, like Andrew Carnegie and John D. Rockefeller, moved from relatively humble origins to fabulous wealth and impressive social standing. Each symbolized the possibility of rising from

rags to riches. New opportunities created new wealth, and the important older American families were forced to make room for the new. As a result, wealthy Americans went to extraordinary lengths to display their status. J. P. Morgan bought yachts and works of art, while still other industrialists built mansions along the rocky shore of Newport, Rhode Island. Both the boats and houses marked the owners as men who had "arrived." The clubs, restaurants, and resorts of the late nineteenth century were part of the attempt to define the new American aristocracy.

Other people suffered during this time of change. For example, the social and economic positions of farmers declined during the late nineteenth century. Once considered the "salt of the earth" and "the backbone of America," they were viewed now as ignorant rubes and country bumpkins. Outmatched by unpredictable weather, expanding railroads, and declining prices produced by overexpansion, they consistently tried to overcome their problems by working harder, organizing cooperatives, and forming political parties. They labored heroically, but most of their efforts and organizations ended in failure.

Minority and ethnic Americans similarly faced difficult battles. Most of them were locked out of the opportunities available to educated white male Americans. Nor could women easily improve their social and economic positions. They experienced the excitement of the period from a distance, but the pain and frustration they knew firsthand.

AMERICAN ASSASSIN:
CHARLES J. GUITEAU

James W. Clarke

Abraham Lincoln, James Garfield, William McKinley, Huey Long, John Kennedy, Robert Kennedy, Martin Luther King, Jr.—our history has been too often altered by an assassin's bullet. Some of America's political assassins were clearly insane, others were motivated by political beliefs or dark personal desires. Normally it is difficult to determine where political partisanship ends and insanity begins. In "American Assassin," James W. Clarke recounts the case of Charles J. Guiteau, a tireless self-promoter who shot President James A. Garfield on July 2, 1881. Guiteau was certainly unusual; part con man, part religious fanatic, he believed he was destined for some sort of greatness. But was he insane? And if so, was his insanity a legal defense for his actions? These and other questions had to be answered by the jurors who sat in judgment of Guiteau. In an age before Sigmund Freud's work, when each person was assumed to be responsible for his actions, these questions were difficult, if not impossible, to fully answer.

With the single exception of Richard Lawrence, there has been no American assassin more obviously deranged than Charles Guiteau. Unlike Lawrence [who attempted to assassinate Andrew Jackson], however, who could be described as a paranoid schizophrenic, Guiteau was not paranoid. Indeed, he possessed a rather benign view of the world until shortly before he was hanged. On the gallows, he did lash out at the injustice of his persecutors, but even then his anger was tempered by a sense of martyrdom, glories anticipated in the next world, and a dying man's belief that in the future a contrite nation would erect monuments in his honor.

That Lawrence was confined in mental hospitals for the remainder of his life and Guiteau hanged can be attributed primarily to two facts: Jackson survived; Garfield did not. For certainly the symptoms of severe mental disturbance in Guiteau's case, although of a different sort, were as striking as in Lawrence's. As we will see, the convenient label and implied motive—"disappointed office-seeker"—that has been attached to Guiteau by writers and historians confuses symptoms with causes.

Religion, Law, and Politics

Charles Julius Guiteau was born on September 8, 1841 in Freeport, Illinois. His mother, a quiet, frail woman, died seven years and two deceased infants later of complications stemming from a mind-altering "brain fever" she had initially contracted during her pregnancy with Charles. In addition to Charles, she was survived by her husband, Luther, an intensely religious man and Charles' older brother and sister, John and Frances.

James W. Clarke, *American Assassins: The Darker Side of Politics.* Copyright © 1982 by Princeton University Press. Excerpt, pp. 198–214, reprinted with permission of Princeton University Press.

From the beginning, people noticed that little Julius, as he was called (until he dropped the name in his late teens because "there was too much of the Negro about it"), was different. Luther Guiteau soon became exasperated with his inability to discipline his unruly and annoying youngest son and, as a result, Julius was largely raised by his older sister and her husband, George Scoville. Years later, in 1881, Scoville would be called to represent the accused assassin at his trial.

Although plagued by a speech impediment, for which he was whipped by his stern father, Guiteau was, in his fashion, a rather precocious youngster who learned to read quickly and write well. An annoying aversion to physical labor was observed early and remained with him the rest of his life. At the age of eighteen, Charles became interested in furthering his education and, against his father's will, used a small inheritance he had received from his grandfather to enter the University of Michigan.

His father, who was scornful of secular education, had urged his son to seek a scripture-based education at the utopian Oneida Community in New York. The curriculum there focused on study of the Bible. The elder Guiteau had hopes that his errant son might also acquire some self-discipline in a more authoritarian God-fearing environment.

After a couple of semesters at Ann Arbor, Charles, as he was now called, decided to heed his father's advice and transfer to Oneida where, in addition to religious instruction, he had recently learned that they practiced free love. With sex and the Lord on his mind, he enthusiastically entered the New York commune in June 1860. Like his father, Charles now believed that Oneida was the first stage in establishing the Kingdom of God on Earth.

Not long after his arrival, Charles came to believe that he had been divinely ordained to lead the community because, as he announced with a typical lack of humility, he alone possessed the ability. Since no one else had received this revelation, Charles soon found himself at odds with the community leadership. Moreover, the Oneida leaders believed that Charles' vigorously protested need of increasing periods for contemplative pursuits was merely evidence of the slothfulness his father had hoped they would correct.

Other tensions also began to build. Young Charles was becoming increasingly frustrated because the young women of the community were not responding to his amorous overtures. Convinced of his personal charm, this nervous, squirrel-like little man was annoyed because these objects of his intended affection were so unresponsive. Adding insult to injury they soon laughingly referred to him as Charles "Gitout."

As his position within the community continued to deteriorate, Charles became more isolated and alienated until, in April 1865, he left for New York City. He wrote to his father to explain his decision after arriving in Hoboken:

Dear Father:

I have left the community. The cause of my leaving was because I could not conscientiously and heartily accept their views on the labor question. They wanted to make a hard-working businessman of me, but I could not consent to that, and therefore deemed it expedient to quietly withdraw, which I did last Monday. . . .

I came to New York in obedience to what I believed to be the call of God for the purpose of pursuing an independent course of theological and historical investigation. With the Bible for my textbook and the Holy Ghost for my schoolmaster, I can pursue my studies without interference from human dictation. In the country [Oneida] my time was appropriated, but now it is at my own disposal, a very favorable change. I have procured a small room, well furnished, in Hoboken, opposite the city, and intend to fruitfully pursue my studies during the next three years.

Then he announced a new scheme:

And here it is proper to state that the energies of my life are now, and have been for months, pledged to God, to do all that within me lies to extend the sovereignty of Jesus Christ by placing at his disposal a powerful daily paper. I am persuaded that theocratic presses are destined, in due time, to supersede to a great extent pulpit oratory. There are hundreds of thousands of ministers in the world but not a single daily theocratic press. It appears to me that there is a splendid chance for some one to do a big thing for God, for humanity and for himself.

With a new suit of clothes, a few books, and a hundred dollars in his pocket, he planned to publish his own religious newspaper that would, he was convinced, spearhead a national spiritual awakening.

In another lengthy letter to his father, Charles continued to detail his plans for the "Theocratic Daily" that would "entirely discard all muddy theology, brain philosophy and religious cant, and seek to turn the heart of men toward the living God." Buoyed with an ill-founded sense of well-being and enthusiasm, Charles went on euphorically: "I claim that I am in the employ of Jesus Christ and Co., the very ablest and strongest firm in the universe, and that what I can do is limited only by their power and purpose." And knowing full well that *he* would edit the paper, he announced confidently:

Whoever edits such a paper as I intend to establish will doubtless occupy the position of Target General to the Press, Pulpit, and Bench of the civilized world; and if God intends me for that place, I fear not, for I know that He will be "a wall of fire round me," and keep me from all harm.

Confidently expecting to promote the Kingdom of God without the restrictions of the Oneida Community and, not incidentally, also enjoy wealth and fame in the process, Guiteau sought financial backing for the paper in New York City. In a flurry of optimistic salesmanship, he scurried about presenting his proposal to prospective subscribers and advertisers; they, as it turned out, were not impressed with this odd little entrepreneur and his religious views. Soon finding himself short of money, somewhat discouraged, and tiring of a diet of dried beef, crackers, and lemonade that he ate in his dingy Hoboken room, Charles returned to Oneida after only three months in the big city.

But his return only confirmed his original reservations about the place, and he soon left again—this time more embittered by his experiences there than ever before. Again without money, Charles wrote to the Community requesting a $9,000 reimbursement—$1,500 a year for the six years he had spent there. When the community refused to pay, Charles sued, threatening to make public the alleged sexual, as well as financial, exploitation employed by the Oneida leadership—especially its founder, John Humphrey Noyes.

Undoubtedly bitter about the rejection he had endured in this sexually permissive environment, Charles lashed out in an unintentionally amusing attack on both Noyes and the Oneida women. Charging that Noyes lusted after little girls, Guiteau angrily told a reporter: "All the girls that were born in the Community were forced to cohabit with Noyes at such an early period it dwarfed them. The result was that most of the Oneida women were small and thin and homely."

Obviously stung by such criticism, Noyes threatened to bring extortion charges against Guiteau. In a letter to Charles' father, who was mortified by his son's behavior, he advised that Charles had admitted to, among other sins, stealing money, frequenting brothels, and being treated for a venereal ailment. Noyes added that Charles also had apparently thrown in the towel, so to speak, in an uninspired battle with masturbation. Such appraisals confirmed his father's sad suspicion that Charles' real purpose in going to Oneida was "the free exercise of his unbridled lust." Charles' "most shameful and wicked attack" and subsequent episodes convinced Luther Guiteau that his prodigal son was "absolutely insane." In

despair, he wrote to his oldest son John that, unless something stopped him, Charles would become "a fit subject for the lunatic asylum."

Having thus incurred his father's anger and facing the prospects of a countersuit for extortion, Charles abandoned his legal claim and left New York for Chicago. There, given the standards of the day, he began to practice law, after a fashion. In 1869, he married a young woman he had met at the Y.M.C.A., a Miss Annie Bunn. After only one memorably incoherent attempt to argue a case, his practice of law was reduced to collecting delinquent bills for clients. By 1874, the law practice and marriage had both failed, the latter as a result of his adultery with a "high toned" prostitute and the occasional beatings he used to discipline his beleaguered wife.

When his marriage ended, Charles wandered back to New York. Continually borrowing small sums of money that he never repaid voluntarily, Guiteau soon found himself, as usual, in trouble with creditors. Resentful of such unseemly harassment, he wrote an indignant letter to his brother John addressing him as "Dear Sir." This and other letters reveal the unfounded arrogance and unintentional humor of a man with only the most tenuous grasp of the reality of his position:

Your letter from Eaton . . . dated Nov. 8, '72, received. I got the $75 on my supposed responsibility as a Chicago lawyer. I was introduced to Eaton by a gentleman I met at the Young Men's Christian Association, and it was only incidentally that your name was mentioned.

I wrote to Eaton several times while at Chicago, and he ought to have been satisfied, but he had the impertinence to write you and charge me with fraud, when he knew he let me have the money entirely upon my own name and position. Had he acted like a "white" man, I should have tried to pay it long ago. I hope you will drop him.

> *Yours truly,*
> *CHARLES J. GUITEAU.*

A few days after this letter was written,

Charles' exasperated brother himself became the target of an angry response when he requested a repayment of a small loan:

J.W. GUITEAU: NEW YORK, March 13th, 1873

Find $7 enclosed. Stick it up your bung-hole and wipe your nose on it, and that will remind you of the estimation in which you are held by

CHARLES J. GUITEAU

Sign and return the enclosed receipt and I will send you $7, but not before, and that, I hope, will end our acquaintance.

Disdainful of the pettiness of such small lenders, Charles confidently launched another major venture in the publishing business: he wanted to purchase the Chicago *Inter-Ocean* newspaper. But businessmen and bankers, from whom he sought financial backing, were unimpressed and not a little skeptical about this seedy little man with a confidential manner. Frustrated but ever the undaunted optimist, Charles turned again to religion.

Impressed with the bountiful collection plates at the Chicago revival meetings of Dwight Moody where he served as an usher in the evening services, Charles decided to prepare himself for the ministry. After a short period of voracious reading in Chicago libraries, he soon had himself convinced that he alone had ascertained the "truth" on a number of pressing theological questions. With familiar enthusiasm, he launched his new career with pamphlets and newspaper advertisements. Adorned with sandwich board posters, Charles walked the streets inviting all who would listen to attend his sermons on the physical existence of hell, the Second-Coming, and so forth. The self-promotion campaign was repeated in one town after another as he roamed between Milwaukee, Chicago, New York, and Boston.

In handbills, Charles proclaimed himself "the Eloquent Chicago Lawyer." His performances, in fact, followed a quite different pattern: a bombastic introduction that soon deteriorated into a series of incoherent nonsequiturs,

whereupon he would end inconclusively and abruptly dash from the building amid the jeers and laughter of his audiences—the whole episode lasting perhaps ten to fifteen minutes. With his dubious reputation as an evangelist growing, Charles darted from one town to another leaving in his path a growing accumulation of indignant audiences and unpaid bills. Often arrested, he was periodically jailed for short periods between 1877 and 1880 when he again turned his attention to politics.

The Garfield Connection

Describing himself as a "lawyer, theologian, and politician," Guiteau threw himself into the Stalwart faction's fight for the 1880 Republican presidential nomination in New York. When a third term was denied the Stalwart's choice, Ulysses S. Grant, the nomination went to a darkhorse, James A. Garfield. Guiteau quickly jumped on the Garfield bandwagon. In New York, he began to hang around the party headquarters and, as he was to remind people later, he did work on the "canvass" for the candidate. In his view, his most noteworthy contribution to the campaign and Garfield's subsequent election, however, was an obscure speech he wrote (and may have delivered once in Troy, New York) entitled, "Garfield vs. Hancock." A few weeks before, the same speech had been entitled "Grant vs. Hancock." Undeterred by the change in candidates, the speech, Guiteau later claimed, originated and developed the issue that won the election for Garfield. That issue, in brief, was the claim that if the Democrats gained the presidency it would mean a resumption of the Civil War because the Democrats had only sectional, rather than national, loyalties. In a personal note, dated March 11, 1881, to the newly appointed secretary of state, James G. Blaine, Guiteau explained his claim:

I think I have a right to claim your help on the strength of this speech. It was sent to our leading editors and orators in August. It was the first shot in the rebel war claim idea, and it was their idea that elected Garfield. . . . I will talk with you about this as soon as I can get a chance. There is nothing against me. I claim to be a gentlemen and a Christian.

Indeed, from the moment the election results were in, Guiteau had begun to press his claims in letters to Garfield and Blaine. He also became a familiar figure at the Republican party headquarters in New York, confident that he would be rewarded for his efforts with a consulship appointment; the only question remaining, he believed, was the location. Would it be Paris, Vienna, or some other post of prominence? With this in mind, he moved from New York to Washington on March 5, 1881, where he began to badger not only the President's staff but Blaine and the President himself in the corridors of the White House. Striking a posture of gallingly unwarranted familiarity with those he encountered, he also let loose a barrage of "personal" notes written in the same annoying style. Typical is the following:

[Private]
GEN'L GARFIELD
From your looks yesterday I judge you did not quite understand what I meant by saying "I have not called for two or three weeks." I intended to express my sympathy for you on account of the pressure that has been on you since you came into office.

I think Mr. Blaine intends giving me the Paris consulship with your and Gen. Logan's approbation, and I am waiting for the break in the Senate.

I have practiced law in New York and Chicago, and presume I am well qualified for it.

I have been here since March 5, and expect to remain some little time, or until I get my commission.

Very respectfully,
CHARLES GUITEAU.

AP'L 8.

Shortly before he had written to the secretary of state to inquire whether President Hayes' appointments to foreign missions would expire in March 1881, as he expected. Learning that they would, Guiteau became more persistent in pressing his claims for an appointment to the missions of either Vienna, Paris, or possibly Liverpool. Earlier he had written again to Garfield, whom he had never met, to advise him of his plans to wed a wealthy and cultured woman (whose acquaintance, also, he had not at that time, or ever, made). Such unknowingly ludicrous acts were intended, in the bizarre judgment of Charles J. Guiteau, to enhance his already eminent qualifications for a foreign ministry.

In the meantime, the newspapers were filled with the controversy that had developed between the new President and the boss-dominated Stalwart faction of the Republican party over patronage appointments in New York. Finally, on May 13, 1881, the two most powerful of the Stalwart bosses, Roscoe Conkling and Tom "Me Too" Platt of New York, resigned their Senate seats in protest over the President's failure to follow their preferences in his patronage appointments. In so doing, they discounted the fact that Garfield had accepted their man, "Chet" Arthur, as his running mate and vice-president. Angrily condemning the beleaguered Garfield's disloyalty and traitorous tactics, the resignations triggered numerous editorial attacks and denunciations of the President and his mentor Blaine, which were to continue until July 2, 1881.

On the same day the resignations were announced, Guiteau once again approached Blaine with his by now familiar blandishments, only to have the exasperated secretary roar, "Never bother me again about the Paris consulship as long as you live!" But Guiteau persisted. A week later, he wrote again to the President:

[Private]
General GARFIELD:

I have been trying to be your friend; I don't know whether you appreciate it or not, but I am moved to call your attention to the remarkable letter from Mr. Blaine which I have just noticed.

According to Mr. Farwell, of Chicago, Blaine is "a vindictive politician" and "an evil genius," and you will "have no peace till you get rid of him."

This letter shows Mr. Blaine is a wicked man, and you ought to demand his immediate resignation; otherwise you and the Republican party will come to grief. I will see you in the morning, if I can, and talk with you.

Very respectfully,
CHARLES GUITEAU.
May 23.

If past behavior is any clue to the future, at this point Guiteau would have begun to consider yet another occupational change, returning again perhaps with his typical enthusiastic optimism to theology or law. Previously, Guiteau had accepted failure with remarkable equanimity, sustained always by the exalted opinion he had of himself. As one scheme after another collapsed—his leadership aspirations at Oneida, his journalistic ventures, the law practice, and the evangelistic crusade—his bitterness and disappointment were short-lived as he moved on to other careers. His confidence in his own ability and the Horatio Alger-like opportunities that abounded in nineteenth-century America remained unshaken. Even his angry exchanges with the Oneida establishment possessed the tone of someone who enjoyed the battle as well as the spoils; certainly these exchanges reflected none of the desperation of the all-time loser that he, in fact, was. In Guiteau's delusional world, these frustrations were merely temporary set backs in a career that was, he remained convinced, destined for wealth and fame.

Now, for the first time in his oddly chaotic life, Guiteau found himself sharing his outsider status with men he admired: Conkling and Platt and the other Stalwarts. And it was in this

■ ■ *Charles J. Guiteau, assassin of President James Garfield (1881). Much of the public viewed his insanity plea as a dodge, arguing that Guiteau's methodical planning and self-seeking motives could not be the product of a disturbed mind.*

realization—not the denial of the various appointments he had sought—that his assassination scheme germinated. Indeed, a month later, on June 16, he wrote in his "Address to the American People":

I conceived of the idea of removing the President four weeks ago. Not a soul knew of my purpose. I conceived the idea myself. I read the newspapers carefully, for and against the administration, and gradually the conviction settled on me that the President's removal was a political necessity, because he proved a traitor to the men who made him, and thereby imperiled the life of the Republic. At the late Presidential election, the Republican party carried every Northern State. Today, owing to the misconduct of the President and his Secretary of State, they could hardly carry ten Northern States. They certainly could not carry New York, and that is the pivotal State.

Ingratitude is the basest of crimes. That the President, under the manipulation of his Secretary of State, has been guilty of the basest ingratitude to the Stalwarts admits of no denial. . . . In the President's madness he has wrecked the once grand old Republican party; and for this he dies. . . .

I had no ill-will to the President.

This is not murder. It is a political necessity. It will make my friend Arthur President, and save the Republic. I have sacrificed only one. I shot the President as I would a rebel, if I saw him pulling down the American flag. I leave my justification to God and the American people.

I expect President Arthur and Senator Conkling will give the nation the finest administration it has ever had. They are honest and have plenty of brains and experience.

[signed] *Charles Guiteau* [Emphasis added.]

Later, on June 20, he added this even more bizarre postscript:

The President's nomination was an act of God. The President's election was an act of God. The President's removal is an act of God. I am clear in my purpose to remove the President. Two objects will be accomplished: It will unite the Republican party and save the Republic, and it will create a great demand for my book, "The Truth," This book was written to save souls and not for money, and the Lord wants to save souls by circulating the book.

Charles Guiteau

It is unlikely that Guiteau would have chosen the course of action he did without the sense that he was in good company—"a Stalwart of the Stalwarts," as he liked to describe himself. In his distorted mind, to "remove" the President, as he euphemistically described it, would provide the same status and recognition he had sought in a consulship appointment, and, more importantly, in every hare-brained scheme he had botched since the time he first entered the Oneida Community to establish the Kingdom of God on Earth. In this last grandly deluded plan, his aspirations in theology, law, and politics were to culminate in a divinely inspired and just act "to unite the Republican party and save the Republic" and, not incidentally, launch a new career for Charles Guiteau not only as a lawyer, theologian, and politician, but as a national hero with presidential aspirations.

With this in mind, on June 8, Guiteau borrowed fifteen dollars and purchased a silver-mounted English revolver. He planned to have it, along with his papers, displayed after the assassination at the Library of the State Department or the Army Medical Museum. To prepare for the big event, he began target practice on the banks of the Potomac. After stalking the President for several weeks and bypassing at least two opportunities to shoot him, Guiteau rose early on Saturday, July 2, 1881. He had rented a room a few days before at the Riggs House and, on this morning, began preparations to meet the President at the Baltimore and Potomac Railroad Station. The President was scheduled to leave that morning for a vacation trip. Downing a hearty breakfast, which he charged to his room, he pocketed the last of a series of bizarre explanations:

July 2, 1881

To the White House:

The President's tragic death was a sad necessity, but it will unite the Republican party and save the Republic. Life is a fleeting dream, and it matters little when one goes. A human life is of small value. During the war thousands of brave boys went down without a tear. I presume the President was a Christian, and that he will be happier in Paradise than here.

It will be no worse for Mrs. Garfield, dear soul, to part with her husband this way than by natural death. He is liable to go at any time anyway.

I had no ill-will towards the President. His death was a political necessity. I am a lawyer, a theologian, a politician. I am a Stalwart of the Stalwarts. I was with General Grant and the rest of our men in

*New York during the canvass. I have some papers
for the press, which I shall leave with Byron
Andrews and his co-journalists at 1440 N.Y. Ave.,
where all the reporters can see them.*

I am going to jail.

[signed] Charles Guiteau

Guiteau then walked to the banks of the
Potomac where after taking a few final practice
shots he proceeded to the railroad station to
await the President's arrival. Once at the station, he used the men's room, had his shoes
shined, and, after estimating that his assignment would be completed shortly before the
President's train was scheduled to leave, he
reserved a hackman for an anticipated 9:30
arrest and departure to the District Prison. He
had already checked the prison's security, lest
in the emotion of the moment he might be
attacked by crowds who had not had time to
realize what a great patriotic service he had
just rendered. He was convinced that after his
explanation was published the wisdom and
justice of his act would be appreciated. Until
such time, however, he had taken a further
precaution of drafting a letter requesting that
General Sherman see to his safekeeping in jail.
The letter, which fell from his pocket during
the scuffle that followed the shooting, read as
follows:

TO GENERAL SHERMAN:

*I have just shot the President. I shot him several
times, as I wished him to go as easily as possible.
His death was a political necessity. I am a lawyer,
theologian and politician. I am a Stalwart of the
Stalwarts. I was with General Grant and the rest of
our men in New York during the canvass. I am
going to jail. Please order out your troops and take
possession of the jail at once.*

Very respectfully,

[signed] Charles Guiteau

So it was with this completely distorted
view of reality that Charles Guiteau fired two
shots into the President's back as he walked
arm-in-arm with Secretary Blaine toward the
waiting train. The President, failing to respond
to treatment, lingered two and a half months
before dying on September 19, 1881.

The Trial

Throughout his lengthy seventy-two-day trial,
Guiteau's delusional state was apparent to
anyone inclined to acknowledge it. His brother-in-law, George Scoville, represented him at
the trial and entered a plea of insanity. In
Scovilles' opening statement for the defense, he
described in some detail the history of mental
illness in the Guiteau family: at least two
uncles, one aunt, and two cousins, not to mention his mother who died of "brain fever" but
was probably insane. He went on to mention
the highly eccentric behavior of his father that,
at least one physician thought, properly qualified him for this category. It should also be
noted that Guiteau's sister, Frances, the wife of
George Scoville, behaved so strangely during
her brother's trial that her probable insanity
was noted by one participating physician who
had occasion to observe her closely. And
indeed, her husband later had her declared
insane and institutionalized in October 1882,
after her brother's execution.

This seemingly overwhelming evidence of
an hereditary affliction was ignored or discounted by expert witnesses and finally the
jury. Also discounted were the defendant's
own delusional symptoms evident in the past
schemes, bizarre letters to prominent persons
he had never met, and his distorted conception
of reality, which was apparent in his remarks
throughout the trial and to the day he was executed. Scoville's line of defense was rejected by
the defendant himself and greatly resented by
John W. Guiteau, Charles' older bother. In a
letter to Scoville, dated October 20, 1881, shortly after the trial began, John denied the history
of family insanity described by the defense.
Rather than heredity, he argued indignantly,
most of the cases Scoville cited could be
explained by self-induced factors such as inso-

briety and "mesmerism"; the others, specifically his parents' symptoms, he categorically denied. Falling into line with previous diagnoses of the causes of Charles' problems, most notably that of leaders of the Oneida Community, John Guiteau wrote: "I have no doubt that masturbation and self-abuse is at the bottom of his [Charles'] mental imbecility."

As for Charles himself, thoroughly contemptuous of his brother-in-law's legal abilities, he drafted his own plea, which read as follows:

I plead not guilty to the indictment and my defense is threefold:

1. Insanity, in that it was God's act and not mine. The Divine pressure on me to remove the President was so enormous that it destroyed my free agency, and therefore I am not legally responsible for my act.

Throughout his trial, Guiteau would acknowledge only this interpretation of insanity; that is, he was insane only in the sense that he did something that was not his will but God's. He did not accept the idea that he was in any way mentally deficient. Typical of his remarks on this issue made throughout the trial is the following:

. . . the Lord interjected the idea [of the President's removal] into my brain and then let me work it out my own way. That is the way the Lord does. He doesn't employ fools to do his work; I am sure of that; he gets the best brains he can find.

His plea continued describing two rather novel circumstances that, he claimed, were the Lord's will just as the assassination:

2. The President died from malpractice. About three weeks after he was shot his physicians, after careful examination, decided he would recover. Two months after this official announcement he died. Therefore, I say he was not fatally shot. If he had been well treated he would have recovered.

The third circumstance had to do with the court's jurisdiction:

3. The President died in New Jersey and, therefore, beyond the jurisdiction of this Court. This malpractice and the President's death in New Jersey are special providences, and I am bound to avail myself of them in my trial in justice to the Lord and myself.

He went on to elaborate:

I undertake to say that the Lord is managing my case with eminent ability, and that he had a special object in allowing the President to die in New Jersey. His management of this case is worthy of Him as the Deity, and I have entire confidence in His disposition to protect me, and to send me forth to the world a free and innocent man.

The jury's guilty verdict notwithstanding, it was clear that Guiteau had no grasp of the reality of his situation. Almost to the last, he believed he would be acquitted, at which point, he planned to begin a lecture tour in Europe and later return to the United States in time to re-enter politics as a presidential contender in 1884. He was confident that the jury, like the great majority of Americans, would recognize that Garfield's "removal" was divinely ordained and that the Almighty himself was responsible. He was convinced they would recognize that he was only an instrument in the Master's hands.

Contrary to some assessments, there was no evidence of paranoia in his behavior. Buoyed by a delusion-based optimism, he mistook the crowds of curious on-lookers at the jail as evidence of respect and admiration: bogus checks for incredible sums of money and ludicrous marriage proposals that were sent to him by cranks were sincerely and gratefully acknowledged; and promotional schemes evolved in his distorted mind to market his ridiculous books and pamphlets—all this while anticipating a run for the presidency in 1884! Meanwhile, in high spirits, the poor wretch ate heartily and slept well in a small cell located both literally and figuratively in the shadow of the gallows.

The Execution

When at the very last he realized that there was no hope for survival, his anger was, considering the circumstances, tempered much as it had been during his dispute with the Oneida Community. There were warnings of divine retribution for the ungrateful new president, Chester Arthur, the unfair prosecuting attorneys, and the jury, but again his anger lacked the intensity and desperation of someone facing death. As the execution date approached, Charles, realizing failure once again, simply set his sights elsewhere as he had on many previous occasions. Eschewing politics, the presidency, the Stalwarts, and the law that had failed him, the lawyer and politician once again became the theologian. Anticipating an other-worldly position at the side of the Almighty, Charles walked serenely to the gallows. Earlier he had given the letter below to the chaplain who stood by him at the last:

Washington, D.C.
June 29, 1882

TO THE REV. WILLIAM W. HICKS:

I, Charles Guiteau, of the City of Washington, in the District of Columbia, now under sentence of death, which is to be carried into effect between the hours of twelve and two o'clock on the 30th day of June, A.D., 1882, in the United States jail in the said District, do hereby give and grant to you my body after such execution; provided, however, it shall not be used for any mercenary purposes.

And I hereby, for good and sufficient considerations, give, deliver and transfer to said Hicks my book entitled "The Truth and Removal" and copyright thereof to be used by him in writing a truthful history of my life and execution.

And I direct that such history be entitled "The Life and Work of Charles Guiteau"; and I hereby solemnly proclaim and announce to all the world that no person or persons shall ever in any manner use my body for any mercenary purpose whatsoever.

And if at any time hereafter any person or persons shall desire to honor my remains, they can do it by erecting a monument whereon shall be inscribed these words: "Here lies the body of Charles Guiteau, Patriot and Christian. His soul is in glory."

[signed] Charles Guiteau

Witnesses: Charles H. Reed
James Woodward

Before the noose was placed around his neck, he was given permission to read his "last dying prayer" to the crowd of faces gazing up at him from the prison yard below. Comparing his situation to that of Christ at Calvary, Guiteau condemned President Arthur's ingratitude "to the man that made him and saved his party and land" and warned of divine retribution.

After completing his prayer, he again looked thoughtfully out over the crowd before announcing in a loud clear voice:

I am now going to read some verses which are intended to indicate my feelings at the moment of leaving this world. If set to music they may be rendered effective. The idea is that of a child babbling to his mamma and his papa. I wrote it this morning about 10 o'clock.

Then with childlike mournfulness, Guiteau read:

I am going to the Lordy. I am so glad.
I am going to the Lordy. I am so glad.
I am going to the Lordy. Glory, hallelujah;
    glory hallelujah.
I am going to the Lordy;
I love the Lordy with all my soul; glory,
    hallelujah.
And that is the reason I am going to the Lord.
Glory, hallelujah; glory, hallelujah. I am going
    to the Lord.
I saved my party and my land; glory, hallelujah.
But they have murdered me for it, and that is the
    reason
I am going to the Lordy.
Glory, hallelujah; glory, hallelujah. I am going
    to the Lordy.
I wonder what I will do when I get to the Lordy;

I guess that I will weep no more when I get to the
*   Lordy.*
Glory, hallelujah!
I wonder what I will see when I get to the Lordy,
I expect to see most splendid things, beyond all
*   earthly conception.*

As he neared completion, he raised his voice to a very high pitch and concluded with

When I am with the Lordy, glory, hallelujah!
Glory, hallelujah! I am with the Lord.

Whereupon attendants strapped his legs, adjusted the noose, and placed a black hood over his head as Rev. Hicks prayed, "God the Father be with thee and give thee peace evermore." Guiteau, according to his own request, signaled the hangman by dropping a slip of paper from his fingers. As the trap sprung, Charles Guiteau slipped confidently into eternity with "Glory, Glory, Glory" on his lips.

Conclusions

Although the debate on the true state of Guiteau's mental condition was to continue among physicians for some years afterward, a brief article in the *Medical News* a day after the execution seems to have been representative of the prevailing view of the medical profession. While conceding that the neurologists who testified to the assassin's obvious insanity may have been correct, society would still be better, the editors reasoned, for having rid itself of such persons. As a further practical matter, it is unlikely that in 1881 any jury in the country would have acquitted the President's assassin whatever his mental condition.

■■■

STUDY QUESTIONS

1. Was Guiteau's life before the assassination consistent with his plea of insanity?

2. What were the political motivations for Guiteau's actions?

3. What were the problems with evaluating the evidence presented by the experts on insanity? Did Guiteau, according to the author, actually suffer from paranoia?

4. How would you describe Guiteau's religious beliefs? In your opinion, did those values inhibit his ability to interpret reality?

5. Was the verdict of the jury just? Could any other verdict have been reasonably justified?

BIBLIOGRAPHY

The most thoughtful and thought-provoking exploration of the Guiteau episode is Charles E. Rosenberg, *The Trial of the Assassin Guiteau* (1968). However, some of the contemporary articles also make interesting reading. John P. Gray, a leading late nineteenth-century American expert on insanity and an important witness in the Guiteau trial, presented his conclusions in "The United States vs. Charles J. Guiteau," *American Journal of Insanity*, 38 (1882). Edward C. Spitzka, the other major expert in the case, offered his opinion in "A Contribution to the Question on the Mental Status of Guiteau and the History of His Trial," *Alienist and Neurologist*, 4 (1883).

The most recent work on American political assassinations is James W. Clarke, *American Assassins: The Darker Side of Politics* (1982). Clarke provides a good general bibliography on the subject. For the politics of the period see H. Wayne Morgan, *From Hayes to McKinley: National Party Politics, 1877–1896* (1969) and John M. Taylor, *Garfield of Ohio: The Available Man* (1970).

THE WIZARD OF OZ:
PARABLE ON POPULISM

Henry M. Littlefield

The late nineteenth century was not a period known for its social justice. Angry and exploited workers found little sympathy in the halls of government. Consistently during strikes, federal authorities intervened on the side of management rather than labor, even though strikes were usually responses to wage cuts. In the 1894 Pullman strike, for example, President Grover Cleveland sided with the rights of property over the rights of labor and crushed the strike. Thus the newly formed unions won few concessions for their members. At the end of the century, the work week for the "average" industrial worker was almost 60 hours. The average skilled worker earned twenty cents an hour, twice as much as the average unskilled worker.

Life on the farms in the Midwest and South was probably even worse than life in the northern industries. Technological innovations and scientific farming techniques led to increased production, which in turn sent prices spiraling downward. Discriminatory railroad rates and the government's tight money policies further weakened the economic positions of farmers. As a result, farmers faced an economic depression that cost many their farms. Returning to his midwestern home in 1889, writer Hamlin Garland noted, "Nature was as bountiful as ever . . . but no splendor of cloud, no grace of sunset could conceal the poverty of these people; on the contrary, they brought out, with a more intolerable poignancy, the gracelessness of these homes, and the sordid quality of the mechanical routine of these lives." In the following essay, Henry M. Littlefield takes a fascinating look at Lyman Frank Baum's *The Wonderful Wizard of Oz* and the light it shed on the workers' and farmers' plight in the late nineteenth century.

On the deserts on North Africa in 1941 two tough Australian brigades went to battle singing,

Have you heard of the wonderful wizard,
The wonderful Wizard of Oz,
And he is a wonderful wizard,
If ever a wizard there was.

It was a song they had brought with them from Australia and would soon spread to England. Forever afterward it reminded Winston Churchill of those "buoyant days." Churchill's nostalgia is only one symptom of the worldwide delight found in an American fairy-tale about a little girl and her odyssey in the strange land of Oz. The song he reflects upon came from a classic 1939 Hollywood production of the story, which introduced millions of people not only to the land of Oz, but to a talented young lady named Judy Garland as well.

Ever since its publication in 1900 Lyman Frank Baum's *The Wonderful Wizard of Oz* has been immensely popular, providing the basis for a profitable musical comedy, three movies and a number of plays. It is an indigenous creation, curiously warm and touching, although no one really knows why. For despite wholehearted acceptance by generations of readers, Baum's tale has been accorded neither critical acclaim, nor extended critical examination. Interested scholars, such as Russell B. Nye and Martin Gardiner, look upon *The Wizard of Oz* as the first in a long and delightful series of Oz stories, and understandably base their appreciation of Baum's talent on the totality of his works.

"The Wizard of Oz: Parable on Populism" by Henry M. Littlefield, from *American Quarterly* 16 (Spring, 1964). Published by the American Studies Association. Copyright © 1964. Reprinted by permission of American Quarterly and the author. "We're Off to See the Wizard" by Harold Arlen and E. Y. Harburg. Copyright © 1938, 1939 (Renewed 1966, 1967) Metro-Goldwyn-Mayer, Inc. c/o EMI Feist Catalog Inc. World Print Rights Controlled and Administered by CPP/Belwin, Inc., Miami, FL. All Rights Reserved.

The Wizard of Oz is an entity unto itself, however, and was not originally written with a sequel in mind. Baum informed his readers in 1904 that he had produced *The Marvelous Land of Oz* reluctantly and only in answer to well over a thousand letters demanding that he create another Oz tale. His original effort remains unique and to some degree separate from the books which follow. But its uniqueness does not rest alone on its peculiar and transcendent popularity.

Professor Nye finds a "strain of moralism" in the Oz books, as well as "a well-developed sense of satire," and Baum stories often include searching parodies on the contradictions in human nature. The second book in the series, *The Marvelous Land of Oz,* is a blatant satire on feminism and the suffragette movement. In it Baum attempted to duplicate the format used so successfully in *The Wizard,* yet no one has noted a similar play on contemporary movements in the latter work. Nevertheless, one does exist, and it reflects to an astonishing degree the world of political reality which surrounded Baum in 1900. In order to understand the relationship of *The Wizard* to turn-of-the-century America, it is necessary first to know something of Baum's background.

Born near Syracuse in 1856, Baum was brought up in a wealthy home and early became interested in the theater. He wrote some plays which enjoyed brief success and then, with his wife and two sons, journeyed to Aberdeen, South Dakota, in 1887. Aberdeen was a little prairie town and there Baum edited the local weekly until it failed in 1891.

For many years Western farmers had been in a state of loud, though unsuccessful, revolt. While Baum was living in South Dakota not only was the frontier a thing of the past, but the Romantic view of benign nature had disappeared as well. The stark reality of the dry, open plains and the acceptance of man's Darwinian subservience to his environment served to crush Romantic idealism.

Hamlin Garland's visit to Iowa and South

Dakota coincided with Baum's arrival. Henry Nash Smith observes,

Garland's success as a portrayer of hardship and suffering on Northwestern farms was due in part to the fact that his personal experience happened to parallel the shock which the entire West received in the later 1880's from the combined effects of low prices, . . . grasshoppers, drought, the terrible blizzards of the winter of 1886–1887, and the juggling of freight rates. . . .

As we shall see, Baum's prairie experience was no less deeply etched, although he did not employ naturalism to express it.

Baum's stay in South Dakota also covered the period of the formation of the Populist party, which Professor Nye likens to a fanatic "crusade." Western farmers had for a long time sought governmental aid in the form of economic panaceas, but to no avail. The Populist movement symbolized a desperate attempt to use the power of the ballot. In 1891 Baum moved to Chicago where he was surrounded by those dynamic elements of reform which made the city so notable during the 1890s.

In Chicago Baum certainly saw the results of the frightful depression which had closed down upon the nation in 1893. Moreover, he took part in the pivotal election of 1896, marching in "torch-light parades for William Jennings Bryan." Martin Gardiner notes besides, that he "consistently voted as a Democrat . . . and his sympathies seem always to have been on the side of the laboring classes." No one who marched in even a few such parades could have been unaffected by Bryan's campaign. Putting all the farmers' hopes in a basket labeled "free coinage of silver," Bryan's platform rested mainly on the issue of adding silver to the nation's gold standard. Though he lost, he did at least bring the plight of the little man into national focus.

Between 1896 and 1900, while Baum worked and wrote in Chicago, the great depression faded away and the war with Spain thrust the United States into world prominence. Bryan

Original title page of Frank Baum's populist classic (1900). The spectacularly successful 1939 film based on the Wizard of Oz *came out during another Great Depression and prefigured happiness in "Somewhere Over the Rainbow."*

maintained Midwestern control over the Democratic party, and often spoke out against American policies toward Cuba and the Philippines. By 1900 it was evident that Bryan would run again, although now imperialism and not silver seemed the issue of primary concern. In order to promote greater enthusiasm, however, Bryan felt compelled once more to sound the silver leitmotif in his campaign. Bryan's second futile attempt at the presidency culminated in November 1900. The previous winter Baum had attempted unsuccessfully to sell a rather original volume of children's fantasy, but that April, George M. Hill, a small Chicago publisher, finally agreed to print *The Wonderful Wizard of Oz.*

Baum's allegiance to the cause of Democratic Populism must be balanced against the fact that he was not a political activist. Martin Gardiner finds through all of his writings "a theme of tolerance, with many episodes that poke fun at narrow nationalism and ethnocentrism." Nevertheless, Professor Nye quotes Baum as having a desire to write stories that would "bear the stamp of our times and depict the progressive fairies of today."

The Wizard of Oz has neither the mature religious appeal of a *Pilgrim's Progress*, nor the philosophic depth of a *Candide*. Baum's most thoughtful devotees see in it only a warm, cleverly written fairy tale. Yet the original Oz book conceals an unsuspected depth, and it is the purpose of this study to demonstrate that Baum's immortal American fantasy encompasses more than heretofore believed. For Baum created a children's story with a symbolic allegory implicit within its story line and characterizations. The allegory always remains in a minor key, subordinated to the major theme and readily abandoned whenever it threatens to distort the appeal of the fantasy. But through it, in the form of a subtle parable, Baum delineated a Midwesterner's vibrant and ironic portrait of this country as it entered the twentieth century.

We are introduced to both Dorothy and Kansas at the same time:

Dorothy lived in the midst of the great Kansas prairies, with Uncle Henry, who was a farmer, and Aunt Em, who was the farmer's wife. Their house was small, for the lumber to build it had to be carried by wagon many miles. There were four walls, a floor and a roof, which made one room; and this room contained a rusty-looking cooking stove, a cupboard for the dishes, a table, three or four chairs, and the beds.

When Dorothy stood in the doorway and looked around, she could see nothing but the great gray prairie on every side. Not a tree nor a house broke the broad sweep of flat country that reached to the edge of the sky in all directions. The sun had baked the plowed land into a gray mass, with little cracks running through it. Even the grass was not green, for the sun had burned the tops of the long blades until they were the same gray color to be seen everywhere. Once the house had been painted, but the sun blistered the paint and the rains washed it away, and now the house was as dull and gray as everything else.

When Aunt Em came there to live she was a young, pretty wife. The sun and wind had changed her, too. They had taken the sparkle from her eyes and left them a sober gray; they had taken the red from her cheeks and lips, and they were gray also. She was thin and gaunt, and never smiled now. When Dorothy, who was an orphan, first came to her, Aunt Em had been so startled by the child's laughter that she would scream and press her hand upon her heart whenever Dorothy's merry voice reached her ears; and she still looked at the little girl with wonder that she could find anything to laugh at.

Uncle Henry never laughed. He worked hard from morning till night and did not know what joy was. He was gray also, from his long beard to his rough boots, and he looked stern and solemn, and rarely spoke.

It was Toto that made Dorothy laugh, and saved her from growing as gray as her other surroundings. Toto was not gray; he was a little black dog, with long silky hair and small black eyes that twinkle merrily on either side of his funny, wee nose. Toto played all day long, and Dorothy played with him, and loved him dearly.

Hector St. John de Crèvecoeur would not have recognized Uncle Henry's farm; it is straight out of Hamlin Garland. On it a deadly environment dominates everyone and everything except Dorothy and her pet. The setting is Old Testament and nature seems grayly impersonal and even angry. Yet it is a fearsome cyclone that lifts Dorothy and Toto in their house and deposits them "very gently—for a cyclone—in the midst of a country of marvelous beauty." We immediately sense the contrast between Oz and Kansas. Here there are "stately trees bearing rich and luscious fruits . . . gorgeous flowers . . . and birds with . . . brilliant plumage" sing in the trees. In Oz "a small brook rushing and sparkling along" murmurs "in a voice very grateful to a little girl who had lived so long on the dry, gray prairies."

Trouble intrudes. Dorothy's house has come down on the wicked Witch of the East, killing her. Nature, by sheer accident, can provide benefits, for indirectly the cyclone has disposed of one of the two truly bad influences in the Land of Oz. Notice that evil ruled in both the East and the West; after Dorothy's coming it rules only in the West.

The wicked Witch of the East had kept the little Munchkin people "in bondage for many years, making them slave for her night and day." Just what this slavery entailed is not immediately clear, but Baum later gives us a specific example. The Tin Woodman, whom Dorothy meets on her way to the Emerald City, had been put under a spell by the Witch of the East. Once an independent and hard working human being, the Woodman found that each time he swung his axe it chopped off a different part of his body. Knowing no other trade he "worked harder than ever," for luckily in Oz tinsmiths can repair such things. Soon the Woodman was all tin. In this way Eastern witchcraft dehumanized a simple laborer so that the faster and better he worked the more quickly he became a kind of machine. Here is a Populist view of evil Eastern influences on honest labor which could hardly be more pointed.

There is one thing seriously wrong with being made of tin; when it rains rust sets in. Tin Woodman had been standing in the same position for a year without moving before Dorothy came along and oiled his joints. The Tin Woodman's situation has an obvious parallel in the condition of many Eastern workers after the depression of 1893. While Tin Woodman is standing still, rusted solid, he deludes himself into thinking he is no longer capable of that most human of sentiments,

love. Hate does not fill the void, a constant lesson in the Oz books, and Tin Woodman feels that only a heart will make him sensitive again. So he accompanies Dorothy to see if the Wizard will give him one.

Oz itself is a magic oasis surrounded by impassable deserts, and the country is divided in a very orderly fashion. In the North and South the people are ruled by good witches, who are not quite as powerful as the wicked ones of the East and West. In the center of the land rises the magnificent Emerald City ruled by the Wizard of Oz, a successful humbug whom even the witches mistakenly feel "is more powerful than all the rest of us together." Despite these forces, the mark of goodness, placed on Dorothy's forehead by the Witch of the North, serves as protection for Dorothy throughout her travels. Goodness and innocence prevail even over the powers of evil and delusion in Oz. Perhaps it is this basic and beautiful optimism that makes Baum's tale so characteristically American—and Midwestern.

Dorothy is Baum's Miss Everyman. She is one of us, levelheaded and human, and she has a real problem. Young readers can understand her quandary as readily as can adults. She is good, not precious, and she thinks quite naturally about others. For all of the attractions of Oz Dorothy desires only to return to the gray plains and Aunt Em and Uncle Henry. She is directed toward the Emerald City by the good Witch of the North, since the Wizard will surely be able to solve the problem of the impassable deserts. Dorothy sets out on the Yellow Brick Road wearing the Witch of the East's magic Silver Shoes. Silver shoes walking on a golden road; henceforth Dorothy becomes the innocent agent of Baum's ironic view of the Silver issue. Remember, neither Dorothy, nor the good Witch of the North, nor the Munchkins understand the power of these shoes. The allegory is abundantly clear. On the next to last page of the book Baum has Glinda, Witch of the South, tell Dorothy, "Your Silver

Shoes will carry you over the desert. . . . If you had known their power you could have gone back to your Aunt Em the very first day you came to this country." Glinda explains, "All you have to do is to knock the heels together three times and command the shoes to carry you wherever you wish to go." William Jennings Bryan never outlined the advantages of the silver standard any more effectively.

Not understanding the magic of the Silver Shoes, Dorothy walks the mundane—and dangerous—Yellow Brick Road. The first person she meets is a Scarecrow. After escaping from his wooden perch, the Scarecrow displays a terrible sense of inferiority and self doubt, for he has determined that he needs real brains to replace the common straw in his head. William Allen White wrote an article in 1896 entitled "What's the Matter with Kansas?" In it he accused Kansas farmers of ignorance, irrationality and general muddle-headedness. What's wrong with Kansas are the people, said Mr. White. Baum's character seems to have read White's angry characterization. But Baum never takes White seriously and so the Scarecrow soon emerges as innately a very shrewd and very capable individual.

The Scarecrow and the Tin Woodman accompany Dorothy along the Yellow Brick Road, one seeking brains, the other a heart. They meet next the Cowardly Lion. As King of Beasts he explains, "I learned that if I roared very loudly every living thing was frightened and got out of my way." Born a coward, he sobs, "Whenever there is danger my heart begins to beat fast." "Perhaps you have heart disease," suggests Tin Woodman, who always worries about hearts. But the Lion desires only courage and so he joins the party to ask help from the Wizard.

The Lion represents Bryan himself. In the election of 1896 Bryan lost the vote of Eastern labor, though he tried hard to gain their support. In Baum's story the Lion, on meeting the little group, "struck at the Tin Woodman with his sharp claws." But, to his surprise, "he could

make no impression on the tin, although the Woodman fell over in the road and lay still." Baum here refers to the fact that in 1896 workers were often pressured into voting for McKinley and gold by their employers. Amazed, the Lion says, "he nearly blunted my claws," and he adds even more appropriately, "When they scratched against the tin it made a cold shiver run down my back." The King of Beasts is not after all very cowardly, and Bryan, although a pacifist and an anti-imperialist in a time of national expansion, is not either. The magic Silver Shoes belong to Dorothy, however. Silver's potent charm, which had come to mean so much to so many in the Midwest, could not be entrusted to a political symbol. Baum delivers Dorothy from the world of adventure and fantasy to the real world of heartbreak and desolation through the power of Silver. It represents a real force in a land of illusion, and neither the Cowardly Lion nor Bryan truly needs or understands its use.

All together now the small party moves toward the Emerald City. Coxey's Army of tramps and indigents, marching to ask President Cleveland for work in 1894, appears no more naively innocent than this group of four characters going to see a humbug Wizard, to request favors that only the little girl among them deserves.

Those who enter the Emerald City must wear green glasses. Dorothy later discovers that the greenness of dresses and ribbons disappears on leaving, and everything becomes a bland white. Perhaps the magic of any city is thus self imposed. But the Wizard dwells here and so the Emerald City represents the national Capital. The Wizard, a little bumbling old man, hiding behind a facade of papier mâché and noise, might be any President from Grant to McKinley. He comes straight from the fair grounds in Omaha, Nebraska, and he symbolizes the American criterion for leadership—he is able to be everything to everybody.

As each of our heroes enters the throne

room to ask a favor the Wizard assumes different shapes, representing different views toward national leadership. To Dorothy, he appears as an enormous head, "bigger than the head of the biggest giant." An apt image for a naive and innocent little citizen. To the Scarecrow he appears to be a lovely, gossamer fairy, a most appropriate form for an idealistic Kansas farmer. The Woodman sees a horrible beast, as would any exploited Eastern laborer after the trouble of the 1890s. But the Cowardly Lion, like W. J. Bryan, sees a "Ball of Fire, so fierce and glowing he could scarcely bear to gaze upon it." Baum then provides an additional analogy, for when the Lion "tried to go nearer he singed his whiskers and he crept back tremblingly to a spot nearer the door."

The Wizard has asked them all to kill the Witch of the West. The golden road does not go in that direction and so they must follow the sun, as have many pioneers in the past. The land they now pass through is "rougher and hillier, for there were no farms nor houses in the country of the West and the ground was untilled." The Witch of the West uses natural forces to achieve her ends; she is Baum's version of sentient and malign nature.

Finding Dorothy and her friends in the West, the Witch sends forty wolves against them, then forty vicious crows and finally a great swarm of black bees. But it is through the power of a magic golden cap that she summons the flying monkeys. They capture the little girl and dispose of her companions. Baum makes these Winged Monkeys into an Oz substitute for the plains Indians. Their leader says, "Once . . . we were a free people, living happily in the great forest, flying from tree to tree, eating nuts and fruit, and doing just as we pleased without calling anybody master." "This," he explains, "was many years ago, long before Oz came out of the clouds to rule over this land." But like many Indian tribes Baum's monkeys are not inherently bad; their actions depend wholly upon the bidding of others. Under the control of an evil influence, they do evil. Under the control of goodness and innocence, as personified by Dorothy, the monkeys are helpful and kind, although unable to take her to Kansas. Says the Monkey King, "We belong to this country alone, and cannot leave it." The same could be said with equal truth of the first Americans.

Dorothy presents a special problem to the Witch. Seeing the mark on Dorothy's forehead and the Silver Shoes on her feet, the Witch begins "to tremble with fear, for she knew what a powerful charm belonged to them." Then "she happened to look into the child's eyes and saw how simple the soul behind them was, and that the little girl did not know of the wonderful power the Silver Shoes gave her." Here Baum again uses the Silver allegory to state the blunt homily that while goodness affords a people ultimate protection against evil, ignorance of their capabilities allows evil to impose itself upon them. The Witch assumes the proportions of a kind of western Mark Hanna or Banker Boss, who, through natural malevolence, manipulates the people and holds them prisoner by cynically taking advantage of their innate innocence.

Enslaved in the West, "Dorothy went to work meekly, with her mind made up to work as hard as she could; for she was glad the Wicked Witch had decided not to kill her." Many Western farmers have held these same grim thoughts in less mystical terms. If the Witch of the West is a diabolical force of Darwinian or Spencerian nature, then another contravening force may be counted upon to dispose of her. Dorothy destroys the evil Witch by angrily dousing her with a bucket of water. Water, that precious commodity which the drought-ridden farmers on the great plains needed so badly, and which if correctly used could create an agricultural paradise, or at least dissolve a wicked witch. Plain water brings an end to malign nature in the West.

When Dorothy and her companions return to the Emerald City they soon discover that the

Wizard is really nothing more than "a little man, with a bald head and a wrinkled face." Can this be the ruler of the land?

Our friends looked at him in surprise and dismay.

"I thought Oz was a great Head," said Dorothy. ... "And I thought Oz was a terrible Beast," said the Tin Woodman. "And I thought Oz was a Ball of Fire," exclaimed the Lion. "No; you are all wrong," said the little man meekly. "I have been making believe."

Dorothy asks if he is truly a great Wizard. He confides, "Not a bit of it, my dear; I'm just a common man." Scarecrow adds, "You're more than that . . . you're a humbug."

The Wizard's deception is of long standing in Oz and even the Witches were taken in. How was it accomplished? "It was a great mistake my ever letting you into the Throne Room," the Wizard complains. "Usually I will not see even my subjects, and so they believe I am something terrible." What a wonderful lesson for youngsters of the decade when Benjamin Harrison, Grover Cleveland and William McKinley were hiding in the White House. Formerly the Wizard was a mimic, a ventriloquist and a circus balloonist. The latter trade involved going "up in a balloon on circus day, so as to draw a crowd of people together and get them to pay to see the circus." Such skills are as admirably adapted to success in late-nineteenth-century politics as they are to the humbug wizardry of Baum's story. A pointed comment on Midwestern political ideals is the fact that our little Wizard comes from Omaha, Nebraska, a center of Populist agitation. "Why that isn't very far from Kansas," cries Dorothy. Nor, indeed, are any of the characters in the wonderful land of Oz.

The Wizard, of course, can provide the objects of self-delusion desired by Tin Woodman, Scarecrow and Lion. But Dorothy's hope of going home fades when the Wizard's balloon leaves too soon. Understand this: Dorothy wishes to leave a green and fabulous land, from which all evil has disappeared, to go back to the gray desolation of the Kansas prairies. Dorothy is an orphan, Aunt Em and Uncle Henry are her only family. Reality is never far from Dorothy's consciousness and in the most heartrending terms she explains her reasoning to the Good Witch Glinda,

Aunt Em will surely think something dreadful has happened to me, and that will make her put on mourning; and unless the crops are better this year than they were last I am sure Uncle Henry cannot afford it.

The Silver Shoes furnish Dorothy with a magic means of travel. But when she arrives back in Kansas she finds, "The Silver Shoes had fallen off in her flight through the air, and were lost forever in the desert." Were the "her" to refer to America in 1900, Baum' statement could hardly be contradicted.

Current historiography tends to criticize the Populist movement for its "delusions, myths and foibles," Professor C. Vann Woodward observed recently. Yet *The Wonderful Wizard of Oz* has provided unknowing generations with a gentle and friendly Midwestern critique of the Populist rationale on these very same grounds. Led by naive innocence and protected by good will, the farmer, the laborer and the politician approach the mystic holder of national power to ask for personal fulfillment. Their desires, as well as the Wizard's cleverness in answering them, are all self-delusion. Each of these characters carries within him the solution to his own problem, were he only to view himself objectively. The fearsome Wizard turns out to be nothing more than a common man, capable of shrewd but mundane answers to these self-induced needs. Like any good politician he gives the people what they want. Throughout the story Baum poses a central thought; the American desire for symbols of fulfillment is illusory. Real needs lie elsewhere.

Thus the Wizard cannot help Dorothy, for of all the characters only she has a wish that is selfless, and only she has a direct connection to honest, hopeless human beings. Dorothy supplies real fulfillment when she returns to her aunt and uncle, using the Silver Shoes, and cures some of their misery and heartache. In this way Baum tells us that the Silver crusade at least brought back Dorothy's lovely spirit to the disconsolate plains farmer. Her laughter, love and good will are no small addition to that gray land, although the magic of Silver has been lost forever as a result.

Noteworthy too is Baum's prophetic placement of leadership in Oz after Dorothy's departure. The Scarecrow reigns over the Emerald City, the Tin Woodman rules in the West and the Lion protects smaller beasts in "a grand old forest." Thereby farm interests achieve national importance, industrialism moves West and Bryan commands only a forest full of lesser politicians.

Baum's fantasy succeeds in bridging the gap between what children want and what they should have. It is an admirable example of the way in which an imaginative writer can teach goodness and morality without producing the almost inevitable side effect of nausea. Today's children's books are either saccharine and empty, or boring and pedantic. Baum's first Oz tale—and those which succeed it—are immortal not so much because the "heart-aches and nightmares are left out" as that "the wonder-ment and joy" are retained.

Baum declares, "The story of 'the Wonderful Wizard of Oz' was written solely to pleasure children of today." In 1963 there are very few children who have never heard of the Scarecrow, the Tin Woodman or the Cowardly Lion, and whether they know W. W. Denslow's original illustrations of Dorothy, or Judy Garland's whimsical characterization, is immaterial. *The Wizard* has become a genuine piece of American folklore because, knowing his audience, Baum never allowed the consistency of the allegory to take precedence over the theme of youthful entertainment. Yet once discovered, the author's allegorical intent seems clear, and it gives depth and lasting interest even to children who only sense something else beneath the surface of the story. Consider the fun in picturing turn-of-the-century America, a difficult era at best, using these ready-made symbols provided by Baum. The relationships and analogies outlined above are admittedly theoretical, but they are far too consistent to be coincidental, and they furnish a teaching mechanism which is guaranteed to reach any level of student.

The Wizard of Oz says so much about so many things that it is hard not to imagine a satisfied and mischievous gleam in Lyman Frank Baum's eye as he had Dorothy say, "And oh, Aunt Em! I'm so glad to be at home again!"

STUDY QUESTIONS

1. Why was Lyman Frank Baum in a good position to understand the problems of workers in the late nineteenth century?

2. What sort of picture does *The Wonderful Wizard of Oz* paint of farm life? What was the effect of agrarian labor on the farmers themselves?

3. How does the story detail the complexities of the silver issue? Does Baum seem to feel that the gold standard was the major problem facing the farmers?

4. How does the Tin Woodman dramatize the plight of the northern industrial worker? How does the Scarecrow symbolize the plight of the farmers?

5. In what ways is the Cowardly Lion similar to William Jennings Bryan?

6. What roles do the good and bad witches play in the story?

7. Is *The Wonderful Wizard of Oz* an effective parable?

BIBLIOGRAPHY

Martin Gardiner and Russell B. Nye, *The Wizard of Oz and Who He Was* (1957) examine Baum and his works. The best studies of the Populist movement are John D. Hicks, *The Populist Revolt* (1931); C. Vann Woodward, *Tom Watson: Agrarian Rebel* (1938); Lawrence Goodwyn, *Democratic Promise: The Populist Movement in America* (1976); Robert C. McMath, Jr., *Populist Vanguard: A History of the Southern Farmers' Alliance* (1975); and Stanley B. Parsons, *The Populist Context: Rural Versus Urban Power on a Great Plains Frontier* (1973). Paul W. Glad, *McKinley, Bryan, and the People* (1964) and Robert F. Durden, *The Climax of Populism: The Election of 1896* (1965) examine the crucial election of 1896. For industrial working conditions in the late nineteenth century see Herbert G. Gutman, *Work, Class, and Society in Industrializing America* (1976); David Brody, *Steelworkers in America: The Nonunion Era* (1960); and Albert Rees, *Real Wages in Manufacturing, 1890–1914* (1961). Also see Steven Hahn, *The Roots of Southern Populism* (1983).

SHE COULDN'T HAVE DONE IT, EVEN IF SHE DID

Kathryn Allamong Jacob

There is something infinitely compelling and fascinating about an unsolved murder. England has Jack the Ripper, and although it has been almost one hundred years since the last Ripper murder was committed, historians of the crimes still speculate on the identity of the murderer. The American equivalent to Jack the Ripper is Lizzie Borden, who very likely killed her father and stepmother on August 2, 1892. Although she was judged innocent of the murders, strong circumstantial evidence points toward her guilt. However, in a larger sense the jury was more concerned with the physical and psychological nature of upper-class womanhood than with the actual crimes. As Kathryn Allamong Jacob writes, during the summer of 1893 "the entire Victorian conception of womanhood was on trial for its life." The question most commonly asked that summer was to the point: How could a well-bred woman, who by her very nature was innocent, childlike, and moral, commit such a horrible crime? The answer of most well-bred men, and of all twelve of the prosperous, Yankee jurors, was that she could not. An examination of the case thus illuminates an entire cultural landscape, casting light especially on American attitudes toward women. Were women, as a writer for *Scribner's* believed, "merely large babies . . . shortsighted, frivolous, and [occupying] an intermediate stage between children and men . . ."? Or was there something more to the issue?

During the summer of 1893, Americans riveted their attention on the town of New Bedford, Massachusetts, where Lizzie Andrew Borden was being tried for the gruesome ax murder of her father and stepmother. All other news paled in comparison, for here, in southeastern Massachusetts, not only a particular woman, but the entire Victorian conception of womanhood, was on trial for its life.

The drama began in August of 1892 at Number 92 Second Street in Fall River, Massachusetts, the home of Andrew Jackson Borden, whose family coat of arms prophetically bore a lion holding a battle-ax. The household consisted of Andrew, seventy; Abby Gray Borden, sixty-five, his wife; his two daughters, Lizzie Andrew and Emma Lenora, aged thirty-two and forty-two; and Bridget Sullivan, twenty-six, an Irish servant who had been with the family for nearly three years.

Andrew Borden began his business career as an undertaker. It was rumored that he had cut the feet off corpses to make them fit into undersized coffins, but however ill-gotten his initial profits, Borden invested them wisely. By 1892 he was worth nearly half a million dollars, served as a director of several banks and as a board member of three woolen mills, and had built the imposing A. J. Borden Building on Main Street as a testimony to his business acumen. To keep his fortunes increasing, Borden foreclosed, undercut, overcharged, and hoarded without flinching.

Borden's first wife, Sarah, had died in 1862 after bearing him three daughters, only two of whom survived past infancy. Two years later, he married Abby Gray, a thirty-eight-year-old spinster. Nothing suggests that Abby was anything but kind to the two little girls whose stepmother she became, but they never returned her affection. After her marriage,

Abby became a compulsive eater. Only a little over five feet tall, by 1892 she weighed more than two hundred pounds.

Emma, the older daughter, still lived at home at age forty-two. By all accounts, she was dowdy and narrow-minded. Lizzie Borden, ten years younger, also lived at home. Otherwise tightfisted, Andrew Borden doted on his younger daughter: over the years he lavished on Lizzie expensive gifts—a diamond ring, a sealskin cape, even a Grand Tour of Europe. Lizzie worshiped her father in return, and even gave him her high school ring to wear as a token of her affection.

Like her sister, Lizzie had evidently given up hope of marriage, but she led a more active life, centered around good works and the Central Congregational Church, where she taught a Sunday-school class of Chinese children, the sons and daughters of Fall River laundrymen. Though she loathed doing housework, she enthusiastically helped cook the church's annual Christmas dinner for local newsboys. In addition to being secretary-treasurer of the Christian Endeavor, Lizzie was active in the Ladies' Fruit and Flower Mission, the Women's Christian Temperance Union, and the Good Samaritan Charity Hospital.

Lizzie's Christian charity did not extend to her own home. The Borden family was not happy. While Emma tolerated her stepmother, Lizzie openly disliked her. Ill feelings increased in 1887, when Andrew gave Abby a house for the use of her sister. Seeking peace, Andrew gave his daughters a house of greater value to rent out, but they were not placated. A dressmaker later remembered making the mistake of referring to Abby as Lizzie's "mother," causing Lizzie to snap, "Don't call her that to me. She is a mean thing and we hate her."

Even the house Lizzie lived in vexed her. Its Grant-era furnishings contrasted sharply with her stylish clothes. There was no bath and no electricity, though such conveniences were common elsewhere in town. Beside the water closet in the basement stood a pile of old news-

"She Couldn't Have Done It, Even If She Did" by Kathryn Allamong Jacob, from *American Heritage* 29 (February/March, 1978). Reprinted by permission.

papers for sanitary purposes. No interior space was wasted on hallways. Rooms simply opened into one another, making it difficult for anyone to pass through unnoticed. Lizzie longed to live "on the hill," Fall River's most elegant neighborhood and the symbol of the social prominence she craved. While her father's wealth entitled her to live there, Andrew insisted on living on déclassé Second Street.

On Tuesday, August 2, 1892, strange things began to happen in the Borden house. Mr. and Mrs. Borden and Bridget suffered severe vomiting; Lizzie later claimed she felt queasy the next day. Emma, on vacation in Fairhaven, was spared. Over Andrew's objections, Abby waddled across the street to Dr. Bowen's to tell him she feared they had been poisoned. When he learned that the previous night's dinner had been warmed-over fish, the doctor laughingly sent her home.

The next day, Uncle John Morse, brother of the first Mrs. Borden, arrived unexpectedly on business. Like Andrew, Morse was single-minded in his pursuit of wealth, and the two men had remained friends. That evening, Lizzie visited Miss Alice Russell, a friend of Emma's. Miss Russell later testified that their conversation had been unsettling. Lizzie had spoken of burglary attempts on the Borden home, of threats against her father from unknown enemies. "I feel as if something was hanging over me that I cannot throw off . . . ," she said. "Father has so much trouble. . . ." Though Miss Russell tried to reassure her, Lizzie left on an ominous, but prescient, note: "I am afraid somebody will do something."

On Thursday morning, August 4, Bridget rose about six and lit the breakfast fire. Around seven, the elder Bordens and their guest sat down to eat in the dining room. Lizzie did not appear downstairs till nine. By then, Mrs. Borden had begun dusting the downstairs and Morse had left the house to visit relatives across town. Lizzie told Bridget she did not feel well enough to eat breakfast, but sat in the

kitchen sipping coffee. About twenty after nine, Andrew, too, left the house, setting off downtown to oversee his investments. Perhaps ten minutes later, Abby Borden went upstairs to tidy the guest room, and Bridget went outside to begin washing the downstairs windows. Only Lizzie and Abby remained in the house; Abby was never seen alive again.

Perhaps because of the oppressive heat, Andrew broke his long-established routine by coming home for lunch at a quarter of eleven, an hour and a half early. Bridget later testified that she had just begun scrubbing the inside of the windows when she heard him struggling with the front-door lock and let him in. Lizzie, by her own admission, was coming down the stairs from the second floor where Abby's body lay. (At the Borden trial the following year, the prosecution would produce witnesses who testified that Abby's body, lying on the guest-room floor, was clearly visible from the staircase, while the defense claimed it was almost completely obscured by a bed). Andrew asked Lizzie about Abby's whereabouts, according to Bridget, and Lizzie told him that Abby had received a note asking her to attend a sick friend.

Bridget finished her windows and climbed the back stairs to her attic room to rest at about eleven. Andrew lay down on the parlor sofa to nap. On the guest-room floor above him lay Abby's bleeding corpse. The house was hot and silent. Within minutes, Bridget recalled, she was awakened by Lizzie calling, "Come down quick; father's dead; somebody came in and killed him."

Little was left of Andrew's face. Half an eye hung from its socket. Doctors testified that a single ax blow had killed him; nine others had been gratuitous. Shortly after the police arrived, Bridget and a neighbor ventured upstairs for a sheet to cover the hideous sight, and there they found Abby. Her plump body lay face down in a pool of blood, her head and neck a bloody mass. Those first on the scene noted that Lizzie remained remarkably calm throughout the ordeal. While one woman claimed that there were tears in her eyes, several others testified that Lizzie's eyes were dry and her hands steady.

News traveled fast from neighbor to neighbor, and even before the evening presses rolled, everyone in Fall River seemed to know of the horrifying incident. A local reporter recalled that "The cry of murder swept through the city like a typhoon . . . murder committed under the very glare of the midday sun within three minutes walk of the City Hall. . . ." By the next day, the story was front-page news throughout the country and when, after two days, no crazed ax-wielder was produced, newspapers which had praised the police began to question their competence. Trial transcripts suggest that the police did err on the side of caution. If the victims had not been so prominent, matters would have been simpler. The *New York Times* appreciated this fact, and on August 6 noted that "The police are acting slowly and carefully in the affair giving way, no doubt, to feelings of sentiment because of the high social standing of the parties involved." No systematic search of the Borden house was conducted until thirty-two hours after the murders. Out of deference to the bereaved daughters, neither Lizzie nor Emma, who had been summoned home from her vacation, was closely questioned for nearly three days.

Yet, by Saturday, the day of the funerals, the police felt that they had little choice but to arrest Lizzie. She alone, they felt, had had the opportunity to commit the murders. They found it hard to believe that anyone could have passed through the house unseen by Lizzie, who claimed to have been on the first floor while Abby was being murdered above. It also strained credibility to assert, as Lizzie did, that Abby's 210-pound body had crashed to the floor without a sound. Furthermore, despite a reward offered by the Borden sisters, no sender of the note that Lizzie claimed had called Abby to town could be found.

Lizzie's own contradictory answers to the first questions put to her by police were highly damaging. When asked her whereabouts when her father was killed, she gave different answers to different interrogators: "In the back yard"; " . . . in the loft getting a piece of iron for sinkers"; ". . . up in the loft eating pears." The closed barn loft would have been so insufferably hot that day that few would have visited it voluntarily, much less lingered to eat pears. Furthermore, an officer who claimed to have been the first to examine the loft after the crimes testified that the dust on the floor was undisturbed by footprints or trailing skirts.

In Lizzie's favor was the fact that she had been neat and clean when first seen after the murders. The police were certain that the murderer would have been covered with blood. (Medical experts would later examine the trajectories of the spurting blood and argue otherwise, but belief in a blood-drenched killer persisted.)

Though puzzled by Lizzie's cleanliness, police were certain that they had found the murder weapon. Lying in a box of dusty tools, stored high on a chimney jog in the basement, was a hatchet head. It was neither rusty nor old, though it had been freshly rubbed in ashes, perhaps to make it appear so. Moreover, its wooden handle, from which blood would have been difficult to remove, had been broken off near the head.

When the news broke that Lizzie was under suspicion, newspaper readers were horrified—not over the possibility that Lizzie might have murdered her parents, but that the police would harbor such horrid thoughts. The Boston *Globe* expressed its readers' indignation: "The only person that the government can catch is one whose innocence placed her in its power; the poor, defenseless child, who ought to have claimed by very helplessness their protection."

Angry letters denouncing the police flooded newspaper offices from New York to Chicago. Editorials appeared castigating the brutish officers who would suspect a grieving daughter of such a crime. Americans were certain that well-brought-up daughters could not commit murder with a hatchet on sunny summer mornings. And their reaction was not entirely without rationale.

Throughout the 1890's nearly every issue of *Forum, Arena, Scribner's, North American Review, Popular Science Monthly,* and *Harper's* (one of Lizzie's favorites) carried at least one article attesting to the gentleness, physical frailty, and docility of the well-bred American woman. Many of these articles were written in response to the growing number of women who were demanding equal rights, and were written with the intention of proving women hopelessly unable to handle the sacred privileges of men. After having read many such articles written by "learned gentlemen"—and antifeminist women—by the summer of 1892, men and women, regardless of how they stood on women's rights, felt certain that Lizzie Borden could not have hacked her parents to death. Physical and psychological frailties simply made it impossible.

Popular theories about women's physiological and psychological make-up took on new importance to followers of the Borden case. After detailed anatomical analysis, scientists confidently declared that the women of their era differed little from their prehistoric sisters. They spoke with assurance of women's arrested evolution. The fault, they agreed, lay in her reproductive capacity, which sapped vital powers that in men contributed to ever-improving physique and intellect.

The defects of the female anatomy included sloping shoulders, broad hips, underdeveloped muscles, short arms and legs, and poor coordination. To those who believed Lizzie innocent, evidence was abundant that no short-armed, uncoordinated, weakling of a woman could swing an ax with enough force to crash through hair and bone almost two dozen times.

But there was more to it than that. Having already noted woman's smaller frame, anatomists should hardly have been surprised to find her skull proportionately smaller than man's, yet they held up this revelation, too, as further proof of her inferiority. Rather than follow intellectual pursuits, for which they were woefully ill-equipped, women were advised to accept their intended roles as wives and mothers. After all, they were reminded, "Woman is only womanly when she sets herself to man 'like perfect music unto noble works.' "

Spinsters like Lizzie were, as one author charitably put it, "deplorable accidents," but they were not wholly usesless. The nation's old maids were urged to devote themselves to Christian charities and to teaching—a "reproductive calling." Lizzie's devotion to good works and the church followed this prescription precisely. Compelling indeed was the image of this pious daughter serving steaming bowls of soup to indigent newsboys and diligently trying to bring the gospel to the heathen Chinese of Fall River.

While anatomists studied the size of woman's skull, psychologists examined its contents. Among the qualities found to be essentially female were spiritual sensitivity, a good memory for minutiae, and a great capacity for "ennobling love." These positive attributes, however, could not obscure the psychologists' basic premise; women were illogical, inconsistent, and incapable of independent thought.

It is no accident that these traits bore striking resemblance to those attributed to children. As one psychologist pointed out in *Scribner's:* "Women are merely large babies. They are shortsighted, frivolous and occupy an intermediate stage between children and men. . . ."

Several authors manfully chuckled over woman's inability to plan and think things through. Clearly the murderer of the Bordens had planned things quite well. Not only had "he" managed to murder two people and elude the police, but "he" had shown remarkable tenacity by hiding for more than an hour after murdering Abby in order to do the same to Andrew.

Woman was considered man's superior in one area only: the moral sphere. She was thought to possess more "natural refinement," "diviner instincts," and stronger "spiritual sensibility" than man. She was inherently gentle, and abhorred cruelty—hardly the virtues of an ax murderer. Woman was also truthful, though some authors attributed her inability to lie to a lack of intelligence rather than to innate goodness. When reporters interviewed Lizzie's friends, the young women repeatedly mentioned her honesty.

Lizzie benefited greatly from the prevailing stereotypes of feminine delicacy and docility: her cause was also served by the widely accepted stereotype of the female criminal. Ironically, the same periodicals which carried articles about women's gentle nature also carried enough sordid stories of crimes committed by them to cast considerable doubt on their moral superiority. But writers did not find the situation paradoxical. To them, there were clearly two types of women: the genteel ladies of their own class and those women beneath them. Gentlemen authors believed that the womanly instincts of gentleness and love were the monopoly of upper-class women.

Scientists could hardly charge women of their own class with propensities toward violence without casting doubt on their own good breeding. For lower-class women with whom they had no intimate ties (at least none to which they would admit), the situation was quite different. These writers made it very clear that no woman servant, housekeeper, prostitute, nurse, washerwoman, barmaid, or factory girl could be above suspicion.

Several authors even believed that the female criminal had to look the part. In an article in *North American Review*, August, 1895, one criminologist thoughtfully provided the following description: "[She] has coarse black hair and a good deal of it. . . . She has often a long

face, a receding forehead, overjutting brows, prominent cheek-bones, an exaggerated frontal angle as seen in monkeys and savage races, and nearly always square jaws."

She could also be marked by deep wrinkles, a tendency toward baldness, and numerous moles. Other authors noted her long middle fingers, projecting ears, and overlapping teeth. While Lizzie had a massive jaw, her hair was red, her teeth were straight, and her ears flat. Perhaps fortunately for Bridget, a member of the suspect servant class, she was mole-free and brown-haired, and she did not have protruding middle fingers.

Criminal women supposedly exhibited neither the aversion to evil nor the love of mankind which ennobled their upper-class sisters. Among their vices were said to be great cruelty, passionate temper, a craving for revenge, cunning greed, rapacity, contempt for truth, and vulgarity. Such women were thought to be "erotic," but incapable of devoted love. Certainly the Bordens' murderer had been exceedingly cruel. But, while Lizzie was admittedly fond of money and volunteered her dislike of her stepmother, few would have called her rapacious or vengeful, and erotic was hardly an adjective one would have applied to the chaste treasurer of the Fruit and Flower Mission.

The ferocity of the criminal woman fascinated many authors. A favorite murderess was Catherine Hayes, who, in 1890, stabbed her husband to death, cut off his head with a penknife, and boiled it. But then, Mrs. Hayes was a mill worker. One writer did admit that murders might be committed by well-bred women; their weapon would be poison, however, rather than a penknife or an ax, because its passivity appealed to their nature.

Lizzie's attorneys skillfully exploited these two stereotypes—the genteel young woman and the wart-ridden murderess—to their client's advantage throughout the Borden trial. Even before the case reached court, the press had firmly implanted in the public mind a clear picture of Lizzie as bereaved daughter. The image-making began with the very first—and entirely false—story about Lizzie printed in the Boston *Globe* on the day after the murders; "The young woman, with her customary cheery disposition, evidenced her feelings in the tuneful melody from *Il Trovatore,* her favorite opera, which she was singing as she returned to the house. . . . One glance into the living room changed her from a buoyant-spirited young woman into a nervous wreck, every fiber of her being palpitating with the fearful effects of that look. . . ."

In the dozens of articles that followed, Lizzie became the embodiment of genteel young womanhood. A reporter who interviewed her friends found "not one unmaidenly nor a single deliberately unkind act." Voicing the belief of many, he concluded, "Miss Borden, without a word from herself in her own defense, is a strong argument in her own favor."

The attributes of womanliness which vindicated Lizzie did not apply to Bridget. A servant, semiliterate, nearly friendless, Catholic and Irish, Bridget was the perfect target for suspicion. To the dismay of many, no evidence or motive ever could be found to implicate her in the deaths of her employers. Nevertheless, the police received dozens of letters urging her arrest. One man wrote demanding that Bridget and "her Confessor"—that is, her priest—be thrown into prison until she admitted her guilt.

The inquest began in Fall River on August 9. Two pharmacists from Smith's Drug Store testified that Lizzie had been shopping for poison on the afternoon before the murders. She had not asked for arsenic, which was sold over the counter, they said, but for the more lethal prussic acid, claiming she needed it to clean her sealskin cape. On the stand, Lizzie steadfastly denied the pharmacists' story, even denied knowing where Smith's Drug Store was, though it had been there for fourteen years on a street not five minutes from the house in

which she had lived since childhood.

Lizzie's own testimony was full of contradictions. Discrepancies in her story might have been explained by hysteria or grief, but she had displayed neither. On August 5, a reporter at the murder scene for the Providence *Journal* noted: "She wasn't the least bit scared or worried. Most women would faint at seeing their father dead, for I never saw a more horrible sight. . . . She is a woman of remarkable nerve and self-control."

Such self-control seemed unnatural in an age when women were expected to swoon, and many people were alarmed by it. The Reverend Mr. Buck, Lizzie's minister, reassured her champions that "her calmness is the calmness of innocence." Her lawyer, Mr. Jennings, sought to explain away her inconsistent answers by noting that "she was having her monthly illness" on the day of the murders, thereby evoking embarrassed nods of understanding.

Public sentiment on Lizzie's behalf rose to extraordinary heights. In full agreement with their pastor, her church declared her innocent. Ecclesiastical supporters were joined by several noted feminists. Mary Livermore, Susan Fessenden (president of the Women's Christian Temperance Union), and Lucy Stone took up the cudgels on Lizzie's behalf. Livermore declared her arrest to be another outrage perpetrated by "the tyrant man." Lizzie became the sacrificial lamb, the simple, warmhearted girl offered up by corrupt police to the altar of a power-hungry district attorney.

Nonetheless, the judge ordered her arrest at the inquest's end.

Reporters found Lizzie disappointingly composed after the indictment. With no tears to report, they concentrated on her cherry-trimmed hat and the two ministers on whose arms she leaned as she went off to jail in Taunton, the county seat. The horrible cell that awaited her was described in detail. In fact, Lizzie was not confined to a cell, but spent much of her time in the matron's room. Little mention was made of the flowers that graced the prison's window sill, or the lace-edged pillow slips brought by Emma, or of the meals which Lizzie had sent over from Taunton's best hotel.

When the preliminary hearing before Judge Blaisdell began in late November, reporters from more than forty out-of-town newspapers attended. Police held back huge crowds while ladies and gentlemen from Fall River's elite filed into the courtroom to claim the best seats.

A new piece of evidence, damaging to Lizzie's cause, was introduced. She had turned over to the police a spotlessly clean, fancy, blue bengaline dress that she swore she had worn on the day of the murders. Women in New England were surprised. No one wore party dresses of bengaline, a partly woolen fabric, around the house in the August heat. While witnesses swore that Lizzie was indeed wearing blue that day, none could swear that this dress was the one they had seen. To confound the problem, Alice Russell reluctantly admitted that she had seen Lizzie burn a blue cotton dress in the kitchen stove three days after the murders. The dress was soiled, she said Lizzie had told her, with brown paint—a color, noted the prosecutor, not unlike that of dried blood.

Except for rubbing her shoe buttons together, Lizzie sat quietly and displayed little interest. On the very last day, however, she broke into sobs as she heard her lawyer declare that no "person could have committed that crime unless his heart was black as hell." Delighted newspaper artists sketched a tearful Lizzie listening to Mr. Jennings as he asked: "Would it be the stranger, or would it be the one bound to the murdered man by ties of love? . . . what does it mean when we say the youngest daughter? The last one whose baby fingers have been lovingly entwined about her father's brow? Is there nothing in the ties of love and affection?"

Judge Blaisdell listened to all the evidence. It was no stranger who sat before him, but the daughter of a family he knew well. Jennings'

image of the twining baby fingers was compelling, but so was the evidence prosecutor Hosea Knowlton produced. The judge finally began to speak: "Suppose for a single moment that *a man* was standing there. He was found close by that guestchamber which to Mrs. Borden was a chamber of death. Suppose that *a man* had been found in the vicinity of Mr. Borden and the only account he could give of himself was the unreasonable one that he was out in the barn looking for sinkers, that he was in the yard. . . . Would there be any question in the minds of men what should be done with such a man?" The judge's voice broke, but he continued: ". . . the judgment of the court is that you are probably guilty and you are ordered to wait the action of the Superior Court."

The trial began in New Bedford, Massachusetts, on June 5, 1893. Reporters from all over the East Coast converged on the town. Every hotel room within miles was reserved. Fences had to be erected around the courthouse to control the crowds.

Lizzie's newly inherited fortune of several hundred thousand dollars bought her excellent counsel. George Robinson, former governor of the state, was a masterful orator with a politician's shrewd sense of public opinion: at his suggestion, Lizzie went into mourning for the first time since the murders. Laboring against him were District Attorneys Hosea Knowlton and William Moody (a future U.S. Supreme Court justice), as able as Robinson, but with a distaste for flamboyance. Among the three judges who would hear Lizzie's case was Justice Justin Dewey, whom Robinson had elevated to the bench while governor.

One hundred and forty-eight men awaited jury selection. It was assumed that all had formed opinions; they were asked only if their minds were still open enough to judge the evidence fairly. The first man called claimed he could never convict a woman of a capital offense and was dismissed. Of the final twelve, the foreman was a real estate broker and sometime politician, two were manufacturers, three were mechanics, and six were farmers with considerable acreage. Not one foreign-sounding name was among them. Nearly all were over fifty: all were good Yankees.

The first blow to the prosecution came when Judge Dewey ruled Lizzie's damaging inquest testimony inadmissible and barred evidence regarding the alleged attempt to buy poison. While these rulings made Knowlton's task more difficult, his biggest worry was that jury men believed, as did the Boston *Globe*, in the "moral improbability that a woman of refinement and gentle training . . . could have conceived and executed so bloody a butchery." As he repeatedly reminded the jury, "We must face this case as men, not gallants."

Knowlton produced medical experts from Harvard who testified that any average-sized woman could have swung an ax with force enough to commit the murders, and that the trajectory of blood would have been away from the assailant: Lizzie's tidy appearance minutes after the crimes had no bearing on her guilt or innocence. Robinson blithely discounted their testimony by asking the jurymen whether they put more store in Harvard scientists than in their own New England common sense.

Though Lizzie later professed to be shocked at his bill of $25,000, Robinson was worth every penny. As she sat before the jury, a Sunday-school teacher and loving youngest daughter, the jurymen, nearly all of whom were fathers themselves, heard Robinson conclude: "If the little sparrow does not fall unnoticed, then indeed in God's great providence, this woman has not been alone in this courtroom."

The jury was sent off to deliberate with what one reporter called Judge Dewey's "plea for the innocent." The other two judges were said to have been stunned by his lack of objectivity. Though Dewey was indeed grateful to Robinson for his judgeship, a more compelling reason for his unswerving belief in Lizzie's

■ ■ ■ *Lizzie Borden, accused of the ax murders of her father and stepmother in Fall River, Massachusetts (August 1892), was aquitted by an all-male jury that refused to believe a well-bred woman could be capable of such an act.*

innocence may have been the three daughters he had at home, the eldest of whom was Lizzie's age.

The jurors who filed out with Dewey's plea ringing in their ears were bewhiskered, respectable, family men. If they could believe that a gentlewoman could pick up a hatchet such as surely lay in their own basements, and by murdering her parents become an heiress, what could they think next time they looked into their own girls' eyes?

They returned in one hour. The *New York Times* reported that Lizzie's "face became livid, her lips were compressed as she tottered to her feet to hear the verdict!" Before the clerk could finish asking for it, the foreman cried, "Not guilty!" Lizzie dropped to her seat as an enormous cheer went up from the spectators who climbed onto the benches, waving hats and handkerchiefs and weeping.

It would have been difficult for any jury to convict "beyond all reasonable doubt" on the circumstantial evidence presented. However, in the nearby bar to which the jurors dashed, a reporter learned that there had been no debate at all among the twelve. All exhibits were ignored. Their vote had been immediate and unanimous. It was only to avoid the impression that their minds had been made up in advance that they sat and chatted for an hour before returning with their verdict.

The following morning, Americans found reflected in the headlines their own joy that the jury had been so wise. Lizzie and Emma returned to Second Street.

Fall River society, which had defended her throughout her ordeal, fell away thereafter, and Lizzie was left pretty much alone. Undaunted, she determined to have all the things she had missed in her youth. With what some considered indiscreet haste, she bought a large house on the hill and named it Maplecroft. She also asked to be called Lisbeth and stopped going to the church whose parishioners had defended her so energetically. Matters were not improved when townspeople learned that she had bought and destroyed every available copy of local reporter Edwin Porter's *The Fall River Tragedy*, which had included portions of her inquest testimony.

Lizzie sealed her isolation in 1904 by striking up a friendship with Nance O'Neil, a Boston actress. The following year, to her neighbors' horror, Lizzie gave a party—complete with caterers and potted palms—for Miss O'Neil and her troupe. That night, Emma quietly moved out and never spoke to or saw Lizzie again.

Lizzie continued to live at Maplecroft in increasing isolation. Undoubtedly, she heard the nasty rhyme children began to sing to the tune of "Ta-Ra-Ra Boom-De-Ay!":

Lizzie Borden took an ax
And gave her mother forty whacks;
When she saw what she had done,
She gave her father forty-one!

Lizzie Borden died on June 1, 1927, at the age of sixty-six in Fall River. Emma died ten days later in New Hampshire. Few gravestones conceal a puzzle more intricate than that sealed away by the imposing Borden monument in Oak Grove Cemetery. The truth about the events on Second Street lies buried there along with Andrew, Abby, Emma, and Lizzie, but back then, in the summer of 1893, most Americans knew in their hearts that no young lady like Lizzie could have murdered her parents with an ax. Reputable authors in respectable magazines assured them their intuition was correct. They did not even want to think that it could be otherwise.

■ ■ ■

STUDY QUESTIONS

1. How did Lizzie Borden's class and social standing influence the way she was treated by legal authorities?

2. What were the physical, psychological, intellectual, and moral characteristics that popular magazines in the late nineteenth century attributed to well-bred women? How closely did Lizzie conform to these expectations?

3. What did late nineteenth-century writers mean by such concepts as "arrested evolution" and "deplorable accidents"? How do these concepts indicate a sexually biased society?

4. In what area were women considered superior to men? Why was this so?

5. How did popular attitudes toward upper-class and lower-class women differ? Why were many people more inclined to suspect Bridget Sullivan than Lizzie Borden of the crime?

6. How was Lizzie's behavior during the entire episode interpreted?

7. Why was the trial politically and symbolically significant?

BIBLIOGRAPHY

The Borden murder case has been examined and reexamined. Victoria Lincoln, *Lizzie Borden, a Private Disgrace* (1967) and Robert Sullivan, *Goodbye Lizzie Borden* (1974) argue that she was indeed guilty of the crimes. Edward D. Radin, *Lizzie Borden: The Untold Story* (1961) views the case from a different perspective.

Recent historical scholarship has only begun to explore the complexities of American attitudes toward women. Lois W. Banner, *Women in Modern America: A Brief History* (1974, second edition 1984) presents a fine introduction to the topic and a good bibliography. Other useful studies on women in the late nineteenth century include John S. Haller, Jr., and Robin M. Haller, *The Physician and Sexuality in Victorian America* (1974); G. J. Barker-Benfield, *The Horrors of the Half-Known Life: Male Attitudes Toward Women and Sexuality in Nineteenth-Century America* (1976); Linda Gordon, *Woman's Body, Woman's Right: A Social History of Birth Control in America* (1976); and Lois Banner, *American Beauty* (1983).

Two other books present different views of the role of women in America. Kate Chopin, *The Awakening* (1980) is a wonderful novel written with depth and sensitivity. Questions of isolation and alienation in a small American town are touched upon in Michael Lesy, *Wisconsin Death Trip* (1973).

THE PHYSICIANS' CRUSADE AGAINST ABORTION, 1857–1880

James C. Mohr

Few people will contest the claim that the abortion question is the most difficult and controversial social and political issue in contemporary America. On the religious right, Americans claim that the fetus enjoys the Fifth Amendment right to life, while pro-choice advocates claim that a women's right to privacy takes precedence over fetal needs. The Supreme Court's decision in Roe *v.* Wade in 1973, legalizing most abortions through the second trimester of pregnancy, has sparked a political firestorm whose quenching is still not in sight. Both sides claim the moral and constitutional high ground, and compromise will certainly be extremely difficult to achieve.

It may surprise some to realize that Americans have not always been so passionate about abortion. Throughout the seventeenth, eighteenth, and first half of the nineteenth centuries, abortion was considered, for the most part, to be beyond the law as long as the termination of the pregnancy occurred before "quickening"—the moment when the mother first felt the fetus move within her uterus. At that point, collective opinion believed, the fetus became a human being and abortion was illegal. But if quickening had not yet occurred, abortion was not considered a crime. Abortionists advertised their skills in the newspapers and district attorneys did not prosecute either the women who received abortions or the people who performed them. Abortion did not become legally and morally controversial until the middle decades of the nineteenth century when physicians launched a powerful, and ultimately very effective, political campaign against abortion. In the following essay, historian James C. Mohr discusses that political campaign and the reasons physicians were so determined to outlaw abortion.

Following the bleak period they endured during the 1830s and early 1840s, America's regular physicians, committed to the forward-looking tenets of what would become scientific medicine, began a concerted, self-conscious, and eventually successful drive designed to improve, professionalize, and ultimately control the practice of medicine in the United States. The founding of the American Medical Association in 1847 may be taken as the beginning of this long-term effort, the goals of which were not fully realized until the twentieth century. While this process obviously and profoundly affected the development of medicine itself in this country, it also dramatically affected the evolution of a number of social policies subsequently inherited by twentieth-century Americans; opposition to abortion was definitely one of them. Regular physicians affiliated with the AMA launched an aggressive campaign against abortion on the eve of the Civil War. The pressure of their crusade pushed state legislators beyond expressions of cautious concern about abortion and its possible excesses to straightforward opposition to the practice. Equally important, the doctors' crusade began also to affect the underlying public tolerance of abortion that had remained so common in the United States through the 1850s.

Although regular physicians had been a major force in the creation of anti-abortion statutes since the 1820s, their support for such legislation had been largely ad hoc: as consultants to code revisers, as friends of individual legislators, as members of legislative committees, as individual protesters, and as reactors to court decisions that affected their livelihood. But regular physicians as a group had not seized the offensive against abortion in America on a broad front, probably in large part because they were not sufficiently well

organized to do anything as a group on a front more extensive than their own states, or often their own counties. While the founding of the AMA did not instantly alter that situation, it did provide an organizational framework within which a concerted campaign for a particular policy might be coordinated on a larger scale than ever before. Ten years after its creation a young Boston physician decided to use that framework to launch an attack upon America's ambiguous and permissive policies toward abortion. He very quickly found himself at the head of one of the first and ultimately one of the most successful public policy crusades ever undertaken by the AMA.

The young physician was Horatio Robinson Storer, a specialist in obstetrics and gynecology. Storer, an activist who "kept things stirred up wherever he was," sensed that his elders were growing restive about abortion and that the time was right for a professionally ambitious leader to take advantage of the still unfocused opposition of regular physicians to abortion. Walter Channing, the long-time Harvard professor and brother of William Ellery Channing, lent his prestige to the anti-abortion cause by reporting suspected cases to professional journals early in the 1850s. Experienced physicians who had scoffed at the talk of an abortion problem in the United States twenty years earlier were openly upset by the mid-1850s. The venerable Hugh L. Hodge of Philadelphia, who had spoken out against the consequences of the quickening doctrine in public lectures in 1839, reiterated his criticisms of American abortion policy in 1854, this time in print. In 1855 Horatio Storer's father, the nationally prominent D. Humphreys Storer, then professor of obstetrics and medical jurisprudence at Harvard, joined the nascent movement by lecturing on the physical dangers involved in having an abortion. But the elder Storer feared that publication of such material might still be premature and withheld his paper, despite a request from the *Boston Medical and Surgical Journal* to print it. The

From *Abortion in America: The Origins and Evolution of National Policy* by James C. Mohr. Reprinted by permission of Oxford University Press, Inc.

younger Storer, however, who had already completed a good deal of research on abortion and who still had a reputation to make rather than one to risk, seized the initiative when his father drew back.

Horatio Storer laid the groundwork for the anti-abortion campaign he launched later in the year by writing influential physicians all around the country early in 1857 and inquiring about the abortion laws in each of their states. The responses must have strengthened his resolve to forge ahead. All of his correspondents reported ineffectual legislation or no legislation at all, an many encouraged Storer to try to do something about it. C. W. LeBoutillier reported from Minnesota Territory that "the practice of producing abortion is frequently resorted to in our vicinity, and it is not unfrequent for married women of high social position to apply for medicines which will produce abortion—and I regret to say that Regular physicians have in many instances assisted in these damnable practices. The law as it stands is to us worthless, and unless it is amended, the evil will not soon cease." The law in Missouri, according to Dr. Charles Pope, a former president of the AMA, was worded in a way that actually "screen[ed]" physicians "in the disreputable practice." Dr. J. Berrien Lindsley of Nashville urged Storer to put the matter before the AMA, though Lindsley himself preferred not to sit on any special committees on the subject. "I am glad, right glad, you have got hold of the subject of criminal abortion—a crime which 40 years ago, when I was a young practitioner, was of *rare* and *secret* occurrence has become *frequent* and *bold*," wrote Dr. Thomas Blatchford from Troy, New York. "It is high time it was taken hold of in good earnest, but you will find its roots deep and its branches very spreading. It is so here[,] our enactments to the contrary notwithstanding. The moral sense of community wants correcting; it is all obtundified (I had to make a word) on this subject. Again I say I am glad you have got hold of it. dont [*sic*] let it go until

■ ■ *Horatio Robinson Storer, the most prominent of the crusaders against abortion in the nineteenth century, played a key role in the beginning of the anti-abortion legislation in the United States.*

you have made your exertions tell on [the] community."

In selecting his correspondents, Storer was careful to solicit the backing of those physicians who were already campaigning for anti-abortion policies in their own states. One such was Henry Brisbane, then working to change Wisconsin's abortion policies. Though Brisbane succeeded, he told Storer that he had worked virtually alone because the poorly organized state medical society had proved "worthless" as a professional pressure group. This, of course, was what Storer hoped to change. Alexander Semmes of Washington, D.C., another valuable contact, assured Storer in

March of 1857 that the time had come "to put such an extinguisher upon [the growing practice of abortion] as to prevent its becoming a characteristic feature in American 'civilization.'" Eight days later Semmes reported to the Bostonian that "commissioners are now occupied in codifying and arranging our laws, and when they reach that portion of criminal law relative to 'Coroners' and 'abortion,' they promise to communicate with me, before reducing the law to a statutory form."

After gaining the private support of key physicians around the country by mail, Storer opened his crusade publicly in May 1857 by introducing to the Suffolk County Medical Society a resolution that called for the formation of a committee to "consider whether any further legislation is necessary in this Commonwealth, on the subject of *criminal abortion*, and to report to the Society such other means as may seem necessary for the suppression of this abominable, unnatural, and yet common crime." Storer also added an amendment: "and that said report, when accepted by this Society, shall by it be recommended to the Massachusetts Medical Society as a basis for its further action." The county society accepted these motions, the Suffolk resolves of the anti-abortion cause, and appointed a committee under Storer's leadership to deal with them.

Storer's committee report touched off considerable controversy among Boston's leading physicians. Indeed, what became a great medical crusade against the practice of abortion was almost aborted itself at the outset. Some members of the county society disagreed with the implication in one of Storer's statements that regular physicians occasionally condoned abortion; some considered the issue too ambiguous and too full of thorny possibilities to risk taking a forceful stand upon it; some apparently disliked and distrusted the younger Storer personally. One anonymous physician criticized Storer's efforts as "too hastily got up," and noted that the Storer committee's report "seems to have thrown out of considera-

tion the life of the mother, making that of the unborn child appear of far more consequence, even should the mother have a dozen dependent on her for their daily bread. It cannot be possible that either the profession or the public will be brought to this belief. Argue as forcibly as they may, to their own satisfaction," the critic continued, "the Committee will fail to convince the public that abortion in the early months is a crime, and a large proportion of the medical profession will tacitly support the popular view of the subject." One section of the report urged lawmakers to reverse the burden of proving intent; to place upon the woman and the person suspected of performing an abortion the duty of proving that abortion was not what they had in mind. This, argued the report's critic quite accurately, would not only stand justice upon its head but open the door to all sorts of malpractice suits as well.

Yet the outcome of the debate indicated that Storer's assessment of regular medical opinion had been fundamentally accurate and that his sense of timing had been perfect. The local criticism of his report ignited a surprisingly vigorous counterreaction in his defense, which reached well beyond the local area, and helped solidify Storer's position at the head of the nascent anti-abortion crusade in America. A tumultuous meeting of the Suffolk District Medical Society, for example, condemned the *Boston Medical and Surgical Journal* for printing criticism of Storer's report on the grounds that the critic had falsely implied that regulars countenanced abortion. The *New Hampshire Journal of Medicine* touched off a bitter editorial feud with its Boston rival when it made similar accusations, and some of the New York medical journals joined in on the side of the *New Hampshire Journal*. Medical journals around the nation began to endorse Storer's proposals and some of them, like the *Medical and Surgical Reporter* of New Jersey, urged physicians in their areas "to make a public protest against the practice [of abortion]." The *Boston Medical and Surgical Journal*, very much on the defensive for having printed the criticism, came out foursquare for the Storer report and tried to mend its fences by reminding its readers of its obligation to print the opinions of any member of the local medical society. The critic himself was finally driven to claim that his statements had been misinterpreted and that he had been a long-time personal foe of abortion. Though a medical student wrote home that Storer won only after his local enemies abandoned the floor in disgust, Boston's regular physicians endorsed Storer's report early in the summer of 1857. Storer, Henry I. Bowditch, and Calvin Ellis were appointed to represent the county's position to the state society. Storer had made it safely over what turned out to be the most formidable hurdle he ever encountered among his fellow regular physicians on the subject of abortion.

Storer concentrated not upon the state level, however, where winning another endorsement of his anti-abortion statements would be a relatively easy process after success in the Boston area, but instead upon the possibility of generating medical pressure against abortion on a national scale. He wrote articles on abortion for the *New York Medical Journal*, the *American Journal of the Medical Sciences*, and the *Medico-Chirurgical Review*, all of which had large national circulations. Although he had only joined the young and still struggling American Medical Association in 1856, Storer focused his attention upon that organization. At the AMA's 1857 annual national meeting held that year in Nashville, Storer urged physicians to take a strong stand against abortion in the United States. The assembled delegates, some of whom had already been contacted earlier in the year by the young Boston activist, responded by appointing a committee to draft a position paper for AMA consideration at a future convention. The committee comprised a who's who of the medical crusade against abortion: Dr. Thomas W. Blatchford of New York, the man most responsible for publicizing Madame Restell's activities in 1845; Dr. Hugh L. Hodge

of Pennsylvania, the first of the nation's prestigious medical professors to attack the practice of abortion publicly; Dr. Edward H. Barton of South Carolina, one of the deans of Southern physicians; Dr. Charles A. Pope of St. Louis, an influential former president of the AMA who had considerable power in his state's legislature; Dr. A. Lopez of Alabama, who believed his efforts to persuade legislators in that state to take a harder line on abortion had been frustrated "because politicians usurp the seats intended for *Representatives*, i.e., exponents of the true wants of society at large, based upon not only the protection of property, but the guardianship of human life and the moral law"; Dr. Alexander J. Semmes, whose influence in Washington, D.C., was well known; and Dr. William H. Brisbane, who had already been successful in toughening the abortion policies of Wisconsin. Horatio R. Storer was selected to chair the group.

Reactions around the country continued to bode well for the success of Storer's national project. Still another prominent professor of obstetrics, Dr. Jesse Boring of the Atlanta Medical School, who was at the AMA meeting in 1857, when Storer called for action, came out publicly against the "prevalent laxity of moral sentiment on this subject, as evidenced by the increasing frequency of induced abortions." The Medical Society of Buffalo, New York, called in 1858 for "a united and powerful movement" of the nation's medical societies in opposition to this ancient practice that had suddenly mushroomed into an enormous social threat in the United States. Regulars of the state of Maine immediately endorsed the Buffalo resolves against "this great and growing evil."

Storer wrote his committee's report by himself in 1858, and early in 1859 he solicited suggestions and support from the other members. Brisbane and Barton both hoped for a strong condemnation of abortifacient medicines and their advertisement, but Storer preferred to avoid that subject. He knew that a head-on confrontation with drug manufacturers and advertisers would be disastrous. As Barton himself conceded, such subjects "might be productive of too much discussion—which might jeopardize our [sic] of your objects." Much more to Storer's liking was a suggestion from the venerable Hodge. "Perhaps," the astute Philadelphia professor opined, "the probability of success might be increased, if the general association should strongly recommend that each state med[ical] association should press the subject on the Legislative bodies of their respective states." Given the highly federated nature of the AMA itself, this was good advice, and Storer recognized it as such. Even though his original draft included language along the line Hodge indicated, the chairman made the idea explicit in a separate resolution. Moreover, as he had done in 1857, Storer also wrote many physicians around the country to generate additional backing for his report at the AMA's national convention, scheduled to meet in 1859 at Louisville. Several physicians agreed to co-sponsor the proposal, and some of the committee members, who would not have made the trip west in 1859 under routine circumstances, agreed to go to Louisville and press for the report.

The document cited three chief causes for the country's "general demoralization" regarding abortion practices. First was the "widespread popular ignorance" about the significance, or lack of significance, of quickening as a stage in gestation. Second was the fact "that the profession themselves are frequently supposed careless of foetal life," which was as close to a confession of partial responsibility as Storer or the AMA ever went. Third was "the grave defects of our laws." To remedy the situation and to suppress the "rapidly increasing crime of abortion," three resolutions were appended to the report. In one the AMA was asked to commit itself "publicly to enter an earnest and solemn protest against [the] unwarrantable destruction of human life" occasioned by the quickening doctrine. In the

second the Association, recognizing the traditional duties of its "grand and noble calling," was charged with urging "the several legislative assemblies of the Union" to revise their abortion laws. In the third, which embodied Hodge's suggestion, the AMA formally requested "the zealous co-operation of the various State Medical Societies in pressing this subject upon the legislatures of their respective States." Storer became ill shortly before the convention and could not travel out to Louisville, but the delegates, encouraged by Storer's representatives among them, accepted the report in a unanimous vote. According to Thomas Blatchford, Storer's project had proved a great success at the convention.

From the Louisville convention of 1859 through the rest of the nineteenth century, the steadily growing AMA would remain steadfastly and officially committed to outlawing the practice of abortion in the United States, both inside and outside that organization, and the vigorous efforts of America's regular physicians would prove in the long run to be the single most important factor in altering the legal policies toward abortion in this country. With remarkable persistence, regular state and local medical organizations likewise sustained the crusade that Storer's report had initiated. The Medical Society of Michigan brought forth a major condemnatory statement almost immediately in 1859. In 1860 Henry Miller devoted the first portion of his presidential address before the AMA's annual convention to the subject of abortion. He reported that Storer, in an effort to implement his 1859 resolutions, had volunteered to draft an anti-abortion memorial, which was then sent in the name of the AMA from the national office to each governor and to every state legislature in the country. Miller implored all delegates to the convention to enlist support from the entire medical community, not just that minority affiliated with the AMA, for a massive crusade of public enlightenment, despite the obstacles of "public ignorance" on the one hand and "the jeers of the flippant, the superficial, and the unthinking in your own ranks" on the other. Toward this end the AMA in 1864 approved a suggestion to establish a special prize and to promise publication for "the best popular tract upon the subject of induced abortion."

The origins of that contest are unknown, but it seems no coincidence that the annual convention that approved the scheme met in Boston. It must have been especially difficult for cynics to believe the protestations denying collusion when the results of the competition were made public. The prize committee, made up of prominent Boston physicians and chaired by D. Humphreys Storer, awarded the AMA's gold medal for 1865 to "The Criminality and Physical Evils of Forced Abortion" by none other than Horatio R. Storer; after all, how many physicians were likely to have had a major manuscript on that subject ready to go? Storer's extended essay was published by the AMA in book form under the title *Why Not? A Book for Every Woman*. Scare propaganda aimed at women predominated throughout the volume, but Storer addressed himself to male policymakers at several points as well. *Why Not?* was well received by the popular press and sold briskly for the next five years. In 1867 Storer tried to follow up his success with *Why Not?* by bringing out a companion piece entitled *Is It I? A Book for Every Man*. Though apparently somewhat less influential than its widely disseminated prototype, *Is It I?* was also favorably received by both the medical and the popular press.

In 1868 the prolific leader of the medical crusade against abortion in the United States collaborated with Franklin Fiske Heard on a volume that focused more sharply the arguments Storer wanted to direct at lawmakers. *Criminal Abortion: Its Nature, Its Evidence, and Its Law* was intended explicitly to substantiate in a rigorous fashion the generalizations and exhortations advanced in *Why Not?* and *Is It I?*, and unlike those more popular tracts, *Criminal Abortion* was intended for lawyers and legal scholars. Storer actually studied for a time at Harvard Law School, in part at least to prepare himself for the collaboration on *Criminal Abortion*. The volume explored the law of abortion in detail and offered the best statistical data then available in support of its contentions. That evidence has already been discussed in a previous chapter. From a scholarly point of view, *Criminal Abortion* was the best piece Storer ever wrote on the subject that dominated his career for more than a decade.

By the end of the 1860s Storer's health began to fail badly, and in 1872 he finally left the country for sunnier climates abroad. Though this removed him from medical politics in the United States, the crusade he had launched never foundered. The AMA, concerned that its recommendations had not been enacted in every state, renewed its campaign to win tougher anti-abortion statutes in another major report on the subject in 1871. Even more importantly, state and local medical societies sustained the anti-abortion efforts that Storer had pressed them to begin. Regular medical journals throughout the nation continued to urge their readers to strike whatever blows they could against the widespread practice of abortion in America. Physicians helped keep the issue before the public and dozens of state and local medical societies memorialized their legislatures on the subject. That these activities had a direct impact upon the evolution of abortion policy in the United States will become apparent in subsequent chapters.

America's regular physicians appear to have persisted in their crusade against abortion for a number of complex reasons that may be divided for convenience into two broad categories: professional reasons and personal reasons. The first professional motive underlying the regulars' anti-abortion campaign had been evident in the United States for thirty years before Storer focused and institutionalized the regulars' uneasiness about abortion: by raising the abortion question and by highlighting the abuses and dangers associated with it, regular physicians could encourage the state to deploy its sanctions against their competitors. This would remain a powerful incentive for regulars to keep up their pressure at least until the 1880s and 1890s, when cooperative licensing laws finally brought an end to the era of laissez faire medicine in America.

A special committee on criminal abortion appointed by the East River Medical Association of New York in 1871 expressed this professional concern of American regulars unambiguously:

Your committee deem the unrestricted practice of medicine as the main cause for the existence of professional abortionists, and the want of proper laws to regulate the practice of medicine as encouraging knaves to assume and practice under titles which institutions duly chartered by the State alone have the right to confer.

The parent body endorsed this conclusion unanimously and implored the legislature to enact regulatory statutes as "encouragement to a profession honored and fostered by every civilized government except this."

The Illinois State Medical Society, even though it conceded that there were "members of the regular profession . . . guilty of this crime," still condemned the "irregulars and persons outside of the profession of medicine proper" in 1872 for performing most of the abortions in their area. The Illinois regulars called for stronger enforcement of the state's laws against such people. In 1874 Detroit physicians likewise urged a crackdown against "the inhuman wretches" who produced abortion; "almost every neighborhood or small village," they claimed, "has its old woman, of one sex or the other, who is known for her ability and willingness for a pecuniary consideration" to break the state's abortion statues. They wanted "her" driven from the field. The Southern Michigan Medical Society was reminded again in 1875 of the key point here. Regular physicians were still losing patients,

even long-time patients, to competitors willing "to prevent an increase in the [patients'] families" by performing abortions.

The specific cases of abortion cited in the medical journals almost invariably stressed that the performer was a "quack," a "doctress," an "irregular," or the like, and regular physicians remained openly jealous of the handsome fees abortionists collected for their services. Article after article and editorial after editorial in the medical journals implored authorities to use the law more effectively against those on the margins of medical practice. As one historian of nineteenth-century physicians put it, the founding of the AMA had been "a time of hope . . . a time to gather the righteous under one banner, to seek out and destroy the foe." The anti-abortion crusade launched a decade later was one of the first great manifestations of that spirit.

A second professional reason for sustaining the anti-abortion campaign stemmed, somewhat paradoxically, from the persistent failure of America's regular physicians, even those directly allied with the AMA, to enforce their own code of ethics during the nineteenth century. Many regular doctors believed strongly that their future depended upon rigorous professionalization. But professionalization, the creation of a self-regulated guild with privileged status, depended in large part upon the ability of the group as a whole to enforce standards of behavior upon all of the individuals who wanted to be part of that profession. Since any healer who wanted to practice medicine could do so, the punishment of expulsion from a formally organized medical society was no particular threat. As a result, codes of ethics were largely unenforceable. Under these circumstances many professional-minded physicians looked to the state for help. An anti-abortion law would lend public sanction to the professionals' efforts at disciplining their own organizations. Put somewhat differently, the anti-abortion crusade became at least in part a manifestation of the fact that many physicians wanted to promote, indeed to force where necessary, a sense of professionalism, as they defined it, upon their own colleagues.

The rhetoric of professionalism was striking and obvious in the anti-abortion crusade from 1860 to 1880. Spokesmen invariably claimed to be speaking for the profession, not for themselves. Storer's writings provide a perfect example of this common ploy. He carefully gained official sanction for his positions; he frequently used the device of the committee to make his efforts appear to be those of the profession as a whole; and he sprinkled his public volumes liberally with phrases such as "viewing the matter, as I do, from a professional standpoint," and "the views that I present are those accepted by the physicians of our time most competent to judge." Time and again medical writers demanded punishment for any regular willing to perform abortions, and urged their fellow doctors to testify against erring brethren in court. Also striking was the large number of anti-abortion writers who accused the medical societies of harboring, or at least of tolerating, members known to be frequent aborters. Such tolerance, claimed the professionalizers, harmed the good name of all regular physicians, and those who aborted were regarded as hateful traitors in the prolonged war over the future of American medicine. The crusade to have abortion outlawed thus functioned as a demonstration of one's good faith on the subject of professional ethics.

In the context it is worth noting that the greatest champions of the anti-abortion crusade were also in the forefront of the drive for professionalization generally. The Boston Gynecological Society, for example, whose members had rallied strongly to Storer's original report, went before the national AMA in 1870 and successfully demanded that its parent body, the Massachusetts Medical Society, be purged of homoeopaths. Storer was such a fierce professional himself that he even barred from his lectures "any applicant who was not affiliated with the American Medical Association." William Henry Brisbane, the anti-abortion advocate from Wisconsin, was involved in attempts to reorganize and professionalize the loosely knit and doctrinally flexible Wisconsin Medical Society. When the corresponding secretary of the AMA solicited state-of-the-profession reports from affiliated societies in 1879, nine state organizations mentioned anti-abortion efforts among their professional activities.

A third professional reason why organized regular physicians sustained an anti-abortion crusade involved their desire to recapture what they considered to be their ancient and rightful place among society's policymakers and savants. From ancient times through the end of the eighteenth century, physicians believed, doctors had occupied positions of high status and great influence. As Walter Channing, an early anti-abortion spokesman, phrased it longingly in his lecture to the incoming class at Harvard Medical School in 1845, the physician had been held "in great honor" from Cicero to Dr. Johnson. "The hospital was a temple in which presided a god. . . . The physician had an important place in society, in the literature and science of the time. He had public and private duties to perform. He was a minister of the public health as well as a private practitioner." Doctors of earlier days had "established a claim to the public confidence and respect." Yet physicians in America had fallen into low repute during the period of democratized and wide-open medicine that characterized the first half of the nineteenth century. Channing referred snidely to that "age of reform[,] a word unmusical to many ears," and urged the matriculants to work to restore the status of their chosen profession.

The anti-abortion crusade was nearly perfect for the purposes Channing and countless others like him had in mind. It provided the exhilaration of helping once again to make public policy, as well as the feeling that physicians could begin to "minister" to the larger needs of their society as before. Indeed, the messianic tone of the physicians' crusade was striking. Storer's AMA report of 1859 had a sermon-like quality in its exhortation to try to change society, and so did the numerous articles, reports, and editorials that followed for the next twenty years in the medical journals. Some writers, including E. P. Christian and John P. Stoddard, two of Michigan's anti-abortion stalwarts, stated explicitly on different occasions that what the doctors were doing was in a real sense "missionary" work; it was time for the enlightened once again to come forward and guide the benighted public on a key question of social and moral policy. In that way the medical profession might recapture some of the luster of its golden past, when the physician had been a major voice in his society and enjoyed the status of a "god."

Compelling personal factors certainly added to the substantial professional motives for an anti-abortion crusade on the part of America's regular physicians. The first was a no doubt sincere belief on the part of most regular physicians that abortion was morally wrong. The fact that this belief coincided nicely with their professional self-interest is no reason to accuse physicians of hypocrisy on the issue; instead, the convergence probably helps to explain the intensity of their commitment to the cause. As was pointed out in an earlier context, nineteenth-century physicians knew categorically that quickening had no special significance as a stage in gestation. Hence it is not difficult to grant the genuineness of their uneasiness over the continued use of what they regarded as an unimportant, almost incidental, occurrence during pregnancy to distinguish between legal life and legal non-existence in cases of assault against a fetus. The next step beyond the denial of quickening as an appropriate distinction between being and non-being was the conclusion that no single occurrence during gestation could be pinpointed as the moment at which a fetus in utero became more "alive" than it had been a moment before. Logically, then, if a child could legally exist in utero at some stage

of gestation, say at eight months, when the law recognized it as a victim, it just as logically existed at all other stages of gestation.

Most physicians considered abortion a crime because of the inherent difficulties of determining any point at which a steadily developing embryo became somehow more alive than it had been the moment before. Furthermore, they objected strongly to snuffing out life in the making. Only if a fully realized life—that of the mother—would surely be lost without their intervention could they morally justify the termination of another already developing life. A physician from Metamora, Illinois, cogently expressed this argument in a paper he read to his local county medical society in 1873 on the subject of criminal abortion:

Many, indeed, argue, that the practice is not, in fact, criminal, because, they argue, that the child is not viable until the seventh month of gestation, hence there is no destruction of life. The truly professional man's morals, however, are not of that easy caste, because he sees in the germ the probable embryo, in the embryo the rudimentary foetus, and in that, the seven months viable child and the prospective living, moving, breathing man or woman, as the case may be.

Physicians who personally believed abortion to be morally wrong—and their many fervent writings on this subject must be taken as evidence of their sincerity—must have been frustrated by the persistent lack of public support for their position. They certainly lamented the public's indifference to their moral arguments frequently enough. Only one state court prior to 1880 decided a pre-quickened abortion case, in the absence of explicit legislation, along the lines that the doctors who followed Storer believed morally valid. Even in that case, an 1850 Pennsylvania ruling, the judge asserted: "It is not the murder of a living child which constitutes the offense, but the destruction of gestation by wicked means and against nature;" and he recognized that his decision was against all legal precedent in the United States. Consequently, it was apparent to physicians that the only way to deal with this question of basic morality was to see that their position was embodied in explicit statutes of their own design. Lobbying became holy work for those physicians who believed that the United States was damning itself as a society by continuing to commit mortal sins on a massive scale without even realizing it. The theme of saving America from itself was a common leitmotif throughout the medical campaign against abortion after 1860.

The desire to save America from itself also underlay a second personal reason why regular physicians fought so strongly for anti-abortion laws. Most regular physicians were white, native-born, Protestants of British and North European stock. And so, as they constantly reiterated for twenty years between 1860 and 1880, were most of the women having abortions. The doctors both used and were influenced by blatant nativism.

In his prize essay Storer had made the standard claim that abortion was "infinitely more frequent among Protestant women than among Catholic." He had already made that point forcefully in previous articles, as had many other observers, and he and Heard, using the available demographic data, laid heavy stress on the decline of native birthrates in their 1868 *Criminal Abortion*. Elsewhere around the country other doctors also continued to beat the old nativist drums on behalf of anti-abortion policies. Many physicians treated their colleagues in medical journals and convention speeches to fantasies of reverse Darwinism ruining the nation, or of "the ignorant, the low lived and the alien" taking over by the straightforward process of outbreeding "our own population." As a Michigan physician phrased it two years prior to the nation's hundredth anniversary, "the annual destruction of foetuses" had become so "truly appalling" among native American women that "the Puritanic blood of

'76 will be but sparingly represented in the approaching centenary." There was "more sense than nonsense," he thought, "in the remark of one of our humorists, that it would be a paying investment for some showman to catch and preserve a pure American, for fifty years hence he would be a phenomenon. America is fast losing her national characteristics." There can be little doubt that Protestants' fears about not keeping up with the reproductive rates of Catholic immigrants played a greater role in the drive for anti-abortion laws in nineteenth-century America than Catholic opposition to abortion did.

In their constantly repeated concerns about being outbred, physicians suggested a third personal reason why some of them may have worked so hard for effective anti-abortion laws in the United States: they seem to have been deeply afraid of being betrayed by their own women. Regular physicians were among the most defensive groups in the country on the subject of changing traditional sex roles. Even while state legislators were passing liberalized property and divorce laws, forcing some of the state universities to admit women, and debating women's suffrage in the 1860s and 1870s, most doctors were bitterly and stridently condemning what one of them called the "*non-infanto* mania" that afflicted the nation's women and desperately decrying the unwillingness of American wives to remain in their "places" bearing and raising children.

Horatio Storer, an outspoken opponent of new social roles for women, infused the anti-abortion campaign with his conservative views on that subject virtually from its inception, though he revealed his position most obviously in *Is It I?* in 1867. In that volume he asserted that men had certain justifiable sexual urges, but counseled husbands to temper their "rights" with a sense of "duty" lest their wives take recourse to abortion from too frequent pregnancies. "And let me say," he added, "that I intend no ultra ground; that I am neither a fanatic nor professed philanthrope; and that in loosing, as I hope to do, some of women's chains, it is solely for professional purposes, to increase her health, prolong her life, extend the benefits she confers upon society—in a word, selfishly to enhance her value to ourselves." Elsewhere he was just as blunt. "I am no advocate for unwomanly women," he wrote in an understatement of epic proportions. "I would not transplant them, from their proper and God-given sphere, to the pulpit, the forum, or the cares of state, nor would I repeat the experiment, so patiently tried by myself, and at last so emphatically condemned—of females attempting the practice of the medical profession." True to his word, he fought the entry of women into the regular ranks, though he was hardly alone on the barricades. AMA physicians voted down a recommendation of their national committee on ethics in 1868 to permit female doctors to consult with regulars and rejected an 1871 constitutional amendment that would have permitted delegates "from colleges and hospitals in which women studied medicine." As might be expected, Storer and others like him opposed liberalized divorce laws on the same grounds they opposed abortion, because "the very foundation of all society and civil government would be uprooted."

Storer was not an extremist, however, at least among physicians, on the subject of the proper social role of women. Recognizing that he faced an era of rising consciousness among women, one of the medical crusaders against abortion wrote in 1869: "Woman's rights and woman's sphere are, as understood by the American public, quite different from that understood by us as Physicians, or as Anatomists, or Physiologists." He was right. To many doctors the chief purpose of women was to produce children; anything that interfered with that purpose, or allowed women to "indulge" themselves in less important activities, threatened marriage, the family, and the future of society itself. Abortion was a supreme

example of such an interference for these physicians. What would become of the country when "American women," in the phrase of an oft-reprinted report submitted to the Iowa State Medical Society in 1871, "for selfish and personal ends, butcher or poison their children?"

Some physicians were more generous toward women than others. Poverty, or relative or perceived poverty, was often acknowledged by physicians as an excuse given for abortion, but always rebutted by the doctors themselves. As was clear in the debates between physicians and feminists over who was responsible for the nation's high abortion rates, a number of physicians blamed men, at least to some extent, for driving women, whom they considered weaker persons, to seek abortions. Occasionally a physician would even recognize and acknowledge the deep fear of pregnancy and childbirth instilled in many nineteenth-century women, for whom those processes held a very real prospect of death. As some doctors pointed out, many women considered abortion a cure, an escape from a situation many women themselves considered pathological and frightening. But most medical writers between 1860 and 1880, when the medical crusade against abortion was at its height and making its greatest impact on American abortion policy, continued to direct their sharpest accusatory arrows at women directly. Many physicians were determined to prevent women from risking the future of society as they understood it by denying what these doctors believed to be a biologically determined social imperative. Their determination on this point almost certainly strengthened their resolve to carry forward their great campaign to alter the nation's legal policies toward abortion.

The physicians' crusade against abortion, launched by Horatio Storer under the auspices of the AMA in the late 1850s, had two primary objectives: to sway public opinion generally and to influence the passage of legislation specifically. The next chapter will explore the doctors' limited success with their first goal; the chapter following that will explore their more impressive achievements in pursuit of the second.

■ ■ ■

STUDY QUESTIONS

1. Who was the leading figure in the anti-abortion crusade of the nineteenth century? Describe his background and tactics.

2. Describe the three professional reasons so many physicians opposed abortion.

3. Describe the three personal reasons why so many physicians opposed abortion.

4. To what extent was physician opposition to abortion a gender question involving the status and roles of men and women in American society?

5. To what extent did financial self-interest play a role in the intensity of physician opposition to abortion?

BIBLIOGRAPHY

James C. Mohr's *Abortion in America* (1978) is the best brief survey of the history of abortion in the nineteenth century. For a survey of the philosophical debate over abortion, see John T. Noonan, Jr., *The Morality of Abortion* (1970). The best studies of the professionalization of American medicine are Donald E. Konold, *A History of American Medical Ethics, 1847–1912* (1962); William G. Rothstein, *American Physicians in the Nineteenth Century* (1972), and Paul Starr, *The Social Transformation of American Medicine* (1984). David Kennedy's *Birth Control in America* (1970) is a first-rate discussion of the abortion issue and the life of Margaret Sanger.

Part Three

WAR AND PEACE IN A NEW CENTURY

The period between the assassination of William McKinley in 1901 and America's entry into the Great War in 1917 has been labeled as the Progressive Era. In character and tone the years mirrored the first Progressive president, Theodore Roosevelt. Animated and energetic, T. R. used the presidency as a "bully pulpit," readily giving his opinion on a variety of subjects, ranging from literature and politics to football and divorce. Roosevelt believed that America's greatness was the result of its Anglo-Saxon heritage. Although he hoped to bring a "Square Deal" to all Americans, his reforming impulse was conservative in nature; he maintained that only through moderate reform could America preserve its traditional social, economic, and political structure. He had no sympathy for such "radical fanatics" as socialists or anarchists; nor did he trust the masses of American people who lacked his breeding and education. His answer for any sort of mob action was "taking ten or a dozen of their leaders out, standing . . . them against a wall, and shooting them dead."

Despite their ethnocentricity and self-righteousness, Roosevelt and the next two Progressive presidents—William Howard Taft and Woodrow Wilson—did attempt to curb some of the worst abuses of the urban-industrial society. They saw legislation through Congress that limited the number of hours that women and children could work and enacted the Pure Food and Drug Act (1906) and the Meat Inspection Act (1906). However, other Progressives, often with the support of the president, supported prohibition and antidivorce legislation, thereby seeking to regulate the private lives of millions of Americans.

A major shortcoming of the Progressive movement was the general reluctance to support minority and ethnic groups. Such Progressives as James K. Vardaman and

Theodore G. Bilbo, both from Mississippi, supported forward-looking legislation for whites but were violent race-baiters. Progressives rarely attacked the Jim Crow system in the South or introduced antilynching legislation in Congress. Segregation within the federal government expanded under Woodrow Wilson.

Similarly, vocal and independent labor unions and women's rights organizations seldom found support among influential Progressives. Margaret Sanger's birth control movement met strong opposition from middle-class men and women who saw it as a threat to family and morality. Such radical working-class organizations as the Industrial Workers of the World (the IWW, or "Wobblies") were not embraced by the mainstream of the Progressive movement.

The Progressive movement, however, did not really survive World War I. As a result of the Spanish-American War of 1898, the United States had acquired new territories in the distant Pacific, requiring a two-ocean navy and leaving Americans with global responsibilities. Those responsibilities eventually complicated and compromised the reform spirit. The Great War of 1914–18 damaged the reform impulses of Progressivism. It inspired skepticism, pessimism, and ultimately cynicism, and in the death-filled trenches of Western Europe, the Progressive movement met its demise.

The following essays deal with different characteristics of the Progressive movement. Confronted by the powerful forces of urbanization and industrialization, Americans attempted—sometimes successfully, often unsuccessfully—to come to terms with their changing society. Amidst that attempt, World War I complicated Progressivist dreams with the reality of horror, stupidity, and mass death.

TEDDY ROOSEVELT AND THE ROUGH RIDERS

Robert J. Maddox

Aboard the *Yucatan*, anchored off the coast of Cuba, Theodore Roosevelt received the news on the evening of June 21, 1898. He and his men, a volunteer cavalry regiment dubbed the Rough Riders, had received their orders to disembark from the safety of the ship and join the fighting ashore. It was a welcomed invitation, celebrated with cheers, war dances, songs, boasts, and toasts. "To the officers— may they get killed, wounded, or promoted," urged one toast that captured the mood aboard ship.

Who were these Rough Riders who seemed so bent on winning glory? As one of them told Roosevelt, "Who would not risk his life for a star?" And who was Theodore Roosevelt, the energetic rich kid who lusted after fame and perhaps had his eyes—albeit nearsighted—focused on the presidency? Robert J. Maddox retells this story of Theodore Roosevelt, the Rough Riders, and America's "splendid little war" with Spain. In the process he tells a great deal about the future president and the nation that made him its hero.

The war against Spain in 1898 was one of the more popular conflicts in American history. Victory came easily, there were relatively few casualties, and the cause seemed just in the minds of most people. From it the United States acquired the Philippine Islands, Puerto Rico, Guam, and a virtual protectorate over Cuba. The nation acquired several heroes as well, Admiral Dewey to name one, but none more colorful than the flamboyant Teddy Roosevelt. His exploits in Cuba, at the head of his Rough Riders, made him a legend in his own lifetime and helped make him President of the United States.

Roosevelt was in the prime of his life when the war broke out. Not yet forty years old, he possessed an imposing if somewhat overweight physique which he kept fit by almost daily exercise. In this regard he was a self-made man. Spindly and a trifle owlish as a youngster, Roosevelt, through what one of his biographers termed the "Cult of Strenuosity," had built up his body by relentless physical activity. Only one of his faculties had failed to respond—his eyesight. Cursed from boyhood with extreme nearsightedness, which grew worse over the years, Roosevelt was very self-conscious about this weakness in an otherwise healthy organism. During the war he was so worried it would betray him in combat that he had at least a half-dozen pairs of spectacles sewn in various parts of his uniform as insurance.

Mentally, Roosevelt was a complex individual. Exceedingly bright, he read voraciously, and penned his own books and articles without the help of a ghostwriter. He was, or would become, friendly with some of the leading intellectuals of the era. One side of him, how-

An 1898 photo shows Teddy Roosevelt as colonel of the Rough Riders. Teddy's uniforms, which had extra spectacles sewn into them, were tailored by Brooks Brothers to ensure a proper fit.

ever, remained boyish until the day he died. "You must always remember, " a British diplomat wrote a friend some years later, "that the President [Roosevelt] is about six." Without in any way belittling his patriotism, it seems safe to say that Teddy's enthusiasm for fighting the Spaniards stemmed at least as much from his desire to have a "bully" time doing it.

No one ever accused Roosevelt of being a pacifist. During the 1880s and 1890s the United States had gotten into a number of scrapes with other nations over issues large and small. Almost invariably T.R. had called for the most militant actions in response to these situations, and had denounced those who urged caution. War to him was not a catastrophe to be avoided; it could be a tonic to the nation's blood-

Robert J. Maddox, "Teddy Roosevelt and the Rough Riders." From *American History Illustrated* 12 (November 1977), pp. 8–15, 18–19. Reprinted through the courtesy of Cowles Magazines, publisher of *American History Illustrated*.

stream. A country too long at peace, he believed, tended to grow soft and effeminate, while war encouraged "manliness," a characteristic he prized above all else.

Before 1897 Roosevelt had held no office which dealt directly with military or foreign affairs. He had served in the New York state legislature as federal Civil Service Commissioner, and as a commissioner of the New York City Police Department. Despite having held such prestigious jobs for a man of his years, Roosevelt's political future was clouded by his tendency to alienate some of those who could help him and by the strident views on foreign policy which he never hesitated to voice—often to the great embarrassment of his own party. When, as a reward for his services in the election of 1896, T.R.'s friends began pushing for his appointment as Assistant Secretary of the Navy in the new Republican administration, they encountered stiff opposition. The President-elect himself had reservations about Teddy, but named him anyway. "I hope he has no preconceived plans," McKinley said wistfully, "which he would wish to drive through the moment he got in."

McKinley hoped in vain. Within two months of his appointment, Roosevelt wrote the well-known naval expert, Captain Alfred Thayer Mahan, that:

If I had my way, we would annex those islands [Hawaii] tomorrow. If that is impossible, I would establish a protectorate. . . . I believe we should build the Nicaraguan Canal at once, and should build a dozen new battleships, half of them on the Pacific Coast. I am fully alive to the danger from Japan.

These and similar sentiments clearly demonstrated that T.R. had no intention of vanishing into the bureaucracy. Nor did he. A short time later, when Secretary of the Navy John D. Long went on vacation, one newspaper reported that Roosevelt soon had "the whole Navy bordering on a war footing. It remains only to sand

down the decks and pipe to quarters for action." Teddy did not try to conceal his delight in being left to mind the store. "The Secretary is away," he wrote in one letter, "and I am having immense fun running the Navy." One story had it that when asked about his Assistant Secretary, Long dourly responded "Why 'Assistant'?"

Sticking pins in maps and running around on inspection tours must have amused him, but Roosevelt wanted some real action. Spain provided the most likely source. Once the possessor of a world empire, Spain by this time was a minor power clinging grimly to its few remaining territories. One of these, Cuba, lay less than 100 miles from American shores, and for several years had smoldered with insurrection against Spanish domination. Though he refrained from speaking out publicly, Roosevelt, in private talks and correspondence, recommended war against Spain almost from the day he became Assistant Secretary. American honor demanded it, he said, and a brief war would help rekindle martial instincts which had flagged through years of peace. There would be an additional dividend, he wrote on one occasion, that being "the benefit done our military forces by trying both the Army and Navy in actual practice."

Roosevelt did not bring on the war with Spain, of course, however much he tried. Cuban propaganda, sensationalist American newspapers, and jingoes in and outside Congress, combined to keep talk of war before the public. Still, through 1897, President McKinley refused to be stampeded, and the Spanish Government (which very much wished to avoid war) repeatedly gave in to American demands over the treatment of Cuba.

Then, early in 1898, two events occurred which made war virtually inevitable. First, a letter critical of McKinley, written by the Spanish minister in Washington, was stolen from the mails and reprinted in the American press. Trivial in itself, this blunder enraged many Americans. More important, the warship *Maine* blew up in a Cuban harbor with the loss of more than 200 sailors. Though not a shred of evidence has ever emerged to indicate that the Spanish were responsible, most Americans (abetted by much of the press) assumed that they were and demanded revenge. McKinley simply was not strong enough to stand against this pressure. On April 10 he asked Congress for what amounted to a declaration of war.

Well before the war began Roosevelt had told others that of it came he would not be content to remain in Washington. He was true to his word. By March he was beseeching New York state officials to permit him to raise a regiment of volunteers, which unit, he promised, would be "jim-dandy." That he had never served in the military, let alone seen combat, fazed Teddy not at all. He was greatly miffed when his generous offer was spurned.

Roosevelt, as usual, had other irons in the fire. Due to the minuscule size of the Regular Army, Congress had authorized the recruitment of three volunteer cavalry regiments from the Southwest. Because of his political connections, which he used to the utmost, Roosevelt was offered the command of one of these units. Modesty suddenly descended upon him. Estimating that it might take him a month or so to familiarize himself thoroughly with military procedures and tactics, T.R. asked that his friend, Captain Leonard Wood (at that time a military surgeon), be promoted to colonel and given command of the regiment. He would be satisfied with a mere lieutenant-colonelcy and would serve under Wood. Roosevelt's light could not be hidden, however, and from the start the First Volunteer Cavalry was known as "Roosevelt's Rough Riders."

Teddy was eager to get going. Quickly ordering the appropriate uniforms from Brooks Brothers (to ensure a proper fit), he began complaining that the war might be over before he could get into it—"it will be awful if we miss the fun." At last, in early May, he set out for San Antonio, Texas, where the First

Volunteers were undergoing preliminary training. He arrived to the welcome of a brass band and "his boys."

And what a group it was. "Mingling among the cowboys and momentarily reformed bad men from the West," Henry Pringle has written, "were polo players and steeplechase riders from the Harvard, Yale and Princeton clubs of New York City." Though from time to time Roosevelt protested against the carnival atmosphere which pervaded the camp, he enjoyed himself hugely. After one period of mounted drill, for instance, he told his men to "drink all the beer they want, which I will pay for" and had a few himself. Colonel Wood admonished Teddy for this kind of behavior, which the latter admitted was out of place. "Sir," Roosevelt replied, "I consider myself the damnedest ass within ten miles of this camp."

Two weeks after Teddy arrived in San Antonio, the Rough Riders were ordered to report to the Tampa, Florida staging area for the expedition against Cuba. By this time they had been transformed from an undisciplined group in civilian clothes to an undisciplined group in uniform. Tampa was, if possible, even more chaotic than San Antonio had been. Units of Regulars, National Guard, and volunteers milled about with little over-all direction and inadequate facilities. Some units were without arms, others had arms but no ammunition, still others lacked uniforms, bedding, or tents. It was a mess. "No head," Roosevelt wrote angrily in his diary, "a breakdown of both the railroad and military system of the country."

With an aroused public clamoring for action, the War Department ordered the expedition to sail despite its obvious lack of preparation. At this point the Rough Riders had what amounted to their first engagement of the war—against other American soldiers. Port Tampa lay about nine miles from Tampa, where the troops were quartered, with only a single track railway connecting them. The orders sent to individual regiments included no scheduling, so it was up to each unit to get to the port as best it could. A mad scramble ensued to commandeer whatever rolling stock was available: The Rough Riders were lucky enough to come upon an engine with some coal cars which they promptly seized. But the excitement was not yet over. Arriving at the port, Roosevelt and Wood found that the ship allotted to them was also designated for two regiments and there was not enough space for all three. As Teddy later recounted the episode:

Accordingly, I ran at full speed to our train; and leaving a strong guard with the baggage I double-quicked the rest of the regiment up to the boat just in time to board her as she came into the quay and then to hold her against the 2d Regulars and the 71st, who had arrived a little too late. . . . There was a good deal of expostulation, but we had possession.

It was a false alarm. On the eve of departure another message arrived from the War Department. "Wait until you get further orders before you sail," it read. "Answer quick." As things turned out the officers and men of the expeditionary force spent almost two weeks sweating and cursing in the tightly packed ships at anchor under the Florida sun. At last, on June 14, thirty-two steamers moved out of Port Tampa heading slowly toward Cuba. The Fifth Army Corps, as it was designated, consisted of two divisions and an independent brigade of infantry, a division of dismounted cavalry, four batteries of field artillery, and some auxiliary troops. The Rough Riders were aboard, of course, but like the other cavalry units they had nothing to ride. Because of the lack of space, the only animals brought along were horses for the officers and mules for carrying supplies.

Eventually the flotilla reached Cuba and landings were made virtually unopposed in several places. The debarkations resembled the disorder which had reigned at Tampa Bay. The men and equipment were brought ashore in helter-skelter fashion by an assortment of launches and other small boats. The animals

were even less fortunate: They were driven off the sides of ships and left to fend for themselves. Some reached shore safely, others swam to watery graves. Once again, Teddy was unwilling to trust luck. Recognizing the captain of a small vessel which drew alongside as a man he had known in the Navy Department, Roosevelt directed that the ship be used solely for getting the Rough Riders ashore as quickly as possible. After spending weeks aboard what they referred to as "prison hulks," the men must have appreciated the initiative of their second-in-command.

The course of the Cuban campaign cannot be recounted in detail here. The most charitable single word to describe it is "muddled." The commander of the Fifth Corps was General William R. Shafter, a rather lethargic man who weighed well over 300 pounds. Suffering from the heat since arriving in Florida, Shafter, during the latter part of the fighting, had to be transported reclining on a barn door. His immediate subordinates were three other general officers, who seemed at least as much concerned with outdoing one another as with fighting the Spaniards. One of them, "Fighting Joe" Wheeler, had last seen combat as a Confederate officer during the Civil War. During moments of stress, it was reported, he became confused as to who his opponents were and several times referred to them as "those Yankees." Fortunately for the Americans, the Spanish were in even worse shape. Although some individual Spanish troops and units fought well, they were badly led and defeatism permeated the defending forces.

Once a semblance of order was created on the beach, preparations were made for the expedition's advance against the main target, the harbor city of Santiago, less than twenty miles west along the coastline. The only available overland route, however, swung inland through jungles which provided excellent concealment for defenders. The movement took place in fits and starts and was not without incident—and losses. The Spanish fought a brief rearguard action at a place called Las Guásimas, for instance, during which sixteen Americans were killed and another fifty wounded. The Rough Riders took part in this engagement, as did some regular units, and there is evidence to indicate that Wood and Roosevelt led their men into an ambush. In later years Roosevelt indignantly denied any such thing and claimed that "every one of the officers had full knowledge of where he would find the enemy." In any event, Teddy boasted, " . . . we wanted the first whack at the Spaniards and we got it."

Finally, by the end of June, American forces were within striking distance of Santiago. Their way was blocked by a series of fortifications and trenches located on a chain of hills surrounding the city—the most prominent of which was San Juan Hill. The difficulty in moving supplies and ammunition by pack animal along narrow jungle trails caused the troops to remain before Santiago for several days. The plan of attack was simple. One division would move several miles north to attack a stronghold at El Caney, the rest of the units would march head-on against the San Juan and nearby hills. Both assaults began on the morning of July 1.

From where they had grouped, American troops had to push through several miles of jungle and ford a stream before reaching clear ground in front of the hills. They began taking losses while still in the jungle. There were only two trails they could use and Spanish artillery had these zeroed in. One column had at its head an observation balloon pulled along by men holding guy ropes. It proved to be of little help to the Americans, but showed Spanish artillery-men exactly where the enemy was. Fortunately for the men underneath it, the bag was pierced several times and settled gently to the ground before it could cause even greater damage.

The jungle ended abruptly at a stream which ran along its edge roughly parallel to the Spanish lines on the ridges. Across the stream there were several hundred yards of meadowlands before reaching the slopes. As the troops emerged from the jungle, therefore, they were exposed to withering Spanish rifle fire from above. What little order there was broke down as the advancing columns began clogging up at the jungle's edge. Some units refused to cross the stream, others became disorganized as they tried to move through and get into position. The situation presented a cruel dilemma to American commanders. To attack with insufficient numbers of men would be to risk defeat. To wait until all units were deployed would mean exposing those who crossed the stream first to an extended period under the crippling fire. Finally, a little past noon and before elements in the rear had left the jungle, the assault began.

San Juan Hill was the main objective. Somewhat to the right and much closer to American lines lay Kettle Hill, assigned to the dismounted cavalry. Since Colonel Wood earlier had taken command of a brigade, Roosevelt now led the Rough Riders. This was what he had been waiting for, and he would not be found wanting. Showing complete disdain for enemy bullets, Teddy galloped around on his horse, Little Texas, exhorting his men to form up for attack. They were joined by elements from several other regiments, including black troops from the 10th Cavalry. Roosevelt waved his hat and the men moved forward. "By this time we were all in the spirit of the thing and greatly excited by the charge," he wrote later, "the men cheering and running forward between shots. . . . I . . . galloped toward the hill. . . . "

According to his own account Roosevelt quickly moved ahead of the men, preceded only by his orderly, Henry Bardshar, "who had run ahead very fast in order to get better shots at the Spaniards. . . ." About forty yards from the crest Teddy encountered a wire fence and jumped off Little Texas, letting the horse run free. Almost immediately he saw Bardshar shoot down two Spaniards who emerged from the trenches. Soon Roosevelt and Bardshar were surrounded by the rest of the men as they swarmed over the hill, capturing or killing the few Spanish troops who had not retreated. The charge up Kettle Hill was over.

From their newly won position, Roosevelt and his men had an excellent view of the assault against San Juan Hill. Earlier artillery barrages had failed to cause much damage to the breastworks, and the black powder used in American guns produced smoke which drew Spanish counterfire. Now, however, three Gatling guns opened up with good effect. "They went b-r-r-r, like a lawn mower cutting grass over our trenches," a Spanish officer said later. "We could not stick a finger up when you fired without getting it cut off." Still the Spaniards held their positions as the ragged blue lines moved forward. Despite heavy losses, the Americans pushed doggedly up the hill. At last, just before they reached the top, the Spanish defenders fired a last volley and fled.

Beyond Kettle Hill and to the right of San Juan lay another ridge from which the enemy kept shooting. Rallying his men again, Roosevelt led them down the far side of Kettle, across the intervening valley, and up the slopes. "I was with Henry Bardshar, running up at the double," Teddy later recalled, "and two Spaniards leaped from the trenches and fired at us, not ten yards away. As they turned to run I closed in and fired twice, missing the first and killing the second. My revolver was from the sunken battleship *Maine*." Again the Americans drove the Spanish before them. When they took possession of these crests, "we found ourselves overlooking Santiago."

Although the Americans had won the day, the battle for Santiago was not yet over. The Spanish had about 16,000 men to defend the city, the Americans an equal number to take it. The latter were exhausted from their attacks and lacked reserves, food, and ammunition. By July 3, two days after the initial assaults, the Americans had lost 224 men killed and 1,370 wounded. The result was a stand-off. Spanish units did not attempt to break out of the ring; the Americans were in no shape to move against the city's defenses. "Tell the President for Heaven's sake to send us every regiment and above all every battery possible," Roosevelt wrote a friend. "We have won so far at a heavy cost, but the Spaniards fight very hard and charging these intrenchments against modern rifles is terrible. . . . We *must* have help—thousands of men, batteries, and *food* and ammunition." Fortunately, the Spanish launched no major counter attacks.

While the men dug themselves into the hills, the battle for Santiago was decided by another engagement—at sea. A Spanish fleet had been bottled up in Santiago Harbor for some time: Shafter's expedition was supposed to take the city, thereby forcing the Spanish ships to leave the harbor or surrender. At 9:30 A.M. on July 3, Spanish ships began coming out singly under the guns of the blockaders. It was a courageous but futile effort. Despite some bungling on the part of the U.S. Navy, all the opposing ships were sunk or disabled. After two weeks of negotiation Shafter received the surrender of Santiago, and less than a month after that the Spanish Government sued for peace.

Although the war had ended in complete victory for the United States, it came in for a great deal of criticism in the period following. Charges of incompetence were leveled against the top echelons, there were undignified exchanges between generals and admirals over who deserved credit for which victory, and the condition of the men returning from Cuba caused a public outcry. Many troops died from tropical illnesses, and still others from food poisoning caused by tainted meat.

It was probably for these reasons that Roosevelt's star came to shine so brightly. He had performed heroically, after all, and he was sufficiently subordinate in rank to escape any blame about the war's mismanagement.

Teddy himself was not loath to accept the limelight; indeed, he eagerly sought it. Almost immediately he began campaigning for the governorship of New York state and, lest anyone forget his exploits, kept the Rough Rider bugler at his side during his speeches. Roosevelt had other assets, of course, but being the "Hero of San Juan Hill" (he was not disposed to argue about which hill he had climbed) did him no harm. He had become fixed in the national mind as Colonel Teddy Roosevelt of the Rough Riders.

"I would honestly rather have my position of colonel," Roosevelt had told his men at their mustering-out ceremony, "than any other position on earth." No doubt he meant it at the time. As governor of New York, and later as President of the United States, he looked back fondly on his days in Cuba and the men who had served with him. In both positions he tried to accommodate as many as possible of the former Rough Riders who petitioned him for a job. His loyalty, if not his judgment, could scarcely be questioned. In one case he tried to have appointed as territorial marshal a man who, it was found, was serving time in prison for homicide. Undaunted, Teddy later tried to have the person installed as warden of the very prison in which he had been confined. "When I told this to John Hay," Roosevelt said, "he remarked (with a brutal absence of feeling) that he believed the proverb ran, 'Set a Rough Rider to catch a thief.' "

For once in his life, Teddy was at a loss for a reply.

■■■

STUDY QUESTIONS

1. What character traits inclined Roosevelt toward war? What events led the United States to war with Spain?

2. What sorts of men joined the Rough Riders?

3. What problems did the United States have mobilizing for war?

4. What role did the Battles of Kettle Hill and San Juan Hill play in the war in Cuba?

5. How did Roosevelt capitalize on his newly won fame?

BIBLIOGRAPHY

The best overview of the Spanish-American War is David Trask, *The War with Spain in 1898* (1981). Shorter, but still useful is Frank Freidel, *The Splendid Little War* (1958). Theodore Roosevelt's own account of his moments of glory is *The Rough Riders* (1899). Among the more readable biographies of Roosevelt are Edmund Morris, *The Rise of Theodore Roosevelt* (1979) and David McCullough, *Mornings on Horseback* (1981). More scholarly biographies are G. Wallace Chessman, *Theodore Roosevelt and the Politics of Power* (1969) and Howard K. Beals, *Theodore Roosevelt and the Rise of America to World Power* (1956). On the war also see Gerald F. Linderman, *The Mirror of War: American Society and the Spanish-American War* (1974) and H. Wayne Morgan, *America's Road to Empire* (1965). Also see Stuart C. Miller, *"Benevolent Assimilation": The American Conquest of the Philippines, 1899–1903* (1982).

LIVING AND DYING IN PACKINGTOWN, CHICAGO from *THE JUNGLE*

Upton Sinclair

In the late fall of 1904 Upton Sinclair, a young ambitious novelist imbued with a zealous sense of socialism, traveled to Chicago to gather information about the horrors and abuses of the meatpacking industry. For the next seven weeks, as a cold fall gave way to a brutal winter, Sinclair lived in the workers' ghetto of Packingtown, talked with workers, and studied the meatpacking industry.

On Christmas Day of 1904 he began writing *The Jungle*, the story of Jurgis Rudkus. A Lithuanian immigrant of great strength, Rudkus came to America full of hope—only to be used, abused, and discarded by the unfeeling powers of Packingtown. Sinclair wrote frantically for three months, stopping only occasionally to eat or sleep. He poured all his emotions into Rudkus's story, hoping to show Americans how evil the industry—and by extension, capitalism—had become. He recorded the stench and unhealthy conditions of Packingtown and the dangers of working in the packinghouses. Of the work, one historian wrote, "Each job had its own dangers: the dampness and cold of the packing rooms and hide cellar, the sharp blade of the beef boner's knife, the noxious dust of the wood department and fertilizer plant, the wild charge of a half-crazed steer on the killing floor." The following selection from *The Jungle* describes some of the working and living conditions in Packingtown.

During this time that Jurgis was looking for work occurred the death of little Kristoforas, one of the children of Teta Elzbieta. Both Kristoforas and his brother, Juozapas, were cripples, the latter having lost one leg by having it run over, and Kristoforas having congenital dislocation of the hip, which made it impossible for him ever to walk. He was the last of Teta Elzbieta's children, and perhaps he had been intended by nature to let her know that she had had enough. At any rate he was wretchedly sick and undersized; he had the rickets, and though he was over three years old, he was no bigger than an ordinary child of one. All day long he would crawl around the floor in a filthy little dress, whining and fretting; because the floor was full of draughts he was always catching cold, and snuffling because his nose ran. This made him a nuisance, and a source of endless trouble in the family. For his mother, with unnatural perversity, loved him best of all her children, and made a perpetual fuss over him—would let him do anything undisturbed, and would burst into tears when his fretting drove Jurgis wild.

And now he died. Perhaps it was the smoked sausage he had eaten that morning—which may have been made out of some tubercular pork that was condemned as unfit for export. At any rate, an hour after eating it, the child had begun to cry with pain, and in another hour he was rolling about on the floor in convulsions. Little Kotrina, who was all alone with him, ran out screaming for help, and after a while a doctor came, but not until Kristoforas had howled his last howl. No one was really sorry about this except poor Elzbieta, who was inconsolable. Jurgis announced that so far as he was concerned the child would have to be buried by the city, since they had no money for a funeral; and at this the poor woman almost went out of her senses, wringing her hands and screaming with grief and despair. Her child to be buried in a pauper's grave! And her stepdaughter to stand by and hear it said without protesting! It was enough to make Ona's father rise up out of his grave to rebuke her! If it had come to this, they might as well give up at once, and be buried all of them together! . . . In the end Marija said that she would help with ten dollars; and Jurgis being still obdurate, Elzbieta went in tears and begged the money from the neighbors, and so little Kristoforas had a mass and a hearse with white plumes on it, and a tiny plot in a graveyard with a wooden cross to mark the place. The poor mother was not the same for months after that; the mere sight of the floor where little Kristoforas had crawled about would make her weep. He had never had a fair chance, poor little fellow, she would say. He had been handicapped from birth. If only she had heard about it in time, so that she might have had that great doctor to cure him of his lameness! . . . Some time ago, Elzbieta was told, a Chicago billionaire had paid a fortune to bring a great European surgeon over to cure his little daughter of the same disease from which Kristoforas had suffered. And because this surgeon had to have bodies to demonstrate upon, he announced that he would treat the children of the poor, a piece of magnanimity over which the papers became quite eloquent. Elzbieta, alas, did not read the papers, and no one had told her; but perhaps it was as well, for just then they would not have had the car-fare to spare to go every day to wait upon the surgeon, nor for that matter anybody with the time to take the child.

All this while that he was seeking for work, there was a dark shadow hanging over Jurgis; as if a savage beast were lurking somewhere in the pathway of his life, and he knew it, and yet could not help approaching the place. There are all stages of being out of work in Packingtown, and he faced in dread the prospect of reaching the lowest. There is a

Upton Sinclair, "Living and Dying in Packingtown, Chicago." From Upton Sinclair, *The Jungle*. Chicago, 1905.

ALL STAR FEATURE CORP. PRESENTS IN MOTION PICTURES

—UPTON SINCLAIR'S—
WONDERFUL STORY OF THE BEEF PACKING INDUSTRY

THE JUNGLE

FEATURING
GEORGE NASH — GAIL KANE
AND THE AUTHOR
5 DARING ACTS — 210 ASTOUNDING SCENES

QUICK JURGIS WE MUST RECOVER THE BODY FROM THE LARD VAT

The drama and emotion of Upton Sinclair's 1905 novel held great appeal for the fledgling motion picture industry. This poster for the 1913 film highlights one of the novel's gruesome details.

place that waits for the lowest man—the fertilizer-plant!

The men would talk about it in awe-stricken whispers. Not more than one in ten had ever really tried it; the other nine had contented themselves with hearsay evidence and a peep through the door. There were some things worse than even starving to death. They would ask Jurgis if he had worked there yet, and if he meant to; and Jurgis would debate the matter with himself. As poor as they were and making all the sacrifices that they were, would he dare to refuse any sort of work that was offered to him, be it as horrible as ever it could? Would

he dare to go home and eat bread that had been earned by Ona, weak and complaining as she was, knowing that he had been given a chance, and had not had the nerve to take it?— And yet he might argue that way with himself all day, and one glimpse into the fertilizer-works would send him away again shuddering. He was a man, and he would do his duty; he went and made application—but surely he was not also required to hope for success.

The fertilizer-works of Durham's lay away from the rest of the plant. Few visitors ever saw them, and the few who did would come out looking like Dante, of whom the peasants declared that he had been into hell. To this part of the yards came all the "tankage" and waste products of all sorts; here they dried out the bones—and in suffocating cellars where the daylight never came you might see men and women and children bending over whirling machines and sawing bits of bones into all sorts of shapes, breathing their lungs full of the fine dust, and doomed to die, every one of them, within a certain definite time. Here they made the blood into albumen, and made other foul-smelling things into things still more foul-smelling. In the corridors and caverns where it was done you might lose yourself as in the great caves of Kentucky. In the dust and the steam the electric lights would shine like far-off twinkling stars—red and blue, green and purple stars, according to the color of the mist and the brew from which it came. For the odors in these ghastly charnel-houses there may be words in Lithuanian, but there are none in English. The person entering would have to summon his courage as for a cold-water plunge. He would go on like a man swimming under water; he would put his handkerchief over his face, and begin to cough and choke; and then, if he were still obstinate, he would find his head beginning to ring, and the veins in his forehead to throb, until finally he would be assailed by an overpowering blast of ammonia fumes, and would turn and run for his life, and come out half-dazed.

On top of this were the rooms where they dried the "tankage," the mass of brown stringy stuff that was left after the waste portions of the carcasses had had the lard and tallow dried out of them. This dried material they would then grind to a fine powder, and after they had mixed it up well with a mysterious but inoffensive brown rock which they brought in and ground up by the hundreds of carloads for that purpose, the substance was ready to be put into bags and sent out to the world as any one of a hundred different brands of standard bone-phosphate. And then the farmer in Maine or California or Texas would buy this, at say twenty-five dollars a ton, and plant it with his corn; and for several days after the operation the fields would have a strong odor, and the farmer and his wagon and the very horses that had hauled it would all have it too. In Packingtown the fertilizer is pure, instead of being a flavoring, and instead of a ton or so spread on several acres under the open sky, there are hundreds and thousands of tons of it in one building, heaped here and there in haystack piles, covering the floor several inches deep, and filling the air with a choking dust that becomes a blinding sand-storm when the wind stirs.

It was to this building that Jurgis came daily, as if dragged by an unseen hand. The month of May was an exceptionally cool one, and his secret prayers were granted; but early in June there came a record-breaking hot spell, and after that there were men wanted in the fertilizer-mill.

The boss of the grinding room had come to know Jurgis by this time, and had marked him for a likely man; and so when he came to the door about two o'clock this breathless hot day, he felt a sudden spasm of pain shoot through him—the boss beckoned to him! In ten minutes more Jurgis had pulled off his coat and over-shirt, and set his teeth together and gone to work. Here was one more difficulty for him to meet and conquer!

His labor took him about one minute to learn. Before him was one of the vents of the mill in which the fertilizer was being ground—rushing forth in a great brown river, with a spray of the finest dust flung forth in clouds. Jurgis was given a shovel, and along with half a dozen others it was his task to shovel this fertilizer into carts. That others were at work he knew by the sound, and by the fact that he sometimes collided with them; otherwise they might as well not have been there, for in the blinding dust-storm a man could not see six feet in front of his face. When he had filled one cart he had to grope around him until another came, and if there was none on hand he continued to grope till one arrived. In five minutes he was, of course, a mass of fertilizer from head to feet; they gave him a sponge to tie over his mouth, so that he could breathe, but the sponge did not prevent his lips and eyelids from caking up with it and his ears from filling solid. He looked like a brown ghost at twilight—from hair to shoes he became the color of the building and of everything in it, and for that matter a hundred yards outside it. The building had to be left open, and when the wind blew Durham and Company lost a great deal of fertilizer.

Working in his shirt-sleeves, and with the thermometer at over a hundred, the phosphates soaked in through every pore of Jurgis's skin, and in five minutes he had a headache, and in fifteen was almost dazed. The blood was pounding his brain like an engine's throbbing; there was a frightful pain in the top of his skull, and he could hardly control his hands. Still, with the memory of his four months' siege behind him, he fought on, in a frenzy of determination; and half an hour later he began to vomit—he vomited until it seemed as if his innards must be torn to shreds. A man could get used to the fertilizer-mill, the boss had said, if he would only make up his mind to it; but Jurgis now began to see that it was a question of making up his stomach.

At the end of that day of horror, he could scarcely stand. He had to catch himself now and then, and lean against a building and get his bearings. Most of the men, when they came out, made straight for a saloon—they seem to place fertilizer and rattlesnake poison in one class. But Jurgis was too ill to think of drinking—he could only make his way to the street and stagger on to a car. He had a sense of humor, and later on, when he became an old hand, he used to think it fun to board a street-car and see what happened. Now, however, he was too ill to notice it—how the people in the car began to gasp and sputter, to put their handkerchiefs to their noses, and transfix him with furious glances. Jurgis only knew that a man in front of him immediately got up and gave him a seat; and that half a minute later the two people on each side of him got up; and that in a full minute the crowded car was nearly empty—those passengers who could not get room on the platform having gotten out to walk.

Of course Jurgis had made his home a miniature fertilizer-mill a minute after entering. The stuff was half an inch deep in his skin—his whole system was full of it, and it would have taken a week not merely of scrubbing, but of vigorous exercise, to get it out of him. As it was, he could be compared with nothing known to men, save that newest discovery of the savants, a substance which emits energy for an unlimited time, without being itself in the least diminished in power. He smelt so that he made all food at the table taste, and set the whole family to vomiting; for himself it was three days before he could keep anything upon his stomach—he might wash his hands, and use a knife and fork, but were not his mouth and throat filled with the poison?

And still Jurgis stuck it out! In spite of splitting headaches he would stagger down to the plant and take up his stand once more, and begin to shovel in the blinding clouds of dust. And so at the end of the week he was a fertilizer man for life—he was able to eat again, and though his head never stopped aching, it ceased to be so bad that he could not work.

So there passed another summer. It was a summer of prosperity, all over the country, and the country ate generously of packing-house products, and there was plenty of work for all the family, in spite of the packers' efforts to keep a superfluity of labor. They were again able to pay their debts and to begin to save a little sum; but there were one or two sacrifices they considered too heavy to be made for long—it was too bad that the boys should have to sell papers at their age. It was utterly useless to caution them and plead with them; quite without knowing it, they were taking on the tone of their new environment. They were learning to swear in voluble English; they were learning to pick up cigar-stumps and smoke them, to pass hours of their time gambling with pennies and dice and cigarette-cards; they were learning the location of all the houses of prostitution on the "Levée," and the names of the "madames" who kept them, and the days when they gave their state banquets, which the police captains and the big politicians all attended. If a visiting "country-customer" were to ask them, they could show him which was "Hinkydink's" famous saloon, and could even point out to him by name the different gamblers and thugs and "hold-up men" who made the place their headquarters. And worse yet, the boys were getting out of the habit of coming home at night. What was the use, they would ask, of wasting time and energy and a possible car-fare riding out to the stockyards every night when the weather was pleasant and they could crawl under a truck or into an empty doorway and sleep exactly as well? So long as they brought home a half dollar for each day, what mattered it when they brought it? But Jurgis declared that from this to ceasing to comé at all would not be a very long step, and so it was decided that Vilimas and Nikalojus should return to school in the fall, and that instead Elzbieta should go out and get some work, her place at home being taken by her younger daughter.

Little Kotrina was like most children of the

■ ■ *Chicago's meatpacking industry grew up with little or no governmental control. These sausage makers at Armour & Co. worked in extreme temperatures and without adequate ventilation, causing many to faint or to vomit from the stench.*

poor, prematurely made old; she had to take care of her little brother, who was a cripple, and also of the baby; she had to cook the meals and wash the dishes and clean house, and have supper ready when the workers came home in the evening. She was only thirteen, and small for her age, but she did all this without a murmur; and her mother went out, and after trudging a couple of days about the yards, settled down as a servant of a "sausage-machine."

Elzbieta was used to working, but she found this change a hard one, for the reason that she had to stand motionless upon her feet from seven o'clock in the morning till half-past twelve, and again from one till half-past five. For the first days it seemed to her that she could not stand it—she suffered almost as much as Jurgis had from the fertilizer—and

would come out at sundown with her head fairly reeling. Besides this, she was working in one of the dark holes, by the electric light, and the dampness, too, was deadly—there were always puddles of water on the floor, and a sickening odor of moist flesh in the room. The people who worked here followed the ancient custom of nature, whereby the ptarmigan is the color of dead leaves in the fall and of snow in winter, and the chameleon, who is black when he lies upon a stump and turns green when he moves to a leaf. The men and women who worked in this department were precisely the color of the "fresh country sausage" they made.

The sausage-room was an interesting place to visit, for two or three minutes, and provided that you did not look at the people; the machines were perhaps the most wonderful things in the entire plant. Presumably sausages were once chopped and stuffed by hand, and if so it would be interesting to know how many workers had been displaced by these inventions. On one side of the room were the hoppers, into which men shoveled loads of meat and wheelbarrows full of spices; in these great bowls were whirling knifes that made two thousand revolutions a minute, and when the meat was ground fine and adulterated with potato-flour, and well mixed with water, it was forced to the stuffing-machines on the other side of the room. The latter were tended by women; there was a sort of spout, like the nozzle of a hose, and one of the women would take a long string of "casing" and put the end over the nozzle and then work the whole thing on, as one works on the finger of a tight glove. This string would be twenty or thirty feet long, but the woman would have it all on in a jiffy; and when she had several on, she would press a lever, and a stream of sausage-meat would be shot out, taking the casing with it as it came. Thus one might stand and see appear, miraculously born from the machine, a wriggling snake of sausage of incredible length. In front was a big pan which caught these creatures, and two more women who seized them as fast as they appeared and twisted them into links. This was for the uninitiated the most perplexing work of all; for all that the woman had to give was a single turn of the wrist; and in some way she contrived to give it so that instead of an endless chain of sausages, one after another, there grew under her hands a bunch of strings, all dangling from a single centre. It was quite like the feat of a prestidigitator—for the woman worked so fast that the eye could literally not follow her, and there was only a mist of motion, and tangle after tangle of sausages appearing. In the midst of the mist, however, the visitor would suddenly notice the tense set face, with the two wrinkles graven in the forehead, and the ghastly pallor of the cheeks; and then he would suddenly recollect that it was

time he was going on. The woman did not go on; she stayed right there—hour after hour, day after day, year after year, twisting sausage-links and racing with death. It was piece-work, and she was apt to have a family to keep alive; and stern and ruthless economic laws had arranged it that she could only do this by working just as she did, with all her soul upon her work, and with never an instant for a glance at the well-dressed ladies and gentlemen who came to stare at her, as at some wild beast in a menagerie.

With one member trimming beef in a cannery, and another working in a sausage factory, the family had a first-hand knowledge of the great majority of Packingtown swindles. For it was the custom, as they found, whenever meat was so spoiled that it could not be used for anything else, either to can it or else to chop it up into sausage. With what had been told them by Jonas, who had worked in the pickle-rooms, they could now study the whole of the spoiled-meat industry on the inside, and read a new and grim meaning into that old Packingtown jest—that they use everything of the pig except the squeal.

Jonas had told them how the meat that was taken out of pickle would often be found sour, and how they would rub it up with soda to take away the smell, and sell it to be eaten on free-lunch counters; also of all the miracles of chemistry which they performed, giving to any sort of meat, fresh or salted, whole or chopped, any color and any flavor and any odor they chose. In the pickling of hams they had an ingenious apparatus, by which they saved time and increased the capacity of the plant—a machine consisting of a hollow needle attached to a pump; by plunging this needle into the meat and working with his foot, a man could fill a ham with pickle in a few seconds. And yet, in spite of this, there would be hams found spoiled, some of them with an odor so bad that a man could hardly bear to be in the room with them. To pump into these the packers had a second and much stronger pickle which destroyed the odor—a process known to the workers as "giving them thirty percent." Also, after the hams had been smoked, there would be found some that had gone to the bad. Formerly these had been sold as "Number Three Grade," but later on some ingenious person had hit upon a new device, and now they would extract the bone, about which the bad part generally lay, and insert in the hole a white-hot iron. After this invention there was no longer Number One, Two, and Three Grade—there was only Number One Grade. The packers were always originating such schemes—they had what they called "boneless hams," which were all the odds and ends of pork stuffed into casings; and "California hams," which were the shoulders, with big knuckle-joints, and nearly all the meat cut out; and fancy "skinned hams," which were made of the oldest hogs, whose skins were so heavy and coarse that no one would buy them—that is, until they had been cooked and chopped fine and labelled "head cheese"!

It was only when the whole ham was spoiled that it came into the department of Elzbieta. Cut up by the two-thousand-revolutions-a-minute flyers, and mixed with half a ton of other meat, no odor that ever was in a ham could make any difference. There was never the least attention paid to what was cut up for sausage; there would come all the way back from Europe old sausage that had been rejected, and that was mouldy and white—it would be dosed with borax and glycerine, and dumped into the hoppers, and made over again for home consumption. There would be meat that had tumbled out on the floor, in the dirt and sawdust, where the workers had tramped and spit uncounted billions of consumption germs. There would be meat stored in great piles in rooms; and the water from leaky roofs would drip over it, and thousands of rats would race about on it. It was too dark in these storage places to see well, but a man could run his hand over these piles of meat and sweep off handfuls of the dried dung of rats. These rats were nuisances, and the packers would put poisoned bread out for them; they would die, and then rats, bread, and meat would go into the hoppers together. This is no fairy story and no joke; the meat would be shovelled into carts, and the man who did the shovelling would not trouble to liftout a rat even when he saw one—there were things that went into the sausage in comparison with which a poisoned rat was a tidbit. There was no place for the men to wash their hands before they ate their dinner, and so they made a practice of washing them in the water that was to be ladled into the sausage. There were the butt-ends of smoked meat, and the scraps of corned beef, and all the odds and ends of the waste of the plants, that would be dumped into old barrels in the cellar and left there. Under the system of rigid economy which the packers enforced, there were some jobs that it only paid to do once in a long time, and among these was the cleaning out of the waste-barrels. Every spring they did it; and in the barrels would be dirt and rust and old nails and stale water—and cart load after cart load of it would be taken up and dumped into the hoppers with fresh meat, and sent out to the public's breakfast. Some of it they would make into "smoked" sausage—but as the smoking took time, and was therefore expensive, they would call upon their chemistry department, and preserve it with borax and color it with gelatine to make it brown. All of their sausage came out of the same bowl, but when they came to wrap it they would stamp some of it "special," and for this they would charge two cents more a pound.

Such were the new surroundings in which Elzbieta was placed, and such was the work she was compelled to do. It was stupefying, brutalizing work; it left her no time to think, no strength for anything. She was part of the machine she tended, and every faculty that was not needed for the machine was doomed to be crushed out of existence. There was only one mercy about the cruel grind—that it gave her the gift of insensibility. Little by little she sank into a torpor—she fell silent. She would meet Jurgis and Ona in the evening, and the three would walk home together, often without saying a word. Ona, too, was falling into the habit of silence—Ona, who had once gone about singing like a bird. She was sick and miserable, and often she would barely have strength enough to drag herself home. And there they would eat what they had to eat, and afterwards, because there was only their misery to talk of, they would crawl into bed and fall into a stupor and never stir until it was time to get up again, and dress by candlelight, and go back to the machines. They were so numbed that they did not even suffer much from hunger, now; only the children continued to fret when the food ran short.

Yet the soul of Ona was not dead—the souls of none of them were dead, but only sleeping; and now and then they would waken, and these were cruel times. The gates of memory would roll open—old joys would stretch out their arms to them, old hopes and dreams would call to them, and they would stir beneath the burden that lay upon them, and feel its forever immeasurable weight. They could not even cry out beneath it; but anguish would seize them, more dreadful than the agony of death. It was a thing scarcely to be spoken—a thing never spoken by all the world, that will not know its own defeat.

They were beaten; they had lost the game, they were swept aside. It was not less tragic because it was so sordid, because that it had to do with wages and grocery bills and rents. They had dreamed of freedom; of a chance to look about them and learn something; to be decent and clean, to see their child grow up to be strong. And now it was all gone—it would never be! They had played the game and they had lost. Six years more of toil they had to face before they could expect the least respite, the cessation of the payments upon the house; and how cruelly certain it was that they could never stand six years of such a life as they were

living! They were lost, they were going down—and there was no deliverance for them, no hope; for all the help it gave them the vast city in which they lived might have been an ocean waste, a wilderness, a desert, a tomb. So often this mood would come to Ona, in the night-time, when something wakened her; she would lie, afraid of the beating of her own heart, fronting the blood-red eyes of the old primeval terror of life. Once she cried aloud, and woke Jurgis, who was tired and cross. After that she learned to weep silently—their moods so seldom came together now! It was as if their hopes were buried in separate graves.

Jurgis, being a man, had troubles of his own. There was another spectre following him. He had never spoken of it, nor would he allow any one else to speak of it—he had never acknowledged its existence to himself. Yet the battle with it took all the manhood that he had—and once or twice, alas, a little more. Jurgis had discovered drink.

He was working in the steaming pit of hell; day after day, week after week—until now there was not an organ of his body that did its work without pain, until the sound of ocean breakers echoed in his head day and night, and the buildings swayed and danced before him as he went down the street. And from all the unending horror of this there was a respite, a deliverance—he could drink! He could forget the pain, he could slip off the burden; he would see clearly again, he would be master of his brain, of his thoughts, of his will. His dead self would stir in him, and he would find himself laughing and cracking jokes with his companions—he would be a man again, and master of his life.

It was not an easy thing for Jurgis to take more than two or three drinks. With the first drink he could eat a meal, and he could persuade himself that that was economy; with the second he could eat another meal—but there would come a time when he could eat no more, and then to pay for a drink was an unthinkable extravagance, a defiance of the age-long instincts of his hunger-haunted class. One day, however, he took the plunge, and drank up all that he had in his pockets, and went home half "piped," as the men phrase it. He was happier than he had been in a year; and yet, because he knew that the happiness would not last, he was savage, too—with those who would wreck it, and with the world, and with his life; and then again, beneath this, he was sick with the shame of himself. Afterward, when he saw the despair of his family, and reckoned up the money he had spent, the tears came into his eyes, and he began the long battle with the spectre.

It was a battle that had no end, that never could have one. But Jurgis did not realize that very clearly; he was not given much time for reflection. He simply knew that he was always fighting. Steeped in misery and despair as he was, merely to walk down the street was to be put upon the rack. There was surely a saloon on the corner—perhaps on all four corners, and some in the middle of the block as well; and each one stretched out a hand to him—each one had a personality of its own, allurements unlike any other. Going and coming—before sunrise and after dark—there was warmth and a glow of light, and the steam of hot food, and perhaps music, or a friendly face, and a word of good cheer. Jurgis developed a fondness for having Ona on his arm whenever he went out on the street, and he would hold her tightly, and walk fast. It was pitiful to have Ona know of this—it drove him wild to think of it; the thing was not fair, for Ona had never tasted drink, and so could not understand. Sometimes, in desperate hours, he would find himself wishing that she might learn what it was, so that he need not be ashamed in her presence. They might drink together, and escape from the horror—escape for a while, come what would.

So there came a time when nearly all the conscious life of Jurgis consisted of a struggle with the craving for liquor. He would have ugly moods, when he hated Ona and the whole family, because they stood in his way. He was a fool to have married; he had tied himself down, and made himself a slave. It was all because he was a married man that he was compelled to stay in the yards; if it had not been for that he might have gone off like Jonas, and to hell with the packers. There were single men in the fertilizer-mill—and those few were working only for a chance to escape. Meantime, too, they had something to think about while they worked—they had the memory of the last time they had been drunk, and the hope of the time when they would be drunk again. As for Jurgis, he expected to bring home every penny; he could not even go with the men at noontime—he was supposed to sit down and eat his dinner on a pile of fertilizer dust.

This was not always his mood, of course; he still loved his family. But just now was a time of trial. Poor little Antanas, for instance—who had never failed to win him with a smile—little Antanas was not smiling just now, being a mass of fiery red pimples. He had had all the diseases that babies are heir to, in quick succession—scarlet fever, mumps, and whooping-cough in the first year, and now he was down with the measles. There was no one to attend him but Kotrina; there was no doctor to help him because they were too poor, and children did not die of the measles—at least not often. Now and then Kotrina would find time to sob over his woes, but for the greater part of the time he had to be left alone, barricaded upon the bed. The floor was full of draughts, and if he caught cold he would die. At night he was tied down, lest he should kick the covers off him, while the family lay in their stupor of exhaustion. He would lie and scream for hours, almost in convulsions; and then when he was worn out, he would lie whimpering and wailing in his torment. He was burning up with fever, and his eyes were running sores; in the daytime he was a thing uncanny and impish to behold, a plaster of pimples and sweat, a great purple lump of misery.

Yet all this was not really cruel as it sounds, for sick as he was, little Antanas was the least unfortunate member of that family. He was quite able to bear his sufferings—it was as if he had all these complaints to show what a prodigy of health he was. He was the child of his parents' youth and joy; he grew up like the conjurer's rose bush, and all the world was his oyster. In general, he toddled around the kitchen all day with a lean and hungry look— the portion of the family's allowance that fell to him was not enough, and he was unrestrainable in his demand for more. Antanas was but little over a year old, and already no one but his father could manage him.

It seemed as if he had taken all of his mother's strength—had left nothing for those that might come after him. Ona was with child again now, and it was a dreadful thing to contemplate; even Jurgis, dumb and despairing as he was, could not but understand that yet other agonies were on the way, and shudder at the thought of them.

For Ona was visibly going to pieces. In the first place she was developing a cough, like the one that had killed old Dede Antanas. She had had a trace of it ever since that fatal morning when the greedy street-car corporation had turned her out into the rain; but now it was beginning to grow serious, and to wake her up at night. Even worse than that was the fearful nervousness from which she suffered; she would have frightful headaches and fits of aimless weeping; and sometimes she would come home at night shuddering and moaning, and would fling herself down upon the bed and burst into tears. Several times she was quite beside herself and hysterical; and then Jurgis would go half mad with fright. Elzbieta would explain to him that it could not be helped, that woman was subject to such things when she was pregnant; but he was hardly to be persuaded, and would beg and plead to know what had happened. She had never been like this before, he would argue—it was monstrous and unthinkable. It was the life she had to live, the accursed work she had to do, that was killing her by inches. She was not fitted for it—no woman was fitted for it, no woman ought to be allowed to do such work; if the world could not keep them alive any other way it ought to kill them at once and be done with it. They ought not to marry, to have children; no working-man ought to marry—if he, Jurgis, had known what a woman was like, he would have had his eyes torn out first. So he would carry on, becoming half hysterical himself, which was an unbearable thing to see in a big man; Ona would pull herself together and fling herself into his arms, begging him to stop, to be still, that she would be better, it would be all right. So she would lie and sob out her grief upon his shoulder, while he gazed at her, as helpless as a wounded animal, the target of unseen enemies.

■ ■ ■

STUDY QUESTIONS

1. What was health care like for children in Packingtown?

2. What sort of men worked in the fertilizer plants? What were the hazards of the job?

3. How did the constant demand for money affect families?

4. What were the abuses of the "spoiled-meat" industry?

5. What response was Upton Sinclair hoping to achieve with *The Jungle*?

BIBLIOGRAPHY

On the life of Upton Sinclair see Floyd Dell, *Upton Sinclair: A Study in Social Protest* (1927); Jon Yoder, *Upton Sinclair* (1975); Leon Harris, *Upton Sinclair, American Rebel* (1975); and his own *The Autobiography of Upton Sinclair* (1962). Three good books on the literature of the period are Daniel Aaron, *Writers of the Left* (1969); James Burkhart Gilbert, *Writers and Partisans: A History of Literary Radicalism in America* (1968); and Larzer Ziff, *The American 1890s: Life and Times of a Lost Generation* (1966). On the meatpacking industry, Packingtown, and the lives of the workers, consult Louis Carroll Wade, *Chicago's Pride: The Stockyards, Packingtown, and Environs in the Nineteenth Century* (1987) and James R. Barrett, *Work and Community in the Jungle: Chicago's Packinghouse Workers* (1988).

ROSE SCHNEIDERMAN AND THE TRIANGLE SHIRTWAIST FIRE

Bonnie Mitelman

The progress Americans made during the Progressive Era depended upon one's perspective. For middle-class Americans, progress was everywhere visible. Real income rose and the government worked to ensure order and efficiency in the industrial world. For their part, most large industrialists cooperated with the government's effort to impose order, which often resulted in the elimination of bothersome competition. For example, leading meatpackers supported the Meat Inspection Act of 1906. The act raised inspection standards, thereby driving out small competitors and guaranteeing the quality of American meat on the competitive world market.

America's working class, however, had reason to question the nature of the "progress" that was being made. The men and women who labored in industrial America often performed uncreative, repetitive tasks at a pace set by machines. Possibly worse than the monotony of industrial life was the danger of it. Machines were blind and uncaring; they showed no sympathy for tired or bored workers who allowed their fingers to move too close to moving cogs. Injuries were common, and far too often industrialists were as unsympathetic as their machines. And for most unskilled workers, labor unions were weak and unrecognized by leading industrialists and manufacturers. In the following essay, Bonnie Mitelman discusses the 1911 Triangle Waist Company fire, a tragedy that saw 146 workers die. The fire and its results raise serious questions about the extent and nature of progress during the early twentieth century.

On Saturday afternoon, March 25, 1911, in New York City's Greenwich Village, a small fire broke out in the Triangle Waist Company, just as the 500 shirtwaist employees were quitting for the day. People rushed about, trying to get out, but they found exits blocked and windows to the fire escape rusted shut. They panicked.

As the fire spread and more and more were trapped, some began to jump, their hair and clothing afire, from the eighth and ninth floor windows. Nets that firemen held for them tore apart at the impact of the falling bodies. By the time it was over, 146 workers had died, most of them young Jewish women.

A United Press reporter, William Shepherd, witnessed the tragedy and reported, "I looked upon the heap of dead bodies and I remembered these girls were the shirtwaist makers. I remembered their great strike of last year in which these same girls had demanded more sanitary conditions and more safety precautions in the shops. These dead bodies were the answer."

The horror of that fire touched the entire Lower East Side ghetto community, and there was a profuse outpouring of sympathy. But it was Rose Schneiderman, an immigrant worker with a spirit of social justice and a powerful way with words, who is largely credited with translating the ghetto's emotional reaction into meaningful, widespread action. Six weeks following the tragedy, and after years of solid groundwork, with one brilliant, well-timed speech, she was able to inspire the support of wealthy uptown New Yorkers and to swing public opinion to the side of the labor movement, enabling concerned civic, religious, and labor leaders to mobilize their efforts for des-

perately needed safety and industrial reforms.

The Triangle fire, and the deaths of so many helpless workers, seemed to trigger in Rose Schneiderman an intense realization that there was absolutely nothing or no one to help working women except a strong union movement. With fierce determination, and the dedication, influence, and funding of many other people as well, she battled to regulate hours, wages, and safety standards and to abolish the sweatshop system. In so doing, she brought dignity and human rights to all workers.

The dramatic "uprising of the 20,000" of 1909–10, in which thousands of immigrant girls and women in the shirtwaist industry had endured three long winter months of a general strike to protest deplorable working conditions, had produced some immediate gains for working women. There had been agreements for shorter working hours, increased wages, and even safety reforms, but there had not been formal recognition of their union. At Triangle, for example, the girls had gained a 52 hour week, a 12–15 percent wage increase, and promises to end the grueling subcontracting system. But they had not gained the only instrument on which they could depend for lasting change: a viable trade union. This was to have disastrous results, for in spite of the few gains that they seemed to have made, the workers won no rights or bargaining power at all. In fact. "The company dealt only with its contractors. It felt no responsibility for the girls."

There were groups as well as individuals who realized the workers' impotence, but their attempts to change the situation accomplished little despite long years of hard work. The Women's Trade Union League and the International Ladies' Garment Workers' Union, through the efforts of Mary Dreier, Helen Marot, Leonora O'Reilly, Pauline Newman, and Rose Schneiderman had struggled unsuccessfully for improved conditions: the futility that the union organizers were feeling in late

"Rose Schneiderman and the Triangle Fire" by Bonnie Mitelman, from *American History Illustrated* (July, 1981). Copyright © 1981 by Historical Times, Inc. Reprinted through the courtesy of Historical Times, Inc., publishers of *American History Illustrated*.

1910 is reflected in the WTUL minutes of December 5 of that year.

A scant eight months after their historic waistmakers' strike, and three months before the deadly Triangle fire, a Mrs. Malkiel (no doubt Theresa Serber Malkiel, who wrote the legendary account of the strike, *The Diary of a Shirtwaist Striker: A Story of the Shirtwaist Makers' Strike in New York*) is reported to have come before the League to urge after a devastating fire in Newark, New Jersey killed twenty-five working women. Mrs. Malkiel attributed their loss to the greed and negligence of the owners and the proper authorities. The WTUL subsequently demanded an investigation of all factory buildings and it elected an investigation committee from the League to cooperate with similar committees from other organizations.

The files of the WTUL contain complaint after complaint about unsafe factory conditions; many were filled out by workers afraid to sign their names for fear of being fired had their employers seen the forms. They describe factories with locked doors, no fire escapes, and barred windows. The *New York Times* carried an article which reported that fourteen factories were found to have no fire escapes, twenty-three had locked doors, and seventy-eight had obstructed fire escapes. In all, according to the article, 99 percent of the factories investigated in New York were found to have serious fire hazards.

Yet no action was taken.

It was the Triangle fire that emphasized, spectacularly and tragically, the deplorable safety and sanitary conditions of the garment workers. The tragedy focused attention upon the ghastly factories in which most immigrants worked; there was no longer any question about what the strikers had meant when they talked about safety and sanitary reform, and about social and economic justice.

The grief and frustration of the shirtwaist strikers were expressed by one of them, Rose Safran, after the fire: "If the union had won we would have been safe. Two of our demands were for adequate fire escapes and for open doors from the factories to the street. But the bosses defeated us and we didn't get the open doors or the better fire escapes. So our friends are dead."

The families of the fire victims were heartbroken and hysterical, the ghetto's *Jewish Daily Forward* was understandably melodramatic, and the immigrant community was completely enraged. Their Jewish heritage had taught them an emphasis on individual human life and worth; their shared background in the *shtetl* and common experiences in the ghetto had given them a sense of fellowship. They were, in a sense, a family—and some of the most helpless among them had died needlessly.

The senseless deaths of so many young Jewish women sparked within these Eastern Europeans a new determination and dedication. The fire had made reform absolutely essential. Workers' rights were no longer just socialist jargon: They were a matter of life and death .

The Triangle Waist Company was located on the three floors of the Asch Building, a 10-story, 135-foot-high structure at the corner of Greene Street and Washington Place in Greenwich Village. One of the largest shirtwaist manufacturers, Triangle employed up to 900 people at times, but on the day of the fire, only about 500 were working.

Leon Stein's brilliant and fascinating account of the fire, entitled simply *The Triangle Fire*, develops and documents the way in which the physical facilities, company procedures, and human behavior interacted to cause this great tragedy. Much of what occurred was ironic, some was cruel, some stupid, some pathetic. It is a dramatic portrayal of the eternal confrontation of the "haves" and the "havenots," told in large part by those who survived.

Fire broke out at the Triangle Company at

approximately 4:45 P.M. (because time clocks were reportedly set back to stretch the day, and because other records give differing times of the first fire alarm, it is uncertain exactly what time the fire started), just after pay envelopes had been distributed and employees were leaving their work posts. It was a small fire at first, and there was a calm, controlled effort to extinguish it. But the fire began to spread, jumping from one pile of debris to another, engulfing combustible shirtwaist fabric. It became obvious that the fire could not be snuffed out, and the workers tried to reach the elevators or stairway. Those who reached the one open stairway raced down eight flights of stairs to safety; those who managed to climb onto the available passenger elevators also got out. But not everyone could reach the available exits. Some tried to open the door to a stairway and found it locked. Others were trapped between long working tables or behind the hordes of people trying to get into the elevators or out through the one open door.

Under the work tables, rags were burning; the wooden floors, trim, and window frames were also afire. Frantically, workers fought their way to the elevators, to the fire escape, and to the windows—to any place that might lead to safety.

Fire whistles and bells sounded as the fire department raced to the building. But equipment proved inadequate, as the fire ladders reached only to the seventh floor. And by the time the firemen connected their hoses to douse the flames, the crowded eighth floor was completely ablaze.

For those who reached the windows, there seemed to be a chance for safety. The *New York World* describes people balancing on window sills, nine stories up, with flames scorching them from behind, until firemen arrived: "The nets were spread below with all promptness. Citizens were commandeered into service, as the firemen necessarily gave their attention to the one engine and hose of the force that first arrived. The catapult force that the bodies gathered in the long plunges made the nets utterly without avail. Screaming girls and men, as they fell, tore the nets from the grasp of the holders, and the bodies struck the sidewalks and lay just as they fell. Some of the bodies ripped big holes through the life nets."

One reporter who witnessed the fire remembered how,

A young man helped a girl to the window sill on the ninth floor. Then he held her out deliberately, away from the building, and let her drop. He held out a second girl the same way and let her drop. He held out a third girl who did not resist. They were all as unresisting as if he were helping them into a street car instead of into eternity. He saw that a terrible death awaited them in the flames and his was only a terrible chivalry. He brought around another girl to the window. I saw her put her arms around him and kiss him. Then he held her into space—and dropped her. Quick as a flash, he was on the window sill himself. His coat fluttered upwards—the air filled his trouser legs as he came down. I could see he wore tan shoes.

Those who had rushed to the fire escape found the window openings rusted shut. Several precious minutes were lost in releasing them. The fire escape itself ended at the second floor, in an airshaft between the Asch Building and the building next door. But too frantic to notice where it ended, workers climbed on to the fire escape one after another until, in one terrifying moment, it collapsed from the weight, pitching the workers to their death.

Those who had made their way to the elevators found crowds pushing to get into the cars. When it became obvious that the elevators could no longer run, workers jumped down the elevator shafts, landing on the tops of the cars, or grabbing for cables to ease their descent. Several died, but incredibly, some did manage to save themselves this way. One man was found, hours after the fire, beneath an elevator car in the basement of the building, nearly drowned by the rapidly rising water from the firemen's hoses.

Several people, among them Triangle's two owners, raced to the roof, and from there were led to safety. Others never had that chance. "When Fire Chief Croker could make his way into the [top] three floors," states one account of the fire, "he found sights that utterly staggered him . . . he saw as the smoke drifted away bodies burned to the bare bones. There were skeletons bending over sewing machines."

The day after the fire, the *New York Times* announced that "the building was fireproof. It shows hardly any signs of the disaster that overtook it. The walls are as good as ever, as are the floors: nothing is worse for the fire except that furniture and 14 [*sic*] of the 600 men and girls that were employed in its upper three stories."

The building *was* fireproof. But there had never been a fire drill in the factory, even though the management had been warned about the possible hazard of fire on the top three floors. Owners Max Blanck and Isaac Harris had chosen to ignore these warnings in spite of the fact that many of their employees were immigrants who could barely speak English, which would surely mean panic in the event of a crisis.

The *New York Times* also noted that Leonora O'Reilly of the League had reported Max Blanck's visit to the WTUL during the shirtwaist strike, and his plea that the girls return to work. He claimed a business reputation to maintain and told the Union leaders he would make the necessary improvements right away. Because he was the largest manufacturer in the business, the League reported, they trusted him and let the girls return.

But the improvements were never made. And there was nothing that anybody could or would do about it. Factory doors continued to open in instead of out, in violation of fire regulations. The doors remained bolted during working hours, apparently to prevent workers from getting past the inspectors with stolen merchandise. Triangle had only two staircases where there should have been three, and those two were very narrow. Despite the fact that the building was deemed fireproof, it had wooden window frames, floors, and trim. There was no sprinkler system. It was not legally required.

These were the same kinds of conditions which existed in factories throughout the garment industry; they had been cited repeatedly in the complaints filed with the WTUL. They were not unusual nor restricted to Triangle; in fact, Triangle was not as bad as many other factories.

But it was at Triangle that the fire took place.

The *Jewish Daily Forward* mourned the dead with sorrowful stories, and its headlines talked of "funerals instead of weddings" for the dead young girls. The entire Jewish immigrant community was affected, for it seemed there was scarcely a person who was not in some way touched by the fire. Nearly everyone had either been employed at Triangle themselves, or had a friend or relative who had worked there at some time or another. Most worked in factories with similar conditions, and so everyone identified with the victims and their families.

Many of the dead, burned beyond recognition, remained unidentified for days, as searching family members returned again and again to wait in long lines to look for their loved ones. Many survivors were unable to identify their mothers, sisters, or wives; the confusion of handling so many victims and so many survivors who did not understand what was happening to them and to their dead led to even more anguish for the community. Some of the victims were identified by the names on the pay envelopes handed to them at quitting time and stuffed deeply into pockets or stockings just before the fire. But many bodies remained unclaimed for days, with bewildered and bereaved survivors wandering among them, trying to find some identifying mark.

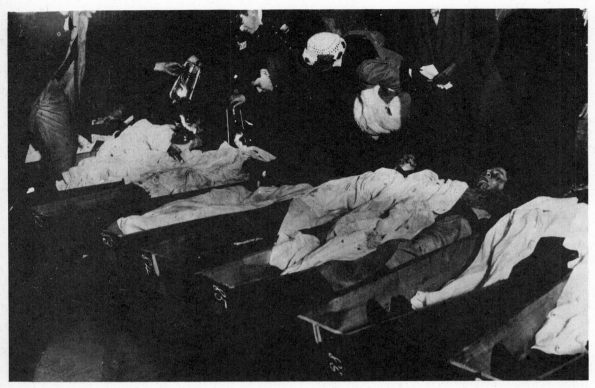

For days after the Triangle Shirtwaist Company fire, family members searched among the burned victims, looking for clues that might help to identify their loved ones.

Charges of first- and second-degree manslaughter were brought against the two men who owned Triangle, and Leon Stein's book artfully depicts the subtle psychological and sociological implications of the powerful against the oppressed, and of the Westernized, German-Jewish immigrants against those still living their old-world, Eastern European heritage. Ultimately, Triangle owners Blanck and Harris were acquitted of the charges against them, and in due time they collected their rather sizable insurance.

The shirtwaist, popularized by Gibson girls, had come to represent the new-found freedom of females in America. After the fire, it symbolized death. The reaction of the grief-stricken Lower East Side was articulated by socialist lawyer Morris Hillquit:

The girls who went on strike last year were trying to readjust the conditions under which they were obliged to work. I wonder if there is not some connection between the fire and that strike. I wonder if the magistrates who sent to jail the girls who did picket duty in front of the Triangle shop realized last Sunday that some responsibility may be theirs. Had the strike been successful, these girls might have been alive today and the citizenry of New York would have less of a burden upon its conscience.

For the first time in the history of New York's garment industry there were indications that the public was beginning to accept responsibility for the exploitation of the immigrants.

For the first time, the establishment seemed to understand that these were human beings asking for their rights, not merely trouble-making anarchists.

The day after the Triangle fire a protest meeting was held at the Women's Trade Union League, with representatives from twenty leading labor and civic organizations. They formed "a relief committee to cooperate with the Red Cross in its work among the families of the victims, and another committee . . . to broaden the investigation and research on fire hazards in New York factories which was already being carried on by the League."

The minutes of the League recount the deep indignation that members felt at the indifference of a public which had ignored their pleas for safety after the Newark fire. In an attempt to translate their anger into constructive action, the League drew up a list of forceful resolutions that included a plan to gather delegates from all of the city's unions to make a concerted effort to force safety changes in factories. In addition, the League called upon all workers to inspect factories and then report any violations to the proper city authorities and to the WTUL. They called upon the city to immediately appoint organized workers as unofficial inspectors. They resolved to submit the following fire regulations suggestions: compulsory fire drills, fireproof exits, unlocked doors, fire alarms, automatic sprinklers, and regular inspections. The League called upon the legislature to create the Bureau of Fire Protection and finally, the League underscored the absolute need for all workers to organize themselves at once into trade unions so that they would never again be powerless.

The League also voted to participate in the funeral procession for the unidentified dead of the Triangle fire.

The city held a funeral for the dead who were unclaimed. "More than 120,000 of us were in the funeral procession that miserable rainy April day," remembered Rose Schneiderman. "From ten in the morning until four in the afternoon we of the Women's Trade Union League marched in the procession with other trade-union men and women, all of us filled with anguish and regret that we had never been able to organize the Triangle workers."

Schneiderman, along with many others, was absolutely determined that this kind of tragedy would never happen again. With single-minded dedication, they devoted themselves to unionizing the workers. The searing example of the Triangle fire provided them with the impetus they needed to gain public support for their efforts.

They dramatized and emphasized and capitalized on the scandalous working conditions of the immigrants. From all segments of the community came cries for labor reform. Stephen S. Wise, the prestigious reform rabbi, called for the formation of a citizens' committee. Jacob H. Schiff, Bishop David H. Greer, Governor John A. Dix, Anne Morgan (of *the* Morgans) and other leading civic and religious leaders collaborated in a mass meeting at the Metropolitan Opera House on May 2 to protest factory conditions and to show support for the workers.

Several people spoke at the meeting on May 2, and many in the audience began to grow restless and antagonistic. Finally, 29-year-old Rose Schneiderman stepped up to the podium.

In a whisper barely audible, she began to address the crowd.

I would be a traitor to these poor burned bodies, if I came here to talk good fellowship. We have tried you good people of the public and we have found you wanting. The old Inquisition had its rack and its thumbscrews and its instruments of torture with iron teeth. We know what these things are today: the iron teeth are our necessities, the thumbscrews the high-powered and swift machinery close to which we must work, and the rack is here in the fireproof structures that will destroy us the minute they catch on fire.

This is not the first time girls have burned alive in the city. Every week I must learn of the untimely death of one of my sister workers. Every year thousands of us are maimed. The life of men and women is so cheap and property is so sacred. There are so many of us for one job it matters little if 140-odd are burned to death.

We have tried you, citizens, we are trying you now, and you have a couple of dollars for the sorrowing mothers and daughters and sisters by way of a charity gift. But every time the workers come out in the only way they know to protest against conditions which are unbearable, the strong hand of the law is allowed to press down heavily upon us.

Public officials have only words of warning to us—warning that we must be intensely orderly and must be intensely peaceable, and they have the workhouse just back of all their warnings. The strong hand of the law beats us back when we rise into the conditions that make life bearable.

I can't talk fellowship to you who are gathered here. Too much blood has been spilled. I know from my experience it is up to the working people to save themselves. The only way they can save themselves is by a strong working-class movement.

Her speech has become a classic. It is more than just an emotional picture of persecution; it reflects the persuasive sadness and profound understanding that comes from knowing, finally, the cruel realities of life, the perspective of history, and the nature of human beings.

The devastation of that fire and the futility of the seemingly successful strike that had preceded it seemed to impart an undeniable truth to Rose Schneiderman: they could not fail again. The events of 1911 seemed to have made her, and many others, more keenly aware than they had ever been that the workers' fight for reform was absolutely essential. If they did not do it, it would not be done.

In a sense, the fire touched off in Schneiderman an awareness of her own responsibility in the battle for industrial reform. This fiery socialist worker had been transformed into a highly effective labor leader.

The influential speech she gave did help swing public opinion to the side of the trade unions, and the fire itself had made the workers more aware of the crucial need to unionize. Widespread support for labor reform and unionization emerged. Pressure from individuals, such as Rose Schneiderman, as well as from groups like the Women's Trade Union League and the International Ladies' Garment Workers' Union, helped form the New York State Factory Investigating Commission, the New York Citizens' Committee on Safety, and other regulatory and investigatory bodies. The League and Local 25 (the Shirtwaist Makers' Union of the ILGWU) were especially instrumental in attaining a new Industrial Code for New York State, which became "the most outstanding instrument for safeguarding the lives, health, and welfare of the millions of wage earners in New York State and . . . in the nation at large."

It took years for these changes to occur, and labor reform did not rise majestically, Phoenix-like, from the ashes of the Triangle fire. But that fire, and Rose Schneiderman's whispered plea for a strong working-class movement, had indeed become the loud, clear call for action.

■■■

STUDY QUESTIONS

1. How successful had workers at the Triangle Waist Company been in gaining better working conditions before the fire? What had been their major successes and failures?

2. What were the major labor concerns of the immigrant women workers?

3. Why did the fire lead to so many deaths? How did the design of the building contribute to the tragedy?

4. What was the reaction to the fire in the Jewish community? How did the funeral help unify reform-minded people in New York City?

5. What role did Rose Schneiderman play in the aftermath of the tragedy? How did the fire influence the American labor movement?

BIBLIOGRAPHY

As Mitelman indicates, the best treatment of the tragedy is Leon Stein, *The Triangle Fire* (1962). Leslie Woodcock Tentler, *Wage-Earning Women: Industrial Work and Family Life in the United States, 1900–1930* (1979), treats the difficulties faced by working women. Useful treatments of the same theme are Susan Estabrook Kennedy, *If All We Did Was to Weep at Home: A History of White Working Class Women in America* (1979), and Barbara Mayer Wertheimer, *We Were There: The Story of Working Women in America* (1977). Two excellent introductions to general issues that concerned workers are Herbert Gutman, *Work, Culture and Society in Industrializing America* (1977), and David Montgomery, *Workers' Control in America: Studies in the History of Work, Technology, and Labor Struggles* (1979). Moses Rischin, *The Promised City: New York's Jews, 1870–1940* (1970); Arthur S. Goren, *New York Jews and the Quest for Community: The Kehillah Experiment, 1908–1922* (1970); and Irving Howe, *World of Our Fathers: The Journey of the Eastern European Jews to America and the Life They Found and Made* (1976), treat the Jewish experience in America.

JACK JOHNSON WINS THE HEAVYWEIGHT CHAMPIONSHIP

Randy Roberts

For the most part, the Progressive movement was a for-whites-only affair. During the first twenty years of the twentieth century, Asian and black Americans faced open and violent discrimination. On the West Coast, Japanese and Chinese immigrants confronted a humiliating series of discriminatory laws, while in the South and even North blacks were equally hardpressed. Neither presidents Theodore Roosevelt nor Woodrow Wilson made any attempt to alter the social structure of the Jim Crow South, where the lives of the blacks were unequal to the lives of the whites. Although blacks retained some political and civil rights in the North, they still suffered from social and economic discrimination.

Some blacks responded to the injustice. Booker T. Washington was willing to forego social and political equality for economic opportunities. W. E. B. Du Bois demanded more; he worked for full equality. Other blacks lodged less articulate protests through their actions. They refused to live within the narrow borders proscribed for them by white society. Often these blacks were labeled "bad niggers." White authorities hated and punished them, but in black communities they were regarded as heroes and legends. The most famous of these real-life renegades was Jack Johnson, the first black heavyweight champion. He defeated white boxers, married white women, enraged white authorities, and lived by his own laws. In the following selection, historian Randy Roberts uses Johnson's fight with Tommy Burns as an opportunity to examine the racial attitudes of the early twentieth century.

Afterwards concerned whites said it should never have taken place. John L. Sullivan, who by 1908 had quit drinking and become a moral crusader, said, "Shame on the money-mad Champion! Shame on the man who upsets good American precedents because there are Dollars, Dollars, Dollars in it." A dejected sports columnist wrote, "Never before in the history of the prize ring has such a crisis arisen as that which faces the followers of the game tonight." The sadness these men felt could only be expressed in superlatives—greatest tragedy, deepest gloom, saddest day, darkest night. The race war had been fought. Armageddon was over. The Caucasian race had lost. Twenty years after the event, and after a few more such Armageddons, Alva Johnston tried to explain the mood of the day: "The morale of the Caucasian race had been at a low ebb long before the great blow fell in 1908. The Kaiser had been growing hysterical over the Yellow Peril. Africa was still celebrating the victory of Emperor Menelik of Abyssinia over the Italians. Dixie was still in ferment because Booker T. Washington . . . had had a meal at the White House. Then . . . Jack Johnson won the World Heavyweight Championship from Tommy Burns. The Nordics had not been so scared since the days of Tamerlane."

Black ghetto dwellers and sharecroppers rejoiced. In cities from New York to Omaha, blacks smiled with delight. "Today is the zenith of Negro sports," observed a *Colored American Magazine* editor. Other black publications felt such qualifications were too conservative. The *Richmond Planet* reported that "no event in forty years has given more genuine satisfaction to the colored people of this country than has the signal victory of Jack Johnson." Joy and pride spilled over into arrogance, or so some whites believed. The cotton-buying firm

Reprinted with permission of The Free Press, a Division of Macmillan, Inc. from *Papa Jack: Jack Johnson and the Era of White Hopes* by Randy Roberts. Copyright © 1983 by The Free Press.

of Logan and Bryan predicted that Johnson's victory would encourage other blacks to enter boxing, thereby creating a shortage of field labor. Independent of Logan and Bryan's report, the black writer Jim Nasium counseled black youths to consider seriously a boxing career—where else could they face whites on an equal footing? In that last week of 1908 social change seemed close at hand. The implication of most reports was that Jack Johnson had started a revolution.

How had it all come about? When Burns arrived in Perth in August 1908, the world did not seem in any immediate danger. He was treated like a conquering hero. From Perth to Sydney he was cheered and fêted. Mayors and members of Parliament courted Burns as if he were visiting royalty. When the train made its normal 6 A.M. stop at Abury, men stood shivering in the cold to greet Burns. And at Sydney, at a more civilized hour, more than 8,000 people cheered the champion. Speeches were made and applause modestly received. An Australian politician, Colonel Ryrie, extolled the virtues of boxing, telling the gathering that the sport produced sturdy young men needed for battle, "not those milksops who cry out against it."

At these August occasions Burns was frequently asked about Johnson. Would he fight the black champion? If so, where? When? Burns patiently answered the questions like a saint repeating a litany. He would fight Johnson when the right purse was offered. The place was not important. In fact, Australia was as good as—if not better than—any other place. As Burns told a Melbourne reporter: "There are a lot of newspaper stories that I don't want to fight Johnson. I do want to fight him, but I want to give the white boys a chance first." And since the early English settlers had exterminated the Tasmanians, there were a lot of white boys in Australia.

Listening to Burns was an ambitious promoter. Hugh D. "Huge Deal" McIntosh was an

American success story with an Australian setting. As a boy he worked in the Broken Hill mines and as a rural laborer, but early in life he realized that a man could make more money using his brain than his back. His fortune was made as a pie salesman in Australian parks and sporting events, but his career included tours as a racing cyclist, a boxer, a waiter, a newspaper publisher, a member of parliament, a theatrical impresario, and other assorted jobs. All these stints equipped him with enough gab and gall to become a first-rate boxing promoter. It was McIntosh who had invited Burns to Australia to defend his title against Aussie boxers. A student of maps and calendars, he knew that when Teddy Roosevelt's Great White Fleet, then cruising about the Pacific, dropped anchor in Australia a heavyweight championship fight would prove a good draw. With this in mind, he rented a market garden at Rushcutter's Bay, on the outskirts of Sydney, and built an open-air stadium on it. By midsummer he was ready for Burns.

In June he matched Burns against Bill Squires, whom the champion had already knocked out twice, once in the United States and once in France. In defense of Squires, however, it was noted by the press that in his second fight with Burns he had lasted eight rounds, seven longer than the first fight. On his home continent Squires did even better. He was not knocked out until the thirteenth round. Though the fight was not particularly good, the overflowing stadium pleased McIntosh mightily. More than 40,000 people showed up for the fight, including American sailors from the Great White Fleet, but only 15,000 could be seated in the stadium. The 25,000 others milled about outside, listening to the noise made by lucky spectators watching the fight.

Less than two weeks later Burns again defended his title, this time against Bill Lang in Melbourne before 19,000 spectators. Like the stadium at Rushcutter's Bay, South Melbourne Stadium had been hurriedly constructed on

McIntosh's orders—it was built in twelve days—and the result had been worth the effort. In the two fights Burns made more than $20,000 and McIntosh grossed about $100,000, half of which was clear profit. In addition, both fights had been filmed, and revenue from this pioneering effort was much greater then anticipated. Burns, McIntosh, and the Australian boxing public were all exceedingly pleased.

In late October Johnson arrived, and the pulse of Australia picked up a beat. The fight had already been arranged. McIntosh guaranteed Burns $30,000. Before such a sum the color line faded. Therefore, when Johnson landed at Perth he was in an accommodating mood. "How does Burns want it? Does he want it fast and willing? I'm his man in that case. Does he want it flat footed? Goodness, if he does, why I'm his man again. Anything to suit; but fast or slow, I'm going to win." After eight years of trying Johnson was about to get his chance to fight for the heavyweight title.

Short of money, Johnson and Fitzpatrick set up their training quarters in the inexpensive Sir Joseph Banks Hotel in Botany, far less plush than the Hydro Majestic Hotel at Medlow Bath, where Burns trained. Yet Johnson, like Burns, trained in earnest. Johnson looked relaxed—he joked, smiled, made speeches, and played the double bass—but the men and women who watched him train failed to notice that he was also working very hard. Each morning he ran; each afternoon he exercised and sparred with Bill Lang, who imitated Burn's style. Johnson knew that Burns—short, inclined toward fatness, addicted to cigars and strong drink—was nonetheless a very good boxer. In Bohum Lynch's opinion, Burns was a "decidedly good boxer" who, though unorthodox, had a loose and easy style. And in the weeks before the fight Johnson showed by his training that he did not take Burns lightly.

Nor did he disregard the power of Australian racism. He feared that in the emotionally charged atmosphere of an interracial championship fight he might not be given an even break. His concern was not unfounded. An editorial in Sydney's *Illustrated Sporting and Dramatic News* correctly indicated the racial temper of Australian boxing fans: "Citizens who have never prayed before are supplicating Providence to give the white man a strong right arm with which to belt the coon into oblivion." But of more concern to Johnson than white men's prayers were his suspicions of McIntosh as promoter and self-named referee. Several times the two quarreled in public, and they nearly came to blows when Johnson greeted the promoter with "How do, Mr. McIntosh? How do you drag yourself away from Tahmy?" McIntosh, a big, burly, muscular man, thereafter began carrying a lead pipe wrapped in sheet music. As he told his friend Norman Lindsay, it was in case "that black bastard" ever "tries any funny business."

As the bout drew closer, the racial overtones destroyed the holiday atmosphere. It seemed as if all Australia were edgy. In the name of civilization, Protestant reformers spoke words that fell on deaf ears. The fight, said the Sydney Anglican Synod, with "its inherent brutality and dangerous nature" would surely "corrupt the moral tone of the community." But the community was worried less about being corrupted than about the implication of a Johnson victory. Lindsay, whom McIntosh hired to draw posters to advertise the fight, visually portrayed the great fear. Across Sydney could be seen his poster showing a towering black and a much smaller white. As Richard Broome has suggested, "This must have evoked the deepest feelings Australians held about the symbols of blackness and whiteness and evoked the emotiveness of a big man versus a small man and the populous coloured races versus the numerically smaller white race." Clearly, the *Australian Star* editors had this in mind when they printed a cartoon showing the fight being watched by representatives of the white and black races. Underneath was a letter that predicted that "this battle may in the future be looked back

upon as the first great battle of an inevitable race war. . . . There is more in this fight to be considered than the mere title of pugilistic champion of the world."

Racial tension was nothing new to Australia. Race had mattered since the colony's founding. Partly it was an English heritage, passed down from the conquerors of Ireland, Scotland, and Wales—an absolute belief in the inferiority of everything and everyone non-English. In Australia, however, it had developed its own unique characteristics. There common English prejudices had been carried to extremes, and when confronted with dark-skinned natives, the Australians did not shrink from the notion of genocide. The most shocking example of racial relations was the case of the small island of Tasmania off the southeast coast of Australia. When the English first settled the island there were perhaps a few thousand Tasmanians. Short but long-legged, these red-brown people were described as uncommonly friendly natives. But the friendliness soon died, as British colonists hunted, raped enslaved, abducted, or killed the Tasmanians. Slowly the race died off, until in 1876 Truganini, the very last survivor, died. Her passing struck many Australians as sad—but inevitable. As a correspondent for the *Hobart Mercury* wrote, "I regret the death of the last of the Tasmanian aborigines, but I know that it is the result of the *fiat* that the black shall everywhere give place to the white."

For Australia the problem was that other darker races had not given way fast enough in the generation after the death of Truganini. Though Social Darwinists preached the virtues of the light-skinned, by 1909 Australians felt threatened by the "lower" races. Increasingly after 1900 Australians demonstrated anxiety over their Oriental neighbors. Immigration restrictions aimed at keeping the country white were proposed and adopted. So bitter had the struggle become that in 1908, the year of the Johnson-Burns fight, the *Australia Bulletin* changed its banner from "Australia for Australians" to "Australia for the white men."

Johnson and Burns became both an example of and a contribution to the fears of white Australians. Small, white Burns became the symbol of small, white Australia, nobly battling against the odds. Burn's defense was his brain and pluck, his desire to stave off defeat through intelligence and force of will. Johnson became the large, vulgar, corrupt, and sensual enemy. Reports said that he ignored training and instead wenched and drank. He had strength and size but lacked heart—in fact, he *should* win but probably would not. This last report gave rise to the rumor that the fight was fixed. Even the *New York Times* endorsed this view, as did the betting line that made Burns a 7 to 4 favorite.

Cool rains washed Sydney on Christmas night, the eve of the fight. To allow filming, the fight was not scheduled to begin until 11 A.M., but by 6 A.M. an orderly crowd of more than 5,000 was waiting at the gate. The stadium would be filled to capacity; yet interest was much more widespread. Throughout Australia men milled around newspaper offices hoping to hear a word about the progress of the fight. Inside the stadium at Rushcutter's Bay all Christmas cheer had vanished. The mood and tone of the day, from the gray, overcast sky to the uneasy quiet of the spectators, was eulogistic.

Johnson entered the ring first. Despite his dull gray robe his mood was almost carefree. There were a few cheers—though not many—as he slipped under the upper strand of the ropes, but calls of "coon" and "nigger" were more common. He smiled, bowed grandly, and threw kisses in every direction. He liked to strut the stage, and the vicious insults did not outwardly affect him. If anything, his smile became broader as he was more abused. In a country exhilarated by the discovery of gold, Johnson's gold-toothed smile ironically attracted only hate. Satisfied that he was not the crowd's favorite, he retired to his corner, where Sam Fitzpatrick massaged his shoulders and whispered words of assurance into an unlistening ear.

By contrast, when Burns climbed into the ring, the stadium was filled with sound. Burns did not seem to notice. For a time it looked as if he had come into the ring expecting something other than a fight. He was dressed in a worn blue suit, more appropriate for a shoe salesman than the heavyweight champion. Methodically he removed the suit, folded it neatly, and put it in a battered wicker suitcase. Yet even in his short, tight boxing trunks he looked out of place. Jack London, covering the fight for the *New York Herald*, wrote that Burns looked "pale and sallow, as if he had not slept all night, or as if he had just pulled through a bout with fever." Pacing nervously in his corner, he avoided looking across the ring at Johnson.

Burns examined the bandages on Johnson's hands. He did this carefully, looking for hard tape or other unnatural objects. Satisfied, he returned to his corner. Johnson, however, was upset by the tape on Burns's elbows. He asked Burns to remove it. Burns refused. Johnson—suddenly serious—said he would not fight until the tape was removed. Still Burns refused. McIntosh tried to calm the two fighters. He was unsuccessful. The crowd, sensing an unexpected confrontation but not aware of the finer details, sided with Burns and used the moment as a pretext to shout more insults at Johnson, who smiled as if complimented on a new necktie but still refused to alter his protest. Finally, Burns removed the tape. Johnson nodded, satisfied.

McIntosh called the fighters to the center of the ring. He went over the do's and don'ts and the business of what punches would or would not be allowed. Then he announced that in the event that the police stopped the fight, he would render a decision based on who was winning at the time. The unpopular "no decision" verdict would not be given. Both Johnson and Burns had earlier agreed to this procedure.

The fighters returned to their corners. A few moments later the bell rang. The color line in championship fights was erased.

Watching films of Johnson boxing is like listening to a 1900 recording of Enrico Caruso played on a 1910 gramophone. When Johnson fought Burns, film was still in its early days, not yet capable of capturing the subtleties of movement. Nuance is lost in the furious and stilted actions of the figures, which move about the screen in a Chaplinesque manner, as if some drunken cutter had arbitrarily removed three of every four frames. When we watch fighters of Johnson's day on film, we wonder how they could have been considered even good. That some of them were champions strains credulity. They look like large children, wrestling and cuffing each other, but not actually fighting like real boxers, no at all like Ali captured in zoom-lensed, slow-motion, technological grace. But the film misleads.

It was no Charlie Chaplin that shuffled out of his corner in round one to meet Tommy Burns. It was a great boxer who at age thirty was in his physical prime. No longer thin, Johnson was well-muscled, with a broad chest and thick arms and legs. His head was shaved in the style of the eighteenth-century bareknuckle fighters, and his high cheekbones gave his face a rounded appearance. Although he had fought often, his superb defensive skills had kept his face largely unmarked. Like his mother he had a broad, flat nose and full lips, but his eyes were small and oddly Oriental when he smiled. He was famous for his clowning, but this stereotype of a black man obscured the more serious reality. He was often somber, and even when he smiled and acted like a black-faced minstrel, he could be serious. What he thought, he believed, was his own affair. His feelings could not be easily read on his face.

Both boxers began cautiously. Johnson flicked out a few probing jabs, designed more to test distance than to do any physical dam-

The first African-American man to gain the heavyweight boxing championship of the world was Jack Johnson, who held the title from 1908 to 1915.

age. Although Burns was much smaller than Johnson, he was considered a strong man with a powerful punch. Johnson clinched, tested Burns's strength, then shifted to long-range sparring. He allowed Burns to force the action, content to parry punches openhanded. Burns tried to hit Johnson with long left hooks, which fell short. Johnson feinted a long left of his own, but in the same motion he lowered his right shoulder, pivoted from the waist, stepped forward with his right foot, and delivered a perfect right uppercut. It was Johnson's finest weapon, and some ring authorities claim there never has been a fighter who could throw the punch as well as Johnson. Burns was caught flatfooted, leaning into the punch. His momentum was stopped and he fell backward. His head hit heavily on the floor. He lay still. The referee started to count.

"The fight," Jack London wrote only hours after it ended, "there was no fight. No Armenian massacre could compare with the hopeless slaughter that took place in the Sydney stadium today." From the opening seconds of the first round it was clear who would win. At least it was clear to London. It was a fight between a "colossus and a toy automation," between a "playful Ethiopian and a small and futile white man," between a "grown man and a naughty child." And through it all, London and the 20,000 white supporters of Burns watched in horror as their worst fears materialized.

"Hit the coon in his stomach." Burns needed no reminder. After surviving the first-round knockdown, he shifted to a different strategy, one he had thought about before. In the days before the fight, when reporters asked about his battle plan, he had smiled knowingly at his white chroniclers and said he would move in close and hit the black fighter where all black fighters were weak—in the stomach. This theory was hardly novel; it had long been considered axiomatic that black boxers had weak stomachs and hard heads. So thoroughly was the view accepted that black boxers took it for granted that white fighters would attack the body. Peter Jackson once told Fred Dartnell, "They are all after my body. Hit a nigger in the stomach and you'll settle him, they say, but it never seems to occur to them that a white man might just as quickly be beaten by a wallop in the same region." Sam Langford agreed: blacks hated to be hit by a hard punch to the stomach, but so too did whites.

Boxing was not immune to the scientific explanations of the day. Polygenists believed—and Darwinists did not deny—that the black race was an "incipient species." Therefore, whites maintained, physically blacks and

whites were very different. Burns, for example, assumed that Johnson not only had a weak stomach but lacked physical endurance. So he believed that the longer the fight lasted the better were his chances. Behind these stereotypes rested the science of the day. Writing only a year before in the *North American Review*, Charles F. Woodruff claimed that athletes raised in Southern climates lacked endurance: "The excessive light prods the nervous system to do more than it should, and in time such constant stimulation is followed by irritability and finally by exhaustion." Only athletes from the colder Northern latitudes had enough stamina to remain strong during the course of a long boxing match. Therefore, Burns, a Canadian, had reason to remain hopeful. By contrast, Johnson, raised about as far south as one could travel in the United States and only a generation or two removed from Africa, had to win quickly or not at all. At least, this was what Burns and his white supporters hoped.

Burns's strategy was thus founded on the racist belief that scientists, armed with physiological and climatological evidence, had proved that blacks were either inferior to whites, or—as in the case of harder heads—superior because of some greater physiological inferiority; that is to say, blacks had thicker skulls because they had smaller brains. Burns never questioned that his abdominal strength and his endurance were superior to Johnson's. Nor did he doubt that his white skin meant that his desire to win and willingness to accept pain were greater than Johnson's. But above all, he was convinced that as a white he could outthink Johnson, that he could solve the problems of defense and offense more quickly than his black opponent. Burns's faith, in short, rested ultimately on the color of his skin.

Burns forgot, however, that he was facing a boxer liberated from the myths of his day. Johnson's stomach was not weak, and, more important, he knew it was not. As the fight progressed, he exposed the fallacy of Burns's theory. He started to taunt Burns. "Go on, Tommy, hit me here," Johnson said pointing to his stomach. When Burns responded with a blow to Johnson's midsection, Jack laughed and said to try again. "Is that all the better you can do, Tommy?" Another punch. "Come on, Tommy, you can hit harder than that, can't you?" And so it continued; Johnson physically and verbally was destroying the white man's myths.

Burns fought gamely, but without success. Johnson did not try for a knockout; he was content to allow the fight to last until the later rounds. Partly his decision was based on economics. The bout was being filmed, and few boxing fans in America would pay to watch pictures of pressmen, seconds, and other boxers for five minutes as a build-up for a fight that lasted only half a minute. But more important was Johnson's desire for revenge. He hated Burns and wanted to punish him. And he did. By the second round Burns's right eye was discolored and his mouth was bloody. By the middle rounds Burns was bleeding from a dozen minor facial cuts. Blood ran over his shoulders and stained the canvas ring. Before the white audience, Johnson badly punished Burns. And he enjoyed every second of it.

But punishment was not enough. Johnson wanted also to humiliate Burns. He did this verbally. From the very first round Johnson insulted Burns, speaking with an affected English accent, so that "Tommy" became "Tahmy." Mostly what Johnson said was banal: "Poor little Tahmy, who told you you were a fighter?" Or, "Say little Tahmy, you're not fighting. Can't you? I'll have to show you how." Occasionally, when Burns landed a punch, Johnson complimented him: "Good boy, Tommy; good boy, Tommy." In almost every taunt Johnson referred to Burns in the diminutive. It was always "Tommy Boy"; or "little Tommy." And always a derisive smile accompanied the words.

Sometimes Johnson sought to emasculate Burns verbally. Referring to Burns's wife,

Johnson said, "Poor little boy, Jewel won't know you when she gets you back from this fight." Once when Burns landed what looked to be an effective punch, Johnson laughed: "Poor, poor Tommy. Who taught you to hit? Your mother? You a woman?" Crude, often vulgar and mean, Johnson's verbal warfare was nevertheless effective.

Burns responded in kind. Bohum Lynch, who was a great fan of Burns, admitted that his champion's ring histrionics included baleful glaring, foot stomping, and mouth fighting. He often called Johnson a "cur" or a "big dog." At other times, when he was hurt or frustrated, he said, "Come on and fight, nigger. Fight like a white man." Burns's comments, however, were self-defeating. When Johnson insulted Burns, the champion lost control and fought recklessly. But Burns's taunts pleased Johnson, who responded by fighting in an even more controlled way than before. Johnson gained particular strength from Burns's racist statements. It was like playing the Dozens, where accepting abuse with an even smile and concealing one's true emotions were the sign of a sure winner.

When Johnson was not insulting Burns, he was talking to ringsiders. Usually he just joked about how easy the fight was and what he would do with the money he won from betting on the bout. That the ringsiders hated Johnson and screamed racial insults did not seem to bother him. Only rarely did Johnson show his disgust with the white audience. Once as he moved from his corner at the start of a round he spat a mouthful of water toward the press row, but such actions were unusual. More common was the smile—wide, detached, inscrutable. In describing the grin, Jack London came closest to the truth: it was "the fight epitomized." It was the smile of a man who has mastered the rules to a slightly absurd game.

After a few rounds the only question that remained unanswered was not who would win but how much punishment Burns could take. By the middle rounds that too was evident—he could survive great amounts of punishment. His eyes were bruised and discolored, his mouth hung open, his jaw was swollen and looked broken, and his body was splotched with his own blood. In the corner between rounds his seconds sponged his face with champagne, which was popularly believed to help revive hurt fighters. It did not help Burns. Yet at the bell he always arose to face more punishment and insults. For the white spectators, Burns's fortitude was itself inspiring. As Bohum Lynch wrote, "To take a beating any time, even from your best friend, is hard work. But to take a beating from a man you abhor, belonging to a race you despise, to know that he is hurting you and humiliating you with the closest attention to detail, and the coldest deliberation . . . this requires pluck."

By the thirteenth round everyone but Burns and Johnson was surfeited with the carnage. Spectators, left with nothing and nobody to cheer, now yelled for the fight to be stopped. After the thirteenth round police entered the ring. They talked with McIntosh, then with Burns. The white champion refused to concede. He insisted that he could win. But in the fourteenth Burns was again severely punished. A hard right cross knocked him to the canvas. He arose at the count of eight but was wobbly. Again policemen climbed into the ring, only this time there was no talking. The fight was stopped, although Burns—dazed, covered with blood, but still game—screamed at the police to give him another chance.

Everywhere was a stunned silence as the spectators accepted that the inevitable was now the actual. It had happened. A black man now wore the crown that had once belonged to Sullivan, Corbett, and Jeffries. As far as Australia was concerned, an "archetypal darkness" had replaced sweetness and light; the barbarian had defeated the civilized man. As the *Daily Telegraph* observed in doggerel:

And yet for all we know and feel,
For Christ and Shakespeare, knowledge, love,

We watch a white man bleeding reel,
We cheer a black with bloodied glove.

The imagery in which the fight was reported clearly reflects the white Australian attitude toward Johnson. He was portrayed as a destructive beast. *Fairplay*, the liquor trades weekly, called Johnson "a huge primordial ape," and the *Bulletin's* cartoons likened him to a shaven-headed reptile. He was the discontented black and yellow masses that haunted the Australian mind. Journalist Randolph Bedford, perhaps the most unabashedly racist reporter at the fight, depicted it in ominous terms: "Yet the white beauty faced the black unloveliness, forcing the fight, bearing the punishment as if it were none . . . weight and reach were ebbing against intrepidity, intelligence and lightness. . . . His courage still shone in his eyes; his face was disfigured and swollen and bloodied. He was still beauty by contrast— beautiful but to be beaten; clean sunlight fighting darkness and losing."

In America the fight was not viewed in quite so maudlin a manner. Certainly the white American press was not pleased by the result, but it generally tried to dismiss it in a light-hearted mood. Perhaps, reporters reasoned, all was not lost. "Br'er Johnson is an American anyway," commented a reporter for the *Omaha Sunday Bee*. Then, too, boxing had declined so much in recent years that some experts wondered if the fight meant anything at all. Though John L. Sullivan criticized Burns for fighting Johnson, he added that "present day bouts cannot truly be styled prize fights, but only boxing matches." A fine distinction, but Sullivan believed it was enough to invalidate Johnson's claim as heavyweight champion. And certainly even if Johnson were the champion, reporters all agreed that he was far below the likes of Sullivan, Corbett, or Jeffries.

Though the mood had not yet reached a crisis stage, the fight's portent was still most unsettling to American whites. This was especially true about the manner in which blacks celebrated Johnson's victory. It was reported that the Manassas Club, a Chicago organization of wealthy blacks who had white wives, hired white waiters to serve the food at their banquet. And one of their members said that "Johnson's victory demonstrates the physical superiority of the black over the Caucasian. The basis of mental superiority in most men is physical superiority. If the negro can raise his mental standard to his physical eminence, some day he will be a leader among men." In other parts of the country blacks were reported as acting rude to whites and being swelled by false pride.

Johnson's actions in Australia did little to calm Caucasian fears. Turning against the sportsmanlike tradition of praising one's opponent, Johnson openly said that Burns was a worthless boxer: "He is the easiest man I ever met. I could have put him away quicker, but I wanted to punish him. I had my revenge." Nor was Johnson discreet about the company with whom he was seen in public. Hattie McClay, his companion who had remained in the background during the weeks before the fight, was now prominently on display. Dressed in silk and furs, she seemed as prized a possession of Johnson's as his goldcapped teeth.

Johnson now seemed more apt to emphasize racial issues that irritated whites. Interviewed during the days after the fight, he told reporters that he had the greatest admiration for the aboriginal Australians. Commenting on their weapons, he said, "Your central Australian natives must have been men of genius to have turned out such artistic and ideal weapons." Nor, he hinted, was he any less a genius. He understood human nature: because he defeated Burns he could expect to be hated by all whites. But, he added, he could find solace in his favorite books—*Paradise Lost, Pilgrim's*

Progress and *Titus Andronicus*. His comments achieved their purpose; everywhere white Australians snorted in disgust. But his choice of books certainly did not reflect his own attitude. Unlike Milton's Adam, Johnson did not practice the standard Christian virtues.

Burns left Australia soon after the fight. A richer man by some $30,000, he nevertheless was bitter and filled with hatred. Johnson, however, decided to stay for a while in Australia. His side of the purse, a mere $5,000, was hardly enough to make the venture profitable. He hoped instead to capitalize on his fame by touring Australia as a vaudeville performer. It was common for any famous boxer to make such tours. In 1908 he had toured in America and Canada with the Reilly and Woods Big Show and had enjoyed the experience. He loved the limelight and, unlike other boxers, put on a good show. He demonstrated a few boxing moves, sang several songs, danced, and played the bass fiddle. During his Australian tour he actually made more money than he had in his fight with Burns. Not until mid-February was he ready to go home.

He had changed. The Johnson who left Australia in February was not the same man who had arrived in October. Inwardly, perhaps, he was much the same. But outwardly he was different. He was more open about his beliefs and his pleasures, less likely to follow the advice of white promoters and managers. Undoubtedly he believed the title of world champion set him apart from others of his race. And in this he was right. He would never be viewed as just another black boxer. But he was wrong in his assumption that the crown carried with it some sort of immunity against the dictates of whites and traditions of white society. Now more than ever Johnson was expected to conform. And now more than ever Johnson felt he did not have to. The collision course was set.

■ ■ ■

STUDY QUESTIONS

1. How did the promoters of the Johnson-Burns fight use racism to build up the gate? How did the racial attitudes of white Australians compare with those of white Americans?

2. How did Burns demonstrate racial stereotypes by the manner in which he fought Johnson?

3. What was the reaction of white Australians and Americans to Jack Johnson's victory?

4. What was Johnson's attitude toward white society?

5. How else might one use sports or popular culture to demonstrate racial attitudes?

BIBLIOGRAPHY

The selection is taken from Randy Roberts, *Papa Jack: Jack Johnson and the Era of White Hopes* (1983). Finis Farr, *Black Champion: The Life and Times of Jack Johnson* (1965), provides a readable popular history of the boxer, and Al-Tony Gilmore, *Bad Nigger! The National Impact of Jack Johnson* (1975), traces the newspaper reaction to Johnson. Johnson's image in black folklore is treated by William Wiggins, "Jack Johnson as Bad Nigger: The Folklore of His Life," *Black Scholar* (1969), and Lawrence W. Levine, *Black Culture and Black Consciousness: Afro-American Folk Thought from Slavery to Freedom* (1977). A number of books trace the evolution of white attitudes toward blacks. Among the best are George M. Fredrickson, *The Black Image in the White Mind: The Debate on Afro-American Character and Destiny, 1817–1914* (1971); Thomas F. Gossett, *Race: The History of an Idea in America* (1965); and John S. Haller, Jr., *Outcasts from Evolution: Scientific Attitudes of Racial Inferiority, 1859–1900* (1971).

THE TRENCH SCENE

Paul Fussell

For the generation that fought it, World War I was the Great War. It came after almost one hundred years of general European peace, and it shattered not only nations and people but also a system of thought, a world view. Before the Great War, intellectuals talked seriously and earnestly about the progress of mankind and the perfectability of societies and individuals. Men and women, they agreed, were reasonable creatures, fully capable of ordering their lives and environment. The terrible slaughter of Verdun and the Somme, the mud and lice and rats of the trenches, the horrors of poison gases and bullet-torn bodies draped over barbed-wire barriers—these unspeakable barbarities silenced talk of progress. Ernest Hemingway spoke for his generation when he wrote about the impact of the Great War: "I was always embarrassed by the words *sacred, glorious,* and *sacrifice* and the expression *in vain* . . . I had seen nothing sacred, and the things that were glorious had no glory and the sacrifices were like the stockyards at Chicago if nothing was done with the meat except to bury it. There were many words that you could not stand to hear and finally only the names of places had dignity. . . . Abstract words such as *glory, honor, courage,* or *hallow* were obscene beside the concrete names of villages, the number of roads, the names of rivers, the numbers of regiments and the dates."

In the following essay literary historian Paul Fussell discusses the Great War as experienced by millions of soldiers who served time in the trenches of the Western Front. In these ditches some 7,000 British soldiers were killed or wounded daily between 1914 and 1918. Though not in such horrendous numbers, Americans too died in the trenches of France, and the experience of mass death transformed American society. The United States went into the war to "make the world safe for democracy" but emerged from the war pessimistic, cynical, and discouraged. As Fussell observes, "To be in the trenches was to experience an unreal, unforgettable enclosure and constraint, as well as a sense of being unoriented and lost." This was the aspect of the Great War that changed the temper of Western culture.

The idea of "the trenches" has been assimilated so successfully by metaphor and myth ("Georgian complacency died in the trenches") that it is not easy now to recover a feeling for the actualities. *Entrenched,* in an expression like *entrenched power,* has been a dead metaphor so long that we must bestir ourselves to recover its literal sense. It is time to take a tour.

From the winter of 1914 until the spring of 1918 the trench system was fixed, moving here and there a few hundred yards, moving on great occasions as much as a few miles. London stationers purveying maps felt secure in stocking "sheets of 'The Western Front' with a thick wavy black line drawn from North to South alongside which was printed 'British Line.' "If one could have gotten high enough to look down at the whole line at once, one would have seen a series of multiple parallel excavations running for 400 miles down through Belgium and France, roughly in the shape of an S flattened at the sides and tipped to the left. From the North Sea coast of Belgium the line wandered southward, bulging out to contain Ypres, then dropping down to protect Béthune, Arras, and Albert. It continued south in front of Montidier, Compiégne, Soissons, Reims, Verdun, St. Mihiel, and Nancy, and finally attached its southernmost end to the Swiss border at Beurnevisin, in Alsace. The top forty miles—the part north of Ypres—was held by the Belgians; the next ninety miles, down to the river Ancre, were British; the French held the rest, to the south.

Henri Barbusse estimates that the French front alone contained about 6250 miles of trenches. Since the French occupied a little more than half the line, the total length of the numerous trenches occupied by the British must come to about 6000 miles. We thus find over 12,000 miles of trenches on the Allied side

alone. When we add the trenches of the Central Powers, we arrive at a figure of about 25,000 miles, equal to a trench sufficient to circle the earth. Theoretically it would have been possible to walk from Belgium to Switzerland entirely below ground, but although the lines were "continuous," they were not entirely seamless: occasionally mere shell holes or fortified strong-points would serve as a connecting link. Not a few survivors have performed the heady imaginative exercise of envisioning the whole line at once. Stanley Casson is one who, imagining the whole line from his position on the ground, implicitly submits the whole preposterous conception to the criterion of the "normally" rational and intelligible. As he remembers, looking back from 1935.

Our trenches stood on a faint slope, just overlooking German ground, with a vista of vague plainland below. Away to right and left stretched the great lines of defense as far as eye and imagination could stretch them. I used to wonder how long it would take for me to walk from the beaches of the North Sea to that curious end of all fighting against the Swiss boundary; to try to guess what each end looked like; to imagine what would happen if I passed a verbal message, in the manner of the parlor game, along to the next man on my right to be delivered to the end man of all up against the Alps. Would anything intelligible at all emerge?

Another imagination has contemplated a similar absurd transmission of sound all the way from north to south. Alexander Aitken remembers the Germans opposite him celebrating some happy public event in early June, 1916, presumably either the (ambiguous) German success at the naval battle of Jutland (May 31–June 1) or the drowning of Lord Kitchener, lost on June 5 when the cruiser *Hampshire* struck a mine and sank off the Orkney Islands. Aitken writes, "There had been a morning in early June when a tremendous tin-canning and beating of shell-gongs had begun in the north and run south down their lines to end, without doubt, at Belfort and Mulhausen on the Swiss

From *The Great War and Modern Memory* by Paul Fussell. Copyright © 1975 by Oxford University Press, Inc. Reprinted by permission.

frontier." Impossible to believe, really, but in this mad setting, somehow plausible.

The British part of the line was normally populated by about 800 battalions of 1000 men each. They were concentrated in the two main sectors of the British effort: the Ypres Salient in Flanders and the Somme area in Picardy. Memory has given these two sectors the appearance of two distinguishable worlds. The Salient, at its largest point about nine miles wide and projecting some four miles into the German line, was notable for its terrors of concentrated, accurate artillery fire. Every part of it could be covered from three sides, and at night one saw oneself almost surrounded by the circle of white and colored Very lights set up by the Germans to illuminate the ground in front of their trenches or to signal to the artillery behind them. The "rear area" at Ypres was the battered city itself, where the troops harbored in cellars or in the old fortifications built by Vauban in the seventeenth century. It was eminently available to the German guns, and by the end of the war Ypres was flattened to the ground, its name a byword for a city totally destroyed. Another war later, in 1940, Colin Perry—who was not born until four years after the Great War—could look at the ruins of London and speak of "the Ypres effect of Holborn." If the character of the Ypres sector was concentration and enclosure, inducing claustrophobia even above ground, the Somme was known—at least until July 1, 1916—for its greater amplitude and security. German fire came generally from only one direction; and troops at rest could move further back. But then there was the Somme mud; although the argument about whether the mud wasn't really worse at Ypres was never settled.

Each of these two sectors had its symbolic piece of ruined public architecture. At Ypres it was the famous Cloth Hall, once a masterpiece of medieval Flemish civic building. Its gradual destruction by artillery and its pathetic final dissolution were witnessed by hundreds of thousands, who never forgot this eloquent emblem of what happens when war collides with art. In the Somme the memorable ruined work of architecture, connoting this time the collision of the war with religion and the old pieties, was the battered Basilica in the town of Albert, or "Bert," as the troops called it. The grand if rather vulgar red and white brick edifice had been built a few years before the war, the result of a local ecclesiastic's enthusiasm. Together with his townsmen he hoped that Albert might become another Lourdes. Before the war 80,000 used to come on pilgrimages to Albert every year. The object of veneration inside the church was a statue of the Virgin, said to have been found in the Middle Ages by a local shepherd. But the statue of the Virgin never forgotten by the hordes of soldiers who passed through Albert was the colossal gilded one on top of the battered tall tower of the Basilica. This figure, called Notre Dame des Brebiéres, originally held the infant Christ in outstretched arms above her; but now the whole statue was bent down below the horizontal, giving the effect of a mother about to throw her child—in disgust? in sacrifice?—into the debris-littered street below. To Colonel Sir Maurice Hankey, Secretary of the War Committee, it was "a most pathetic sight." Some said that the statue had been bent down by French engineers to prevent the Germans from using it to aim at. But most—John Masefield among them—preferred to think it a victim of German artillery. Its obvious symbolic potential (which I will deal with later) impressed itself even on men who found they could refer to it only facetiously, as "The Lady of the Limp."

The two main British sectors duplicated each other also in their almost symbolic road systems. Each had a staging town behind: for Ypres it was Poperinghe (to the men, "Pop"); for the Somme, Amiens. From these towns troops proceeded with augmenting but usually well-concealed terror up a sinister road to the town of operations, either Ypres itself or Albert. And running into the enemy lines out of Ypres and Albert were the most sinister roads of all, one leading to Menin, the other to Bapaume, both in enemy territory. These roads defined the direction of ultimate attack and the hoped-for breakout. They were the goals of the bizarre inverse quest on which the soldiers were ironically embarked.

But most of the time they were not questing. They were sitting or lying or squatting in place below the level of the ground. "When all is said and done," Sassoon notes, "the war was mainly a matter of holes and ditches." And in these holes and ditches extending for ninety miles, continually, even in the quietest times, some 7000 British men and officers were killed and wounded daily, just as a matter of course. "Wastage," the Staff called it.

There were normally three lines of trenches. The front-line trench was anywhere from fifty yards or so to a mile from its enemy counterpart. Several hundred yards behind it was the support trench line. And several hundred yards behind that was the reserve line. There were three kinds of trenches: firing trenches, like these; communication trenches, running roughly perpendicular to the line and connecting the three lines; and "saps," shallower ditches thrust out into No Man's Land, providing access to forward observation posts, listening posts, grenade-throwing posts, and machine gun positions. The end of a sap was usually not manned all the time: night was the favorite time for going out. Coming up from the rear, one reached the trenches by following a communication trench sometimes a mile or more long. It often began in a town and gradually deepened. By the time pedestrians reached the reserve line, they were well below ground level.

A firing trench was supposed to be six to eight feet deep and four or five feet wide. On the enemy side a parapet of earth or sandbags rose about two or three feet above the ground. A corresponding "parados" a foot or so high was often found on top of the friendly side. Into the sides of trenches were dug one- or two-man holes ("funk-holes"), and there were deeper dugouts, reached by dirt stairs, for use as command posts and officers' quarters. On the enemy side of a trench was a fire-step two feet high on which the defenders were supposed to stand, firing and throwing grenades, when repelling attack. A well-built trench did not run straight for any distance: that would have been to invite enfilade fire. Every few yards a good trench zig-zagged. It had frequent traverses designed to contain damage within a limited space. Moving along a trench thus involved a great deal of weaving and turning. The floor of a proper trench was covered with wooden duckboards, beneath which were sumps a few feet deep designed to collect water. The walls, perpetually crumbling, were supported by sandbags, corrugated iron, or bundles of sticks or rushes. Except at night and in half-light, there was of course no looking over the top except through periscopes, which could be purchased in the "Trench Requisites" section of the main London department stores. The few snipers on duty during the day observed No Man's Land through loopholes cut in sheets of armor plate.

The entanglements of barbed wire had to be positioned far enough out in front of the trench to keep the enemy from sneaking up to grenade-throwing distance. Interestingly, the two novelties that contributed most to the personal menace of the war could be said to be American inventions. Barbed wire had first appeared on the American frontier in the late nineteenth century for use in restraining animals. And the machine gun was the brainchild of Hiram Stevens Maxim (1840–1916), an American who, disillusioned with native patent law, established his Maxim Gun Company in England and began manufacturing his guns in 1889. He was finally knighted for his efforts. At first the British regard for barbed wire was on a par with Sir Douglas Haig's understanding of the machine gun. In the autumn of 1914, the first wire Private Frank Richards saw emplaced before the British positions was a single strand of agricultural wire found in the vicinity. Only later did the manufactured article begin to arrive from England in sufficient quantity to create the thickets of mock-organic rusty brown that helped give a look of eternal autumn to the front.

The whole British line was numbered by sections, neatly, from right to left. A section, normally occupied by a company, was roughly 300 yards wide. One might be occupying front-line trench section 51; or support trench S 51, behind it; or reserve trench SS 51, behind both. But a less formal way of identifying sections of trench was by place or street names with a distinctly London flavor. *Piccadilly* was a favorite; popular also were *Regent Street* and *Strand*; junctions were *Hyde Park Corner* and *Marble Arch*. Greater wit—and deeper homesickness—sometimes surfaced in the naming of the German trenches opposite. Sassoon remembers "Durley's" account of the attack at Delville Wood in September, 1916: "Our objective was Pint Trench, taking Bitter and Beer and clearing Ale and Vat, and also Pilsen Lane." Directional and traffic control signs were everywhere in the trenches, giving the whole system the air of a parody modern city, although one literally "underground."

The trenches I have described are more or less ideal, although not so ideal as the famous exhibition trenches dug in Kensington Gardens for the edification of the home front. These were clean, dry, and well furnished, with straight sides and sandbags neatly aligned. R. E. Vernède writes his wife from the real trenches that a friend of his has just returned from viewing the set of ideal ones. He "found he had never seen anything at all like it before." And Wilfred Owen calls the Kensington Gardens trenches "the laughing stock of the army." Explaining military routines to civilian readers, Ian Hay labors to give the impression that the real trenches are identical to the exhibition ones and that they are properly described in the language of normal domesticity a bit archly deployed:

The firing-trench is our place of business—our office in the city, so to speak. The supporting trench is our suburban residence, whither the weary toiler may betake himself periodically (or, more correctly, in relays) for purposes of refreshment and repose.

The reality was different. The British trenches were wet, cold, smelly, and thoroughly squalid. Compared with the precise and thorough German works, they were decidedly amateur, reflecting a complacency about the British genius for improvisation. Since defense offered little opportunity for the display of pluck or swank, it was by implication derogated in the officers' *Field Service Pocket Book*. One reason the British trench system was so haphazard and ramshackle was that it had originally taken form in accord with the official injunction: "The choice of a [defensive] position and its preparation must be made with a view to economizing the power expended on defense in order that the power of offense may be increased." And it was considered really useless to build solid fortifications anyway: "An occasional shell may strike and penetrate the parapet, but in the case of shrapnel the damage to the parapet will be trifling, while in the case of a shell filled with high explosive, the effect will be no worse on a thin parapet than on a thick one. It is, therefore, useless to spend time and labor on making a thick parapet simply to keep out shell." The repeatedly revived hopes for a general breakout and pursuit were another reason why the British trenches were so shabby. A typical soldier's view is George Coppard's:

The whole conduct of our trench warfare seemed to be based on the concept that we, the British, were not stopping in the trenches for long, but were tarrying awhile on the way to Berlin and that very soon we would be chasing Jerry across country. The result, in the long term, meant that we lived a mean and impoverished sort of existence in lousy scratch holes.

In contrast, the German trenches, as the British discovered during the attack on the Somme, were deep, clean, elaborate, and sometimes even comfortable. As Coppard found on the Somme, "Some of the [German] dugouts were thirty feet deep, with as many as sixteen bunk-beds, as well as door bells, water tanks with taps, and cupboards and mirrors." They also had boarded walls, floors, and ceilings; finished wooden staircases; electric light; real kitchens; and wallpaper and overstuffed furniture, the whole protected by steel outer doors. Foreign to the British style was a German dugout of the sort recalled by Ernst Jünger:

At Monchy . . . I was master of an underground dwelling approached by forty steps hewn in the solid chalk, so that even the heaviest shells at this depth made no more than a pleasant rumble when we sat there over an interminable game of cards. In one wall I had a bed hewn out. . . . At its head hung an electric light so that I could read in comfort till I was sleepy. . . . The whole was shut off from the outer world by a dark-red curtain with rod and rings. . . .

As these examples suggest, there were "national styles" in trenches as in other things. The French trenches were nasty, cynical, efficient, and temporary. Kipling remembered the smell of delicious cooking emanating from some in Alsace. The English were amateur, vague, *ad hoc,* and temporary. The German were efficient, clean, pedantic, and permanent. Their occupants proposed to stay where they were.

Normally the British troops rotated trench duty. After a week of "rest" behind the lines, a unit would move up—at night—to relieve a unit in the front-line trench. After three days to a week or more in that position, the unit would move back for a similar length of time to the support trench, and finally back to the reserve. Then it was time for a week of rest again. In the three lines of trenches the main business of the soldier was to exercise self-control while being shelled. As the poet Louis Simpson has accurately remembered:

Being shelled is the main work of an infantry soldier, which no one talks about. Everyone has his own way of going about it. In general, it means lying face down and contracting your body into as small a space as possible. In novels [The Naked and the Dead *is an example*] *you read about soldiers, at such moments, fouling themselves. The opposite is true. As all your parts are contracting, you are more likely to be constipated.*

Simpson is recalling the Second War, but he might be recalling the First. While being shelled, the soldier either harbored in a dugout and hoped for something other then a direct hit or made himself as small as possible in a funk-hole. An unlucky sentry or two was supposed to be out in the open trench in all but the worst bombardments, watching through a periscope or loophole for signs of an attack. When only light shelling was in progress, people moved about the trenches freely, and we can get an idea of what life there was like if we posit a typical twenty-four hours in a front-line trench.

The day began about an hour before first light, which often meant at about 4:30. This was the moment for the invariable ritual of morning stand-to (short for the archaic formal command for repelling attack, "Stand to Arms"). Since dawn was the favorite time for launching attacks, at the order to stand-to everyone, officers, men, forward artillery observers, visitors, mounted the fire-step, weapon ready, and peered toward the German line. When it was almost full light and clear that the Germans were not going to attack that morning, everyone "stood down" and began preparing breakfast in small groups. The rations of tea, bread, and bacon, brought up in sandbags during the night, were broken out. The bacon was fried in mess-tin lids over small, and if possible smokeless, fires. If the men were lucky enough to be in a division whose commanding general permitted the issue of the dark and strong government rum, it was doled out from a jar with the traditional iron spoon, each man receiving about two tablespoonsful. Some put it into their tea, but most swallowed it straight. It was a precious thing, and serving it out was almost like a religious ceremonial, as David Jones recalls in *In Parenthesis*, where a corporal is performing the rite:

O have a care—don't spill the precious
O don't jog his hand—ministering;
do take care.
O please—give the poor bugger elbow room.

Larger quantities might be issued to stimulate troops for an assault, and one soldier remembers what the air smelled like during a British attack:

"Pervading the air was the smell of rum and blood." In 1922 one medical officer deposed before a parliamentary committee investigating the phenomenon of "shell shock": "Had it not been for the rum ration I do not think we should have won the war.

During the day the men cleaned weapons and repaired those parts of the trench damaged during the night. Or they wrote letters, deloused themselves, or slept. The officers inspected, encouraged, and strolled about looking nonchalant to inspirit the men. They censored the men's letters and dealt with the quantities of official inquiries brought them daily by runner. How many pipe-fitters had they in their company? Reply immediately. How many hairdressers, chiropodists, bicycle repairmen? Daily "returns" of the amount of ammunition and the quantity of trench stores had to be made. Reports of the nightly casualties had to be sent back. And letters of condolence, which as the war went on became form-letters of condolence, had to be written to the relatives of the killed and wounded. Men went to and fro on sentry duty or working parties, but no one showed himself above the trench. After evening stand-to, the real work began.

Most of it was above ground. Wiring parties repaired the wire in front of the position. Digging parties extended saps toward the enemy. Carrying parties brought up not just rations and mail but the heavy engineering materials needed for the constant repair and improvement of the trenches: timbers, A-frames, duckboards, stakes and wire, corrugated iron, sandbags, tarpaulins, pumping equipment. Bombs and ammunition and flares were carried forward. All this ant-work was illuminated brightly from time to time by German flares and interrupted very frequently by machine gun or artillery fire. Meanwhile night patrols and raiding parties were busy in No Man's Land. As morning approached, there was a nervous bustle to get the jobs done in time, to finish fitting the timers, filling the sandbags, pounding in the stakes, and then returning mauls and picks and shovels to the Quartermaster Sergeant. By the time of stand-to, nothing human was visible above ground anywhere, but every day each side scrutinized the look of the other's line for significant changes wrought by night.

Flanders and Picardy have always been notorious for dampness. It is not the least of the ironies of the war for the British that their trenches should have been dug where the water-table was the highest and the annual rainfall the most copious. Their trenches were always wet and often flooded several feet deep. Thigh-boots or waders were issued as standard articles of uniform. Wilfred Owen writes his mother from the Somme at the beginning of 1917: "The waders are of course indispensable. In 2 1/2 miles of trench which I waded yesterday there was not one inch of dry ground. There is a mean depth of two feet of water." Pumps worked day and night but to little effect. Rumor held that the Germans not only could make it rain when they wanted it to—that is, all the time—but had contrived some shrewd technical method for conducting the water in their lines into the British positions—perhaps piping it underground. Ultimately there was no defense against the

■ ■ *Front-line trenches in World War I. At some points on the front, a scant 1500 yards separated the Allied and the German lines.*

water but humor. "Water knee deep and up to the waist in places," one soldier notes in his diary. "Rumors of being relieved by the Grand Fleet." One doesn't want to dwell excessively on such discomforts, but here it will do no harm to try to imagine what, in these conditions, going to the latrine was like.

The men were not the only live things in the line. They were accompanied everywhere by their lice, which the professional delousers in rest positions behind the lines, with their steam vats for clothes and hot baths for troops, could do little to eliminate. The entry *lousy* in Eric Partridge's *Dictionary of Slang*

and Unconventional English speaks volumes: "Contemptible; mean; filthy . . . . Standard English till 20th C, when, especially after the Great War, colloquial and used as a mere pejorative." *Lousy with*, meaning *full of*, was "originally military" and entered the colloquial word-hoard around 1915: "That ridge is lousy with Fritz."

The famous rats also gave constant trouble. They were big and black, with wet, muddy hair. They fed largely on the flesh of cadavers and on dead horses. One shot them with revolvers or coshed them to death with pickhandles. Their hunger, vigor, intelligence, and courage are recalled in numerous anecdotes. One officer notes from the Ypres Salient: "We are fairly plagued with rats. They have eaten nearly everything in the mess, including the table-cloth and the operations orders! We borrowed a large cat and shut it up at night to exterminate them, and found the place empty next morning. The rats must have eaten it up, bones, fur, and all, and dragged it to their holes."

One can understand rats eating heartily there. It is harder to understand men doing so. The stench of rotten flesh was over everything, hardly repressed by the chloride of lime sprinkled on particularly offensive sites. Dead horses and dead men—and parts of both—were sometimes not buried for months and often simply became an element of parapets and trench walls. You could smell the front line miles before you could see it. Lingering pockets of gas added to the unappetizing atmosphere. Yet men ate three times a day, although what they ate reflected the usual gulf between the ideal and the actual. The propagandist George Adam announced with satisfaction that "the food of the army is based upon the conclusions of a committee, upon which sat several eminent scientists." The result, he asserted, is that the troops are "better fed than they are at home." Officially, each man got daily: 1 1/4 pounds fresh meat (or 1 pound preserved meat), 1 1/4 pounds bread, 4 ounces bacon, 3 ounces cheese, 1/2 pound fresh vegetables (or 2 ounces dried), together with small amounts of tea, sugar and jam. But in the trenches there was very seldom fresh meat, not for eating, anyway; instead there was "Bully" (tinned corned-beef) or "Maconochie" (ma-coń-o-chie), a tinned meat-and-vegetable stew named after its manufacturer. If they did tend to grow tedious in the long run, both products were surprisingly good. The troops seemed to like the Maconochie best, but the Germans favored the British corned beef, seldom returning from a raid on the British lines without taking back as much as they could carry. On trench duty

the British had as little fresh bread as fresh meat. "Pearl Biscuits" were the substitute. They reminded the men of dog biscuits, although, together with the Bully beef, they were popular with the French and Belgian urchins, who ran (or more often strolled) alongside the railway trains bringing troops up to the front, soliciting gifts by shouting, "Tommee! Bull-ee! Bee-skee!" When a company was out of the line, it fed better. It was then serviced by its company cookers—stoves on wheels—and often got something approaching the official ration, as it might also in a particularly somnolent part of the line, when hot food might come up at night in the large covered containers known as Dixies.

Clothing and equipment improved as the war went on, although at the outset there was a terrible dearth and improvisation. During the retreat from Mons, as Frank Richards testifies, "A lot of us had no caps: I was wearing a handkerchief knotted at the four corners—the only headgear I was to wear for some time." Crucial supplies had been omitted: "We had plenty of small-arm ammunition but no rifle-oil or rifle-rag to clean our rifles with. We used to cut pieces off our shirts . . . and some of us who had bought small tins of vaseline . . . for use on sore heels or chafed legs, used to grease our rifles with that." At the beginning line officers dressed very differently from the men. They wore riding-boots or leather puttees; melodramatically cut riding breeches; and flare-skirted tunics with Sam Browne belts. Discovering that this costume made them special targets in attacks (German gunners were instructed to fire first at the people with the thin knees), by the end they were dressing like the troops, wearing wrap puttees; straight trousers bloused below the knee; Other Ranks' tunics with inconspicuous insignia, no longer on the cuffs but on the shoulders; and Other Ranks' web belts and haversacks. In 1914 both officers and men wore peaked caps, and it was rakish for officers to remove the grommet for a "Gorblimey" effect. Steel helmets were introduced at the end of 1915, giving the troops, as Sassoon observed, "a Chinese look." Herbert Read found the helmets "the only poetic thing in the British Army, for they are primeval in design and effect, like iron mushrooms." A perceptive observer could date corpses and skeletons lying on disused battlefields by their evolving dress. A month before the end of the war, Major P. H. Pilditch recalls, he

spent some time in the old No Man's Land of four years' duration. . . . It was a morbid but intensely interesting occupation tracing the various battles amongst the hundreds of skulls, bones and remains scattered thickly about. The progress of our successive attacks could be clearly seen from the types of equipment on the skeletons, soft cloth caps denoting the 1914 and early 1915 fighting, then respirators, then steel helmets marking attack in 1916. Also Australian slouch hats, used in the costly and abortive attack in 1916.

To be in the trenches was to experience an unreal, unforgettable enclosure and constraint, as well as a sense of being unoriented and lost. One saw two things only: the walls of an unlocalized, undifferentiated earth and the sky above. Fourteen years after the war J. R. Ackerley was wandering through an unfrequented part of a town in India. "The streets became narrower and narrower as I turned and turned," he writes, "until I felt I was back in the trenches, the houses upon either side being so much of the same color and substance as the rough ground between." That lost feeling is what struck Major Frank Isherwood, who writes his wife in December, 1914: "The trenches are a labyrinth, I have already lost myself repeatedly. . . . You can't get out of them and walk about the country or see anything at all but two muddy walls on each side of you." What a survivor of the Salient remembers fifty years later are the walls of dirt and the ceiling of sky, and his eloquent optative cry rises as if he were still imprisoned there: "To be out of this present, everpresent, eternally present misery, this stinking world of sticky, trickling earth ceilinged by a strip of threatening sky." As the only visible theater of variety, the sky becomes all-important. It was the sight of the sky, almost alone, that had the power to persuade a man that he was not already lost in a common grave.

■■■

STUDY QUESTIONS

1. What was the effect of World War I on the landscape of Europe?

2. In theory, how were the trenches supposed to be constructed? What was life supposed to be like in the ideal trench? How did reality differ from theory?

3. What national differences were there in the construction and maintenance of trenches? What do the differences tell us about the different national characters and war aims?

4. Describe the sights, sounds, and smell of life in the trenches. How did trench life affect the soldiers?

5. What does Fussell mean when he describes the experience as "unreal"? How did trench life breed "a sense of being unoriented and lost"?

BIBLIOGRAPHY

The above selection is taken from Fussell's award-winning *The Great War and Modern Memory* (1975), the best discussion of the impact of the war on modern culture. Robert Wohl, *The Generation of 1914* (1979), recreates the experiences of the men who fought and wrote about the war. Three good military overviews of the war are James L. Stokesbury, *A Short History of World War I* (1981); B. H. Liddell Hart, *The Real War, 1914–1918* (1930); and Cyril Falls, *The Great War* (1959). S. B. Fay, *The Origins of World War* (2 vols., 1928–1930); L. Albertini, *The Origins of the War of 1914* (3 vols., 1952–1957); and Fritz Fischer, *Germany's Aims in the First World War* (1967), discuss the complex origins of the war. The best studies of America's entry into the war are E. R. May, *The First World War and American Isolation* (1957); P. Devlin, *Too Proud to Fight: Woodrow Wilson's Neutrality* (1975); and Barbara Tuchman, *The Zimmerman Telegram* (1958). Military studies that give the reader a sense of the problems faced by the typical soldier include Martin Middlebrooks, *The First Day on the Somme* (1971); Alister Horne, *The Price of Glory: Verdun, 1916* (1962); Leon Wolff, *In Flanders Field* (1958); Barrie Pitt, *The Last Act* (1962); and John Keegan, *The Face of Battle: A Study of Agincourt, Waterloo, and the Somme* (1976).

Part Four

HEROES AND SOCIETY IN THE 1920s

The year 1920 ushered in a decade that historians steadfastly refuse to discuss in anything less than superlative terms. The decade brings to mind Charles Dickens's description of the revolutionary years of the eighteenth century in his novel, *A Tale of Two Cities*: "It was the best of times, it was the worst of times . . . it was the season of Light, it was the season of Darkness, it was the spring of hope, it was the winter of despair, we had everything before us, we had nothing before us." If a decade may be said to have a personality, then the 1920s had the personality of a child; sometimes laughing and playful, at other times brooding, brutal, and ugly.

The first and perhaps most widely read book about the decade was Frederick Lewis Allen's *Only Yesterday: An Informal History of the 1920s.* Published in 1931 during the midst of the Great Depression, *Only Yesterday* describes a carefree decade that began with the end of the Great War and ended with the stock market crash. Allen paints a decade that roars with excitement, a decade brimming with bathtub gin, bootleg liquor, and bubbling champagne. Gangsters, movie sex goddesses, athletic heroes, and fabulous moneymakers seem to come alive on the pages of *Only Yesterday*. In sweeping terms, Allen examines the "revolution in manners and morals," the "aching disillusionment" of intellectuals, and the crass materialism of millions of Americans.

Allen was not necessarily wrong. The sexual mores of the youth were changing, and there was evidence of intellectual disillusionment and crass materialism. The

problem with the book is that its sweeping generalizations are simply too sweeping. In addition, too much of the activity of the decade is left out of *Only Yesterday*. The economic plight of rural Americans, the rise of the Ku Klux Klan, urban-rural tensions, racial injustice, nativism, and religious revivalism are just a few of the subjects that Allen does not treat. As a result, *Only Yesterday* is a flawed and unbalanced classic.

In recent years, historians have explored the areas where Allen did not venture. And they have presented a different view of the 1920s, viewing the decade as a period of transition where older rural and newer urban attitudes uneasily coexisted. Although the country was becoming increasingly urban and bureaucratic, many Americans clung tightly to the more traditional values of their parents and grandparents. In an effort to preserve these values, they supported a variety of movements such as the Society for the Preservation of New England Antiquities, the Ku Klux Klan, and the National Origins Act of 1924.

If rural America resisted change, most of urban America accepted it. Spectators filled movie theaters and athletic stadiums to watch others perform, and entertainment became a product that was packaged and marketed by business executives. Millions of Americans worshipped at the altar of business efficiency and organization. Even crime became more organized and efficient. By 1929 the debate between rural and urban America was decided. The future belonged to the cities.

THE REVOLUTION IN MANNERS
AND MORALS

Frederick Lewis Allen

In 1934, Henry Seidel Canby, a noted literary critic and editor, published *The Age of Confidence,* a memoir that spoke frankly about the changes in American society. In the book Canby graphically described the Victorian code that ruled social behavior during most of his life. It was a code that emphasized the values of hard work, sobriety, thrift, and order. It was enforced by laws that prohibited drinking, gambling, and ribald behavior. As for sexual activity, Canby wrote, "except in sin or the reticence of marriage, sexual drives did not exist." Men channeled their energies into useful production, and women emphasized the superiority of the spirit over the body. Writing about the role of the Victorian woman, Canby noted, "one hint of the sexual made her 'common,' which was only one word above 'vulgar.' "

By 1934 Canby believed that a new, more permissive code had gained control of social behavior. He maintained that standards had been relaxed and that self-denial had been replaced by consumption. Other people of his generation agreed with Canby. In the following selection, Frederick Lewis Allen examines what he termed "the revolution in manners and morals." Certainly attitudes were changing, but the grip of Victorianism was perhaps stronger than either Canby or Allen realized. As recent studies have demonstrated, the "revolution" may not have been as all-encompassing as Allen believed. Nevertheless, Allen's discussion of the topic still provides insights into the changing patterns of American behavior.

A first-class revolt against the accepted American order was certainly taking place during those early years of the Post-war Decade, but it was one with which Nikolai Lenin had nothing whatever to do. The shock troops of the rebellion were not alien agitators, but the sons and daughters of well-to-do American families, who knew little about Bolshevism and cared distinctly less, and their defiance was expressed not in obscure radical publications or in soap-box speeches, but right across the family breakfast table into the horrified ears of conservative fathers and mothers. Men and women were still shivering at the Red Menace when they awoke to the no less alarming Problem of the Younger Generation, and realized that if the Constitution were not in danger, the moral code of the country certainly was.

This code, as it currently concerned young people, might have been roughly summarized as follows: Women were the guardians of morality; they were made of finer stuff than men and were expected to act accordingly. Young girls must look forward in innocence (tempered perhaps with a modicum of physiological instruction) to a romantic love match which would lead them to the altar and to living-happily-ever-after; and until the "right man" came along they must allow no male to kiss them. It was expected that some men would succumb to the temptations of sex, but only with a special class of outlawed women; girls of respectable families were supposed to have no such temptations. Boys and girls were permitted large freedom to work and play together, with decreasing and well-nigh nominal chaperonage, but only because the code worked so well on the whole that a sort of honor system was supplanting supervision by

their elders; it was taken for granted that if they had been well brought up they would never take advantage of this freedom. And although the attitude toward smoking and drinking by girls differed widely in different strata of society and different parts of the country, majority opinion held that it was morally wrong for them to smoke and could hardly imagine them showing the effects of alcohol.

The war had not long been over when cries of alarm from parents, teachers, and moral preceptors began to rend the air. For the boys and girls just growing out of adolescence were making mincemeat of this code.

The dresses that the girls—and for that matter most of the older women—were wearing seemed alarming enough. In July, 1920, a fashion-writer reported in the *New York Times* that "the American woman . . . has lifted her skirts far beyond any modest limitation," which was another way of saying that the hem was now all of nine inches above the ground. It was freely predicted that skirts would come down again in the winter of 1920–21, but instead they climbed a few scandalous inches farther. The flappers wore thin dresses, short-sleeved and occasionally (in the evening) sleeveless; some of the wilder young things rolled their stockings below their knees, revealing to the shocked eyes of virtue a fleeting glance of shin-bones and knee-cap; and many of them were visibly using cosmetics. "The intoxication of rouge," earnestly explained Dorothy Speare in *Dancers in the Dark*, "is an insidious vintage known to more girls than mere man can ever believe." Useless for frantic parents to insist that no lady did such things; the answer was that the daughters of ladies were doing it, and even retouching their masterpieces in public. Some of them, furthermore, were abandoning their corsets. "The men won't dance with you if you wear a corset," they were quoted as saying.

The current mode in dancing created still more consternation. Not the romantic violin but the barbaric saxophone now dominated the

Excerpt from '"The Revolution in Manners and Morals" from *Only Yesterday* by Frederick Lewis Allen. Copyright 1931 by Frederick Lewis Allen. Renewed 1959 by Agnes Rogers Allen. Reprinted by permission of Harper & Row, Publishers, Inc.

orchestra, and to its passionate crooning and wailing the fox-trotters moved in what the editor of the Hobart College *Herald* disgustedly called a "syncopated embrace." No longer did even an inch of space separate them; they danced as if glued together, body to body, cheek to cheek. Cried the *Catholic Telegraph* of Cincinnati in righteous indignation, "The music is sensuous, the embracing of partners—the female only half dressed—is absolutely indecent; and the motions—they are such as may not be described, with any respect for propriety, in a family newspaper. Suffice it to say that there are certain houses appropriate for such dances; but those houses have been closed by law."

Supposedly "nice" girls were smoking cigarettes—openly and defiantly, if often rather awkwardly and self-consciously. They were drinking—somewhat less openly but often all too efficaciously. There were stories of daughters of the most exemplary parents getting drunk—"blotto," as their companions cheerfully put it—on the contents of the hip-flasks of the new prohibition régime, and going out joyriding with men at four in the morning. And worst of all, even at well-regulated dances they were said to retire where the eye of the most sharp-sighted chaperon could not follow, and in darkened rooms or in parked cars to engage in the unspeakable practice of petting and necking.

It was not until F. Scott Fitzgerald, who had hardly graduated from Princeton and ought to know what his generation were doing, brought out *This Side of Paradise* in April, 1920, that fathers and mothers realized fully what was afoot and how long it had been going on. Apparently the "petting party" had been current as early as 1916, and was now widely established as an indoor sport. "None of the Victorian mothers—and most of the mothers were Victorian—had any idea how casually their daughters were accustomed to be kissed," wrote Mr. Fitzgerald. ". . . Amory saw girls doing things that even in his memory would

have been impossible: eating three-o'clock, after-dance suppers in impossible cafés, talking of every side of life with an air half of earnestness, half of mockery, yet with a furtive excitement that Amory considered stood for a real moral let-down. But he never realized how widespread it was until he saw the cities between New York and Chicago as one vast juvenile intrigue." The book caused a shudder to run down the national spine; did not Mr. Fitzgerald represent one of his well-nurtured heroines as brazenly confessing, "I've kissed dozens of men. I suppose I'll kiss dozens more"; and another heroine as saying to a young man *(to a young man!)*, "Oh, just one person in fifty has any glimmer of what sex is. I'm hipped on Freud and all that, but it's rotten that every bit of real love in the world is ninety-nine per cent passion and one little *soupçon* of jealousy"?

It was incredible. It was abominable. What did it all mean? Was every decent standard being thrown over? Mothers read the scarlet words and wondered if they themselves "had any idea how often their daughters were accustomed to be kissed." . . . But no, this must be an exaggerated account of the misconduct of some especially depraved group. Nice girls couldn't behave like that and talk openly about passion. But in due course other books appeared to substantiate the findings of Mr. Fitzgerald: *Dancers in the Dark, The Plastic Age, Flaming Youth.* Magazine articles and newspapers reiterated the scandal. To be sure, there were plenty of communities where nice girls did not, in actual fact, "behave like that"; and even in the more sophisticated urban centers there were plenty of girls who did not. Nevertheless, there was enough fire beneath the smoke of these sensational revelations to make the Problem of the Younger Generation a topic of anxious discussion from coast to coast.

The forces of morality rallied to the attack. Dr. Francis E. Clark, the founder and president of the Christian Endeavor Society, declared that the modern "indecent dance" was "an

offense against womanly purity, the very foun-
tainhead of our family and civil life." The new
style of dancing was denounced in religious
journals as "impure, polluting, corrupting,
debasing, destroying spirituality, increasing
carnality," and the mothers and sisters and
church members of the land were called upon
to admonish and instruct and raise the spiritual tone of these dreadful young people.
President Murphree of the University of
Florida cried out with true Southern warmth,
"The low-cut gowns, the rolled hose and short
skirts are born of the Devil and his angels, and
are carrying the present and future generations
to chaos and destruction." A group of
Episcopal church-women in New York, speaking with the authority of wealth and social
position (for they included Mrs. J. Pierpont
Morgan, Mrs. Borden Harriman, Mrs. Henry
Phipps, Mrs. James Roosevelt, and Mrs. E. H.
Harriman), proposed an organization to discourage fashions involving an "excess of nudity" and "improper ways of dancing." The
Y. W. C. A. conducted a national campaign
against immodest dress among high-school
girls, supplying newspapers with printed matter carrying headlines such as "Working Girls
Responsive to Modesty Appeal" and "High
Heels Losing Ground Even in France." In
Philadelphia a Dress Reform Committee of
prominent citizens sent a questionnaire to over
a thousand clergymen to ask them what would
be their idea of a proper dress, and although
the gentlemen of the cloth showed a distress-
ing variety of opinion, the committee proceeded to design a "moral gown" which was
endorsed by ministers of fifteen denomina-
tions. The distinguishing characteristics of this
moral gown were that it was very loose-fitting,
that the sleeves reached just below the elbows,
and that the hem came within seven and a half
inches of the floor.

Not content with example and reproof, legislators in several states introduced bills to
reform feminine dress once and for all. The
New York American reported in 1921 that a bill

A popular, though overdrawn, image of the 1920s was
"six-cylinder love," set in a flashy roadster and featuring a flapper with rolled stockings and a callow colle-
gian sporting a long cigarette holder and a hip flask.

was pending in Utah providing fine and
imprisonment for those who wore on the
streets "skirts higher than three inches above
the ankle." A bill was laid before the Virginia
legislature which would forbid any woman
from wearing shirtwaists or evening gowns
which displayed "more than three inches of
her throat." In Ohio the proposed limit of
decolletage was two inches; the bill introduced
in the Ohio legislature aimed also to prevent
the sale of any "garment which unduly displays or accentuates the lines of the female figure," and to prohibit any "female over fourteen
years of age" from wearing "a skirt which does
not reach to that part of the foot known as the
instep."

Meanwhile innumerable families were torn with dissension over cigarettes and gin and all-night automobile rides. Fathers and mothers lay awake asking themselves whether their children were not utterly lost; sons and daughters evaded questions, lied miserably and unhappily, or flared up to reply rudely that at least they were not dirty-minded hypocrites, that they saw no harm in what they were doing and proposed to go right on doing it. From those liberal clergymen and teachers who prided themselves on keeping step with all that was new, came a chorus of reassurance: these young people were at least franker and more honest than their elders had been; having experimented for themselves, would they not soon find out which standards were outworn and which represented the accumulated moral wisdom of the race? Hearing such hopeful words, many good people took heart again. Perhaps this flare-up of youthful passion was a flash in the pan, after all. Perhaps in another year or two the boys and girls would come to their senses and everything would be all right again.

They were wrong, however. For the revolt of the younger generation was only the beginning of a revolution in manners and morals that was already beginning to affect men and women of every age in every part of the country.

A number of forces were working together and interacting upon one another to make this revolution inevitable.

First of all was the state of mind brought about by the war and its conclusion. A whole generation had been infected by the eat-drink-and-be-merry-for-tomorrow-we-die spirit which accompanied the departure of the soldiers to the training camps and the fighting front. There had been an epidemic not only of abrupt war marriages, but of less conventional liaisons. In France, two million men had found themselves very close to filth and annihilation and very far from the American moral code

and its defenders; prostitution had followed the flag and willing mademoiselles from Armentières had been plentiful; American girls sent over as nurses and war workers had come under the influence of continental manners and standards without being subject to the rigid protections thrown about their continental sisters of the respectable classes; and there had been a very widespread and very natural breakdown of traditional restraints and reticences and taboos. It was impossible for this generation to return unchanged when the ordeal was over. Some of them had acquired under the pressure of wartime conditions a new code which seemed to them quite defensible; millions of them had been provided with an emotional stimulant from which it was not easy to taper off. Their torn nerves craved the anodynes of speed, excitement, and passion. They found themselves expected to settle down into the humdrum routine of American life as if nothing had happened, to accept the moral dicta of elders who seemed to them still to be living in a Pollyanna land of rosy ideals which the war had killed for them. They couldn't do it, and they very disrespectfully said so.

"The older generation had certainly pretty well ruined this world before passing it on to us," wrote one of them (John F. Carter in the *Atlantic Monthly*, September, 1920), expressing accurately the sentiments of innumerable contemporaries. "They give us this thing, knocked to pieces, leaky, red-hot, threatening to blow up; and then they are surprised that we don't accept it with the same attitude of pretty, decorous enthusiasm with which they received it, way back in the 'eighties."

The middle generation was not so immediately affected by the war neurosis. They had had time enough, before 1917, to build up habits of conformity not easily broken down. But they, too, as the let-down of 1919 followed the war, found themselves restless and discontented, in a mood to question everything that had once seemed to them true and worthy and of good report. They too had spent themselves and wanted a good time. They saw their juniors exploring the approaches to the forbidden land of sex, and presently they began to play with the idea of doing a little experimenting of their own. The same disillusion which had defeated Woodrow Wilson and had caused strikes and riots and the Big Red Scare furnished a culture in which the germs of the new freedom could grow and multiply.

The revolution was accelerated also by the growing independence of the American woman. She won the suffrage in 1920. She seemed, it is true, to be very little interested in it once she had it; she voted, but mostly as the unregenerate men about her did, despite the efforts of women's clubs and the League of Women Voters to awaken her to womanhood's civic opportunity; feminine candidates for office were few, and some of them—such as Governor Ma Ferguson of Texas—scarcely seemed to represent the starry-eyed spiritual influence which, it had been promised, would presently ennoble public life. Few of the younger women could rouse themselves to even a passing interest in politics: to them it was a sordid and futile business, without flavor and without hope. Nevertheless, the winning of the suffrage had its effect. It consolidated woman's position as man's equal.

Even more marked was the effect of woman's growing independence of the drudgeries of housekeeping. Smaller houses were being built, and they were easier to look after. Families were moving into apartments, and these made even less claim upon the housekeeper's time and energy. Women were learning how to make lighter work of the preparation of meals. Sales of canned foods were growing, the number of delicatessen stores had increased three times as fast as the population during the decade 1910–20, the output of bakeries increased by 60 per cent during the decade 1914–24. Much of what had once been housework was now either moving out of

the home entirely or being simplified by machinery. The use of commercial laundries, for instance, increased by 57 per cent between 1914 and 1924. Electric washing-machines and electric irons were coming to the aid of those who still did their washing at home; the manager of the local electric power company at "Middletown," a typical small American city, estimated in 1924 that nearly 90 per cent of the homes in the city already had electric irons. The housewife was learning to telephone her shopping orders, to get her clothes ready-made and spare herself the rigors of dress-making, to buy a vacuum cleaner and emulate the lovely carefree girls in the magazine advertisements who banished dust with such delicate fingers. Women were slowly becoming emancipated from routine to "live their own lives."

And what were these "own lives" of theirs to be like? Well, for one thing, they could take jobs. Up to this time girls of the middle classes who had wanted to "do something" had been largely restricted to school-teaching, social-service work, nursing, stenography, and clerical work in business houses. But now they poured out of the schools and colleges into all manner of new occupations. They besieged the offices of publishers and advertisers; they went into tea-room management until there threatened to be more purveyors than consumers of chicken patties and cinnamon toast; they sold antiques, sold real estate, opened smart little shops, and finally invaded the department stores. In 1920 the department store was in the mind of the average college girl a rather bourgeois institution which employed "poor shop girls"; by the end of the decade college girls were standing in line for openings in the misses' sports-wear department and even selling behind the counter in the hope that some day fortune might smile upon them and make them buyers or stylists. Small-town girls who once would have been contented to stay in Sauk Center all their days were now borrowing from father to go to New York or Chicago to seek their fortunes—in Best's or Macy's or Marshall

Field's. Married women who were encumbered with children and could not seek jobs consoled themselves with the thought that home-making and child-rearing were really "professions," after all. No topic was so furiously discussed at luncheon tables from one end of the country to the other as the question whether the married woman should take a job, and whether the mother had a right to. And as for the unmarried woman, she no longer had to explain why she worked in a shop or an office; it was idleness, nowadays, that had to be defended.

With the job—or at least the sense that the job was a possibility—came a feeling of comparative economic independence. With the feeling of economic independence came a slackening of husbandly and parental authority. Maiden aunts and unmarried daughters were leaving the shelter of the family roof to install themselves in kitchenette apartments of their own. For city-dwellers the home was steadily becoming less of a shrine, more of a dormitory—a place of casual shelter where one stopped overnight on the way from the restaurant and the movie theater to the office. Yet even the job did not provide the American woman with that complete satisfaction which the management of a mechanized home no longer furnished. She still had energies and emotions to burn; she was ready for the revolution.

Like all revolutions, this one was stimulated by foreign propaganda. It came, however, not from Moscow, but from Vienna. Sigmund Freud had published his first book on psychoanalysis at the end of the nineteenth century, and he and Jung had lectured to American psychologists as early as 1909, but it was not until after the war that the Freudian gospel began to circulate to a marked extent among the American lay public. The one great intellectual force which had not suffered disrepute as a result of the war was science; the more-or-less educated public was now absorbing a quantity of popularized information about biology and anthropology which gave a general impression that men and women were merely animals of a rather intricate variety, and that moral codes had no universal validity and were often based on curious superstitions. A fertile ground was ready for the seeds of Freudianism, and presently one began to hear even from the lips of flappers that "science taught" new and disturbing things about sex. Sex, it appeared, was the central and pervasive force which moved mankind. Almost every human motive was attributable to it: if you were patriotic or liked the violin, you were in the grip of sex—in a sublimated form. The first requirement of mental health was to have an uninhibited sex life. If you would be well and happy, you must obey your libido. Such was the Freudian gospel as it imbedded itself in the American mind after being filtered through the successive minds of interpreters and popularizers and guileless readers and people who had heard guileless readers talk about it. New words and phrases began to be bandied about the cocktail-tray and the mah jong table—inferiority complex, sadism, masochism, Œdipus complex. Intellectual ladies went to Europe to be analyzed; analysts plied their new trade in American cities, conscientiously transferring the affections of their fair patients to themselves; and clergymen who preached about the virtue of self-control were reminded by outspoken critics that self-control was out-of-date and really dangerous.

The principal remaining forces which accelerated the revolution in manners and morals were all 100 per cent American. They were prohibition, the automobile, the confession and sex magazines, and the movies.

When the Eighteenth Amendment was ratified, prohibition seemed, as we have already noted, to have an almost united country behind it. Evasion of the law began immediately, however, and strenuous and sincere opposition to it—especially in the large cities of the

North and East—quickly gathered force. The results were the bootlegger, the speakeasy and a spirit of deliberate revolt which in many communities made drinking "the thing to do." From these facts in turn flowed further results: the increased popularity of distilled as against fermented liquors, the use of the hip-flask, the cocktail party, and the general transformation of drinking from a masculine prerogative to one shared by both sexes together. The old-time saloon had been overwhelmingly masculine; the speakeasy usually catered to both men and women. As Elmer Davis put it, "The old days when father spent his evenings at Cassidy's bar with the rest of the boys are gone, and probably gone forever; Cassidy may still be in business at the old stand and father may still go down there of evenings, but since prohibition mother goes down with him." Under the new régime not only the drinks were mixed, but the company as well.

Meanwhile a new sort of freedom was being made possible by the enormous increase in the use of the automobile, and particularly of the closed car. (In 1919 hardly more than 10 per cent of the cars produced in the United States were closed; by 1924 the percentage had jumped to 43, by 1927 it had reached 82.8) The automobile offered an almost universally available means of escaping temporarily from the supervision of parents and chaperones, or from the influence of neighborhood opinion. Boys and girls now thought nothing, as the Lynds pointed out in *Middletown,* of jumping into a car and driving off at a moment's notice— without asking anybody's permission—to a dance in another town twenty miles away, where they were strangers and enjoyed a freedom impossible among their neighbors. The closed car, moreover, was in effect a room protected from the weather which could be occupied at any time of the day or night and could be moved at will into a darkened byway or a country lane. The Lynds quoted the judge of the juvenile court in "Middletown" as declaring that the automobile had become a "house

of prostitution on wheels," and cited the fact that of thirty girls brought before his court in a year on charges of sex crimes, for whom the place where the offense had occurred was recorded, nineteen were listed as having committed it in an automobile.

Finally, as the revolution began, its influence fertilized a bumper crop of sex magazines, confession magazines, and lurid motion pictures, and these in turn had their effect on a class of readers and movie-goers who had never heard and never would hear of Freud and the libido. The publishers of the sex adventure magazines, offering stories with such titles as "What I Told My Daughter the Night Before Her Marriage," "Indolent Kisses," and "Watch Your Step-Ins," learned to a nicety the gentle art of arousing the reader without arousing the censor. The publishers of the confession magazines, while always instructing their authors to provide a moral ending and to utter pious sentiments, concentrated on the description of what they euphemistically called "missteps." Most of their fiction was faked to order by hack writers who could write one day "The Confessions of a Chorus Girl" and the next day recount, again in the first person, the temptations which made it easy for the taxi-driver to go wrong. Both classes of magazines became astonishingly numerous and successful. Bernarr McFadden's *True-Story,* launched as late as 1919, had over 300,000 readers by 1923; 848,000 by 1924; over a million and a half by 1925; and almost two million by 1926—a record of rapid growth probably unparalleled in magazine publishing.

Crowding the news stands along with the sex and confession magazines were motion-picture magazines which depicted "seven movie kisses" with such captions as "Do you recognize your little friend, Mae Busch? She's had lots of kisses, but she never seems to grow *blasé.* At least you'll agree that she's giving a good imitation of a person enjoying this one." The movies themselves, drawing millions to their doors every day and every night, played incessantly upon the same lucrative theme. The producers of one picture advertised "brilliant men, beautiful jazz babies, champagne baths, midnight revels, petting parties in the purple dawn, all ending in one terrific smashing climax that makes you gasp"; the venders of another promised "neckers, petters, white kisses, red kisses, pleasure-mad daughters, sensation-craving mothers, . . . the truth—bold, naked, sensational." Seldom did the films offer as much as these advertisements promised, but there was enough in some of them to cause a sixteen-year-old girl (quoted by Alice Miller Mitchell) to testify, "Those pictures with hot love-making in them, they make girls and boys sitting together want to get up and walk out, go off somewhere, you know. Once I walked out with a boy before the picture was even over. We took a ride. But my friend, she all the time had to get up and go out with her boy friend."

A storm of criticism from church organizations led the motion-picture producers, early in the decade, to install Will H. Hays, President Harding's Postmaster-General, as their arbiter of morals and of taste, and Mr. Hays promised that all would be well. "This industry must have," said he before the Los Angeles Chamber of Commerce, "toward that sacred thing, the mind of a child, toward that clean virgin thing, that unmarked slate, the same responsibility, the same care about the impressions made upon it, that the best clergyman or the most inspired teacher of youth would have." The result of Mr. Hays's labors in behalf of the unmarked slate was to make the moral ending as obligatory as in the confession magazines, to smear over sexy pictures with pious platitudes, and to blacklist for motion-picture production many a fine novel and play which, because of its very honesty, might be construed as seriously or intelligently questioning the traditional sex ethics of the small town. Mr. Hays, being something of a genius, managed to keep the churchmen at bay. Whenever the threats of censorship began to become ominous he would promulgate a new series of moral commandments for the producers to follow. Yet of the practical effects of his supervision it is perhaps enough to say that the quotations given above all date from the period of his dictatorship. Giving lip-service to the old code, the movies diligently and with consummate vulgarity publicized the new.

Each of these diverse influences—the postwar disillusion, the new status of women, the Freudian gospel, the automobile, prohibition, the sex and confession magazines, and the movies—had its part in bringing about the revolution. Each of them, as an influence, was played upon by all the others; none of them could alone have changed to any great degree the folkways of America; together their force was irresistible.

■ ■ ■

STUDY QUESTIONS

1. What evidence does Allen offer to demonstrate that a "revolution in manners and morals" was taking place during the 1920s? Does the evidence warrant his conclusions? Is Allen writing about all Americans, or is he referring to a particular class?

2. How did various state legislators try to plug the tide of change? Were they successful? Why or why not?

3. What were the European forces that contributed to the "revolution"?

4. What were the American forces that accelerated the "revolution"?

5. Do you find Allen's argument convincing? Why or why not?

BIBLIOGRAPHY

The best treatments of the 1920s are Roderick Nash, *The Nervous Generation: American Thought, 1917–1930* (1970); William E. Leuchtenburg, *The Perils of Prosperity, 1914–1932* (1958); Paul Carter, *The Twenties in America* (1968), and *Another Part of the Twenties* (1976); and Geoffrey Perrett, *America in the Twenties* (1982). All five books either modify or challenge the conclusions Allen reached. The best study of the changing sexual attitudes of college-educated youth is Paul S. Fass, *The Damned and the Beautiful: American Youth in the 1920s* (1977). Gilman Ostrander, *America in the First Machine Age, 1890–1940* (1970), emphasizes the role of modern technology and consumption on the development of a youth culture. Lary May, *Screening Out the Past: The Birth of Mass Culture and the Motion Picture Industry* (1980), and Lewis A. Erenberg, *Steppin' Out: New York Nightlife and the Transformation of American Culture, 1890–1930* (1981), also discuss changing American attitudes toward sex during the 1920s.

THE MOOD OF THE PEOPLE

Roderick Nash

No decade in American history has been more studded with heroes and idols as the 1920s. Such athletic heroes as Babe Ruth, Jack Dempsey, Red Grange, Bill Tilden, and Bobby Jones are still household names. In Hollywood, they were rivaled by stars such as Rudolph Valentino, Mary Pickford, Douglas Fairbanks, Clara Bow, and Charlie Chaplin. Heroes even came from the worlds of business, finance, and government. Herbert Hoover and Edward Bok demonstrated the appeal of self-made millionaires. The greatest hero, however, was Charles Lindbergh, who captured the public's imagination in 1927 by making the first solo flight across the Atlantic.

Nor has there been a decade that has been more acclaimed for its literary output. Novelists F. Scott Fitzgerald and Ernest Hemingway and poets E. E. Cummings, T. S. Eliot, and Edna St. Vincent Millay are among the most talented America ever produced. More people, however, read the stories of such popular novelists as Gene Stratton-Porter, Harold Bell Wright, Zane Grey, and Edgar Rice Burroughs.

In the following essay historian Roderick Nash probes the meaning behind the heroes people chose and the novels they read. Heroes, Nash claims, reflect the "mood of the people"; they mirror the aspirations, longings, and fears of millions of unheralded Americans. Similarly, popular novelists' success depends on their ability to interpret and tap the mood of the nation. That mood, Nash feels, was not bold and carefree, as Frederick Lewis Allen believed, but rather timid and nervous. Americans chose heroes and read novels that glorified their rural past and eased their minds concerning their urban future.

Heroes abounded in the American 1920s. Their names, especially in sports, have been ticked off so frequently they have become clichés. Less often have commentators paused to probe for explanations. Why were the twenties ripe for heroism? And why did the heroics follow a predictable pattern? Such questions lead to an understanding of the mood of the people, because heroism concerns the public as well as the individual. It depends on achievement but even more on recognition. In the final analysis the hopes and fears of everyday Americans create national heroes.

The nervousness of the post-World War I generation provided fertile soil for the growth of a particular kind of heroism. Many Americans felt uneasy as they experienced the transforming effects of population growth, urbanization, and economic change. On the one hand, these developments were welcome as steps in the direction of progress. Yet they also raised vague fears about the passing of frontier conditions, the loss of national vigor, and the eclipse of the individual in a mass society. Frederick Jackson Turner and Theodore Roosevelt, among others, had pointed to the liabilities of the transformation at the turn of the century. World War I underscored the misgivings and doubts. By the 1920s the sense of change had penetrated to the roots of popular thought. Scarcely an American was unaware that the frontier had vanished and that pioneering, in the traditional sense, was a thing of the past. Physical changes in the nation were undeniable. They occurred faster, however, than intellectual adjustment. Although Americans, in general, lived in a densely populated, urban-industrial civilization, a large part of their values remained rooted in the frontier, farm, and village. Exposure of this discrepancy only served to increase the tightness with

"The Mood of the People" from *The Nervous Generation: American Thought* by Roderick Nash. Copyright © 1970 by Rand McNally College Publishing Company. Reprinted by permission of Roderick Nash.

which insecure people clung to the old certainties. Old-style pioneering was impossible, but Americans proved ingenious in finding equivalents. The upshot in the twenties was the cult of the hero—the man who provided living testimony of the power of courage, strength, and honor and of the efficacy of the self-reliant, rugged individual who seemed on the verge of becoming as irrelevant as the covered wagon.

Sports and the star athlete were the immediate beneficiaries of this frame of mind. The American sports fan regarded the playing field as a surrogate frontier; the athletic hero was the twentieth-century equivalent of the pathfinder or pioneer. In athletic competition, as on the frontier, people believed, men confronted tangible obstacles and overcame them with talent and determination. The action in each case was clean and direct; the goals, whether clearing forests or clearing the bases, easily perceived and immensely satisfying. Victory was the result of superior ability. The sports arena like the frontier was pregnant with opportunity for the individual. The start was equal and the best man won. Merit was rewarded. True or not, such a credo was almost instinctive with Americans. They packed the stadiums of the 1920s in a salute to time-honored virtues. With so much else about America changing rapidly, it was comforting to find in sports a ritualistic celebration of the major components of the national faith.

Writing in the *North American Review* for October 1929, A. A. Brill, a leading American psychologist of the Freudian school, took a closer look at the meaning of athletics. Why, he wondered, do men play and why do they select the particular kinds of play they do? Brill was also interested in the reasons spectators came to games. His main point was that sports were not idle diversions but intensely serious endeavors rooted in the values and traditions of a civilization. "The ancestry of sport," Brill declared, "is written very plainly in the fact that the first games among all nations were simple imitations of the typical acts of warriors and huntsmen." The primary motivation of play, according to Brill, was the "mastery impulse"—and inherent aggressiveness in man stemming from the Darwinian struggle for existence. Modern man had largely transcended direct physical struggle, but the need for it persisted in the human psyche. Sports were contrived as substitutes for actual fighting, mock struggles that satisfied the urge to conquer. Brill did not suggest a relationship between American sports and the American frontier, but his argument suggested one. So did the fact that the rise of mass spectator sports and the decline of the frontier were simultaneous in the United States.

By the 1920s the nation went sports crazy. It seemed to many that a golden age of sport had arrived in America. Football received a large portion of the limelight. As they had in the declining days of Rome, fans thronged the stadiums to witness contact, violence, bloodshed, man pitted against man, strength against strength. The vicarious element was invariably present. For a brief, glorious moment the nobody in the bleachers *was* the halfback crashing into the end zone with the winning touchdown. For a moment he shared the thrill of individual success and fought off the specter of being swallowed up in mass society.

Big-time professional football began on September 17, 1920, when the American Football Association was organized with the great Indian athlete Jim Thorpe as its first president. When the Green Bay Packers joined the Association in 1921, the saga of pro football was solidly launched. Attendance rose dramatically. On November 21, 1925, the presence on the playing field of the fabled Harold "Red" Grange helped draw 36,000 spectators to a game. A week later 68,000 jammed the Polo Grounds in New York to watch Grange in action. The names of the pro teams were suggestive. As on the frontier of old, it was cowboys versus Indians, or giants versus bears— with the names of cities prefixed.

The twenties was also the time of the emergence of college football on an unprecedented scale. Heroes appeared in good supply: Red Grange at Illinois, Knute Rockne's "Four Horsemen" at Notre Dame in 1924, Harold "Brick" Muller who began a dynasty at California that extended through fifty consecutive victories in the seasons 1919 through 1925. Hundreds of thousands attended the Saturday games, an estimated twenty million during the season. Millions more followed the action over their radios and made a Sunday morning ritual of devouring the newspaper accounts of the games of the previous day. To accommodate the crowds colleges and universities built huge new stadiums. Yale's and California's seated eighty thousand; Illinois, Ohio State, and Michigan were not far behind. The number of Americans who attended games doubled between 1921 and 1930. A *Harper's* writer caught the spirit of college football in 1928: "it is at present a religion, sometimes it seems to be almost our national religion." So, once, had been westward expansion.

Despite its popularity, football tended to obscure the heroic individual. It was, after all, a team sport. Even Red Grange received an occasional block on his long runs. But in sports pitting man against man or against the clock the heroism latent in competition achieved its purest expression. Americans in the 1920s had a glittering array of well-publicized individuals from which to choose their idol. In golf Robert T. "Bobby" Jones, Walter Hagen, and Gene Sarazen were the dominant figures. Tennis had "Big" Bill Tilden and "Little" Bill Johnson whose epic duels on the center court at Forest Hills filled the stands. The competition was even more direct in boxing with its "knock out," the symbol of complete conquest. During the twenties promoters like Tex Rickard built boxing into a big business. Jack Dempsey and Gene Tunney proved so attractive to the sporting public that a ticket sale of a million dollars for a single fight became a reality. By the end of the decade the figure was two million. Fifty bouts in the twenties had gates of more than $100,000. More than 100,000 fans came to Soldiers' Field in Chicago on September 22, 1927, to see the second Dempsey-Tunney fight with its controversial "long count" that helped Tunney retain the championship and earn $990,000 for thirty minutes of work. In a nation not oblivious to the approach of middle age, it was comforting to count the heavyweight champion of the world among the citizenry. Here was evidence, many reasoned, that the nation remained strong, young, and fit to survive in a Darwinian universe. Record-breaking served the same purpose, and in Johnny Weismuller, premier swimmer, and Paavo Nurmi, Finnish-born track star, the United States had athletes who set world marks almost every time they competed. Gertrude Ederle chose a longer course when she swam the English Channel in 1926, but she too set a record and was treated to one of New York's legendary ticker-tape parades.

And there was the Babe. No sports hero of the twenties and few of any decade had the reputation of George Herman Ruth. Baseball was generally acknowledged to be the national game, and Ruth played with a superb support-ing cast of New York Yankees, but when he faced a pitcher Babe Ruth stood as an individ-ual. His home runs (particularly the 59 in 1921 and the 60 in 1927) gave him a heroic stature comparable to that of legendary demigods like Odysseus, Beowulf, or Daniel Boone. Ruth's unsavory background and boorish personal habits were nicely overlooked by talented sportswriters anxious to give the twenties the kind of hero it craved. The payoff was public adulation of the Babe and of baseball.

The twenties also saw the public exposure of corruption in baseball and confronted Americans with the necessity of reviewing their entire hero complex. On September 28, 1920, three members of the Chicago White Sox appeared before a grand jury to confess that they and five other players had agreed to throw the 1919 World Series to Cincinnati for a financial consideration. Gradually the unhappy story of the "Black Sox" unfolded. Big-time gamblers had persuaded selected players to make sure that a bet on the underdog Cincinnati team would pay off. Some of the greatest names in the game were involved, pre-eminently that of "Shoeless" Joe Jackson. An illiterate farm boy from South Carolina, Jackson's natural batting eye helped him com-pile a .356 average in ten seasons as a major leaguer. In the process he became one of the most idolized players in baseball. It was Jackson's exit from the grand jury chamber on September 28 that allegedly precipitated the agonized plea from a group of boys: "Say it ain't so, Joe!" According to the newspapers, Jackson, shuffling, head down, replied, "Yes, boys, I'm afraid it is."

Reaction to the Black Sox testified to the importance baseball had for many Americans. One school of thought condemned the "fix" in the strongest terms and agitated for the restoration of integrity to the game. It was a serious matter. The Philadelphia *Bulletin* com-pared the eight players with "the soldier or sailor who would sell out his country and its flag in time of war." Suggesting the link between sports and the national character, the *New York Times* declared that bribing a ballplayer was an offense "which strikes at the very heart of this nation." If baseball fell from grace, what could be honest in America? The question haunted journalists and cartoonists. *Outlook* for October 13, 1920, carried a drawing of a crumpled statue of a ballplayer whose torn side revealed a stuffing of dollar bills. The stat-ue bore the inscription "The National Game." A small boy wept in the foreground; the cap-tion to the cartoon read "His Idol."

Baseball officials and club owners were sim-ilarly dismayed at the revelation of corruption and determined to clean up the game. Charles A. Comiskey, owner of the Chicago White Sox, led the way with a public statement that no man involved in the fix would ever wear the uniform of his club again. Other owners followed suit until all organized baseball, even the minor leagues, was closed to the Black Sox. On November 12, 1920, Kenesaw Mountain Landis, a former federal judge, was appointed commissioner of baseball with full control over the game and a charge to safeguard its integrity.

The everyday fans' response to the fix differed sharply from that of the sportswriters and owners. Many Americans seemed determined to deny the entire affair; more precisely, they didn't *want* to believe anything could be wrong with something as close to the national ideal as baseball. Like the boys of the "say it ain't so" episode, they begged for evidence that the old standards and values still applied. Especially in 1920 in the United States sports heroes were needed as evidence of the virtues of competition, fair play, and the self-reliant individual. Consequently, when confronted with the scandal, the average American simply closed his eyes and pretended nothing was wrong. The heroes remained heroes. When the Black Sox formed an exhibition team, it received enthusiastic support. Petitions were circulated in the major league cities to reinstate the players in organized baseball. But the most remarkable demonstration of the public's feeling came at the conclusion of the Black Sox trial on August 2, 1921. After deliberating two hours and forty-seven minutes, the jury returned a verdict of *not* guilty. According to the *New York Times* reporter at the scene, the packed courtroom rose as one man at the good news, cheering wildly. Hats sailed and papers were thrown about in the delirium. Men shouted "hooray for the clean sox." The bailiffs pounded for order until, as the *Times* reported, they "finally noticed Judge Friend's smiles, and then joined in the whistling and cheering." Finally the jury picked up the acquitted ballplayers and carried them out of the courtroom on their shoulders!

Baseball officials and journalists regarded the acquittal of the Black Sox as a technical verdict secured by the lenient interpretation of the Illinois statute involved. The fans in the courtroom, however, and, presumably, many elsewhere were on the side of the players regardless, and viewed the verdict as a vindication. They were not prepared to believe that baseball or its heroes could become tarnished. The game was too important to the national ego. Following baseball gave Americans an opportunity to pay tribute to what many believed was the best part of their heritage. The game was a sacred rite undertaken not merely to determine the winner of league championships but to celebrate the values of a civilization. As one newspaper account of the scandal put it, to learn that "Shoeless" Joe Jackson had sold out the world series was like discovering that "Daniel Boone had been bought by the Indians to lose his fights in Kentucky."

In the gallery of popular heroes in the United States the only rival of the frontiersman and his athletic surrogate was the self-made man. In the 1920s the archetype was Herbert Hoover, a hero-President hewn out of the traditional rags-to-riches mold. Left an orphan in 1884 at the age of ten, Hoover launched an international career in mining that made him rich. During World War I he became famous, heading the American Relief Commission abroad and the Food Administration at home. A genius in matters of large-scale efficiency, Hoover neatly executed apparent miracles. After the decline of Woodrow Wilson in the wake of the Versailles Treaty, Hoover was easily the foremost American beneficiary of war-caused popularity. In 1922, while Secretary of Commerce under Warren G. Harding, he set forth his creed in a slender book entitled *American Individualism*. Apparently oblivious of the doubts that beset intellectuals at the time, Hoover professed his "abiding faith in the intelligence, the initiative, the character, the courage, and the divine touch in the individual." But he also believed that individuals differed greatly in energy, ability, and ambition. Some men inevitably rose to the top of the

The Mood of the People   147

heap, and for Hoover this was entirely right and proper. It was necessary, moreover, if society were to progress. Hoover's philosophy was the old American one of rugged individualism and free enterprise that the Social Darwinists had decorated with scientific tinsel after the Civil War. Intellectually, Hoover was a bedfellow with Benjamin Franklin and William Graham Sumner.

Hoover's social, political, and economic ideas followed from these assumptions. He staunchly defended the unregulated profit system. Society and government owed the people only three things: "liberty, justice, and equality of opportunity." Competition took care of the rest, carrying the deserving to their just rewards and the failures to deserved defeat. Any interference, such as philanthropy to the poor or favoritism to the rich, only dulled *"the emery wheel of competition."* To be sure, Hoover paid lip service to restricting the strong in the interest of the society, but the main thrust of his thought awarded the victors their spoils. Critics were disarmed with three words— "equality of opportunity." The state should interfere to preserve it; otherwise, hands off! An exponent of the gospel of efficiency in economic affairs, Hoover believed that the road to the good life lay in the direction of more and better production. His mind equated material success with progress.

In the concluding chapter of *American Individualism*, Hoover drew the connection between his philosophy and the frontier. "The American pioneer," he declared, "is the epic expression of . . . individualism and the pioneer spirit is the response to the challenge of opportunity, to the challenge of nature, to the challenge of life, to the call of the frontier." Undismayed by the ending of the geographical frontier in the United States, Hoover declared that "there will always be a frontier to conquer or to hold to as long as men think, plan, and dare. . . . The days of the pioneer are not over."

When Hoover was elected President in 1928, these ideals were accorded the nation's highest accolade. They dominated popular thought as they had for three centuries of American history. In fact, all the men who occupied the Presidency from 1917 to 1930 were distinctly old-fashioned in their beliefs and in their public image. The traits are so familiar as to require listing only: Wilson the moralist and idealist; Harding the exemplar of small-town, "just folks" normalcy; Coolidge the frugal, farm-oriented Puritan; and Hoover the self-made man. If there was any correlation between a people's taste and its Presidents, then the record of this period underscored nostalgia.

Rivalling Hoover in the public mind of the early 1920s as an exponent of self-help and individualism was Edward Bok, the Dutch boy who made good and wrote about it in *The Americanization of Edward Bok* (1920). The book described Bok's immigration from Holland in 1870 at the age of six and his rise from a fifty-cents-a-week window cleaner to editor of the magazine with the largest circulation in the nation, the *Ladies Home Journal.* Bok's autobiography reads as a paean to the American ideal of success. Through luck, pluck, and clean living, he became a confidant and friend of Presidents. Thrift and determination made him rich. Bok played the rags to riches theme to the hilt. "Here was a little Dutch boy," he wrote in his preface, "unceremoniously set down in America . . . yet, it must be confessed, he achieved." His book, Bok promised, would describe "how such a boy, with every disadvantage to overcome, was able . . . to 'make good.' "

In the final chapters of his autobiography, Bok stepped back to comment on the liabilities and advantages of America. He did not slight the former, yet in "What I Owe to America" Bok brushed all debits aside in order to celebrate America's gift of "limitless opportunity: here a man can go as far as his abilities will carry him." For anyone "endowed with honest endeavor, ceaseless industry, and the ability to carry through, . . . the way is wide open to the will to succeed."

The public reception of *The Americanization of Edward Bok* suggests how much Americans in the 1920s wanted to confirm old beliefs. Bok was a hero in the Benjamin Franklin-Horatio Alger mold. His success story demonstrated that passing time and changing conditions had not altered hallowed ideals. His pages suggested no troubling doubts, and, after receiving the Pulitzer Prize for biography in 1921, Bok's book became a best-seller. An inexpensive eighth edition issued in July 1921 enabled it to attain third place on the 1922 lists. But the primary reason for Bok's popularity as hero-author was his ability to tell a nervous generation what it wanted to hear.

It has long puzzled students of the Great Crash of 1929 why even the most informed observers in education and government as well as business did not recognize and heed the prior economic danger signals that in retrospect seem so apparent. Part of the explanation possibly lies in the depth of the general commitment to the ideals of rugged individualism and free enterprise that Hoover and Bok articulated and symbolized. This commitment, in turn, lay in the nervousness of the American people. So much about the twenties was new and disturbing that Americans tended to cling tightly to familiar economic forms. They just could not bear to admit that the old business premises based on individualism and free enterprise might be fraught with peril. With Herbert Hoover leading the way, they chose to go down with the economic ship rather than question and alter its suicidal course.

Respect for the old-time hero was evident in other aspects of postwar thought. The vogue of the Boy Scouts is an example. Although the movement began in 1910, the twenties was the time of its flowering. There were 245,000 Scouts at the beginning of 1917, 942,500 at the end of 1929. In addition, 275,000 adults volunteered their services as leaders. No youth club and few adult organizations matched this record. The Boy Scout Handbook, a manual of ideals and instruction, sold millions of copies. Scouting, apparently, tapped fertile soil in its embodiment of the old-time idea of good citizenship and expertise in the outdoors. The Scout, standing straight in his shorts or knickers and doing the daily good deed that his oath required, was the epitome of the traditional American model of heroic young manhood.

In the late 1920s the Boy Scout Handbook featured an unusual drawing. In the foreground was a clean-cut Scout, eyes fixed on adventure. Behind him, signifying the heritage from which he sprang, were the figures of Daniel Boone, Abraham Lincoln, and Theodore Roosevelt, men who were staples in the annals of American heroism. But there was also a new face, that of Charles A. Lindbergh of Minnesota. At the age of just twenty-five Lindbergh rose to the status of an American demigod by virtue of a single feat. On May 20, 1927, he took off in a tiny single-engine airplane from New York City and thirty-three hours later landed in Paris. The nonstop, solo run across the Atlantic catapulted the average American into a paroxysm of pride and joy. Overnight Lindbergh became the greatest hero of the decade. There was but little exaggeration in the contention of one journalist that Lindbergh received "the greatest ovation in history." Certainly his return from Paris to the United States generated a reception extraordinary even for an age that specialized in ballyhoo. The *New York Times* devoted more space to Lindbergh's return than it had to the Armistice ending World War I. A virtual national religion took shape around Lindbergh's person. A 1928 poll of schoolboys in a typical American town on the question of whom they most wanted to be like produced the following results: Gene Tunney, 13 votes; John Pershing, 14; Alfred E. Smith, 16; Thomas A. Edison, 27; Henry Ford, 66; Calvin Coolidge, 110; Charles A. Lindbergh, 363. If the amount of national adulation is meaningful, adults everywhere would likely have responded in similar proportions.

■ ■ *The New York City ticker-tape parade for aviator Charles Lindbergh on June 14, 1927, attracted more than three million wildly enthusiastic spectators.*

The explanation of Lindbergh's popularity lies less in his feat (pilots had flown across the Atlantic before) and more in the mood of the people at the time it occurred. The typical American in 1927 was nervous. The values by which he ordered his life seemed in jeopardy of being swept away by the force of growth and change and complexity. Lindbergh came as a restorative tonic. He reasserted the image of the confident, quietly courageous, and self-reliant individual. He proved to a generation anxious for proof that Americans were still capable of pioneering. Even in an age of machines the frontier was not dead—a new one had been found in the air.

The reaction to Lindbergh's flight in the national press stressed these ideas. "Lindbergh served as a metaphor," wrote one commenta-

tor in *Century*. "We felt that in him we, too, had conquered something and regained lost ground." A writer in *Outlook* made the point more explicitly: "Charles Lindbergh is the heir of all that we like to think is best in America. He is the stuff out of which have been made the pioneers that opened up the wilderness first on the Atlantic coast, and then in our great West." A newspaper cartoon showed a covered wagon leaving for California in 1849 and next to it Lindbergh's plane taking off for Paris in 1927. Colonel Theodore Roosevelt, the son of the President, remarked that Lindbergh "personifies the daring of youth. Daniel Boone, David Crockett, and men of that type played a lone hand and made America. Lindbergh is their lineal descendant." Calvin Coolidge, who personally welcomed Lindbergh home, simply said that he was "a boy representing the best traditions of this country."

For one journalist the most significant part of the Lindbergh phenomenon was not the flight but the character of the man: "his courage, his modesty, his self-control, his sanity, his thoughtfulness of others, his fine sense of proportion, his loyalty, his unswerving adherence to the course that seemed right." His unassuming manner fit the traditional hero's mold. Many observers of the postflight celebration noted how the hero refused to capitalize financially on his popularity. It was telling evidence as an essayist put it, that the American people "are *not* rotten at the core, but morally sound and sweet and good!" The generalization from the individual to society was easily acceptable because Americans in 1927 desperately wanted to keep the old creed alive. Lindbergh's flight was popularly interpreted as a flight of faith—in the American experience and in the American people.

Looking back over the 1920s F. Scott Fitzgerald remembered in 1931 that "in the spring of 1927, something bright and alien flashed across the sky. A young Minnesotan who seemed to have nothing to do with his generation did a heroic thing, and for a moment people set down their glasses in country clubs and speakeasies and thought of their old best dreams." Also in 1931 Frederick Lewis Allen recalled that Lindbergh had been "a modern Galahad for a generation which had foresworn Galahads." Both Fitzgerald and Allen were right in their assessment of the public reaction to Lindbergh's flight, but wrong about the dreams he engendered being foreign to the 1920s. Fitzgerald notwithstanding, Lindbergh had a great deal to do with his generation. Allen to the contrary, the Lindbergh craze was not a case of Americans returning to ideals they had forsaken; they had never left them.

Popular books as well as heroes revealed the American mind in the 1920s, and the great majority of the best-sellers of the decade were decidedly old-fashioned. Frontier and rural patterns of thought and action dominated the popular novels. Their plots and protagonists operated according to time-honored standards of competition, loyalty, and rugged individualism. Complications were few and usually resolved, in the final pages, with an application of traditional morality. The total effect was a comforting reaffirmation of the old American faith. Such novels, to be sure, made slight contribution to serious American literature. But they were read—by millions! And they both influenced and reflected the mood of Americans who had never even heard of Fitzgerald and Hemingway. Indeed in comparison to best-selling authors, the Fitzgeralds and Hemingways were highly esoteric.

Exact figures are elusive, but it would be difficult to dispute Gene (Geneva) Stratton-Porter's claim to preeminence among popular novelists in the first three decades of the twentieth century. Her vogue began with *Freckles* in 1904 and continued right through the war, into the twenties, and beyond. In 1932 a *Publisher's Weekly* survey of the best-selling novels of the century revealed Porter in the top four positions with *Freckles*, *The Girl of the Limberlost* (1909), *The Harvester* (1911), and *Laddie* (1913). Each had sold well over a million copies. With other titles Porter made the "top ten" list in 1918, 1919, 1921, and 1925. Most of her sales were in fifty-cent reprint editions, suggesting that her public consisted of relatively unsophisticated readers.

Gene Stratton-Porter found a publishing bonanza by articulating the values to which a large part of the American reading public subscribed. Chief among them was a belief in the virtue of close association with nature. As a girl Porter ran in the swamps, woods, and fields around Wabash, Indiana, and the characters in her novels do likewise. The experience was represented as inspirational in the highest sense. Nature was not only a source of beauty and contentment but a repository of moral and religious truth. The outdoors provided a constant backdrop in Porter's stories. Indeed the margins of her books were sometimes adorned with pen and ink drawings of birds, animals, and flowers. *The Harvesters* was dedicated to Henry David Thoreau.

Second only to nature in Porter's scale of values was cheerfulness. Her stories expound the benefits of optimism, confidence, courage, and keeping a stiff upper lip. Typically the plots involve the protagonist, frequently a child, in a series of adversities. But looking for the silver lining and heeding the teachings of nature eventually resolve all problems. *Freckles*, for instance, describes a boy who believes himself an orphan, wanders in the Limberlost swamp, and is ultimately found and claimed by his wealthy father. Eleanora of *A Girl of the Limberlost* defies poverty by selling the moths she collected in the swamp. In *Michael O'Halloran* Porter copied the Horatio Alger formula, taking a little newsboy up the success ladder on the wings of determination and pluck.

Porter's novels appealed to the kind of American whose eyes glazed and even dampened when they thought of the good old days when life was simple and generally lived in close proximity to nature. In Porter one basked momentarily in an uncomplicated world where virtue triumphed and right prevailed. Much of Porter's public seemed to consist of people displaced or crushed by modern American civilization. Letters of appreciation poured in to her from sanitariums, rest homes, reform schools, and jails. But in a larger sense the uncertainties and nervousness of the age in general provided a milieu in which her kind of writing could flourish.

William Lyon Phelps once wrote of Gene Stratton-Porter, "she is a public institution, like Yellowstone Park, and I should not think she would care any more than a mountain for adverse criticism." In fact, Porter did care. She habitually replied to her unfavorable reviewers in lengthy letters. In one she responded to a critic who had labeled her writing "molasses fiction." This was really a compliment, rejoined Porter: "molasses is more necessary to the happiness of human and beast than vinegar. . . . I am a molasses person myself. . . . So I shall keep straight on writing of the love and joy of life . . . and when I have used the last drop of my molasses, I shall stop writing." She closed the letter with a hint of conceit: "God gave me a taste for sweets and the sales of the books I write prove that a few other people are similar to me in this."

Harold Bell Wright rivaled Gene Stratton-Porter as a dispenser of wholesomeness, optimism, and the arcadian myth. His *The Winning of Barbara Worth* (1911) had a half million copies in print within a month of its initial publication and maintained sufficient popularity to rank fifth, behind Porter's four books, in the 1932 best-selling novels of the century poll. After *Barbara Worth* Wright produced a novel every other year for two decades. Americans seemed as eager to buy and read his books after the war as before. His first twelve books enjoyed an average sale of nearly 750,000 each.

A sometime minister, Wright sermonized constantly in his novels. Until the final typing no character in any had a name except that of his main trait—Hypocrisy, Greed, Ambition, and so on. Wright's message was the familiar one: clean living, hard work, and contact with God's great open spaces could save a man from the physical and moral deterioration city life engendered. *When a Man's a Man* of 1916, for example, features a millionaire who goes west to escape the effete, artificial, decadent East. Its setting on an Arizona cattle ranch reflected Wright's own enthusiasm for the Southwest that led him to make his home there. Wright also loved Missouri's Ozark Mountains, and the region figured in a number of his stories. *The Re-Creation of Brian Kent*, third on the best-seller list for 1920, employs an Ozark setting to tell the story of a human wreck who is redeemed by the beauty of nature, the challenge of work, and a woman's love. An elderly schoolmarm, identified only as Auntie Sue, supervises the transformation and extracts the moral.

The stereotyped plots and characters, the wooden dialogue, and the commonplace preaching in Wright's books elicited a barrage of unfavorable criticism. According to one reviewer in 1924, Wright was guilty of perpetuating "the shibboleths and superstitions of our fathers, making old creeds and antique fables sacred in the eyes of all." And so he did. Yet his stories sold millions of copies. A large number of American readers found his message comfortable and meaningful. "Harold," one critic punned, "is always Wright." But for the popular mind of the teens and twenties ethical certainty was highly valued, and traditional mores seemed the most certain. The intellectuals might scoff, but Wright, like Porter, found the goldmine of popular favor.

The western novel, which Owen Wister introduced into American writing in 1902 with *The Virginian*, increased in popularity as the nation moved increasingly further from frontier conditions. The foremost practitioner of the art in the decade after World War I was a onetime dentist from Zanesville, Ohio, named Zane Grey. Blending minor literary talent with a keen sense of the public taste, Grey produced over fifty westerns and provided the basis for dozens of motion pictures, many of which were produced in the early 1920s before the advent of sound tracks. The total sale of all his writings approaches twenty million. From 1917 to 1924 Grey was never *off* the national list of the top ten best-sellers. Twice, 1918 and 1920, he ranked first. He may well have been the most widely read author in the American twenties.

The Zane Grey magic was a blend of violence, heroism, and the frontier. His stories lacked sophistication, but they juxtaposed good and evil in unmistakable terms. Titanic struggles might be waged, but the issues were always clearly defined and the outcome, as Grey fans came to learn, never really in doubt.

A simple code of conduct suffused Grey's books. It emphasized courage, self-reliance, fair play, and persistence—the traditional frontier virtues. Those who violated the code always paid the price.

As a mythmaker for the multitudes in the 1920s, Zane Grey became as legendary as his protagonists. Many people believed he spoke for the best parts of the national heritage. John Wanamaker, the department store mogul, addressed him directly: "never lay down your pen, Zane Grey. . . . You are distinctively and genuinely American. You have borrowed none of the decadence of foreign writers. . . . The good you are doing is incalculable." Even the critics treated Grey more tolerantly than they did Porter and Wright. "We turn to him," one commentator wrote, "not for insight into human nature and human problems nor for refinements of art, but simply for crude epic stories, as we might to an old Norse skald, maker of the sagas of the folk."

The concept of escape from the present, so important in the appeal of many of the bestselling popular novels in the twenties, reached a climax in the writing of Edgar Rice Burroughs. A failure for years in business and pulp magazine writing, Burroughs turned to a new theme in 1914 and struck pure gold. *Tarzan of the Apes* has probably sold more copies to date (over five million) than any other American book. Over thirty other stories of the English orphan reared in the African jungle by apes followed. As early as 1920 the Tarzan cult was nationwide. Burroughs was syndicated in newspapers; his motion pictures reached millions of people. With his superhuman prowess and his mate, Jane, Tarzan entered public thought and speech to an astonishing degree. For people vaguely repressed by civilization, Tarzan was a potent symbol of freedom, power, and individuality. A new wild man on a new frontier, Tarzan helped sustain traditional American values.

American readers seemed to have an insatiable appetite for nature novels for the first three decades of the twentieth century. In addition to Porter, Wright, Grey, and Burroughs, a host of others rode the theme to publishing successes that were minor only in comparison. The names of Rex Beach, Peter B. Kyne, Emerson Hough, and James Oliver Curwood were quite familiar to readers and moviegoers of the postwar decade even if they are not to most literary historians. Curwood, for instance, published between 1908 and 1926 twenty-six novels that dramatized the theme of courage in the wilderness. The motion pictures made from his books, such as *Back to God's Country* (1919), were intended, so an advertisement ran, for those who "love God's great out-of-doors, the land of frozen forests and everlasting snows where the gaunt wolf stalks its prey, where men loom large and life is big." In 1923 Hough's *The Covered Wagon* became the basis for the most famous western movie of the decade. Stewart Edward White rivaled both Curwood and Hough with books such as *The Blazed Trail*, *The Silent Places*, and *The Rules of the Game*. And that was it precisely—the game had rules that were at once easily perceived and rooted in the national character. If changing conditions were eroding the old certainties, that was only more reason to grasp them more tightly.

In popular fiction Americans of the 1920s were still inhabitants of the nineteenth century. The sexy novels of flaming youth and the risqué movies satisfied only part of the taste of the twenties. The other, and larger, part thrilled to old-time heroics such as those provided by the man Douglas Durkin sketched in *The Lobstick Trail* of 1922: "his blood was clean, his body knit of fibre woven in God's out-of-doors, his mind fashioned under a clear sky in a land of wide horizons."

■ ■ ■

STUDY QUESTIONS

1. What caused the nervousness that many Americans experienced in the 1920s?

2. What values were characteristic of America's pioneering past? How did the heroes of the 1920s demonstrate these values?

3. Why were sports so popular during the decade? How did athletic heroes help ease Americans' minds about the national character?

4. How were the popular images of Herbert Hoover and Charles Lindbergh similar? Why were both men considered heroes during the 1920s?

5. What were the characteristics of many popular novels during the 1920s? What type of stories did people enjoy reading about?

6. How were the novels of Gene Stratton-Porter, Harold Bell Wright, Zane Grey, and Edgar Rice Burroughs similar or different?

BIBLIOGRAPHY

The selection comes from Roderick Nash, *The Nervous Generation: American Thought, 1917–1930* (1970), which presents a view of the 1920s vastly different from Frederick Lewis Allen's. A good overview of the role of the hero in American culture is Leo Lowenthal, *Literature, Popular Culture and Society* (1961). The most important athletic heroes of the decade are discussed in Randy Roberts, *Jack Dempsey: The Manassa Mauler* (1979); Robert Creamer, *Babe* (1974); Marshall Smelser, *The Life that Ruth Built* (1975); Paul Gallico, *The Goddess People* (1965); and Frank Deford, *Big Bill Tilden: The Triumphs and the Tragedy* (1975). John W. Ward, "The Meaning of Lindbergh's Flight," *American Quarterly*, 10 (1958), is a classic study of the importance of heroism in the 1920s. On Lindbergh also see Walter S. Ross, *The Last Hero: Charles Lindbergh* (1976).

THE BLACK SOX SCANDAL

Dean Smith

Every few years or so, fat-bellied, middle-aged journalists start complaining that baseball "isn't what it used to be," that the American pastime is "in trouble," that the game is "in a crisis from which it may never recover." And yet, in spite of their nostalgic reflections about "the good old days," baseball is alive and well. Men's and women's softball leagues fill city recreation parks every night of the week, and Little Leaguers are playing more baseball than ever before. Fantasy baseball groups have sprouted in small towns and large cities all over the country, and junior high school boys have turned baseball cards into big business. America still loves baseball.

But there was a time when baseball was in real trouble. In 1921, headlines in newspapers across the country let Americans know that eight members of the Chicago White Sox were accused of conspiring to lose the 1919 World Series. The ensuing investigation and trial became symbolic of American life in the post–World War I years, when doubts about the country's future seemed endemic. It became known as the Black Sox Scandal, and in the following article Dean Smith describes the controversy and its significance in the 1920s.

When Jim Crusinberry, the *Chicago Tribune*'s ace baseball writer, entered the lobby of the Sinton Hotel in Cincinnati that evening of September 30, 1919, he stumbled onto one of the most remarkable scenes of his career.

Perched atop a chair in the lobby was a wildly gesturing man whom he immediately recognized as Abe Attell, former world feather-weight boxing champion and consort of New York gamblers. Attell had $1,000 bills in both hands and he was screaming his head off to anyone who would listen, offering to bet on the Cincinnati Reds to beat the Chicago White Sox—any amount, and at even money—in the World Series which was to open the following day at Redland Park.

Crusinberry's nose for news twitched like a bloodhound's. Even in those free-wheeling days of American sport, gamblers usually exercised more discretion than Attell was displaying. And why was he betting against the White Sox? The awesome Sox, one of the finest teams ever assembled up to that time, were top-heavy favorites to crush the so-so Reds in the Series. in most quarters, one had to offer at least 4-to-1 odds to bet on Chicago. Yet here was Attell betting big on Cincinnati, and at even money!

For most of the next two years, Crusinberry pursued his big story. Although thwarted repeatedly by baseball officialdom, underworld silence, and his cautious sports editor, he put the pieces together at last. With other tenacious reporters, he forced a Chicago grand jury to investigate the case that exploded over the sporting world as the Black Sox Scandal.

For nearly six decades American sports buffs have been discussing and analyzing the Black Sox legend, and still the complete story may never be told. What has been established is that eight members of the 1919 White Sox team conspired with two combinations of gamblers to throw the World Series to the Reds, and that the White Sox did indeed lose, five games to three. None of the sinning players, forever tarred in history as the Black Sox, ever received all the money promised for the fix, and several may have gotten no money at all.

What they did get was lifetime exile from organized baseball—an edict decreed and enforced by Commissioner Kenesaw Mountain Landis—despite the fact that the jury in a Cook County trial found them all innocent.

The Black Sox Scandal had an immense impact on a nation struggling to resume "normalcy" in the wake of World War I. To many Americans in that era of innocence, baseball was an almost religious rite, and the World Series was its most holy sacrament. The heroes of the Great American Game were assumed to be as pure as saints—despite considerable evidence to the contrary—and the heresy of desecrating the game for gamblers' gold was unthinkable. When the stink of the Black Sox sellout fouled the air, an entire nation was sickened.

This early 20th-century scandal did incalculable damage to America's self-image as a moral nation, disillusioned millions of youthful fans, and helped set the tone for the licentious decade of the 1920's. Teapot Dome, the Prohibition era, corruption in high places, and the public acceptance of "everybody's doing it" raised questions about the value of personal integrity that remain to the present.

To reconstruct the story of the Black Sox tragedy, return to the Sinton Hotel and September 30, 1919. Jim Crusinberry was only one of many who had heard the rumor of an impending White Sox sellout. Hugh Fullerton, syndicated columnist of the Chicago *Herald and Examiner*, wired this cryptic warning to his newspaper clients: "Don't bet on Series. Ugly rumors afloat."

Jack Doyle, whose New York billiard acade-

"The Black Sox Scandal" by Dean Smith in *American History Illustrated* 11 (January 1977). pp. 16–25. Reprinted through the courtesy of Cowles Magazines, publisher of *American History Illustrated*.

my was one of the nation's biggest gambling centers, estimated that $2,000,000 was wagered in his establishment the night before the Series opener. "You couldn't miss it . . . the thing had an odor," he said later. "I saw smart guys take even money on the Sox who should have been asking for 5-to-1 odds."

The Series fix was one of the worst-kept secrets in the history of infamy. As the betting odds shifted dramatically, Cincinnati was buzzing with rumors. Chick Gandil, the Chicago first baseman and admitted ringleader of the sellout, recalled in a *Sports Illustrated* confession nearly four decades later that even a clerk in a downtown stationery store whispered to him on the eve of the opener, "I have it firsthand that the Series is in the bag."

Everybody knew, and yet nobody knew for sure. Who was bribing whom—and to do what? To complicate the situation, a story popped up that some Chicago gamblers were out to insure a White Sox victory by getting ace Cincinnati pitcher Dutch Ruether drunk the night before the opener.

The White Sox should have needed no help at all. Owner Charles Comiskey, revered as "The Old Roman," had built a magnificent ball club in Chicago. There was Eddie Collins, probably the best second baseman in baseball, and Buck Weaver, without a peer at third base. "Shoeless Joe" Jackson was a virtual illiterate, but there was no better hitter and left fielder in the game. Happy Felsch in center and Shano Collins in right rounded out a great Chicago outfield. Chick Gandil at first base was so tough he could play his position without a glove. And Swede Risberg was one of the great shortstops of the era. Behind the plate was the superb Ray Schalk.

The pitching staff was a little thin, especially with Red Faber on the injured list, but Eddie Cicotte, Claude Williams, and Dickie Kerr were a match for anything Cincinnati could throw against them. As for manager Kid Gleason, he was a canny veteran who knew the game inside out and did a passable job of welding

his moody and contentious athletes into a team that had dominated the American League.

The first post-World War Series had been lengthened to best five games of nine to insure a bigger box office take (it was returned to best four-of-seven shortly thereafter), and a nation weary of war and sacrifice was eager for the spectacle to begin.

The tragic prelude to the opener at Cincinnati on October 1, 1919 is still difficult to piece together. Conflicting grand jury and court testimony, countless published revelations and "authentic" analyses—but a paucity of reliable source material—combine to create a knotty problem for the historian. Eliot Asinof's *Eight Men Out*, generally regarded as the most comprehensive book on the subject, says the Black Sox plot had its beginning when Gandil contacted Boston gambler Joseph (Sport) Sullivan some three weeks before the 1919 Series and offered to "put the Series in the bag" for $80,000. Gandil, in his 1956 revelation, declared it was Sullivan who first suggested to him that the Series might be fixed.

At any rate, Gandil first enlisted pitcher Eddie Cicotte in the plot and then shortstop Swede Risberg and pitcher Claude Williams. The team's top three hitters—Buck Weaver, Joe Jackson, and Happy Felsch—were reluctant enlistees. Gandil felt sure that those seven could guarantee a White Sox defeat. They could ground out in crucial spots, feed a fat pitch to a slugger with men on base, barely miss a fly ball—all without detection. The seven were soon joined by an eighth conspirator through sheer accident. Utility infielder Fred McMullin, a man hardly in a position to affect the Series outcome, was lying behind a locker one afternoon and overheard Gandil discussing the plan with Risberg. McMullin demanded a part of the action, and he was included to buy his silence.

Consorting with gamblers was not a new occupation for Gandil, who for years had sold information on starting pitchers and other useful baseball tips to the betting fraternity. "We all mixed with gamblers," Gandil explained later, "and most of them were honest." Such shady associations were a fact of baseball life in 1919, and nobody seemed to care very much.

The eight Chicago players assembled in Gandil's room at the Ansonia Hotel in New York City on the evening of September 21st to discuss strategy. The eight were not particularly good friends and were united on only one subject: their common hatred for Comiskey, whom they regarded as a tight-fisted tyrant who paid his players less than did any other owner in major league baseball.

Gandil and Felsch, for example, were earning only a little more than $4,000 a year; Cicotte's 1919 salary was about $5,000 (and he a 29-game winner with an earned run average of 1.82!); and the great Jackson, batting .375 for the season, earned only $6,000—compared with the $10,000 Cincinnati paid its leading hitter, Ed Roush.

The eight agreed to deal with the gamblers, although Weaver is said to have suggested that they take the fix money and win the Series, anyhow. The evidence is conclusive that the superlative third baseman never threw a game or received a dime from the gamblers. He spent the rest of his life protesting his innocence and trying to restore his good name.

Even before arrangements could be made with Sullivan, word of the fix attempt leaked out. Cicotte was approached by gambler William T. (Sleepy Bill) Burns, a former pitcher who had made money in Texas oil, to let him bid on the action. Soon two gambling combinations—unknown to each other—were negotiating with the Chicago eight.

It was common knowledge in the far-flung American gambling community that only one man, Arnold Rothstein of New York City, could put up enough money to engineer a project as grandiose as the fixing of a World Series. Burns hurriedly consulted with a small-time gambler named Billy Maharg in Philadelphia,

and together they rushed to Rothstein with the proposition.

Rothstein would not see them personally, but told his ambitious lieutenant, Abe Attell, to check it out. Attell was entranced with the sheer audacity of the idea, so Rothstein agreed to discuss the matter with Burns. But the gambling king, known far and wide as "The Big Bankroll," turned Burns down flat and advised him to forget this wild scheme.

Attell could not put the lucrative idea out of his mind, however, and he decided to step into the big time on his own. He called Burns and told him a lie that could have bought Abe a concrete casket: Rothstein had changed his mind, said Attell, and would put up $100,000 if Burns could get the eight White Sox to go along. It was sheer bluff on Attell's part. Certainly he could not lay his hands on the money the players were demanding, but he put up a confident front and prayed he could get the cash somewhere.

Meanwhile, Sullivan was busy, too. He also sought out Rothstein and somehow made a better impression on the shrewd New Yorker than had Burns. Rothstein assigned an aide named Nat Evans to work out the details of the Series fix with Sullivan and the players.

So Gandil and his co-conspirators began their comic opera dealings with two sets of gamblers, holding clandestine meetings in hotel rooms and hoping the rival fixers would never meet. The players demanded cash in advance, but the gamblers were untrusting souls who refused payment except after each game Chicago lost. Only Cicotte held out for his money beforehand, so Sullivan gave Gandil $10,000 to clinch the deal. The money mysteriously appeared under Cicotte's pillow at the Sinton Hotel the night before the Series opener.

According to the Black Sox legend, Rothstein demanded that Cicotte "give a sign" that the fix was on by hitting the first Cincinnati batter with a pitch. Whether or not Cicotte agreed, we will never know for sure, but for whatever reason—the heat of the 90-

"Shoeless" Joe Jackson and seven other players on the Chicago White Sox were charged with accepting money to throw the 1919 World Series.

degree afternoon, the screaming throng of 30,500 in Redland Park, nerves made jumpy by his Judas role, or a shouted threat from the stands that "there's a guy looking for you with a rifle"—Cicotte's second pitch to Cincinnati leadoff hitter Maurice Rath strayed inside and hit him in the small of the back.

It was not Cicotte's day. He was driven from the mound in the fourth inning and the Reds waltzed to a 9-1 victory. Even the Cincinnati pitcher, Dutch Ruether, connected for two triples to the humiliation of the proud Sox. The next day Claude Williams, a left-hander famous for his control, was shockingly wild and the Reds won again, 4-2.

Meanwhile, rumors of the fix had reached manager Gleason and owner Comiskey. Late at night after the first game, according to one version of the story, Comiskey woke John Heydler, president of the National League and a member of baseball's National Commission, and poured out his fears that the White Sox had sold out to the gamblers. Heydler then woke Ban Johnson, president of the American League and a bitter enemy of Comiskey's, and relayed the Chicago owner's apprehensions.

"That's the yelp of a beaten cur!" sneered Johnson, who terminated the conversation abruptly and went back to bed.

The gamblers were equally indisposed to conversation. Sullivan disappeared after the first game. Attell was in town, but he was very vague about specifics of the payoff to Gandil.

"The money is all out on bets," he told the ringleader. "You'll have to give me another day."

According to Asinof's version, Attell did come up with $10,000 after the second game, the money going to Gandil. Gandil later denied receiving any of the money for himself, but he did manage somehow to buy a big new car immediately after the Series.

Chicago had lost the first two games and, aside from Gandil and Cicotte, none of the White Sox conspirators had received so much as a "thank you" from either gambling combination. Understandably, they were now ready to forget the entire arrangement and play to win. With rookie Dickie Kerr pitching a three-hit shutout before 29,126 rabid fans at Chicago's Comiskey Park, the White Sox cruised to a 3-0 triumph. Gandil himself drove in two of the Chicago runs.

Unfortunately for Attell, Burns, and their colleagues, the news of the White Sox rebirth of spirit had not reached them. As they ruefully reported later, they lost all their previous winnings betting on the Reds in the third game and had no further participation in the Series machinations. But Sullivan was still very much in the game. Fearful that the White Sox players had revolted, he came up with $20,000, part of the bankroll reportedly supplied by Rothstein.

Now it was time for the fourth game and Cicotte's chance to redeem himself. The spitball ace pitched a strong five-hitter, but his mates were powerless at the plate and Cincinnati walked away with a 2-0 win. Williams gave up only four hits in the fifth game, but again the White Sox bats were silent and the Reds had their fourth victory, 5-0.

At this point Sullivan made the last of the gamblers' payments, this one purportedly $15,000.

Only one game away from losing the Series, the White Sox miraculously returned to their regular season form in the sixth game. Kerr won it, 5-4, with Gandil's hit providing the winning margin in the 10th inning. Cicotte was brilliant in the seventh game, winning 4-1, and suddenly the White Sox looked like winners again.

The gamblers were more than a little nervous, even with the paid-off Williams slated to pitch the eighth game in Chicago. To be sure of his position, Sullivan (according to Williams' wife) employed a professional persuader to remind Williams of the unpleasant consequences in store for him and his family if he should win.

A well-known gambler telephoned reporter Fullerton before the game and told him to "watch out for the biggest first inning you ever saw." It arrived on schedule, with Williams surrendering four runs in the first frame. The fired-up Reds raced off to a 10-1 lead before Chicago scored four in the eighth to close the final Cincinnati victory margin to 10-5.

The lowly Reds had pulled off the baseball upset of the decade. But had they really outplayed the White Sox, or had the eight Chicago conspirators handed the Series to them in return for tainted money?

The debate continues to this day.

One of the leading advocates of the "no fix" theory, Victor Luhrs, in his book The *Great Baseball Mystery,* declares the indications are overwhelming that Cincinnati would have won the Series anyhow. In his summary Luhrs admits that Williams' poor pitching cost the White Sox the second and eighth games and that he quite probably was an intentional loser. Gandil and Risberg, he says, did not give their best efforts and McMullin (who appeared only twice as a pinch hitter) did not play enough to permit a judgment. But he stoutly defends Jackson, Weaver, Felsch, and Cicotte, crediting all four with playing their best.

Dr. Harold Seymour, in his book *Baseball—the Golden Age,* concluded that the box scores do not indicate that the Series was thrown. "In fact," says he, "the Black Sox on the whole actually made a better showing in the games than the Clean Sox (the other

Chicago players)."

Joe Jackson, for example, led both teams at the plate with a .375 average, and Weaver ended with a .324 batting effort. Gandil's timely hitting won two games, and both Weaver and Jackson played errorless ball. Clean Eddie Collins, on the other hand, made two errors and batted an anemic .224; the other unblemished Chicago regulars did little better.

The rumors of a fix continued for many months, despite the best efforts of investigative reporters to dig out the truth. Comiskey offered a $20,000 reward (soon reduced to $10,000) for information on any skullduggery. But he ignored tips supplied by at least one gambler and never answered a letter from the remorseful Jackson, written by his wife, offering to tell what he knew. Apparently baseball officialdom had decided to sweep the dirt under the rug and hope it would be forgotten.

But the Chicago *Tribune's* Jim Crusinberry would not forget.

Crusinberry devoted every spare moment to tracking down leads, and at last—on a rainy New York afternoon in July 1920—the first crack in the wall of silence appeared. The telephone rang in the hotel room when Crusinberry was relaxing with columnist Ring Lardner. It was Kid Gleason, and he spoke in an excited whisper.

"I'm at Dinty Moore's," he told Crusinberry, "and Abe Attell is at the bar, drinking and starting to talk. Come on over and get close enough to listen." Within minutes, Crusinberry and Lardner were eavesdropping on a fascinating conversation.

"So it was Arnold Rothstein who put up the dough for the fix," they heard Gleason say. "That was it, Kid," answered Attell. "You know, Kid, I hated to do that to you, but I thought I was going to make a lot of money and I needed it, and then the big guy double-crossed me, and I never got but a small part of what he promised."

Attell rambled on for half an hour, naming the participants. At last Crusinberry had the information for his block-busting story. But his sports editor, wary of a libel suit, refused to print it. Frustrated and angry, Crusinberry decided to take matters into his own hands. He wrote an open letter to the *Tribune*, demanding a grand jury investigation of the Series fix, and persuaded Chicago businessman Fred M. Loomis to sign it. The strategy worked. The Cook County grand jury agreed to the probe, and on September 21, 1920 subpoenas were sent to baseball owners, managers, players, writers, and gamblers.

Six days later the first sensational revelation hit the newspapers. Enterprising Jimmy Isaminger, a writer for the Philadelphia *North American*, tracked down gambler Billy Maharg —a cohort of Burns and Attell—and got him to talk. Maharg knew only part of the story, of course, but his statement exploded like a bombshell. He implicated Cicotte as the chief fixer, said Attell had betrayed Burns and himself, and declared that the first, second, and eighth Series games had been thrown by the Chicago eight—who immediately became known as the Black Sox.

The ink was still damp on the Isaminger story when Gleason sought out the tormented Cicotte and persuaded him to confess. Weeping through much of his sensational testimony before the grand jury the following day, Cicotte admitted receiving $10,000, confessed that he had served up pitches that anyone could hit, and said he did it for his wife and children.

Jackson next took the stand, nervously admitting that he got $5,000 of the $20,000 promised him. As he was leaving the courthouse following his testimony, the most poignant incident of the whole sordid scandal took place. Several ragged youngsters crowded around him and one asked pleadingly, "Say it ain't so, Joe!"

All America fervently joined in that plea.

Historians may note with some amusement that the original Associated Press quote of the remark was a more grammatical "It isn't true, is it, Joe?" But several other reporters who were there quoted it in the street jargon in which it was probably uttered.

Williams testified next, admitting that he got $5,000 for his part in the fix. Then came Felsch, who also confessed $5,000, but insisted that he had done nothing to throw any of the games.

Although the White Sox were battling for the American League pennant in the final week of the season, Comiskey immediately suspended all seven active players. (Gandil had "retired" from baseball before the start of the 1920 season.) With the Chicago team decimated, Cleveland breezed to the league championship.

The grand jury indicted all eight Chicago players, along with gamblers Attell, Burns, Hal Chase, and "Rachael Brown," the name used by Rothstein aide Nat Evans. Rothstein himself escaped indictment. The New York gambling king made an appearance before the grand jury, storming in outraged innocence, and somehow convinced everyone that he had not participated in any way.

When the Black Sox trial finally began, on June 27, 1921, the prosecution made an electrifying announcement: All the players' signed confessions had mysteriously disappeared from the files! American League President Ban Johnson accused Rothstein of paying $10,000 to arrange the theft, upon which Rothstein threatened him with a $250,000 slander suit. He never carried out the threat.

Free of the damning confessions, the players all denied their earlier testimony and pleaded innocent. None testified during the trial.

All through a blazing hot July the sensational trial dragged on in the sweltering Chicago courtroom. The defense was conducted by several of the most expensive lawyers of the day (who paid them was never proved), and the crowded courtroom was noisily in support of the players. Burns turned state's evidence, and

the other gamblers all avoided prosecution through legal maneuvers.

The outcome teetered in the balance as the mountain of testimony piled up. Then, on August 2d, both legal teams rested their cases and Judge Hugo Friend made his charge to the jury:

The State must prove that it was the intent of the ballplayers and gamblers charged with conspiracy through the throwing of the World Series to defraud the public and others, and not merely to throw ball games.

The tricky bit of semantics was all the jury needed. The judge said taking bribes was not enough—throwing ball games was not enough. To be legally guilty, the players must have intended to defraud the public. How could anybody prove that?

In just two hours, forty-seven minutes the jury brought in "not guilty" verdicts on all concerned. The hushed courtroom erupted in wild cheering and, incredibly, members of the jury hoisted several of the Black Sox to their shoulders and paraded them triumphantly around the courtroom. Flushed with victory, Gandil spotted Ban Johnson, rushed to his side, and declared: "Goodbye, good luck, and to hell with you!"

The Black Sox celebrated their triumph at an Italian restaurant after the verdict was read—the same restaurant, incidentally, where the jurors dined and congratulated themselves—and toasted the immediate resumption of their baseball careers. But they did not reckon with the stern morality of white-haired Judge Kenesaw Mountain Landis, who had been installed as Commissioner of Baseball following the grim days of the grand jury investigation. Landis had said upon taking office that the Black Sox would never play again, but that was before the trial. Surely, the players reasoned, the judge would not dare to overrule a court of law.

But he did just that. Landis' statement after the trial was a verdict of doom:

Regardless of the verdict of juries, no player that throws a ball game . . . [or] sits in a conference with a bunch of crooked players and gamblers where the ways and means of throwing games are planned and discussed, and does not promptly tell his club about it, will ever play professional baseball.

He added one more shocker: In addition to the eight Black Sox, he slapped a lifetime ban on Joe Gedeon of the St. Louis Browns, who had told the grand jury he made money betting on Cincinnati at the suggestion of Swede Risberg.

The players screamed, hired lawyers, and got petitions signed—but all to no avail. None of them ever played in organized baseball again. Landis was as unbending as iron, and many years later he went so far as to deny Jackson's petition to manage the Greenville, South Carolina, club in the low-low minors.

Part of the Black Sox legend is that Landis' stiff punishments saved baseball in its darkest hour. A glance at the soaring major league gate receipts in 1920 and 1921, however, seems to show that the sporting public would have supported the game whether or not the Black Sox had been punished. But the old judge's decision undoubtedly discouraged future cozy dealings between players and gamblers. Baseball never has suffered another scandal.

So the chastened Black Sox were cast out to make a living the best way they could. Weaver ran a Chicago drug store. Cicotte farmed near Detroit and then worked at an automobile plant. Williams ran a Chicago poolroom for a time and then started a nursery business in California. Felsch opened a tavern in Milwaukee. Risberg worked on a Minnesota dairy farm before opening a tavern in northern California. Gandil became a plumber in California. McMullin took one job and then another. Jackson operated a restaurant, and later a liquor store, in South Carolina.

All eight are now dead.

Though most of them protested varying degrees of innocence throughout their lives, Gandil declared in his 1956 confession, "To this day, I feel that we got what we had coming."

Baseball survived and thrived, but it was never again the gloriously pure American rite it once had been. Too many little boys—of all ages—had suffered sobering disillusionment.

Perhaps Nelson Algren, who had idolized Swede Risberg, said it best many years later in his superb short story "The Silver-Colored Yesterday":

I traded off my Risberg bat . . . and I flipped the program from that hot and magic Sunday when Cicotte was shutting out everybody forever, and a triumphant right-hander's wind had blown all the score cards across home plate, into the Troy Street gutter. I guess that was one way of learning what Hustletown, sooner or later, teaches all its sandlot sprouts. "Everybody's out for The Buck. Even big leaguers."

Even Swede Risberg.

■■■

STUDY QUESTIONS

1. Why did the little boy's comment "Say it ain't so, Joe" come to symbolize the public's reaction to the entire scandal?

2. What actually happened? Did the players really throw the World Series?

3. Who were the major characters in the scandal?

4. What decision did Judge Landis reach? Do you agree with the decision?

5. How would you compare the punishment given to the players in 1921 with contemporary professional athletes who gamble or find themselves with drug problems?

BIBLIOGRAPHY

In recent years the history of sport in the United States has enjoyed increasing scholarly respectability. For a general survey, see Benjamin Rader, *American Sports: From the Age of Folk Games to the Age of Spectators* (1983). Stephen Reiss, *Touching Base: Professional Baseball and American Culture in the Progressive Era* (1980) is an especially useful examination of baseball in early twentieth-century America. Also see David Q. Voigt, *American Baseball. Vol. 1: From Gentlemen's Sport to the Commissioner System* (1966). On the scandal itself, see Eliot Asinof, *Eight Men Out: The Black Sox and the 1919 World Series* (1963). For a discussion of the mood of the 1920s in the United States, see Roderick Nash, *The Nervous Generation: American Thought, 1917–1930* (1970). Organized crime in the 1920s has also generated a scholarly literature. Herbert Asbury, *Sucker's Progress: An Informal History of Gambling in America* (1938) is a good, if dated, survey. Also see Jenna Joselit, *Our Gang: Jewish Crime and Politics in One American Community* (1983) and Humbert S. Nelli, *The Business of Crime: Italians and Syndicate Crime in the United States* (1981).

ORGANIZED CRIME IN URBAN SOCIETY: CHICAGO IN THE TWENTIETH CENTURY

Mark Haller

In 1919 Congress adopted the Eighteenth Amendment, which prohibited "the manufacture, sale, or transportation of intoxicating liquors." Prohibition, however, did not stop Americans from manufacturing, selling, or transporting alcohol; it simply made the actions illegal. During the 1920s and early 1930s, criminals rather than businessmen supplied the public's thirst, and often the distinction between the two occupations grew fuzzy. As "Scarface" Al Capone once noted, "I make my money by supplying a public demand. If I break the law, my customers, who number hundreds of the best people in Chicago, are as guilty as I am. . . . Everybody calls me a racketeer. I call myself a businessman. When I sell liquor it's bootlegging. When my patrons serve it on a silver tray on Lake Shore Drive, it's hospitality."

For many Americans, Capone's point was well taken. As a result, criminals achieved a certain social respect and were able to spread their influence into legitimate business. A 1926 congressional investigation demonstrated that organized crime had made significant inroads into the worlds of labor unions, industry, and city governments. By 1933 when Congress repealed the Eighteenth Amendment, organized crime had become a permanent part of the American scene.

In the following essay, historian Mark H. Haller examines the role of crime in ethnic communities and urban society. Like sports and entertainment, crime served as an avenue out of the ethnic ghettoes and played an important role in the complex urban environment.

Many journalists have written exciting accounts of organized crime in American cities and a handful of scholars have contributed analytical and perceptive studies. Yet neither the excitement in the journalistic accounts nor the analysis in the scholarly studies fully captures the complex and intriguing role of organized criminal activities in American cities during the first third of the twentieth century. The paper that follows, although focusing on Chicago, advances hypotheses that are probably true for other cities as well. The paper examines three major, yet interrelated, aspects of the role of organized crime in the city: first, the social worlds within which the criminals operated and the importance of those worlds in providing social mobility from immigrant ghettos; second, the diverse patterns by which different ethnic groups became involved in organized criminal activities and were influenced by those activities; and third, the broad and pervasive economic impact of organized crime in urban neighborhoods and the resulting influence that organized crime did exert.

Crime and Mobility

During the period of heavy immigrant movement into the cities of the Northeast and Midwest, organized crime provided paths of upward mobility for many young men raised in ethnic slums. The gambling kings, vice lords, bootleggers and racketeers often began their careers in the ghetto neighborhoods; and frequently these neighborhoods continued to be the centers for their entrepreneurial activities. A careful study of the leaders of organized crime in Chicago in the late 1920s found that 31 percent were of Italian background, 29 percent

"Organized Crime in Urban Society: Chicago in the Twentieth Century" by Mark Haller, from *Journal of Social History* (Winter, 1971–1972). Copyright © 1971 by The Regents of the University of California. Reprinted by permission.

of Irish background, 20 percent Jewish, and 12 percent black; none were native white of native white parents. A recognition of the ethnic roots of organized crime, however, is only a starting point for understanding its place in American cities.

At a risk of oversimplification, it can be said that for young persons in the ethnic ghettos three paths lay open to them. The vast majority became, to use the Chicago argot, "poor working stiffs." They toiled in the factories, filled menial service and clerical jobs, or opened mom-and-pop stores. Their mobility to better jobs and to homeownership was, at best, incremental. A second, considerably smaller group followed respectable paths to relative success. Some of this group went to college and entered the professions; others rose to management positions in the business or governmental hierarchies of the city.

There existed, however, a third group of interrelated occupations which, although not generally regarded as respectable, were open to uneducated and ambitious ethnic youths. Organized crime was one such occupational world, but there were others.

One was urban machine politics. Many scholars have, of course, recognized the function of politics in providing mobility for some members of ethnic groups. In urban politics, a person's ethnic background was often an advantage rather than a liability. Neighborhood roots could be the basis for a career that might lead from poverty to great local power, considerable wealth, or both.

A second area consisted of those businesses that prospered through political friendships and contacts. Obviously, construction companies that built the city streets and buildings relied upon government contracts. But so also did banks in which government funds were deposited, insurance companies that insured government facilities, as well as garbage contractors, traction companies and utilities that sought city franchises. Because political contacts were important, local ethnic politicians and their friends were often the major backers of such enterprises.

A third avenue of success was through leadership in the city's labor unions. The Irish in Chicago dominated the building trade unions and most of the other craft unions during the first 25 years of this century. But persons of other ethnic origins could also rise to leadership positions, especially in those unions in which their own ethnic group predominated.

Another path of mobility was sports. Boxing, a peculiarly urban sport, rooted in the neighborhood gymnasiums, was the most obvious example of a sport in which Irish champions were succeeded by Jewish, Polish and black champions. Many a fighter, even if he did not reach national prominence, could achieve considerable local fame within his neighborhood or ethnic group. He might then translate this local fame into success by becoming a fight manager, saloon keeper, politician or racketeer.

A fifth area often dominated by immigrants was the entertainment and night life of the city. In Chicago, immigrants—primarily Irish and Germans—ran the city's saloons by the turn of the century. During the 1920s, Greek businessmen operated most of the taxi-dance halls. Restaurants, cabarets and other night spots were similarly operated by persons from various ethnic groups. Night life also provided careers for entertainers, including B-girls, singers, comedians, vaudeville and jazz bands. Jewish comedians of the 1930s and black comedians of our own day are only examples of a larger phenomenon in which entertainment could lead to local and even national recognition.

The organized underworld of the city, then, was not the only area of urban life that provided opportunities for ambitious young men from the ghettos. Rather, it was one of several such areas. Part of the pervasive impact of organized crime resulted from the fact that the various paths were interrelated, binding together the worlds of crime, politics, labor

leadership, politically related businessmen, sports figures and the night life of the city. What was the nature of the interrelationships?

To begin with, organized crime often exerted important influences upon the other social worlds. For aspiring politicians, especially during the early years after an ethnic group's arrival in a city, organized crime was often the most important source of money and manpower. (By the turn of the century, an operator of a single policy wheel in Chicago could contribute not only thousands of dollars but also more than a hundred numbers writers to work the neighborhoods on election day.) On occasion, too, criminals supplied strongarm men to act as poll watchers, they organized repeat voters, and they provided other illegal but necessary campaign services. Like others engaged in ethnic politics, members of the organized underworld often acted from motives of friendship and common ethnic loyalties. But because of the very nature of their activities, criminal entrepreneurs required and therefore sought political protection. It would be difficult to exaggerate the importance of organized crime in the management of politics in many of the wards of the city.

Furthermore, it should not be thought that the politics of large cities like Chicago was peculiarly influenced by organized crime. In a large and heterogeneous city, there were always wards within which the underworld exercised little influence and which could therefore elect politicians who would work for honest government and law enforcement. But in the ethnic and blue-collar industrial cities west or southwest of Chicago, the influence of organized crime sometimes operated without serious opposition. In Cicero, west of Chicago along major commuting lines, gambling ran wide open before the 1920s; and after 1923 Capone's bootlegging organization safely had its headquarters there. In other towns, like Stickney and Burnham, prostitution and other forms of entertainment often operated with greater openness than in Chicago. This symbiotic relationship, in which surrounding blue-collar communities provided protected vice and entertainment for the larger city, was not limited to Chicago. Covington, Kentucky, had a similar relationship to Cincinnati, while East St. Louis serviced St. Louis.

The organized underworld was also deeply involved in other areas of immigrant mobility. Organized criminals worked closely with racketeering labor leaders and thus became involved in shakedowns, strike settlements and decisions concerning union leadership. They were participants in the night life, owned many of the night spots in the entertainment districts, and hired and promoted many of the entertainers. (The comedian Joe E. Lewis started his career in Chicago's South Side vice district as an associate and employee of the underworld; his case was not atypical.) Members of the underworld were also sports fans and gamblers and therefore became managers of prize fighters, patrons at the race tracks and loyal fans at ball games. An observer who knew many of Chicago's pimps in the 1920s reported:

The pimp is first, last and always a fight fan. He would be disgraced if he didn't go to every fight in town. . . .

They hang around gymnasiums and talk fight. Many of them are baseball fans, and they usually get up just about in time to go to the game. They know all the players and their information about the game is colossal. Football is a little too highbrow for them, and they would be disgraced if they played tennis, but of late the high grade pimps have taken to golf, and some of them belong to swell golf clubs.

However, criminals were not merely sports fans; some ran gambling syndicates and had professional interests in encouraging sports or predicting the outcome of sports events. Horse racing was a sport conducted primarily for the betting involved. By the turn of the century, leading gamblers and bookmakers invested in and controlled most of the race tracks near Chicago and in the rest of the nation. A number of successful gamblers had stables of horses and thus mixed business with pleasure while becoming leading figures in horse race circles. At a less important level, Capone's organization in the late 1920s owned highly profitable dog tracks in Chicago's suburbs.

The fact that the world of crime exerted powerful influences upon urban politics, business, labor unions, sports and entertainment does not adequately describe the interrelations of these worlds. For many ambitious men, the worlds were tied together because in their own lifetimes they moved easily from one area to another or else held positions in two or more simultaneously. In some ways, for instance, organized crime and entertainment were barely distinguishable worlds. Those areas of the city set aside for prostitution and gambling were the major entertainment districts of the city. Many cabarets and other night spots provided gambling in backrooms or in rooms on upper floors. Many were places where prostitutes solicited customers or where customers could find information concerning local houses of prostitution. During the 1920s, places of entertainment often served liquor and thus were retail outlets for bootleggers. In the world of entertainment, the distinction between legitimate and illegitimate was often blurred beyond recognition.

Take, as another example, the career of William Skidmore. At age fourteen, Billie sold racing programs at a race track near Chicago. By the time he was twenty-one, in the 1890s, he owned a saloon and cigar store, and soon had joined with others to operate the major policy wheels in Chicago and the leading handbook syndicate on the West Side. With his growing wealth and influence, he had by 1903 also become ward committeeman in the thirteenth ward and was soon a leading political broker in the city. In 1912 he was Sergeant-at-Arms for the Democratic National Convention and, afterwards, aided Josephus Daniels in running the Democratic National Committee. Despite his success as gambler and politician, his

■ ■ *The lavishly bedecked casket and banners in the funeral cortege of a not-very-famous Chicago gangster of the 1920s. Bootlegging and racketeering in life gave way to ritual and pageantry in death.*

by interlocking careers; the worlds also shared a common social life. At local saloons, those of merely local importance met and drank together. At other restaurants or bars, figures of wider importance had meeting places. Until his death in 1920, Big Jim Colossimo's restaurant in the South Side vice district brought together the successful from many worlds; the saloon of Michael (Hinky Dink) Kenna, first ward Alderman, provided a meeting place in the central business district. Political banquets, too, provided opportunities for criminals, police, sports figures and others to gather in honor of a common political friend. Weddings and funerals were occasions when friends met to mark the important passages through life. At the funeral of Colossimo—politician, vice lord and restauranteur—his pallbearers included a gambler, two keepers of vice resorts, and a bailbondsman. Honorary pallbearers were five judges (including the chief judge of the criminal courts), two congressmen, nine resort keepers or gamblers, several aldermen and three singers from the Chicago Opera. (His good friend, Enrico Caruso, was unable to be present.) Such ceremonial events symbolized the overlapping of the many worlds of which a man like Colossimo was a part.

Thus far we have stressed the social structure that linked the criminal to the wider parts of the city within which he operated. That social world was held together by a system of values and beliefs widely shared by those who participated in crime, politics, sports and the night life of the city. Of central importance was the cynical—but not necessarily unrealistic—view that society operated through a process of deals, friendships and mutual favors. Hence the man to be admired was the smart operator and dealer who handled himself well in such a world. Because there was seen to be little difference between a legal and an illegal business, there was a generally tolerant attitude that no one should interfere with the other guy's racket so long as it did not interfere with one's own. This general outlook was, of course,

saloon, until well into the 1920s, was a hangout for pickpockets and con men; and "Skid" provided bail and political protection for his criminal friends. In the twenties Skidmore branched into the junk business and made a fortune selling junk obtained through contracts with the county government. Not until the early 1940s did he finally go to prison, the victim of a federal charge of income tax evasion. In his life, it would be impossible to unravel the diverse careers to determine whether he was saloon keeper, gambler, politician or businessman.

The various social worlds were united not simply by the influence of organized crime and widely shared, in whole or in part, by other groups within American society so that there was no clear boundary between the social world of the smart operators and the wider society.

In a social system held together by friendships and favors, the attitude toward law and legal institutions was complex. A basic attitude was a belief that criminal justice institutions were just another racket—a not unrealistic assessment considering the degree to which police, courts and prosecutor were in fact used by political factions and favored criminal groups. A second basic attitude was a belief that, if anyone cooperated with the law against someone with whom he was associated or to whom he owed favors, he was a stoolpigeon whose behavior was beneath contempt. This does not mean that criminal justice institutions were not used by members of organized crime. On a day-to-day basis, members of the underworld were tied to police, prosecutors and politicians through payments and mutual favors. Criminal groups often used the police and courts to harass rival gangs or to prevent the development of competition. But conflicts between rival groups were also resolved by threats or violence. Rival gambling syndicates bombed each others' places of business, rival union leaders engaged in bombing and slugging, and rival bootlegging gangs after 1923 turned to assassinations that left hundreds dead in the streets of Chicago. The world of the rackets was a tough one in which a man was expected to take his knocks and stand up for himself. Friendship and loyalty were valued; but so also were toughness and ingenuity.

Gangsters, politicians, sports figures and entertainers prided themselves for being smart guys who recognized how the world operated. They felt disdain mixed with pity for the "poor working stiffs" who, ignorant of how the smart guys operated, toiled away at their menial jobs. But if they disdained the life of the working stiff, they also disdained the pretensions of those "respectable" groups who looked askance at the world within which they operated. Skeptical that anyone acted in accordance with abstract beliefs or universalistic principles, the operators believed that respectable persons were hypocrites. For instance, when Frank J. Loesch, the distinguished and elderly lawyer who headed the Chicago Crime Commission, attacked three criminal court judges for alleged political favoritism, one politician declared to his friends:

Why pick on these three judges when every judge in the criminal court is doing the very same thing, and always have. Who is Frank Loesch that he should holler? He has done the same thing in his day. . . . He has asked for plenty of favors and has always gotten them. Now that he is getting older and is all set and doesn't have to ask any more favors, he is out to holler about every one else. . . . There are a lot of these reformers who are regular racketeers, but it won't last a few years and it will die out.

In short, the world view of the operators allowed them to see their world as being little different from the world of the respectable persons who looked down upon them. The whole world was a racket.

Ethnic Specialization

Some have suggested that each ethnic group, in its turn, took to crime as part of the early adjustment to urban life. While there is some truth to such a generalization, the generalization obscures more than it illuminates the ethnic experiences and structure of crime. In important respects, each ethnic group was characterized by different patterns of adjustment; and the patterns of involvement in organized crime often reflected the particular broader patterns of each ethnic group. Some ethnic groups—Germans and Scandinavians, for instance—appear not to have made significant contributions to the development of organized crime. Among the ethnic groups that did contribute, there was specialization within crime that reflected broader aspects of ethnic life.

In Chicago by the turn of the century, for example, the Irish predominated in two areas of organized crime. One area was labor racketeering, which derived from the importance of the Irish as leaders of organized labor in general.

The second area of Irish predominance was the operation of major gambling syndicates. Irish importance in gambling was related to a more general career pattern. The first step was often ownership of a saloon, from which the owner might move into both politics and gambling. Many Irish saloon keepers ran handbooks or encouraged other forms of gambling in rooms located behind or over the saloon. Those Irishmen who used their saloon as a basis for electoral politics continued the gambling activities in their saloons and had ties to larger gambling syndicates. Other saloon keepers, while sometimes taking important but backstage political positions such as ward committeeman, developed the gambling syndicates. Handbooks required up-to-the-minute information from race tracks across the country. By establishing poolrooms from which information was distributed to individual handbooks, a single individual could control and share in the profits of dozens or even hundreds of handbooks.

The Irish also predominated in other areas of gambling. At the turn of the century they were the major group in the syndicates that operated the policy games, each with hundreds of policy writers scattered in the slum neighborhoods to collect the nickels and dimes of the poor who dreamed of a lucky hit. They also outfitted many of the gambling houses in the Loop which offered roulette, faro, poker, blackjack, craps and other games of chance. Furthermore, many top police officers were Irish and rose through the ranks by attaching themselves to the various political factions of the city. Hence a complex system of Irish politicians, gamblers and police shared in the profits of gambling, protected gambling interests and built careers in the police department or city politics. Historians have long recognized the importance of the Irish in urban politics. In Chicago, at any rate, politics was only part of a larger Irish politics-gambling complex.

The Irish politics-gambling complex remained intact until about World War I. By the 1920s, however, the developing black ghetto allowed black politicians and policy operators to build independent gambling and political organizations linked to the Republicans in the 1920s and the Democratic city machine in the 1930s. By the 1920s, in addition, Jewish gamblers became increasingly important, both in the control of gambling in Jewish neighborhoods and in operations elsewhere. Finally, by the mid-1920s, Italian bootleggers under Capone took over gambling in suburban Cicero and invested in Chicago gambling operations. Gambling had become a complex mixture of Irish, Negro, Jewish and Italian entrepreneurship.

Although the Irish by the twentieth century played little direct role in managing prostitution, Italians by World War I had moved into important positions in the vice districts, especially in the notorious Levee district on the South Side. (Political protection, of course, often had to be arranged through Irish political leaders.) Just as the Irish blocked Italians in politics, so also they blocked Italians in gambling, which was both more respectable and more profitable than prostitution. Hence the importance of prohibition in the 1920s lay not in initiating organized crime (gambling continued both before and after prohibition to be the major enterprise of organized crime); rather, prohibition provided Italians with an opportunity to break into a major field of organized crime that was not already monopolized by the Irish.

This generalization, to some extent, oversimplifies what was in fact a complex process. At first, prohibition opened up business opportunities for large numbers of individuals and groups, and the situation was chaotic. By 1924, however, shifting coalitions had emerged. Some bootlegging gangs were Irish, including one set of O'Donnell brothers on the far West Side and another set on the South Side. Southwest of the stockyards, there was an important organization, both Polish and Irish, coordinated by "Pollack" Joe Saltis. And on the Near North Side a major group—founded by burglars and hold-up men—was led by Irishmen . . . and Jews. . . . There were, finally, the various Italian gangs, including the Gennas, the Aiellos, and, of course, the Capone organization.

The major Italian bootlegging gang, that associated with the name of Al Capone, built upon roots already established in the South Side vice district. There John Torrio managed houses of prostitution for Big Jim Colossimo. With Colossimo's assassination in 1920, Torrio and his assistant, Capone, moved rapidly to establish a bootlegging syndicate in the Loop and in the suburbs south and west of the city. Many of their associates were persons whom they had known during humbler days in the South Side vice district and who now rose to wealth with them. Nor was their organization entirely Italian. Very early, they worked closely with Irishmen like Frankie Lake and Terry Druggan in the brewing of beer, while Jake Guzik, a Jew and former South Side pimp, became the chief business manager for the syndicate. In the bloody bootlegging wars of the 1920s, the members of the Capone organization gradually emerged as the most effective organizers and most deadly fighters. The success of the organization brought wealth and power to many ambitious Italians and provided them with the means in the late 1920s and early 1930s to move into gambling, racketeering and entertainment, as well as into a broad range of legitimate enterprises. Bootlegging allowed Italians, through entrepreneurial skills and by assassination of rivals, to gain a central position in the organized underworld of the city.

Although Jewish immigrants in such cities as Cleveland and Philadelphia were major figures in bootlegging and thus showed patterns similar to Italians in Chicago, Jews in Chicago were somewhat peripheral figures. By World War I, Chicago Jews, like Italians, made important inroads into vice, especially in vice districts on the West Side. In the 1920s, with the dispersal of prostitution, several Jewish vice syndicates operated on the South and West Sides. Jews were also rapidly invading the world of gambling. Although Jews took part in vice, gambling and bootlegging, they made a special contribution to the organized underworld by providing professional or expert services. Even before World War I, Jews were becoming a majority of the bailbondsmen in the city. By the 1920s, if not before, Jews constituted over half the fences who disposed of stolen goods. (This was, of course, closely related to Jewish predominance as junk dealers and their importance in retail selling.) Jews were also heavily overrepresented among defense attorneys in the criminal courts. It is unnecessary to emphasize that the entrepreneurial and professional services of Jews reflected broader patterns of adaptation to American urban life.

Even within relatively minor underworld positions, specialization by ethnicity was important. A study of three hundred Chicago pimps in the early 1920s, for instance, found that 109 (more than one-third) were black, 60 were Italian, 47 Jewish and 26 Greek. The large proportion of blacks suggests that the high prestige of the pimp among some elements of the lower-class black community is not a recent development but has a relatively long tradition in the urban slum. There has, in fact, long been a close relationship of vice activities and Negro life in the cities. In all probability, the vice districts constituted the most integrated aspect of Chicago society. Black pimps and madams occasionally had white girls working for them, just as white pimps and madams sometimes had black girls working for them. In addition, blacks held many of the jobs in the vice districts, ranging from maids to entertainers. The location of major areas of vice and entertainment around the periphery and along the main business streets of the South Side black neighborhood gave such activities a pervasive influence within the neighborhood.

Black achievements in ragtime and jazz had their roots, at least in part, in the vice and entertainment districts of the cities. Much of the early history of jazz lies among the talented musicians—black and white—who performed in the famous resorts in the Storyville district of New Orleans in the 1890s and early 1900s. With the dissolution of Storyville as a segregated vice district, many talented black musicians carried their styles to Chicago's South Side, to Harlem, and to the cabarets and dance halls of other major cities. In the 1920s, with black performers like King Oliver and Louis Armstrong and white performers like Bix Beiderbecke, Chicago was an important environment for development of jazz styles. Just as Harlem became a center for entertainment and jazz for New Yorkers during prohibition, so the black and tan cabarets and speakeasies of Chicago's South Side became a place where blacks and whites drank, danced and listened to jazz music—to the shock of many respectable citizens. Thus, in ways that were both destructive and productive, the black experience in the city was linked to the opportunities that lay in the vice resorts, cabarets and dance halls of the teeming slums. In the operation of entertainment facilities and policy rackets, black entrepreneurs found their major outlet and black politicians found their chief support.

Until there has been more study of comparative ethnic patterns, only tentative hypotheses are possible to explain why various ethnic groups followed differing patterns. Because many persons involved in organized crime initiated their careers with customers from their own neighborhood or ethnic group, the degree to which a particular ethnic group sought a particular illegal service would influence opportunities for criminal activities. If members of an ethnic group did not gamble, for instance, then ambitious members of that ethnic group could not build gambling syndicates based upon local roots. The general attitude toward law and law enforcement, too, would affect opportunities for careers in illegal ventures. Those groups that became most heavily involved in organized crime migrated from regions in which they had developed deep suspicions of government authority—whether the Irish fleeing British rule in Ireland, Jews escaping from Eastern Europe, Italians migrating from southern Italy or Sicily, or blacks leaving the American South. Within a community suspicious of courts and government officials, a person in trouble with the law could retain roots and even respect in the community. Within a community more oriented toward upholding legal authority, on the other hand, those engaged in illegal activities risked ostracism and loss of community roots.

In other ways, too, ethnic life styles evolved differently. Among both Germans and Irish, for instance, friendly drinking was part of the pattern of relaxation. Although the Irish and Germans by 1900 were the major managers of Chicago's saloons, the meaning of the saloon was quite different for the two groups. German saloons and beer gardens were sometimes for family entertainment and generally excluded gambling or prostitution; Irish saloons, part of an exclusively male social life, often featured prostitution or gambling and fit more easily into the world of entertainment associated with organized crime. Finally, it appears that south Italians had the highest homicide rate in Europe. There was, in all probability, a relationship between the cultural factors that sanctioned violence and private revenge in Europe and the factors that sanctioned the violence with which Italian bootleggers worked their way into a central position in Chicago's organized crime.

There were, at any rate, many ways that the immigrant background and the urban environment interacted to influence the ethnic experience with organized crime. For some ethnic groups, involvement in organized crime was not an important part of the adjustment to American urban life. For other groups, involvement in the organized underworld both reflected and influenced their relatively unique patterns of acculturation.

Economic Impact

The economic role of organized crime was an additional factor underlying the impact of organized crime upon ethnic communities and urban society. Organized crime was important because of the relatively great wealth of the most successful criminals, because of the large numbers of persons directly employed by organized crime, and because of the still larger numbers who supplemented their income through various part-time activities. And all of this does not count the multitude of customers who bought the goods and services offered by the bootleggers, gambling operators and vice lords of the city.

During the first thirty or forty years after an immigrant group's arrival, successful leaders in organized crime might constitute a disproportionate percentage of the most wealthy members of the community. (In the 1930s at least one-half of the blacks in Chicago worth more than $100,000 were policy kings; Italian bootleggers in the 1920s may have represented an even larger proportion of the very wealthy among immigrants from southern Italy. The wealth of the successful criminals was accompanied by extensive political and other contacts that gave them considerable leverage both within and outside the ethnic community. They had financial resources to engage in extensive charitable activities, and often did so lavishly. Projects for improvement of ethnic communities often needed their support and contacts in order to succeed. Criminals often invested in or managed legitimate business enterprises in their communities. Hence, despite ambiguous or even antagonistic relations that they had with "respectable" members of their ethnic communities, successful leaders in organized crime were men who had to be reckoned with in the ethnic community and who often represented the community to the outside world.

In organized crime, as in other economic activities, the very successful were but a minority. To understand the economic impact of crime, it is necessary to study the many persons at the middle and lower levels of organization. In cities like Chicago the number of persons directly employed in the activities of organized crime was considerable. A modest estimate of the number of fulltime prostitutes in Chicago about 1910 would be 15,000—not counting madams, pimps, procurers and others in managerial positions. Or take the policy racket. In the early 1930s an average policy wheel in the black ghetto employed 300 writers; some employed as many as 600; and there were perhaps 6,000 policy writers in the ghetto. The policy wheels, in this period of heavy unemployment, may have been the major single source of employment in the black ghetto, a source of employment that did not need to lay off workers or reduce wages merely because the rest of the economy faced a major depression. Finally, during the 1920s, bootlegging in its various aspects was a major economic activity employing thousands in manufacture, transportation and retailing activities.

Yet persons directly employed constituted only a small proportion of those whose income derived from organized crime. Many persons supplemented their income through occasional or parttime services. While some prostitutes walked the streets to advertise their wares, others relied upon intermediaries who would direct customers in return for a finder's fee. During certain periods, payments to taxi drivers were sufficiently lucrative so that some taxi drivers would pick up only those passengers seeking a house of prostitution. Bellboys, especially in the second-class hotels, found the function of negotiating between guests and prostitutes a profitable part of their service.

(Many of the worst hotels, of course, functioned partly or wholly as places of assignation.) Bartenders, newsboys and waiters were among the many helpful persons who provided information concerning places and prices.

Various phases of bootlegging during the 1920s were even more important as income supplements. In the production end, many slum families prepared wine or became "alky cookers" for the bootlegging gangs—so much so that after the mid-1920s, explosions of stills and the resulting fires were a major hazard in Chicago's slum neighborhoods. As one observer reported:

During prohibition times many respectable Sicilian men were employed as "alky cookers" for the Capone's, the Aiello's or for personal use. Many of these people sold wine during prohibition and their children delivered it on foot or by streetcar without the least fear that they might be arrested. . . .
During the years of 1927 to 1930 more wine was made than during any other years and even the "poorest people" were able to make ten or fifteen barrels each year—others making sixty, seventy, or more barrels.

Other persons, including policemen, moonlighted as truck drivers who delivered booze to the many retail outlets of the city. Finally, numerous persons supplemented their income by retailing booze, including bellboys, janitors in apartment buildings and shoe shine boys.

The many persons who mediated between the underworld and the law were another group that supplemented its income through underworld contacts. Large numbers of policemen, as well as bailiffs, judges and political fixers, received bribes or political contributions in return for illegal cooperation with the underworld. Defense attorneys, tax accountants and bailbondsmen, in return for salaries or fees, provided expert services that were generally legal.

For many of the small businessmen of the city, retailing the goods or services of the underworld could supplement business income significantly. Saloons, as already mentioned, often provided gambling and prostitution as an additional service to customers. Large numbers of small businesses were outlets for handbooks, policy, baseball pools, slot machines and other forms of gambling. A substantial proportion of the cigar stores, for example, were primarily fronts for gambling; barber shops, pool halls, newsstands, and small hotels frequently sold policy or would take bets on the horses. Drug stores often served as outlets for cocaine and, during the 1920s, sometimes sold liquor.

The organized underworld also influenced business activity through racketeering. A substantial minority of the city's labor unions were racketeer-controlled; those that were not often used the assistance of racketeer unions or of strongarm gangs during strikes. The leaders of organized crime, as a result, exercised control or influence in the world of organized labor. Not so well known was the extensive racketeering that characterized small business organizations. The small businesses of the city were generally marginal and intensely competitive. To avoid cutthroat competition, businessmen often formed associations to make and enforce regulations illegally limiting competition. The Master Barbers Association, for example, set minimum prices, forbad a shop to be open after 7:30 P.M., and ruled that no shop could be established within two blocks of another shop. Many other types of small businesses formed similar associations: dairies, auto parts dealers, garage owners, candy jobbers, butcher stores, fish wholesalers and retailers, cleaners and dyers, and junk dealers. Many of the associations were controlled, or even organized, by racketeers who levied dues upon association members and controlled the treasuries; they then used a system of fines and violence to insure that all businessmen in the trade joined the association and abided by the regulations. In return for control of the association's treasury, in short, racketeers performed illegal services for the association and thereby regulated much of the small business activity of the city.

Discussion of the economic influence of organized crime would be incomplete without mentioning the largest group that was tied economically to the underworld, namely, the many customers for the illegal goods and services. Like other retailers in the city, some leaders of organized crime located their outlets near the center of the city or along major transportation lines and serviced customers from the entire region; others were essentially neighborhood businessmen with a local clientele. In either case, those providing illegal goods and services usually attempted to cultivate customer loyalty so that the same customers would return on an ongoing basis and advertise among their friends. Organized crime existed because of wide customer demand, and a large proportion of the adult population of the city was linked to organized crime on a regular basis for purchase of goods and services.

Heroism and Ambiguity

Because of the diverse ways that successful criminal entrepreneurs influenced the city and ethnic communities, many of them became heroes—especially within their own communities. There were a variety of reasons for the admiration that they received. Their numerous philanthropies, both large and small, won them reputations as regular guys who would help a person in need. Moreover, they were often seen as persons who fought for their ethnic communities. They aided politicians from their communities to win elections in the rough and often violent politics of the slums and thereby advanced their ethnic group toward political recognition. Sometimes they were seen as fighters for labor unions and thus as friends of labor. And, on occasion, they fought directly for their ethnic group. There was, for instance, the case of the three Miller brothers from Chicago's West Side Jewish ghetto. In typical

ghetto pattern, one became a boxer, one a gangster and one a policeman. The boxer and gangster were heroes among Jews on the West Side, where for many years Jewish peddlers and junk dealers had been subjected to racial slurs and violent attacks by young hoodlums from other ethnic groups. "What I have done from the time I was a boy," Davy Miller told a reporter,

was to fight for my people here in the Ghetto against Irish, Poles or any other nationality. It was sidewalk fighting at first. I could lick any five boys or men in a sidewalk free-for-all.

When the Miller brothers and their gang protected the Jews of the West Side, the attacks against them abated.

Particularly for youngsters growing up in the ghettos, the gangsters were often heroes whose exploit were admired and copied. Davy Miller modestly recognized this when he said:

Maybe I am a hero to the young folks among my people, but it's not because I'm a gangster. It's because I've always been ready to help all or any of them in a pinch.

An Italian student at the University of Chicago in the early 1930s remembered his earlier life in the Italian ghetto:

For 26 years I lived in West Side "Little Italy," the community that has produced more underworld limelights than any other area in Chicago. . . .

I remember these men in large cars, with boys and girls of the neighborhood standing on the running board. I saw them come into the neighborhood in splendor as heroes. Many times they showered handfuls of silver to youngsters who waited to get a glance at them—the new heroes—because they had just made headlines in the newspapers. Since then I have seen many of my playmates shoot their way to the top of gangdom and seen others taken for a ride.

Nevertheless, despite the importance of gangsters and the world within which they moved, their relations to ethnic groups and the city were always ambiguous. Because many of their activities were illegal, they often faced the threat of arrest and, contrary to common belief, frequently found themselves behind bars. Furthermore, for those members of the ethnic community who pursued respectable paths to success, gangsters gave the ethnic group a bad name and remained a continuing source of embarrassment. St. Clair Drake and Horace R. Cayton, in their book on the Chicago black ghetto, describe the highly ambiguous and often antagonistic relations of the respectable black middle class and the policy kings. In his book on Italians in Chicago, Humbert S. Nelli explains that in the 1920s the Italian language press refused to print the name of Al Capone and covered the St. Valentine's Day massacre without suggesting its connection with bootlegging wars.

The respectable middle classes, however, were not the only ones unhappy about the activities or notoriety of gangsters. Organized crime sometimes contributed to the violence and fear of violence that pervaded many of the ghetto neighborhoods. Often local residents feared to turn to the police and lived with a stoical acceptance that gangs of toughs controlled elections, extorted money from local businesses and generally lived outside the reach of the law. Some immigrant parents, too, resented the numerous saloons, the open prostitution and the many gambling dens—all of which created a morally dangerous environment in which to raise children. Especially immigrant women, who watched their husbands squander the meager family income on liquor or gambling, resented the activities of organized crime. Within a number of neighborhoods, local churches and local leaders undertook sporadic campaigns for better law enforcement.

Organized crime, then, was an important part of the complex social structure of ethnic communities and urban society in the early twentieth century. For certain ethnic groups, organized crime both influenced and reflected the special patterns by which the groups adjusted to life in urban America. Through organized crime, many members of those ethnic groups could achieve mobility out of the ethnic ghettos and into the social world of crime, politics, ethnic business, sports, and entertainment. Those who were successful in organized crime possessed the wealth and contacts to exercise broad influence within the ethnic communities and the city. The economic activities of the underworld provided jobs or supplemental income for tens of thousands. Despite the importance of organized crime, however, individual gangsters often found success to be ambiguous. They were not always able to achieve secure positions or to translate their positions into respectability.

■ ■ ■

STUDY QUESTIONS

1. What were the primary occupational paths out of the ghetto for uneducated but ambitious ethnic youths? How were the paths interrelated?

2. How did organized crime exert influence upon other social worlds? What in particular was the relationship between organized crime and urban politics?

3. What social values did criminals share with the leaders in politics, sports, labor unions, entertainment, and business? What was the attitude of the men in these professions toward law and legal institutions?

4. What does Haller mean by "ethnic specialization" in crime? What factors account for the criminal specialization of the different ethnic groups?

5. What was the economic impact of organized crime on the ethnic and urban environment?

6. Why did a number of criminals become ethnic heroes? What role did the "criminal heroes" play in their ethnic neighborhoods?

BIBLIOGRAPHY

Because of the secretive nature of organized crime, it has proven an elusive subject for scholars. Nevertheless historians and sociologists have produced several valuable studies. Andrew Sinclair, *Prohibition: The Era of Excess* (1962), examines the impact of the Eighteenth Amendment on the rise of organized crime. Humbert S. Nelli, *The Italians in Chicago, 1880–1930: A Study in Ethnic Mobility* (1970), and *The Business of Crime* (1976) deal admirably with the subject of ethnic crime. John A. Gardiner, *The Politics of Corruption: Organized Crime in the American City* (1970), is also valuable. William F. Whyte, *Street Corner Society: The Social Structure of an Italian Slum* (1955), is a classic sociological study of an ethnic urban environment. Finally, Daniel Bell, *The End of Ideology* (1961), considers crime as a means of social and economic mobility.

Part Five

DEPRESSION AND WAR

Despite all the talk about prosperity and progress in the 1920s, there were disturbing signs that the economy was not as healthy as people assumed. Throughout the decade agricultural prices steadily declined as production rose, in what many called a "poverty of abundance." In face of high protective tariffs, foreign trade gradually declined and the production of durable, domestic goods peaked in 1927. When the bubble burst with the crash of the stock market in October 1929, most Americans were shocked. The shock soon turned to despair as banks failed in record numbers, small businesses closed their doors, and unemployment reached unheard-of levels. How could it have been? For three centuries the world viewed America as the land of opportunity. Suddenly, people were losing their jobs, homes, and life savings. The American dream had become a nightmare.

Bewildered with their plight, most Americans were desperate for answers. Socialists and communists blamed capitalism, arguing that, just as Karl Marx had predicted, the system was collapsing under the weight of its own corruption and exploitation. The technocrats claimed that industrialization had run its course and that a new social order, based on science and technology, would soon emerge out of the rubble of the depression. Businessmen blamed politicians for the trouble. Farmers saw bogeymen in bankers and commodities speculators. Some Americans even blamed Jews for the collapse. Abandoning laissez-faire economics, Hoover modestly tried to reorganize the federal government to fight the depression, but his efforts failed. In the next presidential election Americans put Franklin D. Roosevelt into the White House.

Roosevelt was an unlikely hero for an impoverished nation. Born to old wealth and raised in splendor, he had little understanding of economics and no empathy for

poverty. But he did have keen political instincts and few philosophical inhibitions. In a whirlwind of activity, the New Deal greatly increased relief spending, attacked specific problems in the money markets, and tried, usually in a haphazard way, to stimulate an industrial recovery. Although it took World War II to finally lift the country out of the depression, Franklin D. Roosevelt nevertheless became one of the most beloved presidents in American history, popular enough to win reelection in 1936, 1940, and 1944. People remembered him for the spark in his eye, his smiling face and cocked head, and his uncompromising exuberance. To men working on government projects, it was Roosevelt who took them away from the soup lines. To farm wives living in poverty, it was Roosevelt who brought the electric transmission lines, the subsidy check, and the refinanced mortgage. To mass production workers, it was Roosevelt who sanctioned their labor unions and brought minimum wages. And to old people, it was Roosevelt who provided for their futures with Social Security.

But just as Roosevelt was easing fears about the economic future, political developments in Europe were bringing new tensions to a weary nation. Adolf Hitler's designs on Austria, Czechoslovakia, and Poland in 1938 and 1939 convinced many that another war was imminent and that the problems of the depression, as bad as they were, would only be child's play compared to a new global conflagration. Hitler's conquest of France and the Low Countries in 1940, the assault on Great Britain, and the invasion of the Soviet Union in 1941 only confirmed those fears. For a brief time, the United States was caught between its historic need for isolation and its responsibilities as a global leader. On December 7, 1941, Japan resolved America's uncertain position.

F.D.R.'s EXTRA BURDEN

Bernard Asbell

When President Franklin D. Roosevelt collapsed and died of a stroke on April 12, 1945, the nation went into a state of depression unknown since the death of Abraham Lincoln. Like Lincoln, Roosevelt had become inseparably linked with a series of national crises—in his case the Great Depression and World War II. And like Lincoln, Roosevelt was viewed as a savior, a man who had redeemed his people, first from starvation and then from the spector of fascist oppression. Put simply, FDR enjoyed the elusive charisma so prized by politicians. Blessed with enormous self-confidence and an ingratiating personality, he inspired tremendous loyalty among most Americans. They loved him and put him in the White House on four separate occasions—1932, 1936, 1940, and 1944. But like all charismatic leaders, Roosevelt also generated tremendous hostility in some circles, particularly in corporate boardrooms and the parlors of the well-to-do. They viewed him as a "traitor to his class," a politician so seduced by power that he posed a threat to property and the social order.

Franklin D. Roosevelt was a complicated man, a beloved acquaintance of thousands but an intimate of very few. Born rich and raised in pampered splendor, he nevertheless led a virtual revolution in public policy, giving ethnic minorities, labor unions, and poor people their first taste of influence at the federal level. Although Roosevelt inspired a legion of intellectuals to invest their energies in public service, he was not an innovative thinker himself. He preferred the give and take of politics, and the inherent excitement of its risks, to the intricate nuts and bolts of social and economic policy. His public persona was overwhelming, but there was also a private side to his life that the American people understood only superficially. During the summer of 1921, little more than a decade before he became president, Roosevelt contracted polio, or infantile paralysis, a disease that crippled him for the rest of his life. In "F.D.R.'s Extra Burden," Bernard Asbell describes that paralysis and how Roosevelt, the press, and the nation handled it.

Every campaigner, especially for leadership of a large and complex state or for national office, is a cripple.

His legs are bound against running faster than his constituents are able to keep in step. His hands are tied by the limited powers of the office he seeks; he had better not promise what he knows he cannot deliver. His tongue is gagged against pronouncements that may make new friends if those pronouncements will also make new enemies. His balance is threatened by the pulls and tugs of conflicting demands for justice—shall money go for this urgent need or that one?—shall this group's freedom be expanded at the expense of that one's?

Immobilized by these paralyzing constraints, the candidate has to make himself appear able-bodied, attractive, confident, and powerful. At least more so than his opponent.

Being crippled—not in metaphor, but in reality—is perhaps good schooling for politics.

To this day, more than a quarter century after his death, people keep wondering aloud and speculating, "If Roosevelt had not been a cripple, would he have been the same kind of President?" Of course not. "If a different kind, how?" Impossible to say. "If he had not been a cripple, would he have become President at all?" Again, imponderable.

Did F.D.R.'s private battle teach him to identify with those who suffer? Unquestionably. Moreover it taught him the uses of patience (never a strong suit with crusaders who relied upon him, upon whom he relied, yet who continually harassed him). It heightened his sense of time and timing. "It made him realize"—an observation of Egbert Curtis, a Warm Springs companion—"that he was not infallible, that everything wasn't always going to go his way." More than anything, it forced him to study the uses of handicap, paradoxically giving him a leg up in a profession of able-bodied crippled men.

Let's not carry theory and speculation too far. Instead, let's try to observe firsthand, insofar as the written word permits, the connections between suffering and Roosevelt's acquired capacity for patience, for tolerance and respect of the wills and ambitions of others, for turning handicap into power.

We begin with his own words. A sufferer identifies with sufferers; and "Doctor" Roosevelt of Warm Springs also identified with other doctors. In F.D.R's early days at Warm Springs a South Carolina physician wrote to Roosevelt for a personal case report that might help him treat any polio patients who came his way. Roosevelt's reply is the only detailed personal account of what he had recently endured. The letter, dictated to Missy LeHand, his private secretary, during their first stay at Warm Springs, says in part:

. . . I am very gllad to tell you what I can in regard to my case and as I have talked it over with a great many doctors can, I think, give you a history of the case which would be equal to theirs.

First symptoms of the illness appeared in August, 1921. . . . By the end of the third day practically all muscles from the chest down were involved. Above the chest the only symptom was a weakening of the two large thumb muscles making it impossible to write. There was no special pain along the spine and no rigidity of the neck.

For the following two weeks I had to be catheterized and there was slight, though not severe, difficulty in controlling the bowels. The fever lasted for only 6 or 7 days, but all the muscles from the hips down were extremely sensitive to the touch and I had to have the knees supported by pillows. This condition of extreme discomfort lasted about 3 weeks . . . [but] disappeared gradually over a period of six months, the last remaining point being the calf muscles.

As to treatment—the mistake was made for the

"F.D.R.'s Extra Burden" by Bernard Asbell, from *American Heritage* (June, 1973). Reprinted by permission of Curtis Brown, Ltd. Copyright © 1973 by Bernard Asbell.

first 10 days of giving my feet and lower legs rather heavy massage. This was stopped by Dr. Lovett, of Boston, who was, without doubt, the greatest specialist on infantile paralysis. In January, 1922, 5 months after the attack, he found that the muscles behind the knees had contracted and that there was a tendency to footdrop in the right foot. These were corrected by the use of plaster casts during two weeks. In February, 1922, braces were fitted on each leg from the hips to the shoes, and I was able to stand up and learned gradually to walk with crutches. At the same time gentle exercises were begun, first every other day, then daily, exercising each muscle 10 times and seeking to avoid any undue strain by giving each muscle the correct movement with gravity. These exercises I did on a board placed on the bed.

The recovery of muscle paralysis began at this time, though for many months it seemed to make little progress. In the summer of 1922 I began swimming and found that this exercise seemed better adapted than any other because all weight was removed from the legs and I was able to move the legs in the water far better than I had expected. . . .

I still wear braces, of course, because the quadriceps are not yet strong enough to bear my weight. One year ago I was able to stand in fresh water without braces when the water was up to my chin. Six months ago I could stand in water up to the top of my shoulders and today can stand in water just level with my arm pits. This is a very simple method for me of determining how fast the quadriceps are coming back. Aside from these muscles the waist muscles on the right side are still weak and the outside muscles on the right leg have strengthened so much more than the inside muscles that they pull my right foot forward. I continue corrective exercises for all the muscles.

To sum up I would give you the following "Don'ts":

Don't use heavy massage but use light massage rubbing always towards the heart.

Don't let the patient over-exercise any muscle or get tired.

Don't let the patient feel cold, especially the legs, feet or any other part affected. Progress stops entirely when the legs or feet are cold.

Don't let the patient get too fat.

The following treatment is so far the best, judging from my own experience and that of hundreds of other cases which I have studied:

1. Gentle exercise especially for the muscles which seem to be worst affected.

2. Gentle skin rubbing—not muscle kneading— bearing in mind that good circulation is a prime requisite.

3. Swimming in warm water—lots of it.

4. Sunlight—all the patient can get, especially direct sunlight on the affected parts. It would be ideal to lie in the sun all day with nothing on. This is difficult to accomplish but the nearest approach to it is a bathing suit.

5. Belief on the patient's part that the muscles are coming back and will eventually regain recovery of the affected parts. There are cases known in Norway where adults have taken the disease and not been able to walk until after a lapse of 10 or even 12 years.

I hope that your patient has not got a very severe case. They all differ, of course, in the degree in which the parts are affected. If braces are necessary there is a man in New York . . . who makes remarkable light braces of duraluminum. My first braces of steel weighed 7 lbs. apiece—my new ones weigh only 4 lbs. apiece. Remember that braces are only for the convenience of the patient in getting around—a leg in a brace does not have a chance for muscle development. This muscle development must come through exercise when the brace is not on—such as swimming, etc.

At Hyde Park, before discovering Warm Springs, this powerful man, to the shock of his children and friends, practiced dragging himself crablike across the floor, explaining that the one fear he ever knew was that of being caught in a fire. Then, showing off his inordinately strong shoulders and arms, he filled the house with laughter, wrestling his boys on the floor two at a time. His mother ordered an electric tricycle from Europe, but F.D.R. used it only once. He didn't want his muscles worked;

he wanted to work them himself.

John Gunther describes Roosevelt's determination to get from floor to floor unaided: "Day after day he would haul his dead body weight up the stairs by the power of his hands and arms, step by step, slowly, doggedly; the sweat would pour off his face, and he would tremble with exhaustion. Moreover he insisted on doing this with members of the family or friends watching him, and he would talk all the time as he inched himself up little by little, talk, talk, and make people talk back. It was a kind of enormous spiritual catharsis—as if he had to do it, to prove his independence, and had to have the feat witnessed, to prove that it was nothing."

At Warm Springs in 1924 he concentrated on the day he would be able to walk unaided with braces. Braces, which he once said he "hated and mistrusted," which he could not put on or take off by himself, made him like a man on stilts. Unable to flex his toes, he had no balance. In 1928, after seven years of immobility and more than four years of daring and persevering, one day, finally, triumphantly, he hobbled most of the way across the living-room floor of his cottage—with braces, but without human help. The achievement was exhausting—and was never to be accomplished again. Years later, according to Grace Tully, "Missy's eyes filled up when on occasions she reminisced about those days." Roosevelt liked to maintain the belief that if he had had another year before the demand that he run for governor, he'd have mastered walking with a single brace.

In the summer of 1928 at Warm Springs, shortly after Roosevelt agreed to address the Democratic National Convention at Houston, son Elliott, eighteen, was visiting. One evening Roosevelt was lost in concentrated thought when suddenly he burst out:

"With my hand on a man's arm, *and one cane*—I'm sure. Let's try it!"

A fellow polio victim, Turnley Walker, Roosevelt's dinner guest, described what then

A 1924 photo of FDR taken three years after he was stricken with polio, shows him standing with crutches and leg braces. In later years, as governor of New York and president of the United States, he was rarely photographed in a full-length view.

happened and was repeated over and over:

First Roosevelt would get over to the wall and balance there with his cane. It was an ordinary cane but he held it in a special way, with his index finger extended down along the rod from the handle. This finger acted as a rigid cleat . . . so that the strength of the massive arm and shoulder rammed straight along the cane to its tip against the floor.

"Now, Elliott, you get on the left, my weak side." Elliott watchfully took his place and [Helena] Mahoney [a physiotherapist] came forward to show him how to hold his right arm against his middle at the proper angle and lock it there with a clenching of his biceps.

"Remember that a polio needs more than a fingertip of guidance—he needs an iron bar," said Mahoney, "Make a habit of holding that arm

there. *Never forget the job it's got to do."*

"Let's go," said Roosevelt, and he reached out to find the proper grip. *Elliott had never felt his father's hand touching him that way. He had been grabbed and hugged, and even tossed and caught with wild energy when he was younger. But now the fingers sought their grip with a kind of ruthless desperation. . . . The pressure became stronger than he had expected as his father pressed down to hitch one braced leg forward for the first step.* "You must go right with him," *said Mahoney sternly.* "Watch his feet. Match your strides with his." *Elliott stared down as the rigid feet swung out slowly, and through the pressing hand he could feel the slow, clenching effort of his father's powerful body.*

"Don't look at me, Son. Keep your head up, smiling, watching the eyes of people. Keep them from noticing what we're doing."

The cane went out, the good leg swung, the pressure came, the weak leg hitched up into its arc and then fell stiffly into the proper place against the floor. Elliott carefully coordinated his own legs, and they moved across the room.

Roosevelt set his hips against the far wall and told Elliott to rest his arm. "We'll do beautifully," *he said.*

They went across the room and back again. It was becoming somewhat easier.

"As soon as you feel confident, Son, look up and around at people, the way you would do if I weren't crippled."

"But don't forget," Mahoney warned, *"if he loses his balance, he'll crash down like a tree."*

"Don't scare us," said Roosevelt.

. . . The cane, the swing, the pressure, the swing. Elliott found that he could look up now and then as they advanced. He caught his father's eyes, the broad smile which was held with a very slight rigidity. . . . Only then did he notice that his father was perspiring heavily.

Yet except when a public show required such extraordinary exertion, Roosevelt was as helpless as a baby. When no strangers were around to see, he let himself be carried by practiced attendants. When F.D.R. became gover-

nor, his cousin Nicholas Roosevelt spent a weekend at Hyde Park and later recalled: "His mother and I stood on the veranda watching his son Elliott and Gus Gennerich, the state trooper who acted as his personal bodyguard, carry him down the steps and place him in the car. As they turned and left him, he lost his balance (his powerful torso was much heavier than his crippled legs), and he fell over on the car seat. I doubt if one man in a thousand as disabled and dependent on others would have refrained from some sort of reproach, however mild, to those whose carelessness had thus left him in the lurch. But Franklin merely lay on his back, waved his strong arms in the air and laughed. At once they came back and helped him to his seat behind the wheel, and he called me to join him."

Louis Howe, F.D.R.'s indispensable factotum, set an iron rule—one that F.D.R. was not inclined to resist—that he never be carried in public.

Frances Perkins remembered the gubernatorial campaign.

I saw him speak in a small hall in New York City's Yorkville district. The auditorium was crowded. . . . The only possible way for any candidate to enter the stage without being crushed by the throng was by the fire escape. I realized with sudden horror that the only way he could get over that fire escape was in the arms of strong men. That was how he arrived.

Those of us who saw this incident, with our hands on our throats to hold down our emotion, realized that this man had accepted the ultimate humility which comes from being helped physically. . . . He got up on his braces, adjusted them, straightened himself, smoothed his hair, linked his arm in his son Jim's, and walked out on the platform as if this were nothing unusual. . . . I began to see what the great teachers of religion meant when they said that humility is the greatest of virtues, and that if you can't learn it, God will teach it to you by humiliation.

Was humility—or humiliation—Roosevelt's

great teacher? Many have speculated. Harold Ickes, after a day in a campaign car with press secretary Steve Early:

"[Early] recalled the campaign trips that he had made with Roosevelt when the latter was a candidate for Vice President in 1920. He said that if it hadn't been for the President's affliction, he never would have been President of the United States. In those earlier years, as Steve put it, the President was just a playboy. . . . He couldn't be made to prepare his speeches in advance, preferring to play cards instead. During his long illness, according to Steve, the President began to read deeply and study public questions."

Perkins: ". . . He had become conscious of other people, of weak people, of human frailty. I remember thinking that he would never be so hard and harsh in judgment on stupid people—even on wrongdoers. . . . I remember watching him [as governor] in Utica. . . . Certainly some of the Democratic rank-and-file were pretty tiresome, with a lot of things to say that were of no consequence. However, he sat and nodded and smiled and said, 'That's fine,' when they reported some slight progress. I remembered, in contrast, how he had walked away from bores a few years earlier when he was in the State Senate.

"Now he could not walk away when he was bored. He listened, and out of it learned . . . that 'everybody wants to have the sense of belonging, of being on the inside,' that 'no one wants to be left out,' as he put it years later in a Columbus, Ohio, speech. . . ."

A considerably more speculative observation by Noel F. Busch, childhood neighbor of the Oyster Bay Roosevelts who grew up to be a *Time* correspondent and avid F.D.R.-watcher: "Loss of the use of one's legs has several effects on the human psyche. One is that, when deprived of the power to move around, the mind demands a substitute or compensation for this power, such as the ability to command other people to move around. That is why almost all invalids tend to be peevish and

demanding. However . . . Roosevelt sublimated and refined the pardonable peevishness of the normal invalid into an administrative urge which would have had profound consequences for him even if he had never become President."

Biographer Emil Ludwig: "The privilege of remaining seated, which everyone concedes him because of his affliction, starts him off with an advantage in his intercourse with others, in the same way as the smallness of Napoleon's stature compelled everyone standing before him to bend his back a little. Certainly giants like Bismarck or Lincoln had an advantage when they appeared before men, but the same effect can be produced by the opposite, by a weakness, and as Roosevelt looks up at everyone standing in front of him, he has accustomed himself to an upward and therefore very energetic gesture of the chin which counteracts the danger of his conciliatory smile."

While never mentioning his paralysis in public (until his last speech to Congress in 1945) and seldom privately, F.D.R. could come down fiercely on those he felt mentioned it unfairly. Huey Long's tapping a straw hat on the useless Presidential knee he could take as bad manners—the other fellow's problem, not his. But when Fulton Oursler brought him a manuscript of a profile of F.D.R. by Jay Franklin to be published in *Liberty*—the editor courteously seeking F.D.R.'s reaction—Oursler saw "a red flush rise on his neck like the temperature in a thermometer." Assuming that Roosevelt was angered over some political needling, he learned otherwise:

"Mr. Oursler, there is only one statement in this article that I want corrected. The author says in this line here that I have 'never entirely recovered from infantile paralysis.' *Never recovered what?* I have *never recovered* the complete use of my knees. Will you *fix* that?"

His reticence to mention it—and the released heat that accompanied exceptions—were shared by Mrs. Roosevelt. At an Akron,

Ohio, lecture she was asked: "Do you think your husband's illness has affected his mentality?" Betraying no emotion as she read the written question aloud, she paused for an extra cooling moment and replied: "I am glad that question was asked. The answer is Yes. Anyone who has gone through great suffering is bound to have a greater sympathy and understanding of the problems of mankind." The audience rose in an ovation.

He was frequently torn between keeping his silence and protesting his case. On April 6, 1938, he wrote to an "old friend"—Elliott's description—mentioning his affliction. The important thing is not what he wrote but his decision not to mail it. Instead, he marked it "Written for the Record" and filed it away. It said in part:

. . . I do not mind telling you, in complete 100% confidence, that in 1923, when I first went to Florida . . . my old running mate, Jim Cox, came to see me on my house-boat in Miami. At that time I was, of course, walking with great difficulty— braces and crutches. Jim's eyes filled with tears when he saw me, and I gathered from his conversation that he was dead certain that I had had a stroke and that another one would soon completely remove me. At that time, of course, my general health was extremely good. . . .

Jim Cox from that day on always shook his head when my name was mentioned and said in sorrow that in effect I was a hopeless invalid and could never resume any active participation in business or political affairs.

As late as 1931—I think it was—when I was coming back from the Governors' Conference in Indiana, I stopped off at Dayton to see Jim Cox. He had had a very serious operation, followed by a thrombosis in his leg, and was very definitely invalided. His whole attitude during the two hours I spent with him alone was the same—that it was marvelous that I could stand the strain of the Governorship, but that in all probability I would be dead in a few months. He spent the greater part of

the time asking me solicitously how I was, though he was a much sicker man than I was.

He made a fine come-back and is furious today if anybody ever refers to the thrombosis he had in his leg—but I still think he expects me to pop off at any moment.

While deciding not to mail that letter, at other times he could be as open as a billboard. Son Jimmy recalls that on one of Madame Chiang Kai-shek's visits to the White House the grande dame thoughtlessly told the President not to stand up as she rose to leave the room. He gently replied, "My dear child, I couldn't stand up if I had to."

In a wheelchair or an automobile, getting F.D.R. into or out of an overcoat was an awkward exercise. With a stage sense of costume, F.D.R. took to a velvet-collared, braid-looped regulation Navy cape that, along with his cigarette holder, became a personal mark. Again, disadvantage was the fabric from which, with flair and style, he fashioned advantage.

Out of deference to his office as well as personal affection, newsmen virtually never mentioned the President's disability. So effective was their conspiracy even upon themselves, that, as John Gunther recalled, "hard-boiled newspaper men who knew that he could not walk as well as they knew their own names could never quite get over being startled when F.D.R. was suddenly brought into a room. The shock was greater when he wheeled himself and, of course, was greatest when he was carried; he seemed, for one thing, very small. . . . During the 1930s when I lived in Europe I repeatedly met men in important positions of state who had no idea that the President was disabled."

The people of the United States—his constituents, those from whom he drew strength and, more importantly, those who drew strength from him—knew, yet didn't know. They, too, waiting at tiny railroad depots, straining to see through the autumn sunshine the commanding figure of their President, froze at the sight of the painfully slow-motion, brace-supported step-pause-step across what seemed a torturous mile of observation platform from the train's rear door to the microphone.

It was an unexpected, unforgettable drama of frailty and strength.

■■■

STUDY QUESTIONS

1. Did Roosevelt's illness give him the capacity to identify with the suffering of others? How much? Why?

2. Describe the physical course of Roosevelt's disease? How physically restricted was he in his activities?

3. What would you say about his mental attitude? What does it reveal about his personality?

4. How did the press handle the illness? Why were they so respectful of Roosevelt's privacy? Would today's press be equally respectful? Why or why not?

5. Why was Roosevelt so secretive of his illness? What were the possible political ramifications of the public understanding the extent of his handicap?

BIBLIOGRAPHY

The best survey of the era of Franklin D. Roosevelt is William E. Leuchtenburg, *Franklin D. Roosevelt and the New Deal, 1932–1940* (1963). For a critical approach to the Roosevelt administration, see Paul Conkin, *The New Deal* (1967). Arthur M. Schlesinger, Jr.'s pro-Roosevelt trilogy still makes for outstanding reading. See *The Crisis of the Old Order* (1957), *The Coming of the New Deal* (1959), and *The Politics of Upheaval* (1960). An excellent political biography of Roosevelt is James Macgregor Burns, *Roosevelt: The Lion and the Fox* (1956). Also see Burns's *Roosevelt: The Soldier of Freedom* (1970) for a discussion of World War II. Joseph Lasch, *Eleanor and Franklin* (1971) describes the relationship between the president and his wife. For descriptions of opposition to Roosevelt and the New Deal, see George Wolfskill, *Revolt of the Conservatives* (1962); Donald McCoy, *Angry Voices* (1958); and Alan Brinkley, *Voices of Protest: Huey Long, Father Coughlin, and the Great Depression* (1982). Also see Robert McElvaine, *The Great Depression: America 1929–1941* (1984).

THE SAD IRONS

Robert A. Caro

For millions of older Americans, the Great Depression remains a vivid memory, a haunting reminder of the time when the promise of prosperity failed. For their descendants, the Great Depression is a chapter or two in a textbook, marked by pictures of gaunt faces and skinny Texas panhandle farmers leaning into the fierce winds of the Dust Bowl. Most descriptions of the Great Depression and New Deal revolve around images of what was lost and what was regained, of how the nation underwent the glittering but superficial prosperity of the 1920s, the poverty of the 1930s, and the boom years of World War II, and how public policymakers struggled to gain control of vast economic forces.

But there is another side of the New Deal. While economic recovery was the primary objective of the Roosevelt administration, the New Deal also introduced some sections of the country to modern technology. In the nineteenth century the Industrial Revolution began its transformation of American life, bringing people together in large cities, organizing life into bureaucracies and interest groups, and relieving drudgery through technology. By the 1920s, the nation had become intoxicated with the marvels of the light bulb, the internal combustion engine, and the electric motor, all of which revolutionized the way people lived. But millions of people were still unable to take advantage of the new gadgets. Instead, they lived as their ancestors had, tied to the soil in backbreaking, relentless labor. In "The Sad Irons" Robert Caro describes the Hill Country of Central Texas before the Rural Electrification Administration brought farm families into the modern age. The extension of electric transmission lines into the remote corners of the Hill Country transformed their lives, and for the next fifty years they remembered the New Deal as their savior.

Obtaining the financing and the authorization for the four dams being built along the Lower Colorado had been difficult. Now Lyndon Johnson undertook a task more difficult still. By ensuring completion of the dams, he had ensured the creation of electric power, which would be generated by the fall of water through dam penstocks. Now he was going to try to get the power to the people. He was going to try to bring electricity to the Hill Country.

Electricity had, of course, been an integral part of life in urban and much of small-town America for a generation and more, lighting its streets, powering the machinery of its factories, running its streetcars and trolleys, its elevated trains and subways, moving elevators and escalators in its stores, and cooling the stores with electric fans. Devices such as electric irons and toasters (which were in widespread use by 1900), refrigerators (which were widely sold beginning in 1912), and vacuum cleaners, dishwashers, hot plates, waffle irons, electric stoves and automatic washing machines for clothes had freed women from much of the drudgery of housework. In the evenings, thanks to electricity, there were the movies, and by 1922, forests of radio antennae had sprouted on tenement roofs. By 1937, when Lyndon Johnson went to Congress, electricity was so integral a part of life that it was hard to remember what life had been like without it.

It was not a part of life in the Hill Country. In Lyndon Johnson's congressional district, the sole source of power had been Texas Power & Light, a subsidiary of the New York-based utility holding giant, Electric Bond & Share. TP&L had, in 1927, agreed to "electrify" a handful of Hill Country towns (Johnson City was one), but not with power from its central generating station at Marble Falls; according to the TP&L,

which put the cost of building electric lines at $3,000 per mile, the limited use such small communities would make of electric power would never justify the investment required to build lines across the wide spaces of the Edwards Plateau. The TP&L "power plant" in each of these towns was, therefore, no more than a single thirty-horsepower diesel engine; it generated only enough voltage for ten-watt bulbs, which were constantly dimming and flickering—and which could not be used at all if an electric appliance (even an electric iron) was also in use. Since the "power plant" operated only between "dark to midnight," a refrigerator was useless. To most of the residents in these towns, such problems were academic: so high were TP&L's rates that few families hooked up to its lines. And in any case, the diesel engine was constantly breaking down under the strain placed on it. On the rare occasions on which a movie was shown, there was as much suspense in the audience over whether the electricity would hold out to the end of the film as there was in the film itself. Recalls Lucille O'Donnell of Burnet: "I'd be watching *The Perils of Pauline* and I'd just be about to see whether or not the train was going to run over her and the lights would go out." And the residents of these towns were the only inhabitants of the Hill Country with any electricity at all. TP&L refused even to consider building lines to the area's tens of thousands of individual farms and ranches.

As a result, although the electric milking machine had been invented almost two decades before, the Hill Country farmer had to milk his cows by hand—arising at three-thirty or four o'clock in the morning to do so, because milking was a time-consuming chore (more than two hours for twenty cows) and it had to be finished by daylight: every hour of daylight was needed for work in the fields. Milking was done by the dim light of kerosene lanterns; although Sears, Roebuck was boasting in 1937 that a new, deluxe kerosene lamp provided as much illumination as a forty-watt electric bulb,

From *The Years of Lyndon Johnson: The Path to Power* by Robert A. Caro. Copyright © 1982 by Robert A. Caro. Reprinted by permission of Alfred A. Knopf, Inc.

the lamps in use in the Hill Country furnished—at most—twenty-five watts of light. Or it was done in the dark. And there was a constant danger of fire with kerosene lamps, and even a spark could burn down a hay-filled barn, and destroy a farmer's last chance of holding on to his place, so many farmers were afraid to use a lantern in the barn. "Winter mornings," recalls one, "it would be so dark . . . you'd think you were in a box with the lid shut." Because without electricity there could be no refrigerator, the milk was kept on ice. The ice was expensive and farmers had to lug it from town at enormous cost in time. Though they kept it underground—covered with sawdust—it still, as farmer Chester Franklin of Wimberley puts it, "melted away so quick." And often even the ice didn't help. Farmers would have to take the milk out of their pit and place it by the roadside to be picked up by the trucks from Austin dairies, but often—on those unpaved Hill Country roads on which flat tires were a constant occurrence—the trucks would be late, and the milk would sit outside in the Hill Country heat. Even if it was not actually spoiled, the dairy would refuse to accept it if its temperature was above fifty degrees Fahrenheit—and when the truck driver pulled his thermometer out of the milk, a farmer, seeing the red line above fifty, would know that his hours of work in the barn in the dark had been for nothing.

Because there was no electricity, moreover, a Hill Country farmer could not use an electric pump. He was forced not only to milk but to water his cows by hand, a chore that, in dry weather, meant hauling up endless buckets from a deep well. Because he could not use an electric auger, he had to feed his livestock by hand, pitchforking heavy loads of hay up into the loft of his barn and then stomping on it to soften it enough so the cows could eat it. He had to prepare the feed by hand: because he could not use an electric grinder, he would get the corn kernels for his mules and horses by sticking ears of corn—hundreds of ears of

corn—one by one into a corn sheller and cranking it for hours. Because he could not use electric motors, he had to unload cotton seed by hand, and then shovel it into the barn by hand; to saw wood by hand, by swinging an axe or riding one end of a ripsaw. Because there was never enough daylight for all the jobs that had to be done, the farmer usually finished after sunset, ending the day as he had begun it, stumbling around the barn milking the cows in the dark, as farmers had done centuries before.

But the hardness of the farmer's life paled beside the hardness of his wife's.

Without electricity, even boiling water was work.

Anything which required the use of water was work. Windmills (which could, acting like a pump, bring water out of a well into a storage tank) were very rare in the Hill Country; their cost—almost $400 in 1937—was out of the reach of most families in that cash-poor region, and the few that had been built proved of little use in a region where winds were always uncertain and, during a drought, non-existent, for days, or weeks, on end. And without electricity to work a pump, there was only one way to obtain water: by hand.

The source of water could be either a stream or a well. If the source was a stream, water had to be carried from it to the house, and since, in a country subject to constant flooding, houses were built well away from the streams, it had to be carried a long way. If the source was a well, it had to be lifted to the surface—a bucket at a time. It had to be lifted quite a long way: while the average depth of a well was about fifty feet in the valleys of the Hill Country, in the hills it was a hundred feet or more.

And so much water was needed! A federal study of nearly half a million farm families even then being conducted would show that, on the average, a person living on a farm used 40 gallons of water every day. Since the average farm family was five persons, the family used 200 gallons, or four-fifths of a ton, of water each day—73,000 gallons, or almost 300

■ ■ *Members of the Peterson family in Travis County, Texas. These farm women of the Hill Country had to haul wood and*
water for washing and cooking day in and day out until the end of the 1930s.

tons, in a year. The study showed that, on the average, the well was located 253 feet from the house—and that to pump by hand and carry to the house 73,000 gallons of water a year would require someone to put in during that year 63 eight-hour days, and walk 1,750 miles.

A farmer would do as much of this pumping and hauling as possible himself, and try to have his sons do as much of the rest as possible (it was Lyndon Johnson's adamant refusal to help his mother with the pumping and hauling that touched off the most bitter of the flareups with his father during his youth). As soon as a Hill Country youth got big enough to carry the water buckets (which held about four gallons, or thirty-two pounds, of water apiece), he was assigned the job of filling his mother's wash pots before he left for school or the field. Curtis

Cox still recalls today that from the age of nine or ten, he would, every morning throughout the rest of his boyhood, make about seven trips between his house and the well, which were about 300 feet apart, on each of these trips carrying two large buckets, or more than sixty pounds, of water. "I felt tired," he says. "It was a lot of water." But the water the children carried would be used up long before noon, and the children would be away—at school or in the fields—and most of the hauling of water was, therefore, done by women. "I would," recalls Curtis' mother, Mary Cox, "have to get it, too—more than once a day, more than twice; oh, I don't know how many times. I needed water to wash my floors, water to wash my clothes, water to cook. . . . It was hard work. I was always packing [carrying] water."

Carrying it—after she had wrestled off the heavy wooden lid which kept the rats and squirrels out of the well; after she had cranked the bucket up to the surface (and cranking—lifting thirty pounds fifty feet or more—was very hard for most women even with a pulley; most would pull the rope hand over hand, as if they were climbing it, to get their body weight into the effort; they couldn't do it with their arms alone). Some Hill Country women make wry jokes about getting water. Says Mrs. Brian Smith of Blanco: "Yes, we had running water. I always said we had running water because I grabbed those two buckets up and ran the two hundred yards to the house with them." But the joking fades away as the memories sharpen. An interviewer from the city is struck by the fact that Hill Country women of the older generation are noticeably stooped, much more so than city women of the same age. Without his asking for an explanation, it is given to him. More than once, and more than twice, a stooped and bent Hill Country farm wife says, "You see how round-shouldered I am? Well, that's from hauling the water." And, she will often add, "I was round-shouldered like this well before my time, when I was still a young woman. My back got bent from hauling the water, and it got bent when I was still young."

The Hill Country farm wife had to haul water, and she had to haul wood.

Because there was no electricity, Hill Country stoves were wood stoves. The spread of the cedar brakes had given the area a plentiful supply of wood, but cedar seared bone-dry by the Hill Country sun burned so fast that the stoves seemed to devour it. A farmer would try to keep a supply of wood in the house, or, if he had sons old enough, would assign the task to them. (Lyndon Johnson's refusal to chop wood for his mother was another source of the tension between him and Sam). They would cut down the trees, and chop them into four-foot lengths that could be stacked in cords. When wood was needed in the house, they would cut it into shorter lengths and split the pieces so

they could fit into the stoves. But as with the water, these chores often fell to the women.

The necessity of hauling the wood was not, however, the principal reason so many farm wives hated their wood stoves. In part, they hated these stoves because they were so hard to "start up." The damper that opened into the firebox created only a small draft even on a breezy day, and on a windless day, there was no draft—because there was no electricity, of course, there was no fan to move the air in the kitchen—and a fire would flicker out time after time. "With an electric stove, you just turn on a switch and you have heat," says Lucille O'Donnell, but with a wood stove, a woman might have to stuff kindling and wood into the firebox over and over again. And even after the fire was lit, the stove "didn't heat up in a minute, you know," Lucille O'Donnell says—it might in fact take an hour. In part, farm wives hated wood stoves because they were so dirty, because the smoke from the wood blackened walls and ceilings, and ashes were always escaping through the grating, and the ash box had to be emptied twice a day—a dirty job and dirtier if, while the ashes were being carried outside, a gust of wind scattered them around inside the house. They hated the stoves because they could not be left unattended. Without devices to regulate the heat and keep the temperature steady, when the stove was being used for baking or some other cooking in which an even temperature was important, a woman would have to keep a constant watch on the fire, thrusting logs—or corncobs, which ignited quickly—into the firebox every time the heat slackened.

Most of all, they hated them because they were so hot.

When the big iron stove was lit, logs blazing in its firebox, flames licking at the gratings that held the pots, the whole huge mass of metal so hot that it was almost glowing, the air in the kitchen shimmered with the heat pouring out of it. In the Winter the heat was welcome, and in Spring and Fall it was bearable, but in the

Hill Country, Summer would often last five months. Some time in June the temperature might climb to near ninety degrees, and would stay there, day after day, week after week, through the end of September. Day after day, week after week, the sky would be mostly empty, without a cloud as a shield from the blazing sun that beat down on the Hill Country, and on the sheet-iron or corrugated tin roofs of the box-like kitchens in the little dog-run homes that dotted its hills and valleys. No matter how hot the day, the stove had to be lit much of the time, because it had to be lit not only for meals but for baking; Hill Country wives, unable to afford store-bought bread, baked their own, and all-day task. (As Mrs. O'Donnell points out, "We didn't have refrigerators, you know, and without refrigerators, you just about have to start every meal from scratch.") In the Hill Country, moreover, Summer was harvest time, when a farm wife would have to cook not just for her family but for a harvesting crew—twenty or thirty men, who, working from sun to sun, expected three meals a day.

Harvest time, and canning time.

In the Hill Country, canning was required for a family's very survival. Too poor to buy food, most Hill Country families lived through the Winter largely on the vegetables and fruit picked in the Summer and preserved in jars.

Since—because there was no electricity—there were no refrigerators in the Hill Country, vegetables or fruit had to be canned the very day they came ripe. And, from June through September, something was coming ripe almost every day, it seemed; on a single peach tree, the fruit on different branches would come ripe on different days. In a single orchard, the peaches might be reaching ripeness over a span as long as two weeks; "You'd be in the kitchen with the peaches for two weeks," Hill Country wives recall. And after the peaches, the strawberries would begin coming ripe, and then the gooseberries, and then the blueberries. The tomatoes would become ripe before the

okra, the okra before the zucchini, the zucchini before the corn. So the canning would go on with only brief intervals—all Summer.

Canning required constant attendance on the stove. Since boiling water was essential, the fire in the stove had to be kept roaring hot, so logs had to be continually put into the firebox. At least twice during a day's canning, moreover—probably three or four times—a woman would have to empty the ash container, which meant wrestling the heavy, unwieldy device out from under the firebox. And when the housewife wasn't bending down to the flames, she was standing over them. In canning fruit, for example, first sugar was dropped into the huge iron canning pot, and watched carefully and stirred constantly, so that it would not become lumpy, until it was completely dissolved. Then the fruit—perhaps peaches, which would have been peeled earlier—was put in the pot, and boiled until it turned into a soft and mushy jam that would be packed into jars (which would have been boiling—to sterilize them—in another pot) and sealed with wax. Boiling the peaches would take more than an hour, and during that time they had to be stirred constantly so that they would not stick to the pot. And when one load of peaches was finished, another load would be put in, and another. Canning was an all-day job. So when a woman was canning, she would have to spend all day in a little room with a tin or sheet-iron roof on which a blazing sun was beating down without mercy, standing in front of the iron stove and the wood fire within it. And every time the heat in that stove died down even a bit, she would have to make it hotter again.

"You'd have to can in the Summer when it was hot," says Kitty Clyde Ross Leonard, who had been Johnson's first girlfriend. "You'd have to cook for hours. Oh, that was a terrible thing. You wore as little as you could. I wore loose clothing so that it wouldn't stick to me. But the perspiration would just pour down my face. I remember the perspiration pouring down my mother's face, and when I grew up and had my own family, it poured down mine. That stove was so hot. But you had to stir, especially when you were making jelly. So you had to stand over that stove." Says Bernice Snodgrass of Wimberley: "You got so hot that you couldn't stay in the house. You ran out and sat under the trees. I couldn't stand it to stay in the house. Terrible. Really terrible. But you couldn't stay out of the house long. You had to stir. You had to watch the fire. So you had to go back into the house."

And there was no respite. If a bunch of peaches came ripe a certain day, that was the day they had to be canned—no matter how the housewife might feel that day. Because in the fierce Hill Country heat, fruit and vegetables spoiled very quickly. And once the canning process was begun, it could not stop. "If you peeled six dozen peaches, and then, later that day, you felt sick, you couldn't stop," says Gay Harris. "Because you can't can something if it's rotten. The job has to be done the same day, no matter what." Sick or not, in the Hill Country, when it was time to can, a woman canned, standing hour after hour, trapped between a blazing sun and a blazing wood fire. "We had no choice, you see," Mrs. Harris says.

Every week, every week all year long—every week without fail—there was washday.

The wash was done outside. A huge vat of boiling water would be suspended over a larger, roaring fire and near it three large "Number Three" zinc washtubs and a dishpan would be placed on a bench.

The clothes would be scrubbed in the first of the zinc tubs, scrubbed on a washboard by a woman bending over the tub. The soap, since she couldn't afford store-bought soap, was soap she made from lye, soap that was not very effective, and the water was hard. Getting farm dirt out of clothes required hard scrubbing.

Then the farm wife would wring out each piece of clothing to remove from it as much as possible of the dirty water, and put it in the big vat of boiling water. Since the scrubbing would not have removed all of the dirt, she would try to get the rest out by "punching" the clothes in the vat—standing over the boiling water and using a wooden paddle or, more often, a broomstick, to stir the clothes and swish them through the water and press them against the bottom or sides, moving the broom handle up and down and around as hard as she could for ten or fifteen minutes in a human imitation of the agitator of an automatic—electric—washing machine.

The next step was to transfer the clothes from the boiling water to the second of the three zinc washtubs: the "rinse tub." The clothes were lifted out of the big vat on the end of the broomstick, and held up on the end of the stick for a few minutes while the dirty water dripped out.

When the clothes were in the rinse tub, the woman bent over the tub and rinsed them, by swishing each individual item through the water. Then she wrung out the clothes, to get as much of the dirty water out as possible, and placed the clothes in the third tub, which contained bluing, and swished them around in *it*—this time to get the bluing all through the garment and make it white—and then repeated the same movements in the dishpan which was filled with starch.

At this point, one load of wash would be done. A week's wash took at least four loads: one of sheets, one of shirts and other white clothing, one of colored clothes and one of dish towels. But for the typical, large, Hill Country farm family, two loads of each of these categories would be required, so the procedure would have to be repeated eight times.

For each load, moreover, the water in each of the three washtubs would have to be changed. A washtub held about eight gallons. Since the water had to be warm, the woman would fill each tub half with boiling water from the big pot and half with cold water. She did the filling with a bucket which held three or four gallons—twenty-five or thirty pounds. For the first load or two of wash, the water would have been provided by her husband or her sons. But after this water had been used up, part of washday was walking—over and over—that long walk to the spring or well, hauling up the water, hand over laborious hand, and carrying those heavy buckets back. Another part of washday was also a physical effort: the "punching" of the clothes in the big vat. "You had to do it as hard as you could— swish those clothes around and around and around. They never seemed to get clean. And those clothes were heavy in the water, and it was hot outside, and you'd be standing over that boiling water and that big fire—you felt like you were being roasted alive." Lifting the clothes out of the vat was an effort, too. A dripping mass of soggy clothes was heavy, and it felt heavier when it had to be lifted out of that vat and held up for minutes at a time so that the dirty water could drip out, and then swung over to the rinsing tub. Soon, if her children weren't around to hear her, a woman would be grunting with the effort. Even the wringing was, after a few hours, an effort. "I mean, wringing clothes might not seem hard," Mrs. Harris says. "But you have to wring every piece so many times—you wring it after you take it out of the scrub tub, and you wring it after you take it out of the rinse tub, and after you take it out of the bluing. Your arms got tired." And her hands—from scrubbing with lye soap and wringing—were raw and swollen. Of course, there was also the bending—hours of bending—over the rub boards. "By the time you got done washing, your back was broke," Ava Cox says. "I'll tell you—of the things of my life that I will never forget, I will never forget how much my back hurt on washdays." Hauling the water, scrubbing, punching, rinsing: a Hill Country farm wife did this for hours on end—while a city wife did it by pressing the button on her electric washing machine.

Washday was Monday. Tuesday was for ironing.

Says Mary Cox, in words echoed by all elderly Hill Country farm wives: "Washing was hard work, but ironing was the worst. Nothing could be as hard as ironing."

The Department of Agriculture finds that "Young women today are not aware of the origin of the word 'iron,' as they press clothes with light-weight appliances of aluminum or hollow stainless steel." In the Hill Country, in the 1930s an iron was *iron*—a six- or seven-pound wedge of iron. The irons used in the Hill Country had to be heated on the wood stove, and they would retain their heat for only a few minutes—a man's shirt generally required two irons; a farm wife would own three or four of them, so that several could be heating while one was working. An iron with a wooden handle cost two dollars more than one without the handle, so Hill Country wives did their weekly loads of ironing—huge loads because, as Mary Cox puts it, "in those days you were expected to starch and iron almost everything"—with irons without handles. They would either transfer a separate wooden handle from one iron to another, or they would protect their hands with a thick pot holder.

Since burning wood generates soot, the irons became dirty as they sat heating on the stove. Or, if any moisture was left on an iron from the sprinkled clothes on which it had just been used, even the thinnest smoke from the stove created a muddy film on the bottom. The irons had to be cleaned frequently, therefore, by scrubbing them with a rag that had been dipped in salt, and if the soot was too thick, they had to be sanded and scraped. And no matter how carefully you checked the bottom of the irons, and sanded and scraped them, there would often remain some little spot of soot—as you would discover when you rubbed it over a clean white shirt or dress. Then you had to wash that item of clothing over again.

Nevertheless, the irons would burn a woman's hand. The wooden handle or the potholder would slip, and she would have searing metal against her flesh; by noon, she might have blister atop blister—on hands that had to handle the rag that had been dipped in salt. Ironing always took a full day—often it went on into Tuesday evening—and a full day of lifting and carrying six- or seven-pound loads was hard on even these hardy Hill Country women. "It would hurt so bad between the shoulders," Elsie Beck remembers. But again the worst aspect of ironing was the heat. On ironing day, a fire would have to be blazing in the wood stove all day, filling the kitchen, hour after hour, with heat and smoke. Ironing had to be done not only in the Winter but in the Summer—when the temperature outside the kitchen might be ninety or ninety-five or one hundred, and inside the kitchen would be considerably higher, and because there was no electricity, there was no fan to so much as stir the air. In a speech in Congress some years later, Representative John E. Rankin described the "drudgery" a typical farm wife endured, "burning up in a hot kitchen and bowing down over the washtub or boiling the clothes over a flaming fire in the summer heat." He himself remembered, he said, "seeing his mother lean over that hot iron hour after hour until it seemed she was tired enough to drop." Rankin was from Mississippi, but his description would have been familiar to the mothers of the Edwards Plateau. The women of the Hill Country never called the instruments they used every Tuesday "irons," they called them "sad irons."

Washing, ironing—those were chores that were performed every week. Then, of course, there were special occasions—harvest time and threshing time, when a woman had to cook not just for her family but for a crew of twenty or thirty men; the shearing, when, because there was no electricity and her husband had to work the shears, she had to crank the shearing machine, pedaling as if she were pumping a bicycle up a steep hill, pedaling, with only brief pauses, hour after hour; "He was always yelling 'Faster, faster,' Mrs. Walter Yett of

Blanco recalls. "I could hardly get up the next morning, I was so tired after that." Washing, ironing, cooking, canning, shearing, helping with the plowing and the picking and the sowing, and, every day, carrying the water and the wood, and because there was no electricity, having to do everything by hand by the same methods that had been employed by her mother and grandmother and great-great-great-grandmother before her—"They wear these farm women out pretty fast," wrote one observer. In the Hill Country, as many outside observers noted, the one almost universal characteristic of the women was that they were worn out before their time, that they were old beyond their years, old at forty, old at thirty-five, bent and stooped and tired.

A Hill Country farm wife had to do her chores even if she was ill—no matter how ill. Because Hill Country women were too poor to afford proper medical care, they often suffered perineal tears in childbirth. During the 1930s, the federal government sent physicians to examine a sampling of Hill Country women. The doctors found that, out of 275 women, 158 had perineal tears. Many of them, the team of gynecologists reported, were third-degree tears, "tears so bad that it is difficult to see how they stand on their feet." But they *were* standing on their feet, and doing all the chores that Hill Country wives had always done—hauling the water, hauling the wood, canning, washing, ironing, helping with the shearing, the plowing and the picking.

Because there was no electricity.

The lack of electricity meant that the days of the people of the Hill Country were filled with drudgery; at night they were denied the entertainment—movies, radio—that would have made the drudgery more bearable. The radio could, moreover, have ended the area's isolation. The feeling of the Hill Country youngsters of the 1920s—Lyndon Johnson's generation—that "we were completely cut off out here," that "we were back in the woods, compared to the rest of the world," that "everything had already happened before we found out about it," was the feeling of the 1930s generation as well. Because there was no electricity, the only radios in the Hill Country were the occasional crystal sets with earphones and poor reception. Amos 'n' Andy, Lum 'n' Abner, Ma Perkins—theirs were voices familiar to most of America; it was a rare inhabitant of the Edwards Plateau who had not heard them even once. "What we missed most was the fireside chats," says Mary Cox. "I mean, we loved Franklin D. Roosevelt in this country, and we kept reading about these wonderful fireside chats. But we never got to hear them."

Even reading was hard.

Evening was often the only time in which Hill country farm couples could read ("There was no other time," says Lucille O'Donnell. "There was never a minute to read during the day, it seemed"), but the only light for reading came from kerosene lamps. In movies about the Old West, these lamps appear so homey that it is difficult for a city dweller to appreciate how much—and why—some farm dwellers disliked them so passionately.

Lighting the kerosene lamp was a frustrating job. "You had to adjust the wick just right," says Curtis Cox of Bryan. "If you turned it too high, it would flame up and start to smoke. The chimney—that's the glass part—would get all black, and your eyes would start to smart." Keeping it lit was even more frustrating. It burned straight across for only a moment, and then would either flare up or die down to an inadequate level. Even when the wick was trimmed just right, a kerosene lamp provided only limited illumination. The approximately twenty-five watts of light provided by most such lamps was adequate for children doing their homework—although surveys would later find that the educational level of rural children improved markedly immediately upon the introduction of electricity—but their parents, whose eyes were not so strong, had more difficulty. Mary Cox says that she

couldn't read with their lamp for more than a short period: "I always loved to read," she recalls. "But I couldn't enjoy it on the farm. It was hard on the eyes, a strain on the eyes. I had to force myself to read at night." Lucille O'Donnell came to Burnet from Virginia, where she had liked to read in bed; she couldn't do that on her farm, she says, because she couldn't afford the kerosene. When she did read at night, she couldn't read in bed. Her husband, Tom, "would be asleep," she recalls, "and I would put the lamp beside him on the bed, and sit on that little stool and read in the most awkward position." Pointing to deep vertical lines between her eyebrows, more than one Hill Country farm wife says: "So many of us have these lines from squinting to read."

The circle of light cast by a kerosene lamp was small, and there were seldom enough lamps in the home of an impoverished farm family. If a family had so many children that they completely surrounded the one good lamp while studying, their mother could not do her sewing until they were finished. And outside the small circles of light, the rooms of a farmhouse were dark. "The house looked scary," says Mary Cox. "If I was alone at night, it was awfully lonely." And, of course, there were no lamps in the outhouse. Many a Hill country farm wife echoes the words of Betty MacDonald: "I had a horrible choice of either sitting in the dark and not knowing what was crawling on me or bringing a lantern and attracting moths, mosquitoes, nighthawks and bats."

No radio; no movies; limited reading—little diversion between the hard day just past and the hard day just ahead. "Living was just drudgery then," says Carroll Smith of Blanco. "Living—just *living*—was a problem. No lights. No plumbing. Nothing. Just living on the edge of starvation. That was farm life for us. God, city people think there was something fine about it. If they only knew . . ."

So many conveniences taken for granted in

American cities were unknown on the Edwards Plateau: not just vacuum cleaners and washing machines but, for example, bathrooms, since, as a practical matter, indoor plumbing is unfeasible without running water, which requires an electric pump. In the Summer, bathing could be done in the creek (when the creek wasn't dry); in the Winter, it entailed lugging in water and heating it on the stove (which entailed lugging in wood) before pouring it into a Number Three washtub. Because bathing was so hard, "you bathed about once a week," Bernice Snodgrass says. Children went barefoot, so "we'd make them wash their feet [at the pump outside] you know. We [adults] would wash our face and hands and ears in washpans but we didn't take a bath but once a week." There were few toilets, and most Hill Country outhouses were the most primitive sort. Many had no pit dug under them. "It would just drop on the ground," Guthrie Taylor recalls. "No, it wouldn't be cleared away"; every so often the flimsy little shelter would just be moved to another spot. Since toilet paper was too expensive, pages from a Sears, Roebuck catalogue, or corncobs, were used. And some families did not have outhouses. When the Snodgrasses moved to Mount Gaynor from Austin, Bernice Snodgrass says, "We were the only people in the neighborhood that had one. You know what everybody else did? They went out behind the barn, or behind a tree, or something." Frederick Law Olmsted had found the same situation—houses at which there was "no other water-closet than the back of a bush or the broad prairies"—on his journey through the Hill Country in 1857. He had been shocked then, because the America he knew had advanced beyond such primitive conditions. Now it was 1937; four more generations had been living in the Hill Country—with no significant advance in the conditions of their life. Many of the people of Lyndon Johnson's congressional district were still living in the same type of dwelling in which the area's people had been living in 1857: in rude "dog-run" shelters one board thick, through which the wind howled in the winter. They were still squatting behind a bush to defecate. Because of their poverty, they were still utterly bereft not only of tractors and feed grinders, but of modern medical assistance—and were farming by methods centuries out of date.

Although they understood that, as Louise Casparis says, "we were behind the rest of the world," natives of the Hill Country did not realize how *far* behind the rest of the world.

How could they be expected to realize? Without many books to read—or, in general, newspapers, either, except for those pathetic four-page local weeklies; without radio to listen to, with only an occasional movie to watch—how was news of advances in the rest of the world to reach them? Since many of them never saw that world for themselves—an astonishing high proportion of Hill Country residents would never visit even Austin or San Antonio—the Hill Country's awareness of the outside world was dim. The life of Hill Country natives was, moreover, the same life that their mothers and fathers—and grandmothers and grandfathers—had lived; how were they to know, except in general, vague terms, that there was another kind of life? When they heard about the wonders of electricity, they thought electricity was the electricity they saw in Johnson City, the dim, flickering lights hardly better than lamplight; the wonders they imagined were the electric iron and the radio, little more; "I remember when someone started telling me about these washing machines," recalls Ava Cox. "A machine that *washed*? I couldn't picture that *at all!*" Even the concept of the toilet was difficult for them to accept completely; when Errol Snodgrass, newly arrived in Mount Gaynor, began not only to build an outhouse but to dig a pit underneath it, a neighbor asked him: "What do you want that pit for?" And when he explained, Bernice Snodgrass recalls, the reaction of the neighborhood was, "They're so highfalutin that they have to have a toilet.' They thought an outhouse with a pit under it—they thought that that was what people meant when they spoke about a toilet!" Natives of the Hill Country couldn't understand why families that had moved away from the Hill Country never returned. It is not, therefore, by lifelong residents of the Hill Country that the contrast between life there and in the outside world is most clearly enunciated, but by newcomers: from families which, due to economic necessity, moved to the Hill Country in the 1930s.

The Depression had cost Brian and Mary Sue Smith their home and their once-profitable automobile-repair shop in Portland, Texas, a town near Corpus Christi. In 1937, they moved with their three children to the Hill Country—to a fifty-three-acre farm near Blanco—because "that was the only place where land was cheap enough so we could buy a farm."

Portland had electricity—had had it for years. "You never even thought about electricity," Mrs. Smith says. "I just accepted it. I mean, if I thought about it, I suppose I would have thought, 'Doesn't *everyone* have electricity?'"

Now she found out that not everyone did.

The Smiths had brought their radio, a big black Atwater Kent with an amplifying horn on top, to their new home, but it could not be played. "You know, it was very lonely on that farm," Mrs. Smith says. "The quiet was nice sometimes. But sometimes it was so quiet it hurt you." They had brought their washing machine, but that could not work, either. Mrs. Smith loved to read, but "The light was hard on your eyes. My eyes just weren't good enough to read at night." In Portland, she had crocheted at night, but she found the light was too dim for her to do that at night. And, of course, there was no time to do it during the day; what time wasn't consumed by her household chores was taken up husking, shelling and grinding corn by hand for feed for the 150 hens whose eggs she was selling; by cranking the sheep-shearing machine. Soon after she arrived on the farm, her husband became very ill, and for more than a year she had to care for the livestock too, and to plow behind a pair of mules—although she had never plowed before. "Up before daylight. Build the fire in the wood range. Put on the biscuits. Go out and milk the cows. Breakfast. Work was all there was. It was a bare existence."

Getting the water, from a well some 200 yards from the house, was the chore that bothered her most. "The children had had running water in Portland, of course, and they acted like they still had it," she says. When she started meeting other Hill Country women, she noticed that many of them were round-shouldered, and they told her it was from carrying heavy buckets of water. She didn't want to be round-shouldered. But there seemed no solution. "Carry and carry. Back and forth. Sometimes I would get awfully discouraged. When I first moved there [to the Hill Country], I felt like a pioneer lady, like one of the women who had come here in covered wagons. I said, if they could do it, I could, too. But it was very hard. After you spent all morning lugging those big buckets back and forth, you felt more like an ox or a mule than a human being. Portland was just a little town. It was no great metropolis. But moving from Portland into the Hill Country was like moving from the twentieth century back into the Middle Ages."

■■■

STUDY QUESTIONS

1. Why had electric transmission lines never been built in large areas of the Hill Country?

2. Why was the lot of these women so difficult before the arrival of electricity?

3. Why was water such a critical item to Hill Country women? Describe the efforts required to get water into the typical home in this area.

4. Why did Hill Country women hate their stoves?

5. How did these women iron clothes? Why did they hate the chore of ironing?

6. When electricity arrived at a Hill Country farm, what changes did it bring in the way people lived?

BIBLIOGRAPHY

For the best description of the Hill Country, see Robert A. Caro, *The Years of Lyndon Johnson. The Path to Power* (1982). Also see John Graves, *Hard Scrabble* (1974) and *Texas Heartland: A Hill Country Year* (1975). The best descriptions of southern agriculture during the New Deal years are Richard S. Kirdendall, *Social Scientists and Farm Politics in the Age of Roosevelt* (1966) and David Conrad, *The Forgotten Farmers* (1965). The latter deals with those who did not benefit from the Agricultural Adjustment Administration. On the problem of poverty in the South, see Paul Mertz, *The New Deal and Southern Rural Poverty* (1978). The best discussion of the Rural Electrification Administration is D. Clayton Brown, *Electricity for Rural America: The Fight for REA* (1980).

NIGHT OF THE MARTIANS

Edward Oxford

It's a truism today that the mass media influences the lives of Americans. Society is constantly barraged with questions and criticisms about such issues as the quality of children's programming, the political bias of newscasters, the ethics of television advertising, the domination of political campaigns by the media, and the decline of literacy and the written word. More than any other technological innovation, the development first of radio and then of television has transformed American life, changing the way people live and relate to one another. The first radio station in the United States began broadcasting out of Pittsburgh in 1920. Three years later there were more than 500 stations doing the same thing, and by 1929 more than 12 million families listened to the radio at home every night. The communications revolution that radio stimulated contributed to the creation of a mass, national culture.

The influence of the radio, however, did not immediately dawn on people. In 1927 the National Broadcasting Company became the first national network, and by 1933 President Franklin D. Roosevelt was effectively using the radio for his famous "fireside chats." But it was not until 1938, when Orson Welles broadcast his famous "War of the Worlds" program, that Americans realized the potential of radio to shape public attitudes. With Adolf Hitler making his designs on Czechoslovakia well known, Americans were worried that another global conflict was in the making. Battered by the frustration of the Great Depression and nervous about the safety of the world, millions of people panicked when Orson Welles described over national radio an invasion of the East Coast by Martians. In the following essay, historian Edward Oxford describes the broadcast and the controversy it inspired.

A little after eight P.M. on Halloween eve 1938, thirteen-year-old Dick Stives, his sister, and two brothers huddled around their family's radio. They were in the dining room of their grandfather's farmhouse near the hamlet of Grovers Mill, four miles east of Princeton, New Jersey. Their mother and father had dropped them off there and gone to the movies.

Dick worked the radio dial, hunting for the station that carried the *Chase and Sanborn Hour*, his—and the nation's—favorite Sunday evening program. As he scanned the airwaves, Dick tuned in the local affiliate of the Columbia Broadcasting System (CBS). A commanding voice—that of Orson Welles—riveted his attention.

". . . across an immense ethereal gulf, minds that are to our minds as ours are to the beasts of the jungle, intellects vast, cool, and unsympathetic, regarded this earth with envious eyes and slowly and surely drew their plans against us. . . ."

Dick Stives turned the dial no further. Instead, during the next hour he and millions of other listeners sat glued by their radios, convinced by an alarming series of "news bulletins" that monster aliens from Mars were invading America. Dick's village of Grovers Mill—the supposed landing site for these invaders—became the focal point of a panic wave that rapidly swept across the nation.

The program—the *Mercury Theatre on the Air* adaptation of H.G. Wells's *The War of the Worlds*—would later be remembered as the most extraordinary radio show ever broadcast. And Orson Welles, its brilliant young producer, director, and star, would be catapulted to nationwide fame overnight.

As the wonder boy of the performing arts, Orson Welles had by age twenty-three already appeared on the cover of *Time* magazine; built a considerable reputation as a radio actor; set the stage-world on its ear with a *Julius Caesar* set in Fascist Italy, an all-black *Macbeth*, and a production of Marc Blitzstein's opera *The Cradle Will Rock*; and founded—with his partner-in-drama John Houseman—the revolutionary and often controversial Mercury Theatre.[1]

In midsummer 1938, the Columbia Broadcasting System, impressed by Welles's meteoric success, offered him and his repertory company a grand stage, radio—"the Broadway of the entire United States"—on which to deliver a sixty-minute dramatization each week.

Broadcast from the twenty-second floor of the CBS building in midtown Manhattan, the *Mercury Theatre on the Air* had no commercial sponsor. The show was subsidized by the CBS network, and its bare-bones budget provided no money for expensive, original plays. "We offered the audience classic works from the public domain—*Julius Caesar, Oliver Twist, The Heart of Darkness, Jane Eyre*, and such," recalls John Houseman. "Orson and I would select the book. Sometimes it was my task to fashion the original into a workable radio script."

For the last program of October, the seventeenth in their series, Welles and Houseman wanted to "throw in something of a scientific nature." They settled on an adaptation of *The War of the Worlds*, a science-fiction novel written in 1898 by British author H.G. Wells. Houseman assigned the script to a recent addition to the company, writer Howard Koch.

From "Night of the Martians" by Edward Oxford in *American History Illustrated* 23, October 1988, pp. 14–23, 47–48. Reprinted through the courtesy of Cowles Magazines, publisher of *American History Illustrated*.

[1] *Up to this time Welles was probaly best known to radio audiences as "Lamont Cranston," alias "The Shadow," on the popular Sunday afternoon mystery program of the same name. But he also appeared frequently on many other shows, including The March of Time, and was said to be earning $1,000 a week from his radio commitments alone.*

For the fall season CBS had moved the *Mercury Theatre on the Air* from Monday evening to the Sunday-night eight-to-nine-o'clock slot, an "unsold" time period. During this hour much of America tuned in to the competing NBC Red network for the *Chase and Sanborn Hour*, which featured ventriloquist Edgar Bergen and his wooden-headed "dummy" Charlie McCarthy. The Crossley ratings of listenership gave Charlie McCarthy a "thirty-five" (roughly 35 percent of radio listeners at that hour tuned in), while the *Mercury* usually scored about "three."

During the week before the October 30 broadcast, Welles nonchalantly put in his own typically frantic week while Houseman, Koch, and the cast struggled to ready the show. Welles spent much of his time not in the CBS studios at 485 Madison Avenue, but on the stage of the Mercury Theatre on West 41st Street, rehearsing his repertory company for the opening of a new play. He hurried back to CBS at odd hours to try out some of his lines, listen to run-throughs by the radio show's cast, and render his inimitable revisions.

Welles and his company spent much of Sunday amid a litter of sandwiches and coffee cups in Studio One, adding final touches to their version of *The War of the Worlds* and conducting a dress rehearsal with full music and sound effects.

Just before 8 P.M., Eastern Standard Time, Welles, conductor-like, stood poised on his platform in the middle of the studio. He had at his command not only his loyal band of actors, but also a small symphony orchestra. Wearing a headset, the multifaceted genius was prepared to read his own lines, cue the other actors, signal for sound effects, summon the orchestra, and also keep in touch with the control room.

At the stroke of eight o'clock, he gave the cue for the start of the *Mercury* theme—the Tchaikovsky Piano Concerto No. 1 in B-Flat Minor.

For the next unforgettable hour, Dick Stives at Grovers Mill, along with several million other Americans, sat transfixed as the airwaves brought word of weird and almost incomprehensible events that seemed to unfold with terrifying reality even as they listened.

It was not as though listeners hadn't been warned. Most simply didn't pay close attention to the program's opening signature (or tuned in a few seconds late and missed it altogether): "The Columbia Broadcasting System and its affiliated stations present Orson Welles and the Mercury Theatre on the Air in *The War of the Worlds* by H.G. Wells. . . ."

Many in the radio audience failed to associate what they heard with prior newspaper listings of the drama. And, by the time a single station break came late in the hour with reminders that listeners were hearing a fictional story, many others were too agitated to comprehend that they had been deceived.

Skillfully choreographed by Welles and Houseman, the program—a play simulating a montage of real-life dance band "remotes" and news bulletins—began with deliberate calm. Millions of listeners, conditioned by recent news reports of worldwide political turmoil—and by their inherent trust in the medium of radio—believed what they heard.

Just two minutes into the show, audience perception between fantasy and reality began to blur when, following Welles's dramatic opening monologue, the microphone shifted to a "network announcer" reading an apparently routine report from the "Government Weather Bureau."

Programming then shifted to "Ramon Raquello and his orchestra" in the "Meridian Room" at the "Hotel Park Plaza" in downtown New York City.

During rehearsals for the show, Welles had insisted—over the objections of his associates—on increasing the broadcast time devoted to the fictional orchestra's soothing renditions of "La Cumparsita" and "the ever-popular

'Stardust.'" As he had anticipated, the resulting "band remote" had a disarming air of reality—and provided emotional contrast to the intensity of later news bulletins.[2]

Just when Welles had calculated that listeners might start tuning out the music in search of something more lively, an announcer broke in with a bulletin from the "Intercontinental Radio News": "Professor Farrell of the Mount Jennings Observatory" near Chicago had reported observing "several explosions of incandescent gas occurring at regular intervals on the planet Mars. . . . The spectroscope indicates the gas to be hydrogen and moving towards the earth with tremendous velocity."

The dance music resumed, only to be interrupted repeatedly during the next several minutes by other bulletins. The tempo of events—and listeners' interest—began to intensify.

From a "remote pickup" at the "Princeton Observatory," reporter "Carl Phillips" interviewed famous astronomer "Richard Pierson" (played by Welles). As the clockwork of mechanism of his telescope ticked in the background, Professor Pierson described Mars as a red disk swimming in a blue sea. He said he could not explain the gas eruptions on that planet. But skeptical of anything that could not be explained by logic, the astronomer counted the chances against living intelligence on Mars as being "a thousand to one."

Then Phillips read a wire that had just been handed to Pierson: a seismograph at the "Natural History Museum" in New York had registered a "shock of almost earthquake intensity occurring within a radius of twenty miles of Princeton." Pierson played down any possible connection with the disturbances on Mars: "This is probably a meteorite of unusual size

and its arrival at this particular time is merely a coincidence."

Again the program returned to music, followed by yet another bulletin: an astronomer in Canada had observed three explosions on Mars, confirming "earlier reports from American observatories."

"Now, nearer home," continued the announcer, "comes a special announcement from Trenton, New Jersey. It is reported that at 8:50 P.M. a huge, flaming object, believed to be a meteorite, fell on a farm in the neighborhood of Grovers Mill, New Jersey, twenty-two miles from Trenton. The flash in the sky was visible within a radius of several hundred miles and the noise of impact was heard as far north as Elizabeth."

Listeners leaned closer to their sets. In Grovers Mill, Dick Stives stared at the radio and gulped.

Again the broadcast returned to dance music—this time to "Bobby Millette and his orchestra" at the "Hotel Martinet" in Brooklyn. And again the music was interrupted by a news flash. Having just arrived at the scene of "impact" on the "Wilmuth farm" near Grovers Mill, reporter Carl Phillips, accompanied by Professor Pierson, beheld police, state troopers, and onlookers crowding around what appeared to be a huge metallic cylinder, partially buried in the earth.

About this time, some twelve minutes into the broadcast, many listeners to the *Chase and Sanborn Hour*, momentarily bored by a guest musical spot, turned their dials. A lot of them stopped in sudden shock as they came upon the CBS wavelength. The events being described seemed real to listeners—quite as real to them as reports, not many months before, that Adolf Hitler's troops had marched into Austria.

"I wish I could convey the atmosphere . . . the background of this . . . fantastic scene," reported Phillips. "Hundreds of cars are parked in a field back of us. . . . Their head-

---

[2]*The format was a familiar one to radio listeners. "Big band remotes"—network broadcasts featuring America's best-known dance bands as they played at one-night stands in ballrooms from coast to coast—were a staple of broadcasting during the 1930s.*

lights throw an enormous spot on the pit where the object is half-buried. Some of the more daring souls are venturing near the edge. Their silhouettes stand out against the metal sheen. . . ."

Professor Pierson described the object as "definitely extraterrestrial . . . not found on this earth. . . . This thing is smooth and, as you can see, of cylindrical shape." Then Phillips suddenly interrupted him:

"Just a minute! Something's happening! Ladies and gentlemen, this is terrific! The end of the thing is beginning to flake off! The top is beginning to rotate like a screw! The thing must be hollow! [shouts of alarm] Ladies and gentlemen, this is the most terrifying thing I have ever witnessed. . . . Wait a minute! Someone's crawling out of the hollow top. Someone or . . . something. I can see peering out of that black hole two luminous disks—are they eyes? Good heavens, something's wriggling out of the shadow like a gray snake. . . . I can see the thing's body. It's large as a bear and it glistens like wet leather. But that face. It . . . it's indescribable. I can hardly force myself to keep looking at it. The eyes are black and gleam like a serpent. The mouth is V-shaped with saliva dripping from its rimless lips that seem to quiver and pulsate. . . ."

Thirty state troopers, according to the reporter, now formed a cordon around the pit where the object rested. Three policemen carrying a white handkerchief of truce walked toward the cylinder. Phillips continued:

"Wait a minute . . . something's happening. [high-pitched, intermittent whine of machinery] A humped shape is rising out of the pit. I can make out a small beam of light against a mirror. . . . What's that? There's a jet of flame springing from the mirror, and it leaps right at the advancing men! It strikes them head on! Good Lord, they're turning into flame! [screams and shrieks] Now the whole field by the woods has caught fire! [sound effects intensify] The gas tanks, tanks of automobiles . . . it's spreading everywhere! It's coming this way

now! About twenty yards to my right [abrupt silence]."[3]

Now terror was afoot. A series of voices—fictional "announcers," "militia commanders," "network vice presidents," and "radio operators"—took up the narrative. At least forty people, according to the radio bulletins, lay dead at Grovers Mill, "their bodies burned and distorted beyond all possible recognition." And in a Trenton hospital, "the charred body of Carl Phillips" had been identified.

A current of fear flowed outward across the nation. Real-life police switchboards, first in New Jersey, then, steadily, throughout the whole Northeast, began to light up: "What's happening?" "Who's attacking America?" "When will they be here?" "What can we do?" "Who are they—these Martians?"

By now, according to the broadcast, "eight battalions of infantry" had surrounded the cylinder, determined to destroy it. A "Captain Lansing" of the Signal Corps—calm and confident at first, but with obviously increasing alarm—described what happened next:

"Well, we ought to see some action soon. One of the companies is deploying on the left flank. A quick thrust and it'll all be over. Wait a minute, I see something on top of the cylinder. No, it's nothing but a shadow. . . . Seven thousand armed men closing in on an old metal tube. Tub, rather. Wait, that wasn't a shadow. It's something moving . . . solid metal. Kind of a shield-like affair rising up out of the cylinder! It's going higher and higher! Why, it's . . . standing on legs! Actually rearing up on a sort of metal framework! Now it's reaching above the trees and searchlights are on it! Hold on [abrupt silence]."

---

[3]*Phillips's narrative bore a perhaps-not-coincidental resemblance to a famous eyewitness report by Chicago radio newsman Herb Morrison, who on May 6, 1937, had described the explosion and destruction of the German dirigible Hindenburg as it was about to moor at Lakehurst, New Jersey.*

In a matter of moments, a studio "announcer" gave America the incredible news:

". . . Those strange beings who landed in the Jersey farmlands tonight are the vanguard of an invading army from the planet Mars. The battle which took place tonight at Grovers Mill has ended in one of the most startling defeats ever suffered by an army in modern times; seven thousand men armed with rifles and machine guns pitted against a single fighting machine of the invaders from Mars. One hundred and twenty known survivors. The rest strewn over the battle areas from Grovers Mill to Plainsboro crushed and trampled to death under the metal feet of the monster, or burned to cinders by its heat ray. . . ."

Grovers Mill's couple of hundred real-life residents hardly knew what to make of it all. Young Dick Stives was stunned. He and his sister and brothers pulled down the shades in the farmhouse. Their grandfather shoved chairs against the doors.

Teen-aged Lolly Dey, who heard about the "invasion" while attending a church meeting, consoled herself by saying: "I am in the Lord's House." Another resident, seeing what he thought to be a Martian war machine among the trees (actually a water tower on a neighbor's property), peppered it with shotgun blasts. One man packed his family into the car, bound for parts unknown. He backed right through his garage door. "We're never gonna be needing that again anyway," he muttered to his wife.

"The monster is now in control of the middle section of New Jersey," proclaimed the voice on the radio. "Communication lines are down from Pennsylvania to the Atlantic Ocean. Railroad tracks are torn and service from New York to Philadelphia discontinued. . . . Highways to the north, south, and west are clogged with frantic human traffic. Police and army reserves are unable to control the mad flight. . . ."

Life was soon to imitate art. A wave of terror, unprecedented in its scope and rapidity, swept across New Jersey. A New Brunswick man, bound for open country, had driven ten miles when he remembered that his dog was tied up in the backyard of his home. Daring the Martians, he drove back to retrieve the dog.

A West Orange bar owner pushed customers out into the street, locked his tavern door, and rushed home to rescue his wife and children.

Twenty families began to move their belongings out of a Newark apartment house, their faces covered by wet towels to repel Martian rays. Doctors and nurses volunteered to come to hospitals to help handle the "war casualties."

At Princeton University, the chairman of the geology department packed his field equipment and headed into the night to look for whatever it was that was out there. The governor of Pennsylvania offered to send troops to help New Jersey. A Jersey City man called a bus dispatcher to warn him of the fast-spreading "disaster." He cut their conversation short with: "The world is coming to an end and I have a lot to do!"

Meanwhile, on the radio, the "Secretary of the Interior," speaking in a voice much like that of President Franklin D. Roosevelt, announced that he had faith in the ability of the American military to vanquish the Martians.[4] He solemnly intoned:

". . . placing our trust in God we must continue the performance of our duties each and every one of us, so that we may confront this destructive adversary with a nation united, courageous, and consecrated to the preservation of human supremacy on this earth."

A Trenton store owner ran out screaming, "The world is ending! The world is ending!"

---

[4]Network censors, concerned that the drama might sound too factual, had earlier requested more than thirty changes in the script. Thus, although he still sounded like Franklin Roosevelt, the"President" became the "Secretary of the Interior." The "U.S. Weather Bureau" was changed to the "Government Weather Bureau," the "National Guard" became the "State Militia," etc.

Another man dashed into a motion-picture theater in Orange, crying out that "the state is being invaded! This place is going to be blown up!" The audience hurriedly ran out to the street.

A woman in a Newark tenement just sat and cried. "I thought it was all up with us," she said. A man driving westward called out to a patrolman: "All creation's busted loose! I'm getting out!"

More grim reports issued from the radio. Scouting planes, according to the broadcast, had sighted three Martian machines marching through New Jersey. They were uprooting power lines, bridges, and railroad tracks, with the apparent objectives of crushing resistance and paralyzing communications. In swamps twenty miles south of Morristown, coon hunters had stumbled upon a second Martian cylinder.

In the Watchung mountains, the "22nd Field Artillery" set down a barrage against six tripod monsters—to no avail. The machines soon let loose a heavy black poisonous gas, annihilating the artillerymen. Then eight army bombers from "Langham Field, Virginia," attacked the tripod machines, only to be downed by heat rays.

Thousands of telephone calls cascaded into radio stations, newspaper offices, power companies, fire houses, and military posts throughout the country. People wanted to know what to do . . . where to go . . . whether they were safer in the cellar or the attic.

Word spread in Atlanta that a "planet" had struck New Jersey. In Philadelphia, all the guests in one hotel checked out. Students at a college in North Carolina lined up at telephones to call their parents for the last time. When a caller reached the CBS switchboard, the puzzled operator, asked about the end of the world, said: "I'm sorry, we don't have that information."

Radio listeners soon heard an "announcer," said to be atop the "Broadcasting Building" in Manhattan, describe a doomed New York City:

"The bells you hear are ringing to warn the people to evacuate the city as the Martians approach. Estimated in last two hours three million people have moved out along the roads to the north. . . . No more defenses. Our army wiped out . . . artillery, air force, everything wiped out. . . . We'll stay here to the end."

Something like madness took hold among radio listeners in New York City. People stood on Manhattan street corners hoping for a glimpse of the "battle." Thirty men and women showed up at a Harlem police station wanting to be evacuated. A woman had her husband paged at a Broadway theater and told him of the Martian landings; word spread quickly and a throng of playgoers rushed for the exits.

The radio voice continued: "Enemy now in sight above the Palisades! Five great machines. First one is crossing the river . . . wading the Hudson like a man wading through a brook. . . . Martian cylinders are falling all over the country. One outside Buffalo, one in Chicago, St. Louis. . . . Now the first machine reaches the shore! He stands watching, looking over the city. His steel, cowlish, head is even with the skyscrapers. He waits for the others. They rise like a line of new towers on the city's west side. . . ."

A Bronx man dashed into the street and saw people running in all directions. One New Yorker claimed he heard the "swish" of Martian flying vehicles. Another told of machine-gun fire. Atop a midtown Manhattan building, a man with binoculars "saw" the firing of weapons. In Brooklyn, a man called the police station: "We can hear the firing all the way here, and I want a gas mask. I'm a taxpayer."

An NBC executive was upset because *his* network wasn't carrying the ultimate news event. One man sped at eighty-miles-an-hour to reach a priest before the "death rays" overtook him; his car flipped over twice, but he lived.

The program played out the drama of doom

right to its end.

From atop his fictional building, the "broadcaster" continued his "eyewitness" report: "Now they're lifting their metal hands. This is the end now. Smoke comes out. . . . People in the streets see it now. They're running towards the East River . . . thousands of them, dropping in like rats. . . . It's reached Times Square. . . . People trying to run away from it, but it's no use. They . . . they're falling like flies. . . ."

Meanwhile, in real life, Boston families gathered on rooftops and thought they could see a glow in the sky as New York burned. A horrified Pittsburgh husband found his wife with a bottle of poison, screaming: "I'd rather die this way than that!"

People called the electric company in Providence, Rhode Island, to turn off all the city lights to make it a less visible target. A motorist rode through the streets of Baltimore, Paul Revere-fashion, blowing his horn and warning of the Martian invasion.

The staff of a Memphis newspaper readied an extra edition on rumored landings in Chicago and St. Louis. In Minneapolis, a woman ran into a church yelling: "This is the end of the world! I heard it on the radio!"

Back on the broadcast, the forlorn announcer carried on: "Now the smoke's crossing Sixth Avenue . . . Fifth Avenue . . . [coughing] a hundred yards away . . . it's fifty feet . . . [thud of falling body, then only sound of ships' whistles]."

In Salt Lake City, people started to pack before heading into the Rocky Mountains. One man, in Reno for a divorce, started to drive east, hoping to aid his estranged wife. A man and woman who'd run out of gas in northern California just sat and held hands, expecting any minute to see the Martian war machines appear over the tops of trees. Electric power failed in a village in Washington; families started to flee.

In Hollywood, John Barrymore downed a drink, went to his kennels and released his Great Danes. "Fend for yourselves!" he cried.

Then, from the radio, came the mournful call of a "radio operator": "2X2L calling CQ . . . New York. Isn't there anyone on the air? Isn't there anyone?"

Forty minutes into the broadcast, Welles gave his distraught audience a breather—a pause for station and program identification.

In the control room, CBS staffer Richard Goggin was startled as telephones there began to ring. That would only happen in an emergency. "Tension was becoming enormous in Studio One," he later recalled. "They had a tiger by the tail and couldn't let go."

For those brave enough to stay tuned, Welles was able to match the program's stunning first portion with an equally remarkable concluding sequence. In what amounted to a twenty-minute soliloquy, he, in the role of Professor Pierson, chronicled the events that followed the Martians' destruction of New York City. Welles's spellbinding voice—magnetic, doom-filled, stirring—held listeners mesmerized.[5]

In the script, a stoic Pierson, still alive in the rubble, made his solitary way toward the ruins of New York, hiding from the invaders as he went.

Along the way he met a "stranger," a former artilleryman. This survivor feared that the Martians would cage and enslave any humans still alive. The stranger was determined to outwit and outlast the Martians and, in time, to turn the heat-rays back on the invaders and even—if need be—upon other humans. And so, one day, new leaders would rule a new world.

Pierson, unwilling to join the stranger's cause, continued his lonely journey. Entering Manhattan through the now-empty Holland

---

[5]*Welles's closing narrative, fictionally dramatic in style and compressing months of events into twenty minutes, contrasted sharply with the realism of the first portion of the program. Nevertheless, many listeners apparently remained convinced that Martians had landed.*

Tunnel, he found a lifeless city:

"I wandered up through the Thirties and Forties . . . stood alone on Times Square. I caught sight of a lean dog running down Seventh Avenue with a piece of dark brown meat in his jaws, and a pack of starving mongrels at his heels . . . . I walked up Broadway. . . past silent shop windows, displaying their mute wares to empty sidewalks . . . ."

There seemed to be little hope left for the human race. Then Pierson "caught sight of the hood of a Martian machine, standing somewhere in Central Park, gleaming in the late afternoon sun":

"I rushed recklessly across Columbus Circle and into the park. I climbed a small hill above the pond at Sixtieth Street, and from there I could see standing in a silent row along the mall, nineteen of those great metal Titans, their cowls empty, their steel arms hanging listlessly by their sides. I looked in vain for the monsters that inhabit those machines. Suddenly my eyes were attracted to the immense flock of black birds that hovered directly below me. . .and there before my eyes, stark and silent, lay the Martians, with the hungry birds pecking and tearing brown shreds of flesh from their dead bodies."

The mighty Martians had fallen: ". . . it was found that they were killed by the putrefactive and disease bacteria against which their systems were unprepared . . . slain, after all man's defenses had failed, by the humblest thing that God in His wisdom put upon this earth."

In a sprightly epilogue, Welles then explained away the whole unsettling broadcast as the Mercury Theatre's "way of 'dressing up in a sheet and saying Boo!' . . . We annihilated the world before your very ears, and utterly destroyed the CBS. You will be relieved, I hope, to learn that we didn't mean it, and that both institutions are still open for business."

He tried cheerily to dispel the darkness: "So goodbye everybody, and remember . . . the terrible lesson you learned tonight. . . . And if your doorbell rings and nobody's there, that

was no Martian . . . it's Hallowe'en."

The joke was on the listeners. More than one hundred and fifty stations affiliated with CBS had carried the broadcast. About twelve million people had heard the program. Newspapers estimated that at least a million listeners, perhaps many more, had thought the invasion real.

Back in Grovers Mill, disenchantment began to take hold. Twenty-year-old Sam Goldman and three pals had been playing cards when they heard that the Martians were on the move down by the mill. They had thrown down their cards and jumped into a car, ready to face the invaders. "We got there and looked around," Sam said, "and nothing was going on."

A squad of New Jersey state troopers equipped with riot guns had deployed near the crossroads. They found little more than the dilapidated old mill itself.

Nearby, in their grandfather's farmhouse, Dick Stives, his sister, and brothers talked excitedly about the "men from Mars." Then their mother and father came home from the movies and told the children about the "make believe" on radio that everyone was talking about. Dick, more confused than ever, went upstairs to go to sleep, still half-sure that what he heard was "really real."

For the players who had inadvertently just made radio history, the next hours turned into a nightmare. As soon as Welles left the twenty-second-floor studio, he was called to a telephone. He picked it up, to hear the irate mayor of Flint, Michigan, roar that his city was in chaos because of the program and that he, the mayor, would soon be on his way to New York to punch one Orson Welles in the nose.

"By nine o'clock several high-ranking CBS executives had arrived or were in full flight toward 485 Madison. We were in trouble," recalled Larry Harding, a CBS production supervisor for the Mercury Theatre show.

Policemen hurried into the CBS building. Welles, Houseman, and the cast were held under informal house arrest. Staffers hastily stashed scripts, memoranda, and the sixteen-inch acetate disks upon which the show had been recorded.

Welles was taken to a room on the seventeenth floor, where reporters battered him with questions about whether he knew of the deaths and suicides his broadcast had caused (none have ever been documented), whether he knew ahead of time how devastating an effect his show would have (he said he didn't), and whether he had planned it all as a publicity stunt (he said he hadn't).

Finally, at about one o'clock Monday morning, Welles and the cast were "released," free to go out into the streets of New York where not a Martian was stirring. Welles walked a half-dozen blocks to the Mercury Theatre, where, even at that hour, members of the stage company were still rehearsing their new play.

Welles went up on stage, where news photographers were lurking. They caught him with his eyes raised, his arms outstretched. The next day his photograph appeared in newspapers throughout the country, over a caption that blurted: "I Didn't Know What I Was Doing!", or words to that effect.

The next morning headlines in major city newspapers reported the hoax: "Radio Listeners in Panic, Taking War Drama as Fact" (*New York Times*); "U.S. Terrorized by Radio's 'Men From Mars' (*San Francisco Chronicle*); "Radio Drama Causes Panic" (*Philadelphia Inquirer*); "Listeners Weep and Pray, Prepare for End of World" (*New Orleans Times-Picayune*).

Many of the listeners who had been deluded laughed good-naturedly at one another—and at themselves. Some professed not to have been taken in by what one woman called "that Buck Rogers stuff." But others turned their wrath on Welles, on the network, and on the medium that had turned their Sunday evening into a time of unsolicited terror.

CBS apologized to the public, but also pointed out that during the program no fewer than

four announcements had been made stating that it was a dramatic presentation, not a news broadcast.

A subdued Welles, believing his career was ruined, dutifully followed suit. "I don't think we will try anything like this again," he stated.

For two or three days, the press would not let Welles, nor radio, off the front page. Media rivalry played its part; newspaper publishers seemed anxious to portray radio—and Welles—as villains. The clipping bureau that served CBS delivered condemnatory editorials by the pound.

While newsmen "tsk-tsked," government officials fumed. Senator Clyde Herring of Iowa, reflecting the anger of many citizens, stated his support for legislation to curb such "Halloween bogymen." The Federal Communications Commission (FCC), flooded with complaint letters, tried to find a philosophical stance somewhere between imposing severe censorship and permitting unbridled expression.

Novelist H.G. Wells cabled his disregards from London. Although he had given CBS permission to air his novel, he complained that "it was not explained to me that this dramatization would be made with a liberty that amounts to a complete reworking of *The War of the Worlds*."

But some columnists and editorialists began to perceive significant merit in the program. Essayist Heywood Broun interpreted the broadcast as a cautionary tale: "Jitters have come home to roost. The peace of Munich hangs heavy over our heads like a thundercloud." *Variety*, under a headline stating "Radio Does U.S. A Favor," described the program as a warning to Americans of the danger of unpreparedness.

In a column that turned the tide of public opinion in favor of Welles and company, Dorothy Thompson called the broadcast "the news story of the century—an event which made a greater contribution to an understand-

■ ■ *Orson Welles, besieged by reporters the day after the 1938 broadcast of the "War of the Worlds." Welles expressed amazement and regret that his dramatization had created panic among millions of radio listeners.*

ing of Hitlerism, Mussolinism, Stalinism, anti-Semitism, and all the other terrorism of our time than all the words about them that have been written by reasonable men."

Welles, to his relief, soon learned that he would not be consigned to durance vile. "Bill Paley, the head of CBS, brought Orson and me up on the carpet and gave us a reprimand," Houseman later recalled. "But there was ambivalence to it. The working stiffs thought we were heroes. The executives thought of us as some sort of anarchists. But reason—and revenues—prevailed. A few days after the broadcast, when it was announced that Campbell's Soup had become a sponsor, the boys at the top began to think of us as heroes, or at least as employable persons, as well."

Some critics continued to decry the credulity of the American people. They spoke of the compelling power of the human voice emanating from the upper air. Radio, ominously, seemed able to reduce an entire country to the size of one room; it exerted unexpected power over susceptible millions.

For a book-length study titled *The Invasion from Mars*, Princeton University psychology professor Hadley Cantril interviewed scores of persons who had listened to the program. Speaking with them shortly after "that night," he received responses ranging from insecure to phobic to fatalistic.

"The coming of the Martians did not present a situation where the individual could preserve one value if he sacrifices another," Professor Cantril concluded from his research. "In this situation the individual stood to lose all his values at once. Nothing could be done to save any of them. Panic was inevitable."

Did Welles intend the panic? Had he hoped, by means of his magnificent dramatic powers, to gain all those headlines?

Houseman dismisses such conjecture as "rubbish." He declares: "Orson and I had no clear pre-sense of the mood of the audience. *The War of the Worlds* wasn't selected as a parable of invasion and war in the 1930s, but just as an interesting story unto itself. Only after the fact did we perceive how ready and resonant the world was for the tale. Our intent was theatre, not terror."

Welles and his players could not know that they had portrayed the shape of things to come. The program was, in a way, quite prophetic. Barely two weeks later, German foreign minister Joachim von Ribbentrop chillingly commented: "I would not be surprised if in the United States eye-witness reports are under consideration in which the 'Giants from Mars' marched up in brown shirts waving swastika flags."

Sooner than the peoples of the world could guess, a true nightmare—that of World War II —would be upon them.

Welles, of course, went on to memorable successes in motion pictures and theater. And his *War of the Worlds* broadcast became the most famous radio program of all time.

These days, the crossroads village of Grovers Mill is much the way it was that spectral night half a century ago. There are, however, signs of strangers nearby—new homes sprouting up among what had been potato fields. And futuristic shapes—sleek, glass-walled, high-technology industrial buildings—stand amid the trees.

But the old mill itself is still at the intersection of Millstone and Cranbury roads—a dot east of Princeton on the highway map. The weatherworn wooden structure, with a few of its millstones scattered about, stands lonely vigil.

Here fate tossed its random lightning-bolt. Here the "Martians" made their landing on what is now a municipal park. Nearby, ducks glide on a big, placid pond.

The former Wilson farm (the script spoke of the "Wilmuth" farm, but sightseers made do with the Wilson place) has long since been cut up into smaller properties. Here Martian-hunters once tramped across the cornfields looking for traces of the invaders.

Wayfarers from all parts of the world still occasionally wander the roads and fields of Grovers Mill. They know they will see no Martians, find no burn-marks on the earth left by war machines from outer space, nor come upon charred ruins wrought by the aliens' devastation. Still, drawn by curiosity, they come and look and wonder.

Not all Grovers Mill residents find such doings fascinating. The proprietor of a nearby gas station, for example, remembers the night of the "invasion", but didn't think much of it then and thinks as little of it now. "It doesn't make sense," he says with disdain. "Never has. Never will."

But for Dick Stives, now sixty-three, the "panic broadcast" till holds disquieting memories. Not long ago he walked around the "Martian landing ground."

"When I was a kid," he recalled, "I would crawl down near the wheel of the old mill, just by the pond there, and shuck my clothes and go in swimming. It was just a pond on a farm. But now, looking at it, I have to wonder why people still come so far to find a place where something that was supposed to happen didn't happen.

"I still remember," he said, "how I felt that night, up there in the bedroom in my grand-dad's place, in the dark, trying to sleep, thinking about what we had heard on the radio. The nighttime would make me think about how almost anything, just about anytime, could happen anywhere—even in Grovers Mill. Things in the shadows. Things I didn't understand."

■■■

STUDY QUESTIONS

1. Describe the early career of Orson Welles. Did he realize that his "War of the Worlds" broadcast would create such a controversy?

2. Describe how the show was structured to create tension and heighten suspense.

3. How did Americans react to the broadcast? What do their reactions suggest about the power of radio?

4. In your opinion, was the broadcast unethical or dangerous?

5. How did the struggles going on in Europe affect how Americans received the broadcast?

BIBLIOGRAPHY

For discussions of the role of advertising in the 1920s, see Stuart Ewen, *Captains of Consciousness* (1976). The influence of films on American culture is ably portrayed in Robert Sklar, *Movie-Made America* (1975) and Larry May, *Screening Out the Past* (1980). Paul Carter's *Another Part of the Twenties* (1977) is an excellent description of popular social attitudes during the infancy of the radio industry. Although there is not much literature on the history of radio, see Erik Barnouw, *A Tower of Babel: A History of Broadcasting in the United States* (1966) and Francis Chase, *Sound and Fury: An Informal History of Broadcasting* (1942). The broadcast itself is discussed in Howard Koch, *The Panic Broadcast* (1970) and Barbara Leaming, *Orson Welles* (1985).

HITLER'S LEGIONS IN AMERICA

Arnold Krammer

After a decade of poverty, unemployment, and economic uncertainty, the United States was transformed by the Nazi invasion of France in June 1940. Considered at the time to be one of the premier military powers on earth, France succumbed in less than a month to the German assault, and suddenly the United States was lifted out of its isolationist malaise. The country also left behind the Great Depression. In Franklin D. Roosevelt's words, "Dr. New Deal" gave way to "Dr. Win the War." Employment and government spending increased enormously because of military production. After the Japanese attack on Pearl Harbor in December 1941, the country entered a period of massive mobilization. Men marched off to war and women marched off to the factories. Unprecedented population shifts occurred as people moved to where they could work or be close to loved ones.

One great challenge had given way to another. World War II had a moral clarity about it that sanctioned sacrifice. Arrayed against the United States were the forces of evil, symbolized in Adolf Hitler's outstretched hand, Benito Mussolini's arrogant demeanor, or Hideki Tojo's tight smile. World War II seemed a global struggle between good and evil, and Americans spent a great deal of time between 1941 and 1945 convincing themselves of their own virtue as well as of the malignancy of fascism and its supporters. But amidst that great ideological crusade, some Americans had the opportunity to confront the enemy firsthand. By the end of World War II, there were more than 400,000 German prisoners of war in American camps. Their presence in small towns and cities across the country gave Americans a different image of the Axis "supermen." In "Hitler's Legions in America," historian Arnold Krammer describes those German POWs in the United States.

In the early morning in a small town, people might have been eating breakfast, businesses opening their doors for their first customers, and traffic coming to life. In the distance, people might have heard crisp guttural commands being shouted in German, and they might have shaded their eyes against the bright morning sun to stare at the columns of young men—blond, deeply-tanned, and healthy—as they marched through town to harvest the crops in the surrounding fields. A rural town in Nazi Germany? People across the United States who remember World War II know better. This scene could have taken place in Trinidad, Colorado; Algona, Idaho; Dermott, Arkansas; West Ashley, South Carolina; Evelyn, Michigan; or in any of several hundred other cities and towns across the country.

The scene would have been enacted by Americans by the second year of war, 1943, when the population was adjusting to the scarcity of certain products and to the daily influx of war news. People were exhorted to produce at extraordinary levels; farmers were moving to the city for higher-paying jobs in war industries; the scarcity of tires, gasoline, and batteries was patriotically endured; OPA ration books were the housewives' bibles; and "Mairzy Doats" was at the top of the charts. Young boys avidly followed the course of the war by shifting pins on their bedroom wall maps. People were amused to find that "Kilroy" (whoever he was) had gotten there ahead of them, and every advertisement reminded readers to "Buy War Bonds." The war touched everyone by then. But for most civilians the first contact with the enemy came when large numbers of German prisoners of war appeared in their communities.

"Hitler's Legions in America," by Arnold Krammer from American History Illustrated (June, 1983).
Copyright © 1983 by Historical Times, Inc.
Reproduced through the courtesy of Historical Times, Inc., publisher of American History Illustrated.

When the United States entered the war, the question of enemy prisoners was among the last consideration of a country recovering from a Japanese attack in the Pacific and feverishly preparing for a war in Europe. We had never held large numbers of foreign POWs in our history and were unprepared for the problems of managing them. But prepared or not, we suddenly found ourselves receiving captured German soldiers. More than 150,000 men arrived after the North African campaign in the spring of 1943, and between May and October of that year, an average of 20,000 POWs arrived each month. The Normandy invasion the following June sent the numbers soaring to 30,000 prisoners a month, and by the end of the year, they poured in at the rate of 60,000 a month. By the end of the war, the United States held more than 400,000 enemy captives in 511 camps across the country.

Some of the problems dealing with the POWs were minor, others nearly fatal to the program. No initial attempt was made, for example, to segregate hardened Nazis (many of whom were among the early prisoners from the elite Afrika Korps) from the anti-Nazis, which made later control and re-education of the POWs extremely difficult. German-speaking interpreters among the American guards were scarce since qualified linguists were immediately transferred to intelligence units overseas. This not only prevented the authorities from monitoring the political activities of their prisoners, but it made it easy for the POWs to playfully take advantage of the guards, or interchange identities and ranks when the opportunities arose.

In Washington, government agencies jealously competed for jurisdiction over the POW program. The Justice Department demanded responsibility for the prisoners' security, the War Department for control of the camps, the State Department for control over their eventual repatriation, and the War Production Board for issues involving their labor. Meanwhile, prisoners were already arriving from the battlefields of North Africa and Sicily, and the War Department, together with the Army Corps of Engineers, began scouring the country for camp sites.

Every available country fairground, municipal auditorium, and abandoned CCC camp was held in readiness, and military bases were ordered to prepare a section of the installation for arriving POWs. Construction began on hundreds of POW camps, designed for between 2,000 and 4,000 men and built to standard specifications. The major considerations in site selection were that the area have plenty of available land and that the camp be as far as possible from any critical war industries. As a result, two-thirds of all camps in the United States were located in the south and southwest. The camps had to be located two to three miles from towns and railroad lines—close enough to transport prisoners and provide work projects, but far enough from populated areas to minimize escapes and acts of sabotage. Each camp was made up of two to four compounds of about five hundred men each, and these compounds were surrounded by a heavy wire fence, as was the entire camp. The barracks were designed for utility, not comfort: a concrete slab floor, a structure covered with tarpaper or corrugated tin, rows of cots and footlockers, and a potbellied stove in the center aisle. Stark as they were, many Americans felt that the camps were too good for the prisoners and referred to their local camp as the "Fritz Ritz."

Local communities seldom had more than ten or twelve weeks to adjust to the prospect of hosting a POW camp. Most received word during late autumn of 1942, and while speculation ran high regarding the nationality of the prospective prisoners—relocated Nisei Japanese, German, or Italian military captives—both townspeople and farmers were generally optimistic about the economic and labor potential. The camps were quickly completed by the Corps of Engineers, and the com-

munities settled back to await their new "neighbors."

"When the day arrived for the first trainload of prisoners to reach Hearne," recalled Norman L. McCarver, a local Texas chronicler, "the roadways leading from the outskirts of town to the main entrance of the camp were lined with curious citizens waiting to get a good look at the German prisoners. They were still wearing the clothes they had on when captured several weeks previous. Bloodstains were still visible on those who had been wounded during the fighting in North Africa." In West Ashley, South Carolina, townspeople lined up along Main Street to stare at the 3,250 men in desert-khaki uniforms who disembarked from the train. "Holy Cow!" exclaimed septuagenarian resident Val Horn in recalling that November afternoon. "The line of prisoners stretched the whole distance from town, along Highway 61, all the way out to camp. Remember, we were a town of only 6,000 people!" The community of Rockford, Illinois, hosted 3,865 Germans at the nearby army training installation at Camp Grant; at Camp Como, Mississippi, more than 7,000 German prisoners were isolated on a section of the army base out of the way of the more than 60,000 G.I.s who passed through that training camp; at Camp Indianola, Nebraska, some 4,800 Germans spent the war years in relative comfort; and Somerset, Maryland, nearly tripled its population with the arrival of 3,760 Afrika Korps veterans. Even such tiny towns as Jerome, Arkansas; Ashwood, Virginia; Ysleta, Texas; and Worland, Wyoming, found themselves caught up in the POW program when small work camps of 100–300 prisoners sprang up nearby.

While every community contained some people who were disturbed at having Germans in their midst while their sons and husbands were overseas fighting Nazism, their animosity softened as the war progressed to victory and as the "humanness" of the prisoners became

■ ■ *Education played a key role in every compound, with English classes usually the most popular courses. At Camp Blanding, Florida, the prisoners' senior officer served as the instructor in English classes held daily.*

evident. Eventually, most people realized the logic of the POW program and the potential advantage of the prisoners to labor-starved farmers.

The prisoners themselves were relieved and somewhat astonished at the conditions and treatment which greeted them. Unlike the more security-conscious British, the American War Department allowed incoming prisoners to retain most of their personal belongings. At their first meal they saw foods that most had not tasted in years: beef, tomatoes, green veg-

etables, milk, even ice cream. To their delight they found that cigarettes and, in some camps, even beer and wine were available at the camp PX, purchasable with the canteen coupons that the government paid to them for daily work. "We thought we were in heaven," recalled a former POW. "Food which was not even found in our Mothers' kitchens at home! White bread, and real coffee! We were dumbstruck!" Such treatment caused some grumbling among Americans who resented the quality and quantity of food being fed to the POWs.

The government, however, realized that the better we treated the enemy prisoners in our custody, the better our own soldiers—some 90,000—in enemy hands might be treated. The logic worked. While Russian prisoners in Germany drank melted snow and ate rodents, and French prisoners were humiliated and kept on short rations, American POWs, while certainly not comfortable, received adequate, if not decent, treatment. Unfortunately the War Department never disclosed these motives to an anxious public living with red meat stamps and counting up ration points.

The German prisoners began settling into a daily routine. Following the Geneva Convention of 1929 as the only guideline, the POW camps were separated into different compounds for officers and enlisted men. High-ranking German officers were provided with individual rooms and the use of their enlisted valets. Like American officers in German camps, they were not required to work, seldom volunteered, and received a standard monthly salary: lieutenants received $20.00 a month; captains received $30.00; and majors and higher received $40.00. Enlisted men lived less luxuriously in barracks and were paid 10¢ per day in canteen coupons, plus an additional 80¢ in coupons for every day of mandatory labor. "That may not sound like much today," recalled a former German prisoner, "but that 80¢ would buy us 8 beers or 8 packs of cigarettes!"

The prisoners themselves maintained camp discipline. Long lines of Germans moved to and from their work without resistance or disorganization, led only by several noncommissioned German officers. German enlisted men snapped to attention whenever one of their officers strolled by, and there is no case on record of a German enlisted POW refusing to obey an order from his officer. Washington was greatly relieved that the combat-hardened veterans continued their iron discipline throughout the war, since they required fewer guards and allowed more G.I.s to be shipped overseas. Townspeople were also pleased and gratefully relaxed their vigilance as their earlier fears of mass escapes faded away.

In their spare time, the POWs had a variety of programs in which they could participate. They preferred sports as the most popular pastime, and both officers and enlisted men organized soccer games on the camp parade grounds at every opportunity. Families out for a Sunday afternoon drive often stopped beside their local POW camp to join the cheering crowds of POWs and guards watching young Germans aggressively kicking a soccer ball across a makeshift field. Some prisoners took up weightlifting, others participated in handball, and still others, curious about the customs of their hosts, learned to play baseball. Those prisoners who preferred intellectual to physical exercise had more than enough to occupy their time. Each camp contained men who had been carpenters, mechanics, linguists, or professors of history before the war, and they jumped at the opportunity to conduct classes in their specialties. Regular courses were taught in everything from physics and chemistry to American government, English, and journalism. Some camps even offered piano lessons and such courses as the history of American comic strips. These mini-universities required examinations, encouraged discussion, and issued final grades and even graduation certificates.

For those prisoners who showed an interest in subjects unavailable inside their camps, the War Department arranged for them to enroll in extension courses through local sponsoring universities. While there is no way of knowing how many POWs became dedicated fans of the Wisconsin Badgers, Texas Longhorns, or the Missouri Tigers, many prisoners of war did return to Germany with substantially improved educations.

As the war progressed through 1944, the War Department arranged for these POW students to receive university credit through the German Ministry of Education, and some of the men eventually graduated from German universities after finishing part of their undergraduate work at POW camps in the United States. Many have become successful German businessmen and professionals following their return. Today, Willibald Bergmann is a manufacturer in Nuremburg; Dan Kwart von Arnim is the director of a medical clinic; Carl Amery became a well-known writer, as did Hans Werner Richter; Werner Baecker is the New York representative for a German television network; and Heinrich Matthias is a high official in the Import-Export Department of Germany's second largest financial institution, the Dresdener Bank. Alfred Klein went back into the military when the *Bundeswehr* was authorized in 1956, and today he is a lieutenant colonel in the German air force and head of the Air Warfare Department at the German air force academy at Fürstenfeldbrück. Scratch many an influential German, and you may find an ex-POW who learned his basic English in Pennsylvania, Virginia, Oklahoma, or Tennessee. The two most important German officials in the United States today—Baron Rüdiger von Wechmar, president of the General Assembly of the United Nations, and Brigadier General Hans A. Link, German military representative to the United States and Canada—finished their service in the Afrika Korps in Camps Carson and Trinidad, Colorado.

Prisoners with additional spare time or who did not care to study or play soccer pursued personal hobbies or made handicrafts. Officers, in particular, were fond of gardening, while other prisoners built furniture, painted murals on the walls of camp theaters, mess halls, and clinics, or sculpted statues to be placed outside of the prisoners' canteen buildings. One enterprising prisoner at Camp Ruston, Louisiana, made a clock from some tin cans and used two soda bottles for weights, and it kept perfect time. At Camp Hearne, Texas, a group of Germans painstakingly constructed a waist-high replica of an old German castle complete with detailed turrets and moats. A curious visitor can still examine a medieval *schloss* rising just above the weeds in a corner of the empty landscape of the long-abandoned Texas camp site.

Too much leisure time is the deadly enemy of any prisoner, and prison memoirs are replete with stories of devices to keep prisoners occupied. Without sufficient work the military prisoner in particular, feeling abandoned by his country and despised by his captors, could become increasingly frustrated, hostile, and, in response to his training as a soldier, aggressive against his captors. The best solution was daily and tiring work. Fortunately, the government desperately needed agricultural labor, and the needs of the prisoners coincided with the needs of the government. Following a long period of bureaucratic debate involving the War Department, Department of Labor, Provost Marshal General's Office, union representatives, and lobbyists from a number of industries and agricultural pressure groups, the government hammered out a series of directives in the fall of 1943 outlining the use of POW labor in accordance with the restrictions laid out in the Geneva Convention.

The forced labor of enemy personnel had been a time-honored practice, and while the Geneva Convention did not prevent their employment, it did restrict their use. The prisoners had to be physically able, and the work neither dangerous nor unhealthy. Most important, no work projects would be directly related to the war effort or instrumental in the defeat of the prisoners' homeland. Consequently, the men could work in two areas: at military installations, and as labor contracted out to private businesses, farms, and small industries.

Within weeks of the labor directive, thousands of prisoners were assigned to various military bases to replace American personnel as administrative clerks, bakers, carpenters, electricians, garbage collectors, sign painters, and in many other capacities. Returning American soldiers were startled and often angered to find themselves being processed by indifferent clerks wearing Wehrmacht uniforms with the letters "PW" stenciled across the back. Wounded G.I.s recovering at Halloran General Hospital in New York or Glennan Hospital in Oklahoma were no less outraged to be helped by German-speaking orderlies whose Afrika Korps uniforms were visible beneath their open white smocks. Security was understandably heavy during the first few months because army officials feared the damage that POWs might accomplish when allowed to work inside active military bases and hospitals.

Despite the lack of incidents and the apparent ease with which the prisoners accepted their tasks, the army issued an official *Handbook for Work Supervisors of Prisoner of War Labor* which instructed American guards to "be aloof, for the German only respects firm leadership. . . . Allow them to rest only when necessary. DRIVE!" The American General Wilhelm D. Styer put it more succinctly. When his aide questioned some aspect of prisoner labor, General Styer grunted, "We must overcome the psychology that you cannot do this or that. I want to see these prisoners work like ants!"

And work they did. Within a year of the beginning of the war, the domestic labor market was already feeling the pinch, especially in the agricultural sector since so many able-bodied young men were being drafted into the armed forces. By mid-1942 even the government admitted that the situation was alarming. The practical decision was to provide POWs to the labor-starved market on a contract basis.

This bureaucratic rat race eventually entangled itself, and by mid-1944 the requirements for POW labor became so informal that in many cases a telephone call or personal visit to the county agent's office would be sufficient to obtain a truckload of POWs. Soon even the most skeptical farmers were waiting in line to

get their share of these efficient and inexpensive workers. Harly any eligible industry failed to use at least a few truckloads of prisoners during the war, and the POWs saw "action" in jobs that ranged from logging, food processing, flood control, and quarrying to their ironic but far from unenjoyable assignment as Kosher meat packers in Farmington, New Jersey. Their greatest contribution, however, was in agriculture.

In Louisiana, prisoners worked in the rice, cotton, and sugar cane fields, harvesting more than 246,000 acres of cane in 1944 alone. In Missouri, they dug potatoes, shocked oats, and harvested wheat. They picked tomatoes in Indiana, potatoes and sugar beets in Nebraska, wheat and seed crops in Kansas, and peanuts in Georgia.

They were young, farmers recalled, about twenty years old on the average and very eager to learn. The prisoners worked a steady ten-hour day, broken only by a lunch of bologna sandwiches supplied by the farmers and eaten out in the fields. They were guarded by a minimum number of armed G.I.s from the camp, and due to the low incidence of escapes, supervision was negligible. "I remember a number of occasions when we were being trucked out of Camp Rucker, Alabama," said former POW Alfred Klein, "and the guard would ask me to hold his rifle until he had climbed in or out of the truck. Almost as an after-thought, he would ask me to hand it up to him a few minutes later."

There were some difficulties, to be sure. Many prisoners were inexperienced in farm work and, as a result, did not produce as much as "free" labor. Another problem voiced by American farmers concerned the fact that they would train one group of POW laborers only to be assigned a different group the following day. Finally, there was the language barrier, and the resulting difficulties were more often humorous than not. One day in the spring of 1944, an American sergeant was marching a large group of prisoner-laborers the several miles from a farm to the prisoner compound at Camp Reynolds, Pennsylvania, when he found himself groping in his vocabulary for the German equivalent of "Halt!" (which happens to be "Halt!"). He threw up his arm to stop them, and the entire platoon of prisoners came to attention, shot their arms upward, and chorused, "Heil Hitler!"

The stories and anecdotes about the prisoners are as varied and numerous as the men and tasks involved, and without a doubt, readers of these pages who used POW labor or lived near a camp will smile as they recall an amusing incident.

Despite the extensive work, education, and recreation programs, prisoners escaped, approximately 100 per month or slightly more than three per day. Working on agricultural sites under the minimal supervision, some prisoners walked away from their work parties to find female company. Others wanted to shop in local stores, or mingle with people, or only wanted to be alone. Indeed, prisoner escapes were as varied as imagination and circumstances allowed. They dug tunnels under the wire fences, jumped from barracks roofs, hung under laundry trucks, and posed as American guards. Whatever the method of escape, the prisoners were almost always rounded up within hours of their disappearance.

Sheriff Harold Ellsworth of Lewiston, Illinois, near Camp Ellis, described his feelings about the escapees. "They made us feel kind of sorry for them, these German escapees," recalled the sheriff. "We would find them there in the streets, without a word of English, in Bloomington, in Peoria, in Galesburg; or else in the woods, completely lost like strayed sheep. Yes, I tell you, it was rather pitiful. Besides, local people weren't afraid of them. When they met up with one, they called us; we came, put a hand on their shoulder, and gently brought them back to camp."

Unlike American prisoners in Germany who had the help of the French underground and could escape to Switzerland, German prisoners in the United States found little sympathy among Americans. Even if they did, there was no place for them to go. Such logic, however, did not stop 2,222 men from trying.

In Wyoming, two German escapees succeeded in getting almost three miles from their camp and were already celebrating their newfound freedom when they ran headlong into a detachment of American troops on maneuvers. They were returned to Camp Douglas at gun point and presented to the startled camp authorities who were not yet aware of their escape. On another occasion, a German was captured outside of Lisbon, New Hampshire, when he accepted an automobile ride from the local police chief. On another occasion, an escapee made it from Camp Grant, Illinois, to Chicago in time to celebrate New Year's Eve 1945 in a tavern. When the party moved to a private home for sandwiches, Paul Stachowiak went along too. Everybody thought he was the guest of somebody else, but when he began to boast that he had just escaped from the POW camp in nearby Rockford, one of the more sober partygoers called the police. Another prisoner was captured by a Pennsylvania railroad detective in Oil City, Pennsylvania, when he failed to understand that his ticket did not entitle him to remain in the parlor car. Five others were captured in a hen house outside of Indianola, Nebraska, by several country boys armed with shotguns. Still another escapee was captured near Camp Como, Mississippi, as he sat down in the back of a southern bus directly beneath the sign that read: "Colored Only."

A few prisoners had greater success. Georg Gaertner was a former draftsman who escaped from his POW compound at Deming Army Air Corps Base, New Mexico, on September 21, 1945. The last statement he made to his comrades before his escape was that he had no intention of returning home to the devastation of postwar Germany, and he apparently made good on his promise. Gaertner simply melted into the mainstream of American life. Despite an intensive search by the FBI and his photo appearing in post offices across the country, he has never been located. In 1963, on the authority of the U.S. Attorney General, the FBI ended its search for Georg Gaertner, and at the moment of this writing, the now sixty-two-year-old German is the only former POW who remains at large.

As the war drew to a close, the question of repatriation became an immediate and thorny problem, and the United States was torn between two opposing points of view. One segment of public opinion warned that to send the German prisoners home so soon would be detrimental to our labor situation and dangerous to the Allied occupation effort to prevent the rise of Neo-Nazism. The other side argued that with the war over, the country no longer had any legal right to hold or work the POWs. The latter position prevailed. Repatriation finally began in November 1945, and the POWs were returned to Germany at the rate of 50,000 a month. The final boatload of 1,500 German prisoners sailed from Camp Shanks, New Jersey, on July 22, 1946, "waving an indifferent farewell." The commander of Camp Shanks, Colonel Harry W. Maas, echoed the feelings of the country at large, sighing, "Thank God, that's over!" With the exception of 188 German prisoners still in hospitals, psychiatric wards, military prisons, or on the run in the United States, it was indeed over.

People living in communities that had once hosted large numbers of German prisoners have forgotten the experience as nearby camps gradually disappeared. One by one, they were shut down during the postwar months and the facilities sold at auction. But if the townspeople have forgotten about those days, the prisoners have not.

Announcements appear periodically in German newspapers and military journals reminding former POWs from particular camps about an upcoming reunion or social function. More than 300 former prisoners from Camp Mexia, Texas, gathered for such a reunion in Heidelberg in June 1978. They crammed their signatures on several 6" x 8" photo postcards and mailed them to favorite guards and townspeople. Some even return with their families to their old camp sites to stroll through the "old neighborhood," noting changes, taking photographs, and reminiscing with welcoming friends, farmers, and even community dignitaries.

During one of these visits, a former POW named Wilhelm Sauerbrei best summarized the experience of the prisoners. Driving from Houston to Hearne, Texas, in a car full of reporters and friends, the former Afrika Korps corporal regaled the occupants with stories and recollections about his camp days.

"You must have had it pretty easy," a Houston reporter commented.

"I'll tell you, pal," Sauerbrei said confidently, "if there is ever another war, get on the side that America isn't, then get captured by the Americans—you'll have it made!"

■■■

STUDY QUESTIONS

1. What problems did the United States have in administering the prisoner of war program?

2. How did the government decide where to build the prisons? How did American communities react to the POWs? Did their reactions change over time? Why or why not?

3. In general, what kind of treatment was extended to the POWs? How did the Germans feel about their care? Why?

4. What was the day-to-day routine in the camps? Why did the camps require relatively little security?

5. What kind of work did the POWs do? How did they respond to the work?

6. Why did relatively few German POWs try to escape? How successful were they? Why?

BIBLIOGRAPHY

An excellent study of the impact of World War II on American society is John Morton Blum, *V Was for Victory* (1976). Also see Richard Polenberg, *War and Society* (1972). Phillip Knightley treats the effect of World War II on American journalism and culture in *The First Casualty* (1975), as does Alan Winkler in *The Politics of Propaganda* (1978). An excellent study of Franklin D. Roosevelt as a wartime leader is James MacGregor Burns, *Roosevelt: The Soldier of Freedom* (1970). The impact of World War II on the American economy is treated in Donald Nelson, *Arsenal of Democracy* (1946) and Bruce Catton, *The War Lords of Washington* (1946).

JOHN WAYNE GOES TO WAR

Randy Roberts

More than a decade after his death, John Wayne's movies are still enjoyed by millions of Americans. The individual names of the films are hardly important. A John Wayne western says it all, evoking a world divided between the forces of good and evil where one man, steely-eyed and leathered by the sun, stands ready to preserve order and punish lawbreakers. From his first major film in 1930 to his last leading role in 1976, John Wayne played the same role. He was the hero—sometimes gruff and occasionally flawed, but always there when the fighting began. He was Davy Crockett at the Alamo, the Ringo Kid on the stagecoach, the Quiet Man in Ireland, and the man who shot Liberty Valance. On screen, he fought Indians and Outlaws in the West, Nazis and Japanese in World War II, communists in the Cold War, and North Vietnamese and Viet Cong in the Vietnam War. And he always won, even if he died in the process.

But John Wayne was also part of Hollywood, part of the dream factory that catered to American fantasies and myths. His wars were fought and his victories won only in front of the cameras. During World War II when he was eligible for the draft, he chose to accept a deferment and remain in Hollywood and make movies. Like many other people in the motion picture industry, he decided that he could support America's war effort—and his own career—best by starring in movies. In the following essay, Randy Roberts examines John Wayne and Hollywood during the early years of World War II.

December 7, 1941. The news reached Hollywood at 11:26 on a calm Sunday morning. The Japanese had attacked American naval and air bases in Honolulu. A few people refused to believe the news. It seemed impossible, almost like another "War of the Worlds" broadcast, and they waited for the soothing voice of an announcer to tell them that it was only make believe. Everything about the day clashed with the brutal facts. The weather was perfect, even for a city where ideal weather was the norm. A cool night breeze blew off the desert from the northeast, but by 11:00 it was already in the low 70s. For the Hollywood elite, many of whom had gone to their vacation retreats in Malibu, Palm Springs, or the High Sierras, golf and swimming, not war, was on the day's agenda. Before the news reached Los Angeles, harmony reigned. Only the day before, the UCLA Bruins and the USC Trojans had played to a 7–7 tie, and that very morning a *Los Angeles Times* headline announced "FINAL PEACE MOVE SEEN."

The attack stunned Los Angeles. Responses varied. Some followed normal schedules. Thousands turned up at the "little world championship" football game and watched the undefeated Hollywood Bears, led by Kenny Washington and Woody Strode, defeat the Columbus Bulls. During the game, news updates reminded the spectators that the Bears' victory would probably not be remembered as the day's most important event. In another part of town, several hundred spectators watched Paramount Studio's baseball team defeat an "all-Jap aggregation." After the game, the FBI took the Japanese team into custody. The attack, however, disrupted most schedules. Golfers finished the holes they were playing and returned to the clubhouse. Gossips ended their conversations about Harry Warner's new granddaughter or the removal of Eddie Albert's tonsils or the antiaircraft men who had set up shop at Hollywood Park, and turned to more urgent topics. Thousands simply got into their automobiles—tanks full and rubber treads still good—and drove aimlessly through the city, leading to traffic jams in downtown Los Angeles and Hollywood.

Soon the rumors started to ricochet like bullets. Air defense men had known the attack was imminent. Two squadrons of airplanes—that's thirty planes—had been sighted over the California Coast. Japanese airplanes had reconnoitered the Bay Area. Bombed the Golden Gate Bridge. Pearl Harbor was only a stepping stone. California was next. There would be an uprising of Japanese Americans. Sabotage was certain. Moved to action by the rumors as well as sound precaution, policemen went on 12-hour shifts and sent extra security guards to dams, bridges, and power stations. Most others waited for FDR's announcement that the United States was now at war.

Hollywood and the entertainment industry responded to the attack with sincere feelings of patriotism mixed with an equally sincere desire to cash in on the event. Studios abandoned a few films already in production with poorly timed themes or poorly chosen titles—the musicals *Pearl Harbor Pearl* and *I'll Take Manila* and the comedy *Absent Without Leave*, about a GI who goes AWOL. Just as quickly studios secured the copyrights for more promising titles—*Sunday in Hawaii, Wings Over the Pacific, Bombing of Honolulu, Remember Pearl Harbor, Yellow Peril, Yellow Menace, My Four Years in Japan,* and *V for Victory.* Tin Pan Alley produced topical songs within days of the attack. Although none muscled onto the Hit Parade, such songs as "Let's Put the Axe to the Axis," "We're Going to Find the Fellow Who Is Yellow and Beat Him Red, White and Blue," "They're Gonna Be Playin' Taps on the Japs," "The Sun Will Soon Be Setting for the Land of the Rising Sun," "To Be Specific, It's Our Pacific," "When Those Little Yellow Bellies Meet the Cohens and the Kelleys," and "You're

---

"John Wayne Goes to War," by Randy Roberts.
Copyright © 1993 by Randy Roberts.

a Sap, Mr. Jap" expressed the angry mood of the country. The Metropolitan Opera Company, sensing that Americans did not want to see a sympathetic portrayal of any Japanese, dropped their production of "Madame Butterfly." The Greenwich Village Savoyards followed the Met's lofty example and dumped their production of "The Mikado."

While Tin Pan Alley turned out their topical tunes and opera companies pruned their repertoires, Americans huddled close to their radios. On Monday morning and Tuesday night FDR delivered his impassioned war speeches before Congress. For a few days, America—and particularly the West Coast—moved through a fog of air raid alarms, blackouts, and tense expectations. They listened as America's foreign commentators broke the news that Germany and Italy had declared war on the United States. They listened to the news that the Germans had sunk two British ships and that the Japanese had followed up Pearl Harbor with attacks in the Philippines, Hong Kong, Wake Island, Guam, and other Pacific strongholds.

Hollywood moaned that the war was a killer at the box office. Certainly flights of parochialism were the standard Hollywood reaction to any event. In 1935 when Mussolini's troops stormed into Ethiopia and the world focused on the League of Nations, a Hollywood producer asked a friend, "Have you heard any late news?" Yes, the friend replied hotly, "Italy just banned *Marie Antoinette!*" This episode of tunnel vision was surpassed in 1939 when Italy ruthlessly invaded Albania. Louella Parsons, Hollywood's leading gossip writer, began her column that week: "The deadly dullness of the past week was lifted today when Darryl Zanuck announced he had bought all rights to *The Bluebird* for Shirley Temple."

By mid-December Hollywood spokesmen complained that Americans were too interested in the war to go to the movies. Attempting to demonstrate that Hollywood *was* concerned with other events, *Variety* observed that the war had also hurt Christmas shopping, but clearly the box office crisis overshadowed all other concerns. The Wolf Man's *Variety* advertisement announced "Listen to That Box Office Howl!" but the only noise was the studio's howl of financial pain. The same was true for *The Great Dictator, Sergeant York, Citizen Kane,* and the season's other top pictures. Amidst considerable hand wringing, Hollywood leaders speculated on the long-term impact of the war on the industry.

John Wayne shared the industry's general concern, although his worries focused more specifically on the effect the war would have on his own career. After years of struggle with bad scripts and tight budgets, by late 1941 he was moving closer to the fringes of stardom. The reviews he had received for *Stagecoach* and *The Long Voyage Home* had pushed his career to a new level. Republic's head Herbert Yates responded by searching for better scripts, assigning first-line directors, and increasing the budgets for Wayne films. *The Dark Command,* Wayne's first film for Republic under the contract his new agent had negotiated for him, reflected Wayne's new status. Yates allocated $700,000 for the film—more than any previous Republic project—and hired Raoul Walsh to direct it. He also arranged for Claire Trevor and Walter Pidgeon to star in the film with Wayne. And less than four months before the attack on Pearl Harbor, Wayne had finished his work on Cecil B. DeMille's *Reap the Wild Wind,* which Paramount had scheduled for a March 1942 release.

New agents, new contracts, better directors, better films—at the age of thirty-four Duke was a player in Hollywood. But he was not yet a major star. In late December 1941, *Variety* issued its annual review of the stars. It set down clearly where an actor or actress stood in the complicated Hollywood pecking order. At the summit of the hierarchy were the performers whose pictures earned the most money for the year: Gary Cooper, Abbott and Costello, Clark Gable, Mickey Rooney, Bob Hope, Charlie Chaplin, Dorothy Lamour, Spencer Tracy, Jack Benny, and Bing Crosby. They had helped make 1941 the best year ever for domestic box office receipts.

Next came the individual studio reports. The stars and featured performers of the individual studios were listed and briefly discussed. The major studios controlled the major talent. MGM led the pack; its stars included Gable, Rooney, Tracy, Robert Taylor, Lana Turner, James Stewart, Hedy Lamarr, Judy Garland, Myrna Loy, William Powell, Joan Crawford, Nelson Eddy, Jeanette MacDonald, Greta Garbo, Norma Shearer, the Marx Brothers, and a host of other leading performers. If the other studios could not match MGM, they could all boast of their proven box office attractions. Warner Brothers, king of the gangster genre, had James Cagney, Humphrey Bogart, Edward G. Robinson, John Garfield, and George Raft, as well as Erroll Flynn, Bette Davis, Merle Oberon, and Ronald Reagan. Twentieth Century Fox had a group of attractive leading men and women which included Tyrone Power, Betty Grable, Gene Tierney, Henry Fonda, Randolph Scott, Maureen O'Hara, and Linda Darnell. Paramount had its comedians—Hope, Crosby, and Benny—as well as Lamour, Claudette Colbert, Veronica Lake, Paulette Goddard, Fred MacMurray, and Ray Milland. RKO featured Ginger Rogers, Orson Welles, Cary Grant, Carole Lombard, Ronald Coleman, and Gloria Swanson. Universal had a great year in 1941 thanks to the success of Abbott and Costello. And Columbia featured Peter Lorre, Boris Karloff, Fay Wray, and the recently acquired Rita Hayworth.

At the bottom of the hierarchy were the smaller studios and their performers. There dwelled Monogram. "No pretenses. No ambitious production. Just bread and butter," noted *Variety*. Its older cowboy and action stars—Jack LaRue, Buck Jones, Tim McCoy, and Bela Lugosi—kept the studio afloat. Finally came Republic. *Variety* listed Gene Autry and John Wayne as Republic's "two corking box-office assets." Wayne's reputation derived from his "loanout" status. Like Monogram, Republic produced films for theaters outside of the major distribution circles, and a star like Wayne who was used by the major studios gave prestige to the Poverty Row studio.

Wayne, always a clear-thinking realist, knew where he stood in the Hollywood hierarchy. He was a star in the third-and-fourth-run theaters in the South and Southwest, in areas with more cattle than people. His success following *Stagecoach* introduced him to the first-and-second-run palaces of the East, Midwest, and West. At the end of 1941 he was nowhere near the summit of the hierarchy, far from the status of such leading men as Clark Gable, Robert Taylor, Tyrone Power, Cary Grant, Gary Cooper, or Henry Fonda. But Wayne was ambitious, and no one in the industry had his capacity for work. The facts were indisputable: his reputation was growing but not yet firmly established, and he was a thirty-four year old leading man. If he enlisted, would his fragile reputation survive two, three, four years in the service? How many years did he have left as a leading man? Enlistment, in the final analysis, would probably end his career.

While Wayne pondered his future and prepared for his next picture, other Hollywood stars put their careers on hold and their lives on the line. Pearl Harbor aroused deep emotions in Hollywood. During the next four years journalists and politicians would accuse the film industry of being cynical, opportunistic, greedy, and worse. The charges were often accurate. But in late 1941 and early 1942 scores of actors, directors, producers, and technicians enlisted out of a deep sense of patriotism. Like millions of other Americans, they were shocked by the Japanese attack and wanted to help win the war.

Henry Fonda, one of Duke's boon companions on the vacations to Mexico, felt the pull of patriotism. He was thirty-seven—three years older than Wayne—and had a wife and three children. For all practical purposes, he was exempt from the draft. But he had a baby face, and he did not want the wives and mothers of soldiers and sailors to see him on the screen and ask, "Why isn't he out there?" Besides, as he told his wife, "this is my country and I want to be where it's happening. I don't want to be in a fake war in a studio or on location. . . . I want to be on a real ocean not the back lot. I want to be with real sailors and not extras." After he finished *The Ox-Bow Incident*, the film in which he was then starring, Fonda drove to the Naval Headquarters in Los Angeles and enlisted. No screen photographers were present; his press agent had not tipped off any reporters. Fonda wanted it simple, no different than other Americans.

John Ford, the man Duke admired the most, also felt the pull. During the late-1930s he had followed with growing uneasiness the spread of fascism in Europe. When Ford's leading writer Dudley Nichols sent him a wire of congratulations for winning the 1940 Academy Award for his direction of *The Grapes of Wrath*, Ford wrote back, "Awards for pictures are a trivial thing to be concerned with at times like these." That spring he organized the Naval Field Photographic Reserve unit, which Washington officially recognized. The forty-six year old Ford was ordered to report to Washington for active duty in the month before Pearl Harbor. Immediately and without publicity he left Hollywood. He left the money, the fame, the career, the glamour.

When the Japanese attacked Pearl Harbor, Ford was eating lunch at the eighteenth-century Alexandria, Virginia, home of Admiral William Pickens. He watched the Admiral take the urgent phone call. He saw the blood drain from his face. After they heard the news, Pickens' wife, Darrielle, showed Ford a scar on their home where a Revolutionary War musket ball had torn through a wall. "I never let them plaster over the hole," she said. Throughout the war and for the rest of his life Ford would remember the story. He wanted to be part of that tradition.

Tradition and patriotism pulled Jimmy Stewart into the war. Stewart's grandfather had fought for the union during the Civil War. Stewart's father had fought in the Spanish-American War and World War I. In February 1941, Stewart attempted to enlist in the Army Air Corps but was rejected because his 147 pounds was ten pounds too light for his six feet four inch frame. He went on a diet of candy, beer, and bananas. In a month he had put on the ten pounds and he was sworn into the Army. He left his $1,500-a-week movie salary for a private's wages.

Other leading men and Hollywood personalities also felt the pull. Wayne's fellow star at Republic, Gene Autry, joined the Army Air Corps. Robert Montgomery enlisted in the Navy. Tyrone Power joined the Marines. William Holden went into the Army. After the death of his wife Carole Lombard in January 1942, Clark Gable also enlisted in the Army. David Niven, Laurence Olivier, and Patrick Knowles returned to their native Britain and enlisted. Ronald Reagan, Sterling Hayden, Burgess Meredith, and Gilbert Roland all signed up. So too did directors Frank Capra, William Wyler, Anatole Litvak, John Huston, and William Keighley; producers Hal Roach, Jack Warner, Gene Markey, and Darryl F. Zanuck; writers Garson Kanin and Budd Schulberg; cameraman Gregg Toland; and thousands of other Hollywood workers. By October 1942 over 2,700—or 12%—of the men and women in the film industry had entered the armed forces. Some like Fonda and Stewart enlisted quietly and without fanfare. Others like Reagan and Zanuck and Gable made the process of enlistment and service an act of Hollywood. But quietly or loudly they did serve.

In 1941 professional baseball players were the only men who received as much attention and adulation as Hollywood stars. When the war started they laid down their bats and picked up service issue weapons. Joe DiMaggio, Hank Greenberg, Bob Feller, Ted Williams, Bill Dickey, Peewee Reese, and most of the other baseball legends from the 1930s entered the service. More than 4,000 of the roughly 5,700 players in the major and minor leagues served in the armed forces during the war. Some were killed or seriously injured during the conflict. Others experienced the loss of crucial skills because of a lack of practice. And even the players who returned to the big leagues after the war lost several years from a career which at best was painfully short.

Even America's popular comic book heroes enlisted in the war effort. Joe Palooka and Snuffy Smith joined the Army; Mickey Flynn enlisted in the Coast Guard; Dick Tracy received a commission in naval intelligence. Batman, Robin, the Flash, Plastic Man, Captain America, Captain Marvel, the Green Lantern, the Spirit—the cream of the super heroes—fought German and Japanese in the pages of thousands of comic books. The only important super hero who did not enlist was Superman—and he stayed at home for a very good reason. His creators, Jerry Siegel and Joe Schuster, reasoned that Nazis and Japs would be no match for the Man of Steel, and with real Americans fighting and dying in the war it might denigrate their efforts if Superman defeated the Axis. To keep Superman out of the war but still show his patriotism, Siegel and Schuster had Clark Kent—a.k.a. Superman—declared 4-F. Superman's famed X-ray vision malfunctioned during his preinduction physical; instead of reading the eye chart in front of him, Superman accidentally looked through the wall and focused on the one in the next room. Shazam—4-F. Instead of fighting abroad, Superman battled Fifth Columnist activities in the States.

Movie stars and baseball stars, superheroes and boxing champions—they took their place with millions of other less famous Americans. More than any other war in America's history,

World War II was a popular, democratic war. In the five years between December 1941 and December 1946, 16.3 million Americans entered the armed forces. All males between the ages of 18 and 64 had to register for the draft, although the upper age limit for service was set at 44 and later lowed to 38. One out of every six American men wore a uniform during the war. The wealthy fought along side the poor, the single beside married men with children. Unlike the Vietnam War, relatively few men tried to avoid military service. For a man in his twenties or thirties not in uniform, the central question was, "Why not?"

It was a question John Wayne had to face for the next four years. Wayne's case was not a matter of draft dodging. Although by late 1941 Wayne's marriage was falling apart and his visits to his home and children were becoming more infrequent, he was technically married and had four children. This coupled with his age meant that he was not a prime candidate for the draft. And in February 1942 General Lewis B. Hershey, Director of Selective Service, called the motion picture industry "an activity essential in certain instances to the national health, safety and interest, and in other instances to war production." In accordance with his statement, he instructed Selective Service officials in California to grant deferments to men vital to the industry. Although Hershey's order was not meant as a blanket deferment, and although the Screen Actors Guild announced that it did not want any privileged status, the California draft board was liberal in its application of the ruling. Many Washington and California officials argued that Gary Cooper was more valuable to the war effort as Sergeant York—a role he played in the top money grosser in 1941 which oozed patriotism—than as Sergeant Cooper.

The most visible Hollywood commodity in need of protection during the war was the leading man. Out of sincere feelings of patriotism or the fear of being branded as a slacker, many of Hollywood's youngest and most famous leading men enlisted. The shortage created a ticklish problem for studio public relation staffs. Leading men were supposed to project youth, sexuality, virility, and strength. But a movie star projecting those traits on the screen during the war faced the painful question, "Why isn't he in the army?" As *Daily Variety* commented, "No more he-man build up of young men as in the past, for these might kick back unpleasant reverberations. If the build up is too mighty, [the] public may want to know if he's that good why isn't he in the Army shooting Japs and Nazis. This is a particularly touchy phase and p-r has to be subtle about it." The irony of the situation was best expressed by an agent who told a producer about his latest discovery: "I've got a great prospect for you—a young guy with a double hernia."

A leading man during the war needed a good profile and an adequate voice, but more importantly he had to be either over forty, married with two or more children, or 4-F. Gary Cooper, Bing Crosby, James Cagney, John Garfield, Don Ameche, and Joel McCrea all "had a brood at home to call [them] 'pop'." Warner Baxter, Neil Hamilton, and Nils Aster—all forty to fifty—led the new crop of "semi-romantic" leading men. Sonny Tufts, the handsome, ex-Yale football player who starred in the hit *So Proudly We Hail*, was safely classified as 4-F.

John Wayne's draft status was a family present. Like other actors with two or more children, he could have enlisted. Like his friends Henry Fonda or John Ford, he could have placed his concern for his nation above his concern for his family, status, and career. There were some aspects of his life that Wayne never spoke to the press about; some that he rarely ever even spoke to his family or closest friends about. His decision not to enlist was a part of his life that he did not discuss. Pilar Wayne, whom Duke met and married a decade after the war, said that the guilt he suffered over his failure to enlist influenced the rest of his life.

Mary St. John, who worked at Republic during the war and became Wayne's personal secretary after the war, agreed. She recalled that Wayne suffered "terrible guilt and embarrassment" because of his war record. The fact that his brother Robert served in the Navy only exasperated Wayne's sensitivity. His mother, who always openly favored Robert, was not above reminding Wayne that Robert, and not Duke, had served his country during the great crisis. On the screen, Wayne was the quintessential man of action, one who took matters into his own powerful hands and fought for what he believed. Never had the chasm between what he projected on the screen and his personal actions been so great.

Throughout 1942 and 1943, as he made one picture after another and as his reputation as a leading man soared, Wayne flirted with the idea of enlistment. He was particularly concerned about his stature in Ford's eyes, and he suspected that Ford had little respect for Celluloid soldiers. His suspicion was dead right. In early October 1941, shortly after he went on active duty, Ford wrote his wife that Wayne and Ward Bond's frivolous activities were meaningless in a world spinning toward total war. "They don't count. Their time will come." Three months after Pearl Harbor, Ford again mentioned Wayne in a letter to his wife. In a letter soaked in contempt, he remarked that he was "delighted" to hear about Wayne and Bond sitting up all night on a mountain top listening through earphones for signs that the Japanese were attacking California: "Ah well—such heroism shall not go unrewarded—it will live in the annals of time."

A pattern developed in Wayne's letters to Ford during the first two years of the war. Again and again, Wayne told Ford that he wanted to enlist—planned to enlist—as soon as he finished just one or two pictures. In the spring of 1942, Wayne inquired if he could get in Ford's unit, and if Ford would want him. If that option were closed, what would Ford suggest? Should he try the Marines? Plaintively,

Wayne insisted that he was not drunk and that he hated to ask for favors, adding, "But for Christ's sake, you can suggest can't you?" A year later, Wayne was still considering enlistment in his letters to Ford. After he finished one more film he would be free: "Outside of that [film] Barkus [sic] is ready, anxious, and willin'."

But Barkus never did enlist. Toward the end of his life, Wayne told Dan Ford, John Ford's grandson, that his wife Josie had prevented him from joining Ford's outfit. According to his story, OSS head and Ford's superior William J. Donovan had sent a letter to Wayne explaining when Duke could join the Field Photographic Unit, but Josie never gave him the letter. He also confessed that he considered enlisting as a private, but rejected the idea. How, he pondered, could he fight along side seventeen and eighteen year old boys who had been reared on his movies? For them, he said, "I was America." In the end he concluded that he could best serve his country by making movies and going on an occasional USO tour.

The problem with any discussion of Wayne's "war record" is that it depends too much on statements made by Duke and others long after the war ended. Did his wife hide Donovan's letter? There is no such letter in Donovan's public and private papers. Did he believe that he was such an American institution by 1942 that he could not enlist as a private? This statement is difficult to take at face value when one considers that Gable, Power, Fonda, and Stewart—far more important stars than Wayne—were willing to share a foxhole or a cockpit or a ship deck with seventeen and eighteen year old American soldiers or sailors. Did, in fact, Wayne try to enlist? Catalina Lawrence, a script supervisor at Republic during the war who sometimes doubled as Wayne's secretary, remembers writing letters for Wayne attempting to get him in the service. "He felt so bad," she recalled, "especially after Robert was drafted into the Navy. Duke wanted to get in, but he just never could."

The closest one can come to the truth is Wayne's Selective Service record, and even here there are a few problems. The government has destroyed full individual records; all letters between Wayne and his draft board have long since been turned into ashes in official government incinerators. The skeleton of Wayne's record, however, remains. When the war started, Marion Mitchell Morrison—Selective Service Serial Number 2815, Order Number 1619—was classified 3-A, "deferred for dependency reasons." A continuation of that classification was requested and granted on November 17, 1943. Local draft boards periodically reviewed all classifications, and depending on their needs the government changed some classifications. To maintain a deferment or obtain a different deferment, a person or his employer had to file an official request. After returning the initial Selective Service Questionnaire, Wayne never personally filed a deferment claim, but a series of claims were filed "by another." Although the records have been destroyed, Republic Pictures almost certainly filed the claims. After Republic's leading money earner Gene Autry enlisted in 1942, studio president Herbert Yates was determined to keep Wayne out of uniform and in front of the camera. Therefore, in April 1944 another deferment claim was filed and granted reclassifying Wayne 2-A, "deferred in support of national health, safety, or interest." A month later Wayne was once again reclassified. With the war in Europe and the Pacific reaching a critical stage, Duke received a 1-A classification, "available for military service." This reclassification generated a series of new deferment claims, and on May 5, 1945, Wayne was once again classified 2-A. His last classification came after the war when he received a 4-A deferment on the basis of his age.

At any time during the war Wayne could have appealed his classification. At no time did he file an appeal. Always an active man, the war years were particularly frantic for Wayne. With his career bolting forward, he worked at four different studios and starred in thirteen pictures. In addition, he divorced his first wife, met and married his second wife, and led an active social life. When he was not working, the absence of a uniform gnawed into Wayne's self-respect and sense of manhood. It was then that he wrote Ford that "Barkus was ready." But then would come another movie, another delay, another link in a chain of delays that stretched from Pearl Harbor to Hiroshima.

Perhaps in his own mind his single-minded pursuit of his career meshed with his sense of patriotism. If so, Wayne was not the only person in Hollywood who expressed such beliefs. In March 1942, shortly after the premiere of *Reap the Wild Wind,* Wayne attended a luncheon for the Associated Motion Picture Advertisers. Cecil B. DeMille addressed the audience on the subject of the role Hollywood should play in the war. DeMille, his voice charged with moral urgency, remarked, "The job of motion pictures is to help bring home a full realization of the crisis and of the deadly peril that lurks in internal squabbles. Ours is the task of holding high and ever visible the values that everyone is fighting for. I don't mean flag waving, but giving the embattled world sharp glimpses of the way of life that we've got to hang on to in spite of everything." In DeMille's mind, the civilians who worked in the motion picture industry had a job and a duty every bit as important to the war effort as the American Marines fighting on Pacific islands or American sailors battling the Germans on the Atlantic. Victory demanded unity and dedication by all Americans—at home and abroad, civilian and military.

The Roosevelt Administration agreed with DeMille. Only weeks after the war began, FDR announced that Hollywood had an important role to play in the war effort: "The American motion picture is one of our most effective media in informing and entertaining our citizens. The motion picture must remain free in so far as national security will permit." Unlike steel, automobiles, and other vital American industries, which were heavily controlled by the government during the war, the controls on the film industry were comparatively light. Although several of FDR's advisors counseled him to take over Hollywood production, he believed that the industry leaders would perform their duty better if they remained in charge. But the subtext of Roosevelt's message to Hollywood was clear. The studio heads could continue to make money, but their product had to serve the war effort. They had to combine propaganda within the entertainment. If they did not, then the government would take over the industry.

Washington's liaison with Hollywood was Lowell Mellett, a former editor of the *Washington Daily News* who had the good looks of an older Hollywood character actor. After considerable bureaucratic reorganization in June 1942, Mellett was placed in charge of the Bureau of Motion Pictures (BMP) which was nominally under the Domestic Branch of the Office of War Information (OWI). While Mellett, dubbed the "white rabbit" for his less than forceful character, administered the BMP from his Washington office, the bureau's Hollywood office was run by Nelson Poynter. A close friend of Mellett's as well as a newspaper man, the dark-haired, frail looking Poynter had unassailable New Deal and interventionist credentials but lacked even basic knowledge of Hollywood and film making. Nevertheless, FDR charged the team of Mellett and Poynter with making sure Hollywood produced the kind of pictures deemed important to the war effort.

If he were uncertain about the process of making pictures, Poynter was very explicit about what kind of films he expected Hollywood to produce. From his tiny office in Hollywood, Poynter and his small staff compiled a blueprint to guide the motion picture industry's wartime behavior. Officially titled *The Government Informational Manual for the Motion Picture Industry,* it set down the official—and ideological—government line. The central question every producer, director, and writer should ask was "Will this picture help win the war?" Every film should contribute to that end by presenting America's effort and cause, its allies and friends, in the most generous possible terms. The manual emphasized that the United States was engaged in nothing less than "a people's war" to create a "new world" where want and fear were banished and freedom of religion and speech were a birthright. Social democratic and liberal internationalist in its intent, the manual was designed to move Hollywood toward its ideological position.

In practical terms, *The Government Informational Manual for the Motion Picture Industry* codified a long list of "do's" and "don'ts" for Hollywood. Whenever possible, for example, films should "show people making small sacrifices for victory"—"bringing their own sugar when invited out to dinner, carrying their own parcels when shopping, travelling on planes or trains with light luggage, uncomplainingly giving up seats to servicemen or others travelling on war priorities." Americans on the homefront should be portrayed as happy, busy, productive, rationing-loving patriots, planting victory gardens, taking public transportation even when they could afford to drive, and generally pitching in to win the war. Heading the list of "don'ts" was disunity on the homefront or the battlefront. America was not to be presented as divided by any racial, class, or gender issue. Scenes of strikes or labor conflict critical of labor were frowned upon; plots which suggested that the United States was anything less than a paradise for black Americans were verboten; and resorts to ethnic or religious bigotry were censored. Similarly, the allies of the United States had to be presented as paragons of national virtue. Hollywood was instructed to use its magic to manufacture a classless Britain, an efficient and incorruptible China, and a democratic Russia. Noting the irony of Hollywood's whitewash of the Soviet Union, *Variety* commented, "War has put Hollywood's

traditional conception of the Muscovites through the wringer, and they have come out shaved, washed, sober, good to their families, Rotarians, brother Elks, and 33rd Degree Mason."

During the war, John Wayne starred in movies which fit comfortably within the parameters defined by Mellett, Poynter, and the BMP. To be sure, the producers of the Wayne films occasionally clashed with the BMP, but the conflicts were usually caused by the BMP's narrow ideological interpretation of individual scenes or insistence that a specific propaganda message appear in the film's dialogue. In a larger sense, *The Government Information Manual for the Motion Picture Industry* described an America—if not a world—that Wayne already held dear. Perhaps the physical world of Hollywood was closer to the ideal presented by the BMP than any other American community. The motion picture industry was populated by WASPs, and immigrants, Catholics and Jews, whites and blacks, men and women. A communist might write a screenplay which a liberal would produce and a reactionary direct, but for a time all three would be unified by a common bond—the movie. In Hollywood some of the highest paid stars were women, and a few blacks—very few—earned incomes higher than Southern cotton planters. And nowhere in America was the Horatio Alger ideal of rags to riches so religiously enshrined. Hollywood was an industry that literally manufactured modern American folk heroes. It was America's "last frontier." It was the crossroads where luck, looks, and talent intersected. And in a strange way, it was the America described in the pages of the BMP official manual. Of course Wayne believed in its message. He was its message.

John Wayne's wartime movies portrayed the BMP's message even before the bureau was created and the manual written. During the first four months of 1942, as American forces experienced painful losses in the Pacific and the Atlantic, Wayne made two pictures—*The*

Spoilers and *In Old California*. Both films have similar plots. *The Spoilers*, based on the Rex Beach novel, is set in Nome in 1900 during the Alaskan Gold Rush, centers on a claim jumping scheme, and features a love triangle between Wayne, a society woman, and a dance-hall girl. During the course of the film, Wayne thwarts the claim jumping scheme as he discovers that the society woman is heartless and the dance-hall girl has a heart as pure as a Klondike nugget. *In Old California* is set in Sacramento in 1848–1849 during the California gold rush, features a land grabbing scheme, and highlights a love triangle between Wayne, a society woman, and a dance-hall girl. By the end of the film, not only does Wayne foil the land grabbing scheme and discover that the society woman is heartless and the dance-hall girl has a heart as pure as a nugget from Sutter's Mill, but he also saves the entire region from a particularly nasty typhoid epidemic.

The message of both films was also similar: defend your property with every fiber of your being. Neither film expresses any sympathy for men who traffic in appeasement or legal niceties. In *The Spoilers* two prospectors announce in a saloon that they were "just working along kinda peaceful like" when at least twenty claim jumpers forced them off their stake. What could we do, they ask. "Ya still have five fingers on your gun hand, ain't ya," comes the immediate reply. All at the bar nod in agreement to the sage advise. Even the sexual innuendo revolves around claim jumping and force. Crooked gold commissioner Alexander McNamara (Randolph Scott) plans to jump both Roy Glennister's (John Wayne) Midas Gold Mine and his woman, Cherry Malotte (Marlene Dietrich). He tells Cherry that he might "move into [Glennister's] territory." "Could be tough going," Cherry cautions. "But worth it," McNamara replies. Glennister's use of brutal force defeats both forms of aggression. In one of the longest fist fights in film history, Glennister outlasts McNamara. Force—not the impotent and even dishonest

representatives of the law—proves the only solution to aggression.

The same conclusion is expressed in *In Old California*. When the good but timid citizens of Sacramento are attacked, Tom Craig (John Wayne), the otherwise peace-loving town pharmacist, asks, "Doesn't anybody fight back around here?" "Angry men defending their home," he asserts, can never be defeated. And, of course, they do triumph. Lead by the forceful Craig, "the people" overcome both the land grabbers and the typhoid epidemic. For Americans embroiled in a war to prevent land-grabbing aggression, the message of *The Spoilers* and *In Old California*—both released in the dark month of May 1942—reinforced official government statements about the causes of the war.

In Old California was little more than an inexpensive Republic formula picture. Without John Wayne, wrote the *New York Times'* reviewer Bosley Crowther, the picture "would be down with the usual run of strays." *The Spoilers*, however, received favorable reviews. "The he-men are back," noted the *New York Times*. "John Wayne is . . . virile," commented *Variety*. "John Wayne is a valuable piece of property," was the judgment of the *Chicago Tribune*. The acting characteristics which Wayne had spent a decade perfecting—the sideways glance and smile at his female lead, the tight-lipped, shark-eyed stare at his evil rival—found worthy recipients in *The Spoilers*. Dietrich's seething sexuality and Scott's oily villainy contrasted nicely with Wayne's cocky masculinity.

Wayne was maturing as an actor, and he knew it. On the set he was more self-confident. He was occasionally rude and impatient with Scott, who took a more artistic approach to his craft than Wayne. Scott, a Southerner with courtly manner, disliked Duke. On and off the set of *The Spoilers*, Dietrich occupied Wayne's attentions. The affair which had begun when Wayne and Dietrich were starring together in *Seven Sinners* had not yet run its passionate course. On and off the set they were constantly together. They dined at Ciros, the Brown Derby, Mocambo, and the Trocadero, Hollywood's trendiest restaurants. They went to sporting events and on weekend hunting and fishing trips together. Dietrich "was the most intriguing woman I've ever known," Wayne later told his wife Pilar. She shared her bedroom and ideas with Duke. And this combination of sexual and intellectual stimulation bolstered Wayne's belief in himself.

At Republic Pictures, Herbert Yates was not as interested in Wayne's emotional and intellectual growth as in his burgeoning box office power. Paramount released *Reap the Wild Wind* in March 1942, and it opened in the first-run theaters and music halls throughout the country. Respected *New York Times* reviewer Bosley Crowther saw the Technicolor epic in Radio City Music Hall. Always a generous reviewer for DeMille's films, he was particularly lavish in his praise for *Reap the Wild Wind*. It was "the essence of all [DeMille's] experience, the apogee of his art and as jam-full a motion picture as has ever played two hours upon a screen. It definitely marks a DeMillestone," Crowther wrote. The review, and others like it, echoed like gold coins in Yates's mind. *Reap the Wild Wind* was a hit—reviewers' compared it with that other breezy film, *Gone With the Wind*—and John Wayne was one of its stars, even if he were killed in the movie by a giant squid and therefore failed to win the heroine. And Wayne belonged to Yates and Republic. If Yates had been unimpressed by Duke's success in *Stagecoach* and *The Long Voyage Home*, he now fully understood the worth of his star attraction.

With profits and the war in mind, Yates put Wayne into his first war film. If it were not for the fact that *Flying Tigers* was a shameless rip off of *Only Angels Have Wings*, the film might be considered as the prototype for World War II combat films. It possessed everything but originality, a point that did not cause serious concern for an action oriented studio

like Republic. Howard Hawks's *Only Angels Have Wings* (1939) contained all the motifs that film scholar Robert B. Ray has labeled as basic to Hollywood's World War II combat films: "the male group directed by a strong leader, the outsider who must prove himself by courageous individual action, the necessity for stoicism in the face of danger and death, the premium placed on professionalism, and the threat posed by women."

Only Angels Have Wings centers on a group of pilots in a South American jungle contracted to deliver the mail over a range of dangerous, stalactite mountains of unearthly appearance. In this group of flying mercenaries is a brave leader called "Pappy" who emphasizes teamwork, a man branded as a coward who has to prove his courage to win acceptance, a woman who threatens to destroy the chummy fraternity atmosphere, and pilots who share a common Hemingwayesque code of life and language. They speak with their actions, resist expressing their emotions, and demonstrate their dependency and even love in such nonverbal ways as asking for a cigarette or a match.

Flying Tigers contains all the same elements. This time the mercenary pilots are part of Colonel Claire Lee Chennault's "American Volunteer Group," flying against the Japanese for China on the eve of Pearl Harbor. Once again, the leader stresses the value of teamwork and is called "Pappy" by his men. Once again, there is a suspected coward who must prove himself, a flamboyant individualist who on the surface seems to only care about himself, and a woman who threatens the harmony and effectiveness of the male unit. There is even the same language of cigarettes and matches and painful grimaces when talk turns to matters of the heart. The similarities of plot and structure are so striking that Ray commented that "Hawks should have sued for plagiarism."

But for all the similarities—and there were many—there was a major difference. *Flying Tigers* went into production shortly after Pearl

Harbor during America's darkest months in the Pacific War and dealt with the most urgent topic in the world: the war. It was filmed from May to July, 1942, months that saw the Japanese take Corregidor and the United States win the Battles of Coral Sea and Midway. *Flying Tigers* capitalized on the national mood. At a moment when the nation demanded a hero, Republic responded with John Wayne. At a time when the Americans longed for good news from the Pacific, *Flying Tigers* recounted the heroics of Chennault's "American Volunteer Group." During a crisis when the country wanted to believe the best of its allies and the worst of its enemies, the film presented Chinese straight from the pages of Pearl S. Buck's *The Good Earth* and automatous Japanese fresh from hell. In addition, the film touched the rawest of American nerves—Pearl Harbor. FDR's full war speech is replayed in the film, and the climactic scene occurs after the Japanese attack on Pearl Harbor.

The film was an ideal vehicle for Wayne. The role of the solid, quiet leader around whom all the action and all the other parts revolved played to Duke's strengths. Increasingly in his recent films he was developing a palpable screen presence. Without talking, often without moving, he dominated a scene. In one scene, for example, the pilots listen to FDR's war speech on the radio. Slowly the camera moves in for a close-up on Wayne, who stands silent, listening to the FDR's message, a cigarette in his left hand. During the entire message, Wayne never moves. His eyes and mouth do not change expression. The only movement is the smoke drifting upward from Wayne's unsmoked cigarette. At the end of the speech, he takes a deep breath and walks off screen. Roosevelt had said it all; Wayne could only have added a trite cliché. Duke played the scene with controlled passion and complete sincerity. It is a powerful scene which underscored Wayne's screen presence.

Republic believed *Flying Tigers* conveyed the message advocated by the Office of War Information's Bureau of Motion Pictures. The film emphasized teamwork. Woody Jason (John Carroll) tells his fellow mercenaries early in the film that he is in China for the $600 a month and the $500 bonus for every Japanese plane he shoots down: "This is not our home. It's not our fight. It's a business. And, boy, I hope business is good." "It's every man for himself, isn't it," he asks just before he bums a cigarette from one man and a match from another. But by the end of the film Woody sacrifices his life in a suicide mission to save Jim "Pappy" Gordon (John Wayne). After Pearl Harbor, he realizes that China is as important as his "home street." Scenes that emphasize the importance of non-flying personal and mechanics similarly stress the themes of teamwork and cooperation. And if that did not provide enough propaganda content, *Flying Tigers* is filled with good-hearted, loyal Chinese and cold, ruthless Japanese.

Government officials, however, had mixed reactions to the film. Harry B. Price, a government consultant on China, noted that although the film was generally of a high caliber, it left "much to be desired from the standpoint of an adequate portrayal of our Allies, the Chinese." Like so many other Hollywood films, wrote Price, *Flying Tigers* presented the Chinese as "likable, but slightly ludicrous," and there is "little in the picture to suggest that the Chinese people are human beings just as varied and many sided in their natures as Americans." In addition, the film did not explore Chennault's tactical innovations. The Bureau of Motion Picture staffer who reviewed *Flying Tigers* agreed with Price's assessment. Marjorie Thorson complained that the film's glorification of individual heroics muted its theme of teamwork and cooperation, that the Chinese are presented as harmless and slightly incompetent people, and that the major issues of the war are not discussed. She notes that although there are Chinese nurses and doctors in the movie, only American nurses are shown changing bandages and "the final decision in any matter of a flier's health is left to the *non-professional* American squadron leader . . . just being an American presumably qualifies him to make medical decisions over the head of the trained Chinese." Even worse, "no Chinese men are shown fighting." "Altogether," she concluded, the "picture attempts a great deal more than it accomplishes."

Official complaints often demonstrated an ignorance both of filmmaking and the war. Members of the "American Volunteer Group" charged that *Flying Tigers* was "unbelievably bad" because it contained several factual errors and employed two former members of the AVG as technical advisors who had been dishonorably discharged for being "suspected of perversion." Contentions that filmmakers distort history by focusing on the individual or the small group at the expense of historical reality reveal a deep misunderstanding of the industry. As for *Flying Tigers'* treatment of Chiang Kai-shek and the Chinese, blindly generous is the best description. Divided by warlordism and civil war, plagued by corruption and inefficiency, Chiang's Kuomintang government dismissed "aggressive action" against the Japanese before Pearl Harbor and after December 7, 1941, left any serious fighting to the United States. As one American military official noted in late 1941, "The general idea in the United States that China has fought Japan to a standstill and has had many glorious victories is a delusion." If *Flying Tigers'* portrayal of the Chinese is historically inaccurate, it was closer to reality than the line adopted by the BMP. And the assertion in the film that Americans provided the combat muscle in the war did reflect actual conditions.

The entire debate was irrelevant at Republic. Yates was not interested in the veracity of *Flying Tigers*. Republic was a bottom line studio, and its only concern was ticket sales. From its first preview, the film exceeded Republic's usual modest expectations. The *Hollywood Reporter* announced, "*Flying Tigers* marks an all-time production high for Republic. It is a

smashing, stirring, significant film. . . . It will be a record grosser in all engagements, and no theater in the land should hesitate about proudly showing it." *Variety* agreed: In *Flying Tigers,* Republic has its best picture." Even though the film was released late in the year, *Flying Tigers* became one of 1942's leading box office successes and the only picture in the top twenty not produced in one of the major studios.

No one at Republic had to search for the reason. It was John Wayne. If Republic executives needed confirmation, they found it in every major review. *Hollywood Reporter:* "John Wayne is at his peak. . . . " *Variety:* "John Wayne matches his best performance. . . . " *New York Times:* "Mr. Wayne is the sort of fellow who inspires confidence. . . . " Republic had a hit and a star. Yates was now convinced. So was the rest of the industry. And during the next three years of war, Wayne would reconfirm again and again his star status as his name alone came to guarantee box office success.

Now more than ever, Yates was determined to keep Wayne. Shortly after the release of *Flying Tigers* the film's producer, Edmund Grainger, and director, David Miller, entered the armed service. Neither would make another picture until the late 1940s. Wayne believed that he too should enlist. Yates refused to release Wayne. The loss of Gene Autry, whose contract to make eight straight pictures for Republic had to be shelved when the singing cowboy enlisted in the Army air service, devastated Yates. He told Wayne that he would sue him for breach of contract if Duke enlisted. Furthermore, Yates announced, if Wayne enlisted he would make certain that Duke would never work for Republic or any other studio again. Although Yates's threat violated government policy—every person in uniform was guaranteed their civilian job once the war ended—Wayne did not press the issue. He feared poverty and unemployment, and perhaps more, he feared losing the status he had achieved and sinking into obscurity. Always a man haunted by the ghosts of his own insecurity, he stayed out of uniform, secure in his home at Republic.

Wayne's home was Republic, but his contract allowed him to make pictures for other studios. With the scarcity of leading men becoming more pressing every month, Duke was never in greater demand. It was an ideal situation for Wayne. He was a man who never made peace with inactivity. He loved his work and he hated the time between pictures. Mary St. John, who worked as Wayne's personal secretary for over twenty-five years, said that part of his problem was that he had no hobbies, nothing to do to fill the empty days. His daughter Aissa commented that he "was a slave to his energy." On location he always awoke by four-thirty or five A.M., and even when he was not working on a picture he was up at dawn. "He never slept late. Ever," Aissa remembered. Once up, and wired by his morning coffee, he was ready for work, and when there was no work, he simply had to endure long periods of restless rest. And in 1942, such stretches were intolerable. His home life was empty, his marriage almost over, many of his friends in uniform. When he worked, his life had structure and purpose. When he was not working, he had time to mull over the irony that without serving a day in the armed forces he was becoming a World War II hero. It was during these periods that he penned "Barkus" letters to Ford.

Throughout 1942 Duke worked at a hectic pace. *The Spoilers* was shot in January and February, *In Old California* in March and April, and *Flying Tigers* in May, June, and July. While *Flying Tigers* was in post-production, Wayne moved on to other films. Between the end of July and September he starred in *Reunion in France* for MGM, and in September and October he starred in *Pittsburgh*, another Universal film with Marlene Dietrich and Randolph Scott. Both *Reunion in France* and *Pittsburgh* were released in December. In one year Wayne had made five films, all released

that same year. In addition, *Lady for the Night* and *Reap the Wild Wind* had also premiered in 1942. There were few empty periods.

Like *Flying Tigers, Reunion in France* and *Pittsburgh* were war films. *Reunion in France*, however, was a peculiar sort of war film, the product of MGM's odd but predictable slant on life. MGM, noted Warner Brothers' executive Milton Spalding, "was a studio of white telephones." Quality—or at least the illusion of quality—mattered, and studio head Louis B. Mayer spent money to obtain it. As a result, at MGM nothing was what it seemed, everything was idealized. Reality never entered the MGM lot. Women especially had to look perfect. Cameramen "had to photograph the movie queens and make them look damn good," said MGM director George Cukor. If such MGM women as Greta Garbo, Joan Crawford, Jean Harlow, Norma Shearer, Lana Turner, Greer Garson, and Myrna Loy had individual styles, they all shared a common glamour and elegance. Regardless of the role they were called on to play, they always projected beauty and glamour.

After Pearl Harbor and the start of the war, Hollywood wags exchanged jokes about how the conflict would be portrayed at MGM. "The Japs may take California but they'll never get in to see Louis B. Mayer," quipped one wit. When an industry personality remarked that the United States needed a positive slogan that articulated what the country was fighting for, a less earnest listener replied, "Lana Turner." There was a truth in both jokes. As long as Louis B. Mayer called the shots at MGM, only movies that presented a highly stylized version of World War II would be made. And as long as Mayer approved all projects, MGM would fight a war to make the world safe for Lana.

Reunion in France brought America face to face with the stark glamour of war. The film centers on the trials and clothes of Michele de la Becque (Joan Crawford), a wealthy French socialite who loses her mansion and carefree life when the Germans invade France in 1940.

■■■ *John Wayne achieved superstardom making war movies during the 1940s. Here he is pictured with Anna Lee in the "Flying Tigers," a 1942 production.*

With the swiftness of the Nazi blitzkrieg, her comfortable, insulated world is shattered. Her industrialist fiancé turns collaborationist, her wealth is confiscated, and she is forced to work for her former dressmaker—a job that pays poorly but allows her to remain the best dressed woman in Paris—to pay her bills. Resisting Nazi domination, she befriends Pat Talbot (John Wayne), an American RAF Eagle Squadron flier who has been shot down and wounded behind enemy lines, and helps him escape. The film ends with Michele's reunion with her fiancé, who turns out to be a resistance fighter in collaborationist clothing. Far from helping Germany, the industrialist had been sending the Nazis faulty war materials to foil their efforts to dominate Europe.

The BMP reacted angrily to MGM's sanitized version of the war. "If there were ever a perfect argument for OWI reading of scripts before they are shot, this picture is it," wrote BMP staffer Marjorie Thorson in her review of the film. The picture failed the war effort on a number of counts. Count one: the film presented the Gestapo as "cruel, suspicious, and sadistic" but contained a favorable portrayal of all other Germans. The German military governor of Paris is depicted as a courtly, sweet, and charming older gentleman, an echo of a European aristocracy of decency and integrity. Furthermore, the German soldiers were disciplined and polite. Count two: the film suggests that any greedy, opportunistic collaborationist may really be an upstanding, patriotic member of the French Resistance. "It is a well known fact," the reviewer reported, "that many of the great French industrialists were pro-fascist long before the present war began; that they helped the Nazis conquer France; that they are now reaping the blood-stained rewards of their betrayal." Count three: the film shows nothing of the misery that the Germans have brought to the French people. MGM portrays a France that "falls with great elegance. Everyone we see is beautifully gowned, comfortably housed, and apparently well fed." Nazi occupation of Paris, the film insinuates, only means that the swastika hangs on the railroad stations and dumpy German women get the first crack at the latest Parisian fashions. Count four: the film misses the chance to contrast Nazi and democratic ideologies. Beyond the heroine saying that democracy is not dead and will live again in France, the film fails to explore the vital issue. In the context of the film, democracy suggests only that thin French women will someday reclaim their own fashions.

The serious charges led to the final verdict: *Reunion in France* "is a very poorly conceived picture. It misrepresents France, the French underground, the Nazis. Far more serious, it unintentionally gives aid and comfort to the enemy in the peace offensive that will surely, and perhaps soon, be launched." That was the crux of the matter. The Office of War Information predicted a German peace offensive in January 1943, and it believed *Reunion in France* would work to the benefit of the Germans. At the time when the Office of War Information was pressing the BMP to get pro-

ducers to seriously discuss the issues of the war in their films, MGM suggested that the war was between fat German and thin French women with fashion hanging neatly pressed in the balance. Reviewing the film, the Office of War Information's Bureau of Intelligence commented, "the most striking feature of France as shown in the picture is a genius for designing and wearing women's clothes. . . . The preservation of this genius from the bad taste of the Germans is the big issue."

Newspaper reviews agreed with the government's assessment. One review commented that Joan Crawford behaves in the film "like nobody except an MGM movie star," and the *New York Times* found Wayne "totally unconvincing as an American flyer." Most reviews emphasized that the war was a serious affair and should not be used as an MGM costume drama. The reviews, however, did not kill *Reunion in France* at the box office. It was one of MGM's top fifteen grossers for 1943. Once again, Wayne had demonstrated his worth. The message in Hollywood was clear: even a bad Wayne film made money.

Wayne's last film of 1942 was his most ambitious attempt to aid the war effort. As originally planned by agent Charles K. Feldman, *Pittsburgh,* like *The Spoilers,* was to be a vehicle for three of his clients—Dietrich, Wayne, and Scott. But it soon turned into a tribute to the industrial home front. Associate Producer Robert Fellows worked closely with the BMP to ensure that the film conveyed the government's exact propaganda message. It focuses on the Markham-Evans Coal Company, and its heroes are industrialists and workers in the coal and steel industries. In the film, Wayne plays the flawed hero Charles "Pittsburgh" Markham, a man who rose from the depths of a coal mine to the ownership of the company. In a role that Wayne was to develop more fully in such films as *Red River, Hondo, The Sea Chase, The Searchers,* and *The Man Who Shot Liberty Valance*, he portrays a man obsessed, driven by his own inner demons. Pittsburgh willingly uses anything and anyone to acquire power. On his way to the top, he abandons the woman who loves him (Marlene Dietrich) and his trusted partner (Randolph Scott). But the same ruthlessness that allowed him to rise in the coal business leads to his downfall, causing him to lose his wife, his company, and his self-worth. World War II provides a rebirth for Pittsburgh. Once again, he rises from the mines to manage the company. Only this time he works for his nation, not himself. He is redeemed by submerging his own ego into his nation's crusade for a better world.

When Nelson Poynter and his BMP staff previewed *Pittsburgh* at Universal Studio on December 1, 1942, they were delighted. The picture was a preachy epic of coal and steel that appealed to the BMP's wordy sense of effective propaganda. It contained long semi-documentary sections of the coal and steel industries, and it rarely said anything visually that could be put into flat dialogue. But there was no mistaking its message: every American—soldier and industrial worker alike —can and should contribute to the war effort; victory would only result if "all the people" work and fight as one. The BMP applauded the results. "*Pittsburgh* succeeds in making many excellent contributions to the war information program," noted the BMP review of the film. In fact, much of the dialogue "appears to have been culled directly from the OWI Manual of Information for the picture industry. . . ." Nevertheless, the picture was "highly commended for an earnest and very successful contribution to the war effort." As far as the BMP was concerned, *Pittsburgh* was "one of the best pictures to emerge to date dealing with our vital production front. . . ."

Poynter, who had worked so closely with Bob Fellows on *Pittsburgh,* thought he had scored a real coup. Often ignored by the more important producers, Poynter actually believed that *Pittsburgh* was a good film and that his contributions to the film had been significant.

As soon as he saw the final cut, he shot off a series of letters complimenting everyone involved with the movie including himself. "Magnificent. . . . It shows what can be done if the creative unit sets out to help interpret the war and at the same time put on a helluva good show," he wrote Fellows, Faldman, and several Universal executives. Poynter wrote Lowell Mellett, his BMP superior in Washington, telling him to see *Pittsburgh* and to take other Office of War Information and War Production Board people with him.

Mellett went, but he did not share Poynter's enthusiasm. "The propaganda sticks out disturbingly," Mellett responded to Poynter. Most newspaper reviewers shared Mellett's opinion. "This business of instructing and informing intrudes at times at the expense of the entertaining," noted the *Motion Picture Herald*, but the film "yields realistic results when not hampered by dialogue freighted with purpose." From West Coast to East, the reviews were the same. *Pittsburgh* was not exactly a bad film, but it was certainly "not in the inspired class," or, more to the point, it was "routine entertainment at best." In a New York theater, a cartoon entitled *Point Rationing*, which explained the use of the new rationing book, drew a more positive review than *Pittsburgh.*

The critical and financial failures of *Pittsburgh* reinforced the belief in Hollywood that if FDR and alphabet agencies could get America out of the Depression, they certainly could not make a hit movie. The resistance against Poynter and his staff that was present in the industry from the beginning stiffened even more in the months after the release of *Pittsburgh.* Hollywood was right. The BMP was not film-literate. Both Mellett and Poynter were newspaper men who thought in terms of words. They wanted dialogue that sounded like it was straight off an editorial page. As far as they were concerned, if a movie did not use dialogue to present the government's message, then the message was not delivered. They had difficulty thinking visually. The major studio executives realized the government approach toward propaganda would mean death at the box office. They were willing to make propaganda pictures that served the interest of the country, but they wanted to make them in their own way.

No film better demonstrates Washington's lack of understanding of movies than *Casablanca*. The classic film ran into trouble in Washington. Various sections of the Office of War Information were disappointed by the movie. Most were upset with Rick's (Humphrey Bogart's) cynicism. Others were dissatisfied with the treatment of the French, the Germans, and the North Africans. And the last line—"This could be the beginning of a beautiful friendship"—well, as far as the OWI was concerned, it said nothing about the Atlantic Charter or why the United Nations were fighting Fascism. As film historians Gregory D. Black and Clayton R. Koppes observed, Washington "was not content to let meaning emerge from the interaction of the characters and the overall story line . . . it would have preferred a two-paragraph sermonette explaining Nazi aggression and the justice of the Allied cause."

The battle between Washington and Hollywood would drag into 1943 and would last in a more limited way for the rest of the war. It was a war fought by studio heads and producers, not actors, and as in the larger war, Wayne avoided the conflict. But his hectic activity of 1942 had begun to undermine his health. On January 21, 1943, he collapsed on a movie set and was rushed to the hospital. Doctors told him he had influenza and needed rest. That was the bad news. The good news was that his collapse was reported in the *New York Times*. Duke was a star.

■■■

STUDY QUESTIONS

1. How did the entertainment industry react to the Japanese attack on Pearl Harbor? How did the event affect Hollywood?

2. Why did John Wayne decide not to enlist when so many other leading actors enlisted in the service?

3. What role did the Roosevelt administration believe that Hollywood should play during the war?

4. Describe the goals and work of the Bureau of Motion Pictures. How did that organization try to influence the movie industry?

5. Discuss John Wayne's early war pictures. How were the enemy and the home front portrayed in these films?

BIBLIOGRAPHY

The above essay is from *Show Me a Hero: The World of John Wayne,* a forthcoming biography by Randy Roberts and James S. Olson. Two standard biographies of John Wayne are Donald Shepard and Robert Slatzer, *Duke: The Life and Times of John Wayne* (1985) and Maurice Zolotow, *Shooting Star: A Biography of John Wayne* (1974). Two outstanding books that survey the movie industry are Garth Jowett, *Film: The Democratic Art* (1976) and Robert Sklar, *Movie-Made America: A Cultural History of American Movies* (1975). For a closer look at Hollywood during World War II see Clayton R. Koppes and Gregory D. Black, *Hollywood Goes to War: How Politics, Profits, and Propaganda Shaped World War II Movies* (1987) and Bernard F. Dick, *The Star-Spangled Screen: The American World War II Film* (1985). Richard R. Lingeman, *Don't You Know There's a War On* (1970) is an outstanding look at the home front during World War II.

Part Six

AMERICA IN THE AGE OF ANXIETY: 1945–1960

The fallout of Hiroshima lasted many years. The most immediate result of the atomic bombs that America dropped on Japan on August 6 and August 9, 1945 was the end of World War II. V-J Day was celebrated with an emotional outpouring of relief. Most Americans believed that the United States had saved the world from the totalitarian threat of the Axis Powers. They also assumed that America would now return to its traditional foreign policy posture of isolationism. Such was not the case. World War II had made the United States the most powerful country in the world. Retreat into isolationism was impossible. During the next few years, America accepted the responsibilities that went with being a world power and replaced Great Britain as the globe's policeman.

Almost as soon as the war was over, the Soviet Union emerged as America's leading rival. Joseph Stalin, Russia's leader, was by nature suspicious, and the complexities and uncertainties of Soviet politics made him even more so. He resented America and Great Britain for delaying the second front against Germany during World War II. He was also upset that the United States refused to share its nuclear secrets with the Soviet Union. Fears, anxieties, and ambitions degenerated into a new type of power conflict. Called the cold war, the object was to control, either through economic or military means, as much of the world as possible.

America originated the policy of containment as a strategy for the cold war. The policy was essentially defensive in nature, and it forced America to react to Soviet movements. Although the policy scored several notable successes—particularly in Turkey, Greece, and Western Europe—it had a number of real weaknesses. Most

important, it committed American troops to prevent the expansion of Communism. In Korea and later in Vietnam, Americans came to understand the limitations and constraints of the containment doctrine.

The cold war and the fear of a nuclear confrontation shaped domestic politics as well as foreign affairs. If Americans distrusted Stalin's motives, they also questioned the actions of their own leaders. They asked pointed and complex questions, yet sought simple answers. Why had Stalin gained so much territory at Yalta? How was Russia able to develop its own atomic weapons so rapidly? Who lost China? Politicians such as Senator Joseph McCarthy of Wisconsin and Congressman Richard Nixon of California provided easy answers. They said that Communist sympathizers in the American government had worked to ensure the success of the Soviet Union. The publicity lavished on the trials of Alger Hiss and Julius and Ethel Rosenberg and the activities of McCarthy and the House Un-American Activities Committee increased the public's distrust of its own officials.

In the following section the essays deal with the fallout of Hiroshima and the cold war. Although they examine very different subjects—television scandals, Korean War POWs, science fiction movies, and investigations of sexual behavior—they contain a unifying theme. They all discuss Americans' attitudes toward themselves. The underlying assumption was that something deep and troubling was wrong, that the American character had changed for the worse. The search for exactly what was wrong took many different turns and helped illuminate the psychological, cultural, and social landscape of the 1950s.

THE SCIENTIST AS SEX CRUSADER: ALFRED C. KINSEY AND AMERICAN CULTURE

Regina Markell Morantz

During the late 1940s and early 1950s a series of unsettling events shocked Americans and disturbed their sense of postwar complacency and optimism. Communism—its spread and increased dangerousness—inspired much of the fear. In late 1949 the Nationalist leader Chiang Kai-shek and his followers fled mainland China for sanctuary on Formosa. In Chiang's place came Communist Mao Tse-tung. Although Mao's victory was predictable and the result of internal Chinese forces, Americans tended to view the fall of China as a victory for Soviet foreign policy. Other shocks came rapidly. In September 1949 President Truman announced that the Russians had detonated a nuclear device, thus ending the American monopoly of the bomb. And throughout the period, the trials of Alger Hiss raised questions about the loyalty of American government officials.

No less sensational and disturbing was the publication of Alfred Kinsey's *Sexual Behavior in the Human Male* (1948), which quickly sold over 275,000 copies. For many Americans, Kinsey's message was as insidious as those of Marx and Lenin. He told Americans about themselves, about their sexual practices, fears, and desires. And what Kinsey said was not what most Americans wanted to believe. In the following essay historian Regina Markell Morantz discusses the reception, influence, and implications of Kinsey's scientific pioneering work. She demonstrates the limits of Kinsey's scientific objectivity and the nature of his liberalism. More importantly, however, Morantz uses the findings of Kinsey and more recent sex researchers to explore the changing character and behavior of millions of Americans. As she suggests, sex has become less a liberating, revolutionary force than simply another aspect of America's consumer economy.

In January 1948, Robert Latou Dickinson, noted gynecologist and sex researcher, dashed off a note to his friend and colleague Alfred Charles Kinsey. Dickinson's copy of the newly published *Sexual Behavior in the Human Male*, which he had awaited "with one of the keenest anticipations of a lifetime," had arrived. "I have my copy at last of SBHM!" he informed Kinsey. "Glory to God!" In a lively correspondence throughout the 1940s the two men shared enthusiasm for Kinsey's studies in human sexuality, their mutual respect enhanced by appreciation of the social significance of this work. Given the chance to see Kinsey's labors in print, Dickinson's excitement grew: "Dear ACE:" he wrote Kinsey in February, "In sex education, and marriage counsel [sic] and v.d. and prostitution attacks . . . we would, in America, hereafter, speak of the Pre-Kinsey and Post-Kinsey eras."

The press, the public, and expert opinion subsequently confirmed Dickinson's assessment. Writers dubbed *Sexual Behavior in the Human Male* "the most talked about book of the twentieth century." Others ranked it with *Das Kapital, The Origin of Species,* and *Wealth of Nations.* Indeed, the reception accorded Kinsey's work was unprecedented. Although Kinsey's publishers authorized an inadequate first printing of 5,000 copies, less than two months after publication *Sexual Behavior in the Human Male* had sold 200,000 copies and stood in second place on the non-fiction best-seller list. George Gallup reported that one out of every five Americans had either read or heard about the book, while five out of six of those interviewed judged its publication "a good thing." Multiple reviews appeared in literary periodicals. Medical and lay organizations held

symposia to assess its impact. Overnight "Kinsey" became a household word, his name forever embedded in popular culture.

Response to the Kinsey report testified more than anything else to the revolution in sexual mores that its text, charts, and statistical tables so laboriously documented. No one would now dispute that a generation of Americans who had come of age in the first decades of the twentieth century had begun to lift the mantle of fear and shame from their sexual activities. Since 1913 American newspapers had been hailing what one headline writer called "sex o'clock in America." Even the scientific study of sex had gotten underway years before Kinsey: The Male Report cites 19 prior investigations of human sexuality. But journalists who wrote about America's sex obsession before World War I rarely elaborated on what factors underlay the new freedom in manners, while post-war professionals who had begun to analyze its components increasingly avoided sharing their findings with a popular audience. What made Kinsey different—indeed, what made him unique—was his confidence that Americans were ready for a confrontation with their own sexuality. In dispassionate prose he laid bare the facts.

Most of his contemporaries understood Kinsey's research to be a monumental achievement of twentieth-century science. He managed where others had failed to discuss sexual matters before a public still ignorant and uncomfortable with the subject. His own liberalism was grounded in the conviction that nothing human should be alien to the realm of science.

Of course Kinsey's detractors were vindictive. Some disputed his findings, questioning his evidence and doubting his methods; others condemned him for publicizing his facts. But though Kinsey may have underestimated the reaction of those ill-equipped to handle his candor, his faith in the American people was not misplaced. Accepting the legitimacy of his research with respect they afforded all science,

"The Scientist as Sex Crusader: Alfred C. Kinsey and American Culture" by Regina Markell Morantz, from *American Quarterly XXIX* (Winter, 1977). Published by the American Studies Association. Copyright © 1977. Reprinted by permission of *American Quarterly* and the author.

■ ■ *Dr. Alfred C. Kinsey, shown here with his family, pioneered sex research in two studies (1948 and 1953) that brought sex out of the bedroom and into America's parlor.*

they rapidly made his work part of the conventional wisdom. After summarizing the origins of sex research in America, this essay will attempt to analyze this process of acceptance. It will focus on Kinsey the man, the content of his reports and the critical response they evoked, and the larger cultural meaning of Kinsey's work.

Victorian aversion to the investigation of sexual matters relegated sex to the backroom almost as effectively in 1900 as in the previous century. Scientists and physicians either shared their society's view of what was proper, or else kept quiet about it. Research into the socially taboo took courage; chastisement was often swift and forceful. When the distin-

guished Chicago physician, Denslow Lewis, proposed in 1899 to speak to the American Medical Association on the "Gynecological Consideration of the Sexual Act," he was denounced by Howard A. Kelly of Johns Hopkins. "The discussion of the subject," Kelly asserted, "is attended with filth and we besmirch ourselves by discussing it in public." Characteristically, the Association refused to publish Lewis' paper.

Nineteenth-century moralism gradually succumbed in the first decades of the twentieth century to the combined attack of purity advocates (including feminists, clergymen, and social reformers), idealistic physicians inspired by bacteriological discoveries facilitating the control of venereal disease, and the diverse but insistent proponents of the Freudian revolution. Social and economic factors also underlay the emergence of new sexual attitudes. As early as 1907 Simon Patten predicted the gradual economic shift away from austerity and production to a concern with consumption. An interest in leisure and luxury fostered pleasure and personal fulfillment as positive goods, and undermined Victorian prescriptions of thrift, self-denial, and personal control. Urbanization eroded community and religious controls on behavior. In addition, the increasingly visible women joining the labor force were freed from some of the constraints of home and family.

Though sex was discussed in the Progressive era, sex research remained controversial. Not until 1921 did scientists and social reformers organize a two-day conference under the auspices of the National Research Council to examine the status of American sex research. Acknowledging the importance of such investigation, conference members decried the "enshrouding of sex relations in a fog of mystery, reticence and shame." Sensing the national faith in science, participants argued that scientists were best qualified to study sex because "their standing in the community would prevent fears that their findings would be put to propaganda purposes." The meetings resulted in the formation of a Committee for Research on Problems in Sex chaired by Yale psychologist Robert Yerkes and connected with the National Research Council. Funded largely by the Rockefeller Foundation, and working closely with the Bureau of Social Hygiene, another Foundation project, the Committee directed most sex studies in the next two decades. Alfred Kinsey turned to this committee for financial support in 1939. Aid for this project opened the door to a new and controversial era in sex research.

While the Committee for the Study of Problems in Sex quietly encouraged research on sexuality in the 1920s and 1930s, Kinsey built his career as a leading expert on the gall wasp. Twenty-six years old in 1920, Kinsey

came to Indiana University as an assistant professor of zoology. For the next two decades he taught courses in entymology, general biology, and insect taxonomy, and by the mid-thirties he had published two specialized books, numerous articles, and an innovative high school biology text.

Few facts are available to explain Kinsey's subsequent interest in sex. His own sexual history, like those of the people he interviewed, will presumably remain locked forever in the confidential files at the Institute for Sex Research. Though he spoke little of his past, it is clear that his parents were strict and puritanical. The product of a deeply religious home, Kinsey suffered as a youngster because of his proficiency in the natural sciences and his fascination with Darwinian evolution. When Kinsey rebelled, science offered him a set of values which emotionally rivaled his juvenile commitment to religion. His sympathetic attitude toward the sexual dilemmas of the young may have grown out of the memories of his own pain, frustration, and ignorance; science granted him the tools to make his sympathy more objective. But cloaked in the unbiased empiricism of the dispassionate scientist lay the emotional preferences of a moral crusader.

Kinsey's involvement with sex research began quietly in 1938 when he was chosen as the faculty coordinator of a newly established marriage course. The course consisted of interdisciplinary guest lecturers, with Kinsey lecturing on biology. His class notes reveal sophistication with published works on sex. Indeed, in a letter to Robert Latou Dickinson written in 1941, he admitted: "It was your own work which turned my attention to the purposes of research in this field some ten or twelve years ago although circumstances were not propitious for starting the work until three years ago." In a talk he delivered in 1935 to a faculty discussion club he had proved himself familiar with previous sex studies by G. V. Hamilton and Katherine B. Davis. The lectures displayed his concern with both the influence of social institutions on sexual behavior and the "sexual conflicts of youth." Significantly, he reflected that such conflicts arose because of the "long frustration of the normal sexual activities."

Kinsey emphasized the central importance of sexual adjustment to stable unions. "I know of no evidence," he stated flatly, "that this biological basis can be completely sidestepped and still lead to a successful home." He accused modern education "through its system of mores, laws, and ethics," of conditioning attitudes toward sex which were "wrong in the sense that they interfere with the successful consummation of the marriage . . . [and] develop the sexual maladjustments that appear most often after marriage. Our ignorance of copulatory techniques," he continued, "which is the direct outcome of the impressions that are imprinted on the young, our ignorance of satisfactory contraceptive devices above all, produce attitudes which make our concepts of sex wrong." By delaying sexual activity until marriage, he argued, young people only made the achievement of successful marriage more problematic. Responses repressed for ten or twelve years after an individual is first capable of sexual activity could hardly be changed by a marriage ceremony. Distorted attitudes formed in adolescence required years of adjustment after marriage. "Why offer a marriage course?" Kinsey asked his listeners. "Society," he answered, "has been responsible for interfering with what would have been normal biological development. . . . It behooves us to make amends to society by taking you as you approach the time of marriage and giving you the results of scholarly thinking on these several problems." Repeatedly, Kinsey the scientist would side with biology when it conflicted with accepted social mores.

In the summer of 1938 Kinsey began taking the sex histories of his students and within a year had scheduled interviews outside the university to vary his sampling. Aware of their potential significance, he termed these histories "a scientific goldmine" and wondered to a colleague if they would not account "for the largest volume of research I will yet publish." Under mounting pressure from conservative elements of the community, Kinsey terminated his connection with the marriage course in 1940. Soon afterward he received his first grant from the Committee for Research in Problems of Sex. Abandoning his interest in the gall wasp, he prepared to devote himself solely to the study of human sexual behavior.

The current permissiveness surrounding sex research should not obscure the fact that thirty years ago Kinsey's findings disturbed, shocked, and threatened not just ordinary men and women but professionals as well. A good deal of the hostile criticism directed at Kinsey's work had little to do with its scientific value. Princeton University president Harold Dodds likened the Male volume to "the work of small boys writing dirty words on fences." The Chicago *Tribune* termed Kinsey a "menace to society." The Reverend Henry Van Dusen, president of Union Theological Seminary and a member of the Rockefeller Foundation, called for a "spontaneous ethical revulsion from the premises of the study," and chided the Foundation for its sponsorship. Kinsey's work, he lamented, revealed "a prevailing degradation of American morality approximating the worst decadence of the Roman era." Harvard sociologist Carle C. Zimmerman labeled the Male volume an "attack on the Western family," and accused Kinsey of irresponsibility in making it public. Millicent McIntosh, indomitable president of Barnard College and mother of five, worried in 1954 that Kinsey's books had already contributed "to the difficulties encountered by young people in establishing a good relationship between the sexes."

Hysteria reached Congress when New York Representative Louis B. Heller called upon the Postmaster General to bar the Female Report from the mails until it could be investigated, charging Kinsey with "hurling the insult of the century against our mothers, wives, daughters and sisters." Soon rumors spread that the Special House Committee founded during the McCarthy era to inquire into the use of funds by tax-exempt foundations would ask Kinsey to testify regarding financial aid from the Rockefeller Foundation. Others accused Kinsey of aiding communism. Shortly thereafter the Rockefeller Foundation informed Kinsey that his grant would not be renewed.

Much of the criticism of Kinsey's work, however, was not hysterical. Most commentators admired his research and welcomed its publication. Yet serious critics also offered objections. The debate centered on two issues: the possibility of conducting a scientific investigation that was value-free (and whether Kinsey had done so); and the extent to which a behavioristic approach could solve fundamental questions of human existence.

Kinsey never admitted publicly that scientists based their investigations on cultural assumptions. He remained deaf to the charge that his work reflected his own biases. Yet his objectivity was itself polemical: his research subverted the status quo specifically because it examined individual deviance dispassionately. Many critics were repelled by the idea of studying sexual nonconformity objectively. By definition norms are not always rational. Kinsey's non-judgmental approach aligned him with the twentieth-century rebels against Victorian repression. Though many critics shared the Progressive faith that the truth would make men free, they resisted applying this conviction to sex research. In this instance the truth was dangerous and might help destroy the American value system. Reinhold Niebuhr passionately argued this point of view when he declared that Kinsey's assumptions represented "a therapy which implies a disease in our culture as grievous or more grievous than the sickness it pretends to cure."

Soon after the publication of the Male volume, Lionel Trilling wrote of Kinsey and his coauthors that "nothing comes more easily to their pens than the criticism of the subjectivity of earlier writers on sex, yet their own subjectivity is sometimes extreme." A retrospective reading of both volumes reveals why Kinsey was an easy mark for Trilling's pen. In neither book did he disguise either his admiration for the sexually active or his suspicion of the sexually repressed. His statistical interpretations fell invariably on the side of sexual liberalism. In a chapter on the onset of male puberty, for example, he recorded his approval of men who began their sexual activities early. On scant evidence he asserted that early-adolescent males were often "the more alert, energetic, vivacious, spontaneous, physically active, socially extrovert, and/or aggressive individuals in the population," while late-maturing males tended to be "slow, quiet, mild in manner, without force, reserved, timid, taciturn, introvert, and/or socially inept." He revealed his own biases most clearly when he linked the aggressive, success-oriented personality type— and American paragon—to vigorous sexuality.

Equally controversial were Kinsey's interpretations of the data concerning the relationship between premarital intercourse and marital adjustment. Although he admitted that premarital petting contributed "definitely to the effectiveness of the sexual relations after marriage," he nevertheless remained contemptuous of the hypocrisy involved in adolescent petting behavior. "It is amazing," he wrote,

to observe the mixtures of scientifically supported logic, and utter illogic, which shapes the petting behavior of most of these youths. That some of them are in some psychic conflict over their activities is evidenced by the curious rationalizations which they use to satisfy their consciences. They are particularly concerned with the avoidance of genital union. The fact that petting involves erotic contacts which are as effective as genital union, and that it may even involve contacts which have been more taboo than genital union, including some that have been considered perversions, does not disturb the youth so much as actual intercourse would. By petting, they preserve their virginities, even though *they may achieve orgasm by doing so.*

Coupled with his disdain for this hypocrisy was his finding of a "marked, positive correlation between experience in orgasm obtained from premarital coitus [for women], and the capacity to reach orgasm after marriage." Over half the female sample who had experienced premarital coital orgasm had reached sexual climax in nearly all of their coitus during the first year of marriage. Only 29 percent of women without such premarital experience were able to achieve regular orgasm during the first year.

Kinsey dismissed selective factors as accounting for the correlation, and emphasized that almost half of those women sampled who had premarital intercourse had it exclusively with their fiancés. This figure led some critics to question whether such behavior could properly be termed "premarital coitus" at all. Kinsey found that the overall number of women achieving orgasm *at least occasionally* within the first year of marriage was as high as 75 percent. Indeed, the percentage rose steadily according to the number of years married. What Kinsey's statistics seemed to indicate was that reaching orgasm for women was a *learned* skill that took time to develop. Kinsey's data, critics argued, could or could not be interpreted to justify premarital intercourse.

Kinsey nevertheless used his findings to suggest that traditional mores regarding premarital intercourse were outmoded. In an impassioned paragraph, he made his sympathies clear. His carefully selected phrases, typical of numerous passages in the books, bristled with an aggressive undertone barely couched in the language of scientific neutrality: "The attempt," he wrote

to ignore and suppress the physiologic needs of the sexually most capable of the population, has led to more complications than most persons are willing to recognize. This is why so many of our American youth, both females and males, depend upon masturbation instead of coitus as a premarital outlet.

Restraints on premarital heterosexual contacts appear to be primary factors in the development of homosexual activities among both females and males. . . .

The considerable development of petting, which many foreigners consider one of the unique aspects of the sexual pattern in this country, is similarly an outgrowth of this restraint on premarital coitus.

The law specifies the right of the married adult to have regular intercourse, but it makes no provision whatsoever for the approximately 40 per cent of the population which is sexually mature but unmarried. Many youths and older unmarried females and males are seriously disturbed because the only sources of sexual outlet are either legally or socially disapproved.

Such statements challenged the 1950s social and sexual standards. Most marriage manuals still preached the virtues of premarital chastity, while only a few professionals had given serious thought to the problems of sexual adjustment for the unmarried.

Kinsey's detractors feared that his premises implied an animalistic philosophy of sex devoid of emotional and social content. They accused him of a crude behaviorism that failed to place sexual activity within the larger context of human values. Thoughtful reviewers, many of them psychiatrists and psychologists, chided him for his recurrent neglect of the psycho-dynamics of sex. Denying that as a biologist Kinsey was equipped to examine complex psycho-social questions, analysts decried his measure of sex activity in terms of outlet and orgasm. By reducing sex to the mechanistic Kinsey ignored motivation. Should orgasm in and of itself, they asked, be the goal of human sexual behavior? Where was the place of love in Kinsey's universe? Speaking of sex solely in terms of outlet negated its relationship to the creative, integrative, and inspirational aspects of human life. Sexuality, though important, remained only one dimension of the human personality. "It was Freud's idea," wrote Karl

Menninger, "that sexuality in the broad sense, the life instinct, was represented not nearly so much by orgasm as by human love, and that the goal of all sexual behavior was better integration, better inter-human concern, and thereby less mutual destructiveness."

The psychoanalytic case against Kinsey extended beyond his failure to consider the emotional content of the sex act. Kinsey avoided placing sexuality within a developmental framework. Except for confirming infantile sexuality, he refused to see any substantiation for other central tenets of psychoanalytic theory. His animus toward psychoanalysts remained clear. He denied that "normal" psychosexual development preceded from narcissism through homosexual to heterosexual activities. In a final affront to Freudian theory, he questioned the significance to women of such concepts as penis envy, castration fear, defense against incestuous wishes, and fixation at the clitoral stage. "The psycho-sexual pattern in the human animal," he wrote, "originates in indiscriminate sexual responses which as a product of conditioning and social pressures, become increasingly restricted in the directions of traditional interpretations of what is normal or abnormal in sexual behavior. . . . It is simply a picture of physiologic response and psychologic conditioning in terms that are known to the biologist and psychologist." Psychoanalysts found this approach simplistic. "Frigidity," argued Marie Robinson, "is in the vast majority of cases, essentially a psychological problem. No amount of mechanical manipulation can make a difference. Anybody who tells you differently," she cautioned her patients, "is . . . wrong." "Kinsey's credo," wrote Edmund Bergler and William S. Kroger, "amounts to naiveté of the first order. . . . It overlooks the complex mechanisms of inner-unconscious-conscious. . . . Sex, though biologically present in every human being, goes through complicated (not simple) transformations before maturity is reached."

While psychoanalysts worried over Kinsey's

behaviorism, theologians accused him of materialism. Kinsey's animal analogy represented a conscious tool in his revolt against Victorian sexual attitudes which for a century had exalted ecstasy of the spirit and devalued the pleasures of the flesh. In contrast, Kinsey embraced man's mammalian heritage. Admiring Freud for reasserting the primacy of physical drives, Kinsey believed that man's pretensions to uniqueness had accounted for untold sexual unhappiness. As a biologist he took for granted that, in the long run, physiological factors were more effective than man-made regulations in determining patterns of human behavior. Reinhold Niebuhr read him correctly when he charged Kinsey with referring consistently to analogies between man and the sex practices of infrahuman species "without once calling attention to uniquely human characteristics of man's sexual life."

This alleged materialism led Kinsey to the controversial assumption that the prevalence of certain types of behavior indicated both their mammalian origins and their biological normality. The frequency of types of behavior socially labelled "deviant" testified to the persistence of biologic over cultural determinants. Such a view demanded a reevaluation of homosexuality. Regarding the "normality" of such behavior Kinsey wrote:

In view of the data which we now have on the incidence and frequency of the homosexual, in particular on its coexistence with the heterosexual in the lives of a considerable portion of the male population, it is difficult to maintain the view that psychosexual reactions between individuals of the same sex are rare and therefore abnormal or unnatural, or that they constitute within themselves evidence of neuroses or even psychoses.

Theologians and other humanists united in their revulsion against this view of sex. Man, they reminded their readers, was not just a little above the apes, but a little below the angels. The difference between human beings and animals lay in the capacity of men to control their instincts, to use language, and to develop creativity, imagination, and culture. In the end, critics maintained, sex was a social activity, culturally and psychologically influenced.

Many of Kinsey's difficulties with the humanists may have arisen from his narrow philosophy of science. He often argued that as a scientist he reserved the right to limit his investigation in any way he saw fit. Though he never denied the significance of the social and psychologic components of human behavior, he insisted that science was "by its method limited to the consideration of material phenomena. The accumulation of scientific data depends upon the reduction of such material to quantifiable units which can be measured." He implied that any other order of facts or values than his could be explored only by non-scientific or ultra-scientific means. He accused psychiatrists studying Freudian stages in psychosexual development of investigating "mystic impulses." Theologians, and those "concerned with the moral values of sexual behavior" he considered to be antagonistic to science altogether.

Kinsey's refusal to answer the criticism of the humanists also revealed his shortcomings as a sexual theorist. Kinsey's work is peculiarly joyless. "If someone," wrote Karl Stern in *Commonweal*, "attempted to set the stage for a dehumanized, de-personalized society, for the great beehive—he would start out with things like the Kinsey Report." Ironically, the Victorians themselves had been accused of joylessness, though for different reasons. Kinsey, it seemed to some, represented a new kind of puritan. "There is in all this," Stern remarked with considerable irony, "a subtle, hidden despising of nature."

In the present period of sexual permissiveness, the arguments of the humanists loom more salient than they did thirty years ago. A general theory of sexuality cannot remain grounded in only one academic discipline, but must seek to integrate the methods and findings of many. Undoubtedly Kinsey would have renounced the role of sexual theorist. He died too soon for us to speculate on whether subsequent research would have led him beyond a crude empiricism. Yet in stubbornly labelling even thoughtful critics as Victorian moralists in disguise, perhaps Kinsey had a point. His findings may not have helped to cure the sexually neurotic, but, given the prevailing atmosphere surrounding the public discussion of sex, his behavioristic approach may have liberated sexually active men and women still haunted with Victorian prudery. *Look* magazine recognized this therapeutic effect: "What they [the authors] have learned and will learn may have a tremendous effect on the future social history of mankind. For they are presenting facts. They are revealing not what *should be*, but what *is*. For the first time data on human sex behavior is entirely separated from questions of philosophy, moral values, and social customs."

The fact that Kinsey himself had been raised under the canons of sexual puritanism probably made him sensitive to the problems of ordinary men and women. Certainly his democratic tendencies convinced him that for most people questions concerning the ultimate significance of sexuality were not only unimportant, they were irrelevant. The first task was to unshackle a generation from its repressive past. Relieving guilt and reassuring readers that everyone had similar sexual impulses, Kinsey's books contributed to a changing sexual climate in which ordinary people lived and worked. They probably had the same emancipating effect on the unpsychoanalyzed masses that Freud's work achieved for generations of intellectuals.

Not long after the publication of the Female volume, Kinsey's health began to deteriorate. For over a decade he had maintained a schedule which left him little free time. The emotional criticism that accompanied the release of his second book hurt him deeply. Cessation of foundation backing left the future of his research in the balance; for three years he struggled to reestablish the Institute for Sex Research on a solid financial footing. In 1956, at the age of 64, he died of a heart attack.

In the years between the publication of the Male Report and his premature death, Kinsey grew petrified of yellow journalism and the danger of misinterpretation. The importance of his scientific approach in achieving acceptance for his work cannot be overstressed. Indeed, his insistence on the legitimacy of his research and his scientific credentials eventually made him a heroic figure, even in the eyes of his enemies. Nowhere was this fact more poignantly demonstrated than in the following obituary published in the *Catholic Record*, one of his most severe critics:

The death of Dr. Kinsey, famous Indiana University zoologist, and compiler of the controversial studies on human sex life, removes a truly dedicated scholar from the Bloomington campus. Few could disagree more strongly than we with Dr. Kinsey's views or deplore more deeply the evil influence such views could have on individuals and society. Yet one cannot deny that Dr. Kinsey's unremitting efforts, his patient, endless search, his disregard for criticism and ridicule, and his disinterest in financial gain should merit him high marks as a devoted scholar. While we have hurled our share of brick-bats at some of Dr. Kinsey's ideas when he was living, and still hold these ideas to be poisonously wrong, we must admit that we would welcome on our side many more scholars with something of Kinsey's devotion to knowledge and learning.

Kinsey hoped that his work would be widely publicized and that its effect would be educational, not trivializing. Contemporary observers credited him with achieving his goal. Donald B. Hileman's study of magazine coverage of the Female volume in 1953 found that Kinsey had already forced a reorientation of attitudes toward sexual matters among journalists. *Time* magazine agreed. Kinsey's biggest impact, they argued, was "conversational."

Despite the increase in talk about sex after World War I, printed and public discussion remained taboo. "No single event," they concluded, "did more for open discussion of sex than the Kinsey Report, which got such matters as homosexuality, masturbation, coitus and orgasm into most papers and family magazines."

Though some critics feared that the reports would have an immediate adverse effect on public behavior, there is little evidence that such fears were justified. On the other hand, studies undertaken soon after publication suggested that Kinsey's work did liberalize attitudes, especially among the young. His findings publicized not only the sexual diversity but also the gap between ideals and reality in America. Such information about the prevalence of certain "questionable" practices tended to alter attitudes in the direction of tolerance. In this sense Kinsey's books probably were a catalyst. With consummate skill he dispelled ignorance about changes in sexual mores which had already taken place, *sub rosa*, since World War I. In presenting Americans with a *fait accompli*, his work demanded more realistic, more human sex mores. He forced a public debate over the meaning of sex in modern life as no other author had except Freud.

Marriage counselors and sex therapists hailed the report's role in alleviating guilt and promoting understanding between the sexes. For over a generation liberal therapists had struggled with their own ignorance and the greater ignorance of their patients. Lack of sexual harmony was deemed the most frequent cause of family disruptions. Dr. Lena Levine, director of the Margaret Sanger Research Bureau, recalled the early period of marriage counseling "with no nostalgia whatever."

We had no authorities to turn to, no reference books to give the women. We listened to the same story over and over again, and we counseled patients as best we could on technique. The worst job was to get the message across to the husbands, who were usually at fault, chiefly because they hadn't the slightest idea how a woman was put together and what she needed in the way of stimulation.

Kinsey paved the way for modern approaches to sex therapy. Masters and Johnson built on the groundwork laid by their more controversial predecessor.

Ironically, Kinsey's friends as well as his enemies responded only to the obvious Kinsey: the broad-minded, democratic rebel, the sexual libertarian. While he was surely all of these things, there was another side to this complex and subtle man, more easily understood only in historical retrospect. In many ways Kinsey remained bound to his Victorian past. Despite his studied neutrality concerning the various forms of sexual outlet, his acceptance of homosexuality, and his tolerance of extramarital sexuality, Kinsey was not a social revolutionary. His revolt against his society's outmoded sexual mores did not lead him to question other aspects of the value structure. Like most of his contemporaries, he had an attachment to happy, stable marriages, and he expected his research to ease the majority of Americans into a permanent monogamy so satisfying that social stability would be guaranteed. His data suggesting that sexual liberation had *not* destroyed cherished social institutions should have reassured his detractors, had they been composed enough to pay careful attention. It was no accident that Kinsey admired other personality traits of sexually precocious youths—their aggressive energy, their drive and spontaneity. Here he is most candid and also most reactionary: sexual abandon is coupled with the time-honored assumptions of enterprising capitalistic society.

Kinsey's faith in this social order is evident in his lecture notes for the 1938 marriage course, and in his special relationship with the American Association of Marriage Counselors. For many years an associate member, Kinsey was made an affiliate in 1952. Many critics erroneously interpret the failure to treat reproductive issues in the two reports as evidence of Kinsey's lack of interest. Yet approximately ten percent of Kinsey's standard interview was devoted to this subject and his silence on these matters reflects anything but indifference. He withheld his statistics on pregnancy, contraception, and abortion because the AAMC had convinced him to devote an entire book to these questions. Thus Masters and Johnson have only followed in the direction that Kinsey led. Like him they emerge as resolute foes of guilt and shame; like him they do not champion the cause of premarital chastity. But their ideal sexual order, like Kinsey's, leads to a retreat into privatism. They link greater sexual permissiveness with happier marriages, and they conceive of sexual life in terms of "enduring, heterosexual relationships of substantial affection."

Thus the cultural and intellectual revolution that Kinsey touched off was archetypically American: its purpose was to keep basic institutions the same, especially at a time when, in the aftermath of world war, they might have been fundamentally altered.

In the thirty years since Kinsey published his volumes, his data have become a rich potential source for measuring social change. Unfortunately, historians have yet to mine his findings with any persistence. Used primarily to verify the "sexual revolution" in the first decades of this century, Kinsey's work has been virtually ignored by students interested in broader social and cultural issues. Few commentators, for example, have explored the implications of Kinsey's discovery that men from different classes exhibit divergent sexual behaviors. The report maintained that lower- and working-class males had a decidedly higher incidence of premarital intercourse than college-educated men, tended to frown on extended foreplay in intercourse as "unnatural," were less likely to make love in the nude, masturbated less frequently, and viewed sex more as an uncontrollable impulse, less as a question of right and wrong. Middle-class and college-educated youths were moralistic; they tended to be virgins at marriage, although they petted and masturbated more often. The upwardly or downwardly mobile male, moreover, tended to form such attitudinal and behavioral patterns *long before he moved into his destined class.*

Kinsey's findings raise questions about the relationship of sex behavior, character structure, social mobility, and class, some of which might be read back into the past. Indeed, his data suggest a connection between twentieth-century middle-class behavior patterns and the emergence of the "modern" temperament, a primary attribute of which seems to be, at least for the nineteenth century, the ability to defer present gratification for future rewards. Historians of the nineteenth century have been struggling to link Victorian sexual repression to the emergence of a personality type comfortable with industrial capitalism. Thrift in semen, they argue, mirrored the injunction to be frugal materially. The ability to control passion and the denigration of personal pleasure as a goal created men and women who fit the demands of the take-off period of industrialization, when production, economy, and austerity took precedence over consumption. Marx eloquently characterized this stage in capitalistic growth:

Political economy, the science of wealth, is therefore, at the same time, the science of renunciation, of privation and of saving. . . . The science of a marvelous industry is at the same time the science of asceticism. . . . The less you eat, drink, buy books, go to the theater or to balls, or to the public house, and the less you think, love, theorize, sing, paint, fence, etc. the more you will be able to save. . . .

Historians have based their theories about nineteenth-century sexuality on evidence drawn from the prescriptive literature—advice books, political and social writings, medical treatises. Surely Kinsey's statistics give us some hard evidence that the repressive Victorian sexual theory was somehow linked to the behavior patterns of an upwardly mobile middle class.

Yet when we examine Kinsey's data more closely we must qualify Marx's contention that deferred gratification was always a prerequisite for capitalistic growth. By the 1920s, at least, it seems clear that middle-class youths were no longer deferring *gratification;* they were merely delaying *copulation.* The upwardly mobile petted and masturbated frequently despite guilt. Kinsey's figures for *total* sexual outlet (achieving orgasm by any means) showed only minor class differences. Presumably, the mature industrial economy no longer requires the full repression of sexual desires, it merely demands that those desires be gratified in particular ways. Thus, middle-class youths, in order to contribute to the system, deferred not necessarily sexual pleasure, but intercourse, marriage, children, and family obligations. Lower-class men, on the other hand, postponed neither early copulation, nor marriage, nor large families, all of which probably helped to insure their docility, if not contentedness, in the factory.

Recent sex surveys report that the behavioral gap between men of different classes has substantially narrowed since Kinsey. Probably because of the widespread dissemination of effective contraceptive devices, premarital intercourse has increased among college-educated males, while sex behavior among the lower classes has differentiated to include nudity, extended foreplay, and increasing oral-genital contacts. Indeed, it appears that in an economy characterized by abundance and oriented toward the production of luxury items and consumer goods, sexual pleasure has become a means of recreation for all classes. Character structure and child rearing practices have shifted accordingly, away from an emphasis on autonomous self-control and toward the rational acceptance of pleasure, personal fulfillment, and happiness. Education, mass media, and the increase in leisure time among all social strata have tended to homogenize popular culture and narrow behavioral differences between social groups.

These developments suggest that we have entered a third phase of capitalistic growth. As yet we have proved incapable of dealing with problems of overproduction. The goal of the system remains consumption, and sexual liberation is encouraged primarily through advertising, as a means of orienting people toward new *things,* new ideas, new forms of luxury and pleasure. The encouragement of hedonism in all spheres seems essential for the affluent society. Thus sexual freedom has not been tied to social revolution. Championing privatism and the concern with individual adjustment, the new permissiveness has focused on self-fulfillment, not social change. Social historians interested in generational shifts in personality structure would do well to explore the implications of these changes in sexual behavior.

Kinsey's findings also indicate that knowledge of female sexuality has gradually become more sophisticated. If a sexual revolution has occurred, its base has been changes in female attitudes and behavior. While male trends shifted only minimally between generational cohorts in Kinsey's sample, women moved steadily toward the male standard. The evidence of the Female Report that women born after 1900 were more likely to reach orgasm in marriage, and that educated middle-class women achieved greater sexual satisfaction than their lower-class sisters deserves special attention. It would seem that sexual liberation, fostered by greater educational opportunities, presupposes and encourages the development of individuality and autonomy among women.

On the other hand, students of lower-class sexual patterns have found that among the less educated "both husbands and wives feel that sexual gratification for the wife is much less important than for the husband." Lower-class lovemaking tends to be less "technically versatile," lacking in the extended foreplay intended to facilitate the wife's satisfaction. Lower-class women, perhaps as a consequence, view sex primarily as a duty. Yet although they enjoy sex less they rarely refuse intercourse. Sociologist Lee Rainwater links these sexual patterns to a patriarchal family structure, a radical separation between male and female spheres, and a lack of meaningful communication between sexual partners, all characteristic of lower-class groups. Recent work on nineteenth-century sex roles has pictured a similar family structure exhibiting the same well-defined differentiation between male and female culture. One is tempted to use Kinsey's statistics to posit the prevalence among the middle class in the last century of contemporary lower-class patterns of lovemaking, oriented toward male satisfaction. For an age which barely accepted the legitimacy of female pleasure and still linked intercourse with reproduction, such a thesis appears plausible and is borne out by Kinsey's data revealing a gradual increase in female orgasm in the twentieth century.

The evolution of consciousness over the last century has altered expectations concerning what is sexually natural and possible. Human needs diversify with changing social and cultural conditions, and things become desirable merely because they are suddenly possible. Kinsey's data offer us an insight into this transformation in the meaning of marriage and sexual relations. His findings suggest that this century has witnessed a merging of spiritual love and passion in a novel way. His evidence indicates that middle-class lovemaking techniques are a recent dimension of the popular imagination. The emergence of almost universal petting in the 1920s and 1930s represents a new psycho-sexual intimacy. The increasing sexual responsiveness of middle-class women may be a function of this.

It has become fashionable to mourn the passing of the old sexual order in which the omnipresence of guilt, anxiety, and dread over the violation of taboos guaranteed at least that life would be interesting. "If . . . nothing is grave," a recent commentator has written, "satire cannot bite and tragedy gives way to the social illness of maladjustment. For many, human life under such conditions would lose its music." Such an attitude offers further proof of the distance we have travelled from the sexual culture of Kinsey's generation. Privy to the tragic ways in which people's sexual lives were blighted by society, Kinsey welcomed a new order while he helped bring it about. We are the richer for Kinsey's conviction that human beings should get more joy out of all sexual activity.

Yet Kinsey was no revolutionary. Though he wished that the world would be a better place because of his books, his vision required no fundamental social or economic changes. He understood neither the revolutionary nor the disintegrative potentialities inherent in sexual liberation. In the end, Kinsey's hedonism has become a conservative force, and he himself the unwitting agent of an increasingly callous and wasteful society.

■ ■ ■

STUDY QUESTIONS

1. What factors explain the remarkable popular success of *Sexual Behavior in the Human Male?*

2. What characterized the study of sexual behavior before Kinsey? How did Kinsey's study change people's beliefs and attitudes?

3. What does Regina Morantz mean when she describes Kinsey as "the scientist as sex crusader"? Did the passionate or dispassionate side of Kinsey's personality influence his life?

4. How did the American people react to the publication of *Sexual Behavior in the Human Male?* What were the major issues raised by the debate over Kinsey's book?

5. How were Kinsey's research and results culturally biased? How was his sexual liberalism demonstrated in his work? How did he challenge the 1950s social and sexual standards? What place did love play in Kinsey's study of sexual relations?

6. How did Kinsey's work set the stage for dehumanized, depersonalized society? What long-range effects did Kinsey's writing have on society? Was Kinsey a social revolutionary? Why or why not?

7. What links are there between sexual activity and economic and class behavior?

BIBLIOGRAPHY

Sexual Behavior in the Human Male (1948) and *Sexual Behavior in the Human Female* (1953) are the classic sexual studies by Alfred C. Kinsey. Gay Talese, *Thy Neighbor's Wife* (1980), is a popular and useful examination of changing sexual behavior in America. Reay Tannahill, *Sex in History* (1980), discusses changing sexual behavior and attitudes in world history. A number of useful articles deal with the subject of American and English sexual attitudes. Among the best are John Burham, "The Progressive Era Revolution in American Attitudes Toward Sex," *Journal of American History*, 59 (1973); Charles Rosenberg, "Sexuality, Class, and Role," *American Quarterly*, 25 (1973); and Peter Cominos, "Late Victorian Sexual Respectability and the Social System," *International Review of Social History*, 8 (1963). Two other innovative books are Steven Marcus, *The Other Victorians: A Study of Sexuality and Pornography in Mid-Nineteenth Century England* (1974), and John S. Haller and Robin M. Haller, *The Physician and Sexuality in Victorian America* (1974). Also see Kristin Luker, *Abortion and the Politics of Motherhood* (1984).

AMERICAN PRISONERS OF WAR IN KOREA: A SECOND LOOK AT THE "SOMETHING NEW IN HISTORY" THEME

H. H. Wubben

Contrary to what most people had anticipated, the end of World War II did not bring a feeling of security to the United States. The war was barely over when the Soviet Union replaced the Germans and Japanese as mortal enemies of the Americans. The Soviet threat seemed particularly ominous because of the Marxist prediction of revolutionary upheavals in capitalist countries. In the late 1940s, United States foreign policy revolved around the idea of containment, an economic and military commitment to keep Russian influence behind the Iron Curtain. The Truman Doctrine of 1946, the Marshall Plan of 1947–48, the North Atlantic Treaty Organization, and the Berlin Airlift of 1948–49 were all directed at stopping Soviet expansion in Western Europe. To secure congressional funding of that foreign policy, the Truman administration talked unceasingly of the international communist conspiracy, and in the process created a tense, suspicious political atmosphere inside the United States. Many Americans became convinced there was a subversive, internal Communist plot to overthrow the United States government.

The American fear of the Soviet Union and Communism intensified in 1950 with the outbreak of the Korean War. North Korean troops poured across the 38th parallel into South Korea, and the United States implemented the containment policy by sending hundreds of thousands of troops into the peninsula. When the armistice was reached three years later, the United States had had its first taste of undeclared war—a "police action." And when the prisoners of war began filtering home with their horror stories of deprivation, torture, and "brainwashing," Communism became even more sinister to the American people. The experiences of the POWs also gave rise to serious doubts about the "American character." In the following selection, historian H. H. Wubben discusses the significance of the POW problem in the context of the cold war.

Americans have long been intrigued by speculations about their national character. In particular they have been receptive to assessments which credit them with immunity against certain human frailties, an immunity not possessed by most other peoples. Out of the Korean War came a controversy which impinged annoyingly upon such assessments and which provided grist for the mill of those who now preferred to believe that in recent decades the character had deteriorated.

Throughout the conflict reports coming out of North Korea indicated that the communists were subjecting American prisoners of war to a reeducation process popularly described as "brain washing." Prisoner returnees during Operation Little Switch in May and Operation Big Switch in August and September 1953 corroborated some of these reports. But it also became clear that such re-education was largely ineffective. Nevertheless, 21 prisoners chose not to return home. A few who did return admitted that they were "progressives," that is, men partially converted by the Chinese re-education program. Some who did not confess to such leanings faced accusations from other prisoners that they had taken the "progressive" line.

In addition it became apparent that a number of men had engaged in collaborative or criminal behavior detrimental to the welfare of their fellows. Consequently, the armed services made special efforts to find out what had happened. Psychiatrists and psychologists interviewed the newly-freed prisoners during the repatriation process and on the journey home. Intelligence officers also interviewed them, compiling dossiers on each man. Information acquired by these specialists eventually pro-vided the data upon which subsequent formal studies of the prisoners and their behavior in captivity were based.

In 1955 came the official government view of the POW behavior issue, the report of the Secretary of Defense's Advisory Committee on Prisoners of War. But the committee's judgment was hardly definitive. On the one hand, the group declared, "the record [of the prisoners] seems fine indeed . . . they cannot be found wanting." On the other it concluded, "The Korean story must never be permitted to happen again." Then in 1956 the Army issued a training pamphlet on the subject of POW behavior. It was even more ambiguous. Readers learned that the Chinese "lenient policy" designed to lessen resistance "resulted in little or no active resistance to the enemy's indoctrination." Later, however, they read that the "large majority . . . resisted the enemy in the highest tradition of the service and of our country."

Findings of the major formal studies, financed by or undertaken by the armed services in most cases, are much more satisfying to the scholar who desires more consistency in both raw material and analysis. These include research projects done for the Department of the Army, the Surgeon General's Office, the Air Force and the Walter Reed Army Institute of Research. Also engaged in examination of POW experiences was the Society for the Investigation of Human Ecology. The studies never achieved wide circulation although the research scientists who engaged in them reported their substance in professional journals. Eventually one scholarly book-length treatment appeared, Albert Biderman's *March to Calumny*. Biderman, a sociologist who was active in several of these projects, demolished in a convincing manner those interpretations which accused the prisoners of being singularly deficient in the attributes expected of American servicemen unfortunate enough to become prisoners of war.

The work of such specialists, however, has

"American Prisoners of War in Korea: A Second Look at the 'Something New in History' Theme" by H. H. Wubben, from *American Quarterly*, *XXII* (Spring, 1970). Published by the American Studies Association. Reprinted by permission of *American Quarterly* and the author.

had little impact compared with that of those whose reports convey a largely, if not exclusively, negative version of the prisoners' actions during captivity. That version, in general, declares that American prisoners of war in Chinese and North Korean hands were morally weak and uncommitted to traditional American ideals. Consequently, some, though not a majority, were infected to a degree with the virus of communism. Furthermore, they were undisciplined. They were unwilling to aid each other in their travail. And they succumbed too easily under limited duress or no duress at all to the pressures of their captors to engage in collaborative behavior, including informing on each other. Their death rate, 38%, was the highest in history, and most deaths resulted from "give-up-itis" and lack of concern for one another among the prisoners themselves, not from communist mistreatment. Also, no prisoners successfully escaped from communist prison camps, a "first" in U.S. military experience. Other nationality groups, particularly the Turks, successfully resisted communist blandishments, and only the Marines among the Americans consistently adhered to patterns of honorable conduct. Finally, the POWs in Korea were the first Americans in captivity to so act, a "fact" which calls for a reassessment of mid-century American values and the culture which spawned them.

Among those who accepted this as history, in part or in whole, were President Dwight Eisenhower, FBI Director J. Edgar Hoover and Senator Strom Thurmond of South Carolina. Political scientist Anthony Bouscaren saw the "record" as evidence that American education had flunked a significant test. Another critic of education, Augustin Rudd, viewed the prisoner performance as evidence that the chickens of progressive education had come home to roost. The editors of *Scouting* magazine in 1965 cited it in urging continued efforts to implant the ideals of the Boy Scout Code among youth in that organization. And as late as 1968, California educator and political figure Max

Rafferty employed it in some of his campaign literature during his senatorial race.

These individuals, however, have not been so influential as two others in promoting this "history." They are the late Eugene Kinkead, a freelance writer, and Lt. Col. William E. Mayer, one of the psychiatrists who participated in the interviewing of the repatriates. Kinkead's major contribution was a book entitled *In Every War But One* which sold around fifteen thousand copies. Col. Mayer's contributions, mainly public addresses, have won even wider circulation than Kinkead's, thanks to the tape recorder and the mimeograph. Both men have modified from time to time their indictment of the prisoners, if not of recent trends in American society. Mayer, for instance, toward the end of one of his speeches said, "Finally, the great majority of men didn't become communists, didn't suffer any kind of moral breakdown, no matter what the communists did to them." But by then the negative point had been so strongly stressed that few listeners were aware of his significant caveat.

That they were not aware resulted from a number of circumstances. Many conservative Americans were disgruntled at the absence of a decisive American victory in the war. They blamed communist subversion at home for the result. This subversion in turn they blamed on "socialistic" influences originating in the 1930s which, they charged, had weakened the capacity and will of home, church and school to develop good character among the nation's youth. Thus, the prisoners served as evidence to verify their beliefs. Many liberals accepted the prisoners as examples of societal sickness also, although they rejected the communist subversion theme. They claimed that American materialism lay at the root of the problem. Both groups professed to view the prisoners with pity rather than scorn, as men who through no fault of their own were simply unfortunate products of a society on the verge of decay. Both were impressed by Mayer's credentials and the literate, entertaining manner in which he employed tendentious illustrations to document a general picture of moral and morale breakdown resulting from defective precaptivity nurture. Given these general dispositions on the part of many Mayer listeners, it is no wonder that they let his muted but significant qualifier slip by. They weren't interested in it. Finally many Americans, including academicians who would ordinarily have demanded more intellectual rigor in their own disciplines, simply took Mayer's and Kinkead's revelations at face value because they seemed to meet the test of reasonableness.

Historians have long known a great deal about the behavior of Americans in prisoner camps prior to the Korean War, particularly about prison behavior in World War II camps. As Peter Karsten wrote in the spring of 1965 issue of *Military Affairs,* the motivation and conduct of American servicemen, in or out of prison camps, have been a source of concern from the American Revolution to the Present. George Washington had numerous unkind words for defectors, mutineers and those of his forces who lacked "public spirit." The activities of the reluctant warriors of the War of 1812, the defectors and the short-term volunteers who departed the service when their time was up—if not sooner—wherever they were during the Mexican and Civil Wars, are a matter of record. "Give-up-itis," called "around the bends," was not unknown at Andersonville and Belle Isle. Draft dodgers and deserters numbered over 170,000 in World War I. By the early 1940s, "around the bends" had several new names, the most common being "Bamboo disease" and "fence complex."

Even in a "popular" war, World War II, the Army worried about the lack of dedication among its troops. Indoctrination programs were overhauled and beefed up with negligible success. A Social Science Research Council team which analyzed data collected by the Army during the war, concluded that the average soldier "gave little concern to the conflicting values underlying the military struggle. . . .

[and] Although he showed a strong but tacit patriotism, this usually did not lead him in his thinking to subordinate his personal interests to the furtherance of ideal aims and values."

As to moral and morale breakdown under severe conditions, two military physicians reported that in Japanese POW camps "moral integrity could be pretty well judged by inverse ratio to one's state of nutrition." And, they added, "Although some of these prisoners sublimated their cravings by giving aid to their fellows, there was, in general, a lowering of moral standards. Food was often obtained by devious means at the expense of other prisoners." Though a buddy system did function to some extent, particularly among small cliques who shared both companionship and food, there were few group activities, and most men tended to be taciturn and seclusive. Being unable to defy their captors and survive, they expressed considerable verbal resentment toward each other. In particular they disparaged their own officers and their behavior. Another physician, who was a prisoner himself in the Philippines and Japan, write that most POWs, whether sick or well, suffered periods of apathy or depression which, if not countered forcefully, would lead to death. "Giving up" occurred earliest and easiest among younger men as in Korea. In a sentence strikingly reminiscent of the Kinkead-Mayer critique, except that he omitted the "something new in history" theme, the physician wrote, "Failures in adjustment were most apparent in the 18-to-23-year-old group who had little or no previous experience and much overprotection. These men demonstrated marked inability to fight physical diseases and the initial shock of depression of captivity."

Dr. Harold Wolff, a consultant to the Advisory Committee, reported that in World War II German prison camps where the pressures were much less severe than in Japanese and Korean camps, about 10% of the Americans "offered remarkably little resistance, if not outright collaboration." Wolff also noted that the escape record of Americans in World War II was not exceptional. Less than a dozen prisoners of the Japanese out of twenty-five to thirty thousand escaped from permanent camps, all in the Philippines. Less than one hundred out of ninety-four thousand Americans captured by the Nazis successfully escaped from camps, of which less than half returned to Allied control.

Autobiographical accounts of former World War II prisoners also tell much which shows that the Korean POW behavior was not unique. Edward Dobran, an airman held by the Germans, reported that a G.I.. mess hall crew at his camp took care of itself well but skimped on the rest of the men's rations. Nor could those who apportioned food in the squads be trusted to do their job honestly more than a few days at a time. Dobran concluded, "In a place such as this, every man is strictly for himself. This sort of living and hardships showed what a human being is really made of. If you didn't look out for yourself here, nobody else did."

Physician Alfred Weinstein's book-length recital of prison-camp life in the Philippines and Japan tells about a Marine officer's extensive collaboration with the Japanese and about the stealing of medicine by the same officer and some enlisted men medics at Cabanatuan. Some POW mechanics and truck drivers, put to work by the Japanese, lived high, using their positions to smuggle from Manila desperately needed food and medicine which they then sold for outrageous prices to the rest of the prisoners who were in dire need of both. Nor was Weinstein complimentary about behavior in an officers' ward at a prisoner hospital at Cabanatuan. These officer-patients demanded so many special privileges, food and medicine because of their rank that the senior American officer had to break up the group by distributing the men throughout the other wards. Also not complimentary about the self-seeking of a few officers incarcerated in Japan is Hugh Myers in a recently published memoir. Myers

has described how four veteran Navy chiefs from the garrison at Guam assumed control over prison life at one stage in his POW experience when it became apparent that the officers were too concerned about their privileges, too inexperienced, or both, to do the job fairly or well.

Nevertheless, in all the accounts discussed above which were written by men who had been POWs there is no tendency to denigrate American civilization because of the failings of a greater or lesser number of men in prison camps. Nor is it assumed by them that men under conditions of stress will uniformly conduct themselves in exemplary fashion. Weinstein, for instance, wrote, "Hard living, disease, and starvation made heroes out of few men. More frequently does it make animals out of men who, in the normal course of living would go through life with a clean slate."

Two aspects of the Korean POW story, then, should be of particular interest to the historian. First, there is the fact that a poorly understood historical experience is interpreted in such a way that it makes a thoroughly inaccurate comparison between Americans past and Americans present. Second, there is the acceptance by the general public of this "nonhistory" as history, largely without the aid of historians. Critical to the development of these two aspects is the misuse of the data derived from the prisoner's experiences. This data, largely collected at the time of their repatriation, was not originally intended to provide raw material for behavioral or historical studies per se. It was, rather, gathered with the intention of providing information for possible court martial action against men accused of collaboration or criminal activity while in captivity, to identify men who merited commendation and decoration, and to identify repatriates who needed psychiatric care.

Consequently, the generally accepted percentage classification of POWs by behavior, 5% resistor, 15% participator (or collaborator), and 80% middlemen, needs to be viewed more as suggestive than as absolutely definitive. Biderman, for instance, reports that placement of a POW in the collaborator category required only that he be "accused of committing isolated but serious acts in collaboration" which could be corroborated. Placement in this category remained firm, moreover, even if the prisoner were otherwise regarded as having been a hard-case resistor throughout his captivity, as some of them were.

With regard to the evidence that the POWs were peculiarly weak in moral fibre, uncommitted to American ideals and ignorant of the institutions and history of their country, a change in perspective is revealing. If one accepts the idea that it takes moral fibre to resist, actively *and* passively, ideological conversion attempts by a captor who is very concerned about "correct thoughts" and who has overwhelming power which he uses as it suits his purpose, then one must grant that most prisoners had it to some meaningful degree. The Chinese regarded passive resistance to indoctrination, including "going through the motions," as "insincere" and "stupid," if not actually reactionary behavior, as many of the scholars of POW behavior have noted. They made strenuous efforts to overcome such "insincerity" and "stupidity." But in May of 1952 they abandoned compulsory indoctrination, keeping classes only for the relatively small number of progressives. Their extensive efforts had resulted in disappointing returns among their stubborn captives.

Many prisoners did supply evidence that there was often a lack of discipline in their ranks. Autobiographies, both American and British, speak of a dog-eat-dog system prevailing during several of the "death marches" and in the temporary holding camps during the harsh winter of 1950–51. They also tell of prisoners in need being refused assistance by other prisoners. In these respects, however, they differ little from World War II POW memoirs which described the same kind of reaction to stress during those periods in which captivity

conditions were the worst. Conversely, those who give testimony to such animalistic behavior also testify to behavior of a different order. Morris Wills, one of the original 21 who refused repatriation, only to return over a decade later, has written: "You really can't worry about the other fellow; you are at the line of existence yourself. If you go under that, you die. You would help each other if you could. Most would try; I wouldn't say all."

"Reactionary" Lloyd Pate wrote in a similar, if more positive, vein. "After the first shock of our capture wore off, the G.I.'s with me on those Korean mountain roads began to act like soldiers this country could be proud of." He told of prisoners helping each other to keep up the pace when dropping out meant death; and he credited two such good Samaritans with saving his life. Captive British journalist Philip Deane in one poignant passage revealed the context within which many prisoners faced life or death under brutal march conditions. In it he inadvertently answers many who charge that the prisoners "shamefully" abandoned their weaker fellows en route. A young American lieutenant, faced with a bitter choice, allowed five men to drop out, in effect "abandoning" them, contrary to the orders of the North Korean march commander. He could not, he told the North Korean, order them carried because "That meant condemning the carriers to death from exhaustion." For this decision, the lieutenant's captors executed him on the spot.

The same kinds of sources, supplemented again by the studies of research scientists and journalists, reveal that the physical duress to which prisoners allegedly succumbed so easily, presumably leading to widespread collaboration, ranged all the way from calculated manipulation of necessities of life to murder. One former prisoner labeled a reactionary by his captors told the author of many instances of physical brutality practiced by the Chinese. Among those brutalized were Chinese-appointed squad leaders who couldn't or wouldn't promote group compliance with the indoctrination program. Some, he maintained, were murdered. Others were subjected to severe beatings and then denied medical treatment for the injuries inflicted; death sometimes resulted. Some bad treatment, he declared, resulted from caprice, citing a case of one man in his squad, a "middleman" who underwent several nighttime beatings over a period of one month for no apparent reason. Nevertheless, those who disparage prisoner behavior tend to take at face value the Chinese contention that they did not commit atrocities or torture their captives. An official U.S. Army report issued in June 1953, however, declared that after Chinese entrance into the war they were "fully as active as the North Koreans" in commission of war crimes.

So far as the POW death rate, 38%, is concerned, this figure is speculative. It does not include atrocity deaths, which numbered over a thousand. Nor does it include well over two thousand missing in action. The Chinese kept no dependable records, and throughout much of the first year of the war the prisoners were in no position to do so themselves. Whatever the true death rate, critics of the prisoners and of the alleged "softness" of American society see it as "too high." By implication they blame most of the deaths on prisoner negligence, or worse, on loss of will to live. Five prisoner physicians, however, reported otherwise shortly after the war. They wrote:

The erroneous impression has been created that prisoners of war who were in good physical health gave up and died; this is not true. Every prisoner of war in Korea who died had suffered from malnutrition, exposure to cold, and continued harassment by the Communists. Contributing causes to the majority of deaths were prolonged cases of respiratory infection and diarrhea. Under such conditions, it is amazing not that there was a high death rate, but that there was a reasonably good rate of survival.

Another example of misuse of data to demonstrate weakness on the part of the POWs

and their nurture is the "no escape" theme. While it is true that no American successfully escaped from permanent prison camps in the Yalu River region, several hundred did escape before permanent camps were established, some after several months of captivity. From these camps, furthermore, at least 46 verifiable escape attempts involving nearly 4% of the POWs have been authenticated. Nevertheless, both Mayer and Kinkead have insisted that failure to escape from permanent camps is significant. Mayer, in one speech, praised American prisoners in the Philippines for attempting and completing escapes despite the Japanese practice of putting prisoners in blood-brother groups of ten. If one escaped the rest were to be shot. But, according to Weinstein, the POWs took the Japanese at their word and established MP patrols to halt just such escape attempts.

The assumption of Turkish superiority in POW camps also rests on a misreading of evidence. Turkish prisoners were, in the first place, a select group of volunteers. Furthermore, half of them were captured after the worst period of captivity was over, the winter of 1950–51. Well over 80% of the American POWs were not so fortunate. Turkish prisoners, unlike the Americans, were not split up. Officers and enlisted men remained together most of the time, an aid to maintenance of discipline. Nor were the Turks the objects of intense re-education efforts as the Americans were. Yet, one Turk served on a peace committee. One refused to accept repatriation until he had a late change of heart. And some communist propaganda materials show Turkish involvement in communist-sponsored POW programs. In 1962, Brigadier General S. L. A. Marshall (ret.), military historian and author of *The River and the Gauntlet* and *Pork Chop Hill* bluntly told a Senate subcommittee that the Trunks were overrated. Said Marshall, "The story about the Turks being perfect prisoners is a continuation of the fable that they were perfect soldiers in the line which was not true at all."

The assumption of Marine superiority to soldiers in prisoner-camp behavior also rests upon misreading of evidence. Marines may have retained more esprit de corps as prisoners, but they, like the Turks, were more of an elite unit. However, at Kangyye in 1951, some Marines made speeches, signed peace petitions (often with illegible signatures and wrong or misspelled names), and wrote articles for a "peace camp" paper called *The New Life*. Told by the Chinese that rewards for being a "good student" could include early release, some made up stories of hungry childhood and living on relief. Others said they joined the Corps in order to get decent food and clothing. Two described the criteria for a satisfactory article: "All you had to do was string stuff together in fairly coherent sentences, such words as 'warmongers' . . . 'Wall Street big shots' . . . 'capitalistic bloodsuckers' and you had it made." Eighteen Marines and one soldier who convinced the Chinese of their "sincerity" eventually were selected for early repatriation. Taken close to the front, they crossed up their captors by escaping ahead of schedule.

The experience of the eighteen Marines is discussed in a University of Maryland history master's thesis on Marine POWs in Korea by Lt. Col. Angus MacDonald. MacDonald notes with disapproval that the Marines gave far more information to their captors than name, rank, and serial number. But he correctly views these as gambits designed to secure release from captivity. The Army, however, seems to have taken a less pragmatic, and, consequently, more humorless view of similar efforts by its enlisted men. MacDonald, on the other hand, does not deal adequately with the joint investigations of all services which, when concluded, revealed that only 11% of the Army repatriates compared with 26% of the Marine repatriates warranted further investigation on possible misconduct charges. Instead he quotes with approval an address by Col. Mayer which praised Marine performance, and by implica-

tion, criticized that of Army POWs. Eventually both services made the further investigations suggested, the Army possibly applying a broader set of standards to define misconduct, since it initially cleared only 58% of the 11% thought to warrant further investigation. The Marines cleared 94%. Finally, only fourteen cases came up for trial, all Army cases, out of which eleven convictions resulted.

In view of the commonly accepted belief that the Marines performed better than soldiers as POWs, it is interesting to note the comment by retired Air Corps Major General Delmar T. Spivey in a John A. Lejeune Forum on prisoner behavior. In this Marine-sponsored forum, Spivey, who while imprisoned in Germany during World War II was senior officer in the Center Compound of Stalag III, made the unrebutted statement that:

Even with all these things ["survival courses, physical conditioning programs, instruction in our American heritage, information about the enemy, courses and exercises designed to instill pride and self-respect and belief in one's service and country, and the assurance that our country will stand by an individual, both in combat and as a prisoner"] . . . we cannot assume that every fighting man will be completely prepared for his responsibilities as a prisoner. History is not on our side, and neither is human nature when we consider the past conduct of prisoners of war.

The conclusions of professional and semiprofessional scholars and writers about American POW behavior are mixed. Stanley Elkins in his search for suggestive experience to support his description of the effects of a closed system on slave psychological development turned to the POWs. Unfortunately he exaggerated some of the findings of his source, Edgar Schein, one scholar involved in the POW studies. Elkins wrote of "profound changes in behavior and values" being "effected without physical torture or extreme deprivation" and of "large numbers" of American informers and men who cooperated in the indoctrination program.

But Schein said only that mandatory discussion and mutual criticism sessions which followed communist indoctrination lectures probably created "considerable doubt concerning ideological position in some of the men." They were, as a whole, he declared, "not very effective." Nor did he give any estimates of the numbers of informers or cooperators relative to the total POW population.

Betty Friedan has seen the average Korean prisoner as an "apathetic, dependent, infantile, purposeless being . . . a new American man . . . reminiscent of the familiar 'feminine' personality." Edgar Friedenberg described the POW as a new model of being, but an international one, not just American. He wrote, "this sort of young man is a character in existentialist novels and post-World War II Italian films." Miss Friedan, however, discovered parallels closer to home. She found them in the youth of the 1950s, in their "new passivity," bored and passionless, demonstrated variously in: the annual springtime collegiate riots at Fort Lauderdale; a teenage call girl service in a Long Island suburb; adolescent grave defiling in Bergen County, New Jersey; drug-taking parties in Westchester County, New York, and Connecticut; and the "helpless, apathetic state" of the female student body at Sarah Lawrence College.

It is doubtful whether the typical Korean POW would recognize himself in all this. His schooling averaged somewhat less than nine years. His social class was hardly comfortable middle. And his withdrawal from activity was certainly in part a shrewd way of fending off the ubiquitous Chinese indoctrinators.

Among historians, Walter Hermes, author of the second volume of a projected five-volume official history of the war, took note of the Kinkead book. But he accepted Biderman's view, calling it a "convincing rebuttal" of Kinkead's thesis. Robert Leckie, however, relied heavily on Kinkead and called the POW record "sorry . . . the worst in American history." Apathy, he declared, was responsible for

the failure of any men to escape. But in the same paragraph he asserted that the Caucasian appearance of the Americans was the "more likely reason for this failure." T. R. Fehrenbach, too, has generally taken a dim view of the prisoners' behavior. "Chemistry and culture," the Doolittle Board's democratization reforms and American education, among other culprits, were at fault, he wrote. His analysis of sources, like Leckie's, was less than rigorous.

Harry Middleton, while acknowledging that the percentage of collaborators was small, also looked askance at the prisoners' record. His book, though published later (1965) than Fehrenbach's narrative, displayed less acquaintance with or close reading of the available literature on the subject. An English scholar, David Rees, in *Korea: the Limited War*, after devoting a lengthy chapter to the subject, leaned to the point of view that POW behavior was not unusual considering the fallible nature of man and considering the unique nature of the prisoners' experiences. S. L. A. Marshall, a consultant to the Advisory Committee, is a defender of the prisoners. And Russell Weigley in his *History of the United States Army* also concluded that the Korean POWs were not a discredit to the nation.

In 1962, 21 scholars familiar with the POW behavior materials signed a paper entitled "Statement: to Set Straight the Korean POW Episode." This paper, drawn up by two of the signers, Edgar Schein and Raymond Bauer, who had worked extensively on the subject, directly refuted the popular version of the POW story expounded by Kinkead and Mayer. The "Statement" included these challenging assertions:

The behavior of the Korean prisoners did not compare unfavorably with that of their countrymen or with the behavior of people of other nations who have faced similar trials in the past.

Instances of moral weakness, collaboration with the enemy, and failure to take care of fellow soldiers in Korea did not occur more frequently than in

*other wars where comparable conditions of physical
and psychological hardship were present. Indeed,
such instances appear to have been less prevalent
than historical experience would lead us to
expect. . . .*

*It is our opinion that any serious analysis of
American society, its strengths and weaknesses,
should rest on historically correct data. It is unfortunate that the Korean POW episode has been distorted to make the case for one view of American
society. We hope that this Statement will be the first
step toward setting the historical facts of this
episode straight.*

Historically correct data, however, were
insufficient for many Americans in the 1950s
and 1960s. They seemed to feel that any communist success at eliciting collaborative behavior or inducing ideological doubt among any
American soldiers, no matter how small the
number, signified a general American failure.
Such failure to them was not to be taken lightly. It might reflect, after all, the existence of a
more dangerous cancer in the American character than even they had suspected.

What is really "new in history," then, about
the whole Korean POW episode?

First, never before Korea were American
POWs confronted by a captor who worked
hard to change their ideological persuasion.
This point is worth a brief examination. Had
American POWs of the Germans, for instance,
been subjected to ideological thought reform
efforts designed to inculcate virulent racist attitudes or to inculcate the idea that Germany
was fighting the West's battle against communism, had these efforts taken place over the
length of time and under circumstances comparable to those endured by the Korean POWs,
there might be a rough basis for comparison.
But those American POWs weren't so subjected. Dobran did report some anti-Semitism
among his POW group upon which the
Germans might have capitalized. But one can
speculate a little in the other direction that the
American reaction to this divisive ploy might

■ ■ *American GIs returning from North Korean prison
camps after the end of the Korean War. Contrary to
popular opinion, which was gripped by fear of
Communist subversion, Korean War POWs did not
conduct themselves much differently than did POWs of
earlier wars.*

have been similar to that in one group of
Negro POWs in Korea among whom the
Chinese tried to foment ideological change by
hammering upon the existence of racial discrimination in the United States. Wrote Lloyd
Pate, "A few colored guys got up and said it
was our business what we did in the United
States and for the Chinks to mind their own
damn business."

Second, never before had the American public been so gullible as to believe that such a

chimera as the enemy's self-proclaimed "lenient policy" was, in fact, lenient. During the first year of the war in particular the Chinese and North Koreans, often in systematic fashion, fostered brutalizing captivity conditions which were in significant part responsible for prisoner behavior which did not measure up to "ideal" standards.

And, finally, for the first time the public seemed to assume that such selfish, undisciplined behavior as existed among the POWs was something new in American military experience and that it was a direct consequence of a characterological deterioration in the nation itself.

Whether or not such a deterioration has been taking place in American society, from the advent of the New Deal and the impact of progressive education as the critics strongly imply, is not under contention here. What is being contended, rather, is that if one really believes this and wants evidence to prove it, one will have to find examples other than among those Americans who died and those who survived in the prison camps of North Korea, 1950–53.

■■■

STUDY QUESTIONS

1. What is the meaning of "brainwashing" and "reeducation"?

2. By the mid-1950s, what was the prevailing opinion about the behavior of American POWs in Korea? Why did that issue seem to be so important to the American public? How did Americans explain the behavior and "failure" of the POWs?

3. Compare the behavior of American POWs in German prison camps during World War II with the Americans in Japanese or Korean prisoner of war camps. Was there much difference? Why or why not?

4. Does POW behavior reveal anything about American civilization? Why or why not?

5. Did large numbers of POWs die because of a "loss of the will to live"? Why or why not? Was the behavior of U.S. Marines any different from other groups of POWs? Why or why not?

6. Summarize Wubben's feelings about the behavior of American POWs during the Korean War.

BIBLIOGRAPHY

For a general discussion of the Korean War, see Joseph C. Goulden, *Korea: The Untold Story of the War* (1982). Also see Bruce Cummings, *The Origins of the Korean War* (1980). Ronald Caridi's *The Korean War and American Politics* (1969), analyzes the domestic impact of the conflict. The internal tension inspired by the cold war is discussed in Edward Shils, *The Torment of Secrecy* (1956); David Caute, *The Great Fear* (1978); and Alan Harper, *The Politics of Loyalty* (1969). The most critical account of American POW behavior during the Korean War is Eugene Kinkead, *In Every War But One* (1959). For a devastating critique of Kinkead's book, see Albert D. Biderman, *March to Calumny: The Story of American POWs in the Korean War* (1963). Also see Louis J. West, "Psychiatry, 'Brainwashing,' and the American Character," *American Journal of Psychiatry* CXX (1964). Also see Robert J. Donovan, *Tumultuous Years* (1982).

INTELLECT ON TELEVISION: THE QUIZ SHOW SCANDALS OF THE 1950s

Richard S. Tedlow

In 1854, Henry David Thoreau wrote, "We are in great haste to construct a magnetic telegraph from Maine to Texas; but Maine and Texas, it may be, have nothing important to communicate." More than one hundred years later, Thoreau's observation, greatly expanded, is still valid. Possessing the technological means of communication is no guarantee of meaningful communication. Nowhere is this situation more evident than in the commercial television industry. In the following essay, Richard S. Tedlow examines the problems inherent in commercial broadcasting, especially as they relate to the television quiz scandals of the late 1950s. The picture he presents is not a flattering one; the object of commercial television is quite simply to sell products, not to educate or uplift its audience. The result is an industry dominated by monetary values and generally oblivious to all ethical or moral consideration. In the specific case of quiz shows, television has produced an additional side effect: it has cheapened the meaning of education and intelligence. As Tedlow cogently observed, "If any crime had been committed in the quiz show episode, it was surely the broad conspiracy to portray as genuine intellectual activity the spouting of trivia." In today's America where books of lists and trivia make the best-sellers list, Tedlow's discussion of the quiz shows has a haunting familiarity.

On the 7th of June, 1955, *The $64,000 Question* made its debut on the CBS television network. No programming idea could have been more thoroughly foreshadowed by previous shows. Since the mid-1930s radio had been exploiting the American passion for facts with contests and games. For years, small amounts of cash or manufacturer-donated merchandise had been given away through various formats. What was new about *Question* was the size of the purse. The giveaway had taken a "quantum jump"; losers received a Cadillac as a consolation prize.

Question's format was simple. The producers selected a contestant who chose a subject about which he or she answered increasingly difficult questions which were assigned monetary values ranging from $64 to $64,000. The contestants could quit without attempting the succeeding plateau, but if he chose to continue and missed, he forfeited his winnings and was left with only his Cadillac.

By a few deft touches, the producers heightened the aura of authenticity and tension. The questions used were deposited in a vault of the Manufacturers Trust Company and brought to the studio by a bank officer flanked by two armed guards. As the stakes increased, the contestant entered a glass-enclosed "isolation booth" on stage to the accompaniment of "ominous music which hinted at imminent disaster" in order to prevent coaching from the audience. Since the contestant returned week after week rather than answering all the questions on one broadcast, the audience was given time to contemplate whether he would keep his winnings or go on to the next plateau and also a chance to worry about how difficult the next question might be.

"Intellect on Televison: The Quiz Show Scandals of the 1950s" by Richard S. Tedlow, from *American Quarterly* (Fall, 1979) Volume XXVIII No. 4. Published by the American Studies Association. Copyright © 1976. Reprinted by permission of *American Quarterly* and the author.

The program became an immediate hit. In September, an estimated 55 million people, over twice as many as had seen the Checkers speech, viewing 84.8% of the television sets in operation at the time, saw Richard S. McCutchen, a 28-year-old marine captain whose category was gourmet foods, become the first grand prize winner.

Most early contestants were seemingly average folks who harbored a hidden expertise in a subject far removed from their workaday lives. Thus McCutchen was asked about *haute cuisine* rather than amphibious assault. This separation was no accident. Its purpose was not only to increase the novelty of the show by providing something odd to the point of being freakish but also to integrate the viewer more intimately into the video melodrama. Everyone who had ever accumulated a store of disconnected, useless information could fantasize about transforming it into a pot of gold.

In a few months, *Question* had created a large new "consumption community," Daniel Boorstin's label for the nonideological, democratic, vague, and rapidly shifting groupings which have characterized twentieth-century American society. Suddenly, a third of the country had a common bond about which total strangers could converse. Paradoxically, in order to belong to this community, the individual had to isolate himself physically from others. Families stayed at home to watch the show, rather than celebrating it in the company of a large crowd. Movie theaters reported a precipitous decline in business, and stores and streets were empty when it came on the air.

Everyone whose life was touched by the show seemed to prosper. In addition to their prize money, some contestants received alluring offers to do public relations work for large companies or to star in movies. *Question's* creator, an independent program packager named Louis Cowan, became president of CBS-TV, an indication of how pleased the network executives were to present so successful a show. Even the banker who brought the sealed questions from the vault found himself promoted to a vice presidency. But the greatest beneficiary was the sponsor.

In March of 1955, the show was purchased by Revlon, which soon began reaping the rewards of well-constructed advertising on a popular television program. Several products quintupled their sales, and advertising for one had to be discontinued because it sold out nationally. George F. Abrams, the company's vice president in charge of advertising, gloated that *Question*". . . is doing a most fantastic sales job. It certainly is the most amazing sales success in the history of the cosmetics industry. There isn't a single Revlon item that hasn't benefitted. . . ." Net sales for 1955 increased 54% over the previous year, and in 1956 they soared another 66%. When Revlon shares were first offered on the New York Stock Exchange at the end of 1955, the issue's success was "so great it was almost embarrassing."

Question's greatest liability was its own success; it spawned imitators around the world. In the United States, a spate of programs featuring endless variations of gift-giving for answering questions further retarded "TV's already enfeebled yearning to leaven commercialism with culture." Most of these have mercifully been consigned to oblivion, but one rivaled *The $64,000 Question* in the impact it made upon the nation.

The *21* program was developed by another firm of independent program packagers, Barry and Enright, Inc. The format was different, especially in having two contestants compete against each other and no limit on their winnings, but the basic idea was the same. Questions were given point values, and the points were worth money. Once again, the "wiles of a riverboat gambler" were combined with the memory of sundry bits of information which was passed off as intellectual acumen, with the result a spectacularly profitable property.

Barry and Enright leased the show to Pharmaceuticals, Inc., now known as the J. B.

Williams Company, and it first appeared on NBC on October 12, 1956. Pharmaceuticals, whose most well-known product was Geritol, soon had good reason to be pleased with its quiz show. *21* did not attain quite the ratings of *Question*, but it competed successfully against *I Love Lucy*, one of the most popular programs in television history, and attracted much notice. Although its advertising director was reluctant to give complete credit to the program for the increased sales of Geritol, it could hardly have hurt. Sales in 1957 bettered the previous year's mark by one-third.

Unlike *Question*, *21* did not shun the highly educated, and one of its contestants became a symbol to the nation of the profitability of intellectual achievement. Charles Van Doren provided evidence that an intellectual could be handsome, that he could get rich, and that he could be a superstar. Like a football player, the intellectual athlete could win fame and wealth. Van Doren's family could lay genuine claim to membership in an American aristocracy of letters. Descended from seventeenth-century Dutch immigrants, Van Doren's uncle Carl was a literary critic whose 1939 biography of Benjamin Franklin won a Pulitzer Prize. His father Mark won the Prize for poetry the following year, and he was equally famous for his accomplishments in the classroom as a professor of English at Columbia. The wives of the Van Doren brothers were also literary, rounding out a remarkably cultivated quartet. Van Doren's family divided its time between a country estate in Connecticut and a Greenwich Village townhouse where guests over the years included Sinclair Lewis, Mortimer Adler, Joseph Wood Krutch, and Morris Ernst. The family was the symbol of intellectual vitality.

Van Doren established himself on the program by defeating the swarthy, seemingly impoverished previous champion Herbert Stempel on December 5, 1956, after having played three tie matches with Stempel on November 28. It was smooth sailing for the weeks that followed.

*On the TV screen [Eric Goldman has written] he
appeared lanky, pleasant, smooth in dress and manner but never slick, confident but with an engaging
way of understating himself. The long, hard questions would come at him and his eyes would roll up,
squeeze shut, his forehead furrow and perspire, his
teeth gnaw at his lower lip. Breathing heavily, he
seemed to coax information out of some corner of his
mind by talking to himself in a kind of stream-of-
consciousness. Like a good American, he fought
hard, taking advantage of every rule. . . . Like a good
American, he won without crowing. And, like a
good American, he kept on winning, drowning corporation lawyers or ex-college presidents with equal
ease on questions ranging from naming the four
islands of the Balearic Islands to explaining the
process of photosynthesis to naming the three baseball players who each amassed more than 3,500 hits.
Charles Van Doren was "the new All-American
boy," the magazines declared, and to millions he
was that indeed. . . .*

Van Doren's victories on the quiz show
brought him greater rewards than had accrued
to any of his predecessors. He received thousands of letters from parents and teachers
around the world, thanking him for populariz-
ing the life of the mind. Little services such as
dry cleaning, which he had had to pay for
when supporting himself on his $4,400 yearly
salary as an English instructor at Columbia,
were now donated *gratis* by star-struck shop-
keepers. Several colleges expressed an interest
in hiring him away from Columbia, and he
found himself referred to in print as "Doctor"
despite not yet having earned his Ph.D. And
then, of course, there was the money. Van
Doren won $129,000 during his 14 weeks on *21*.
Soon after he left, he was awarded a $50,000
contract to appear on the *Today* show, where
for five minutes each morning he would speak
of science, literature, history. "I think I may be
the only person," he once remarked, "who ever
read 17th century poetry on a network television program—a far cry from the usual diet of
mayhem, murder, and rape."

Rumors of improper practices surfaced soon
after the quiz shows made their debut. By the
end of 1956, articles were appearing in the
trade and general circulation press discussing
the "controls" exercised by the producers to
keep popular contestants alive and eliminate
the unpopular. "Are the quiz shows rigged?"
asked *Time* magazine in the spring of 1957, a
year in which the networks were investing a
small fortune in them. The answer: producers
could not "afford to risk collusion with contestants," and yet, because of pretesting, they
were able to ask questions which they knew
the contestants would or would not know.
They could thus manipulate the outcome "far
more effectively than most viewers suspect."
The report noted, however, that Van Doren
"feels certain that no questions were being
formfitted to his phenomenal mind."

A number of contestants had been disappointed at their treatment on the shows. The
most important of these, and the John Dean of
this piece, was the man Van Doren first defeated Herbert Stempel.

Stempel's motives were very mixed. One
was money. He had quickly squandered his
winnings and had failed in an attempt to black-
mail more out of producer Dan Enright. A
more important reason was his bruised ego.
Stempel had been forced to portray himself as
a poor boy from Brooklyn, when in fact he had
married into a well-to-do family and was from
Queens. Enright insisted that he wear ratty
suits and a cheap wristwatch to project this
image and that he address the emcee, Jack
Barry, deferentially as Mr. Barry while other
contestants called him Jack. He had an I.Q. of
170 and was infuriated by having to "miss"
answers he knew "damn well." And he was
beside himself at the unearned praise accorded
to Van Doren. Here was ". . . a guy that had a
fancy name, Ivy League education, parents all
his life, and I had the opposite. . . ." He would
hear passing strangers remark that he was the
man who had lost to this child of light, and he

could not stand it. But it was more than greed or envy that prompted Stempel to turn state's evidence. Even before he was ordered to "take a dive" and before he had ever heard of Charles Van Doren, he was telling friends that the show was fixed. Stempel knew all the real answers about the quiz shows, and he was bursting to show the nation how smart he was.

In 1957, Stempel tried to interest two New York newspapers in the truth, but both papers refused to print what would have been one of the biggest scoops of the decade because they feared libel action. It is a commentary on the state of investigative journalism at the time that not until August, 1958, after the discovery that a giveaway show called *Dotto* was fixed, was Stempel able to make his charges in public. At this time also, New York County District Attorney Frank Hogan began an investigation, and the inexorable process of revelation had been set in motion. For almost a year, the grand jury interviewed about 150 witnesses. The producers tried to arrange a cover-up by persuading the show's alumni to perjure themselves. Many of the most well known did just that. It was one thing to fix a quiz show, however, and quite another to fix a grand jury probe. Realizing that the day of reckoning was at last approaching, the producers hurried back to change their testimony. This they did without informing the contestants, leaving them, to put it mildly, out on a limb.

For reasons which remain unclear, the judge sealed the grand jury's presentment, but the Subcommittee on Legislative Oversight (over the FCC) of the House Interstate and Foreign Commerce Committee determined to get to the bottom of the matter. Its public hearings, held in Washington in October and November of 1959, attracted worldwide attention.

On October 6, a bitter Herbert Stempel exposed the whole sordid story of *21*. He had originally applied to take part in what he thought was an honest game but was approached by Enright who talked him into becoming an actor rather than a riverboat gambler. Every detail of his performances was pre-arranged: his wardrobe, his diffidence, his hesitations, and his answers. He was instructed on the proper way to mop his brow for maximum effect, and he was guaranteed to sweat because the air conditioning in the isolation booth was purposely kept off. From his testimony, it became clear that Van Doren was implicated as well. On the following two days, other contestants, producer Enright, and his assistant Albert Freedman testified to the fix. No one contradicted Stempel.

In the months preceding the hearings Van Doren had consistently and ever more vehemently proclaimed that no matter what others had done, his appearances on *21* had been strictly legitimate. When Stempel's charges were first published in the papers, Van Doren was ". . . horror struck. . . . I couldn't understand why Stempel should want to proclaim his own involvement." A representative of D.A. Hogan interviewed him toward the end of the year, and he denied everything. He retained a lawyer, to whom he lied about his involvement, and then proceeded to perjure himself before the New York County Grand Jury in January, 1959. He was assured by Enright and Freedman that they too would cover up.

Van Doren's day of reckoning came on November 2, 1959, before the subcommittee. Herb Stempel hurried down from New York City to get a seat from which he could clearly see his former adversary. Pale and jittery, Van Doren walked into the crowded hearing room and delivered himself of one of the most pathetic confessions in the history of American public speech.

He wished that he could erase the past three years but realizing the past may be immutable resolved to learn from it. When he had first contacted Barry and Enright, he had assumed that their programs were honest. Before his appearance on *21*, Albert Freedman summoned him to his apartment and, taking him into the bedroom, explained that Stempel had to be defeated in order to make the show more popular. Van Doren asked to go on the air honestly, but Freedman said he had no chance to defeat the brilliant Stempel. "He also told me that the show was merely entertainment and that giving help to quiz contestants was a common practice and merely a part of show business." Besides, said Freedman, Van Doren had an opportunity to help increase respect for intellectual life and education. "I will not," said Van Doren, "bore this committee by describing the intense moral struggle that went on inside me." The result of that struggle was history. Freedman coached him on how to answer questions to increase suspense and several times gave him a script to memorize. When Van Doren missed the questions which were slated for the evening, Freedman ". . . would allow me to look them up myself. A foolish sort of pride made me want to look up the answers when I could, and to learn as much about the subject as possible."

As time went on the show ballooned beyond my wildest expectations. . . . [F]rom an unknown college instructor I became a celebrity. I received thousands of letters and dozens of requests to make speeches, appear in movies, and so forth—in short, all the trappings of modern publicity. To a certain extent this went to my head.

He realized, however, that he was misrepresenting education and was becoming more nervous about the show. He urged the producers to let him quit, but it was only after they could arrange a sufficiently dramatic situation that he was defeated.

Van Doren's brief testimony was the climax of the subcommittee's investigation as it was of this scandal as a whole. Nevertheless, the hearings continued, including an investigation of *The $64,000 Question. Question* was also fixed, and although the details differed from the *21* case, the deception was no less pervasive.

It is no exaggeration to say that the American public was transfixed by the revelation of quiz show fraud. A Gallup poll found the highest level of public awareness of the event in the history of such surveys. Questioned about the shows at successive news conferences, President Eisenhower said he shared "the American general reaction of almost bewilderment" and compared the manipulations to the Black Sox scandal of 1919. The quiz show episode affords an opportunity to discuss feelings toward Van Doren, the hero unmasked, and also the general arguments which swirled around television at decade's turn.

For Van Doren, humiliation came in the wake of confession. Just as institutions had been happy to associate themselves with quiz show geniuses, they hurried to dissociate themselves when the geniuses turned out to be hustlers. NBC fired Van Doren, while Columbia "accepted his resignation." The actions of these two institutions were scrutinized along with those of Van Doren in the period following his confession.

From the first, both NBC and CBS had maintained the highly implausible stand that they were fooled about the shows along with the public. They unquestionably could have uncovered the rigging had they really wanted to, and in the end they were left holding the bag. They had lost millions of dollars and, what was worse, had suffered what at the time loomed as a potentially mortal blow to a very pleasant way of making a lot of money. The popular uproar threatened to force government to restrict the broadcasting prerogatives of management. In this state of affairs, Van Doren had to go. CBS took the next step eliminating quiz shows altogether, from which NBC refrained.

Few were surprised by NBC's stand. The network was, after all, a business, and Van Doren had become a liability. Columbia's treatment of him aroused different issues. Some students had no patience with him, but hundreds rallied to his defense with petitions and demonstrations. They pointed out that his teaching was excellent and that having made public relations capital out of his victories, Columbia would be craven to desert him now. The Columbia College dean, however, maintained, "The issue is the moral one of the honesty and integrity of teaching." The dean found Van Doren's deceptions contrary to the principles a teacher should have and should try to instill in his students.

The academic community holds in especial contempt, as *Love Story* author Eric Segal was to discover, those "willing to play the fool" for limitless publicity. In defense of Columbia's action, political scientist Hans J. Morgenthau published two essays purporting to show that Van Doren had actually violated "the moral law" as handed down from Moses, Plato, Buddha, and other worthies. Apparently no such law would have been violated had Van Doren's participation in what thinking people very well knew was a cheap stunt been unrigged. If any crime had been committed in the quiz show episode, it was surely the broad conspiracy to portray as genuine intellectual activity the spouting of trivia. But while the shows were on and winning high ratings, there was neither from Morgenthau nor Columbia a peep of protest.

The most devastating but also perhaps the fairest indictment of Van Doren's role was penned by a Columbia colleague, Lawrence S. Hall, who demonstrated that Van Doren's confession had been as thoroughly fraudulent as his conduct on *21*. He had not confessed because of a letter from a fan of his on the *Today* show as he had claimed but only because of a congressional subpoena. "To the very end he never did perform the ethical free act of making up his mind. . . .Van Doren did not *decide* to tell the truth; what he did was adapt himself to the finally inescapable necessity of telling it." Worst of all, asserted Hall, was his "concealing under [the] piously reflexive formulas" of his silken prose "the most maudlin

and promiscuous ethical whoredom the soap opera public has yet witnessed."

Unlike Hall the average American seemed rather sympathetic. A Sindlinger poll asked respondents to rate those most blameworthy for the fixes. Asked to assess the responsibility of network, sponsor, producer, and Van Doren, only 18.6% blamed Van Doren the most while 38.9% blamed him the least. A substantial number even favored a continuation of the shows rigged or not. Many man-in-the-street interviewees said they would have done no differently, and most newspaper editorials treated him extraordinarily gently.

Investigators discovered not a single contestant on *21*, and only one on *The $64,000 Question*, who refused to accept money once they learned the shows were fixed. Most were quite "blithe" about it. Pollsters at the end of the 1950s were finding the belief widespread that the individual did not feel it was his place to condemn. Moral relativism, it seemed, rather than adherence to Professor Morgenthau's moral absolutism, was the rule. So many people lived polite lies that though it may have been titillating to discover them, they were hardly worth preaching about.

Other factors, in addition to this general willingness to partake in a fraud such as the quiz shows, help explain why the outrage was muted and transient. First, as Boorstin has pointed out, television unites many people in a community, but their union is tenuous and easily forgotten. Secondly, although many were taken in by the seeming reality of the shows, they had believed and been disabused so many times in the past that the shock soon wore off. For underneath the belief in the shows there probably lingered skepticism. Robert Merton observed in 1946 that cynicism about public statements from any source, political or commercial, was pervasive. Television was a new medium which some may have thought was simply too big to play by the rules of the old-time newspaper patent medicine advertiser. The quiz shows taught them that it was not, and some critics asserted that it was the naked selfishness of commercial radio and television, more than the machinations of particular producers or contestants, that was truly to blame. The quiz shows excited to a new pitch of intensity long-running arguments about commercial broadcasting and the public interest.

The growth of commercial broadcasting cannot be explored here at length, but suffice it to say that it was opposed every step of the way by intellectuals, educators, and journalists who deplored what they saw as the perversion of a medium of great potential for the sake of the desire of private business to push products. As early as the 1920s, when radio was first coming into its own, articulate voices spoke up against its use for advertising. Bruce Bliven thought such "outrageous rubbish" should be banned from the air, and at least one congressman considered introducing legislation to that end. Herbert Hoover, whose Commerce Department supervised the granting of broadcast licenses, felt that radio would die if it allowed itself to be "drowned in advertising chatter," but he favored self-regulation rather than government action. The Radio Act of 1927 demanded that licensees operated their stations not solely for profit but with due regard for the "public interest, convenience, and necessity."

As charted by broadcasting's foremost historian, Erik Barnouw, the ascendancy of commercial programming was established in a fit of absence of mind. "If such a system [as exists today] had been outlined in 1927 or 1934, when our basic broadcasting laws were written," he concluded, "it certainly would have been rejected." Critics believed that the quiz shows and the radio "payola" scandals that followed proved that broadcasting was too important to be left in the hands of those whose primary, if not sole, motive was to turn a profit for the stockholders.

Television executives insisted that the scandals were the exception in a generally well run industry, but critics thought they were the tip

of the iceberg. In themselves, the scandals were relatively unimportant, held the *New Republic*. "A real investigation would center on the simple question: why is television so bad, so monstrous?" It was the thirst for profit which forced the industry to a state of thralldom to the ratings. It was profit which mandated such dreadful children's programming. Advertising agencies and their clients, with profit always uppermost in mind, forced absurd restrictions on what could be broadcast. When commentators complained about the astounding amount of violence on the tube, defenders warned of the danger of censorship. Critics replied that the most stultifying censorship was already being exercised in behalf of the manufacturers of the pointless nostrums of an overindulgent society. In its quest for ratings, television seemed consistently to avoid satisfying the intelligent minority.

The industry had now been caught redhanded, Walter Lippmann wrote, in ". . . an enormous conspiracy to deceive the public in order to sell profitable advertising to the sponsors." The situation which had made this shameful occurrence possible could not be allowed to survive intact. Television had "to live up to a higher, but less profitable, standard." What America needed was prime time TV produced "not because it yields private profits but because it moves toward truth and excellence." What was needed, said Lippmann, was public service television.

Industry spokesmen had traditionally defended themselves as true democrats. The president of CBS, Frank Stanton, soon after *The $64,000 Question* was first aired, declared, "A program in which a large part of the audience is interested is by that very fact. . . in the public interest." By such a standard, the quiz shows can be seen not as "cynical malpractices. . . in one corner of television," as Robert Sarnoff tried to represent them, but rather as the perfect expression of the industry.

Sarnoff recognized the charges being hurled at TV in 1959 and 1960 as the "long-familiar

■ ■ *Charles Van Doren, winner of $129,000 in a rigged TV quiz show, pleaded guilty to perjury in his testimony to the New York County Grand Jury and received a suspended sentence in 1962.*

[ones] of mediocrity, imbalance, violence, and overcommercialism." These charges had been unjustified in the past and were unjustified in 1960, but because ". . . those who press them are now armed with the cudgels represented by the quiz-show deceptions" they could not be sloughed off. Sarnoff's response was to promise careful scrutiny of such programs in the future and vigorous self-regulation. As a special bonus to the viewing public in a gesture to wipe the slate clean, he offered to donate time for series of debates between the major Presidential candidates of 1960, which eventually resulted in the televised confrontations between Kennedy and Nixon.

Sarnoff's offer was enthusiastically welcomed by such politicians as Stewart Udall, who had been working for a suspension of

equal time regulations in order to permit broadcast debates between Democratic and Republican Presidential nominees in the upcoming election. Paradoxically, the four "Great Debates" which ensued showed unmistakably the influence of the supposedly discredited quiz programs. The similarity in formats was obvious. As in *21*, two adversaries faced each other and tried to give point-scoring answers to questions fired at them under the glare of klieg lights. The debates bore as little relationship to the real work of the presidency as the quiz shows did to intellectuality. Boorstin has remarked on how successful they were ". . . in reducing great national issues to trivial dimensions. With appropriate vulgarity, they might have been called the $400,000 Question (Prize: a $100,000-a-year job for four years)." No President would act on any question put to him by the reporters without sustained and sober consultation with trusted advisors. But the American people, conditioned by five years of isolation booth virtuosity, expected the "right" answer to be delivered pithily and with little hesitation. They did not want to be told that some questions did not have simple answers—or any answers at all.

The technological advances which led to radio and television grew out of the tinkerings of amateur experimenters. These two new forms of mass communication, with unprecedented drama and immediacy, developed independently of the desire to say anything. In 1854, Henry David Thoreau wrote, "We are in great haste to construct a magnetic telegraph from Maine to Texas; but Maine and Texas, it may be, have nothing important to communicate." This observation has been yet more relevant during the last half century. Except for the military, which was always seeking more direct means for locating ships at sea and soldiers on the battlefield, no one knew what to broadcast and telecast. The federal government, dominated by the ideology of free enterprise, declined to fill this void. To be sure, regulations did prohibit certain messages over the air, but there has never been a national statement on the positive purposes of the new media which the industry was obliged to take seriously.

Businessmen soon discovered that broadcasting was a powerful instrument for increasing sales. Those advertisers who had financed the print media, including manufacturers of patent medicines, cosmetics, and cigarettes, quickly adopted the same role with radio and television. Left to their own devices, they sought programs which would constitute a congenial frame for their selling message. They soon hit upon the idea, among others, of parlor games, of which the quiz shows were direct descendants.

Such programs had been popular since the thirties, but in the 1950s, clever producers learned how to make them even more so. They combined large sums of money with the American fondness for facts, dressed up as intellectuality, and the result was *The $64,000 Question* and *21*. When these programs were exposed as frauds, a jaded public, inured to mendacity, was quick to forgive.

Critics have often complained, as they did with vigor after the scandals, that television—"a medium of such great potential"—was being so ill-used. But no one seems to have a clear vision of what that potential is. The lack of direction which characterized the early years of American broadcasting has never been overcome. Commentators such as Lippmann have won their public broadcasting system, but commercial television has not upgraded its fare in order to compete. If anything, public TV may act as a lightning rod deflecting complaints about the commercial industry by providing an outlet for those demanding alternative viewing.

For its part, the industry has usually ignored what enlightened guidance has been available in favor of traditional forms of entertainment guaranteed not to distract the viewer from the advertisements. Thus, recently, quiz and game shows have made a comeback. There has even been talk of resurrecting *The $64,000 Question*, despite the risk of reviving along with it memories of past chicanery. Such programming represents a distressing devotion to Philistinism and a failure of imagination, the solution for which is not in sight.

■ ■ ■

STUDY QUESTIONS

1. What is implied by the concept of a "consumption community"? How is this sort of a community different from any other community?

2. Compare how Charles Van Doren and Herbert Stempel were presented on the television quiz show *21*. Why was Stempel told to appear poor and deferential on the show? Is there a political statement in the images of both men?

3. How did most Americans respond to the disclosure that *21* and other quiz show were rigged?

4. What does Tedlow mean by the concept of "moral relativism"? Is morality ever absolute?

5. What issues are involved in the debate between advocates of commercial broadcasting and proponents of public service broadcasting?

6. How were the Nixon-Kennedy television debates in 1960 similar to or different from the format of the television quiz show *21*? What does this say about the importance of television in a political campaign?

BIBLIOGRAPHY

The television industry has received far less historical attention than the film industry. This is perplexing, considering that television "touches" more people—American as well as non-American—than the movies. The fact that some movie directors have consciously cultivated reputations as "artists" undoubtedly has something to do with academic interest in their product that is not apparent with television. There are, however, several very good books on television. Among the best are Erik Barnauw, *The Golden Web* (1968), and *The Image Empire: A History of Broadcasting in the United States* (1970); Raymond Williams, *Television: Technology and Cultural Form* (1975); and Robert Sklare, *Prime-Time America: Life on and Behind the Television Screen* (1980). Also of interest are two books by Daniel Boorstin, *The Americans: The Democratic Experience* (1974), and *The Image: A Guide to Pseudo-Events in America* (1961).

The Van Doren case is dealt with in Kent Anderson, *Television Fraud* (1978), and Eric Goldman, *The Crucial Decade and After: America, 1945–1960* (1960). Douglas Miller and Marian Novak discuss social and cultural developments in the 1950s in *The Fifties: The Way We Really Were* (1977).

THE AGE OF CONSPIRACY AND CONFORMITY: INVASION OF THE BODY SNATCHERS

Stuart Samuels

During the late 1940s and early 1950s several investigations by the House Un-American Activities Committee (HUAC) focused on the subversive nature of Hollywood films. Walt Disney told HUAC that screenwriters had tried to make Mickey Mouse follow the Communist party line, and committee members criticized such openly pro-Soviet films as Warner Brothers' *Mission to Moscow* (1943) and MGM's *Song of Russia* (1943). Given the anticommunist mood of the period, it was clear that heads would have to roll. And roll they did. In 1947 a group of filmmakers, the Hollywood Ten, challenged HUAC's authority to pry into their personal and political beliefs. As a result, the members of the Hollywood Ten found themselves on a blacklist and for more than a decade the heads of the major studios refused to hire them. In 1951 HUAC resumed their investigation of Hollywood. Many producers, screenwriters, actors, and directors were called before the committee. About one-third cooperated with HUAC. The two-thirds that refused to cooperate were blacklisted.

This disruption of the Hollywood community spilled over into the films made during the period. Most studios, eager to publicize their anticommunist credentials, turned out violently anticommunist films. The result was such movies as *My Son John* (1952) and *I Was a Communist for the FBI* (1951). Other films reflected the political and cultural mood of the country in a less overt manner. In the following essay, Stuart Samuels demonstrates that *Invasion of the Body Snatchers* (1956) is far more than a class "B" science fiction film. Rather, it is a film that exemplifies the fear and anxieties of the 1950s.

In what way can a seemingly absurd science fiction/horror film, *Invasion of the Body Snatchers*, give us insight into the history and culture of America in the mid-1950s? How is a film about people being taken over by giant seed pods "reflective" of this critical period in our history?

Films relate to ideological positions in two ways. First, they *reflect*, embody, reveal, mirror, symbolize existing ideologies by reproducing (consciously or unconsciously) the myths, ideas, concepts, beliefs, images of an historical period in both the film content and film form (technique). Secondly, films *produce* their own ideology, their own unique expression of reality. Films can do this by reinforcing a specific ideology or undercutting it.

All films are therefore ideological and political insomuch as they are determined by the ideology which produces them. Fictional characters are only prototypes of social roles and social attitudes; every film speaks to some norm. Some behaviors are deemed appropriate, others not. Some acts are condemned, others applauded. Certain characters are depicted as heroic, others as cowardly. Film is one of the products, one of the languages, through which the world communicates itself to itself. Films embody beliefs, not by a mystic communion with the national soul, but because they contain the values, fears, myths, assumptions, point of view of the culture in which they are produced.

While films relate to ideology, they also relate to specific historical and social events, most obviously when the content of a film deals directly with a subject that is identifiable in its own period. In the 1950s, for example, such films as *I Was a Communist for the FBI*

"The Age of Conspiracy and Conformity: Invasion of the Body Snatchers" from *American History/American Film: Interpreting the Hollywood Image* by Stuart Samuels. Copyright © 1979 by Frederick Ungar Publishing Co., Inc. Reprinted by permission.

(1951) and *My Son John* (1952) spoke to a society increasingly concerned with the nature of the internal communist threat. Similarly, in the previous decade such films as *The Best Years of Our Lives* (1946) attempted to analyze some of the problems and confusions of the immediate post-World War II period and *The Snake Pit* (1948) addressed a society trying to deal with the tremendous increase in the hospital treatment of the mentally ill. As far back as Griffith's *Intolerance* (1916), which relayed a pacifist message to a nation struggling to stay out of war, films have reflected society's attempts to come to grips with contemporary problems.

Film "reflects" an agreed-upon perception of social reality, acceptable and appropriate to the society in question. Thus, in the 1950s when a conspiracy theory of politics was a widely accepted way of explaining behavior (being duped), action (being subversive), and effect (conspiracy), one would expect the films of the period to "reflect" this preoccupation with conspiracy. But *Invasion of the Body Snatchers* is not *about* McCarthyism. It is about giant seed pods taking over people's bodies. Indirectly, however, it is a *statement about* the collective paranoia and the issue of conformity widely discussed in the period.

The idea for the film came from Walter Wanger, the producer, who had read Jack Finney's novel of the same name in serial form in *Collier's Magazine* in 1955. Wanger suggested the project to his friend Don Siegel, who in turn assigned Daniel Manwaring to produce a screenplay from Finney's book.

The story of the film is contained within a "framing" device—a seemingly insane man, Miles Bennell (Kevin McCarthy), telling a bizarre story to a doctor and a policeman. In flashback we see Bennell's tale—of giant seed pods taking over the minds and bodies of the people of Santa Mira, a small town in California, where Bennell was the local doctor. Returning home after a medical convention, Miles finds the pretty little town and its peaceful inhabitants in the grip of a "mass hysteria." People seem obsessed by the conviction that relatives and friends are not really themselves, that they have been changed. Despite the outward calm of Santa Mira, there is a creeping contagion of fear and paranoia, of wives not knowing their husbands, children fleeing from their parents.

Miles's friend Becky (Dana Wyntner) struggles against this delusion, tends to dismiss it as improbable, but nevertheless finds her own Uncle Ira slightly changed: "There's no emotion in him. None. Just the pretense of it." The improbable becomes real when Miles's friend Jack calls him to report something fantastic: a semihuman body, without features, has been found on Jack's billiard table. From this point on events move rapidly. The unformed body is clearly growing into an exact duplicate of Jack, and in the greenhouse Miles stumbles upon giant seed pods, each containing a half-formed body. In Becky's basement Miles finds still another embryonic shape—this time a model of Becky herself. Now Miles believes the fantastic stories, and determines to escape and warn the world of this danger.

But escape is not simple. The town of Santa Mira has nearly been taken over by the pods, who while the inhabitants sleep form themselves into precise replicas of human beings—even-tempered, peaceful, but soulless automatons. Miles is terrified and drags Becky from her bedroom, to flee in his auto. But the town has now mobilized against them; the pod-people cannot allow the story to be told, and the "people" of Santa Mira organize to catch Miles and Becky. In a desperate escape attempt, they flee over the mountains, pursued by those who had once been friends and neighbors.

The horror mounts when, in a tunnel, Becky succumbs to the pods. She falls asleep and soon her mind and body are taken over, cell by cell. In a moment of utmost panic, Miles looks into her eyes and realizes the awful truth. Continuing on alone, he comes to a highway where he makes wild attempts to flag down

motorists who are terrified by his insane behavior. Eventually, he is picked up by the police, who naturally consider him mad, and taken to a hospital for medical examination. The doctors agree that he is psychotic, but then fate intervenes. An intern reports an accident to a truck from Santa Mira, and in a casual aside, he tells how the driver of the wreck had to be dug out from under a pile of strange giant seed pods. The truth dawns on the police inspector, who orders the roads to Santa Mira closed, and in the final shot tells his assistant to "call the FBI."

The political, social, and intellectual atmosphere of the era that created *Invasion* must be understood in light of several preoccupations: the "Red Menace," which crystallized around the activities of Senator Joseph McCarthy and the somewhat less spectacular blacklisting of figures in the communications and entertainment industry, who were seen as a nefarious, subversive element undermining the entire fabric of American society; learning to cope with the consequences of a modern, urban, technologically bureaucratized society; and the pervasive fear of atomic annihilation. All these factors undermined the traditional American myth of individual action. The experience of the Depression, the rise and threat of totalitarianism, the loss of American insularity, the growth of technocracy all in one form or another challenged the integrity of the individual. It is therefore not surprising to note that film genres like science fiction or horror films proliferated in the 1950s. The central themes of these films show a preoccupation with depersonalization and dehumanization. Moreover, as Susan Sontag has suggested, it is by no means coincidental that at a time when the moviegoing public had over ten years been living under the constant threat of instant atomic annihilation, films of the 1950s should be concerned with the confrontation of death. As Sontag expressed it: "We live[d] under continued threat of two equally fearful, but seemingly opposed destinies: unremitting banality and inconceivable terror." On the surface there existed a complacency that disguised a deep fear of violence, but conformity silenced the cries of pain and feelings of fear.

In response to the threats of social banality and universal annihilation, three concepts dominated the decade: (1) conformity, (2) paranoia, (3) alienation. Each concept had its keywords. *Conformity:* "silent generation," "status seekers," "lonely crowds," "organization men," "end of ideology," "hidden persuaders." *Paranoia:* "red decade," "dupes," "front organization," "blacklisting," "un-Americanism," "fifth column," "fellow travelers," "pinkos." *Alienation:* "outsiders," "beats," "loners," "innerdirected men," "rebels." For the most part, the decade celebrated a suburbanized, bureaucratized, complacent, secure, conformist, consensus society in opposition to an alienated, disturbed, chaotic, insecure, individualistic, rebel society. Each of those three concepts dominating the 1950s finds obvious expression in *Invasion of the Body Snatchers.* First—conformity.

During the 1950s a concern for respectability, a need for security and compliance with the system became necessary prerequisites for participation in the reward structure of an increasingly affluent society. Conformism had replaced individuality as the principal ingredient for success. This standard extended to all aspects of life. Tract-built, identical, tidy little boxlike ranch houses on uniform fifty-foot plots bulldozed to complete flatness were the rage. Conformity dictated city planning in the form of Levittowns, the same way it silenced political dissidents in Congress. Creativity meant do-it-yourself painting-by-numbers. One created great artistic masterpieces by following directions.

The concern with conformity grew out of a need to escape from confusion, fear, worry, tension, and a growing sense of insecurity. It was accentuated by a sense of rootlessness and increased mobility. Consensus mentality offered a refuge in an anxious and confusing world. It represented an attempt to shift the burden of individual responsibility for one's fate to an impersonal monolithic whole. Excessive conformity, as in the 1950s, was a salve to smooth over obvious conflict and turmoil. A country that emerged from war victorious around the globe feared internal subversion at home; a society powered by a new technology and a new structure (corporate bureaucracy) feared a loss of personal identity. In the White House was a person whose great appeal was that he represented a politics of consensus, classlessness, and conformism— Eisenhower.

By the time *Invasion* was released (May, 1956) the intensity of the drive for consensus politics had diminished—the Korean War had ended, McCarthy had been censored, Stalin was dead, the spirit of Geneva had thawed the Cold War, the imminent threat of atomic annihilation had subsided, witch hunting had lost its appeal, and the threat of internal subversion had lessened. But the context of fear was still active. The political reality might not seem as frightening, but the mind-set of the period was always ready at any moment to raise its repressive head. To many people, the fact that the enemy appeared less threatening only meant that he was better at concealing his subversion and that the eternal vigilance of good Americans had to be even more effective.

David Riesman's *The Lonely Crowd* (1955) spoke of a society obsessed by conformity. His now-famous formulation about inner-directed and other-directed men, focuses on the same conflicts outlined by Siegel in *Invasion.* Miles Bennell is "inner directed"—a self-reliant individualist who has internalized adult authority, and judged himself and others by these internalized self-disciplined standards of behavior. The "pods" are "other-directed" beings whose behavior is completely conditioned by the example of their peers. While inner-directed individuals like Miles felt concern and guilt about violating their inner ideals—in fact, were driven by them—the other-directed pods had no inner ideals to violate. Their morality came from the compulsion to be in harmony with the crowd. Their guilt developed in direct proportion to how far they deviated from group consensus. The other-directed pods were uncritical conformists. It was no coincidence that the most popular adult drug of the 1950s was not alcohol or aspirin, pot or cocaine—but Miltown and Thorazine—tranquilizers.

The second basic concept in 1950s America, the natural corollary to the drive toward conformity, was the notion of conspiracy. Conformity is based on the idea that there is a clear-cut division between *them* and *us*. In periods of overt conflict, like wars or economic crises, the division between the good and the bad is obvious. But in periods of confusion, the identification of enemies becomes more problematic. Covert expressions of subversion are more common than overt challenges; the enemy attacks—whether real or imagined—through subversion and conspiracy rather than war. In the 1950s subversion seemed to be everywhere. Appearances were deceptive; to many, nothing was what it appeared to be. Schools named after American heroes like Jefferson, Lincoln, Walt Whitman, Henry George were rumored to be fronts for communists, calls for free speech were seen as pleas for communism, and racial unrest as being fomented by party activists. To many, taking the Fifth Amendment in order not to incriminate oneself was just another way of disguising one's political treason.

Threats to social order in the 1950s were not so much associated with personal violence as with an indefinable, insidious, fiendishly cold undermining of the normal. Conspiracy theories feed off the idea of the normal being deceptive. In *Invasion*, the pods, the alien invaders, take on the appearance of normal people. It becomes physically impossible to tell the difference between the aliens and the normals. In *Invasion* all forms of normalcy are inverted. Friends are not friends, "Uncle Ira" is not Uncle Ira, the police do not protect, sleep is not revivifying, telephones are no longer a way of calling for help but a device to tell the pod-people where the remaining non-pod-people are. Even the name of the town is paradoxical. Mira in Spanish means "to look," but the people of Santa Mira refuse to look; they stare blankly into the unknown. A patina of normalcy hides a deepseated violence. A man holds a giant seed pod and calmly asks his wife, "Shall I put this in with the baby?" "Yes," she replies, "then there'll be no more crying." In another scene, what appears to be a quiet Sunday morning gathering in the town square turns out to be a collection point where fleets of trucks filled with pods quietly dispense these "vegetables" to people who carry them to their cars and buses, ready to spread the invasion to neighboring towns. It is during a typical home barbeque among friends that Miles finds the pods in his greenhouse.

At the end of the film, when all avenues of help seemed closed, Miles and Becky, hiding in an abandoned cave, hear sweet, loving music—a Brahms lullaby. Miles decides that such beauty and feeling could not possibly be the singing of unemotional pods. He scrambles off to find out where this music is coming from—only to discover that its source is a radio in a large truck being loaded by robotlike people with seed pods destined for far-off towns. The familiar is fraught with danger. It is no wonder that Miles comes to the edge of madness, no wonder that he treats people with a paranoid suspicion. Paranoia becomes the logical alternative to podlike conformism.

Finally, conformism and conspiracy signaled a new age of personal alienation. From the very beginning of our history, one of the most persistent myths about American society has been the myth of natural harmony. The idea is derived from the notion made popular by Adam Smith and John Locke that there is a *natural* and harmonious relationship between the desires of individuals and the demands of social necessity, that individuals who act out of self-interest will automatically move the society as a whole in the direction of natural perfection. At the heart of this notion was the belief that nothing in the system prevented people from achieving their own individual goals, and that the traditional barriers of class, religion, and geography were absent in the American experience. The concept of natural harmony is further based on the belief of abundance. Individual failure had to be due to personal shortcomings because a society of abundance offered opportunity to anyone capable of grasping it—conflict was not built into the system. People were basically good. Solutions were always within grasp. Control was inevitable. Progress was assured.

This underlying belief in natural harmony was one of the casualties of the post-1945 world. In the 1930s American films had portrayed people ordering their environment. "The people," the Mr. Smiths, the Mr. Deeds, the Shirley Temples, and the Andy Hardys saw to it that control and harmony were restored. Individual "good acts" reinforced "social good" in the desire to control life. In the 1940s the theme of conquest, control, and restoration of the natural was the underlining statement of war films. Commitments to courage, self-sacrifice, and heroism were shown instead of Senate filibusters, talks with Judge Hardy, or faith in "the people." Depictions of failure, helplessness, and feelings of inadequacy were introduced as muted themes in the postwar films. Although we had won the war, conquered the Depression, and tamed nature by splitting the atom, things seemed out of control in the 1950s as conflict emerged between the desire for personal autonomy and the pressures for collective conformity. Individual acts of heroism were suspect. Group work and group think were the ideals. Success was measured by how much individuals submerged themselves into some larger mass (society, bureaucracy) over which they had little individual control. The rewards of status, popularity, and acceptance came with conformity to the group. In the films of the period, people who did not sacrifice

individual desires for general social needs were fated to die, commit suicide, be outcast, or simply go mad.

Popular books like Riesman's *The Lonely Crowd*, William Whyte's *The Organization Man*, and Vance Packard's *The Status Seekers* showed how the traditional model of the hard working, rugged individualist was being rejected for a world of the group—big universities, big suburbs, big business, and big media. Such harmony as existed resulted from the artificial ordering to an agreed upon surface norm. After the scarcity of the Depression came the affluence of the 1950s—complete with its never-ending routine of conspicuous consumption. Out of the victory for democracy and freedom came a society more standardized, less free, more conformist, and less personal. Out of splitting the atom came the threat of instant annihilation.

The mid-1950s films portrayed people trying desperately to ward off failure in the face of overwhelming destructive forces of nature (horror films), technology (science fiction films), and human imperfection *(film noir)*. There were films about people being taken over or reincarnated: *The Search for Bridie Murphy* (1956), *I've Lived Before* (1956), *Back from the Dead* (1957), *The Undead* (1957), *Vertigo* (1956), *Donovan's Brain* (1953); about individuals in conflict with their societies: *High Noon* (1952), *The Phoenix City Story* (1955), *No Place to Hide* (1956), *Not on this Earth* (1957); about superior forces beyond man's control: *Them* (1954), *Tarantula* (1956), *The Beast from 20,000 Fathoms* (1953), *This Island Earth* (1955), *Earth versus the Flying Saucers* (1956); about the apocalypse: *20,000 Leagues Under the Sea* (1954), *On the Beach* (1959), *The Thing* (1951). In these films, the world seemed menacing, fluid, chaotic, impersonal, composed of forces which one seldom understood, and certainly never controlled. Fear is centered on the unknown, unseen terrors that lurk beneath the surface normality.

Invasion's podism is depicted as a malignant evil, as a state of mind where there is no feeling, no free will, no moral choice, no anger, no tears, no passion, no emotion. Human sensibility is dead. The only instinct left is the instinct to survive. Podism meant being "reborn into an untroubled world, where everyone's the same." "There is no need for love or emotion. Love, ambition, desire, faith—without them, life is so simple." A metaphor for communism? Perhaps! But, more directly, podism spoke to a society becoming more massified, more technological, more standardized.

The motto of the pods was "no more love, no more beauty, no more pain." Emotionless, impersonal, regimented, they became technological monsters. But they were not the irrational creatures of blood lust and power—they were just nonhuman. They became tranquil and obedient. They spoke to the fear of the 1950s—not the fear of violence, but the fear of losing one's humanity. As Susan Sontag argued, "the dark secret behind human nature used to be the upsurge of the animal—as in *King Kong* (1933). The threat to man, his availability to dehumanization, lay in his animality. Now the danger is understood to reside in man's ability to be turned into a machine." The body is preserved, but the person is entirely reconstituted as the automated replica of an "alien" power.

The attraction of becoming a pod in the 1950s was all too real. But although dangling the carrot of conformity, *Invasion* opts ultimately for the stick of painful individuality. The possibility of moral uncertainty was the price we must pay for continued freedom. As Miles says: "Only when we have to fight to stay human do we realize how precious our humanity is." Podism, an existence without pain or fear or emotion, is seen as no existence at all. The fear of man becoming a machinelike organism, losing his humanity, was centered around the ambiguous dual legacy of an increasingly technological civilization. The atomic bomb was both a testament to man's increased control over his universe and a clear symbol of man's fallibility. *Invasion* mirrors

this duality. It praises the possibility of a society without pain, yet it raises the spectre of a society without feeling. Security at what price?—the price of freedom and individualism. The rise of technology at what costs?—the cost of humanness itself. Although *Invasion* is ambiguous on the issue, demonstrating the positive effects of "podism" at the same time as condemning its consequences, this confusion, this ambiguity, is very much at the heart of the American cultural issues of the period—the internal conflict between the urge for conformity and the painful need for individuality, between an antiheroic loner and an institutionalized, bureaucratized system of mindless automated pods.

In his struggle to remain his own master, Miles fights against control by first falling back on the traditional notions inherited from the past. He appeals to friends—only to be betrayed. He appeals to the law—only to be pursued by it. He appeals to the system—only to be trapped by it. He appeals to love—only to be disappointed by losing it. All betray him. All become his enemy. Not because they are corrupt, or evil, but because they have become pods, because they have given up their individuality, their ability to choose.

If there is a 1950 vision of historical reality in *Invasion*, there is also a system of film technique designed to reinforce this vision. The language and technique of *Invasion* come out of the social reality of the period and speak directly to that context.

One of the major themes of life in the 1950s was the feeling of constraint—people feeling enclosed within boundaries. People were cut off from options, limited in their choices. There was a closing down of dissent, a shrinking of personal freedom. Silence became the acceptable response to oppression.

Invasion is a film about constraints. It is the story of a man whose ability to make sense of the world decreases and diminishes to the point of madness and frenzy. The film's action takes place within enclosed physical spaces

■ ■ *Still photo from the film* Invasion of the Body Snatchers. *This movie was made in 1956, a time when Hollywood began taking a look at the push for conformity and the collective paranoia about conspiracies that characterized the era.*

and the physical spaces in the film induce a sense of isolation and constraint. The sleepy California town of Santa Mira is surrounded by hills. When Miles tries to escape he must run up a series of ladder-like stairs to flee the pod-people and reach the open highway that separates the town from the outside world. Miles and Becky are constantly running—in and out of small rooms, darkened cellars illuminated only by matches, large but empty nightclubs, miniature greenhouses, closets, low-ceilinged dens, abandoned caves. The giant seed pods are found in basements, closets, car trunks, greenhouses. The main actors are claustrophobically framed by doorways and windows photographed from low angles, and spend much of their time running down and up endless stairs, into locked doors, and beneath towering trees. The narrative structure of *Invasion* resembles a series of self-contained Chinese boxes and is designed to tighten the tension of the story at every step. Though Miles returns from his convention on a sunny morning and the film ends in a confused mixture of daylight and darkness, the main section of the film takes place in darkness—at night.

The whole film is enclosed within a framing device of prologue and epilogue. Siegel's original version had not included this frame, but the addition of a prologue and epilogue, making the film narrative appear as an extended flashback, has the unintended effect of constricting the narrative—itself contained in a rigidly enclosed time frame—even further. Within this framing device, Siegel also uses the technique of repeating a situation at the end of the film that mirrors a sequence presented at the beginning. In the final flashback episode, Siegel has Miles running in panic down the road and being pursed by a whole town of pod-people. This scene mirrors the opening scene when we see little Jimmy Grimaldi running down the road being pursued by his "podized" mother.

The effect of these devices is to keep the narrative tight in order to heighten tension and suspense. The use of flashback, prologue and epilogue, repeated scenes, interplay of lightness and darkness, all keep the narrative constrained within a carefully defined filmic space. The unbelievable tension is released only in the epilogue, when Miles finally finds someone who believes his story. The ending is not about the FBI's ability to counteract the threat of the pods but about the fact that Miles has finally made contact with another human—and that he is not alone. The film is more about being an alien, an outsider, an individualist, than about the "invasion" by aliens. When Dr. Bassett and his staff finally believe Miles's story, the enclosing ring of constraint is broken, and Miles collapses, relaxing for the first time in the film, knowing that at least he has been saved from a horror worse than death—the loss of identity. The final line— "Call the F.B.I."—is the signal that he is not alone and acts as an affirmative answer to the shout heard at the opening of the film—"I'm not insane." Up to the point when the doctor finally believes Miles's story, the film is actually about a man going insane.

Time is also a constant constraint on humanity, and Siegel emphasizes the fact that time is running out for Miles. The whole film is not only a race against madness, but also against time—of time slipping away. Time in *Invasion* is circumscribed by the fact that sleep is a danger. Miles needs to escape Santa Mira before he

falls asleep. He takes pills, splashes his and Becky's face in a constant battle to stay awake. Sleep is not comfort and safety but the instrument of death.

Siegel uses a whole arsenal of filmic techniques to reinforce the feelings of enclosure, isolation, and time running out. His shot setups focus on isolated action. People are photographed in isolation standing beneath street lamps, in doorways, alone at crowded railway stations. A background of black velvet darkness and a direct artificial light are used to highlight objects which in isolation take on an "evil clarity." In the film, objects are always illuminated, people's faces are not. Shadows dominate people's space and obscure personality. Diagonal and horizontal lines pierce bodies.

Darkness is combined with a landscape of enclosure to increase the feeling of fear. There is a stressed relationship between darkness and danger, light and safety. Those who wish to remain free of the pods must not only keep awake, but must constantly keep themselves close to direct light. For example, when Miles discovers Becky's pod-like double in the basement of her home, he hurries upstairs into her darkened bedroom and carries her out of the dark house into his car which is parked directly beneath a bright street lamp.

Tension in the film is not only created by lighting techniques and camera setups, but most significantly by the contrast in how the actors play their roles. Miles is frenzied, harried, hard-driving, always running. The robot-like, affectless pod people stare out at the camera with vacant eyes, openly unemotional, unbelievably calm, rational, logical. They appear to be normal, and Miles appears to be insane; however, the reverse is true. The pod's blank expression, emotionless eyes mask their essential deadness.

The whole film texture is based on the internal contrast between normal and alien. The hot dog stands, used-car lots, small office buildings, friendly cops, sleepy town square, and neighborhood gas stations only create the illusion of normalcy played against the mounting terror.

The mise-en-scéne, lighting, acting styles, physical presence, props, and Carmen Dragon's unrelenting, spine-chilling musical score keep the audience in a constant state of tension. The same is true of the constant introjection of siren sounds, cuckoo clocks, screams in the middle of the night, and the use of distorting lenses, claustrophobic close-ups, juxtaposed long shots, and low-angled shots that establish a mood of vague disquiet. All help to create a basic tension between the normal and the fearful, the familiar and the sinister, and to result in a film designed to give the audience a sense of isolation, suspense, and feeling of constraint.

Historians will debate the actual nature of the 1950s for a long time. But through the films of a period we can see how a particular society treated the period, viewed it, experienced it,

and symbolized it. Few products reveal so sharply as the science fiction/horror films of the 1950s the wishes, the hopes, the fears, the inner stresses and tensions of the period. Directly or indirectly, *Invasion* deals with the fear of annihilation brought on by the existence of the A-bomb, the pervasive feeling of paranoia engendered by an increasing sense that something was wrong, an increasing fear of dehumanization focused around an increased massification of American life, a deep-seated expression of social, sexual, and political frustration resulting from an ever-widening gap between personal expectation and social reality, and a widespread push for conformity as an acceptable strategy to deal with the confusion and growing insecurity of the period. It is a film that can be used by historians, sociologists, and psychologists to delineate these problems and demonstrate the way American society experienced and symbolized this crucial decade.

■ ■ ■

STUDY QUESTIONS

1. How can films be viewed as ideological statements? Does a film have to be overtly political to be ideological?

2. Out of what sort of political, social, and intellectual atmosphere did *Invasion of the Body Snatchers* emerge? Why were science fiction and horror films popular in the 1950s?

3. How does *Invasion* suggest the theme of conformity in the 1950s? What made Americans retreat from individualism during the decade? What is meant by the shift from "inner-directed" to "outer-directed" individual?

4. How does *Invasion* suggest the themes of conspiracy and paranoia in the 1950s?

5. How does *Invasion* suggest the theme of alienation in the 1950s? Why was podism a very real fear during the decade?

6. How did director Don Siegel shoot the film in order to emphasize the feeling of constraint? What technical duties did he use to reinforce this general theme?

BIBLIOGRAPHY

A number of books deal intelligently with movies and the film industry during the cold war. The most thoughtful and provocative is Victor Navasky, *Naming Names* (1980). Nancy Lynn Schwartz, *The Hollywood Writers' War* (1982), discusses the role of the Screen Writers Guild in the political battles in Hollywood. The blacklisting of film artists is treated in David Cants, *The Great Fear: The Anti-Communist Purge Under Truman and Eisenhower* (1978); Larry Ceplair and Steven Englund, *The Inquisition in Hollywood* (1980); Bruce Cook, *Dalton Trumbo* (1977); Sterling Hayden, *Wanderer* (1963); Lillian Hellman, *Scoundrel Time* (1976); Stefan Kanfer, *A Journal of the Plague Years* (1973); and Robert Vaughn, *Only Victims: A Study of Show Business Blacklisting* (1972). Two recent books that discuss the films themselves in a lively manner are Peter Biskind, *Seeing is Believing: How Hollywood Taught Us to Stop Worrying and Love the Fifties* (1983), and Nora Sayre, *Running Time: Films of the Cold War* (1982). Finally, Stuart A. Kaminsky, *Don Siegel: Director* (1974), and Alan Lovell, *Don Siegel: American Cinema* (1975), discuss the director of *Invasion of the Body Snatchers*.

Part Seven

COMING APART: 1960–1990

The era began innocently enough. In an extremely close election, John F. Kennedy defeated Richard M. Nixon for the presidency and quickly became one of the most admired men in the country. Blessed with brains, charisma, money, and a lovely young family, Kennedy epitomized America, particularly the rise and triumph of the immigrant. In public rhetoric, he cultivated a tough idealism, one that offered a courageous challenge to the Russians and hope for democracy and prosperity in the rest of the world. When Kennedy assumed the presidency in 1961, Americans believed their moral hegemony would last forever. They believed that their values deserved to govern the world by virtue of their success—an equality of opportunity and a standard of living unparalleled in human history. In closing his inaugural address, Kennedy even invoked the divine by claiming that "God's work must truly be our own."

What few people realized was that Kennedy was sitting on a powder keg, both at home and abroad. His liberal idealism, so self-righteous and yet so naive, barely survived his own life. From the mid-1960s through the mid-1970s, the country passed through a period of intense turmoil and doubt. Smug convictions about the virtues of equality and opportunity in the United States succumbed to the shrill criticisms of racial, ethnic, and sexual groups. Beliefs in the virtues, safeguards, and stability of the American government were shattered by the lies exposed in the controversies over Watergate and the Pentagon Papers. By the late 1960s and early 1970s the explosion in oil prices, the appearance of stagflation, and the worries about the future of the environment all undermined the prevailing confidence about the American econ-

omy. Finally, the moral complacency so endemic to Kennedy liberalism died in the jungles of Southeast Asia. Like few other events in American history, the Vietnam War tore the country apart. At home, America was characterized by bitterness, demonstrations, and widespread disaffection from the country's leaders. A counterculture of young people scornful of conventional values appeared, and the symbols of their rebellion were drugs and rock and roll. As far as world opinion was concerned, the country seemed to be a superpower out of control, employing the latest military technology in a futile effort to impose democracy on a nation barely out of the stone age.

Between 1964 and 1977, four American presidents struggled with these overwhelming problems. Lyndon Johnson's Great Society was eventually destroyed by what he called "that bitch of a war." Richard Nixon left the White House in disgrace after the Watergate tapes proved his complicity in perjury and obstructing justice. Gerald Ford failed in his WIN campaign—whip inflation now—and then watched helplessly as the last Americans, fleeing the invading North Vietnamese and Viet Cong troops, took off in helicopters from the roof of the United States embassy in Saigon. Jimmy Carter left the White House in 1977 after trying unsuccessfully to get Americans to accept the idea of austerity, shortages, and reduced expectations. The hostage crisis in Iran seemed the final symbol of American impotency. Not until the late 1980s, with Vietnam receding into history, oil prices dropping, inflation subsiding, Ronald Reagan in the White House, did the United States recapture its legendary optimism about the future.

KENNEDY LIBERALISM

David Burner and Thomas R. West

On the morning after his election in 1960, no one had any idea of how completely John F. Kennedy would capture the American imagination. When he stated in his inaugural address that "the torch has been passed to a new generation of Americans," he became the symbol of a youth culture that would soon come to dominate American society and politics. By the early 1960s the first of the post–World War II baby boomers graduated from high school. Soon they filled colleges and universities, spearheading the crusades against racism, environmental pollution, and the Vietnam war. Raised during a time of unprecedented prosperity, and extraordinarily idealistic in outlook, they needed a political figure they could idolize.

John Fitzgerald Kennedy, for a brief period of time, became that idol. He had been tested in battle against the Japanese during World War II, and his exploits as commander of PT–109 had made him a hero. Kennedy had all the ingredients for stardom. Young and athletic, he exuded sexuality, at least for a major politician. His wife Jacqueline also enjoyed star qualities. Sexually appealing herself, she was at the same time refined and elegant. Small children romped in the White House for the first time since the administration of Theodore Roosevelt, and the public loved it. JFK's tragic death in 1963 only further endeared him to the American public.

However, by the early 1970s, Kennedy's image was changing. He was accused of having been lukewarm on civil rights, a belligerent "cold warrior," and a friend of the business community. Rumors of his sexual escapades with several women became national gossip. Instead of the young hero trying to shape a new world, Kennedy began to look like a calculating politician obsessed with the possibility of his own greatness. In "John F. Kennedy and the Black Revolution," David Burner looks at the record of the Kennedy administration in the area of civil rights, analyzing the political environment in which the young president operated and the extent to which his own views shaped—and limited—the federal response to the civil rights movement.

It was so sudden. The front of a bus where no black person had dared to sit, a lunch counter operated by and for the South's master race, a white southern high school class—each had a black occupant free in that instant of centuries of subordination. The country had seldom known such freedom: the stepping across of an invisible line that had been a chasm, a moment astonishing in its revelation that a new thing could happen so quickly.

In 1960, before Kennedy's election, black and white students defied segregation ordinances by drinking coffee together at southern lunch counters. A year later freedom riders were assaulted on their peaceable, though morally revolutionary, bus journey through the South. In the fall of 1962 the governor of Mississippi raged, for Mississippi public consumption at any rate, and mobs took over the campus of Ole Miss in answer to the enrollment of the first black student, and Kennedy, who delivered a speech that denounced not prejudice but the violation of the Constitution, sent marshals and troops to the campus. In Birmingham the following spring fire hoses and police dogs were turned upon children, and in September a fire bombing killed four black children in a Sunday school class in the basement of a Baptist church. Even before that bombing civil rights activists had compelled segregation to disgrace itself so publicly that a President with any claim to Democratic liberalism had to call for a legislated end to the discredited system. Southern white liberals, meanwhile, having finally encountered a movement that forced them to choose between their regional loyalty and their consciences, between their doubts about the efficacy of efforts for social change and their hopes for it, were turning with relief to desegregation. They, like the black community, were among

the liberated. John Kennedy responded as circumstances, politics, and morality required.

Television brought the civil rights movement before the public, and without it the 1960s would be unimaginable. That medium is faulted today for replacing the most subtle, analytical, and elegant means of conversation, the written word. But for a time two decades ago television became an instrument of analysis, making possible one of the most remarkable experiences of self-awareness and self-criticism in the nation's history. The nineteenth-century abolitionists, in contrast, had been forced to rely on a religious and Victorian moral rhetoric that defined the evil of slavery but seldom could describe its psychological and moral corruptions as precisely as do the best parts of *Uncle Tom's Cabin*. And for generations after abolition, white American politics rarely discussed racism at all except, of course, to approve of it. When the advent of television as a mass medium almost exactly coincided with the earlier days of the civil rights movement, it gave to a whole nation, perhaps even to blacks and to southern whites as never before, clear images of the racial issue as immediate, national, morally inescapable. That is not to say that television itself is the best vehicle of criticism and analysis; brief, violent images on a screen—black protesters falling under the force of fire hoses, white mobs screaming at black children entering public schools—are not in themselves more conducive to intelligent political thought than the images of Iranian crowds that in 1980 endangered rational discussion of foreign policy in this country. But in the early 1960s the images on the screen worked with the civil rights movement itself, with a responsiveness on the part of politicians, and with such reflective writers as James Baldwin to elevate rather than to degrade the public consciousness.

Television, meanwhile, made for the ersatz familiarity with which the Kennedy family entered millions of American homes, and it was just the right family: beautiful, well man-

"Kennedy Liberalism" from *The Torch is Passed: The Kennedy Brothers and American Liberalism* by David Burner and Thomas R. West. Reproduced by permission of the authors.

nered, well favored. TV allowed Kennedy to be so visible to the public as a whole that he seemed to be outside the party structures and the backroom maneuverings that his people managed so well.

It is easy to forget that during the early days of television another older visual medium was in its prime. Photojournalism, along with photography in general, can be at once brief and analytical; it can study the exact placement of individuals in a crowd, the look on a black child's face, the twist of hatred on the face of a white woman. During the Birmingham civil rights crisis President Kennedy commented that a photograph of a German shepherd leaping at a black woman made him "sick." Photojournalism, like television, cannot look into the ambiguities that the word can explore; it needs dramatic events, striking figures, exact moments of pain and triumph, or larger cultural events that express themselves flamboyantly. And in the 1960s Selma, Vietnam, Haight-Ashbury, and the photogenic Kennedys supplied precisely the materials with which it could do its most effective work.

The Kennedy forces knew the power of a good visual image. John Kennedy had seen Democratic governor Paul Dever of Massachusetts go down to defeat in 1952 because on television he came across as a cartoonist's rendering of an old pol, and the President knew what his own election had owed to the television debates. The administration was friendly to the press cameras. Kennedy opened his press conferences to live television coverage. The Executive Mansion initiated ideas for picture stories. It was at the suggestion of the White House that during the missile crisis a photographer snapped the reassuring picture through a rainy window of the President in thought.

In this early time of the image, President Kennedy and the civil rights movement were the most important subjects of television and photojournalism, and while the media were studying both, each was doing something for the other. At the push and tug of events, President Kennedy lent to the movement enough of the protection of the federal government to make it slightly freer to operate in the South, and his presidency made the preliminary decisions that would grow into the important legislation of the Johnson years. And civil rights would eventually bestow on the Kennedy administration a moral meaning beyond anything the government had at first planned for.

Kennedy liberalism was born in the presumption, which turned itself into a fact, that there was in John Kennedy's person and programs a force for social reformation. Black leaders increasingly looked to him for whatever he had to offer, whether it was the tangible support of marshals and federal troops in the South when their presence was essential, the partial symbolic desegregation in 1962 of federally funded public housing, or in 1963 Kennedy's espousal of civil rights legislation. Opponents of the civil rights movement, in their very fear that the President favored the rights cause, contributed to defining him as the embodiment of a liberalism that would go beyond the established New Deal programs. Liberal intellectuals could think that a youthful Harvard graduate with a beautiful and socially accomplished wife must be one of them.

Apart from Kennedy's major activities in foreign affairs, it is his performance in the civil rights controversies that has led to the most extensive judgments of him, favorable and condemnatory. That this should be so is a commentary on the early sixties. No President before John Kennedy, Abraham Lincoln included, could meet more than the smallest test for racial justice, or for forthright public discussion of the racial issue, on the terms that are now acceptable. But then no President had been put to the test by any movement as highly visible as the civil rights forces of the sixties. Kennedy's presidency coincided with the early years of a rights activism that demanded an absolute and uncompromised equality, a disappearance of private as well as official discrimination, an end to stereotypes and to the whole range of cruelties that had attended racism in this country. The Kennedy administration connected with that movement—furthering it, Kennedy's supporters say, dragged along, as more skeptical commentators insist, or growing with it. But it is at least beyond dispute that the administration's activity for civil rights differed fundamentally in character from that of the protesters in the southern streets and the rights workers in the southern back country. Not one but two forces were arrayed against segregation, one of them hesitant, legalistic, calculating, while the other acted out of a simple and relentless moral witness. The result of the administration's caution is that in the presence of the rights workers and demonstrators it looked timid and temporizing; the result of its activity is that the rights movement gained a solid body of federal practices to supplement the sit-ins, the freedom rides, and the marches.

Kennedy brought to his presidency a record of compromise and expediency on civil rights. As a senator coming to national prominence he had seemed scarcely aware of the Supreme Court desegregation decision of 1954 and the Montgomery bus boycott. For a northern liberal, Kennedy's record in the Senate was, even on balance, unsatisfactory. He said of Little Rock that a greater planning and leadership on Eisenhower's part could have prevented the trouble. In his vice presidential and presidential campaign he sought support from the South's most truculent segregationist governors. Kennedy omitted civil rights from a list of the "real issues of 1960" that he presented near the beginning of his presidential contest. His sympathy call to Coretta Scott King while her husband sat in a Georgia jail was a gesture of great political value, but there is no evidence that it was anything more. During the weeks after the election he created a number of task forces to make recommendations on pressing national problems, but he appointed none on

civil rights. The pessimism of a conservative oddly coexisted, even in Kennedy's words, with the vocabulary of will and action. "There is always some inequality in life," he observed at a press conference in Greenfield, Massachusetts, on March 21, 1962. "Some men are killed in war, and some are wounded, and some men never leave the country, and some men are stationed in the Antarctic and some men are stationed in San Francisco. It is very hard in military or personal life to assure complete equality." Such pessimism Kennedy could also bring to the rights question.

Harris Wofford was, by Robert Kennedy's explanation, "so committed to civil rights emotionally" that the administration decided against appointing him assistant attorney general in charge of civil rights in the Justice Department. Wofford instead became a White House assistant on civil rights. He was to say of the position in retrospect that what President Kennedy had most liked about it, and he had least liked, was his task of serving as a buffer between the President and the civil rights forces. For the civil rights position in the Justice Department Byron White, the conservative Rhodes scholar from Yale, friend of Kennedys, and future Supreme Court justice, recommended Burke Marshall, another Yale Law School graduate and a member of a distinguished corporate law firm in Washington, D.C.

Marshall, like so many educated Americans, understood the moral problem and was a patient negotiator. He also brought to the job a liberal record; he had been a member of the American Civil Liberties Union and an originator of the idea of federal registrars who could insure enrollment of southern black voters. But he believed in the ways of compromise and agreement and despaired of addressing the question of civil rights with the means available to a federal system of government. Marshall later opposed the Civil Rights Commission's plan to hold hearings in Mississippi that would publicize conditions there, and he opposed the commission's wish for a halt in all federal money to that and other states. He was also to observe that a major nationwide effort for integrated housing would have been too frightening. In *Federalism and Civil Rights,* published in 1964, Marshall concludes that the central government's police power cannot deal effectively with the complex race problem. And for generations, legal and social conservatives, following similar reasoning, had refrained from using governmental power to challenge unjust social institutions, so the injustice, in all its complexity, remained. The moralistic and relentless Robert Kennedy was making use of legal power, first against radicals in the Redbaiting days of the early 1950s and then against labor racketeers, long before he discovered a real "enemy within" that had long made a mockery of American ideas of justice. Yet even Burke Marshall could draw limits to compromise. He was later to observe that while some liberals were too aggressive for civil rights, others, such as Hubert Humphrey, were too conciliatory.

The earliest of the administration's measures were symbolic acts of integration. Having seen no blacks in the Coast Guard contingent of the inauguration march, Kennedy instructed the academy to recruit more. The government increased the number of blacks at social functions, desegregated the White House press and photography pools, multiplied the appointment of Negroes to important government posts. In the spring of 1961 Secretary of Labor Arthur Goldberg attacked the practice of racial segregation in private clubs. Afterward the economist John Kenneth Galbraith, Kennedy's ambassador to India, resigned from Washington's Cosmos Club, an association of writers, scientists, and other professional people, when the club, which at the time had no black members, refused to admit the columnist Carl Rowan. At the resignation the name of John Kennedy, whom Galbraith had been sponsoring for membership, was automatically withdrawn. When for a time later in the sixties

a scornful anger became the moral fashion among leftists, black and white, the well-meaning social gestures of white liberals fell victim to a studied contempt. But that has gone the way of other fashions, and it is perhaps now safe to suggest that the efforts of the Kennedy liberals to extend the common civilities had some role in the rights revolution.

Soon after two black students had integrated the University of Georgia, Attorney General Robert Kennedy in 1961 gave a speech there depicting the two as freedom fighters. (The phrase recalls the Hungarian insurgents of 1956; that is how strongly the struggle against communism gripped the imagination of the times and the Kennedys.) At the university Kennedy announced his intention to work for racial justice, and his speech decried inequities in the North as well as in the South. It was the first time a modern attorney general had spoken in the South for civil rights. Robert Kennedy's Justice Department made or was forced to make many of the day-to-day decisions bearing on civil rights. He brought in a handful of black attorneys, along with Archibald Cox as solicitor general, Ramsey Clark, John Doar, John Seigenthaler, and many others of note. But Robert shared Burke Marshall's caution about sudden federal assaults on local customs. It was the demonstrators and the rights workers, and more particularly the assaults on them, that pushed the Justice Department forward.

The freedom riders, organized by James Farmer's Congress of Racial Equality, pressed the cause of civil rights. CORE's northern black and white demonstrators, beginning in the spring of 1961, went through the South in busloads, defying segregation of terminals enforced by state and local officials. Farmer, before the trek through the South, sent an itinerary to the President, Robert Kennedy, and the FBI, in addition to Greyhound and Trailways, and got no response. The attorney general did not like the freedom rides and tried to discourage them. Possibly the lawyer and politician in him, which in other cases his anger could overwhelm, predominated at the moment, recoiling from tactics of confrontation and defiance of local officials. If so, freedom riders would have had a ready response. Their intention was to compel the enforcement of the law, for the Supreme Court decision in *Boynton* v. *Virginia* had declared illegal any segregation in interstate bus and train terminals. The freedom riders were aware of the violence their journey might provoke but calculated that the violence would make the federal government intervene. That is precisely what Robert Kennedy did not want forced upon him.

The attorney general did not get the peace he had wished for. When a freedom bus was fire-bombed in Anniston, Alabama, he ordered the FBI to investigate the arson. Bull Connor, the hostile chief of the Alabama police, was directed to protect the riders in Birmingham. On May 21 patrolmen and police helicopters escorted them to Montgomery. Governor John Patterson had promised continuing protection. The governor was not an unenlightened southern politician. He had acquired his political prominence when, upon becoming Alabama attorney general in 1954, he finished cleaning up vice-ridden Phenix City, completing the work for which his father as a district attorney had been murdered. More recently he has revealed sufficient contrition, or at least embarrassment, about racism to observe that while he did use the race issue in campaigning for governor, he would have preferred not to do so. Yet he was sufficiently of his own culture that he could not bring himself to act promptly in defense of the riders. When the riders arrived in Montgomery, a mob set upon them. John Seigenthaler, the Justice Department official and friend of Robert Kennedy, was clubbed as he was trying to protect a female demonstrator, and he lay unconscious for about twenty-five minutes. The FBI, meticulously staying within the letter of its mandate, as it sometimes did to its own advantage, stood by and took comprehensive notes. (Therein the

bureau acted consistently with its inconsistent conduct during the civil rights years, when it was censorious of the movement, legalistically slow to discover violations of racial justice, and at times energetic in support of civil rights.) That evening some fifty marshals tried to protect Martin Luther King and civil rights supporters as King led a vigil in the city's First Baptist Church until Patterson at length discovered his responsibilities, declared martial law, and sent the National Guard. Nicholas Katzenbach, an assistant attorney general in Robert Kennedy's Justice Department, has remarked in another connection that neither he nor his chief liked to take away from local officers the job of protection, for they knew how much that is resented. But local authority, in Montgomery and elsewhere in these violent times, refused to act on its obligations, so there was to be street war, of sorts, between the Justice Department and the segregationists.

But in 1961 Robert Kennedy remained aloof from the tactics of confrontation and peaceful rebellion that gave to the civil rights movement its distinctive character. Byron White, who thought that blacks needed a higher standard of living rather than civil rights, explained at a press conference in Birmingham that marshals would not intervene if the police arrested the freedom riders: "I'm sure they would be represented by competent counsel." Robert actually countenanced the arrest of riders in Jackson, Mississippi, on whatever charge the local officers used against violators of segregation. Apparently he thought that the arrests would rescue the riders from the dangers they were inviting upon themselves. "Do you know," he exclaimed to Wofford, "that one of them is against the atom bomb—yes, he even picketed against it in jail!" After the arrests the attorney general urged a cooling-off period; he cited the forthcoming summit conference between the United States and the Soviet Union. Martin Luther King, Jr., agreed to a momentary respite. But hundreds of arrests followed later in the summer.

The administration was unwilling to make demands on Congress. The President appointed to southern federal districts, especially in the deep South, judges so traditionalist that they obstructed the work of his brother's civil rights lawyers. He was, of course, constrained in his selections by the custom almost never violated, of obtaining approval from the states' Democratic senators. The political commentator Tom Wicker has argued that Kennedy could have risked presenting Congress with a civil rights bill early in his administration. Republicans, he contends, would have had no good reason to oppose it, and southerners were already as alienated as they could be, antagonized by the liberal rhetoric of the presidential campaign, by the administration's support of the fight to widen the membership of the House Rules Committee, and by liberal legislation having the endorsement of the White House. But when Senator Joseph Clark of Pennsylvania and Representative Emanuel Celler of New York introduced six bills to implement the Democratic platform of 1960 on civil rights, the White House disavowed the very bills Kennedy had asked for during the campaign.

Almost as cautious about the use of executive power, the administration canceled no contracts for reasons of job discrimination. Speaking of such new regulations as withholding federal funding from highway construction that practiced discrimination in working conditions, the President once urged that the rules be enforced only when essential. In 1961 the NAACP had proposed that the government withhold funds from states using them in a discriminatory way. The report of the Civil Rights Commission recommended that Kennedy explore his authority to hold back funding from Mississippi. The President, calling the idea "unbelievable" and "almost irresponsible," urged the commission not to make its statement public. At a press conference he said that he neither had nor should have the authority to stop funds going to recalcitrant

states. "They ran away from it," Roy Williams said of the scheme, "like it was a rattlesnake." Yet the Civil Rights Act of 1964 was to give the President the power Kennedy had rejected. In 1960 Kennedy had attacked the previous administration for tolerating segregation in federally funded housing. But it was almost two years before he acted on his promise to eliminate it with "a stroke of the presidential pen" (he had received thousands of pens and floods of ink through the mail), and even then he acted circumspectly, burying the order in the midst of public announcements covering other subjects and phrasing it to apply only to future FHA and VA mortgages. Probably he knew that the desegregation of suburban housing was a dangerous issue; it took Lyndon Johnson until 1968 to get any legislation on the subject, and suburban desegregation is still notoriously slow to proceed.

Three times the Civil Rights Commission was ready to hold hearings in Mississippi, and three times Robert Kennedy stopped the hearings, claiming that impending legislation would be endangered. Even while pushing voter registration, the attorney general feared race riots in the South and thought that hearings might set them off. He complained, Wofford recalls, that the commission was not objective: "It was almost like the House Un-American Activities Committee investigating Communism." The commission, disregarding the wishes of the President and the attorney general, published a report on violations of civil rights in Mississippi.

Robert Kennedy and his Justice Department did take or respond to initiatives in the furtherance of civil rights. When King and other civil rights leaders involved in the freedom rides complained to him that the Interstate Commerce Commission was not enforcing the Supreme Court declaration in terminals, he had explained to them that the commission was both independent and slow to move, but in the wake of the rides, he disproved his claim, persuading the ICC to forbid discrimination. By the end of the year every airport and nearly every bus and railroad station had been desegregated. Hoping that the voter registration movement for black southerners would bring less violence than the freedom rides, the attorney general joined in the call for the project, which the NAACP announced to the press in a statement that included the phrase "ask what you can do for your country." The need was plain: in Mississippi the percentage of blacks registered to vote had been declining for seventy years even as literacy among Negroes had been steadily rising. When the question of voter registration became central, Burke Marshall's civil rights division sent lawyers into the South to investigate violations of voting rights, and in another innovation he permitted them to initiate actions, which numbered about seventy by late 1963. Government lawyers went into Fayette County in Tennessee to sue landlords who had forced black sharecroppers off their land for trying to register for the vote, and the Agriculture Department gave food to the dispossessed.

The voter registration campaign, which put the administration at odds with white supremacists it had appointed to federal courts, was in its defense of traditional constitutional rights an eminently conservative program; and even Americans relatively indifferent to race issues could acknowledge its justice. It therefore accorded with the streak of caution that had marked Robert Kennedy's initial management of the race problem. But in the self-consciousness and militancy it awakened in black southerners, in the political organization it spawned among them, and in the power base it ultimately provided, the voter registration project was revolutionary.

John Kennedy's administration as a whole was moving incrementally and yet at a rate unprecedented within this century on the issue of civil rights. In the early sixties motor travelers between Washington and the Northeast still had to use Route 40 in Maryland, and those travelers sometimes included diplomats from the new African nations. The government, its attention fixed on international politics, successfully urged the state of Maryland to pass a public accommodations law and persuaded the governor to apologize to a black diplomat who had been turned away from a restaurant. In the days when the District of Columbia still practiced much de facto segregation, the President appointed the first black District commissioner. He also made some notable selections of blacks elsewhere, choosing for the court of appeals Thurgood Marshall, who had argued the great school desegregation case of 1954. Kennedy strengthened the President's Commission on Equal Employment Opportunity, charged with working for more equitable hiring in the government and in the firms with which the government did business. It won some voluntary agreements from businesses contracting with the government to survey and improve their hiring practices. President Kennedy asked Congress to forbid literacy tests for voting, and at his behest the national legislature sent to the states the Twenty-fourth Amendment, outlawing the poll tax. The government warned universities receiving federal money for language institutes that the program funding would be contingent on an absence of discrimination; as a result, a half dozen schools withdrew. Washington also resolved to withhold federal aid from segregated school districts in areas "impacted" by federal installations. The President appointed Robert C. Weaver as housing administrator and worked hard but unsuccessfully to have his office raised to cabinet status. To the Civil Rights Commission, which President Eisenhower had made a more effective body than had been expected, Kennedy made some appointments that strengthened its activist character, and the commission, of all government agencies the most aggressive on the rights issue, was a goad to the administration.

The administration, in sum, was sending contradictory signals, and that may have given hope to elements in the South of winning a battle that they had already lost. The presidency had chosen to act with some responsiveness to that first moment in American history when it appeared possible that racial equality could actually prevail, and now rather than in an indefinite future to which Americans of good will could look wistfully. That may explain both the activity and the reticence of the administration. It was active because an increasingly insistent segment of the black population and numbers of white allies were urging it into action and because a growing number of white Americans were showing that they would not, at the slightest progress toward integration, turn into a mob. And the administration could afford to be reticent, prepared to compromise for the sake of keeping its friendship with white southerners, because it believed that the revolution in attitudes and practices had its own momentum. Every small gesture on the part of the government made the revolution appear, and therefore be, all the more an irresistible reality. The Kennedy presidency might have gone its entire tenure in the way it and events had set, forceful enough to win popularity among black Americans, politic enough to keep the popularity among southern whites that opinion polls registered for it until mid-1963. But in the end violence by southern bigots brought the President to speak and act against racial injustice with a militancy that he may once have intended only for confrontation with communism.

In the autumn of 1962 James Meredith pursued his plans to enter the University of Mississippi, its first black student. He has recalled that he might not have applied to the University of Mississippi had Kennedy lost the 1960 election. Meredith worked out his plan on his own, claiming later to have received inspiration from the cadences of John Kennedy's inaugural address—which said not a word about civil rights. At least not intentionally. The famous Lincolnesque phrase borrowed by Kennedy—"We shall have to test anew

whether a nation organized and governed such as ours can endure"—looked to foreign affairs, but events played it out in the deep South.

After resistance from the state a federal court ordered Meredith's admission. On the night preceding his enrollment Assistant Attorney General Nicholas Katzenbach was on the campus at Oxford, Mississippi, along with Justice Department marshals armed with tear gas. For several hours marshals were under siege in a pitched battle, while Governor Ross Barnett, instead of sending sufficient police or militia forces, declined to deviate from his public posture of antagonism to integration—though his phone conversation with the President in the evening reveals a worried and hesitant man hoping for some solution: he told Kennedy that his defiant words were directed "just to Mississippi."

The President, still unaware of the violence, went on television, urging compliance with the court order, appealing to sportsmanship on the gridiron and to southern honor won in battle. That evening—that terrible evening, in Robert Kennedy's memory—Washington learned that two people had been killed on a campus in anarchy. The White House waited and fretted while federal troops sent by the President took much longer to arrive at Ole Miss than he had expected. Katzenbach asked over the phone whether the marshals could fire on the rioters. No, answered Kennedy, except to protect Meredith. That evening Bobby thought of the killing that might take place, and he thought of the Bay of Pigs. So did the President. "I haven't had such an interesting time since the Bay of Pigs," he said. And Robert composed a bulletin: "The attorney general announced today he's joining Allen Dulles at Princeton University." John Kennedy spoke of *Seven Days in May*, the taut 1962 thriller about a general who tries to overthrow a President to prevent a conciliatory arrangement with the Soviet Union. "The only character that came out at all was the general," said Kennedy. "The president was awfully vague." The novel's general reminded Robert of General Edwin Walker, who had been retired from a European command after his broodings about communism seemed to be prodding him toward making his own separate war on it. Robert's association was apt on that night of Ole Miss: Walker, by now connecting communism with integration or both with the crumbling of Western civilization, was among the rioters. In the end the federal soldiers quelled the mob. Walker was arrested on a federal warrant charging him with seditious conspiracy and insurrection for spurring the rioters, but the government did not get an indictment. The army remained on the campus for months. It had taken some 23,000 troops to do the job.

Robert Kennedy was to remember that after Ole Miss the President said that he would never again believe stories about terrible federal troops in the Reconstruction era. Yet the federal government was so new to the task of enforcing civil rights that Burke Marshall had worried about whether the President had the constitutional authority to send troops without first calling on the governor to act.

The following spring Vivian Malone and James Hood entered the University of Alabama under the protection of federal soldiers. In Alabama, where the attorney general went to prepare for the integration, a state trooper jabbed him with a nightstick, and he was asked at a press conference if he was a member of the Communist party. In a remarkable effort that recalls the administration's earlier mobilizing of its resources in a war with the steel industry, cabinet members and directors of agencies called 375 business executives in Alabama to request that there be no more trouble. Similar calls were to be made to Birmingham businessmen later in 1963 with reminders that the economies of Little Rock and Oxford had suffered after racial troubles there.

The impending riot at Ole Miss had put President Kennedy for the first time before the national television audience on the subject of civil rights. Yet conceivably for strategic reasons at a moment when the threat of violence was the immediate problem, he had stressed not racial justice but obedience to the Constitution. Events the next spring so intruded the race issue into the national consciousness that a moral vocabulary was at last inescapable.

Federal efforts in deeply segregated Birmingham had been virtually unavailing; aside from the post office and Veterans Administration hospital, blacks held fewer than one percent of federal jobs in the area. George Wallace, now Alabama governor, was moving into the leadership of southern segregationists. The strategy of the rights workers in 1963, the only workable one, was to confront the city with massive demonstrations. What transpired placed an overwhelming demand on the national conscience: police dogs, electric cattle prods, fire hoses, and rioting. Burke Marshall, at his best when the patient arts of negotiation were required, talked endlessly with white business leaders and won at least a segment of civic opinion to the cause of peace. The administration, meanwhile, had entreated King to call off the demonstrators on the ground that they were hindering the negotiations with the whites, as the two Kennedys, never pleased with the tactics of confrontation, had wanted him in 1962 to ease off in Albany, Georgia, so that a moderate Democratic candidate for governor might win. Kennedy, foreseeing the "fires of frustration and discord . . . burning in every city, North and South," responded as the occasion demanded. By now he, the churches, a majority in Congress, and much of the nation had awakened. Kennedy on June 11 gave an eloquent address on television: "I ask you to look into your hearts—not in search of charity, for the Negro neither wants nor needs condescension—but for the one plain, proud and priceless quality that unites all as Americans: a sense of justice."

That same night in Mississippi a white racist murdered the civil rights leader Medgar Evers. His was only one of innumerable murders of

■ ■ *In 1963, civil rights leaders from around the country assembled in Washington, D.C., to demand an end to segregation and discrimination against African-Americans. The major civil rights leaders appear here with President John Kennedy in the White House.*

black people since the coming of slavery to the continent, but now there were awakened media to give the killing nationwide prominence.

Shortly after his television talk the President, who had presented to Congress a mild civil rights bill after Ole Miss but before Birmingham, requested the national legislature to place a partial ban on discrimination in public places, empower the Justice Department to sue for school desegregation upon a request that it do so, and give the executive broader authority to withhold funds from federally assisted programs in which discrimination occurred. The President, who had been politic enough not to want Johnson to speak out inor-

dinately on the race issue, was bold enough to deliver his historic speech against the judgment of most of his White House advisers. Johnson had argued for some preparatory work to soften up Congress. Afterward civil rights leaders persuaded Kennedy to strengthen the proposed legislation to give the attorney general power to intervene in all civil rights cases. The Civil Rights Acts that followed his death were to go well beyond the initial Kennedy program.

Though the President never perhaps came to see the issue as absolutely and morally central—he told a press conference that tax reform was more important than anything else—he did work hard to pass the legislation, meeting with some 1,700 people that summer. After House liberals tried to revise his legislation with provisions that the administration feared would bring its defeat, Kennedy persuaded conservative Republican leader Charles Halleck to agree to a moderate version and thereby, according to the recollections of Robert Kennedy and Burke Marshall, presented the liberals with a political situation so promising that holdouts came over. If they had compromised their virtue, Halleck in the view of many conservatives had compromised his. He found a furled umbrella on his desk in the House. Senator Everett Dirksen made passage nearly certain by agreeing on November 2 that the Republican leadership would not support a filibuster. By the time of the President's death the bill had already cleared its most difficult hurdle, the House Judiciary Committee.

Martin Luther King, Jr., was to comment privately in an oral history that at the President's directions Robert Kennedy had done much more than his office of attorney general obliged him to do. But he remarked before Kennedy's June 1963 speech that while the President had perhaps done "a little more" for blacks than Eisenhower, "the plight of the vast majority of Negroes remains the same." When 250,000 people under King's leadership marched on Washington that August in support of the proposed legislation, John Kennedy first tried to dissuade them and then avoided addressing the assembly. Burke Marshall, however, has claimed that the attorney general did much of the real work of organizing the march: providing water and toilets (which a government is virtually obligated to do anyway) and insuring—whatever this means—"that the character of the people who were coming was in close touch with the police." Upon learning that John Lewis of the Student Nonviolent Coordinating Committee was going to give an inflammatory speech—"It attacked the President," Robert laments—the theologically conservative but socially progressive Roman Catholic archbishop of Washington, Patrick

O'Boyle, was going to decline to participate. Marshall went to Walter Reuther, who enlisted the help of King, James Farmer of CORE, and others to persuade Lewis to temper his speech, which satisfied O'Boyle. The final version omitted the announcement that the civil rights forces would "march through the South, through the Heart of Dixie, the way Sherman did." The contrast is inviting: the heroic and visionary rights activists in a triumphant moment; the worried administrators who rushed about to keep everything safe and orderly. The generation of the sixties reveled in such contrasts. But if the movement that called the march could reach beyond the caution that guided the administration, the government, by keeping O'Boyle in the march, rendered the demonstration a service.

On August 28 King addressed the marchers: "I have a dream that one day on the red hills of Georgia the sons of former slaves and the sons of former slaveholders will be able to sit down together at the table of brotherhood. I have a dream that one day even the state of Mississippi, a desert state sweltering with the heat of injustice and oppression, will be transformed into an oasis of freedom and justice. . . . I have a dream that one day the state of Alabama . . . will be transformed [and] little black boys and black girls will be able to join hands with little white boys and white girls and walk together as sisters and brothers." John Kennedy never gave voice to such a dream. But he allied himself with King's, and the alliance brought forth after his death the great civil rights legislation of the mid-sixties. Congress approved the first law in 1964, and others followed in 1965 and 1966.

Robert Kennedy's later commentary on the administration's race policies gives a plausible, though self-interested, justification of the caution. State by state, he was to claim, the government had to accommodate southern senators on federal judicial appointments. The reason the administration did not send more civil rights legislation to Congress, by his explanation, is that there was so little effective demand for it. In 1962 the attorney general went to the Hill to testify for a bill that would insure voting rights for people literate at the sixth-grade level, but interest in it was insufficient. Robert was wary of expanding the power of the federal government to defend civil rights, believing that a gradual resolution of issues was healthier than sudden confrontations of the South by rights workers under federal protection. His idea of a well-managed policy was the federal pressure and discussion that brought about the desegregation of rail and air terminals. The strategy-tempered idealism of the administration, as Robert's recollections present it, was typified in the determination to protect the right to vote: the federal government had the authority, accomplishment would bring much good, and there could be relatively small opposition to so clearly fundamental a right.

Robert Kennedy's observations in his oral history on the House liberals who tried to stiffen the administration's civil rights bill (which include his comment that the epithet sons of bitches that his father had applied to businessmen applied also to liberals) put neatly the difference between two perceptions of morality. The liberals preferred failure to a reasonable bill. "An awful lot of them, as I said then, were in love with death," the motive, perhaps, that some of them had for liking Adlai Stevenson; they thought only of their own goals, not of the needs of others. This moralistic denunciation of liberal moralism comes from a man in whom virtuous anger seemed forever close to eruption. It may not be a just interpretation of the House liberals of 1963, and it does not take into account the demonstration provided by the civil rights activists that a will to strain beyond the limits of the sensible and the possible may have the practical effect of widening the limits. But Robert Kennedy makes a good moral case against the virtuousness that thirsts after purity. The argument is also applicable to those right-wingers who were offended at President Kennedy's attempts to reach accommodations with the Soviet Union. And it is applicable later in the decade to the seekers after purity whose antiwar, antiliberal, antigovernment, and anti-American convictions could express themselves only in superlatives chasing after superlatives. In those days could be heard the most tremendous denunciations of the United States as genocidal country and of its people as rotting in corruption, as if any accusation more measured would be a compromise.

George McGovern has commented that President Kennedy's respect and desire for power led him to conserve it for essential uses and to refrain from expending it on anything that could dissipate it. If the observation does not describe the President who agreed to the Bay of Pigs, it does suggest the administration that finally spoke for a sophisticated understanding of the architectures of world power. Kennedy had something of the sense of federal power as a force to be calculatingly and subtly deployed against racism. And the other, contradictory component of John Kennedy's feeling for power, his tendency to react to crisis rather than to the stubborn detail of a problem, may be further explanation for the peculiar pace of his dealings with the race question: conciliatory, slow, incremental reform punctuated in the end by dramatic televised responses to the great civil rights events of the day.

■■■

STUDY QUESTIONS

1. Why was television so important to the success of the civil rights movement in the 1960s?

2. During his presidency, John F. Kennedy was extraordinarily popular with African Americans. Why? Did his record on civil rights justify that popularity?

3. What role did Robert Kennedy play in the administration's approach to civil rights?

4. Explain the major achievements of the Kennedy administration in civil rights.

5. Historians and critics have labeled John F. Kennedy as a conservative, a radical, or a moderate. Based on his civil rights record, what would you say about Kennedy's political philosophy?

BIBLIOGRAPHY

For favorable portraits of Kennedy and his administration, see Arthur M. Schlesinger, Jr., *A Thousand Days* (1965); Theodore M. Sorensen, *Kennedy* (1973); Herbert Parment, *Jack: The Struggles of John F. Kennedy* (1980); and *JFK: The Presidency of John F. Kennedy* (1983). Also see Henry Farlie, *The Kennedy Promise* (1973). For harsh criticisms of the Kennedy administration, see Bruce Miroff, *Pragmatic Illusions: The Presidential Politics of John F. Kennedy* (1976) and Garry Wills, *The Kennedy Imprisonment* (1982). For views of the Kennedy family, see Doris Kearns Goodwin, *The Fitzgeralds and the Kennedys: An American Saga* (1987) and Nancy Gager Clinch, *The Kennedy Neurosis: A Psychological Portrait of an American Dynasty* (1973). David Burner's *John F. Kennedy and a New Generation* (1987) is a short but excellent biography.

For studies of the civil rights movement of the 1960s, see Carl Bauer, *John F. Kennedy and the Second Reconstruction* (1977) and Harris Wofford's *Of Kennedys and Kings* (1980). Also see Robert E. Gilbert, "John F. Kennedy and Civil Rights for Black Americans," *Presidential Studies Quarterly* 12 (Summer 1982), pp. 386–99.

VIETNAM IN THE COMIC BOOKS

Bradford Wright

Recent American historians view the Vietnam War as one of the seminal events in United States history—a period that shaped American military and foreign policy as well as American culture. Even the most cursory survey of books, films, and television programs over the past twenty years, to say nothing of the news media, illustrates how influential the Vietnam War has been in shaping American thought. Like no event since the Civil War, Vietnam divided Americans into opposing camps and inspired a sharp, acrimonious debate about national values and the nation's destiny. On many levels, that debate continues today. What is becoming increasingly clear is just how deeply the Vietnam War has affected American life. Perhaps the best way of demonstrating the impact of Vietnam is to look at popular culture—and no dimension of popular culture is more popular than comic books. In the following essay, Bradford Wright discusses how the comic book industry in the United States dealt with the war in Vietnam.

The comic book industry thrived during the early 1950s, largely due to the popularity of crime and horror comic books that featured graphic violence, sexual overtones, and other adult themes. Parents, psychologists, government officials, and other concerned groups suspected that comic books contributed to a rise in juvenile delinquency. The public crusade against comic books resulted in a U.S. Senate investigation into the industry in 1954, after which the publishers established the self-censoring Comics Code Authority. In order to ensure the national distribution of their comic books, the code required publishers to adhere to the standards, which have been described by one of the code's proponents as "the most stringent for any media." The code was intended to uphold the principles of "good taste" in comic books and to preserve the medium as a "wholesome form of entertainment." Among the code's standards was the provision that "policemen, judges, government officials and respected institutions shall never be presented in such a way as to create disrespect for established authority." The code, therefore, dictated that comic book stories after 1954 would be not only sanitized and juvenile, but devoid of social and political criticism as well.

The establishment of the Comics Code Authority had an immediate and depressing effect on the comic book industry as a whole. Many publishers who had relied upon themes forbidden by the code were unable to distribute their comic books and went out of business within a few years. The industry was further hurt by the rise of television, which had more to offer discerning teenagers and young adults than the code-approved comic books. The *New York Times* reported that by 1962 annual comic book sales had dropped from 800,000,000 in 1952 to 350,000,000 in 1962. The comic book industry, which had once consisted of over fifty publishers, began the 1960s with fewer than a dozen publishing houses.

The code did not affect all publishers equally, however, and some were not hurt by it at all. DC Comics survived the 1950s in good shape, and by 1962 it had acquired 30 percent of the market. DC had never participated heavily in the controversial crime of horror trends, and the content of its comic books was restrained even before the code, featuring such widely recognizable characters as Superman, Batman, and Wonder Woman. Throughout the 1950s these titles remained targeted at an unsophisticated juvenile readership and were, therefore, unchanged by the editorial standards of the code. DC was also probably hurt less by television than other publishers because the popularity of the televised "Adventures of Superman" may have actually boosted the sales of Superman comic books. In 1956 DC initiated what comic book historians have termed the "silver age" of superhero comic books by reviving some of its stock superheroes from the 1940s and giving them revised origins with more contemporary settings. The popularity of titles like *The Flash, Green Lantern,* and *The Justice League of America* helped reestablish the superhero comic book as the industry's most popular genre of the 1960s.

The Dell Publishing Company was one comic book publisher that may have actually benefited from the establishment of the code. Dell's top-selling comic books were its "funny animal" titles that featured characters from the cartoons of Walt Disney and Warner Brothers. The company was proud of its reputation for producing clean, wholesome comic books that were held up as positive examples by those who criticized the rest of the industry. The president of Dell was one of the few publishers who refused to submit their comic books to the Code Authority, because Dell already maintained its own code for decency and good taste. The company thrived during the late 1950s, selling more comic books worldwide than any

"Vietnam in the Comic Books" by Bradford Wright. Copyright © 1992 James Olson. Reprinted by permission.

other publisher, but circulation dropped dramatically in the early 1960s. Dell's attempt to diversify its publishing operation by producing titles in genres such as war and science fiction failed to capture a large audience, and the company remained a second-rate publisher until it left the comic book field in 1973.

Marvel Comics had been among the most prolific of comic book publishers since its entry into the field in 1939. During its first two decades, Marvel followed changing industry trends, publishing titles in every comic book genre. Marvel's war and horror comic books were its most visible titles prior to the code. The former were inspired by the Korean War and have been described by one writer as perhaps the most anti-communist of all 1950s war comics. The latter were among those specifically condemned by the U.S. Senate investigation into the industry. Marvel entered the 1960s as a much smaller publishing operation, whose most notable comic books were fantasy stories inspired by Saturday matinee monster films. That the *New York Times* failed even to mention Marvel in its report on the status of the industry in 1962 attests to the publisher's small share of the market.

The publisher of Marvel Comics noticed the success of DC's superhero titles and asked his staff to put out a comic book featuring a team of superheroes modeled after DC's *The Justice League of America*. Stan Lee, who served as Marvel's comic book editor, art director, and head writer, conceived a comic book that actually bore little resemblance to any DC comic. Lee, working with writer Jack Kirby, created an experimental group of superheroes who displayed a depth of characterization beyond anything that had yet been attempted in the genre. The "Fantastic Four" were portrayed as human beings with diverse personalities and human failings who had accidentally acquired superpowers. One member of the group, Ben Grimm, gained his superstrength at the expense of his humanity, when "cosmic rays" transformed him into a hulking, orange, rock-skinned monster. Grimm, calling himself simply "the Thing," was overtly envious of, and hostile toward, his friends and teammates who retained their human appearance. The Thing was a new kind of superhero for the 1960s—one who was deeply alienated from and resentful of, the society that he was sworn to protect.

The success of *The Fantastic Four* prompted Marvel to produce another innovative superhero comic book. *The Incredible Hulk* featured Dr. Bruce Banner, a mild-mannered physicist reminiscent of Dr. Jekyll, who periodically transforms into a tremendously strong, green-skinned brute. The Hulk's bestial nature and his hatred of the human race, which constantly hounds him, make him an outsider far removed from the traditional ideal of a superhero.

Spider-Man was destined to become Marvel's most popular character. Peter Parker is a shy, socially inept high school science student whose only family and friends are his elderly aunt and uncle. He accidentally gains the proportionate powers of a spider when he is bitten by a radioactive spider at a science demonstration. Upon discovering his powers, however, he is not inspired to use them to help mankind, but instead seeks personal fame and wealth. After his debut performance on television, Spider-Man witnesses a fugitive escape from a pursuing police officer. When the angry policeman asks him why he did not help stop the criminal, Spider-Man replies that he is looking out only for himself. Soon thereafter, Parker discovers that his beloved Uncle Ben has been killed by a burglar. He tracks the murderer down only to discover that the killer is the very fugitive whom he had allowed to escape earlier. Only then does he realize that "with great power comes great responsibility," and he pledges himself to a life of crime fighting. Here was a young superhero whose service to society was motivated not by a noble heroic ideal, but rather by an intense sense of personal obligation born of guilt. This set the tone for the *Spider-Man* comic book series, in which the hero had to contend with society's problems, phobias, and his own self-pity as often as he had to battle supervillains.

These and other comic books injected a renewed vitality into the industry, which had stagnated since the establishment of the code. Working within the constraints of the code, Stan Lee brought a sense of contemporary realism to superhero comic books despite the obviously fantastic premise of the genre. In this sense, the Marvel comic books were very different from DC's. While DC stories were set in such mythical locations as "Metropolis," "Gotham City," and "Star City," Marvel superheroes operated in and around New York City. DC editorial policy dictated that its comic books would appeal almost exclusively to a juvenile audience, but Stan Lee searched for an older readership. Lee maintained that it was possible to capture a postadolescent audience without alienating the younger readers by presenting comic book stories on two levels: "color, costumes, and exaggerated action for the kids, [and] science-fiction, satire, and sophisticated philosophy for the adults and near-adults."

This creative strategy brought success to Stan Lee and Marvel Comics. Although Marvel remained well behind DC in overall sales, the gap between the two publishers narrowed considerably throughout the 1960s. Marvel also won a devoted following among older readers. The popularity of Marvel Comics on college campuses was noted by *Esquire* magazine, which reported in 1966 that Stan Lee had become a popular visiting lecturer. Another issue noted that Spider-Man and the Hulk ranked alongside Bob Dylan, Che Guevara, and Malcolm X as the most popular revolutionary figures among the collegiate New Left.

Marvel Comics employed a realism in both characterization and setting in its superhero titles that was unequaled in the comic book industry. Marvel Comics were the most popular among college students—a socially aware audience that Marvel strove to retain. For these reasons, the Marvel comic books, more than any other, serve as a barometer of the changing political and social mood during the Vietnam War. They will be dealt with in greater detail later in this chapter.

The Dell Publishing Company was the first to portray the Vietnam War in comic books. *Jungle War Stories* featured tales set in South Vietnam as early as July 1962, marking one of the war's earliest appearances in American popular culture. Unlike most Dell titles, which were targeted at young children, this war comic book aimed at a slightly older readership. Each issue of *Jungle War Stories* consisted of three or four short war stories that usually featured soldiers of the U.S. Special Forces. The emphasis of these stories was not on characterization—of which there was virtually none—or even on action. Above all, they sought to educate the audience about America's increasing involvement in the Vietnam conflict. Because the series ran during the earliest stage of American military involvement, it is likely that many of the teenagers who read the comic book gleaned from it their initial knowledge of the Vietnam situation. *Jungle War Stories* merits a careful and deliberate propaganda effort for American policy in Vietnam.

The early issues of *Jungle War Stories* were devoted primarily to an explanation and justification of the U.S. presence in South Vietnam. One such story, entitled "Day of Reckoning," was unusual in that it was told from the viewpoint of a Russian military advisor to the Vietcong. The protagonist, who is referred to only as "Comrade," recounts the history of his life to some of his Vietcong troops. His life has been endless frustration. As a boy he was chosen by the "Party" for special training in guerrilla warfare. It was a promising start for a career, because "this was the first step of the communist ladder." He was given his first great opportunity to prove himself when "the movement swept over China." He leads an attack against some of Chiang Kai-shek's supply junks, but his ambush is defeated when the supposedly "helpless" ships return fire with American-supplied machine guns. "Curse the Yankee. . . . Curse him!" exclaims the Comrade. Later he seeks to redeem himself in the eyes of his superiors by aiding the Communist guerrillas in Greece, but again he is frustrated by "American weapons speaking from the hands of Greek Government troops." Likewise, his efforts in the Malayan insurrection fail due to "Yankee arms." The Comrade angrily concludes, "It was the Yankee weapons that ended all hopes!" The Soviet's ravings are cut short by a Green Beret airborne assault on his position. The Vietcong are defeated, and the Comrade meets a fitting end when he himself is killed by American soldiers. The message in this story is that American military aid to South Vietnam is needed to confront the Communist Menace, which must be contained. The story supports the Truman Doctrine and suggests that Communism is a monolithic threat. It even hints that defeat in Vietnam might compel the Soviet "comrades," who are apparently directing the insurrection, finally to realize the futility of their efforts.

South Vietnam, however, needed more than just American weapons to stop the Vietcong. American military advisors were needed to instruct and lead the Army of the Republic of Vietnam (ARVN), which could not do anything right on its own. *Jungle War Stories* made this point clear as early as issue number one. In the first story, American Green Berets parachute into Phu-Yen province in order to lead some ARVN troops and soon conclude that "these people got no belly for fighting the Viet Cong guerrillas." Under American leadership, however, the South Vietnamese score their first success against the Communists.

The South Vietnamese civilian population similarly needed American guidance to put them on the path to victory and peace. In "A Walk in the Sun," some Green Berets come to a village with orders to move the inhabitants to a nearby strategic hamlet. Upon arriving in the village, one American soldier comments to another that "it's a crazy mixed-up war." His friend agrees, adding, "Half the peasants want no part of it . . . either side." He concludes that "there'll always be folks who figure the world owes them a living." Later, the Americans are confronted by the village leader, who tells them, "The sides of this cursed war are like grains of rice . . . no difference!" As the villagers are led through the jungle by the Americans, they witness some scenes that make a strong impression upon them: entire villages burned and destroyed by the Communists, contrasted by scenes of Green Berets giving medical attention and food to injured peasants. When the group finally arrives at the strategic hamlet, the Vietnamese peasants have undergone a profound change of attitude. The village leader acknowledges: "We were fools. You [Americans] showed us today that as you fed our hungry, buried our dead and saved our children from [the Vietcong's] horrors." He pledges the villagers' allegiance to the South and the American leadership, promising to "do our part to fight the Red dogs." The Green Berets had won the hearts and minds of the Vietnamese people.

Not all Vietnamese were so quick to come to this conclusion, however. The South Vietnamese population remained deeply divided, and this was reflected in the comic book as well. "The Year of the Cat" is set in a village that is about to be turned into a strategic hamlet. It features two villagers—a female Songtoi and her lover, Van Xuan. Songtoi is angered by the Americans' presence in her village. Moreover, she is unhappy with the Saigon regime. She tells her lover: "Those with intelligence realize how evil the [South] Vietnamese are! And unworthy of our allegiance." Van Xuan remains committed to the South, arguing that "the government helps arm us so that we can defend ourselves against the raids of the Viet Cong!" Songtoi defends the ruthless tactics of the Communists by claiming that "people must be forced to accept what is just for them!" She eventually leaves her lover, joins the Vietcong, and is killed when they launch an unsuccessful attack on the village. Van Xuan mourns her death, but he is pleased with the battle's outcome: "It is good that the [South] Vietnamese armed us for such a time!"

It is interesting to note that both the loyalist Vietnamese and the Vietcong refer to those loyal to the Saigon regime as simply "the Vietnamese." South Vietnam is simply "Vietnam." In this sense the Vietcong are portrayed not as Vietnamese but as an exterior threat to the legitimate government and people of the South—the only true Vietnam.

In addition to the regular war stories, *Jungle War Stories* often contained pages of straightforward information on the Vietnam conflict. One such page, entitled "The Enemy in Vietnam," described the Vietcong guerrilla as a "scrawny, unkempt 100-pounder who barely comes up to the average G.I.'s shoulders." Despite his diminutive size, though, the enemy is "cruel, cunning and tough" and capable of traveling "up to forty miles a day on fabric rubber-soled shoes." This "fact page" went on to describe some of the tactics employed by the Vietcong. According to the comic book, the Communists would have children play "for days on end" near a fort that is targeted for an attack so that "the coming and going of its personnel can be carefully noted." Supposedly innocent Vietnamese children, therefore, may actually work for the enemy—an ambiguous foe indeed. Information pages like this one usually contained a combination of established facts and unsupported assertions. One, entitled "Viet Cong: The Face of the Enemy," introduces the reader to Vo Nguyen Giap, "the little-known author of the master plan for conquest by subversion." Vietcong tactics, as directed by Giap, include "a brutal succession of village burnings, road minings and bridge burnings . . . together with the capture of vital rice barges and incessant extortion of money and food from Vietnamese peasants." According to the comic book, "Viet Cong sol-

diers are frequently hard to distinguish from the rest of the Vietnamese population because of the typical black pajamas which they wear." While this information could have been read in the *New York Times*, the next panel states: "Reminiscent of the brutal war in North Korea is the 'Human Wave' technique practiced by the Viet Cong. Accompanied by the wild blowing of bugles, the North Vietnamese Communists attack in overwhelming numbers." This claim bore less resemblance to the true military situation in Vietnam than to the racist notion that Asians, whether they be Japanese, Chinese, North Korean, or North Vietnamese, must employ their "overwhelming numbers" on the battlefield in order to compensate for their inferiority as individual soldiers and human beings. In any case, this juxtaposition of fact and assertion in *Jungle War Stories* would have made it difficult for the otherwise uninformed reader to distinguish what is true and what is false about the situation in Vietnam.

The Vietcong in *Jungle War Stories* are portrayed as a dangerous and treacherous foe, more likely to cut their adversary's throat from behind than assault him frontally. In one story, the Vietcong take over a village and masquerade as the inhabitants in order to fool the U.S. Special Forces and the ARVN. In the next issue the Communists again disguise themselves, this time as ARVN soldiers, in order to deceive an American pilot. The next issue's story, entitled "The Enemy Has Many Faces," tells how the Vietcong, disguised as Buddhist monks, try to infiltrate a strategic hamlet. This absurd premise is taken even further in another story when the Vietcong kidnap some Vietnamese children and masquerade as their teachers in order to sneak into a school on the outskirts of Saigon. The point, which is overstated in these stories, is that the enemy in Vietnam can appear in any number of forms. What appears to be a harmless villager, teacher, or other Vietnamese civilian may well be a Communist waiting to stab a trusting American in the back.

The series suggested that it was difficult to tell friend from foe in the Vietnam War.

The American soldier in *Jungle War Stories* exhibited superior qualities of military prowess, humanitarianism, and leadership. The troops of the U.S. Special Forces were usually featured as the protagonists in the stories. Several Green Berets, in particular, appeared as recurring characters, but their individual personalities are so shallow and indistinguishable from one another that the reader is not able to identify with any of them. Their deeds are not portrayed as individual accomplishments, but rather are representative of the entire American military effort in Vietnam. A page entitled "Vietnam Battle Facts," which appeared in a 1963 issue, stated simply that "our job in Vietnam is to supply and instruct [the South Vietnamese] in ways of halting the Red guerrillas' terror." The Green Berets pursue this directive successfully, whether they are organizing militarily incompetent ARVN troops or winning the hearts and minds of the population with the Strategic Hamlets program.

"The Attack Begins," proclaimed the cover of the January-March, 1965, issue of *Jungle War Stories*. The inside cover of the comic book displayed a picture of the USS *Maddox*, flanked by North Vietnamese gunboats. It briefly described the Tonkin Gulf incident as "the first major naval engagement of the Vietnam conflict."

The nature of the war had clearly changed, and the increasing American involvement in Vietnam was reflected in *Jungle War Stories*. The Green Berets were no longer as concerned with training and leading the South Vietnamese as they were with winning the war. American GIs were now fighting alongside the Special Forces. As early as 1965, the comic book drew attention to difficulties that would continue to frustrate the American military effort for the duration of the war. In one story an American pilot is forced to abandon his pursuit of retreating Vietcong soldiers when they cross the border into Laos. The Vietcong laugh at the American's predicament, noting "a little thing like a border . . . saps their strength and turns them into cowards." When the pilot returns to headquarters, he complains that "if that crazy [border is] gonna stop us every time we chase . . . well that's a dang fool way to fight a war!" ("Pinch the Devil"). As early as 1965, the series hinted that the war might be lost because government policy tied the hands of our troops.

The South Vietnamese themselves were portrayed as a significant obstacle to victory. The ARVN had always appeared as confused and inept in the series, but by 1965 the South Vietnamese leadership was seen to be dangerously corrupt, incompetent, and jealous of their American allies. In "Frontal Assault," the South Vietnamese military commanders devise a plan that they keep secret from the Americans because they want to "show our American colleagues that we Vietnamese can work out a battle scheme just as clever as [the Americans] might suggest." The plan, of course, fails miserably. Later, the American commanders discover that this and other ARVN military fiascos have come about because the plans were leaked to the enemy by a spy among the ARVN planning staff in Saigon. If the United States was going to win the war in Vietnam, according to this comic book, it would have to do so not with the help of its South Vietnam allies, but in spite of them.

A curious item appeared in the April-June 1965 issue of *Jungle War Stories*. "A Letter from Vietnam" was a one-page letter from "Jim," an American serviceman in South Vietnam, to his teenage brother, "Billy." There were no accompanying pictures or explanation for the letter, and it is not clear whether it was fictional or an actual, reprinted letter. In it the soldier writes of his close friend Johnny, who, while stationed in Vietnam, spent his free time studying in order to earn his high school diploma. The soldier then describes an incident in which Johnny was killed in action before he had received his diploma. Jim urges his young brother to stay in high school until he earns his diploma and then to go to college. The last line of the letter reads, "I just don't want my kid brother to waste his life when it isn't necessary."

This downbeat letter was highly uncharacteristic of the usual content of *Jungle War Stories*. In one page, Dell offered a pessimistic account of a war that was crueler than anything that had been depicted in its comic books. The first comic book publisher to come out in support of the American effort in Vietnam was also the first to discourage enlistment, however obliquely. With the rapidly escalating U.S. presence in Vietnam in 1965, it is possible that the staff at Dell feared the possible success of their own propaganda.

Because Dell did not give public credit to its comic book writers, it is not known whether there was a change of view in one writer's mind or a change in the creative staff behind *Jungle War Stories*. Whichever the case, the tone of the comic book shifted slightly after 1965. "Face of the Enemy," appearing in the same issue as "A Letter from Vietnam," tells of an American pilot who is forced to bail out over North Vietnam. He encounters a Communist soldier, who does not capture or kill the American but instead leads him safely back to the South Vietnamese border. The Communist returns to the North, where he maintains that he is doing his best to end the war, "for the benefit of all Vietnam." Never before in the comic book had the enemy been depicted with such humane characteristics.

Another story, "Big Surprise," features no Americans. It is about a South Vietnamese member of the Civilian Irregular Defense group, who is portrayed as a hero—albeit a reluctant one—who defeats a company of Vietcong single-handedly. His success is a result of accidental circumstances—he deceives the enemy because his appearance is identical to that of their commander—but, nevertheless, for the first time the South Vietnamese have

demonstrated that, with a little luck, they can defeat the enemy without American help.

With the July-September 1965 issue, Dell changed the title of *Jungle War Stories* to *Guerrilla War*, a more appropriate title for a Vietnam War comic book, but the series was canceled by the beginning of 1966. The contribution of *Jungle War Stories* and *Guerrilla War* to the comic book field was marginal. The series lasted only fourteen issues and was greatly overshadowed and outsold by the more popular superhero titles of Marvel and DC. Still, the series was significant for several reasons. It represented the first attempt by a publisher to portray the Vietnam conflict in comic books, and it did so several years before the Gulf of Tonkin Resolution truly made Vietnam an American war. The comic book was also the closest that the industry came to a propaganda effort in support of American policy in Vietnam. It should be noted that *Jungle War Stories*, like all privately published comic books, was in no way licensed by the U. S. government for propaganda purposes. Indeed, the comic book contained some themes and ideas, such as the unfavorable portrayal of our South Vietnamese allies, that would not have been encouraged by the Johnson administration. Still, by incorporating an impressive amount of information into the comic books—whether it was true or not—the creators of *Jungle War Stories* gave even their fictional features an air of authority that could lead the reader to believe that these stories, which usually followed the official government line, were an accurate reflection of the situation in Vietnam. It is impossible to determine what influence this series had upon its adolescent audience, but it is likely that many readers who came of age during the height of the Vietnam War initially learned of the conflict in the pages of this comic book.

The last significant point to make about *Jungle War Stories* is that it was the first Vietnam War comic book to fail commercially. Although the series lasted for over three years, a run of only fourteen issues is a fair to poor one by industry standards. That the title was canceled at the same time that the American military presence in Vietnam was nearly 200,000 strong and growing is probably not a coincidence. The more that people were bombarded by images and information about the war in the mass media, the less they wanted to be exposed to it in escapist popular entertainment. Whether its cancellation was a result of a conscious editorial decision or falling sales or a combination of both, the demise of *Jungle War Stories* was an early indication that the Vietnam War would be difficult to sell to the American people.

Subsequent efforts to portray the Vietnam War in comic form were also short-lived. *The Green Berets* continued to be the popular protagonist for Vietnam War comic books. Robin Moore's well-received novel *The Green Berets* and Sgt. Barry Sadler's hit song "Ballad of the Green Berets" seemed to demonstrate the marketability of the U.S. Special Forces. According to Robin Moore, he was approached in 1966 by General Yarborough, the commander of the J.F.K. Special Warfare Center at Fort Bragg, to start a comic strip "extolling the heroism of the Green Berets." Moore, working with artist Joe Kubert, an illustrator who had done work for DC's line of war comic books, produced a syndicated newspaper strip entitled "Tales of the Green Beret," which was based upon Moore's novel. Although Kubert maintained that he and Moore were not "taking any side, either hawk or dove," the strip read like propaganda for the Johnson administration's Vietnam policy.

The "Tales" strip was not well received. Newspapers that carried it began to drop the strip when they received complaints from readers. Some deplored the strip's "paramilitary bloodthirstiness," while others complained that it played "propaganda on the comic page." Newspaper editors also feared reader indifference. As the managing editor of the *Charlotte Observer* put it: "People were read-ing about the war on the front page and throughout the newspaper. By the time they got to the comic page they wanted relief." Joe Kubert admitted that portraying the Vietnam War in comics created problems of reader empathy, because the United States in Vietnam was "the big guy fighting the little guy and the American has always been for the underdog."

"Tales of the Green Beret" was terminated by the end of 1967. Robin Moore blamed the cancellation of his strip on "the left-leaning portion of the academic community [who] . . . waged a vituperative campaign against the newspapers carrying [it]." Efforts by the comic book industry to portray the Vietnam War in its publications, however, met with a similar lack of success. Dell tried once again to sell the war to readers with its own comic book adaptation of Moore's "Tales" strip. Dell's *Tales of the Green Beret* depicted the bitter fighting in Vietnam in a more grim and realistic manner than *Jungle War Stories*. In one story a Green Beret is even prepared to kill innocent Vietnamese civilians in order to get at the Vietcong, claiming that there was "no such thing as a non-combatant in this war!" The comic book, which proclaimed on the cover of its first issue that "if we must fight . . . we will win!" It was a loser with readers. Dell published only five issues of *Tales* over a period of two and a half years before it canceled the title.

The Milson Publishing Company was a short-lived operation that tried in 1967 to capitalize on the public fascination with the Green Berets and the popularity of superhero comic books. Milson's *Super Green Beret* featured a teenager who turns into a full-grown superpowered Green Beret soldier when he dons a magical green beret. This, the most absurd of all Vietnam War comic books, failed miserably. It lasted only two issues, and Milson folded shortly thereafter.

DC and Marvel, the two leading publishers by 1968, avoided the Vietnam War for the most part. DC published five war comic books, but only one of them ever featured stories set in

Vietnam. From the start of 1966 to the middle of 1967, *Our Fighting Forces* starred Captain Hunter, a retired Green Beret who has been captured by the Vietcong. Although Captain Hunter frequently encounters the Vietcong, the search for his brother, not the war itself, motivates him and serves as the dramatic focus of the series. The published reader response to the "Captain Hunter" feature was generally favorable, but some maintained that the Vietnam War belonged in the newspapers and not in comic books. Others criticized the writers for portraying Captain Hunter as being too preoccupied with finding his brother at the expense of helping America win the war. Hunter, ultimately unable to appeal to either hawks or doves, found his brother and was banished from *Our Fighting Forces*. Such a theme was consistent with the other DC war comic books featuring stories set during World War II, a more popular war with a clearly defined purpose.

Marvel's only 1960s war comic book was also set in World War II. *Sgt. Fury and His Howling Commandos* featured a cast a diverse characters who starred in action-packed adventures that, as one writer has noted, "read like an unintentional parody of bad war movies." The 1967 *Sgt. Fury King-Size Special*, however, was set during contemporary times and featured Fury and his commandos in Vietnam. Fury, now the head of SHIELD—a high-tech espionage agency modeled after television's "UNCLE"—is approached by President Johnson to undertake a secret mission into North Vietnam in order to prevent what Washington believes is an attempt by Hanoi to build a hydrogen bomb. Fury then recruits the old members of his World War II commando unit from their civilian lives. Johnson insists that the mission must be performed by civilians, because "we cannot afford to risk escalation of the war by having our troops invade North Vietnam."

The reunited "Howling Commandos," now middle-aged but apparently still capable of taking on the Vietnamese, parachute into Haiphong in order to sabotage the suspected nuclear weapons plant. Outside the factory, two North Vietnamese sentries are having a conversation; one asks the other if he thinks that the Americans might invade the North. The soldier laughs and replies: "But of course not . . . .I hear that many of them would rather invade Washington!" While the comic book implied that the American war effort might be threatened by domestic dissent, it was certainly not in danger of being defeated militarily by the enemy. The North Vietnamese soldiers in the story are hopelessly inept. An entire North Vietnamese battalion is unable to prevent the escape of any one of the seven Americans who successfully complete their mission. Indeed, the Vietnamese enemy is remarkably similar to the bungling Germans who were the prototypical antagonists in the regular Sgt. Fury series. While the idea of American civilians conducting covert missions in Vietnam was revived with popular success in the 1980s with movies like *Rambo* and *Missing in Action*, the comic book audience was not ready for it in 1967. Marvel, highly conscious of its sales figures and reader response, was not impressed enough with the reaction to the story to publish a similar comic book. Sergeant Fury returned permanently to the more familiar and more marketable Second World War.

The failure of Vietnam War comic books to command the interest and support of readers was similar to the trouble that the Johnson administration had rallying popular support for its Vietnam policy. The Vietnam conflict was a grim struggle for unclear objectives against an enemy that was not well defined. The American Green Beret was marketed in comics as the ideal heroic figure in an otherwise inglorious war. Readers, however, identified more with the superpowered comic book heroes who at times seemed more believable than their counterparts in the war comic books. While Vietnam War comic books represented only a very marginal portion of the industry's output during the 1960s, the war itself had a tremendous impact on American society that was, in turn, reflected in the more popular and prolific superhero comic books.

Marvel comic books are the most useful for the purpose of this chapter, because they differed from those of DC and other publishers in some key respects. Marvel was the first to publish code-approved comic books that appealed to an audience that was more sophisticated than the code presumed. Feedback from this older readership, which included an avid following among college students, was an important factor determining the content of the comic books. Unlike the DC superheroes who remained entrenched within the realm of fantasy for much of the 1960s, the Marvel superheroes were placed in identifiable contemporary settings like New York City, the New Mexican desert, or even Vietnam. Marvel was also the first publisher to give any of its superhero comic books a political focus during the Vietnam War period. An analyses of these Marvel comic books and the reader response to them will illustrate the degree to which they reflected the contemporary American political and social mood between 1963 and 1975.

Stan Lee wrote in 1975 that "Marvel Comics has never been very much into politics. . . . We have no official party line—I issue no editorial edicts as to what the political tone of our stories should be." Marvel comic books of the early 1960s, however, frequently had a political focus that followed the line of the Johnson administration. The early superhero plots, which were written almost exclusively by Lee, regularly featured the hero as the defender of American interests against evil Communist forces.

The Hulk in his first appearance prevents a spy named Igor from stealing the formula for America's secret "Gamma-ray bomb." In subsequent issues the Hulk battles both Soviet troops that seek to capture him and Red Chinese forces under "General Fang" that try to overrun a peaceful Himalayan nation.

Comic book historians have pointed out that these stories were inappropriate for this comic book because "the [Hulk] was cast as an anti-hero with no concern for human society [but] Lee insisted upon pitting him against evil communists." Thor was another Marvel superhero who was made to endure a series of implausible adventures laden with the clichés of cold war propaganda. In one issue, the Norse God of Thunder helps the inhabitants of a fictional Latin American nation overthrow a ruthless Communist dictator. Later he thwarts a Soviet plot to capture some top American scientists. In another story, Thor even defends an Indian outpost against an attack by the Red Chinese.

On one occasion, in 1965, Thor's adventures took him to the jungles of Vietnam. After being knocked unconscious by a Vietcong mortar shell, the Thunder God wakes up to find himself in the hut of a Vietnamese family. The villagers think that Thor is a "messenger of Buddha" who has been sent in answer to their prayers to "destroy the guerrillas" who have been terrorizing them. Looking about the village, Thor observes that "there is little food. . . . The Red guerrillas have brought famine to the land." He sees some American helicopters on patrol but notes that "they are so few, and the communist foe is so many . . . and so cunning."

The villain in the story is a ruthless Vietcong commander whose troops routinely round up hostages from captured Vietnamese villages. Among those captured is the family that aided Thor. It is revealed that the Vietcong officer is actually the family's eldest son, who had abandoned them years earlier in order to join the Communist cause. The younger brother, who remains loyal to the Saigon regime, accuses the elder of betraying his family by "serving the Red terrorists." The Communist shoots and kills his brother in a fit of rage, shouting: "You do not matter! Nobody matters! Only the communist cause is important! People mean nothing! Human lives mean nothing!" Thor eventually rescues the family and defeats the Vietcong. The commander, overcome with grief as a result of his actions, comes to his senses, renounces Communism, and commits suicide. His last words are: "It was communism that made me what I am . . . that shaped me into a brutal, unthinking instrument of destruction . . . may it vanish from the face of the earth and the memory of mankind!"

At the end of the story Thor vows, "I shall return, and when I do, the hammer of Thor shall be heard in every village . . . in every home . . . in every heart throughout this tortured land!" Despite his dramatic pledge, however, the Thunder God never did return to Vietnam. It is possible that even at this early stage of the conflict, comic book readers understood that the situation was far more complex than this cliché-ridden plot suggested. Perhaps the 1960s readership was too sophisticated to accept the kind of simplistic scenarios that had been popular in the comic books of World War II. In any case, the Thor comic book with its trappings of Norse mythology was a highly appropriate vehicle for conveying political messages.

Another Marvel superhero was much better suited for this. Stan Lee created "Iron Man" in 1973 and gave the character and the series a political focus that it would retain, in one way or another, throughout the Vietnam War years. A brief analysis of the "Iron Man" series during this period will illustrate how the political tone of the comic book changed according to the evolving political and social mood of America.

The origin of Iron Man was set in South Vietnam. Anthony Stark is introduced as a millionaire industrialist and scientist who invents and manufactures weapons for the U.S. government. He travels to South Vietnam in order to demonstrate his latest invention to some high-ranking American military advisors. While accompanying a group of ARVN soldiers into the jungle to observe his weapons in action, Stark accidentally sets off a Vietcong land mine, which leaves him critically wounded. When he awakens, Stark discovers that he

has been captured by Vietcong forces led by a ruthless tyrant named Wong Chu. The Communists know that a piece of shrapnel lodged near Stark's heart gives him only days to live, but they convince him to construct a weapon for them in return for an operation that will save his life. Stark agrees to build a weapon, but he secretly plans not to turn it over to the Communists, but to use it for himself. The "weapon" that Stark constructs is actually a suit of armor that keeps his heart beating and gives him augmented strength, among other powers. Taking the name "Iron Man," Stark escapes, defeats the Vietcong, kills Wong Chu, and destroys the Communist base. Like other Marvel superheroes, however, Iron Man pays a price for his new powers—he must forever wear the metal chest plate under his clothes in order to keep his heart beating.

The elements in this story set the tone for future Iron Man comic books. The Communist villain Wong Chu is the epitome of evil: ugly, rotund, and smoking cigarettes, he has no concern whatsoever for human life. The Red guerrilla cares nothing about the Vietnamese people. Even the advancement of Communism is important only as a means to achieving personal power. Tony Stark, meanwhile, is the very symbol of America, a noble hero helping the South Vietnamese with his superior wealth and technology. Marvel's portrayal of the Vietnam conflict is not only childishly simplistic, but ethnocentric as well. The war is not so much a Vietnamese phenomenon as it is a battleground in the greater global struggle between the democratic West and the Communist East. Vietnam is a domino that America must now allow to fall.

Tony Stark devoted both of his lives to keeping the United States ahead in the cold war. As Stark the industrialist and inventor, he builds new weapons like his "atomic naval cannon" for the Defense Department. In his Iron Man identity, he battles "America's enemies from within and without." His efforts as both Stark and Iron Man were appreciated by the government officials with whom he often worked. In one story, Iron Man is thanked by an FBI agent for thwarting a "commie spy ring." Later, a general at the Pentagon compliments Stark on his latest invention: "The Reds would probably give up half of Asia if they could steal the plans of what you've invented so far." No other superhero was so closely associated with the U.S. government.

Iron Man fought a series of Communist villains in battles symbolic of the struggle between the West and the East. Among these adversaries were the Red Barbarian—a Soviet general who works directly for Comrade K; the Crimson Dynamo—Iron Man's armor-clad Soviet counterpart; the Black Widow—a Soviet spy and seductress; and the Titanium Man—another armored Soviet supersoldier. Even Nikita Khrushchev made an occasional appearance; he once worked out a plan to sabotage Stark industries so that "the U.S. would lag behind . . . in the arms race." In each of these stories, Iron Man triumphs on behalf of the U.S. government. Even when things went badly, the armored hero maintained his patriotic zeal. Once, when he was captured, he defiantly exclaimed: "If this is to be my finish, I'll show how an American faces death! I'll show that nothing can shatter the faith of a man who fights for freedom!"

From time to time Iron Man would return to the war-torn country where his heroic career was born. In a 1967 story he thwarts a plot by the Titanium Man and a Red Chinese villain called Half-Face to score a Communist propaganda victory by destroying a peaceful Vietnamese village at night and making it appear that American bombers were responsible for the carnage. Iron Man saves the village, preserves America's good international reputation, and takes the opportunity to smash some Vietcong in the process.

For the most part, though, Iron Man left the fighting in Vietnam to the American military, while he engaged Communist enemies in a more symbolic show of support for U.S. policy.

When the Titanium Man issued a public challenge to Iron Man, Stark felt compelled to accept, because it was a "matter of national pride and prestige." He defeats his much larger Soviet foe and exclaims: "You thought you'd just have to flex your muscles and show your strength, and your enemies would fall by the wayside! . . . You made the worst mistake any Red can make . . . you challenged a foe who isn't afraid of you!" Iron Man's stand underscored the need to preserve American prestige by containing the Communist menace however and wherever it threatens American interests.

Two things happened in 1968 that forever changed the political tone of the *Iron Man* series. One was the Tet Offensive. The other was the expansion of the Marvel Comics publishing operation. The magnitude of the National Liberation Front offensive stunned the American people and called into serious question the administration's entire Vietnam policy, which had been so doggedly defended by Iron Man. Disillusioned Americans, especially among the young generation, felt that they had been misled and misinformed by the government. It would have been commercially unwise to present the same government line in a comic book. At the same time, Marvel's financial success allowed the publisher to expand and hire new writers and artists. *Iron Man* was one of the titles that was handed over to these new young comic book writers, who tended to be politically liberal. The content of *Iron Man* comic books was thereafter affected by change in both the Marvel staff and the mood of comic book readers.

After 1968 all cold war themes were abandoned in the *Iron Man* series. Even when Soviet foes like the Crimson Dynamo returned, they acted more like other apolitical supervillains than the Communist stereotypes that they had once been. Iron Man himself spent less time working for the U.S. government and turned his attention inward toward such domestic issues as race relations and pollution control. The new writers played upon the Tony

Stark/Iron Man character as a well-meaning but misdirected defender of the establishment. He is pitted against a new enemy called the Firebrand, who claims to have been "an all-American boy who started out to make this nation a better place . . . sat in for civil rights, marched for peace, and demonstrated on campus, and got spat on by bigots, [and] beat on by 'patriots'". Firebrand whips up riots and hysteria among young demonstrators because he has concluded that America "doesn't want to be changed. The only way to build anything decent is to tear down what's here and start over."

Although Firebrand was portrayed as a dangerous villain, his message elicited some reader empathy. One letter pointed out that "while Firebrand was marching, trying to bring about a more peaceful world, Stark Industries was probably building weapons for Vietnam where we 'destroyed a city in order to save it'". Before 1968, most of the printed response to the series did not comment on the hero's politics, although an occasional letter praised his patriotism: "Not since George M. Cohan has anyone so waved their country's flag—and it wouldn't hurt if there were more of this sort of thing." By the early 1970s, however, *Iron Man*'s readers became increasingly concerned with the character's political stance. One wrote that "Tony Stark is going to have to do some pretty big restructuring of his life to avoid being classified as an enemy of the people." Another insisted that "the time is right for Tony Stark to quit being a weapons manufacturer." Although some conservative readers did not object to Iron Man's role as a defender of authority, most of the printed mail demanded a change.

Anthony Stark was, according to one reader, "a profiteering, capitalistic, war-mongering defense contractor . . . .[who] produces devices to kill people." Recognizing that the political mood of their readership had shifted, *Iron Man*'s writers tried to improve the hero's image. In one issue, Iron Man argues with a right-wing U.S. senator who claims that "there's a new breed of people in this country today. . . . who want to destroy the government that made America great." Iron Man counters that the American people, not the government, makes the country great. The senator then calls him an anarchist. This was change, indeed, from the superhero who once claimed that "no one has the right to defy the wishes of his government."

Iron Man's political about-face is confirmed after a student demonstration outside of Stark Industries turns into a riot, and the crowd is fired on by Stark's own security force. The demonstrators cry out, "it's another Kent State!" and stone Iron Man when he arrives on the scene. He criticizes the students for "preaching peace while resorting to violence," but one of them justifies their action as "the only way we can make your generation hear us." These events leave the hero deeply disturbed. He later reevaluates his image as a defender of government policy and a weapons manufacturer: "I designed . . . weapons that can be used to kill one people . . . to save another. . . . I find myself pondering every action I ever made." Finally, Stark resolves to end his corporation's association with weapons research and development and to diversify into areas such as pollution control and consumer goods.

A powerful story entitled "Long Time Gone" serves as a fitting epilogue for the political metamorphosis of Iron Man. Published in 1975 simultaneously with the fall of Saigon, the story opens with Tony Stark sitting alone in his office, pondering his own experiences in Vietnam. Looking into a mirror, he questions himself and searches his soul for the answers: "As Iron Man you beat the commies for democracy without ever questioning just whose democracy you were serving . . . or just what those you served intended to do with the world once you'd saved it for them. Vietnam raised all those questions . . . like: what right had we to be there in the first place?"

Stark relives through a flashback sequence a time when, as Iron Man, he observed the horrors of the Vietnam War firsthand. He sees confused and weary American troops fight and die. He sees a high-tech artillery piece of his own design lay waste to a village, killing enemy and innocent alike. He comes across a blind Vietnamese boy who has been orphaned by the day's fighting. Moved to tears by the death and carnage that have resulted in part from his own action, Iron Man buries the dead in a mass grave and marks it with the epitaph "Why?" Returning to the present, Tony Stark dons his Iron Man armor, strikes a dramatic pose, and pledges "to avenge those whose lives have been lost through the ignorance of men like the man I once was . . . or I will die trying!" The end of the Vietnam War brings with it Iron Man's final repudiation of the government actions that he had once so zealously defended.

It would seem that a comic book featuring a star-spangled hero named Captain America should have been an appropriate series for a political focus. In 1964, Marvel revived this World War II comic book hero, who was a living symbol of patriotism and the American ideal. Stan Lee, though, seemed unsure of what to do with the Captain America character. Captain America confronts apolitical villains in New York for a few issues. Then he travels to Vietnam—not to fight alongside American troops as he did in the Second World War, but to rescue a friend who has been captured by the Vietcong. While American objectives in the war remained ambiguous, a rescue mission presented the hero with a clear and attainable goal. While he's there, of course, he battles some Communists, who are portrayed much like the other evil Red caricatures of early Marvel Comic books. Beyond this, however, there is no mention of the need to defend South Vietnam from the Communist threat, a message that was overstated in the *Iron Man* comic book.

After his brief adventure in Vietnam, Captain America is sent back to World War II,

where he once again battles Hitler's hordes for nine issues, before returning to contemporary times. In an effort to find the proper tone and setting for Captain America, Stan Lee had unintentionally portrayed the patriotic hero as an appropriate symbol of a confused America that preferred to relive past glories, rather than recognize and adapt to the new world situation.

Captain America, more than any other comic book, generated a political controversy among its readers. As early as 1965, a letter from an American serviceman suggested that "the war in Vietnam would make an endless amount of adventures for . . . Cap." Lee responded, though, that other readers wanted Captain America to stay out of Vietnam. After 1968 the difference in opinion over the hero's role became more pronounced. Some readers argued that Cap should stop being a defender of the Establishment. One letter asserted, "It would fit the standards of today . . . if [Captain America was] more liberal." Another, more sophisticated response pointed out that Cap "is a very strange mixture of individualism and statism, in that when he lectures on freedom, he seems to be talking about the nation rather the people who make it up"

Marvel also printed letters from those who continued to urge Captain America to go to Vietnam. One of these stressed that "Captain America should be devoted to uniting our nation against foes who are killing our soldiers in Vietnam. Regardless if . . . our foreign policy is right or wrong, we should stand behind the men who are dying to preserve our liberty." Stan Lee maintained, however, that informal polls taken by Marvel over the years indicated that the great majority of readers wanted Cap to stay out of the fighting in Vietnam.

Stan Lee wrote most of the *Captain America* comic books until 1972. By then the tone of the character had changed in a way similar to that of Iron Man's. Lee wrote in 1971 that Captain America "simply doesn't lend himself to the John Wayne-type character he once was. . . .

We just cannot see any of our characters taking on a role of super-patriotism in the world as it is today." Consequently, Captain America went through a period of soul-searching and self-doubt about his role in the Vietnam era:

Throughout the world, the image of Captain America has become a symbol . . . a living embodiment of all that democracy stands for. But now . . . there are those who scorn love of our flag . . . love of country . . . those to whom patriotism is just a square, out-moded word. Those who think of me . . . as a useless relic . . . of a meaningless part. . . . This is the day of the antihero . . . the age of the rebel and the dissenter. It isn't hip to defend the establishment . . . only to tear it down. And in a world rife with injustice, greed, and endless war . . . who's to say the rebels are wrong? . . . I've spent a lifetime defending the flag . . . and the law. Perhaps . . . I should have battled less . . . and questioned more.

Stan Lee maintained that because Americans could not agree on a common enemy in Vietnam and because the administration's objectives were unclear, "Captain America would not be serving America by taking sides. For the sake of unity, Cap [remained] on the home front." Therefore, when Captain America does go to Vietnam in one story, he avoids conflict with either side and tries only to facilitate the peace negotiations. Captain America, instead, turned his attention toward America's domestic concerns. Together with his black, superhero sidekick the Falcon, who leads a civilian life as a social worker in Harlem, Captain America tackled such problems as inner-city crime, poverty, and social dislocation. The Captain America of the 1970s symbolized a nation, weary of confusing and painful overseas adventures, that had turned inward to confront serious domestic ills, brought on, in part, by a decade of war.

Captain America's disassociation from the U.S. government was completed after the revelations of the Watergate scandal. The hero discovers that an organization called CRAP—the Committee to Regain America's Principles—

■ ■ *In the following sequence from Marvel comics, the American hero "Iron Man" battles the Vietcong in Vietnam.*

led by a man named Quentin Harderman, is actually a front for the "Secret Empire," a fascist organization that seeks to overthrow the U.S. government. Tracking down the mysterious leader of the Secret Empire leads Captain America to the White House and the Oval Office. Although the face of the villain is obscured in shadow, the reader is left with little doubt as to the true identity of the man who sought to overthrow the U.S. Constitution. Captain America is so stunned and disillusioned that he temporarily changes his name to "Nomad—the man without a country." He later readopts the name Captain America, however, and pledges to help restore legitimacy to the perennial American ideals of freedom and democracy that have been corrupted by a self-serving government.

The radical shift in the political tone and character of *Iron Man* and *Captain America* was a result of changes in popular American values and changes in the comic book industry itself. After 1968 it became fashionable among the younger generation to oppose the Establishment, which had brought America the Vietnam War. The culture of dissent, which was reflected in popular music and film, was also mirrored in comic books. Cognizant of the views held by the majority of their readers, Stan Lee and the new generation of comic book creators abandoned the cold war clichés of early Marvel stories. Evil communist caricatures were replaced by villainous right-wing authority figures. Before this could happen, however, Marvel had to confront an authority figure of its own—the Comic Code Authority.

By the beginning of the 1970s it had become clear that the comic book audience had outgrown the naive presumptions of the code. The code's insistence that "in every instance good shall triumph over evil" and that "policemen, judges, government officials and respected institutions shall never be presented in such a way as to create disrespect for established authority" could not be taken seriously by a generation that had watched the Chicago police riot of 1968, read about the Pentagon Papers, and followed a war that defied such simplistic concepts as "good" and "evil."

Adapting to growing reader sophistication led Marvel to brush against certain code restrictions. A character called Tribune, who appeared in the *Daredevil* comic book, was typical of the new right-wing comic book villains. The Tribune is a self-styled judge, jury, and executioner who "convicts" and sentences to death antiwar demonstrators, draft dodgers, and anyone else whom he judges to be a "commie pinko." In the *Spider-Man* comic book, a character named Sam Bullitt is introduced as a retired police officer who runs for New York City district attorney. His platform is one of "law and order" that promises to stamp out "left-wing anarchists who are trying to destroy this great proud nation of ours." It is revealed that Bullitt is not only a crypto-fascist, but also a crook with ties to organized crime. Although these story lines were not technically in violation of the code, because the Tribune is not really a judge and Bullitt is not an acting policeman or an elected official, they clearly presented the authority figure as an antagonistic element and thus ran contrary to the spirit of the code.

In 1971 Stan Lee wrote several issues of *The Amazing Spider-Man* that dealt with the problem of drug abuse. The code implicitly forbade any mention of drugs in comic books, and the stories were rejected by the Code Authority. Lee published the comic books without the authority's seal of approval, and they sold well in spite of it. Marvel's successful defiance compelled the Code Authority to revise its outdated standards. Among the provisions that were dropped was one that forbade the unfavorable portrayal of authority figures. Comic book writers at both Marvel and DC, which together accounted for about two-thirds of all comic books sold at that time, took advantage of the liberalized guidelines to produce stories that were more reflective of the concerns of American society.

The Comics Code Authority was established in 1954, when it was unpopular and unwise to criticize traditional American values and institutions. By 1971 the cold war consensus had broken down, and it had become popular to question authority and to challenge the Establishment. The young generation's disillusionment and alienation during the Vietnam War years gave rise to the culture of dissent, which was reflected in the superhero comic books of Marvel and, by this time, of DC as well. The contemporary media took notice of the comic book industry's trend toward relevance but pointed out that its new social awareness was self-conscious and self-serving as well. Slumping sales by the end of the 1960s led the major publishers to do market surveys of their collegiate readership. Whatever their motivations, the comic book creators' attempts to reflect contemporary values and concerns forced a revision of the code, which ultimately broadened the potential of comic books as a medium and an art form.

Comic books since the end of the Vietnam War have tended to deal with the conflict in a manner similar to that of other popular entertainment media. The Vietnam veteran in comic books has generally been portrayed as a figure who is left alienated from society by his Vietnam experience. The first veteran to return from the war was Flash Thompson, a supporting character in the *Spider-Man* comic book. Flash, a friend of Peter Parker (Spider-Man), is an all-American boy—a high school football star, voted most likely to succeed, popular with his classmates and with women in particular. He forsakes a college football scholarship to serve his country in the Vietnam War. When he returns, Flash is a very different character. He has trouble adjusting to civilian life. He keeps to himself and snaps at his friends when they offer to help him. Later, it is revealed that Flash is deeply disturbed by his participation in a war that had victimized the peaceful Vietnamese people. Flash never really could readjust to American society after the war. By 1986 he had bounced "from one dead-end job to the next," suffered a failed relationship with a Vietnamese American woman, and felt betrayed by his friends who had stayed at home during the war and enjoyed more happiness and success then himself.

While Flash Thompson's war experience left him embittered and depressed, another comic book veteran has suffered an even deeper alienation. Frank Castle was a captain in the U.S. Marine Corps who served in Vietnam for five years. Soon after the end of the war, his wife and children are murdered by the mob after they accidentally witness a gangland killing. The traumatized marine hunts down and kills the murderers himself, and thereafter, armed with a Vietnam-era M-16, assorted pistols, knives, and grenades and calling himself "the Punisher," he wages a one-man war against crime. The Punisher's ruthless and sometimes psychotic vigilantism frequently brought him into conflict with superheroes as well as criminals during the 1970s, when he was first introduced. In the 1980s the Punisher was revised slightly into a more heroic and sympathetic figure, and he had become one of Marvel's most popular character. Mirroring popular films like *Rambo* and *Missing in Action,* the Punisher acts outside of the law, because his experience in Vietnam has taught him that the government cannot or will not get the job done. The streets of New York become a war zone, criminals are the elusive enemy, and the Punisher is the soldier who is forever fighting his own personal war against crime.

Compared with World War II and Korea, the Vietnam War itself elicited a marginal response from the publishers. Few Vietnam War comic books were published, and none succeeded commercially. To avoid alienating any segment of their politically divided readership, Marvel and DC rarely mentioned the Vietnam War in their contemporary comic books. The impact that the war had on American society, however, was reflected in the content of these comic books and was ultimately recognized by the revised Comics Code Authority. The national consensus that had united America during World War II and cold war dissolved during the Vietnam War. The diversity of view on the war was mirrored in the comic books, ranging from the propaganda of *Jungle War Stories* to the antiwar and anti-Establishment Marvel comic books of the early 1970s. Considering the preponderance of the Vietnam War in the American media overall, though, the comic book industry's treatment of the conflict was quite restrained. In final analysis, comic books, indeed, reflected America's subconscious wishes: some endorsed the war, and others criticized it, but many simply offered readers an escape from the tragedy of Vietnam.

■■■

STUDY QUESTIONS

1. What was "the code" and how did it affect the comic book industry?

2. Describe the publishing objectives of Dell Comics and Marvel Comics in the early 1960s.

3. In the early stages of the Vietnam War, how did Dell Comics and Marvel Comics portray the conflict?

4. How did *Jungle War Stories* change in its portrayal of the Vietnam War in the late 1960s?

5. How was Marvel Comics unique in the comic book industry and how did it portray the Vietnam War from the mid-1960s to mid-1970s?

6. Describe the evolution of the Iron Man character.

7. Describe the political controversy in the comic book industry over Captain America.

BIBLIOGRAPHY

For a general discussion of the history of the comic book in the United States, see Joseph Witek, *Comic Books as History* (1989) and Michael Benton, *The Comic Book in America* (1989). Will Jacobs and Gerard Jones, *The Comic Book Heroes* (1985) is a useful survey of the primary comic characters. Stan Lee, *Origins of Marvel Comics* (1974) provides a history of one of the giants in the industry. There is a wealth of excellent published material on the impact of the Vietnam War on American films, television, and literature. For the best of these materials, see Philip Beidler, *American Literature and the Experience of Vietnam* (1982); Timothy J. Lomperis, *"Reading the Wind": The Literature of the Vietnam War* (1987); Albert Auster and Leonard Quart, *How the War Was Remembered: Hollywood and Vietnam* (1988); Peter T. Rollins, "The Vietnam War: Perceptions Through Literature, Film, and Television," *American Quarterly*, 36 (Fall 1984), 419-32; and Deborah Ballard-Reisch, *"China Beach* and *Tour of Duty:* American Television and Revisionist History of the Vietnam War," *Journal of Popular Culture*, 25 (Winter 1991), 135–50.

THE ELVIS PRESLEY PHENOMENON

Greil Marcus

Elvis. His last name is used only to give balance to his first. There is no need to use it as a point of identification. The history of rock 'n' roll is the story of a series of overnight wonders, performers who rose fast, achieved momentary fame, and then drifted into obscurity, only to be revived years later on golden oldies concerts. But not Elvis Presley. His fame lasted. Even his death has not diminished it. He was one of a kind.

Why? He didn't discover or invent rock 'n' roll. He wasn't the first white singer to blur lines between race and hillbilly music. Elvis's career took off in 1956. Five years earlier, disc jockey Alan Freed began his "Moon-dog's Rock-and-Roll Party" on station WJW in Cleveland. Several years before anyone heard of Elvis, Bill Haley and the Comets reached the Top Ten with "Rock Around the Clock." But Elvis was different, and he was better.

Elvis defies easy description. He was modest and soft-spoken, shy around women, and deferential to his elders. He was raised in the shadow of the Pentecostal First Assembly of God Church, and gospels were the first songs he sang. "He grew up," noted one music critic, "schooled in all the classic virtues of small-town America: diffident, polite, sirring and ma'aming his elders. . . ." But there was another side to Elvis, a wild impulsive side. On stage, his movements shocked middle-class white America, and his voice was hungry and sensual. In the following selection, Greil Marcus beautifully describes the culture and times that produced Elvis.

They called Elvis the Hillbilly Cat in the beginning; he came out of a stepchild culture (in the South, white trash; to the rest of America, a caricature of Bilbo and moonshine) that for all it shared with the rest of America had its own shape and integrity. As a poor white Southern boy, Elvis created a personal culture out of the hillbilly world that was his as a given. Ultimately, he made that personal culture public in such an explosive way that he transformed not only his own culture, but America's. I want to look at that hillbilly landscape for a bit—to get a sense of how Elvis drew on his context.

It was, as Southern chambers of commerce have never tired of saying, A Land of Contrasts. The fundamental contrast, of course, could not have been more obvious: black and white. Always at the root of Southern fantasy, Southern music, and Southern politics, black Americans were poised in the early fifties for an overdue invasion of American life, in fantasy, music, and politics. As the North scurried to deal with the problem, the South would be pushed farther and farther into the weirdness and madness its best artists had been trying to exorcise from the time of Poe on down. Its politics would dissolve into night-riding and hysteria; its fantasies would be dull for all their gaudy paranoia. Only the music got away clean.

The North, powered by the Protestant ethic, had set men free by making them strangers; the poor man's South that Elvis knew took strength from community.

The community was based on a marginal economy that demanded cooperation, loyalty, and obedience for the achievement of anything resembling a good life; it was organized by religion, morals, and music. Music helped hold the community together, and carried the tradi-

tions and shared values that dramatized a sense of place. Music gave pleasure, wisdom, and shelter.

"It's the only place in the country I've ever been where you can actually drive down the highway at night, and if you listen, you hear music," Robbie Robertson once said. "I don't know if it's coming from the people or if it's coming from the air. It lives, and it's rooted there." Elegant enough, but I prefer another comment Robbie made. "The South," he said, "is the only place we play where everybody can clap on the off-beat."

Music was also an escape from the community, and music revealed its underside. There were always people who could not join, no matter how they might want to: tramps, whores, rounders, idiots, criminals. The most vital were singers: not the neighbors who brought out their fiddles and guitars for county picnics, as Elvis used to do, or those who sang in church, as he did also, but the professionals. They were men who bridged the gap between the community's sentimentalized idea of itself, and the outside world and the forbidden; artists who could take the community beyond itself because they had the talent and the nerve to transcend it. Often doomed, traveling throughout the South enjoying sins and freedoms the community had surrendered out of necessity or never known at all, they were ambitious, ornery, or simply different to fit in.

The Carter Family, in the twenties, were the first to record the old songs everyone knew, to make the shared musical culture concrete, and their music drew a circle around the community. They celebrated the landscape (especially the Clinch Mountains that ringed their home), found strength in a feel for death because it was the only certainty, laughed a bit, and promised to leave the hillbilly home they helped build only on a gospel ship. Jimmie Rodgers, their contemporary, simply hopped a train. He was every boy who ever ran away from home, hanging out in the railroad yards, bumming around with black minstrels, push-

From *Mystery Train* by Greil Marcus. Copyright © 1975 by Greil Marcus. Used by permission of the publisher, Dutton, an imprint of New American Library, a division of Penguin Books USA Inc.

ing out the limits of his life. *He* celebrated long tall mamas that rubbed his back and licked his neck just to cure the cough that killed him; he bragged about gunplay on Beale Street; he sang real blues, played jazz with Louis Armstrong, and though there was melancholy in his soul, his smile was a good one. He sounded like a man who could make a home for himself anywhere. There's so much *room* in this country, he seemed to be saying, so many things to do—how could an honest man be satisfied to live within the frontiers he was born to?

Outside of the community because of the way they lived, the singers were tied to it as symbols of its secret hopes, of its fantasies of escape and union with the black man, of its fears of transgressing the moral and social limits that promised peace of mind. Singers could present the extremes of emotion, risk, pleasure, sex, and violence that the community was meant to control; they were often alcoholic or worse, lacking a real family, drifters in a world where roots were life. Sometimes the singer tantalized the community with his outlaw liberty; dying young, he finally justified the community by his inability to survive outside of it. More often than not, the singer's resistance dissolved into sentiment. Reconversion is the central country music comeback strategy, and many have returned to the fold after a brief fling with the devil, singing songs of virtue, fidelity, and God, as if to prove that sin only hid a deeper piety—or that there was no way out.

By the late forties and early fifties, Hank Williams had inherited Jimmie Rodgers' role as the central figure in the music, but he added an enormous reservation: that margin of loneliness in Rodgers' America had grown into a world of utter tragedy. Williams sang for a community to which he could not belong; he sang to God in whom he could not quite believe; even his many songs of good times and good lovin' seemed to lose their reality. There were plenty of jokes in his repertoire,

novelties like "Kaw-liga" (the tale of unrequited love between two cigar store Indians); he traveled Rodgers' road, but for Williams, that road was a lost highway. Beneath the surface of his forced smiles and his light, easy sound, Hank Williams was kin to Robert Johnson in a way that the new black singers of his day were not. Their music, coming out of New Orleans, out of Sam Phillips' Memphis studio and washing down from Chicago, was loud, fiercely electric, raucous, bleeding with lust and menace and loss. The rhythmic force that was the practical legacy of Robert Johnson had evolved into a music that overwhelmed *his* reservations; the rough spirit of the new blues, city R&B, rolled right over his nihilism. Its message was clear: "What life doesn't give me, I'll take."

Hank Williams was a poet of limits, fear, and failure; he went as deeply into one dimension of the country world as anyone could, gave it beauty, gave it dignity. What was missing was that part of the hillbilly soul Rodgers had celebrated, something Williams' music obscured, but which his realism could not express and the community's moralism could not contain: excitement, rage, fantasy, delight—the feeling, summed up in a sentence by W. J. Cash from *The Mind of the South,* that "even the Southern physical world was a kind of cosmic conspiracy against reality in favor of romance"; that even if Elvis's South was filled with Puritans, it was also filled with natural-born hedonists, and the same people were both.

To lie on his back for days and weeks [Cash writes of the hillbilly], storing power as the air he breathed stores power under the hot sun of August, and then to explode, as that air explodes in a thunderstorm, in a violent outburst of emotion—in such a fashion would he make life not only tolerable, but infinitely sweet.

In the fifties we can hardly find that moment in white music, before Elvis. Hank Williams was not all there was to fifties country, but his style was so pervasive, so effective, carrying so much weight, that it closed off the possibilities of breaking loose just as the new black music helped open them up. Not his gayest tunes, not "Move It on Over," "Honky Tonkin'," or "Hey Good Lookin'," can match this blazing passage from Cash, even if those songs share its subject:

To go into the town on Saturday afternoon and night, to stroll with the throng, to gape at the well-dressed and the big automobiles, to bathe in the holiday cacaphony . . . maybe to have a drink, maybe to get drunk, to laugh with the passing girls, to pick them up if you had a car, or to go swaggering or hesitating into the hotels with the corridors saturated with the smell of bicloride of mercury, or the secret, steamy bawdy houses; maybe to have a fight, maybe against the cops, maybe to end, whooping and goddamning, in the jailhouse. . . .

The momentum is missing; that will to throw yourself all the way after something better with no real worry about how you are going to make it home. And it was this spirit, full-blown and bragging, that was to find its voice in Elvis's new blues and the rockabilly fever he kicked off all over the young white South. Once Elvis broke down the door, dozens more would be fighting their way through. Out of nowhere there would be Carl Perkins, looking modest enough and sounding for all the world as if he was having fun for the first time in his life, chopping his guitar with a new kind of urgency and yelling: "Now Dan got happy, and he started ravin'—He jerked out his razor but he wasn't shavin.' "

Country music (like the blues, which was more damned and more honestly hedonistic than country had ever been) was the music for a whole community, cutting across lines of age, if not class. This could have meant an openly expressed sense of diversity for each child, man, and woman, as it did with the blues. But country spoke to a community fearful of anything of the sort, withdrawing into itself, using music as a bond that linked all together for better or for worse, with a sense that what was

shared was less important than the crucial fact of sharing. How could parents hope to keep their children if their kids' whole sense of what it meant to live—which is what we get from music when we are closest to it—held promises the parents could never keep?

The songs of country music, and most deeply, its even narrow sound, had to subject the children to the heartbreak of their parents: the father who couldn't feed his family, the wife who lost her husband to a honky-tonk angel or a bottle, the family that lost everything to a suicide or a farm spinning off into one more bad year, the horror of loneliness in a world that was meant to banish that if nothing else. Behind that uneasy grin, this is Hank Williams' America; the romance is only a night call.

Such a musical community is beautiful, but it is not hard to see how it could be intolerable. All that hedonism was dragged down in country music; a deep sense of fear and resignation confined it, as perhaps it almost had to, in a land overshadowed by fundamentalist religion, where original sin was just another name for the facts of life.

Now, that Saturday night caught by Cash and Perkins would get you through a lot of weekdays. Cash might close it off—"Emptied of their irritations and repressions, left to return to their daily tasks, stolid, unlonely, and tame again"—and he's right, up to a point. This wasn't any revolution, no matter how many cops got hurt keeping the peace on Saturday night. Regardless of what a passport to that Southern energy (detached from the economics and religion that churned it up) might do for generations of restless Northern and British kids, there is no way that energy can be organized. But the fact that Elvis and the rest could trap its spirit and send it out over a thousand radio transmitters is a central fact of more lives than mine; the beginning of most of the stories in this book, if nothing near the end of them.

For we are treading on the key dividing line that made Elvis "King of Western Bop" (they went through a lot of trouble finding a name for this music) instead of just another country crooner or a footnote in someone's history of the blues: the idea (and it was just barely an "idea") that Saturday night could be the whole show. You had to be young and a bit insulated to pull it off, but why not? Why not trade pain and boredom for kicks and style? Why not make an escape from a way of life—the question trails off the last page of *Huckleberry Finn*—into a way of life?

You might not get revered for all time by everyone from baby to grandma, like the Carter Family, but you'd have more fun. Reality would catch up sooner or later—a pregnant girlfriend and a fast marriage, the farm you had to take over when your daddy died, a dull and pointless job that drained your desires until you could barely remember them—but why deal with reality before you had to? And what if there was a chance, just a chance, that you *didn't* have to deal with it? "When I was a boy," said Elvis not so long ago, "I was the hero in comic books and movies. I grew up believing in a dream. Now I've lived it out. That's all a man can ask for."

Elvis is telling us something quite specific: how special he was; how completely he captured and understood what for most of us is only a tired phrase glossing the surfaces of our own failed hopes. It is one thing, after all, to dream of a new job, and quite another to dream of a new world. The risks are greater. Elvis took chances dreaming his dreams; he gambled against the likelihood that their failure would betray him, and make him wish he had never dreamed at all. There are a hundred songs to tell that story, but perhaps Mott the Hoople, chasing the rock 'n' roll fantasy Elvis made of the American dream, said it best: "I wish I'd never wanted then/What I want now twice as much."

Always, Elvis felt he was different, if not better, than those around him. He grew his

sideburns long, acting out that sense of differentness, and was treated differently: in this case, he got himself kicked off the football team. Hear him recall those days in the midst of a near-hysterical autobiography, delivered at the height of his comeback from the stage at the International Hotel in Las Vegas: " . . . Had pretty long hair for that time and I tell you it got pretty weird. They used to see me comin down the street and they'd say, 'Hot dang, let's get him, he's a squirrel, he's a squirrel, get him, he just come down outta the trees.' "

High school classmates remember his determination to break through as a country singer; with a little luck, they figured, he might even make it.

Out on the road for the first time with small-change country package tours, though, Elvis would plot for something much bigger—for everything Hollywood had ever shown him in its movies.

On North Main in Memphis, as Harmonica Frank recalls Elvis, this was nothing to put into words. Talking trash and flicking ash, marking time and trying to hold it off, what did Elvis have to look forward to? A year or so of Saturday nights, a little local notoriety, then a family he didn't quite decide to have and couldn't support? It would be all over.

Elvis fancied himself a trucker (if there weren't any Memphis boys in the movies, there were plenty on the road), pushing tons of machinery through the endless American night; just his version of the train whistle that called out to Johnny B. Goode and kept Richard Nixon awake as a boy. If it is more than a little odd that what to Elvis served as a symbol of escape and mastery now works—as part of his legend—as a symbol of everything grimy and poor he left behind when he did escape, maybe that only tells us how much his success shuffled the facts of his life, or how much he raised the stakes.

You don't make it in America—Emerson's mousetrap to the contrary—waiting for someone to come along and sign you up. You might be sitting on the corner like a Philly rock 'n' roller and get snatched up for your good looks, but you'll be back a year later and you'll never know what happened. Worst of all, you may not even care. What links the greatest rock 'n' roll careers is a volcanic ambition, a lust for more than anyone has a right to expect; in some cases, a refusal to know when to quit or even rest. It is that bit of Ahab burning beneath the Huck Finn rags of "Freewheelin'" Bob Dylan, the arrogance of a country boy like Elvis sailing into Hollywood, ready for whatever kind of success America had to offer.

So if we treat Elvis's words with as much respect as we can muster—which is how he meant them to be taken—we can see the first point at which his story begins to be his own. He took his dreams far more seriously than most ever dare, and he had the nerve to chase them down.

Cash's wonderful line—"a cosmic conspiracy against reality in favor of romance"—now might have more resonance. Still, if the kind of spirit that romance could produce seems ephemeral within the context of daily life, you would not expect the music it produced to last very long either. Not even Elvis, as a successful young rocker, could have expected his new music to last; he told interviewers rock 'n' roll was here to stay, but he was taking out plenty of insurance, making movies and singing schmaltz. You couldn't blame him; anyway, he liked schmaltz.

Within the realm of country music, the new spirit dried up just like Saturday fades into Monday, but since rock 'n' roll found its own audience and created its own world, that hardly mattered. Rock 'n' roll caught that romantic conspiracy on records and gave it a form. Instead of a possibility with a music, it became the essence; it became, of all things, a tradition. And when that form itself had to deal with reality—which is to say, when its young audience began to grow up—when the compromise between fantasy and reality that fills most of this book was necessary to preserve the possibility of fantasy, the fantasy had become part of the reality that had to be dealt with; the rules of the game had changed a bit, and it was a better game. "Blue Suede Shoes" had grown directly into something as serious and complex, and yet still offhand, still take-it-or-leave-it-and-pass-the-wine, as the Rolling Stones' "You Can't Always Get What You Want," which asks the musical question, "Why *are you* stepping on my blue suede shoes?"

Echoing through all of rock 'n' roll is the simple demand for peace of mind and a good time. While the demand is easy to make, nothing is more complex than to try to make it real and live it out. It all sounds simple, obvious; but that one young man like Elvis could break through a world as hard as Hank Williams', and invent a new one to replace it, seems obvious only because we have inherited Elvis's world, and live in it.

Satisfaction is not all there is to it, but it is where it all begins. Finally, the music must provoke as well as delight, disturb as well as comfort, create as well as sustain. If it doesn't, it lies, and there is only so much comfort you can take in a lie before it all falls apart.

The central facts of life in Elvis's South pulled as strongly against the impulses of hedonism and romance as the facts of our own lives do against the fast pleasures of rock 'n' roll. When the poor white was thrown back on himself, as he was in the daytime, when he worked his plot or looked for a job in the city, or at night, when he brooded and Hank Williams' whippoorwill told the truth all too plainly, those facts stood out clearly: powerlessness and vulnerability on all fronts. The humiliation of a class system that gave him his identity and then trivialized it; a community that for all its tradition and warmth was in some indefinable way not enough; economic chaos; the violence of the weather; bad food and maybe not enough of that; diseases that attached themselves to the body like new organs—they all mastered him. And that vulnerability produced—along with that urge to cut loose, along with that lively Southern romance—uncertainty, fatalism, resentment, acceptance, and nostalgia: limits that cut deep as the oldest cotton patch in Dixie.

Vernon Presley was a failed Mississippi sharecropper who moved his family out of the country with the idea of making a go in the city; it's not so far from Tupelo to Memphis, but in some ways, the journey must have been a long one—scores of country songs about boys and girls who lost their souls to the big town attest to that. Listen to Dolly Parton's downtown hooker yearning for her Blue Ridge mountain boy; listen to the loss of an America you may never have known.

They don't make country music better than that anymore, but it's unsatisfying, finally; too classical. This country myth is just one more echo of Jefferson pronouncing that, in America, virtue must be found in the land. I like myths, but this one is too facile, either for the people who still live on the land or for those of us who are merely looking for a way out of our own world, for an Annie Green Springs utopia. The myth is unsatisfying because the truth is richer than the myth.

"King Harvest (Has Surely Come)," the Band's song of blasted country hopes, gives us the South in all of its earthly delight and then snuffs it out. All at once, the song catches the grace and the limbo of the life that must be left behind.

The tune evokes a man's intimacy with the land and the refusal of the land to respond in kind. The music makes real, for the coolest city listener, a sense of place that is not quite a sense of being at home; the land is too full of violence for that. One hears the farmer's fear of separating from the land (and from his own history, which adhering to the land, is not wholly his own); one hears the cold economic necessities that have forced him out. The melody—too beautiful and out of reach for any words I have—spins the chorus into the pastoral with a feel for nature that is *really* hedo-

nistic, and a desperate, ominous rhythm slams the verses back to the slum streets that harbor the refugees of the pastoral disaster: "Just don't judge me by my shoes!" Garth Hudson's organ traces the circle of the song, over and over again.

The earliest picture of Elvis shows a farmer, his wife, and their baby; the faces of the parents are vacant, they are set, as if they cannot afford an unearned smile. Somehow, their faces say, they will be made to pay even for that.

You don't hear this in Elvis's music; but what he left out of his story is as vital to an understanding of his art as what he kept, and made over. If we have no idea of what he left behind, how much he escaped, we will have no idea what his success was worth, or how intensely he must have wanted it.

Elvis was thirteen when the family left Tupelo for Memphis in 1948, a pampered only child; ordinary in all respects, they say, except that he liked to sing. True to Chuck Berry's legend of the Southern rocker, Elvis's mother bought him his first guitar, and for the same reason Johnny B. Goode's mama had in mind: keep the boy out of trouble. Elvis sang tearful country ballads, spirituals, community music. On the radio, he listened with his family to the old music of the Carter Family and Jimmie Rodgers, to current stars like Roy Acuff, Ernest Tubb, Bob Wills, Hank Williams, and to white gospel groups like the Blackwood Brothers. Elvis touched the soft center of American music when he heard and imitated Dean Martin and the operatics of Mario Lanza; he picked up Mississippi blues singers like Big Bill Broonzy, Big Boy Crudup, Lonnie Johnson, and the new Memphis music of Rufus Thomas and Johnny Ace, mostly when no one else was around, because that music was naturally frowned upon. His parents called it "sinful music," and they had a point—it was dirty, and there were plenty of blacks who would have agreed with Mr. and Mrs. Presley—but Elvis was really too young to worry. In this he was no different from hundreds of other white country kids who wanted more excitement in their lives than they could get from twangs and laments—wanted a beat, sex, celebration, the stunning nuances of the blues and the roar of horns and electric guitars. Still, Elvis's interest was far more casual than that of Jerry Lee Lewis, a bad boy who was sneaking off to black dives in his spare time, or Carl Perkins, a musician who was consciously working out a synthesis of blues and country.

The Presleys stumbled onto welfare, into public housing. Vernon Presley found a job. It almost led to the family's eviction, because if they still didn't have enough to live on, they were judged to have too much to burden the county with their troubles. Elvis was a loner, but he had an eye for flash. He sold his blood for money, ushered at the movies, drove his famous truck, and divided the proceeds between his mother and his outrageous wardrobe. Looking for space, for a way to set himself apart.

Like many parents with no earthly future, the Presleys, especially Gladys Presley, lived for their son. Her ambition must have been that Elvis would take all that was good in the family and free himself from the life she and her husband endured: she was, Memphian Stanley Booth wrote a few years ago, "the one, perhaps the only one, who had told him throughout his life that even though he came from poor country people, he was just as good as anybody."

On Sundays (Wednesdays too, sometimes) the Presleys went to their Assembly of God to hear the Pentecostal ministers hand down a similar message: the last shall be first. This was democratic religion with a vengeance, lower class and gritty. For all those who have traced Elvis's music and his hipshake to his religion (accurately enough—Elvis was the first to say so), it has escaped his chroniclers that hillbilly Calvinism was also at the root of his self-respect and his pride: the anchor of his ambition.

■ ■ *One of the sources of Elvis Presley's "rockabilly" rhythms, with their energy, tension, and power, was the intensity of the music of the Assembly of God, a Pentacostal church of Elvis's childhood.*

His church (and the dozens of other Pentecostal sects scattered throughout the South and small-town America) was one part of what was left of the old American religion after the Great Awakening. Calvinism had been a religion of authority in the beginning; in the middle-class North, filtered through the popular culture of Ben Franklin, it became a system of tight money, tight-mindedness, and gentility; in the hillbilly South, powered by traveling preachers and their endless revivals, the old holiness cult produced a faith of grace, apocalypse, and emotion, where people heaved their deepest feelings into a circle and danced around them. Momentum scattered that old authority; all were sinners, all were saints. Self-consciously outcast, the true faith in a land of Philistines and Pharisees, it was shoved into storefronts and tents and even open fields, and no less sure of itself for that.

Church music caught moments of unearthly peace and desire, and the strength of the religion was in its intensity. The preacher rolled fire down the pulpit and chased it into the aisle, signifying; men and women rocked in their seats, sometimes onto the floor, bloodying their fingernails scratching and clawing in a lust for absolute sanctification. No battle against oppression, this was a leap right through it, with tongues babbling toward real visions, negating stale red earth, warped privies, men and women staring from their sway-backed porches into nothingness. It was a faith meant to transcend the grimy world that called it up. Like Saturday night, the impulse to dream, the need to escape, the romance and the contradictions of the land, this was a source of energy, tension, and power.

Elvis inherited these tensions, but more than that, gave them his own shape. It is often said that if Elvis had not come along to set off the changes in American music and American life that followed his triumph, someone very much like him would have done the job as well. But there is no reason to think this is true, either in strictly musical terms, or in any broader cultural sense. It is vital to remember that Elvis was the first young Southern white to sing rock 'n' roll, something he copied from no one but made up on the spot; and to know that even though other singers would have come up with a white version of the new black music acceptable to teenage America, of all that did emerge in Elvis's wake, none sang as powerfully, or with more than a touch of his magic.

Even more important is the fact that no singer emerged with anything like Elvis's combination of great talent and conscious ambition, and there is no way a new American hero could have gotten out of the South and to the top—creating a whole new sense of how big the top was, as Elvis did—without that combination. The others—Perkins, Lewis, Charlie Rich—were bewildered by even a taste of fame and unable to handle a success much more limited than Presley's.

If Elvis had the imagination to come up with the dreams that kept him going, he had the music to bring them back to life and make them real to huge numbers of other people. It was the genius of his singing, an ease and an intensity that has no parallel in American music, that along with his dreams separated him from his setting.

■ ■ ■

STUDY QUESTIONS

1. What role did country music traditionally play in Southern culture?

2. How did the southern singers help to define the boundaries and limits of community life?

3. In what way was Hank Williams a "poet of limits, fears, and failure"? How was he similar to or different from Elvis Presley?

4. What factors explain the success of rock 'n' roll?

5. How did Elvis Presley change the course of American, and particularly southern, music?

6. How was Elvis Presley different from the other southern rock 'n' roll singers of his day?

BIBLIOGRAPHY

The above selection is from Greil Marcus's insightful *Mystery Train* (1975). Throughout the volume, Marcus demonstrates and traces the relationships of rock 'n' roll, blues music, and American culture. There are several readable histories of rock 'n' roll. Among the best are such popular studies as Carl Belz, *The Story of Rock* (1972); Nik Cohn, *Rock from the Beginning* (1969); John Gabree, *The World of Rock* (1968); Ralph Gleason, *The Jefferson Airplane and the San Francisco Sound* (1969); Jerry Hopkins, *The Rock Story* (1970); and Arnold Shaw, *The Rock Revolution* (1970). Charlie Gillett, *The Sound of the City* (1970), is more scholarly and contains a wealth of information about early rock music and the industry of music. Pete Guralnick, *Feel Like Going Home* (1971), is outstanding on the southern origins of rock 'n' roll. The best biography of Elvis Presley is Jerry Hopkins, *Elvis* (1971). Bill Malone, *Country Music U.S.A.* (1968), surveys the world that produced Elvis.

PERFECT BODIES, ETERNAL YOUTH: THE OBSESSION OF MODERN AMERICA

Randy Roberts and James S. Olson

The message comes at Americans from every direction, every hour of the day. Cher appears on television touting the miraculous benefits of the President's First Lady exercise salons. Lynn Redgrave comes on a few minutes later delivering superlatives about Weight Watchers' frozen entree foods. Jane Fonda's exercise videotapes confront shoppers in supermarkets and video stores. Victoria Principal and Raquel Welch write diet and fitness books, both of which become best sellers. Plastic surgeons advertise in newspapers and on television, urging Americans to get rid of what they hate or acquire what they want for their bodies. Every issue of *Family Circle, Woman's Day*, and *The Enquirer* contains some new article about the latest weight-loss panacea.

Sports programming dominates television, as if Americans have an insatiable need to watch football, baseball, basketball, bowling, bodybuilding, and a host of other competitions. Future linguists and anthropologists will study what have become the highlights of contemporary American popular culture—diet sodas, low-calorie beers, Lean Cuisine, sugarless gum, half-the-calories bread, Nautilus, jogging, Iron Man marathons, "fun runs," tennis, bicycling, 10K races, Superbowls, play-offs, World Series, Grand Slams of golf and tennis, Little League, Pop Warner football, and championship after championship.

Modern America is not the first society to indulge in the emptiness of narcissism, but no other society has ever had such resources to spend on a fruitless crusade to prevent aging and deny death. In "Perfect Bodies, Eternal Youth: The Obsession of Modern America," Randy Roberts and James S. Olson examine the preoccupation with health, fitness, and youth in the United States, explaining how and why the members of an entire culture have become infatuated with their own bodies.

Fewer and fewer people these days argue that running shortens lives, while a lot of people say that it may strengthen them. If that's all we've got for the time being, it seems a good enough argument for running. Not airtight, but good enough.

—JIM FIXX

It was a perfect July day in Vermont—clear and cool. Jim Fixx, on the eve of a long-awaited vacation, put on his running togs and headed down a rural road for his daily run, expecting to do the usual twelve to fifteen miles. At fifty-two years of age, Fixx was a millionaire, the best-selling author of *The Complete Book of Running*, and the reigning guru of the American exercise cult. In 1968 he had weighed 214 pounds, smoked two packs of cigarettes a day, and worried about his family health history. Fixx's father had died of a heart attack at the age of forty-three. So Fixx started running and stopped smoking. He lost 60 pounds and introduced America to the virtues of strenuous exercise: longevity, freedom from depression, energy, and the "runner's high." He regularly ran 80 miles a week. When he hit the road on July 21, 1984, Fixx weighed 154 pounds and seemed the perfect image of fitness. Twenty minutes into the run he had a massive heart attack and died on the side of the road. A motorcyclist found his body later that afternoon.

Fixx's death shocked middle- and upper-class America. Of all people, how could Jim Fixx have died of a heart attack? Millions of joggers, runners, swimmers, cyclists, tri-athletes, walkers, weightlifters, and aerobic dancers had convinced themselves that exercise preserved youth and postponed death. It was the yuppie panacea; "working out" made them immune to the ravages of time.

From Randy Roberts and James S. Olson, *Winning Is the Only Thing*. The Johns Hopkins University Press, Baltimore/London, 1989, pp. 213–34. Reprinted by permission.

The autopsy on Fixx was even more disturbing. In spite of all the running, his circulatory system was a shambles. Fixx's cholesterol levels had been dangerously high. One coronary artery was 98 percent blocked, a second one 85 percent blocked, and a third one 50 percent blocked. In the previous two to eight weeks, the wall of his left ventricle had badly deteriorated. On that clear Vermont day, Jim Fixx shouldn't have been running; he should have been undergoing triple-bypass surgery.

Even more puzzling, Fixx had been complaining for months of chest pains while running—clear signs of a deadly angina, the heart muscle protesting lack of oxygen. Friends had expressed concern and urged him to get a check-up. He resisted, attempting to will good health. In January 1984 he had agreed to a treadmill test, but he skipped the appointment that afternoon, running 16 miles instead. Why had someone so committed to health ignored such obvious warnings? How had sports, exercise, and fitness become such obsessions in the United States?

Modern society was the culprit. In an increasingly secular society, church membership no longer provided the discipline to bind people together into cohesive social groups. Well-integrated neighborhoods with long histories and strong identities had given way after World War II to faceless suburbs. Corporate and professional elites tended to be highly mobile, relocating whenever a pay raise was offered. The new American community had become fifty suburban homes and a 7-11 convenience store. New organizations, especially business and government bureaucracies, had assumed power in the United States, but those were hardly places where most Americans could feel comfortable and in control. Blessed with money but deprived of community in the 1970s and 1980s, Americans began to use sports to rebuild their sense of community and fitness and to define individual happiness and individual pleasure, creating a culture of competitive narcissism supported by a host of therapeutic panaceas, such as EST, psychotherapy, Scientology, and strenuous exercise.

For individuals, families, groups, and communities, sports had become a new cultural currency, a common ground upon which a diverse people could express their values and needs. Unlike European society, where such traditional institutions as the church, the aristocracy, and the monarchy had maintained order through established authority, America had been settled by lower-class working people and small farmers. The traditional institutions anchoring European society were absent. Without those same moorings, America had always confronted the centrifugal forces of individualism, capitalism, Protestantism, and ethnicity, using the culture of opportunity to stave off social disintegration. Social mobility, the westward movement, the abundance of land, and ruralism helped stablilize a highly complex society.

But in the twentieth century, when industrialization, urbanization, and the disappearance of the frontier changed the definitions of opportunity and progress, the values of individualism, community, and competition had to find new modes of expression, and sports became a prominent one. At the local, regional, and national levels, sports evolved into one of the most powerful expressions of identity. Outside observers marveled, for example, at the "religion" of high school football in the more than eleven hundred independent school districts of Texas. When viewed simply as sport, of course, the obsession with football seems absurd, but when viewed in terms of community identity, it becomes more understandable. In hundreds of rural areas, where scattered farms surround tiny county seats, the local high school, with its arbitrarily drawn district lines, was the central focus of community life. Rural Texans passionately opposed school district consolidations, even when it made good economic sense, because it threatened the high school, high school football, and community identity. For hundreds of small

Texas towns—and rural areas throughout much of the rest of the country—high school athletics was literally the cement of community life.

It wasn't just high school sports which provided new identities in the United States. After World War II, social and economic pressures worked against the nuclear family. More and more women were working outside the home; more and more men were working at job sites long commutes from the suburbs; and divorce rates were way up. Childhood play became less spontaneous and more organized as schools, government, and communities assumed roles once played by the family. The most obvious consequence was the appearance of organized youth sports. Little League grew by leaps and bounds beginning in the 1950s; child's play, once the domain of the home and immediate neighborhood, became a spectator sport complete with uniforms, umpires, scoreboards, leagues, play-offs, drafts, and championships. By the 1980s, Little League was competing for time with Pop Warner football, Little Dribblers basketball, soccer, and swimming, with organized competition beginning in some sports at the age of three. In 1987 sports sociologists estimated that thirty million children under sixteen years of age were competing in organized sports.

Sports functioned as identity on the regional level as well. In an age when television, movies, and mass culture threatened regional distinctiveness, sports emerged as the single most powerful symbol of localism and community loyalty. That was obviously true of high school and college sports, but even in professional sports, when ownership shifted away from local businesses and entrepreneurs to conglomerates and national corporations, the regional identity of teams remained critically important to gate receipts and television revenues. The rivalries between the Chicago Bears and the Green Bay Packers, or the Boston Red Sox and the New York Yankees, or the Boston Celtics and the Los Angeles Lakers, filled stadiums, arenas, and living rooms with fans desperate for the home team to win. Five hundred years ago, European cities dedicated all their surplus capital over the course of 100 to 200 years to build elaborate cathedrals to God. In the United States during the 1970s and 1980s, the modern equivalent of the medieval cathedral was the domed stadium. For sports, not for God, American communities would sell bonds and mortgage themselves for the next generation.

Even on the national level, sports competition reflected and promoted American nationalism. Sports was a mirror of federalism, at once local in its community loyalties but national in its collective forms. The 1984 Olympic Games in Los Angeles did not just expose a rising tide of patriotism and national pride; they became a major force in stimulating a new American nationalism. Unlike the recent Olympic Games in Montreal, Moscow, and Seoul, the Los Angeles Games did not accumulate billion-dollar deficits and require the resources of national governments to prop them up. In 1984, "free enterprise capitalism" organized and conducted the Games, used existing facilities, and turned a profit. The Los Angeles Coliseum was filled with flag-waving Americans cheering every native athlete winning a medal. On television back home, Europeans watched the proceedings with astonishment and not a little fear, worrying about the burst of American patriotism, nationalism, and even chauvinism. Nearly a decade after the debacle in Vietnam, American pride and optimism were on the rebound, and the 1984 Olympic Games was center stage for the resurrection of the American sense of mission.

Modern sports in the United States also provided a sense of identity cutting across class, racial, and ethnic lines. In penitentiaries throughout the country, intense struggles were waged every evening over television and radio programming, black convicts wanting to watch soul stations and black sit-coms and whites demanding MTV or white sit-coms. But there was no trouble or debate on Sunday afternoon or Monday nights during the fall. It was football, only football, and blacks and whites watched the programs with equal enthusiasm. On Monday evenings in the fall, whether in the poorest ghetto tenement of the South Side of Chicago or the most tastefully appointed living room in the Lake Forest suburbs, televisions were tuned in to football, and discussions at work the next morning revolved around the game, who won and who lost, and why.

For ethnic minorities and immigrants, sports similarly became a way of identifying with the new society, a powerful form of acculturation. During the 1980s, for example, Los Angeles became the second largest Mexican city in the world, behind only Mexico City in Spanish-speaking population and larger now than Guadalajara in terms of Mexican residents. At Dodger Stadium in Los Angeles, Mexicans and Mexican Americans became an increasingly large part of the evening box office, helping to sustain Dodger attendance at its three million-plus levels each year. In September 1986, when Dodger pitcher Fernando Valenzuela won his twentieth game of the season, the Spanish cable network SIN broke into its regular programming nationwide for live interviews. The fact that sports was making its way to the headlines and front pages of major newspapers was no accident in the United States. It had become, indeed, a new cultural currency in modern America, a way to interpret change and express traditional values.

Women, too, used sports as a vehicle in their drive for equality and identity. The development of women's and men's sports in America has varied considerably. From the first, men's sports have emphasized fierce competition and the ruthless pursuit of expertise. Early male and female physical educators, however, believed women were uncompetitive and decided that women's sports should promote a woman's physical and mental qualities and thus make her more attractive to men. They also believed that sports and exercise should sublimate female sexual drives. As renowned nineteenth-century physical educator Dudley A. Sargent noted, "No one seems to realize that there is a time in the life of a girl when it is better for her and for the community to be something of a boy rather than too much of a girl."

But tomboyish behavior had to stop short of abrasive competition. Lucille Eaton Hill, director of physical training at Wellesley College, urged women to "avoid the evils which are so apparent . . . in the conduct of athletics for men." She and her fellow female physical educators encouraged widespread participation rather than narrow specialization. In short, women left spectator and professional sports to men. Indeed, not until 1924 were women allowed to compete in Olympic track and field events, and even then on a limited basis.

During the 1920s the tennis careers of Suzanne Langlen and Helen Wills were used to demonstrate the proper and improper pursuit of victory by athletic women. Tennis, for the great French champion Langlen, was not only a way of life: it was life. Her only object on a tennis court was to win, and between 1919 and 1926, when she turned professional, Langlen lost only two sets of singles and won 269 of 270 matches. But at what cost? Bulimic in her eating habits and subject to dramatic swings in emotions, she suffered several nervous breakdowns and lived in fear of losing. In addition, male critics noted that, far from keeping her looking young, tennis cruelly aged Langlen. Journalist Al Laney remarked that by the mid-1920s Langlen looked thirty years older than she actually was and that her complexion had turned dull and colorless. Her friend Ted Tinling agreed that before she turned twenty-five, "her face and expression had already the traces of deep emotional experiences far beyond the normal for her age."

In contrast, Helen Wills was a champion of great physical beauty. Before Wills, Americans tended to agree with journalist Paul Gallico that "pretty girls" did not excel in sports and that outstanding female athletes were simply compensating for their lack of beauty. Summarizing this school of thought, Larry Engelmann observed: "Athletics was their way of getting attention. If Suzanne Langlen were really beautiful, for instance, she wouldn't be running around like crazy on the tennis courts of Europe. She would have been quietly at home, happily married. Athletics proved a refuge and a last chance for the desperate female ugly duckling."

Yet Wills was beautiful, and she was great, winning every set of singles competition she played between 1927 and 1933. Journalists explained Wills' success and beauty by stressing the fact that tennis was only a game for her, not a way of life and certainly not life itself. Losses did not worry her. She always appeared composed. "My father, a doctor," she explained, "always told me not to wince or screw up my face while I was playing. He said it would put lines on my face." And no victory was worth a line.

Women were not fully emancipated from the older ideal until the 1970s, when they asserted their right to be as ruthless and competitive in athletics as men. Tennis champion Billy Jean King symbolized on the court as well as off this new attitude. Like Langlen, she single-mindedly pursued victory. And she was no more concerned with sweating and grimacing than Pete Rose. Unlike Wills, King was not interested in art or starting a family. When asked why she was not at home, she replied, "Why don't you ask Rod Laver why he isn't at home?" It was as eloquent a statement of athletic liberation as could be asked for.

To develop fully as an athlete, King had to earn money. Along with Gladys Heldman and Philip Morris Tobacco Company, King helped to organize the Virginia Slims women's tennis circuit in 1971. That year she became the first female athlete to earn $100,000 in a single year. More importantly, she labored to get women players a bigger share of the prize money at the major championships. In the early 1970s women's purses at Wimbledon and the U.S.

Open were about 10 percent of the men's. By the mid-1980s the prize money split was equal. As if to punctuate the point that women's tennis had arrived, King defeated the former Wimbledon triple-crown champion (1939) Bobby Riggs 6–4, 6–3, 6–3, in a highly publicized match in the Houston Astrodome in 1973.

Even more important than King for the future of women's athletics was Title IX of the 1972 Educational Amendments Act. It outlawed sexual discrimination by school districts or colleges and universities which received federal aid. Certainly, athletic budgets in high schools and universities are not equally divided between male and female athletics. But women have made significant gains. Before Title IX less than 1 percent of athletic budgets went to women's sports. By the 1980s that figure had increased to over 10 percent. No longer is there a serious argument over the road women's sports should travel. Instead, the battle is over what portion of that pie they should receive.

But it wasn't just countries, cities, colleges, small towns, high schools, and ethnic groups which turned to sports in the 1980s as the most powerful way of defining their values. The most extraordinary development in contemporary popular culture was the extent to which individuals turned to athletics, exercise, and body image as a way of finding meaning in an increasingly dislocated society. In the mid-1980s, a Louis Harris poll indicated that 96 percent of all Americans found something about their bodies that they didn't like and would change if they could. Harris said that the "rampant obsessions of both men and women about their looks have produced an obvious boon for the cosmetics industry, plastic surgery, diet doctors, fitness and shape advisers, fat farms, and exercise clubs." The cult of fitness and the cult of individual happiness went hand in hand. Politicians used international sports at the Olympic level to confirm the superiority of various political systems or prove the equality

of their Third World cultures; they mustered professional sports to project the quality of life in major American cities; collegiate sports touted the virtues of different universities; and in the 1970s and 1980s, millions of Americans embraced the cult of fitness to discover the meaning of life, retreating into the fantasy that they are how they look.

The cult of fitness and preoccupation with physical appearance first emerged in the United States during the John Kennedy administration. In the election of 1960, Kennedy used television as it had never been used before when he challenged Richard Nixon to a series of debates. Kennedy faced formidable odds. Young, handsome, and wealthy, he was considered perhaps too young, too handsome, and too wealthy to make an effective president. His Roman Catholicism seemed another albatross. Behind the polls, Kennedy needed a boost. The televised debates were perfect.

Nixon arrived in Chicago for the first debate looking tired and ill. He had injured his knee six weeks before, and a hospital stay had weakened him. On the eve of the debate a chest cold left him hoarse. He looked like a nervous corpse—pale, twenty pounds underweight, and haggard. Make-up experts suggested covering his heavy beard with a thick powder, but Nixon accepted only a thin coat of Max Factor's "Lazy Shave," a pancake cosmetic.

Kennedy looked better, much better. He arrived at Chicago from California with a suntan. He didn't need make-up to look healthy, nor did he need special lighting to hide a weak profile. He did, however, change suits. He believed that a dark blue rather than a gray suit would look better under the bright lights. Kennedy was right, of course, as anyone who watches a nightly news program must realize. Once the debate started, Kennedy intentionally slowed down his delivery and watered down his ideas. His face was controlled and cool. He smiled with his eyes and perhaps the corners of his mouth, and his laugh was a mere suggestion of a laugh. Although Nixon marshalled a mountain of facts and closely reasoned arguments, he looked bad. Instead of hearing a knowledgeable candidate, viewers saw a nervous, uncertain man, one whose clothes didn't fit and whose face looked pasty and white. In contrast, Kennedy *looked* good, scored a victory in the polls, and went on to win the election by a razor-thin margin.

The first president born in the twentieth century, Kennedy had claimed in his inaugural address that "the torch had been passed to a new generation of Americans . . . tempered by war, disciplined by a hard and bitter peace, proud of our ancient heritage." Life around the White House soon reflected the instincts of a new generation. It wasn't just little Caroline and later John-John frolicking on the White House lawn. The Kennedys were fiercely competitive and obsessed with sports. At the family compound at Hyannisport or Robert Kennedy's "Hickory Hill" home in Virginia, the days were filled with tennis, golf, sailing, isometric exercise, swimming, horseback riding, badminton, and a brutal form of touch football, which overweight and overaged visitors dreaded, since the Kennedys expected everyone to give it a try. An atmosphere of youthful virility surrounded the Kennedy administration. To impress the Kennedys, one associate remembered, you had to "show raw guts, fall on your face now and then. Smash into the house once in a while going after a pass. Laugh off twisted ankles or a big hole torn in your best suit."

The whole country became infatuated with the sense of vitality, and the fifty-mile hike became the symbol of fitness. Marine Corps commandant General David M. Shoup, whom Kennedy especially admired, accepted Kennedy's challenge to see if his marines could duplicate a feat of Theodore Roosevelt's 1908 marines—march fifty miles in less than twenty hours. Shoup met the challenge, as did Attorney General Robert Kennedy, who walked his fifty miles along the path of the C & O canal. Kennedy's secretaries took up the

challenge, and once the newspapers had picked up the story, tens of thousands of Americans tried it too. The spring of 1963 became the season of the fifty-mile hike.

These were also years of giddy infatuation with the Mercury astronauts, whose crew-cut fitness first came to public attention at their introductory press conference in 1959. All of them were military pilots, and John Glenn of Ohio emerged as their leader. Square-jawed with ramrod perfect posture, Glenn had a personality and value system to match. He was the ultimate "goody-goody," and America loved him. The country was also astounded at his daily fitness regimen—vigorous calisthenics followed by a two-mile jog along the beach. Two miles—every day! Even when it rained.

If John Glenn was the leading jogger of the 1960s, the scientific father of running was Kenneth Cooper, an Air Force physician. A high school track star in Oklahoma City, Cooper finished medical school and joined the Air Force as a physician at the School of Aerospace Medicine in San Antonio. He tested fitness levels in thousands of potential Air Force pilots and in the process developed new standards of conditioning. To really benefit from exercise, Americans had to get their heart rate above 130 beats a minute for a sustained period. Jogging, running, racquetball, squash, cycling, walking, and swimming were the best exercises.

To please an increasingly technical, postindustrial clientele whose faith in science was unrivaled, Cooper even charted fitness, providing a quantified methodology to guarantee fitness. An aerobically fit person had to "earn 30 points a week." He or she could do this by walking three miles in no more than forty-one minutes five times a week; by swimming 700 yards in fifteen minutes five times a week; or by running a mile in eight minutes only twice a week. To measure fitness, Cooper recommended the "twelve minutes test." If a person can run or walk less than a mile in twelve minutes, he or she is in "very poor shape"; 1 to 1.25

According to tradition, the marathon commemorates the messenger who, in 490 B.C., ran 20 miles to Athens with news of the Greek victory at Marathon. Running marathons has gained popularity in recent years: In 1986 some 20,000 runners entered New York City's marathon and 19,412 finished it.

miles is "poor"; 1.25 to 1.5 miles is "fair"; 1.5 to 1.75 miles is "good"; and more than 1.75 miles is "excellent." Cooper also warned people to watch out if their pulse rate exceeded 80 beats a minute. Fewer than 60 beats was "excellent." Vigorous exercise would reduce the heart rate. In Cooper's own words, "You might just save your heart some of those 20,000 to 30,000 extra beats you've forced on it every day."

The country was more than ready for Cooper's message. Early in the 1960s the first of the baby-boom generation hit college. The "don't trust anyone over thirty" culture had appeared, protesting war and inequality and proclaiming the virtues of brotherly love and sexual liberation. In 1961 half the American population was under thirty. By 1964 the median age had dropped to twenty-seven and in 1966 to twenty-five. America fell in love with

youth, health, sex, and pleasure. Hippies, protests, "love-ins," "teach-ins," Woodstock, drugs, rebellion, and loud, self-righteous rejections of materialism emanated from college campuses.

But in 1967 the first baby-boom class graduated from college. The transformation of hippies into "yuppies" was underway. By 1971 those 1946 babies were twenty-five years old. The cruel tricks of gravity and heredity commenced. Bellies started to thicken, hairlines to recede. Women with babies looked despairingly at abdominal stretch marks and the faint beginnings of "crow's feet." The youth culture still survived, but individual youth was proving to be a temporary state. Middle age loomed as large as death.

Dr. Kenneth Cooper had the answer. Late in 1968, he coined a new word and wrote a book by the same name—*Aerobics*. By 1972 the book had sold nearly three million copies to anxious yuppies bent on postponing the inevitable. By the early 1970s, Cooper had an estimated eight million Americans, including astronaut John Glenn, adding up their weekly points, counting their pulse, testing their speed, taking their blood pressure, and weighing their bodies.

Throughout the 1970s and 1980s the cult of fitness reached extraordinary dimensions in the United States. More than twenty million Americans regularly exercised, and along with the running boom came a boom in racquetball, tennis, swimming, cycling, weightlifting, and "aerobic" dancing. In 1970 only 125 people entered the first New York City marathon, which took runners over a 26-mile course through all four boroughs; but in the 1986 marathon, 20,000 officially entered the race, and 19,412 finished it. The race was so popular that organizers had to reject thousands of applicants. Marathons became common events on every weekend all across the country.

The triathlon endurance was an even better gauge of the fitness cult. Known as the ultimate of the "ultrasports," the triathlon combined a 2-mile swim with a 112-mile cycle ride and a 26-mile run. In 1986 more than one million Americans competed in triathlon events around the country. And in what can only be considered the absurd limit of the fitness craze, Stu Mittleman won the "Sri Chinmoy 1,000 Mile Marathon" in New York City in 1986. His time of just under fifteen days "was my best ever."

The cult of fitness was rivaled only by the obsession with youth and body image which swept through American culture in the 1970s and 1980s. To be sure, this was nothing new. Americans had long been preoccupied with their bodies, and attempts to stay young had centered on staying thin, as if slenderness were in itself a foundation of youth. In the 1860s Harriet Beecher Stowe had written: "We in America have got so far out of the way of a womanhood that has any vigor of outline or

opulence of physical proportion, that, when we see a woman made as a woman ought to be, she strikes us as a monster. Our willowy girls are afraid of nothing so much as growing stout."

To stay thin, nineteenth-century American women dieted and corseted their bodies. "It ain't stylish for young courting gals to let on like they have any appetite," admitted one female. And through tightlacing their corsets, women could maintain the proper girlish waistline of eighteen inches, with only such acceptable side effects as headaches, fainting spells, and uterine and spinal disorders.

If tightlacing and dieting led to serious health problems, illness was in itself admired. Consumptive women were romanticized and imbued with spiritual qualities. Little Eva in *Uncle Tom's Cabin*, Beth in *Little Women*, Mimi in *La Bohème*—all were thin, romantic consumptives who radiated spirituality and sensuality. Perhaps the ideal was the romantic ballerina—thin, ethereal, pale, pure, as certain to die young as poor broken-hearted Giselle.

Throughout the twentieth century, thinness has largely remained the feminine ideal, although sickliness generally declined as an attractive characteristic. The Gibson Girl of the turn of the century touted athletics, and during the 1920s the flapper exuded energy, vitality, and youth. And if the breast-bound flapper did not survive the 1929 stock market crash, an emphasis on thinness did. Indeed, only during the 1950s, when Marilyn Monroe was at her height was there a serious challenge to the slender ideal.

Post–World War II culture has enshrined both thinness and youth for men as well as women. Advertisers have aided the process. Since photographers maintain that clothes look best on lean bodies, leading fashion models have always been thin and generally young. But since the 1960s, advertisers have used youth and thinness to sell other products as well. The evolution of Pepsi-Cola slogans illustrates this point:

1935: "Twice as Much."

1948: "Be Sociable—Have a Pepsi."

1960: "Now it's Pepsi for those who think young."

1965: "The Pepsi Generation."

1984: "Pepsi: The Choice of a New Generation."

Appeals to abundance ("twice as much") and social interaction ("be sociable") were replaced by the promise of eternal youth. As if to reinforce this appeal, Pepsi paid magnificent amounts to two thin, youthful Michaels as spokesmen: Michael Jackson and Michael J. Fox. Far from being sociable, Jackson is a virtual recluse, obsessed with personality change through plastic surgery. And Fox, as sure as Peter Pan, is the perpetual adolescent.

To fit the culture's procrustean mold, advertisers encourage Americans to binge and purge, consume and diet. Consume because "you are someone special" and "you can have it all." Diet because "you can never be too thin or too rich." In his perceptive book *Never Satisfied*, Hillel Schwartz argues that "dieting is an essentially nostalgic act, an attempt to return to a time when one *could* be satisfied, when one *was* thinner, when the range of choices in the world neither bewildered nor intimidated. To restrict one's range of choices, as all dieters must do, is not so much deficient as it is regressive. . . . Imagining a miraculous future, the dieter is always looking back."

In a secular, materialistic age, dieting has become an ascetic religion. Seventeenth-century poet and preacher John Donne wrote, "The flesh that God hath given us is affliction enough, but the flesh that the devil gives us, is affliction upon affliction and to that, there belongs a woe." To be fat in America has become a religious as well as a secular sin. Christian diet books emphasize John 3:30 "He must increase, but I must decrease."

In 1957 Charlie Shedd in his *Pray Your Weight Away* confessed, "We fatties are the only people on earth who can weigh our sin."

His book inspired some Christians to lose weight and others to write diet books. Such works as Deborah Price's *I Prayed Myself Thin*, John Cavanaugh's *More of Jesus and Less of Me*, Reverend H. Victor Kane's *Devotion for Dieters*, and Francis Hunter's *God's Answer to Fat—Lose It!* emphasized that godliness is in league with thinness. Capturing the temper of her times, columnist Ellen Goodman wrote in 1975 that "eating has become the last bona fide sin left in America." And on this point, religion and secular humanism are in complete accord.

The fitness boom and body-image obsession financed a huge growth industry. To support their new interest in fitness, Americans needed equipment and clothes—shoes, shorts, shirts, racquets, bicycles, balls, paddles, bats, cleats, gloves, goggles, weights, scales, blood-pressure cuffs, timing watches, clubs, socks, headbands, wristbands, and leotards. Between 1975 and 1987 sporting goods sales in the United States increased from $8.9 billion to $27.5 billion. Americans spent $4 billion on athletic shoes alone in 1987. Health clubs, once the domain of the wealthy and a small clique of bodybuilders, multiplied in number from 350 in 1968 to more than 7,000 in 1986. Gross revenues in 1987 exceeded $650 million.

Exercise and fitness revenues were matched by those of the weight loss industry. Jean Nidetch founded Weight Watchers in 1962 and eventually franchised it, making sure that group leaders had been through the diet program and reached "maintenance" levels. Attendance doubled between 1983 and 1987, the gross revenues went past $200 million that year. Sybil Ferguson's Diet Center, Inc., founded in 1969, had two thousand franchises in 1987 and nearly $50 million in gross revenues. Americans spent $6 billion for diet soda in 1986, $5 billion for vitamins and health foods, and $350 million for diet capsules and liquid protein. The President's Council on Physical Fitness estimated that 65 million Americans were dieting in 1987. Diet Coke, Diet Pepsi, Diet Dr. Pepper, Lean Cuisine, Bud Light,

Miller Lite, lite bread, sugarless gum, NutraSweet, Cambridge, and a host of other diet products entered American popular culture.

What dieting and exercise couldn't fix, plastic surgery could. Americans went on a plastic surgery binge in the 1980s—not to repair real damage to their bodies or birth defects, but to improve their appearance cosmetically and recapture the illusion of youth. In 1987 more than 500,000 Americans underwent cosmetic plastic surgery. The most popular procedures were abdominoplasty (tummy tucks), breast augmentation, liposuction (fat removal), blepharoplasty (eyes), and rhinoplasty (nose). Plastic surgeons were also beginning to perform "total body contour" procedures. To postpone middle age, yuppies made plastic surgery a $3 billion industry.

Americans also changed a number of their habits in the 1970s and 1980s. Cigarette consumption began to decline in 1982. In 1965, 52 percent of men and 34 percent of women smoked. By 1985 only 33 percent of men and 28 percent of women smoked, and at the end of 1987 the American Cancer Society estimated that only 27 percent of Americans were still smoking. Per capita whiskey consumption dropped nearly 20 percent between 1976 and 1986 as Americans turned to lower-alcohol-content beer and wine coolers. Beef and pork consumption dropped in favor of chicken and fish when cholesterol-conscious Americans turned away from "red meat." Caffeine was also suspect. Americans under twenty-five drank only a third of the coffee their parents did; sales of decaffeinated coffee and drinks like Pepsi Free and Pepper Free symbolized the new health consciousness.

The results were impressive, even though some of the gains had to be attributed to better drug therapy, the rise of heart bypass surgery, and improvement of cardiac care units in American hospitals. But the bottom line was that between 1950 and 1985, the death rate per 100,000 people from cardiovascular and cerebrovascular disease declined from 511 to 418, a dramatic improvement. The cult of fitness seemed to be paying dividends.

But there was an underside to the cult of fitness, an obsessive perfectionism which was the antithesis of good health. Jim Fixx and his daily runs in spite of chest pains were one example. Kathy Love Ormsby was another. The North Carolina State University junior, who held the U.S. collegiate women's record for 10,000 meters, had difficulty dealing with failure. In the 1986 NCAA championships, after 6,400 meters, she was struggling along in fourth place, running a bad race. Then, as she approached a turn, she decided to keep going straight. She ducked under a railing and ran straight past Wisconsin team coach Peter Tegen. "It was eerie," he said. "Her eyes were focused straight ahead." She kept going—out of Indiana University's track stadium in Indianapolis, across a softball diamond, over a seven-foot fence, down New York Street, toward the bridge that spans the White River. Seventy-five feet onto the bridge she stopped, climbed over the railing, and jumped. After falling thirty-five feet, she landed on the soggy ground close to the river. She broke a rib, collapsed a lung, and fractured a vertebrae. The doctor who attended her said that she would be permanently paralyzed from the waist down: "Given the distance that she fell, she's very lucky she's not a quadriplegic," Dr. Peter Hall noted. "She could have easily died."

Why? Ormsby was a high school valedictorian, a straight-A student, the record holder for the 800, 1,600, and 3,200 meters. At North Carolina State she was a track star and promising premed student. She was raised in a strong Christian family and was deeply religious herself. After her record-breaking 10,000-meter run, she told a reporter: "I just have to learn to do my best for myself and for God and to turn everything over to Him." Her leap had turned everything over to Him.

Some observers blamed Ormsby's consuming pursuit of perfection. Others blamed the pressure of world-class sport competition. Her father commented, "I believe . . . that it had something to do with the pressure that is put on young people to succeed." Certainly society's emphasis on the importance of sports places tremendous strains on young athletes. Often isolated from the world outside gyms and tracks and stadiums, they begin to think that their world has real, lasting meaning. Failure, then, becomes equated with death itself.

Such obsessive perfectionism also affected millions of other people, only a tiny fraction of whom were competitive athletes. For many people, exercise and weight loss became forms of psychological discipline, proof that the individual was in charge of his or her life. A 1986 Gallup Poll estimated that three million Americans, most of them women, suffered from eating disorders—anorexia nervosa and bulimia. In anorexia nervosa, victims virtually starve themselves to death, using laxatives, exercise, and absurdly low calorie intake to lose body weight. Most psychologists attribute the eating disorder to a sense of powerlessness in the victim. They strive for a sense of weightlessness, and in that weightlessness they find a sense of control missing from other areas of their lives. In 1984 the soft-rock vocalist Karen Carpenter brought the disease to national attention when she died of a heart attack induced by extreme weight loss. Even when their weight drops below 85 pounds and they resemble concentration-camp victims, anorectics still look in the mirror and see themselves as fat, with round faces and flabby skin. Breasts disappear, menstruation stops, and their bodies return momentarily, just before death, to preadolescence.

Bulimia is a related disorder. The Gallup Poll concluded that nearly 10 percent of all American women between the ages of sixteen and twenty-five practice bulimia, an eating disorder characterized by huge calorie intake followed by self-induced vomiting. The Food and Drug Administration said that bulimia may

last up to eight hours, with an intake of 20,000 calories (an equivalent of 210 brownies, or 6 layer cakes, or 35 "Big Macs"), involve 25 to 30 vomiting episodes, and cost up to $75 a day for food purchases. If untreated, the disease causes irregular heartbeats, cramps, fatigue, and seizures by destroying the body's electrolyte balance. The gastric acid from vomiting will also erode teeth away.

In a country which historically has been keenly competitive and has periodically affirmed a belief in perfectionism, the idea of a better life through sports has been carried to obsessive lengths. Often the object of physical fitness has not been to produce health and well-being but to test or even to escape the limits of one's body. Ultra-distance runner Stu Mittleman, one of the leaders in his field during the 1980s, was the epitome of this tendency. For him a 26-mile marathon was unsatisfactory, a flat, almost meaningless endeavor. The 100-mile event was better, and in the early 1980s he established the American record with a 12:56:34 run. Better still was the six-day event, in which his 488 miles was also an American record.

In ultra-distance running Mittleman saw man rediscovering his lost past. "Our culture forces us to eliminate sensory input so that we can cope," he observed. "Sports re-sensitizes. I want to live life intensely. . . . Long slow running has a heritage in hunting and gathering. Sprinting is based on retreat, on flight." Life, then, is best experienced at the limits of endurance, well past what is good for one's health. Yet, sometimes even that does not seem enough. As Mittleman told an interviewer, "I plan to do a 12-hour run tomorrow. You know, it seems like so little now."

Among world-class athletes, performance is more important than health. During the nineteenth century athletes occasionally took drugs to enhance their performances. Cyclists, in particular, used drugs to extend their pain and endurance barriers. As early as 1869 some cyclists used "speed balls" of heroin and cocaine to increase endurance. Others used caffeine, alcohol, nitroglycerine, ethyl ether, strychnine, and opium to achieve the same effect.

Of course, not all athletes survived such experimentation. And in the twentieth century, as drug use became more frequent, the casualty rate climbed. In 1960 Danish cyclist Knut Jensen collapsed and died during the Rome Olympics. He had taken amphetamines and nicotinyl tartrate to improve his chances of victory. In 1967 Thomas Simpson died during the ascent of Mount Ventoux in the Tour de France. Amphetamines were discovered in his jersey pockets and luggage.

Since World War II, however, stimulants have done less damage than muscle-building drugs. During the 1920s American scientists isolated the male hormone testosterone. By the 1940s testosterone was being hailed as a potential fountain of youth. Science writer Paul de Kruif in *The Male Hormone* (1945) noted that the newly developed synthetic testosterone "did more than give [the subjects] more energy and a gain in weight. . . . It changed them, and fundamentally. . . after many months on testosterone, their chest and shoulder muscles grew much heavier and stronger. . . . In some mysterious manner, testosterone caused the human body to synthesize protein, it caused the human body to be able to build the very stuff of its own life." There is evidence that during World War II testosterone was administered to German storm troopers to increase their strength and aggressiveness.

In 1945 de Kruif speculated, "It would be interesting to watch the productive power of [a] . . . professional group [of athletes] that would try a systematic supercharge with testosterone." By the 1952 Helsinki Olympics the Soviet Union had embarked on just such a campaign. That year Soviet weightlifters won seven Olympic medals, and U.S. Olympic weightlifting coach Bob Hoffman told reporters, "I know they're taking the hormone stuff to increase their strength."

At the 1954 World Weightlifting Championships in Vienna, a Soviet team physician confirmed Hoffman's belief. Upon returning home, Dr. John Ziegler, the U.S. team physician, acquired some testosterone and tested it on himself, Hoffman, and several American lifters. Concerned about the hormone's side effects—heightened aggression, increased libido, prostatic problems, and hirsutism—Ziegler approached the CIBA pharmaceutical company about producing a drug that would have testosterone's anabolic (muscle-building) effects without its androgenic (masculine characteristics) problems. The unsatisfactory result was the anabolic steroid Dianabol, a drug intended to aid burn victims and certain postoperative and geriatric patients.

Dianabol soon became the candy of the athletic world. By the 1960s nearly every world-class weightlifter was taking some form of anabolic steroid. In fact, steroids became the *sine qua non* of lifting. American superheavyweight weightlifting champion Ken Patera announced in 1971 that he was anxious to meet his Russian counterpart Vasily Alexiev in the 1972 Olympics: "Last year, the only difference between me and him was that I couldn't afford his pharmacy bill. Now I can. When we hit Munich next year, I'll weigh in at about 340, maybe 350. Then we'll see which are better—his steroids or mine."

Track and field athletes, football players, and bodybuilders similarly improved their performances with the aid of drugs. Jay Sylvester, a member of the 1972 U.S. Olympic track and field team, polled his teammates and found that 68 percent had used steroids to prepare for the Games. They believed that without them they would be at a competitive disadvantage. The same was true in football. One San Diego Charger player told team psychiatrist Arnold J. Mandell, "Doc, I'm not about to go out one-on-one against a guy who's grunting and drooling and coming at me with big dilated pupils unless I'm in the same condition."

Testosterone and anabolic steroids have led

to athletes' experimenting with other perfor-
mance-enhancing drugs. One of the more popular recent additions to this drug array is
human growth hormone (hGH), a hormone
manufactured from the pituitary. As the
authors of *The Underground Steroid Handbook*
claimed, hGH could "overcome bad genetics.
. . . We LOVE the stuff." Of course, it may also
cause elongation of the chin, feet, and hands;
thickening of the rib cage and wrists; and heart
problems.

Risk is part of taking drugs. Anabolic
steroids can cause a rare, fatal type of kidney
tumor, high blood pressure, sterility, intestinal
bleeding, hypoglycemia, heart problems, acne,
a deepened voice, and a change in the distribution of body hair. Steroids and testosterone
also make users more aggressive and irritable.
One NFL player confessed that testosterone
"definitely makes a person mean and aggressive. . . . On the field I've tried to hurt people in
ways I never did before. . . . A lot of guys can't
handle it. I'm not sure I can. I remember a
while back five of the guys on our team went
on the juice at the same time. A year later four
of them were divorced and one was separated.
I've lost a lot of hair from using it, but I have to
admit it's great for football. . . . I lost my family, but I think I'm a better player now. Isn't
that a hell of a trade-off?"

By the 1970s steroids had become part of
America's drug culture, and athletes asserted
the right to decide what could or could not go
into their own bodies. Frederick C. Hatfield in
Anabolic Steroids: What Kind and How Many
(1982) wrote: "As pioneers, these athletes carefully weigh the risk-to-benefit ratio and proceed with caution and with open minds. Can
there be much wrong with getting bigger
and/or stronger?" Users, then, have been
transformed into pioneers, "adventurers who
think for themselves and who want to accomplish something noble before they are buried
and become worm food."

Ironically, however, most of the users are
not world-class athletes. In the 1980s use of

steroids expanded out of the realm of world-
class athletes to college and high school playing fields. An estimated one million young
American men and women were consuming
large amounts of anabolic steroids in 1987. The
praise they received for "bulking up" was irresistible. When they reduced steroid use and
lost muscle tissue, friends immediately commented on how "much smaller you are," and
they would return to the pills. Like bulimia
and anorexia nervosa, anabolic steroids were
addictions linked inseparably with body
image.

Steroid use was most pronounced in the
subculture of body building. Most of these men
and women are not competitive athletes trying
to break a world record or win an Olympic gold
metal—"to accomplish something noble"—but
people who want to look "pumped." Like dieting and cosmetic surgery, steroid use has
become a means to a better-looking body, and
looks—not health—is the real objective.

The quest for the "ideal" body has been
taken to its furthest pharmaceutical extremes
by bodybuilders. Not only do they take
steroids to build up muscle mass, but they also
diet and take diuretics to achieve maximum
muscular striation, or the "cut up" look. For
weeks or even months before an important
competition, bodybuilders eat as little as 1,000
calories a day and still work out eight or more
hours a day. The result may be "the picture of
health," but there is no reality behind the
image. As one professional commented,
"When we walk on stage we are closer to death
than we are to life." And after a contest, in a
bulimic binge, bodybuilders "pig out," often
putting on fifteen pounds in one evening of
eating.

Furthermore, to support their quest, many
bodybuilders resort to homosexual "hustling."
In theory, male bodybuilders have enshrined
heterosexuality. Charles Atlas advertisements
emphasized that the prize for the biggest
biceps was the woman in the bathing suit.
Muscle and Fitness, the leading bodybuilder

magazine, reinforces this mythology by always picturing beautiful women hanging onto the biceps and thighs of "pumped," oiled men. "Ya know," said *Muscle and Fitness* editor Joe Weider, "in every age the women, they always go for the guy with the muscles, the bodybuilder. [The women] never go for the studious guy."

In fact, gay men have been a continual source of financial support for bodybuilders. Since serious bodybuilding is a full-time pursuit, the men involved need some source of income. Anthropologist Alan M. Kline estimated that 50 to 75 percent of southern California bodybuilders "hustle" the gay community for living expenses. Hustling ranges from posing for "beefcake" photographers and dancing nude at all-male events to pornography and sexual acts. Most bodybuilders, however, insist that they are not homosexual, that they have to hustle only to finance their bodybuilding habit. And besides, they insist, almost everyone does it. "People don't realize," noted one bodybuilder, "that in any given line-up of twenty competitors ten are hustling."

Many serious bodybuilders sacrifice heterosexual relationships as well as good health for their obsession. As one admitted, "On any given day I can go out with a woman, but it is not very satisfying. . . . Women demand time. I don't have that right now." Time, commitment, women, and even other men—all are obstacles to be mastered or avoided in the pursuit of a narcissistic ideal. To echo Michael Jackson's popular 1988 song, life for these bodybuilders starts and ends with the man in the mirror.

By the end of the 1980s, sports had become the secular religion of America. The stadiums, tanning salons, health spas, and gymnasiums had become the new cathedrals; jogging, running, aerobic dancing, cycling, weightlifting, and dieting the new rituals; and televised events, newspapers, radio talk shows, and sports and health magazines the new liturgies. The most obsessive athletes have a disciplined devotion that even the most ascetic medieval saints would have envied. Alberto Salazar, the world-class marathoner, bragged about his willingness to run 105 miles a week on stress-fractured legs. In the heat of one marathon, he kept running even when his body temperature had reached 108 degrees, collapsed in heat prostration, and while being packed in ice, received the last rites of the Roman Catholic Church.

Sports in the 1980s holds out secular salvation for nations, communities, and individuals. In competition and fitness, they locate the holy grail, the meaning of life in a world where God, church, and state no longer reign supreme. In *The Complete Book of Running*, Jim Fixx wrote: "It is here with my heart banging against my ribs that I discover how far beyond reason I can push myself. Furthermore, once a race has ended, I know what I am truly made of. Who can say how many of us have learned life's profoundest lessons while aching and gasping for breath?" On that Vermont road in 1986, with his body aching, his lungs gasping for breath, and his heart pounding against his ribs, Jim Fixx may have discovered the meaning of life.

∎∎∎

STUDY QUESTIONS

1. Why did sports assume such an important dimension in American culture after World War II?

2. To what extent does sports in America reflect the aggressive, competitive spirit of the larger culture?

3. What are the advantages and disadvantages to the new American obsession with sports?

4. In rural areas, why are high school sports so important to the community?

5. Why has plastic surgery become so popular in modern America?

6. How can anorexia nervosa and bulimia be seen as cultural, not merely physical, extremes?

7. What does the concept *cultural currency* mean? How does sports assist American society in transcending ethnic and religious divisions?

8. What is the connection between the cult of fitness and the post–World War II baby boom generation of yuppies?

BIBLIOGRAPHY

For an extraordinary look at American values in the contemporary period, see Christopher Lasch, *The Culture of Narcissism: American Life in the Age of Diminishing Expectations* (1975). Also see Peter Clecak, *America's Quest for the Ideal Self* (1983). Randy Roberts and James S. Olson analyze the American obsession with sports in *Winning Is the Only Thing* (1989). Studs Terkel's *American Dreams: Lost and Found* (1980) is an oral history of how Americans coped with the social and economic changes of the 1970s and 1980s. Hillel Schwartz's *Never Satisfied: A Cultural History of Diets, Fantasies and Fat* (1986) is an outstanding examination of the American preoccupation with youth and body image. Also see Kim Chernin, *The Obsession: Reflections on the Tyranny of Slenderness* (1981). For the dangerous, pathologic dimension of weight consciousness in history, see Rudolph M. Bell, *Holy Anorexia* (1985).